CORE CONCEPTS OF ORGANIZATIONAL BEHAVIOR

JOHN R. SCHERMERHORN, JR.
Ohio University

JAMES G. HUNT
Texas Tech University

RICHARD N. OSBORN
Wayne State University

www.wiley.com/college/schermerhorn

Project Editor *David Kear*
Marketing Manager *Charity Robey*
Media Editor *Allison Keim*
Managing Editor *Kevin Dodds*
Associate Production Manager *Kelly Tavares*
Designer *Shoshanna Turek*

This book was set in Minion by Leyh Publishing LLC and printed and bound by Malloy Lithograph. The cover was printed by Phoenix Color.

This book is printed on acid free paper.∞

ISBN 0-471-39182-4

Printed in the United States of America

10 9 8 7 6 5 4 3 2 1

Brief Contents

Contents

PART 2   INDIVIDUALS

PART 3   GROUPS

9   THE NATURE OF GROUPS   142

10   TEAMWORK AND HIGH PERFORMANCE TEAMS   158

PART 4   ORGANIZATIONS

11   BASIC ATTRIBUTES OF ORGANIZATIONS   174

12   STRATEGIC COMPETENCY AND ORGANIZATIONAL DESIGN   196

Preface

Along with all the complexities, uncertainties, ethical scandals and global challenges, the advent of the 21st century has ushered in a new era of management and organizational practices. We now live, work, and learn in a society that expects high performance and high quality-of-work-life to go hand in hand; that considers ethics and social responsibility paramount measures of individual and organizational performance; that respects the talents of workforces increasingly rich in demographic and cultural diversity; and that knows the imprint of an interconnected world.

The new workplace is a meeting ground for diverse viewpoints, new ideas, intense problem-solving, and interactive teamwork. It is a place that values teamwork, entrepreneurship, horizontal structures, knowledge management, virtual organizations, work-life balance, and more. This is the world in which today's students must find career success as individual contributors, team members, and group leaders or managers. The landscape of this new emerging world of work is bold, bright, imaginative, and ever changing. It is alive with color and possibilities. So, too, is the learning potential of the discipline we call organizational behavior—the study of individuals and groups in organizations.

Core Concepts of Organizational Behavior has been prepared with these many challenges, needs, and opportunities in mind. It recognizes that the study of organizational behavior is essential for everyone seeking career success in the modern workplace. It doesn't matter whether that career unfolds in the arena of business, government, education, or public service. It does matter that the individual is prepared to perform in organizations challenged by uncertainty, bound for continuous change, affected by the forces of high technology and ultimately held accountable by society for high performance achieved by ethical conduct.

Core Concepts of Organizational Behavior presents the basic foundations of OB through discussions of core theories, concepts, and issues. The clean design provides readers with open page layouts and a professional appearance. Each chapter opens with a set of study questions tied directly to major text headings; end-of-chapter summaries use these questions again to remind readers of core points. In keeping with our commitment to theory-into-practice applications, Effective Manager boxes in each chapter offer action guidelines for using the insights in real work situations.

This book is written for students who want to understand the discipline of OB in full awareness of its practical value and importance to their future careers. It is also written for instructors who want to give their students a solid introduction to the discipline in the form of a concise paperback format. The book is organized in a convenient manner that allows for flexible scheduling of chapters to fit a variety of innovative course designs and supplemental methods, including case studies, experiential exercises, Internet research, group projects, and outside readings. Although chapters can be assigned in any order, we suggest that the first two—1) "Organizational Behavior Today," and 2) "The High Performance Organization"—be used in sequence to set the context for the course.

Core Concepts of Organizational Behavior introduces the essential knowledge foundations of a dynamic discipline that is increasingly relevant as our society and its institutions rush forward into an uncertain future. We hope this introduction to OB will help to inform and enthuse students who will face the challenges of tomorrow's workplace, not yesterday's.

SUPPORT PACKAGE

Core Concepts of Organizational Behavior is supported by a learning package that assists the instructor in creating a motivating and enthusiastic environment (www.wiley.com/college/schermerhorn). Students can benefit from on-line study materials that include cases, self-assessments, PowerPoint reviews, and more. An Instructor's Resource Guide offers resources for course development, sample assignments, innovative instructions designs, teaching tips, and much more. An expanded and revised Test Bank includes approximately 120 questions per chapter, which include approximately 75–100 multiple choice questions, 25 True/False questions, and 4 essay questions with suggested responses. The Computerized Test Bank is available for IBM and compatible computers, and contains an electronic version of the test bank with full custom test design features.

ACKNOWLEDGEMENTS

As always, the staff at John Wiley & Sons, Inc. was most helpful in various stages of developing and producing this book. We would like to thank especially our project editors, David B. Kear and Jessica Bartelt, Charity Robey for leading the marketing campaign, Allie Keim for her work on the Web support, and Kelly Tavares for her production assistance. Our thanks also to the production team at Leyh Publishing, especially Kevin Dodds and Lari Bishop. Thank you everyone!

John R. Schermerhorn, Jr.
Ohio University

James G. (Jerry) Hunt
Texas Tech University

Richard N. Osborn
Wayne State University

CHAPTER 1

Organizational Behavior Today

Study Questions

Chapter 1 introduces the field of organizational behavior as a useful knowledge base for achieving career success in today's dynamic environment. As you read the chapter, keep in mind these key questions.

- What is organizational behavior and why is it important?
- How do we learn about organizational behavior?
- What are organizations like as work settings?
- What is the nature of managerial work?
- How do ethics influence human behavior in organizations?

Core Concepts of Organizational Behavior is about people, everyday people like you and us, who work and pursue careers today in new and highly demanding settings. It is about people who seek fulfillment in their lives and jobs in a variety of ways and in uncertain times. It is about common themes that now characterize the modern workplace, including high performance, ethical behavior, productivity improvement, technology utilization, product and service quality, workforce diversity, work-life balance, and competitive advantage in a global economy. This book is also about how a complex environment challenges people and organizations to change, learn, and continuously develop themselves in the quest for promising futures.

Of all the available advice on high performing organizations, one message stands out to guide them all: "People are an organization's most important assets!"[1] If you act ethically and treat people in organizations well, you can expect them to treat you well in return. The pathways to high performance will always be complex, challenging, and full of pitfalls. Nothing is guaranteed. Yet, you can face the future with confidence. Whether your career unfolds in entrepreneurship, corporate enterprise, public service, or any other occupational setting, one thing remains sure: Success requires flexibility, creativity, learning, and a willingness to change. That is the message of today; it will be the message for tomorrow; and, it is the message of *Core Concepts of Organizational Behavior.*

ORGANIZATIONAL BEHAVIOR TODAY

People at work in organizations today are part of a new era. The institutions of society and the people who make them work are challenged in many and very special ways. The public at large increasingly expects high performance and high quality of life to go hand-in-hand, considers ethics and social responsibility core values, respects the vast potential of demographic and cultural diversity among people, and accepts the imprint of globalization on everyday living and organizational competitiveness. In this new era of work and organizations, the body of knowledge we call "organizational behavior" offers many insights of great value.

WHAT IS ORGANIZATIONAL BEHAVIOR?

Formally defined, **organizational behavior**—OB for short—is the study of individuals and groups in organizations. Learning about OB will help you develop a better work-related understanding about yourself and other people. It can also expand your potential for career success in the dynamic, shifting, complex, and challenging *new* workplaces of today…and tomorrow.

Figure 1.1 shows how *Core Concepts of Organizational Behavior* progresses logically from the current environment—including an emphasis on high performance organizations and implications of globalization, to dimensions of individual and group behavior in organizations, to the nature of organizations themselves, and to core processes of OB—including leadership, power and politics, information and communication, decision making, conflict and negotiation, and change, innovation, and stress.

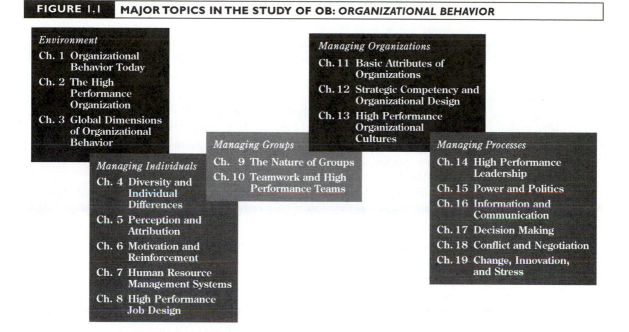

FIGURE 1.1   MAJOR TOPICS IN THE STUDY OF OB: ORGANIZATIONAL BEHAVIOR

Environment
Ch. 1 Organizational Behavior Today
Ch. 2 The High Performance Organization
Ch. 3 Global Dimensions of Organizational Behavior

Managing Individuals
Ch. 4 Diversity and Individual Differences
Ch. 5 Perception and Attribution
Ch. 6 Motivation and Reinforcement
Ch. 7 Human Resource Management Systems
Ch. 8 High Performance Job Design

Managing Groups
Ch. 9 The Nature of Groups
Ch. 10 Teamwork and High Performance Teams

Managing Organizations
Ch. 11 Basic Attributes of Organizations
Ch. 12 Strategic Competency and Organizational Design
Ch. 13 High Performance Organizational Cultures

Managing Processes
Ch. 14 High Performance Leadership
Ch. 15 Power and Politics
Ch. 16 Information and Communication
Ch. 17 Decision Making
Ch. 18 Conflict and Negotiation
Ch. 19 Change, Innovation, and Stress

SHIFTING PARADIGMS OF ORGANIZATIONAL BEHAVIOR

Progressive workplaces today look and act very differently from those of the past. They have new features, they approach work processes in new ways, and they serve different customer and client markets. The last decade of the twentieth century was especially dramatic in both the nature and pace of change. One observer called it a "revolution that feels something like this: scary, guilty, painful, liberating, disorienting, exhilarating, empowering, frustrating, fulfilling, confusing, challenging. In other words, it feels very much like chaos."[2] But what began as a revolution has become everyday reality. Intense global competition, highly interdependent national economies, constantly emerging computer and information technologies, new forms of organizations, and shifting population demographics are now part of the norm. Today we are surrounded by change and uncertainty, and their implications for organizations—just look at the new economic realities and the world of electronic commerce, and for individuals—look also at the demand for competencies with new technologies and commitment to continuous personal improvement.[3] What remains is the struggle to deal best with these changes, individually and institutionally, and to keep up the pace as further challenges emerge in the new workplace.

In an article entitled "The Company of the Future," Brandeis Professor and former Secretary of Labor Robert Reich says: "Everybody works for somebody or something—be it a board of directors, a pension fund, a venture capitalist, or a traditional boss. Sooner or later you're going to have to decide who you want to work for."[4] In making this decision, you will want to join a progressive workplace that reflects values consistent with your own. This book can help you prepare for such choices in full recognition that work in the new century includes these trends:[5]

- Demise of "command-and-control"—increasing competitiveness in organizational environments has made traditional hierarchical structures too unwieldy, slow, and costly to do well.

- Emergence of new workforce expectations—the new generation of workers is less tolerant of hierarchy, more informal, and concerned more for performance merit than status.

- Commitment to ethical behavior—congressional hearings into the collapse of the Enron Corporation and questionable practices by its auditor Arthur Andersen highlight concerns for ethical behavior in the workplace; there is growing intolerance for breaches of public faith by organizations and those who run them.

- Critical role of information technologies—organizations now depend on computers; the consequent implications for workflows and information utilization are far reaching.

- Belief in empowerment—a dynamic and complex environment places a premium on knowledge, experience, and commitment, all of which thrive in high-involvement and participatory work settings.

- Emphasis on teamwork—organizations today are less vertical and more horizontal in focus; driven by complex environments and customer demands, work is increasingly team based with a focus on peer contributions.

- Concern for work-life balance—as society increases in complexity, organizations are paying more attention to how members balance conflicting demands and priorities of work and personal affairs.

ORGANIZATIONAL BEHAVIOR AND DIVERSITY

An important watchword in the twenty-first century is **workforce diversity**—the presence of differences based on gender, race and ethnicity, age, able-bodiedness and sexual orientation.[6] Success in the new workplace requires a set of skills for working successfully with a broad mix of people from different racial and ethnic backgrounds, of different ages and genders, and of different domestic and national cultures. *Valuing diversity* is a core OB theme.[7] It refers to managing and working with others in full respect for their individual differences (see The Effective Manager 1.1). Interpersonal and cultural sensitivity is indispensable to valuing diversity.

Even though valuing diversity is emphasized in our books and classrooms, much remains to be accomplished. A **glass ceiling effect** acts as a hidden barrier limiting the career advancement of minorities and women in some situations.[8] A *Harvard Business Review* forum on "Race in the U.S. Workplace," for example, included these opening statements: "Many people of color themselves still struggle with the closed doors of institutional racism…ignorance and prejudice have by no means disappeared from the U.S. workforce." The article went on to conclude: "Yet there are signs of headway."[9] A study of 860 U.S. companies indicates that the number of African-Americans serving as board directors increased 18 percent in a two-year period; the number of women directors increased 4 percent. Yet, as

---

THE EFFECTIVE MANAGER 1.1

HOW TO MAKE DIVERSITY STICK

- Focus on getting the best talent.
- Develop career plans for *all* employees.
- Provide career mentoring by diversity cohorts.
- Promote minorities to responsible positions.
- Maintain accountability for diversity goals.
- Make diversity part of organizational strategy.
- Build diversity into senior management.

---

one indicator of lingering disparities in diversity representation in the executive ranks, women are reported as holding only about 12.5 percent of corporate officerships in *Fortune* 500 companies. They also earn as senior executives only about 72 cents to the dollar earned by the highest-paid men. In the American workforce overall, the wages of black women trail by 13 percent those of white women.[10]

LEARNING ABOUT ORGANIZATIONAL BEHAVIOR

We live and work in a knowledge-based economy that is continually laced with the winds of change. This places a great premium on "learning" by organizations as well as individuals. Only the learners, so to speak, will be able to maintain the pace and succeed in a constantly changing environment.[11]

ORGANIZATIONAL BEHAVIOR AND THE LEARNING IMPERATIVE

Consultants and scholars emphasize **organizational learning** as the process of acquiring knowledge and utilizing information to adapt successfully to changing circumstances.[12] Organizations must be able to change continuously and positively while searching for new ideas and opportunities. The same is true for each of us. We must strive for continuous improvement to maintain career readiness and keep pace with a dynamic and complex environment.

Life-long learning is a popular concept these days, and the message is relevant. You can and must learn from day-to-day work experiences, conversations with colleagues and friends, counseling and advice from mentors, success models, training seminars and workshops, and the information available in the popular press and mass media. The typical Organizational Behavior course is designed specifically to help you in this learning process. Included are many opportunities for you to analyze readings and cases, participate in experiential exercises, and complete skills-assessment inventories to advance your learning.

SCIENTIFIC FOUNDATIONS OF ORGANIZATIONAL BEHAVIOR

As far back as a century ago, consultants and scholars were giving increased attention to the systematic study of management. Although the early focus was initially on physical working conditions, principles of administration, and industrial engineering principles, the interest had broadened by the 1940s to include the essential human factor. This gave impetus to research dealing with individual attitudes, group dynamics, and the relationships between managers and workers. Eventually, the discipline of organizational behavior emerged as a broader and encompassing approach. Today, it continues to evolve as a discipline devoted to scientific understanding of individuals and groups in organizations, and of the performance implications of organizational structures, systems, and processes.[13]

Interdisciplinary Body of Knowledge   OB is an interdisciplinary body of knowledge with strong ties to the behavioral sciences—psychology, sociology, and anthropology, as well as to allied social sciences such as economics and political science. Organizational behavior is unique, however, in its devotion to applying and integrating these diverse insights. The ultimate goal is to improve the functioning of organizations and the work experiences of their members.

Use of Scientific Methods   OB uses scientific methods to develop and empirically test generalizations about behavior in organizations. Figure 1.2 describes research methodologies commonly used. Scientific thinking is important to OB researchers and scholars for these reasons: (1) the process of data collection is controlled and systematic; (2) proposed

---

FIGURE 1.2   RESEARCH METHODS IN ORGANIZATIONAL BEHAVIOR

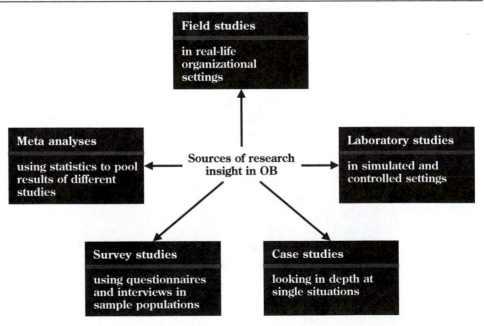

explanations are carefully tested; and (3) only explanations that can be scientifically veri-fied are accepted. Research concepts and designs in OB are explained further in the end-of-book module, "Research Methods in Organizational Behavior."

Focus on Application   The field of organizational behavior focuses on applications that can make a real difference in how organizations and people in them perform. The out-come or dependent variables studied by researchers, for example, include task perform-ance, job satisfaction, job involvement, absenteeism, and turnover. Among the practical questions addressed by the discipline of OB and in this book are: How should rewards such as merit pay raises be allocated? How can jobs be designed for high performance? What are the ingredients of successful teamwork? How can organizational cultures be changed? Should decisions be made by individual, consultative, or group methods? In a negotiation, what is the best way to achieve "win-win" outcomes?

Contingency Thinking   Rather than assume that there is one "best" or universal way to manage people and organizations, OB recognizes that management practices must be tai-lored to fit the exact nature of each situation. Using a **contingency approach**, researchers try to identify how different situations can best be understood and handled. In Chapter 3, for example, we recognize that culture can affect how OB theories and concepts apply in different countries.[14] What works well in one culture may not work as well in another. Other important contingency variables addressed in this book include environment, tech-nology, task, structure, and people.

ORGANIZATIONS AS WORK SETTINGS

The study of organizational behavior must be framed in an understanding of organizations as work settings. An **organization** is formally defined as a collection of people working together in a division of labor to achieve a common purpose. This definition describes a wide variety of clubs, voluntary organizations, and religious bodies, as well as entities such as small and large businesses, labor unions, schools, hospitals, and government agencies. The insights and applications of OB can be applied to help all such organizations perform up to expectations as social institutions.

PURPOSE, MISSION, AND STRATEGIES

The *core purpose* of an organization may be stated as the creation of goods or services for customers. Nonprofit organizations produce services with public benefits, such as health care, education, judicial processing, and highway maintenance. Large and small for-profit businesses produce consumer goods and services such as automobiles, banking, travel, gourmet dining, and accommodations.

Missions and *mission statements* focus the attention of organizational members and external constituents on the core purpose.[15] For example, the pharmaceutical giant Merck states that its purpose is "to preserve human life." The retailer Wal-Mart states that it seeks "to give ordinary folk the chance to buy the same things as rich people."[16] Increasingly, mission statements are written to communicate a clear *vision* in respect to long-term goals and future aspirations. The corporate vision at America West Airlines expresses the desire "to build a winning airline by taking care of our customers."[17] Bold and challenging visions can attract attention and help draw members together in the quest for high performance. As Robert Reich states in his description of the company of the future: "Talented people want to be part of something that they can believe in, something that confers meaning on their work, on their lives—something that involves a mission."[18]

Given a sense of purpose and a vision, organizations pursue action *strategies* to accomplish them. The variety of mergers, acquisitions, restructurings, and divestitures found in business today are examples of corporate strategies to achieve and sustain advantage in highly competitive environments. In this context, strategies must be both well formulated and well implemented for the organization to succeed.[19] A good plan alone is insufficient to achieve the broader strategic goal: To get and stay ahead of the competition. It is here, at the level of action, that the field of organizational behavior becomes especially important. A knowledge of OB is essential to effective strategy implementation. Things happen in organizations because of the efforts of people. How people work and perform together in organizations is what OB is all about.

PEOPLE AND WORK SYSTEMS

Richard Kovacevic, president and CEO of Wells Fargo, once said: "Our success has to do with execution…talented, professional, motivated people who care…that's our competitive advantage."[20] Leaders of today's organizations increasingly recognize the importance of putting people first as they face new and sometimes very difficult times. The very best leaders understand the new significance of an old concept—people are an organization's most critical assets.

One of the important directions in OB today is the emphasis on **intellectual capital** as represented by the sum total of knowledge, expertise, and dedication of an organization's workforce.[21] It recognizes that even in the age of high technology, people are the indispensable **human resources** whose knowledge and performance advance the organization's purpose, mission, and strategies. Only through human efforts can the great advantages be realized from other *material resources* of organizations such as technology, information, raw materials, and money. A *Fortune* survey of America's most-admired firms goes so far as to report that "the single best predictor of overall success was a company's ability to attract, motivate, and retain talented people."[22]

Today's strategic emphasis on customer-driven and market-driven organizations places great significance on understanding the relationship between an organization and its environment. As shown in Figure 1.3, organizations can be viewed as **open systems** that obtain resource inputs from the environment and transform them into outputs that are returned to the environment in the form of finished goods or services. If everything works right, the environment values these outputs and creates a continuing demand for them. This sustains operations and allows the organization to survive and prosper over the long run. But things can and sometimes do go wrong in the organization/environment relationship. If the value chain breaks down and an organization's goods or services become unpopular, it will sooner or later have difficulty obtaining the resources it needs to operate. In the extreme case, it will be forced out of existence.

FIGURE 1.3	ORGANIZATION AND ENVIRONMENT RELATIONSHIPS

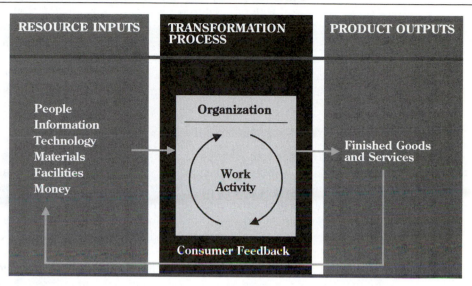

ORGANIZATIONAL BEHAVIOR AND MANAGEMENT

Regardless of your career direction and entry point, the field of organizational behavior will someday become especially important as you try to master the special challenges of working as a **manager.** In all organizations, managers perform jobs that involve directly supporting the work efforts of others. Being a manager is a unique challenge that carries distinct performance responsibilities. Managers help other people get important things done in timely, high-quality, and personally satisfying ways. In the new workplace, this is accomplished more through "helping" and "supporting" than through traditional notions of "directing" and "controlling." Indeed, the word "manager" is increasingly being linked in the new workplace to roles described by such titles as "coordinator," "coach," or "team leader."[23]

THE NATURE OF MANAGERIAL WORK

Anyone who serves as a manager or team leader assumes a unique responsibility for work that is accomplished largely through the efforts of other people. The result is a very demanding and complicated job that has been described by researchers in the following terms.[24] *Managers work long hours.* A work week of more than the standard 40 hours is typical. The length of the work week tends to increase as one advances to higher managerial levels; heads of organizations often work the longest hours. *Managers are busy people.* Their work is intense and involves doing many different things on any given workday. The busy day of a manager includes a shifting mix of incidents that require attention, with the number of incidents being greatest for lower-level managers. *Managers are often interrupted.* Their work is fragmented and variable. Interruptions are frequent, and many tasks must be completed quickly. *Managers work mostly with other people.* In fact, they spend little time working alone. Time spent with others includes working inside the organization with bosses, peers, subordinates, and subordinates of their subordinates. Externally, it includes working with outsiders such as customers, suppliers, and the like. *Managers are communicators.* Managers spend a lot of time getting, giving, and processing information in both face-to-face and electronic communications. They participate in frequent formal and informal meetings, with higher level managers typically spending more time in scheduled meetings.

THE MANAGEMENT PROCESS

An **effective manager** is one whose organizational unit, group, or team consistently achieves its goals while members remain capable, committed, and enthusiastic. This definition focuses attention on two key results. The first is **task performance**—the quality and quantity of the work produced or the services provided by the work unit as a whole. The second is **job satisfaction**—how people feel about their work and the work setting. Just as a valuable machine should not be allowed to break down for lack of proper maintenance, the performance contributions of human resources should never be lost or compromised for lack of proper care. Accordingly, OB directs a manager's attention to such matters as job satisfaction, job involvement, and organizational commitment, as well as measures of actual task performance.

The job of any manager or team leader is largely one of adding value to the work setting by doing things that help others to accomplish their tasks. A traditional and still relevant way of describing this job is as a set of tasks or functions performed constantly and often simultaneously. As shown in Figure 1.4, these four *functions of management* are planning, organizing, leading, and controlling. They form a framework for managerial action that can be described as follows:[25]

- **Planning**—defining goals, setting specific performance objectives, and identifying the actions needed to achieve them.

FIGURE 1.4	**THE MANAGEMENT PROCESS OF PLANNING, ORGANIZING, LEADING, AND CONTROLLING**

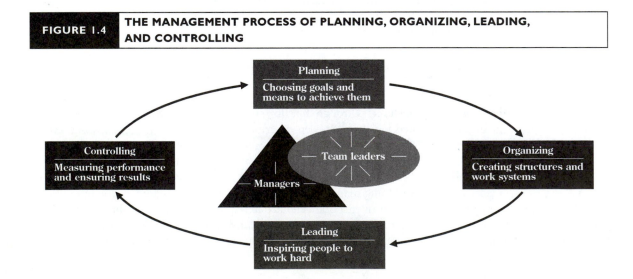

- **Organizing**—creating work structures and systems, and arranging resources to accomplish goals and objectives.
- **Leading**—instilling enthusiasm by communicating with others, motivating them to work hard, and maintaining good interpersonal relations.
- **Controlling**—ensuring that things go well by monitoring performance and taking corrective action as necessary.

MANAGERIAL ROLES AND NETWORKS

In what has become a classic study of managerial behavior, Henry Mintzberg moved beyond this functional approach to describe what managers do. He identified ten roles, falling into three categories as shown in Figure 1.5, that managers must be prepared to perform on a daily basis.[26] The *interpersonal roles* involve working directly with other people. They include hosting and attending official ceremonies (figurehead), creating enthusiasm and serving people's needs (leader), and maintaining contacts with important people and groups (liaison). The *informational roles* involve exchanging information with other people. They include seeking out relevant information (monitor), sharing relevant information with insiders (disseminator), and sharing relevant information with outsiders (spokesperson). The *decisional roles* involve making decisions that affect other people. They include seeking out problems to solve and opportunities to explore (entrepreneur), helping to resolve conflicts (disturbance handler), allocating resources to various uses (resource allocator), and negotiating with other parties (negotiator).

Good interpersonal relationships are essential to success in these roles and to all managerial work. Managers and team leaders should be able to develop, maintain, and work well with a wide variety of people, both inside and outside the organization.[27] They must seek out and work with others in *task networks*—of specific job-related contacts,

---

FIGURE 1.5   TEN ROLES OF EFFECTIVE MANAGERS

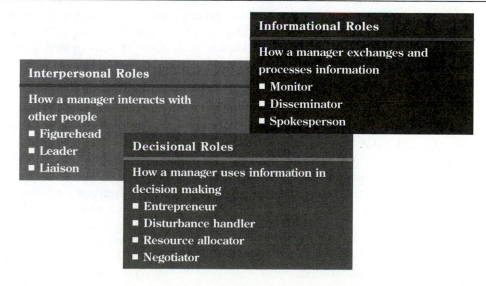

Interpersonal Roles

How a manager interacts with other people
- Figurehead
- Leader
- Liaison

Informational Roles

How a manager exchanges and processes information
- Monitor
- Disseminator
- Spokesperson

Decisional Roles

How a manager uses information in decision making
- Entrepreneur
- Disturbance handler
- Resource allocator
- Negotiator

career networks—of career guidance and opportunity resources, and *social networks*—of trustworthy friends and peers.[28]

MANAGERIAL SKILLS AND COMPETENCIES

A *skill* is an ability to translate knowledge into action that results in a desired performance. Robert Katz divides the essential managerial skills into three categories: technical, human, and conceptual.[29] He further suggests that the relative importance of these skills varies across the different levels of management. Technical skills are considered more important at entry levels of management, where supervisors and team leaders must deal with job-specific problems. Senior executives are concerned more with issues of organizational purpose, mission, and strategy. Broader, more ambiguous, and longer term decisions dominate attention at these higher levels, and conceptual skills gain in relative importance. Human skills, which are strongly grounded in the foundations of organizational behavior, are consistent in their importance across all managerial levels.

Technical Skills   A **technical skill** is an ability to perform specialized tasks. Such ability derives from knowledge or expertise gained from education or experience. This skill involves proficiency at using select methods, processes, and procedures to accomplish tasks. Perhaps the best current example is skill in using the latest communication and information technologies. In the high-tech workplaces of today, technical proficiency in word processing, database management, spreadsheet analysis, e-mail, and communications networks are often hiring prerequisites. Some technical skills require preparatory education, whereas others are acquired through specific training and on-the-job experience.

Human Skills   Central to managerial work and team leadership are **human skills,** or the ability to work well with other people. They emerge as a spirit of trust, enthusiasm, and genuine involvement in interpersonal relationships. A person with good human skills will have a high degree of self-awareness and a capacity for understanding or empathizing with the feelings of others. People with this skill are able to interact well with others, engage in persuasive communications, deal successfully with disagreements and conflicts, and more.

An important new emphasis in this area of human skills is **emotional intelligence (EI).** Defined by Daniel Goleman as the ability to manage both oneself and one's relationships effectively, EI is now considered an important leadership competency.[30] Goleman's research suggests that a leader's emotional intelligence contributes significantly to his or her leadership effectiveness. Important dimensions of emotional intelligence that can and should be developed by any manager are shown in The Effective Manager 1.2. Human skills such as EI are indispensable in the new age of organizations where traditions of hierarchy and vertical structures are giving way to lateral relations and peer structures.

Conceptual Skills   All good managers are able to view the organization or situation as a whole and to solve problems to the benefit of everyone concerned. This capacity to analyze and solve complex and interrelated problems is a **conceptual skill.** It involves the ability to see and understand how the whole organizational system works, and how the parts are interrelated. Conceptual skill is used to identify problems and opportunities, gather and interpret relevant information, and make good problem-solving decisions that serve the organization's purpose.

THE EFFECTIVE MANAGER 1.2

DEVELOPING YOUR EMOTIONAL INTELLIGENCE

- *Self-awareness*—ability to understand your own moods and emotions.
- *Self-regulation*—ability to think before acting and control disruptive impulses.
- *Motivation*—ability to work hard and persevere.
- *Empathy*—ability to understand emotions of others.
- *Social skill*—ability to gain rapport with others and build good relationships.

ETHICS AND ORGANIZATIONAL BEHAVIOR

The word "ethics" is important in OB. **Ethical behavior** is that accepted as morally "good" and "right," as opposed to "bad" or "wrong," in a particular setting. Is it ethical to withhold information that might discourage a job candidate from joining your organization? Is it ethical to ask someone to take a job you know will not be good for his or her career progress? Is it ethical to ask so much of someone that they continually have to choose between "having a 'career' and having a 'life'"? The list of questions can go on and on, but an important point remains: The public is increasingly demanding that people in organizations and the organizations themselves all act in accordance with high ethical and moral standards.

WAYS OF THINKING ABOUT ETHICAL BEHAVIOR

Ethical behavior conforms not only to the dictates of law but also to a broader moral code that is common to society as a whole. Just exactly what moral code governs a person's choice, however, is a subject of debate. At least four ways of thinking about ethical behavior in and by organizations can be identified.[31]

The *utilitarian view* considers ethical behavior to be that which delivers the greatest good to the greatest number of people. Those who subscribe to the results-oriented utilitarian logic assess the moral aspects of their decisions in terms of the consequences they create. Utilitarianism believes that the needs of the many outweigh the needs of the few. From such a perspective, it may be ethical to close a factory in one town in order to keep the parent corporation profitable and operating in several other towns.

The *individualism view* considers ethical behavior to be that which is best for an individual's long-term self-interests. In principle, at least, someone who acts unethically in the short run—such as by denying a qualified minority employee a promotion, should *not* succeed in the long run because the short-run actions will not be tolerated. Thus, if everyone operated with long-term self-interest in mind, their short-run actions would be ethical.

The *moral-rights view* considers ethical behavior to be that which respects fundamental rights shared by all human beings. This view is tied very closely to the principle of basic human rights, such as those of life, liberty, and fair treatment by law. In an organization, this principle is reflected in such issues as rights to privacy, due process, and freedom of speech. Ethical behavior does not violate any of these fundamental human rights.

The *justice view* considers ethical behavior to be that which is fair and impartial in its treatment of people. It is based on the concept of equitable treatment for all concerned. In OB, two issues address this view of ethical behavior.[32] **Procedural justice** is the degree to which the rules and procedures specified by policies are properly followed in all cases under which they are applied. In a sexual harassment case, for example, this may mean that required formal hearings are held for every case submitted for administrative review. **Distributive justice** is the degree to which all people are treated the same under a policy, regardless of race, ethnicity, gender, age, or any other demographic characteristic. In a sexual harassment case, this might mean that a complaint filed by a man against a woman would receive the same consideration as one filed by a woman against a man. A third issue is **interactional justice,** or the degree to which the people affected by a decision are treated with dignity and respect.[33] In a sexual harassment case again, this may mean that both the accused and accusing parties believe they have received a complete explanation of any decision made.

ETHICAL DILEMMAS IN THE WORKPLACE

An **ethical dilemma** is a situation in which a person must decide whether or not to do something that, although benefiting them or the organization, or both, may be considered unethical. It is difficult to predict exactly what ethical dilemmas you will someday face. However, research suggests that people at work often encounter such dilemmas in their relationships with superiors, subordinates, customers, competitors, suppliers, and regulators. Common issues underlying the dilemmas involve honesty in communications and contracts, gifts and entertainment, kickbacks, pricing practices, and employee terminations.[34] More and more organizations are offering ethics training programs that offer advice (see The Effective Manager 1.3) for handling ethical dilemmas. In addition, the training helps participants learn how to identify and deal with these common *rationalizations for ethical misconduct:*[35]

- Pretending the behavior is not really unethical or illegal.
- Excusing the behavior by saying it's really in the organization's or your best interest.
- Assuming the behavior is okay because no one else is expected to find out about it.
- Presuming your superiors will support and protect you if anything should go wrong.

ORGANIZATIONAL SOCIAL RESPONSIBILITY

Closely related to the ethics of workplace behavior is **social responsibility**—the obligation of organizations to behave in ethical and moral ways as institutions of the broader society.[36] This concept suggests that members must ensure that their ethical frameworks extend to the organization as a whole. Managers and leaders should commit organizations to actions that are consistent with both the quest for high productivity and the objective of corporate social responsibility. Unfortunately, it doesn't always turn out this way.

Some years ago, for example, two Beech-nut senior executives were sentenced to jail for their roles in a notorious case of organizational wrongdoing. The scandal involved the sale of adulterated apple juice for infants. Although the bottles were labeled "100% fruit

THE EFFECTIVE MANAGER 1.3
HOW TO DEAL WITH ETHICAL DILEMMAS

1. Recognize and clarify the dilemma.
2. Get all possible facts.
3. List all of your options.
4. Test each option by asking:
   - *Is it legal?*
   - *Is it right?*
   - *Is it beneficial?*
5. Make your decision.
6. Double check your decision by asking:
   - *How will I feel if my family finds out?*
   - *How will I feel if this is printed in the newspaper?*
7. Then, and only then, take action.

juice," the contents turned out to be a blend of chemical ingredients. This case came to public awareness because of a **whistleblower**—someone within the organization who exposes the wrongdoings of others in order to preserve high ethical standards.[37]

Now we have the Enron case.[38] Employees kept buying shares in the firm for their retirement accounts, unaware that a complex series of limited partnerships was creating financial instability. Those who lost most of their retirement savings when Enron went bankrupt are now probably wishing that someone had publicly "blown the whistle" on the firm's questionable practices. They had a right to expect, furthermore, that Enron's auditor Arthur Andersen would have disclosed these practices at the time. By failing to do so and thereby violating its public trust, Andersen—a long-standing and highly reputed accounting firm, lost credibility and its own business viability when major customers canceled contracts with the firm.

Today, the spotlight is on. Corporate executives in America and worldwide will never again be able to so easily hide from public scrutiny. Hopefully, the hard-learned management lessons of Enron and Andersen will have long-term positive consequences for the ethical climates of organizations.

WORK AND THE QUALITY OF LIFE

In many ways, the study of organizational behavior is a search for practical ideas on how to help organizations achieve high performance outcomes while always acting in an ethical and socially responsible manner. A key concern in this quest must be the well being of an organization's entire workforce—this means everyone, not just the managers. The term **quality of work life,** or QWL, is a prominent indicator in OB of the overall quality of human experience in the workplace. It is a reminder that high performance in any work setting can and should be accomplished by high levels of job satisfaction.

A commitment to QWL can be considered a core value of OB. The stage was set very early in the life of the discipline by theorists with a strong human orientation, such as

Douglas McGregor.[39] He contrasted what he called *Theory X assumptions*—that people basically disliked work, needed direction, and avoided responsibility, with *Theory Y assumptions*—that people liked work, were creative, and accepted responsibility. For McGregor, Theory Y assumptions were the most appropriate and tended to create positive *self-fulfilling prophecies.* That is, when people were treated well at work, the likelihood was that they would respond positively and as expected.

Today the many concepts and theories discussed in OB reflect QWL and Theory Y themes. The hallmarks of excellence in management and organizations now include *empowerment*—involving people from all levels of responsibility in decision making; *trust*—redesigning jobs, systems, and structures to give people more personal discretion in their work; *rewards*—building reward systems that are fair, relevant, and consistent, while contingent on work performance; *responsiveness*—making the work setting more pleasant and supportive of individual needs and family responsibilities; and **work-life balance**— making sure that the demands of the job are a reasonable fit with one's personal life and nonwork responsibilities.[40]

A commitment to QWL is consistent with respect for what was earlier called the intellectual capital of an organization. It involves putting people first in any list of organizational priorities. The next chapter will continue to explore how people help to build high performance organizations. For now, consider the leadership challenge posed in these comments made by Jeffrey Pfeffer in his book, *The Human Equation: Building Profits by Putting People First.*[41]

> The key to managing people in ways that lead to profits, productivity, innovation, and real organizational learning ultimately lies in how you think about your organization and its people.... When you look at your people, do you see costs to be reduced?... Or, when you look at your people do you see intelligent, motivated, trustworthy individuals—the most critical and valuable strategic assets your organization can have?

CHAPTER 1 SUMMARY

What is organizational behavior and why is it important?

- Organizational behavior is the study of individuals and groups in organizations.
- Dramatic changes signal the emergence of a new workplace with high technology, global competition, demanding customers, and high performance systems.
- Valuing diversity and respecting differences is a key theme in OB; workforces are increasingly diverse in terms of gender, race and ethnicity, age, able-bodiedness, and sexual orientation.

How do we learn about organizational behavior?

- Organization learning is the process of acquiring knowledge and utilizing information to adapt successfully to changing circumstances.

- Learning about organizational behavior involves more than just reading a textbook; it also involves a commitment to continuous and life-long learning from experience.
- OB is an applied discipline based on scientific methods and that uses a contingency approach recognizing that management practices must fit the situation.

What are organizations like as work settings?

- An organization is a collection of people working together in a division of labor for a common purpose—to produce goods or services for society.
- As open systems, organizations interact with their environments to obtain resources that are transformed into outputs returned to the environment for consumption.
- The resources of organizations are material—such as technology, capital, and information, as well as human (the people who do the required work).

What is the nature of managerial work?

- Managers in the new workplace are expected to act more like "coaches" and "facilitators" than as "bosses" and "controllers."
- An effective manger is one whose work unit, team, or group accomplishes high levels of performance that are sustainable over the long term by enthusiastic workers.
- The four functions of management are (1) planning—to set directions, (2) organizing—to assemble resources and systems, (3) leading—to create workforce enthusiasm, and (4) controlling—to ensure desired results.
- Managers fulfill a variety of interpersonal, informational, and decisional roles while working with networks of people both inside and outside of the organization.
- Managerial performance is based on a combination of essential technical, human, and conceptual skills.

How do ethics influence human behavior in organizations?

- Ethical behavior is that which is accepted as morally "good" and "right" instead of "bad" or "wrong."
- Ways of thinking about an ethical behavior include the utilitarian, individualism, moral-rights, and justice views.
- The workplace is a source of possible ethical dilemmas in which people may be asked to do or are tempted to do things that violate ethical standards.
- Organizational social responsibility is the obligation of organizations as a whole to act in ethical ways.
- The insights of OB can help build and maintain high performance organizations that offer their members a high quality of work life.

CHAPTER 2

The High Performance Organization

Study Questions

Chapter 2 examines trends and directions in high performance organizations, and their implications for the field of organizational behavior. As you read the chapter, keep in mind the following key questions.

- What is the high performance context of organizational behavior?
- What is a high performance organization?
- What are the management challenges of high performance organizations?
- How do high performance organizations operate?

We live and work in an age of increasing global competition, new technologies, shifting demographics, and changing social values. A crucial reaction to these kinds of forces has been the emergence of a new breed of organization, the *high performance organization (HPO)*. These are organizations intentionally designed to bring out the best in people and create an extraordinary organizational capability that delivers sustainable high performance results.[1]

HPOs are fast, agile, and market-driven. They emphasize respect for people, as evidenced by the involvement of workers and managers at all levels and consistent use of teams. Organizations with significant HPO features now make up from one-fifth to one-third of Fortune 1000 companies, and the growth trend will surely continue.[2] Increasingly, future careers will unfold in high performance work settings.

HIGH PERFORMANCE CONTEXT OF ORGANIZATIONAL BEHAVIOR

Organizations today operate in a social context that is unforgiving in its demands for high performance. Critical forces driving organizations toward high performance include changing customer expectations, the changing workforce, and changing organizations.

OB AND CHANGING CUSTOMER EXPECTATIONS

Only those organizations that deliver what customers want in terms of quality, service, and cost will prosper in today's highly competitive environments. This continues to be an age of **total quality management (TQM)**—management dedicated to ensuring that an organization and all of its members are committed to high quality, continuous improvement, and customer satisfaction. Quality in this sense means that customers' needs are met and that all tasks are done right the first time. An important hallmark of the total quality concept is **continuous improvement**—the belief that anything and everything done in the workplace should be continually evaluated by asking two questions: (1) Is this necessary? (2) If so, can it be done better?[3]

Consistent with this approach is the creation of customer-driven organizations that are dedicated to quality and service. Figure 2.1 expresses this notion in the form of an *upside-down pyramid* view of organizations. The figure focuses attention on total quality service to customers and clients by placing them at the top of the organization. Managing from this point of view requires that workers operate in ways that directly affect customers and clients; it requires that team leaders and middle managers do things that directly support the workers; and it requires that top managers clarify the organizational mission and objectives, set strategies, and make adequate resources available.[4]

OB AND THE CHANGING WORKFORCE

The American workforce is becoming more and more diverse with an increasing proportion of women, persons of color, and older employees. Trends in Canada and the European Union are similar.[5] Besides more diversity, two especially important and contradictory workforce characteristics are (1) the impact of **Generation X** or *"Gold-Collar"* workers (those born between 1965 and 1977), and (2) the impact of poor educational preparation

FIGURE 2.1	THE "UPSIDE-DOWN PYRAMID" VIEW OF ORGANIZATIONS AND MANAGEMENT

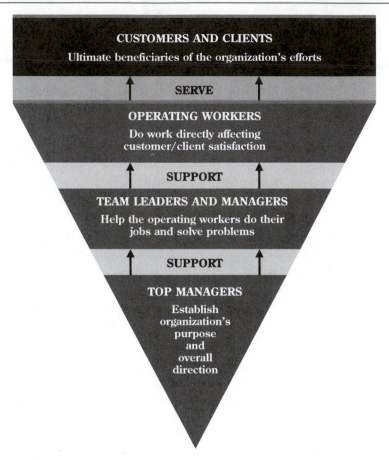

of some high school graduates. In fact, U.S. test scores were the lowest in one comparison of 16 industrialized countries.[6] Both characteristics present a current OB challenge but in very different ways.

Figure 2.2 shows that Gold-Collar Generation X workers demand a lot from a company. They want challenge on the job and flexibility in work schedules; some even want to work at home. But they also want to work in teams, and they are interested in **empowerment**—being allowed as an individual or group to make decisions that affect their work. These needs, wants, and desires are likely to be strongest for **knowledge workers**—employees whose major task is to produce new knowledge, typically through computer-oriented means—and other jobs with workers in high demand and low supply. The level of skills and abilities among many of these workers allows them to function well in highly challenging jobs and work settings.[7]

At the opposite end of the spectrum are those high school graduates who score poorly on standardized tests and enter the workforce with skills deficiencies. In the United States, an alarming number of them require considerable basic skills training in math, writing,

FIGURE 2.2	VALUES AND PREFERENCES OF THE GENERATION X OR "GOLD-COLLAR" WORKFORCE

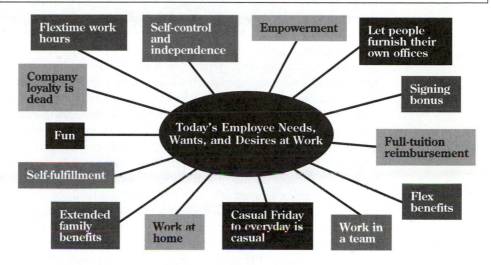

and reasoning to get them up to speed in many of today's organizations.[8] In a knowledge-driven economy, high costs are associated with such remedial training and the individuals can suffer long-term career disadvantages.

OB AND CHANGING ORGANIZATIONS

The last decade may well be remembered as the one that fundamentally changed the way people work.[9] We experienced the stresses of downsizing and restructuring; we gained sensitivity to the peaks and valleys of changing economic times; and we witnessed the advent of the Internet with its impact on both people and organizations. Truly progressive organizations, however, are doing much more than simply cutting employees and adding technology to reduce the scale of operations in the quest for productivity. They are changing the very essence of the way things are done, and they are adding new meaning to the traditional notions of employer-employee relationships.

One characteristic of this new and fast-paced world of organizations is constant change which carries with it an emphasis on reinventing ways of doing things and continuously improving in all aspects of operations. Many organizations have pursued **process reengineering,** which rethinks and radically redesigns business processes to stimulate innovation and change and improve critical performance measures such as cost, quality, service, and speed.[10] Organizations facing these new demands are being asked to "start over"—to forget how things were done in the past and to ask only how they should be done to best meet critical performance measures. Answers to these questions are used to redesign activities and workflows in order to give better value to both internal and external customers.

New information technology has seen an explosion of activity in what may become a benchmark of twenty-first century organizations—**electronic commerce** in which business is transacted through the Internet. The popular Web-based bookseller Amazon.com is but one example of emerging **e-corporations** that utilize the Internet and information technologies to support enterprise-wide computer integration of all aspects of operations.[11] In an increasingly "Net-centric" world, technology-driven *network organizations* operate as virtual alliances of suppliers, customers, and even competitors, who link with the latest electronic information technologies and share such things as skills, costs, and access to global markets.[12] These alliances are formed, utilized, and disbanded with ease, all in quick response to business opportunities.

These and related developments are giving rise to what some call a *free-agent economy,* one in which individuals contract their services to a shifting mix of employers over time.[13] British scholar and consultant Charles Handy describes the career implications of what he calls the **shamrock organization.**[14] A shamrock, the Irish national emblem, has three leaves per stem. Each leaf represents a different group of people. The first leaf is a core group of workers made up of permanent, full-time employees with critical skills, who follow standard career paths. This is a relatively small group, perhaps made up of those who remain after major downsizing of a more traditional organization. The second leaf is a group of outside operators who are engaged contractually by the core group to perform a variety of jobs essential to the daily functioning of the organization. Many of these jobs would be performed by full-time staff (e.g., human resource personnel) in a more traditional organization. The third leaf is a group of part-timers who can be hired temporarily by the core group as the needs of the business grow and who can just as easily be let go when business falls. Today's college graduates must be prepared to succeed in the second and third leaves, not just the first.

WHAT IS A HIGH PERFORMANCE ORGANIZATION?

The free-agent economy and shamrock organization are one aspect of the rapidly changing context of OB. Another is the **high performance organization,** introduced earlier as one intentionally designed to bring out the best in people and thereby produce organizational capability that delivers sustainable organizational results. Instead of treating people as disposable parts of constantly shifting temporary alliances, HPOs place people first.[15] They are regarded as the crucial resource in providing the capability to deliver sustainable high performance results.

EMPHASIS ON INTELLECTUAL CAPITAL

The essential foundation for the high performance organization is **intellectual capital,** defined in Chapter 1, as represented by the sum total of knowledge, expertise, and dedication of an organization's workforce.[16] In this sense, even in the days of high technology, people are the indispensable *human resources* whose contributions advance the organization's purpose, mission, and strategies. To utilize this intellectual capital, HPOs often organize their flow of work around the key business processes and often create work teams within these processes.[17] They follow human-resource policies directed toward enhancing employee flexibility, skills, knowledge, and motivation.[18] At the same time, high performance organizations involve fewer levels of management and change the way managers operate. They become much less directive order-givers and instead emphasize coaching, integrating the work of work teams with each other, and facilitating the work of the teams so that they can best complete their jobs and meet customer expectations.[19]

COMPONENTS OF HIGH PERFORMANCE ORGANIZATIONS

A high performance organization's specific form depends on its setting—for example, an HPO bank would have a form different than an auto manufacturer's.[20] But, high performance organizations often utilize the five components shown in Figure 2.3 in dynamically adjusting to their environment. The key HPO components are: employee involvement, self-directing work teams, integrated production technologies, organizational learning, and total quality management.

Employee Involvement   The amount of decision making delegated to workers at all levels reflects **employee involvement.** This can be visualized as a continuum.[21] At one end is no involvement (workers just do their jobs) or parallel involvement (there are such things as suggestion boxes, roundtable discussions concerning the jobs, and quality circles (members of a quality circle meet regularly to find ways to achieve continuous improvement of quality operations). In the middle is moderate involvement or participative management (there are increased responsibilities for making day-to-day job decisions). At the opposite end from low involvement is high involvement, or what we earlier termed empowerment—where, you will recall, there is worker responsibility for making decisions regarding themselves and their work. Typically, these decisions are of great latitude regarding virtually all aspects of the job. Increased use of employee involvement came from the realization that positive benefits could come from allowing employees input into how their jobs were done. Research shows that employee productivity and various aspects of satisfaction tend to be higher with more involvement.[22]

Self-Directing Work Teams   Teams or workgroups that are empowered to make decisions about planning, doing, and evaluating their work are **self-directing work teams.** They sometimes have other names, such as self-managing or self-leading work teams, or autonomous workgroups. We discuss them thoroughly in Chapter 10. There are at least two reasons for their role in high performance organizations. First, the importance of tapping employee expertise and knowledge is now well-recognized. Second, there has been an

FIGURE 2.3   FIVE COMPONENTS OF A HIGH PERFORMANCE ORGANIZATION

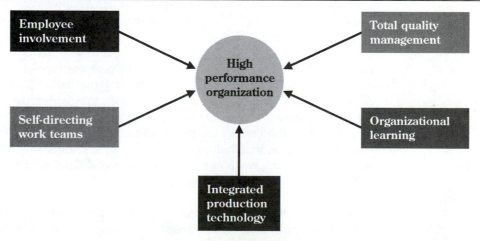

increased need for employees to manage themselves as organizations have downsized and restructured for greater competitiveness.[23] Self-directing work teams strongly affect employee satisfaction and commitment and moderately affect performance.[24]

Integrated Production Technologies   All organizations use technology to combine the use of resources, knowledge, and techniques and create a product or service output. The concept of **integrated production technologies** focuses on providing flexibility in manufacturing and services and involves job-design and information systems. Key aspects of integrated production technologies typically involve the use of just-in-time production or service systems, and a heavy emphasis on computers to assist in designing products or services, controlling equipment in production processes, and integrating the business functions.

Just-in-time systems involve working closely with suppliers to make sure just the right amount of material is available to do the job. At Honeywell, for example, this is done by having the materials suppliers work in the Honeywell plants to see that the inventory level is appropriate. McDonald's does it by keeping only a very small (just-in-time) supply of hamburgers on hand to service its customers.[25]

Computer usage includes integrating such business functions as order entry and accounting with computer-aided design of the product or service and computer-aided production to help control workflow and other product or service aspects. For example, the Technology/Clothing Technology Corporation has developed a computer design process that will allow clothing manufacturers to create "custom" clothing and then to use computers to translate the final design specifications into instructions for manufacturing the item.[26] K2 Corporation, a large U.S. manufacturer of skis, uses these approaches in producing its custom-ordered skis.[27] These design and production functions are often integrated via computer into the just-in-time systems and the integration of business functions so that placing the order, designing it, producing it, and making sure an appropriate level of parts is available are all assisted by computer.

A particularly ambitious attempt at such integration involves the multibillion-dollar VF Corporation, which makes 17 brands of apparel including Wranglers. VF set out to reinvent itself as an integrated e-corporation with a total system tying all components together, from initial design to a "micromarketing system" that would promptly make exact numbers and apparel colors available, on demand, at specific outlets throughout the world. The firm's targeted estimate for rolling out this reinvention has moved from five to seven years. In spite of the difficulties, such integration may well become an important part of numerous HPOs in the future.[28]

Organizational Learning   Chapter 1 introduced *organizational learning* as a way for organizations to adapt to their settings and to gather information to anticipate future changes.[29] High performance organizations with the characteristics in this section are designed for organizational learning. They integrate information into the organization's memory for availability and use in new situations.[30] The need for such learning resulted from the realization that traditional, hierarchically structured organizations were not very good at anticipating environmental changes or at sharing information across functions such as production, marketing, and engineering.

Total Quality Management   As introduced earlier, total quality management involves a total commitment to high-quality results, continuous improvement, and meeting customer needs. The initial push for TQM as far back as the mid-1980s tended to apply it in separate, narrowly focused groups emphasizing various aspects of quality. These groups met separately from the workers' regular jobs. Now total quality management has become a tightly integrated part of HPOs where an emphasis on employee involvement and self-management encourages all workers to do their own quality planning and checking.

MANAGEMENT CHALLENGES OF HIGH PERFORMANCE ORGANIZATIONS

The journey toward becoming an HPO presents many challenges. Responding to these challenges calls for a very strong leadership commitment. For those organizations that have made the HPO commitment, it has been well worth the effort. Studies of some 1,100 companies across a 30-year period show some interesting results. First, bottom-line financial performance tends to increase 30 to 50 percent over a three- to five-year time period. Second, this bottom-line financial performance has increased by a minimum of 3 to 7 percent per year faster than in traditional organizations.[31] These results, however, are dependent upon the mastery of the following challenges.

ENVIRONMENTAL LINKAGES

Like other organizations, high performance organizations are open systems influenced by the rapidly moving *external environment* with its global emphasis and rapidly changing customer expectations. Among the most important *inputs* are the organizational worksite's problems and opportunities and the organization's purpose, mission, and strategy, along with its vision. HPOs typically develop a mission and vision package that ties these elements together and integrates them with the organization's core values.[32] In a true HPO, this vision/direction package must involve employees and managers at all organization levels. This blending is crucial to ensuring a high level of acceptance by everybody in the organization. This high level of mutual acceptance is a key difference between HPOs and other more traditional organizations. The previously mentioned *HPO components*—employee involvement, self-directed work teams, integrated manufacturing technologies, organizational learning, and total quality management—make unique contributions to the transformation of inputs into outputs and to dealing with a dynamic environment.

The *outputs* basically consist of individual, group, and organizational effectiveness and contributions to society. Organizational effectiveness looks at how well the HPO has done financially and what the quality of work life is for members of the organization. The latter includes satisfaction, commitment to the organization, and many other measures of this kind, as indicated in Chapter 1. Contributions to society are those the organization is making to society through charitable contributions, volunteer activities by managers and workers, and many other similar activities.[33]

This open systems perspective therefore means that the inputs, transformation processes, and outputs are all influenced by the external environment and all influence each other. Thus, there is feedback from the outputs to the transformation components and inputs, and there is continual adjustment to meet the environmental demands.

INTERNAL INTEGRATION

A difficult challenge is the integration of all five HPO components. For example, the self-directing teams must include the integrated production system in their plans and operations. Often the teams are heavily involved in the system's design. Similarly the teams also must include total quality management considerations as part of their functioning. At the same time, they must build organizational learning and employee involvement functions and activities. In successful HPOs there is a fit among all these activities and functions, as there is with the open system inputs and outputs.

Unlike traditional organizations, in which design emanates from the top down, the design of an HPO involves a combination of top-down and bottom-up decision making. Successful design calls for a strong and sustained emphasis from the top supported by various deign teams comprised of people from all levels of the organization. It also calls for staying on course in dealing with the inevitable problems introduced by change. Organizations able to do this can reap the kinds of benefits we discuss in the concluding section.

Sometimes **HPO "islands"** exist within a larger, more traditional organization. HPO islands are engulfed by organizations or units that do not function as HPOs and may even be opposed to them. Saturn Corporation within General Motors is one such example. Originally set up to help serve as an example for the rest of the corporation, Saturn has been in a constant struggle to maintain itself as a true HPO.[34] Some influential executives from GM and the United Auto Workers Union have not supported Saturn because they have been concerned about losing the control they maintain elsewhere in GM's more traditional organization.[35]

In spite of these internal pressures, Saturn has had early success as a high performance organization. At the same time, external market forces have made it very difficult for Saturn to continue its success. For example, until a recent SUV addition, Saturn had not had any major changes or new additions to its traditional small car line. A recent larger model, built at a different plant, did not sell well. Therefore, in spite of its early success, the jury is still out on Saturn. Even so, well-run HPOs, in general, have been better able than traditional organizations to withstand negative pressures.[36]

MIDDLE MANAGER ROLES

Middle managers must also address a number of challenges to build a true high performance organization. Many will be asked to help implement one or more of the components described earlier to help move their organization on the journey toward becoming an HPO. As an example, creating self-directing work teams can provide resistance at both manager and employee levels.[37] A key concern is that middle managers in traditional organizations may be asked to implement a change that eliminates some or all of their job.[38] Many of these functions have been shifted to the teams themselves, and the middle managers must carve out new roles and adjust their traditional role as a source of direction.

Although many Generation X employees may welcome new self-managing team environments, other workers, particularly those lacking the appropriate educational skills, may offer resistance. Some employees do not believe that working in teams is a fair way to work, and some do not like the additional challenge of teams. There is also a strong preference among many employees, especially in the United States, to do individual work. A key challenge for middle managers in implementing any of these components (see The Effective Manager 2.1) is to help deal with possible employee resistance.[39]

Another challenge for middle managers is to resolve the tensions that may exist between or among the various components. For example, in an organization on a journey toward becoming an HPO, the total quality management component may reflect the separate, narrowly focused groups emphasizing various aspects of quality. These groups typically have lots of management control. In contrast, an employee involvement component in this same organization involves considerable worker empowerment across a great many issues, and not just quality. To reconcile the demands of these two different HPO components is very difficult for both managers and employees. The middle managers and the employees will need to be extensively trained to handle their new role in an HPO. Middle managers also generally will require lots of training and they must help with the design and implementation of training for other employees.[40] This much or more training is needed for employees to be able to perform their new duties and to keep up with increasing competition.

HIGH LEVEL LEADERSHIP

The first challenge for upper level management is to decide how far to go in becoming an HPO. Many organizations implement only one or two of the components above and are not true HPOs. They are traditional organizations with some HPO components. How far they attempt to go depends on the environment and input factors, as well as on how strongly the top level values and is committed to a true HPO. For example, HPOs are particularly useful in constant, changing environments that demand innovation. Some firms, such as Procter and Gamble, place a strong value on HPOs, and top management has a strong commitment to them.[41] Many managers simply do not want to make this kind of commitment and instead are satisfied with trying to implement one or two components or sometimes just a small portion of a single component.

Another challenge for senior managers is the internationalization of U.S. business practices. In a number of countries where status, power, and prestige are inherent in work-related values (e.g., Malaysia, Italy, Mexico), it can be very difficult to implement HPO components like self-directing teams and employee involvement. In addition, workers with the appropriate abilities and education may not be available.[42] Finally, training and

---

THE EFFECTIVE MANAGER 2.1

MANAGERIAL CHALLENGES OF HIGH PERFORMANCE ORGANIZATIONS

- Employee concern with effectiveness
- Employee self-direction
- Employee concern with organization design
- Challenging jobs and/or work teams
- Intense peer and customer feedback
- Financial rewards and recognition

---

development of middle managers is a challenge. As we have stated, they no longer perform many of the managerial duties in traditional organizations.

GREENFIELD SITES VERSUS REDESIGNS

A final challenge is the question of starting a high performance organization from scratch or redesigning a traditional organization to become one. Those started from scratch at a new site are called **greenfield sites.** Saturn Corporation is an example. It took ten years to develop Saturn from its original conception until its plant opened. During that period, everything was designed from the ground up—typical for greenfield sites.[43] In contrast, redesigns start out as more traditional organizations and try to change these designs to work toward becoming an HPO.

Organizations that have implemented new designs have experienced an average financial increase of about 10 percent a year. In contrast, organizations that have redesigned themselves have realized average increases of 6.8 percent a year. Traditional organizations that have not been redesigned have seen improvements of 3.8 percent a year.[44] So, although all three design types have experienced financial increases in response to external and internal pressures, the HPO designs have done the best.

How High Performance Organizations Operate—The Case of Southwest Airlines

Southwest Airlines is an example of an organization that reflects many features of a high performance organization.[45] Interestingly, the airline demonstrated a number of these features even before its first flight in 1971, before HPOs and their underlying characteristics enjoyed their vogue status of today. The founders and those following them emphasized these features as part of the culture and provided the base that has served and continues to serve Southwest so well. In effect, they established a greenfield site, although no one called it that. Herb Kelleher, the longtime and only recently retired board chair, is given much of the credit for this in the media. However, in keeping with HPO ideals, it was actually a team of several individuals who joined Kelleher in laying the groundwork and strongly reinforcing HPO tenets as part of Southwest's culture.

Let's briefly examine Southwest as an HPO by considering it within the earlier five-component HPO model summarized in Figure 2.3. We start with *employee involvement,* which, you will recall, reflects the amount of decision making delegated to an organization's people at all levels of the organization. From the beginning, Southwest's organizational hierarchy was flat and lean, comprised of a CEO, department heads, managers, supervisors, and employees. There was a heavy team emphasis throughout, starting with a senior management decision-making team, with the board of directors reviewing all major policy areas. This lean-and-mean philosophy permeated the entire organization. Paperwork was minimized, rapid decision making was emphasized, and generally people were empowered to do "whatever it takes" to get the job done. These high-involvement notions were much easier to carry out when the organization started with only three airplanes, but the culture has insisted that they be continued even with the rapid growth that the airline has experienced.

SELF-DIRECTING WORK TEAMS

Often, as especially emphasized in Chapters 10 and 14, these are longer-term manufacturing or service teams, maintaining the same member composition for some time. Wherever called for, there are these kinds of teams at Southwest. At the same time, it is not unusual to find ad-hoc teams that are spontaneously formed to accomplish given projects or duties and then are disbanded until needed again. The culture promotes these kinds of cooperative activities and many of Southwest's self-directing teams are of this nature—a kind of task force.

INTEGATED PRODUCTION TECHNOLOGIES

The operative word here is "integrated." Southwest's heaviest use of information technology has been in distribution, essentially Web site sales. These now account for 27 percent of the airline's revenues, as travel agent sales have dropped to 30 percent of Southwest's total revenue, half their peak. Ticketless travel also was launched several years ago and now accounts for 80 percent of sales.

The above, of course, involves the order entry part of integrated production, at which Southwest has been very aggressive. Until recently, the organization was much more conservative in other IT usage. However, with the airline's recent growth to 29,000 employees, 2,550 daily flights, and more than 300 aircraft, it has been forced to more seriously consider using IT to help provide integrated workflow. A key recent use is for crew pairings across six crew bases, the aircraft, flights, and airports. Until recently this was done manually. Additionally, Web technology is used for dispatching of flights. IT is also used for revenue management in terms of prices and seats. Schedule planning, too, is inching toward IT. IT is also being used for parts replacement. But a key concern in the company is the loss of the intuition, passion, and experience that are key aspects of Southwest's culture—IT minimizes these qualities. Kelleher argues that the very soul of the corporation is at stake.

Given how far some firms, even other airlines, have moved in integrating IT, there appears to be much additional potential for Southwest, which, as suggested above, has tended to be resistant to IT, at least for its own sake. Of course, the more IT that is used, the more integration across the IT is required, and Kelleher's concern about the effect on culture becomes even more crucial.

From its very inception, Southwest has promoted *organizational learning*. Such learning is deeply rooted in its culture. In addition to a plethora of letters to employees and newsletters that discuss details about company business, Southwest has additional learning devices. One of these, a publication called "Cutting Edge Team," is illustrated by the pilots working on the ramp. As another key component of learning, managers encourage employees to spend time regularly at jobs other than their own. Yet another device is the "University for People." This is a multitiered learning facility staffed by a separate department in Southwest. Its primary goal is to equip employees to practice the kind of leadership the airline expects. The University facilitates and teaches courses, does in-house consulting, and provides change agents to ongoing company workgroups. Essentially, it reinforces learning as a way of life.

The airline's culture and the kinds of learning devices mentioned above are used for both individual and organizational learning. As we have argued, such learning is needed to deal with fast-changing environments and information sharing across functions.

Total quality management, in terms of commitment to high-quality results, continuous improvement, and meeting customer needs, is another HPO component emanating from Southwest's culture. It is part of the "Southwest Spirit," which encompasses a strong work ethic, a strong desire for quality work, a desire to go beyond the call of duty, helping others, and doing the "right" thing. These qualities are reinforced by empowerment and the previously mentioned learning and communication devices to provide information on where the company stands and where it wants to go. There is a deluge of this kind of information and a constant push to do better.

A case in point is a recent falling off in monthly on-time competitive performance as revealed by information routinely released to all the airlines. Southwest traditionally has been the industry leader, or close to it. The recent drop in standing led to four initiatives to enhance Southwest's on-time performance. Combined, these initiatives, which involved cooperation from management and employees throughout the airline, appear to have moved Southwest back to its accustomed position.

OTHER HPO CONSIDERATIONS

Some additional important considerations mentioned in this chapter concern the vision/direction-setting package, the people, compensation, dealing with the environment, and outcomes.

Vision/Direction-Setting Package   The airline's mission statement is:

> The mission of Southwest Airlines is dedication to the highest quality of Customer Service delivered with a sense of warmth, friendliness, individual pride, and Company Spirit.[46]

Some key strategic elements in the direction-setting package focus on niche and markets, financial viability, organization structure, customer service, productivity goals, and quality measurements. Core values important in the package are low cost, family, fun, love, hard work, autonomy, ownership, legendary service, egalitarianism, common sense/good judgment, simplicity, and altruism. The airline's culture reflects these values.

The People   Attitude reflecting the "Southwest Spirit" is a key hiring requirement, regardless of other qualifications. Previously mentioned core values, such as hard work and especially fun, are important. It is claimed that it is harder to get hired at Southwest than to be admitted to Harvard.

Compensation   Flight attendants are paid by the trip rather than by the hour, as in other airlines. There are incentives for employee performance and incentives are applied to customers, lenders, suppliers, and investors. Pilots' salaries are comparable to those of other airlines but they fly 40 percent more hours. There is also profit sharing and a 401k pension plan, in addition to the usual airline fringe benefits.

Dealing with the Environment   The industry has been deregulated for some time and Southwest was specifically developed to flourish in such an environment. In this environment, competition from other airlines is fierce and there is constant concern with fuel costs and downturns in pleasure and business flying. Southwest's management culture, communication and learning, and employees, as previously described, continue to serve it well in dealing with this highly competitive environment.

Outcomes   These include highly satisfied employees, strong commitment to the firm, low turnover, and strong performance on various productivity measures such as on-time performance, quick customer turnaround, and various profitability and customer service ratings. Southwest also is active in contributing to the communities in which it operates.

To summarize, by the criteria we have discussed in this chapter, Southwest is an excellent example of a high performance organization. It operates in a highly competitive industry that has suffered through a lot of economic turbulence and has been a consistent high performer on a wide range of outcomes.

Chapter 2 Summary

What is the high performance context of organizational behavior?

- Total quality management deals with meeting the customer's needs, making sure all tasks are done right the first time, and with continuous improvement.

- Customer-driven organizations can be seen as upside-down pyramids where workers operate in ways directly affecting customers, and managers directly support the workers.

- The diverse and changing workforce includes new pressures from "Generation X workers" who want such things as job challenge, job flexibility, and empowerment.

- Organizations are embracing process reengineering, electronic commerce, and free-agent employees with a mix of permanent, part-time, and transitory workers.

What is a high performance organization?

- A high performance organization is designed to bring out the best in people and achieve sustained high performance.

- HPOs tend to organize workflow around key business processes and follow human-resource policies designed to enhance employee flexibility, skills, knowledge, and motivation.

- The key components of HPOs include employee involvement, self-directing work teams, integrated production technologies, organizational learning, and total quality management.

What are the management challenges of high performance organizations?

- Environmental linkages challenge HPOs to be effective open systems whose inputs, transformation processes, and outputs support a clear and relevant vision.

- Internal integration challenges all HPO components to work successfully together in a dynamic and ever-improving fashion.

- Middle manager challenges involve implementing the HPO components, adapting to different managerial roles, and helping with design and implementation of employee training.

- High-level leadership challenges include determining how far to go toward becoming an HPO, training and development of middle managers, and maintaining overall positive momentum during times of great change.

How do high performance organizations operate?

- Southwest Airlines has operated, in effect, as an evolving high performance organization since it was founded.

- Its vision/direction-setting package focuses on the kinds of customer and employee mission, direction, and values that personify HPOs.

- Each of the key HPO components is emphasized in dealing with Southwest Airline's environment and operations.

- Southwest's outcomes in terms of production activity measures, financial measures, employee quality of life measures, and societal contributions have consistently tended to be superior for many years.

CHAPTER 3

Global Dimensions of Organizational Behavior

Study Questions

This chapter will broaden your understanding of people and organizations operating across cultures and in a complex global economy. As you read Chapter 3, keep in mind these key questions:

- Why is globalization significant to organizational behavior?
- What is culture?
- How does globalization affect people at work?
- What is a global view on organizational learning?

This is the age of globalization when corporate success is increasingly linked to worldwide operations and a global staff. Top executive teams have learned first-hand one of the foremost lessons of doing business in international markets—you've got to understand the local culture. All around the globe, people working in large and small businesses alike are facing the many challenges and opportunities associated with business competition in an increasingly complex and "borderless" world.[1] The ability to respect differences and value diversity is an important key to success in managing organizational behavior across cultures.

Today's organizations need managers with global awareness and cultural sensitivity. This doesn't mean that they all must work in foreign lands. But it does mean that they must be aware of how international events may affect the well-being of organizations. They must know how to deal with people from other countries and cultures. Especially for those who cross cultural and national boundaries, understanding these differences is critical for success working in an interconnected world.

Today, managers must be inquisitive and willing to learn quickly from management practices around the globe. Insights into effective management and high performance organizations are not restricted to any one location or culture. Contributions to our understanding about people and organizations can be found from Africa to Asia and from Europe to North and South America. The variety of issues and topics in the present chapter will help you to understand the important global dimensions of organizational behavior.

ORGANIZATIONAL BEHAVIOR AND GLOBALIZATION

Most organizations today must achieve high performance in the context of a competitive and complex global environment.[2] As we begin the twenty-first century, we find ourselves fully in the age of **globalization** with its complex economic networks of competition, resource supplies, and product markets transcending national boundaries and circling the globe.[3] No one can deny its impact on organizations, the people who work in them, and our everyday lives. Consider globalization in terms of your own life and career: (1) You already purchase many products made by foreign firms; (2) you may someday work overseas in the foreign operation of a domestic firm; (3) you may someday work overseas as an expatriate employee of a foreign firm; and (4) you may someday work as a domestic employee of a foreign firm operating in your home country. The field of organizational behavior recognizes these realities and seeks to help you understand the performance implications of work in the global economy.

A GLOBAL ECONOMY

The rapid growth of information technology and electronic communications has heightened the average person's awareness of the global economy. The international news brings the entire world into our homes and our thoughts daily. An explosion of opportunities on the Internet allows us to share and gather information from global sources at low cost and from the convenience of our desktops and laptops—at home, while traveling, or at work. And, always, the transnational movement of products, trends, values, and innovations continues to change lifestyles at a rapid pace. At the same time that valuable skills and investments move from country to country, cultural diversity among the populations is increasing. Immigration is having profound implications for many nations. Tomorrow's employers will have even greater need to deal with *multicultural workforces*—those that draw workers from nontraditional labor sources and from ethnic backgrounds representing all corners of the globe.[4]

Domestic self-sufficiency is no longer a viable option for nations or businesses.[5] Commercial investments travel the trade routes of the world. Canadian businesses, for example, have their sights set on America, with some $30 billion invested in 2000 alone. Germany is a large investor in the United States, with high visibility mergers creating the global giants Daimler Chrysler and Deutsche Bank–Bankers Trust. The Japanese are also large investors with ownership stakes in over 1,500 U.S. factories, employing over 350,000 people.[6] Crossing the Atlantic to Scotland, with its low taxes, excellent infrastructure, and skilled workers, many high-technology firms like IBM have invested heavily in what is now being called "Silicon Glen." Global supplier networks play significant roles in the operations of many industries. The U.S. automobile industry, for example, imports Japanese, Mexican, and Brazilian engines; utilizes German instruments and British electronics; and employs Italian designers. Advances in technology make it possible for software developers in places like Bangalore, India, to work for global employers without ever having to leave home.

REGIONAL ECONOMIC ALLIANCES

The importance of regional economic alliances as forces in the global economy is undeniable.[7] First and foremost, the European Union (EU) is moving forward with its agendas of political, economic, and monetary union among member countries. Remarkably, it has seen the advent of a new world currency, the Euro, which has replaced the traditional currencies of many member nations. Within the EU, businesses from member countries have access to a market of some 400 million customers. Agreements to eliminate border controls and trade barriers, create uniform technical product standards, open government procurement contracts, and unify financial regulations are all designed to bring economic benefit and union to Europe, a region whose economy of some $6.5 trillion closely approaches the U.S.'s $8.0 trillion economy.[8]

The EU's counterpart in North America, the North American Free Trade Agreement (NAFTA), links the economies and customer markets of Canada, the United States, and Mexico in freer trade. NAFTA has been praised for uniting in trade a region with more potential customers than the European Union. It now looks forward to a future of expanded membership to other countries of the Americas. Some business and government leaders even speak of an all-encompassing Free Trade Agreement for the Americas (FTAA) by 2005. At present, the Caribbean Community (CARICOM) is seeking to negotiate free trade agreements with Latin American countries. In addition, the Andean Pact (linking Venezuela, Colombia, Ecuador, Peru, and Bolivia) and Mercosur (linking Brazil, Paraguay, Uruguay, and Argentina) are already active in South America.

Similar regional economic partnerships are being forged in other parts of the globe as well. In Asia, the Asia-Pacific Economic Co-operation Forum (APEC) is designed for joint economic development among member countries. Even with economic challenges worldwide, Asia remains an economic power and is the home of many world-class business competitors. Japan's economic influence is ever-evident, as is China's, whose might may well dominate the twenty-first century. Recent events have further confirmed the importance of other Asian countries, especially Taiwan, Singapore, South Korea, Malaysia, Thailand, and Indonesia. India, with its huge population, is an economy on the move and is recognized as a world-class supplier of software expertise.

Africa, led by developments in post-Apartheid South Africa, has also become an important member of the global economy. Countries like Uganda, Ivory Coast, Botswana, South Africa, and Ghana are recognized for their positive business prospects. Since Apartheid was ended, for example, South Africa has steadily advanced to stand 42nd in the IMD world competitiveness rankings.[9] A report on sub-Saharan Africa concluded that the region's contextual problems are manageable and that the continent presents investment opportunities.[10]

GLOBAL QUALITY STANDARDS

One indicator of the importance of business globalization is the quality designation "ISO," representing quality standards set by the International Standards Organization in Geneva, Switzerland. This mark of quality excellence has become a framework for quality assurance worldwide. The European Union and more than 50 countries, including the United States, Canada, and Mexico, have endorsed the ISO's quality standard. The certification is fast becoming a goal for companies around the world who want to do business in Europe and want to win reputations as total quality "world-class" manufacturers.

GLOBAL MANAGERS

Along with prior developments in globalization, the search is now also on for a new breed of manager—the **global manager,** someone who knows how to conduct business across borders.[11] Often multilingual, the global manager thinks with a world view; appreciates diverse beliefs, values, behaviors, and practices; and is able to map strategy accordingly. If you fit this description (see The Effective Manager 3.1), or soon will, get ready. Corporate recruiters are scrambling to find people with these skills and interests.

The global dimension in business and management, though pervasive, poses many complications to be overcome. Even high performers with proven technical skills at home

---

THE EFFECTIVE MANAGER 3.1

ATTRIBUTES OF THE "GLOBAL MANAGER"

- Adapts well to different business environments
- Respects different beliefs, values, and practices
- Solves problems quickly in new circumstances
- Communicates well with people from different cultures
- Speaks more than one language
- Understands different government and political systems
- Conveys respect and enthusiasm when dealing with others
- Possesses high technical expertise for a job

---

may find that their styles and attitudes just don't work well overseas. Experienced international managers indicate that a "global mindset" of cultural adaptability, patience, flexibility, and tolerance are indispensable.[12] The failure rate for Americans in overseas assignments has been measured as high as 25 percent, and a study criticizes British and German companies for giving inadequate preparation to staff sent abroad.[13]

CULTURES AND CULTURAL DIVERSITY

The word "culture" is frequently used in organizational behavior in connection with the concept of corporate culture, the growing interest in workforce diversity, and the broad differences among people around the world. Specialists tend to agree that **culture** is the learned, shared way of doing things in a particular society. It is the way, for example, in which its members eat, dress, greet, and treat one another, teach their children, solve everyday problems, and so on.[14] Geert Hofstede, a Dutch scholar and consultant, refers to culture as the "software of the mind," making the analogy that the mind's "hardware" is universal among human beings.[15] But the software of culture takes many different forms. Indeed, we are not born with a culture; we are born into a society that teaches us its culture. And because a culture is shared by people, it helps to define the boundaries between different groups and affect how their members relate to one another.

POPULAR DIMENSIONS OF CULTURE

The popular dimensions of culture are those that are most apparent to the individual traveling abroad—for example, language, time orientation, use of space, and religion.[16]

Language   Perhaps the most conspicuous aspect of culture, and certainly the one the traveler notices first, is language. The languages of the world number into the thousands. Some, such as Maltese, are spoken by only a handful of people, whereas others, such as English, Spanish, and Chinese, are spoken by millions. Some countries, such as France and Malaysia, have one official language; others, such as Canada, Switzerland, and India, have more than one; and still others, like the United States, have none.

The centrality of language to culture is represented by the *Whorfian hypothesis,* which considers language as a major determinant of our thinking.[17] The vocabulary and structure of a language reflect the history of a society and can also reveal how members relate to the environment. Arabic, for example, has many different words for the camel, its parts, and related equipment. As you might expect, English is very poor in its ability to describe camels. The fact that many people apparently speak the same language, such as English, doesn't mean that they share the same culture. Some words spoken in one language fail to carry the same meaning from culture to culture or region to region. A "truck" in Chicago is a "lorry" in London; "hydro" in Calgary is "electric power" in Boston; grocery shoppers in the American Midwest put "pop" in their "sacks," East Coast shoppers put "soda" in their "bags."

The anthropologist Edward T. Hall notes important differences in the ways different cultures use language.[18] Members of **low-context cultures** are very explicit in using the spoken and written word. In these cultures, such as those of Australia, Canada, and United States, the message is largely conveyed by the words someone uses, and not particularly by the "context" in which they are spoken. In contrast, members of **high-context cultures** use words to convey only a limited part of the message. The rest must be inferred or interpreted from the context, which includes body language, the physical setting, and past relationships—all of which add meaning to what is being said. Many Asian and Middle Eastern cultures are considered high context, according to Hall, whereas most Western cultures are low context.

Time Orientation   Hall also uses time orientation to classify cultures.[19] In **polychronic cultures** people hold a traditional view of time that may be described as a "circle." This suggests repetition in the sense that time is "cyclical" and goes around and around. In this view time does not create pressures for immediate action or performance. After all, one will have another chance to pass the same way again. If an opportunity is lost today—no problem, it may return again tomorrow. Members of polychronic cultures tend to emphasize the present and often do more than one thing at a time.[20] An important business or government official in a Mediterranean country, for example, may have a large reception area outside his or her office. Visitors wait in this area and may transact business with the official and others who move in and out and around the room, conferring as they go.

Members of **monochronic cultures** view time more as a "straight line." In this "linear" view of time, the past is gone; the present is here briefly; and the future is almost upon us. In monochronic cultures, time is measured precisely and creates pressures for action and performance. People appreciate schedules and appointments and talk about "saving" and "wasting" time. Long-range goals become important, and planning is a way of managing the future. In contrast to the Mediterranean official in the last example, a British manager will typically allot a certain amount of time in her daily calendar to deal with a business visitor. During this time the visitor receives her complete attention. Only after one visitor leaves will another one be received, again based upon the daily schedule.

Use of Space   *Proxemics,* the study of how people use space to communicate, reveals important cultural differences.[21] Personal space can be thought of as the "bubble" that surrounds us, and its preferred size tends to vary from one culture to another. When others invade or close in on our personal space, we tend to feel uncomfortable. Then again, if people are too far away, communication becomes difficult. Arabs and South Americans seem more comfortable talking at closer distances than do North Americans; Asians seem to prefer even greater distances. When a Saudi moves close to speak with a visiting Canadian executive, the visitor may back away to keep more distance between them. But the same Canadian may approach a Malaysian too closely when doing business in Kuala Lumpur, causing her or his host to back away. Cross-cultural misunderstandings due to different approaches to personal space are quite common.

In some cultures, often polychronic ones, space is organized in such a way that many activities can be carried out simultaneously. Spanish and Italian towns are organized around central squares (plazas or piazzas), whereas American towns typically have a traditional "Main Street" laid out in linear fashion. Similar cultural influences are seen in the layout of work space. Americans, who seem to prefer individual offices, may have difficulty adjusting to Japanese employers who prefer open floor plans.

Religion   Religion is also a major element of culture and can be one of its more visible manifestations. The influence of religion often prescribes rituals, holy days, and foods that can be eaten. Codes of ethics and moral behavior often have their roots in religious beliefs. The influence of religion on economic matters can also be significant.[22] In the Middle East, one finds interest-free "Islamic" banks that operate based on principles set forth in the Koran. In Malaysia, business dinners are scheduled after 8:00 p.m. so that Muslim guests can first attend to their evening prayer.

VALUES AND NATIONAL CULTURES

Cultures vary in their underlying patterns of values and attitudes. The way people think about such matters as achievement, wealth and material gain, risk and change, may influence how they approach work and their relationships with organizations. A framework developed by Geert Hofstede offers one approach for understanding how value differences across national cultures can influence human behavior at work. The five dimensions of national culture in his framework can be described as follows.[23]

1. **Power distance** is the willingness of a culture to accept status and power differences among its members. It reflects the degree to which people are likely to respect hierarchy and rank in organizations. Indonesia is considered a high power distance culture, whereas Sweden is considered a relatively low-power distance culture.

2. **Uncertainty avoidance** is a cultural tendency toward discomfort with risk and ambiguity. It reflects the degree to which people are likely to prefer structured versus unstructured organizational situations. France is considered a high-uncertainty avoidance culture, whereas Hong Kong is considered a low-uncertainty avoidance culture.

3. **Individualism-collectivism** is the tendency of a culture to emphasize either individual or group interests. It reflects the degree to which people are likely to prefer working as individuals or working together in groups. The United States is a highly individualistic culture, whereas Mexico is a more collectivist one.

4. **Masculinity-femininity** is the tendency of a culture to value stereotypical masculine or feminine traits. It reflects the degree to which organizations emphasize competition and assertiveness versus interpersonal sensitivity and concerns for relationships. Japan is considered a very masculine culture, whereas Thailand is considered a more feminine culture.

5. **Long-term/short-term orientation** is the tendency of a culture to emphasize values associated with the future, such as thrift and persistence, or values that focus largely on the present. It reflects the degree to which people and organizations adopt long-term or short-term performance horizons. South Korea is high on long-term orientation, whereas the United States is a more short-term-oriented country.

The first four dimensions in Hofstede's framework were identified in an extensive study of thousands of employees of a multinational corporation operating in more than 40 countries.[24] The fifth dimension of long-term/short-term orientation was added from research using the Chinese Values Survey conducted by cross-cultural psychologist Michael Bond and his colleagues.[25] Their research suggested the cultural importance of Confucian dynamism, with its emphasis on persistence, the ordering of relationships, thrift, sense of shame, personal steadiness, reciprocity, protection of "face," and respect for tradition.[26]

When using the Hofstede framework, it is important to remember that the five dimensions are interrelated and not independent.[27] National cultures may best be understood in terms of cluster maps or collages that combine multiple dimensions. For example, Figure 3.1 shows a sample grouping of countries based on individualism-collectivism and power distance. Note that high power distance and collectivism are often found together, as are low power distance and individualism. Whereas high collectivism may lead us to expect a work team in Indonesia to operate by consensus, the high power distance may cause the consensus to be heavily influenced by the desires of a formal leader. A similar team operating in more individualist and low power distance, Great Britain or America might make decisions with more open debate, including expressions of disagreement with a leader's stated preferences.

UNDERSTANDING CULTURAL DIFFERENCES

To work well with people from different cultures, you must first understand your own culture. We are usually unaware of our own culture until we come into contact with a very different one. Knowing your own culture will help guard you against two problems that frequently arise in international dealings. One is the danger of *parochialism*—assuming that the ways of your culture are the only ways of doing things. The other is the danger of *ethnocentrism*—assuming that the ways of your culture are the best ways of doing things.[28] It is parochial for a traveling American businesswoman to insist that all of her business contacts speak English, whereas it is ethnocentric for her to think that anyone who dines with a spoon rather than a knife and fork lacks proper table manners.

A framework developed by Fons Trompenaars offers a useful vantage point for better understanding and, hopefully, dealing with cultural differences.[29] Working from a databank of respondents from 47 national cultures, he suggests that cultures vary in the way

FIGURE 3.1	SAMPLE COUNTRY CLUSTERS ON HOFSTEDE'S DIMENSIONS OF INDIVIDUALISM-COLLECTIVISM AND POWER DISTANCE

	Low Power Distance	**High Power Distance**
Collectivism		Colombia, Peru, Thailand Singapore, Greece, Mexico, Turkey, Japan, Indonesia
Individualism	Israel, Finland, Germany, Ireland, New Zealand, Canada, Great Britain, United States	Spain, South Africa, France, Italy, Belgium

their members solve problems of three major types: (1) relationships with people, (2) attitudes toward time, and (3) attitudes toward the environment.

Trompenaars identifies five major cultural differences in how people handle relationships with other people. The orientations, as illustrated in Figure 3.2, are:

1. *Universalism versus particularism*—relative emphasis on rules and consistency, or on relationships and flexibility.
2. *Individualism versus collectivism*—relative emphasis on individual freedom and responsibility, or on group interests and consensus.
3. *Neutral versus affective*—relative emphasis on objectivity and detachment, or on emotion and expressed feelings.
4. *Specific versus diffuse*—relative emphasis on focused and narrow involvement, or on involvement with the whole person.
5. *Achievement versus prescription*—relative emphasis on performance-based and earned status, or on ascribed status.

With regard to problems based on attitudes toward time, Trompenaars distinguishes between cultures with sequential versus synchronic orientations. Time in a sequential view is a passing series of events; in a synchronic view, it consists of an interrelated past, present, and future. With regard to problems based on attitudes toward the environment, he contrasts how different cultures may relate to nature in inner-directed versus outer-directed ways. Members of an inner-directed culture tend to view themselves separate from nature and believe they can control it. Those in an outer-directed culture view themselves as part of nature and believe they must go along with it.

GLOBALIZATION AND PEOPLE AT WORK

OB scholars are increasingly sensitive to the need to better understand how management and organizational practices vary among the world's cultures. In this sense, we must be familiar with the importance of multinational employers, the diversity of multicultural workforces, and the special demands of international work assignments.

FIGURE 3.2	**SAMPLE COUNTRY CLUSTERS ON TROMPENAARS' FRAMEWORK FOR UNDERSTANDING CULTURAL DIFFERENCES**

Canada, USA, Ireland	**Universalism vs. Particularism**	Indonesia, China, Venezuela
USA, Hungary, Russia	**Individualism vs. Collectivism**	Thailand, Japan, Mexico
Indonesia, Germany, Japan	**Neutral vs. Affective**	Italy, France, USA
Spain, Poland, USA	**Specific vs. Diffuse**	India, Great Britain, Egypt
Australia, Canada, Norway	**Achievement vs. Ascription**	Philippines, Pakistan, Brazil
Great Britain, Belgium, USA	**Sequential vs. Synchronic**	Malaysia, Venezuela, France

MULTINATIONAL EMPLOYERS

A true **multinational corporation (MNC)** is a business firm that has extensive international operations in more than one foreign country. MNCs are more than just companies that "do business abroad"; they are global concerns—exemplified by Ford, Royal-Dutch Shell, Sony, and many others. The missions and strategies of MNCs are worldwide in scope. In the public sector, multinational organizations (MNOs) are those with nonprofit missions whose operations also span the globe. Examples are Amnesty International, the International Red Cross, the United Nations, and the World Wildlife Fund.

The truly global organization operates with a total world view and does not have allegiance to any one national "home." Futurist Alvin Toffler labels them *transnational organizations* that "may do research in one country, manufacture components in another, assemble them in a third, sell the manufactured goods in a fourth, deposit surplus funds in a fifth, and so on."[30] Although the pure transnational corporation may not yet exist, large firms like Nestle, Gillette, and Ford are striving hard to move in that direction. Greatly facilitating those moves are new information technologies, which allow organizations to operate through virtual linkages with components and suppliers located around the world.

The MNCs have enormous economic power and impact. Toffler, in particular, warns that "the size, importance, and political power of this new player in the global game has skyrocketed." Their activities can bring both benefits and controversies to host countries. One example is in Mexico, where many *maquiladoras,* or foreign-owned plants, assemble imported parts and ship finished products to the United States. Inexpensive labor is an advantage for the foreign operators. Mexico benefits from industrial development, reduced unemployment, and increased foreign exchange earnings. But some complain about the downsides of *maquiladoras*—stress on housing and public services in Mexican border towns, inequities in the way Mexican workers are treated (wages, working conditions, production quotas) relative to their foreign counterparts, and the environmental impact of pollution from the industrial sites.

MULTICULTURAL WORKFORCES

What is the best way to deal with a multicultural workforce? There are no easy answers. Styles of leadership, motivation, decision making, planning, organizing, leading, and controlling vary from country to country.[31] Managing a construction project in Saudi Arabia with employees from Asia, the Middle East, Europe, and North America working side by side will clearly present challenges different from those involved in a domestic project. Similarly, establishing and successfully operating a joint venture in Kazakhstan, Nigeria, or Vietnam will require a great deal of learning and patience. In these and other international settings, political risks and bureaucratic difficulties further complicate the already difficult process of working across cultural boundaries.

The challenges of managing across cultures, however, are not limited to international operations. In this connection, a new term has been coined—**domestic multiculturalism,** which describes cultural diversity within a given national population: this diversity will be reflected in the workforces of local organizations.[32] Los Angeles, for example, is a popular home to many immigrant groups. Some 20 percent of the city's school children speak other languages more fluently than they speak English; in Vancouver, British Columbia, Chinese is also the mother tongue of some 20 percent of the population.

EXPATRIATE WORK ASSIGNMENTS

People who work and live abroad for extended periods of time are referred to as **expatriates.** The cost of an expatriate worker can be very expensive for the employer. An executive earning $100,000 per year in the United States, for example, might cost her company more than $300,000 in the first year of an assignment in England—with the added cost tied to compensation, benefits, transfer, and other relocation expenses. Estimates are that a three-year expatriate assignment will cost the employer an average of $1 million.[33] To get the most out of the investment, progressive employers will maximize the potential of expatriate performance success by taking a variety of supportive actions.[34] They carefully recruit employees who have the right sensitivities and skills, provide them with good training and orientation to the foreign culture, actively support them while working abroad, give extra attention to the needs of the expatriate's family members, and pay careful attention to relocation when the expatriate and family return home.

Expatriates usually face their greatest problems when entering and working in a foreign culture, and when experiencing repatriation on the return home. Figure 3.3 illustrates phases in the typical expatriate work assignment, beginning with the initial assignment shock the person experiences upon being informed of a foreign posting. The ways in which recruitment, selection, and orientation are handled during this stage can have an important influence on the assignment's eventual success. Ideally, the employee, along with his or her spouse and family, is allowed to choose whether or not to accept the opportunity. Also ideally, proper pre-departure support and counseling are given to provide "realistic expectations" of what is to come.

FIGURE 3.3	STAGES IN THE EXPATRIATE INTERNATIONAL CAREER CYCLE; POTENTIAL ADJUSTMENT PROBLEMS IN THE HOME AND FOREIGN COUNTRIES

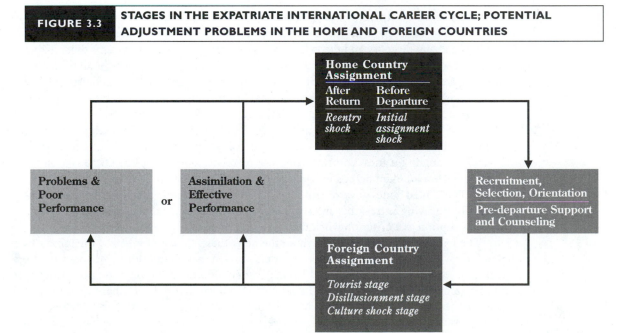

The expatriate undergoes three phases of adjustment to the new country.[35] First is the *tourist stage,* in which the expatriate enjoys discovering the new culture. Second is the *disillusionment stage,* in which his or her mood is dampened as difficulties become more evident. Typical problems include conversing well in the local language and obtaining personal products and food supplies of preference. Third, the expatriate's mood often hits bottom in the stage of *culture shock.* Here confusion, disorientation, and frustration in the ways of the local culture and living in the foreign environment set in. If culture shock is well handled, the expatriate begins to feel better, function more effectively, and lead a reasonably normal life. If it isn't, work performance may suffer, even deteriorating to the point where a reassignment home may be necessary.

At the end of the expatriate assignment, perhaps after two to four years, the reentry process can also be stressful. After an extended period away, the expatriate and his or her family have changed and the home country has changed as well. One does not simply "fall back in"; rather, it takes time to get used to living at home again. In too many instances, little thought may be given to assigning the returned expatriate a job that matches his or her current skills and abilities. While abroad, the expatriate has often functioned with a great degree of independence—something that may or may not be possible at home. Problems caused by reentry shock can be minimized through careful planning. This includes maintaining adequate contact with the home office during the expatriate assignment, as well as having all possible support for the move back. Employers should also identify any new skills and abilities, and assign returned expatriates to jobs commensurate with their abilities. As organizations utilize more and more expatriate assignments, their career planning and development systems must also operate on a global scale.

ETHICAL BEHAVIOR ACROSS CULTURES

The importance of ethical issues in organizational behavior and management was first introduced in Chapter 1. In the international arena, special ethical challenges arise as a result of cultural diversity and the variation in governments and legal systems that characterize our world. Prominent current issues include corruption and bribery in international business practices, poor working conditions and the employment of child and prison labor in some countries, and the role of international business in supporting repressive governments that fail to protect and respect the basic human rights of citizens.[36]

In the United States, the Foreign Corrupt Practices Act of 1977 makes it illegal for firms to engage in corrupt practices overseas, such as giving bribes to government officials in order to obtain business contracts. In 1999, member countries of the Organization for Economic Development agreed to ban payoffs to foreign officials by their countries' businesses. The United States government is pushing for more countries to join the movement against bribe giving and taking, and suggestions have been made that the World Bank consider corruption as a criterion when making loan decisions.[37]

The term *sweatshop* is increasingly in the news these days, and refers to organizations that force workers to labor under adverse conditions that may include long work days, unsafe conditions, and even the use of child labor. A variety of advocacy groups are now active in campaigning against sweatshops, and a number of well-recognized firms have been the targets of their attention—including such prominent multinationals as Nike, Mattel, and Disney. Watchdog groups in Asia, for example, have criticized Disney for allowing some of its contract manufacturers in China to force workers to labor seven days a week, up to 16 hours a day, and at no overtime. Mattel has been accused of engaging subcontractors who run "sweatshop Barbie" assembly lines that include extra-long work hours and heavy fines for workers' mistakes. In response to such criticisms more multinational employers are engaging outside consultants to conduct social audits of their international operations, adopting formal codes of ethical practices governing subcontractors, and backing external codes of conduct such as *Social Accountability 8000*—a certificate awarded by the Council on Economic Priorities. Nike, Disney, and Mattel have each taken steps along these lines to ensure that products made under their name are manufactured under conditions that meet acceptable standards.[38] Worth considering is the following comment by Jack Sheinkman, President Emeritus of the Amalgamated Clothing and Textile Workers Unions, and member of the Council on Economic Priorities Advisory Board:

> As business becomes ever-more global in scope and its links in the chain of production extend further, the task of rating corporate social responsibility has become more complex. So, too, has the safeguarding of workers' rights… especially when responsibility is shared among manufacturers, contractors, subcontractors, buying agents,… and other parties to business agreements which transcend time-zones, language barriers, and developing and industrialized country borders alike.[39]

A continuing issue for debate in this area of international business and management practices is the influence of culture on ethical behavior. Figure 3.4 presents a continuum that contrasts "cultural relativism" with "ethical absolutism."

Business ethicist Thomas Donaldson describes **cultural relativism** as the position that there is no universal right way to behave and that ethical behavior is determined by its cultural context.[40] In other words, international business behavior is justified on the argument: "When in Rome, do as the Romans do." If one accepts cultural relativism, a sweatshop operation would presumably be okay as long as it was consistent with the laws and practices of the local culture. The opposite extreme on the continuum in Figure 3.4 reflects **ethical absolutism,** a universalistic assumption that there is a single moral standard that fits all situations, regardless of culture and national location. In other words, if a practice such as child labor is not acceptable in one's home environment it shouldn't be engaged in elsewhere. Critics of the absolutist approach claim that it is a form of *ethical imperialism* because it attempts to impose external ethical standards unfairly or inappropriately on local cultures and fails to respect their needs and unique situations.

FIGURE 3.4	THE EXTREMES OF CULTURAL RELATIVISM AND ETHICAL ABSOLUTISM IN INTERNATIONAL BUSINESS ETHICS

Cultural relativism   **Ethical absolutism**

◄───►

No culture's ethics are superior.   Certain absolute truths apply everywhere.
The values and practices of the local   Universal values transcend cultures
setting determine what is right or wrong.   in determining what is right or wrong.

When in Rome, do as the Romans do.   *Don't do anything you wouldn't do at home.*

Donaldson suggests that there is no simple answer to this debate and warns against the dangers of both cultural relativism and ethical absolutism. He makes the case that multinational businesses should adopt core or threshold values to guide behavior in ways that respect and protect fundamental human rights in any situation. However, he also suggests that there is room beyond the threshold to adapt and tailor one's actions in ways that respect the traditions, foundations, and needs of different cultures.[41]

A Global View of Organizational Learning

Organizational learning was first defined in Chapter 1 as the process of acquiring the knowledge necessary to adapt to a changing environment. In the context and themes of this chapter, the concept can be extended to **global organizational learning**—the ability to gather from the world at large the knowledge required for long-term organizational adaptation. Simply stated, people from different cultures and parts of the world have a lot to learn from one another about organizational behavior and management.

ARE MANAGEMENT THEORIES UNIVERSAL?

One of the most important questions to be asked and answered in this age of globalization is whether or not management theories are universal. That is, can and should a theory developed in one cultural context be transferred and used in another? The answer according to Geert Hofstede is "no," at least not without careful consideration of cultural influences.[42] Culture can influence both the development of a theory or concept and its application. As an example, Hofstede cites the issue of motivation. He notes that Americans have historically addressed motivation from the perspective of individual performance and rewards—consistent with their highly individualistic culture. However, concepts such as merit pay and job enrichment may not fit well in other cultures where high collectivism places more emphasis on teamwork and groups. Hofstede's point, and one well worth remembering, is that although we can and should learn from what is taking place in other cultures, we should be informed consumers of that knowledge. We should always factor cultural considerations into account when transferring theories and practices from one setting to the next.

A good case in point relates to the interest generated some years ago in Japanese management approaches, based upon the success experienced at the time by Japanese industry.[43] Japanese firms have traditionally been described as favoring *lifetime employment* with strong employee-employer loyalty, seniority pay, and company unions. Their operations have emphasized a *quality commitment,* the *use of teams* and *consensus decision making,* and career development based upon *slow promotions* and *cross-functional job assignments.*[44]

Although the Japanese economy and many of its firms have had problems of their own recently, management scholars and consultants recognize that many lessons can still be learned from their practices. However, we also recognize that cultural differences must be considered in the process. Specifically, what works in Japan may not work as well elsewhere, at least not without some modifications. Japan's highly collectivist society, for example, contrasts markedly with the highly individualistic cultures of the United States and other Western nations. It is only reasonable to expect differences in their management and organizational practices.

BEST PRACTICES AROUND THE WORLD

An appropriate goal in global organizational learning is to identify the "best practices" found around the world. What is being done well in other settings may be of great value at home, whether that "home" is in Africa, Asia, Europe, North America, or anywhere else. Whereas the world at large once looked mainly to the North Americans and Europeans for management insights, today we recognize that potential "benchmarks" of excellence for high performance organizations can be discovered anywhere. For example, as discussed above, the influence of the Japanese approaches as a stimulus to global organizational learning is evident in many of the workplace themes with which you will become familiar in this book. They include growing attention to the value of teams and workgroups, consensus decision making, employee involvement, flatter structures, and strong corporate cultures.

As the field of organizational behavior continues to mature in its global research and understanding, we will all benefit from an expanding knowledge base that is enriched by cultural diversity. Organizational behavior is a science of contingencies, and one of them is culture. No one culture possesses all of the "right" answers to today's complex management and organizational problems. But, a sincere commitment to global organizational learning can give us fresh ideas while still permitting locally appropriate solutions to be implemented with cultural sensitivity. This search for global understanding will be reflected in the following chapters as we move further into the vast domain of OB.

CHAPTER 3 SUMMARY

Why is globalization significant to organizational behavior?

- Globalization, with its complex worldwide economic networks of business competition, resource supplies, and product markets, is having a major impact on businesses, employers, and workforces around the world.

- Nations in Europe, North America, and Asia are forming regional trade agreements, such as the EU, NAFTA, and APEC, to gain economic strength in the highly competitive global economy.

- More and more organizations, large and small, do an increasing amount of business abroad; more and more local employers are "foreign" owned, in whole or in part; the domestic workforce is becoming multicultural and more diverse.

- All organizations need global managers with the special interests and talents needed to excel in international work and cross-cultural relationships.

What is culture?

- Culture is the learned and shared way of doing things in a society; it represents deeply ingrained influences on the way people from different societies think, behave, and solve problems.

- Popular dimensions of culture include observable differences in language, time orientation, use of space, and religion.

- Hofstede's five national culture dimensions are power distance, individualism-collectivism, uncertainty avoidance, masculinity-femininity, and long/short-term orientation.
- Trompenaars's framework for understanding cultural differences focuses on relationships among people, attitudes toward time, and attitudes toward the environment.
- Cross-cultural awareness requires a clear understanding of one's own culture and the ability to overcome the limits of parochialism and ethnocentrism.

How does globalization affect people at work?

- Multinational corporations (MNCs) are global businesses that operate with a worldwide scope; they are powerful forces in the global economy.
- Multiculturalism in the domestic workforce requires everyone to work well with people of different cultural backgrounds.
- Expatriate employees who work abroad for extended periods of time face special challenges, including possible adjustment problems abroad and reentry problems upon returning home.
- Ethical behavior across cultures is examined from the perspectives of cultural relativism and universalism.

What is a global view on organizational learning?

- A global view on learning about OB seeks to understand the best practices from around the world, with due sensitivity to cultural differences.
- Management concepts and theories must always be considered relative to the cultures in which they are developed and applied.
- Interest in Japanese management practices continues, with the traditional focus on long-term employment, emphasis on teams, quality commitment, careful career development, and consensus decision making.
- Global learning will increasingly move beyond North America, Europe, and Japan to include best practices anywhere in the world.

4

Diversity and
Individual Differences

Study Questions

An understanding of individual differences and similarities is crucial in today's diverse organizations. As you read Chapter 4, keep in mind these key questions.

- What is workforce diversity, and why is it important?
- What are demographic differences among individuals, and why are they important?
- What are aptitude and ability differences among individuals, and why are they important?
- What are personality determinants and differences among individuals, and why are they important?
- What are value and attitude differences among individuals, and why are they important?
- What does managing diversity and individual differences involve, and why is it important?

As our society evolves, diversity is, and should be, a major concern of organizations, and valuing diversity in all aspects of operations should be a top priority. With diversity comes differences, and with differences come the potential for problems in relationships. That cannot be denied. But importantly, too, with diversity comes the great potential for new perspectives. Creativity and expanded problem solving can help meet the needs of our complex and dynamic work settings. In this chapter, we examine diversity and differences within the framework of organizational behavior for their workplace implications.

WORKFORCE DIVERSITY

A majority of Fortune 500 companies, including Colgate Palmolive, Corning, and Quaker Oats, are now providing incentives for executives to deal successfully with workforce diversity.[1] **Workforce diversity** refers to the presence of individual human characteristics that make people different from one another.[2] More specifically, this diversity comprises key demographic differences among members of a given workforce, including gender, race and ethnicity, age, and able-bodiedness. Sometimes they also encompass other factors, such as marital status, parental status, and religion.[3] The challenge is how to manage workforce diversity in a way that both respects the individual's unique perspectives and contributions and promotes a shared sense of organization vision and identity.

Workforce diversity has increased in both the United States and Canada, as it has in much of the rest of the world. For example, in the United States, between 1990 and 2005, about 50 percent of the new entrants to the labor force will be women and racial and ethnic groups such as African Americans, Latinos, and Asians. At the same time, those 55 and older are projected to make up nearly 15 percent of the labor force. All of this is in sharp contrast to the traditional, younger, mostly white American male labor force. Canadian and U.K. trends for women are similar.[4]

As the workforce becomes increasingly diverse, the possibility of stereotyping and discrimination increases and managing diversity becomes more important. **Stereotyping** occurs when one thinks of an individual as belonging to a group or category—for instance, elderly person—and the characteristics commonly associated with the group or category are assigned to the individual in question—for instance, older people aren't creative. Demographic characteristics may serve as the basis of stereotypes that obscure individual differences and prevent people from getting to know others as individuals and accurately assessing their performance potential. If you believe that older people are not creative, for example, you may mistakenly decide not to assign a very inventive 60-year-old person to an important task force.

Discrimination against certain people in the organization is not only a violation of U.S., Canadian, and European Union (EU) laws, but it is also counterproductive because it prevents the contributions of people who are discriminated against from being fully utilized. Many firms are increasingly recognizing that a diverse workforce that reflects societal differences helps bring them closer to their customers.

EQUAL EMPLOYMENT OPPORTUNITY

Equal employment opportunity involves both workplace nondiscrimination and affirmative action. Employment decisions are nondiscriminatory when there is no intent to exclude or disadvantage legally protected groups. *Affirmative action* is a set of remedial actions designed to compensate for proven discrimination or correct for statistical imbalances in the labor force (e.g., local workers are 90 percent Hispanic, and your organization employs only 10 percent Hispanics).[5]

The most comprehensive statute prohibiting employment discrimination is Title VII of the Civil Rights Act of 1964. This act prohibits employers from discriminating against any individual with respect to compensation, terms, or conditions of employment because of race, color, religion, sex, or national origin. Affirmative action plans are required of federal government agencies and federal contractors, as well as organizations found to be in noncompliance with equal employment opportunity provisions. Many organizations also have implemented voluntary affirmative action plans.[6]

Affirmative action is legally driven by federal, state and provincial, and local laws, as well as numerous court cases. It requires written reports containing plans and statistical goals for specific groups of people in terms of such employment practices as hiring, promotions, and layoffs.[7]

MANAGING DIVERSITY

The concept of managing diversity in organizations emphasizes appreciation of differences in creating a setting where everyone feels valued and accepted. An organization's success or progress in managing diversity can be monitored by organizational surveys of attitudes and perceptions, among other means. Managing diversity assumes that groups will retain their own characteristics and will shape the firm as well as be shaped by it, creating a common set of values that will strengthen ties with customers, enhance recruitment, and the like. Sometimes, diversity management is resisted because of fear of change and discomfort with differences. To deal with this resistance, some countries, such as Canada, have laws designed to encourage the management of diversity at the provincial level through Employment Equity Legislation.[8]

DEMOGRAPHIC DIFFERENCES

Demographic characteristics are the background characteristics that help shape what a person becomes. Such attributes may be thought of in both current terms—for example, an employee's current medical status—and historical terms—for instance, where and how long a person has worked at various jobs. Demographic characteristics of special interest from equal employment opportunity and workplace diversity considerations include gender, age, race, ethnicity, and able-bodiedness.

GENDER

The research on working women in general tells us that there are very few differences between men and women that affect job performance (see The Effective Manager 4.1). Thus, men and women show no consistent differences in their problem-solving abilities, analytical skills, competitive drive, motivation, learning ability, or sociability. However, women are reported to be more conforming and to have lower expectations of success than men do. And, women's absenteeism rates tend to be higher than those of men. This latter

---

THE EFFECTIVE MANAGER 4.1
TIPS IN DEALING WITH MALE AND FEMALE MANAGERS

- Do not assume that male and female managers differ in personal qualities.
- Make sure that policies, practices, and programs minimize gender differences in managers' job experiences.
- Do not assume that management success is more likely for either females or males.
- Recognize that there will be excellent, good, and poor managers within each gender.
- Understand that success requires the best use of human talent, regardless of gender.

---

finding may change, however, as we see men starting to play a more active role in raising children; absenteeism is also likely to be less frequent as telecommuting, flexible working hours, and the like become more prevalent.[9] In respect to pay, women's earnings have risen slowly from 59 percent of men's in 1975 to 76 percent most recently.[10] Certainly, this rise is not consistent with the doubling of women in the labor force since 1970.[11]

AGE

The research findings concerning age are particularly important given the aging of the workforce. People 50 years old and older account for 85 percent of the projected labor force growth between 1990 and 2005.[12] Older workers are susceptible to being stereotyped as inflexible and undesirable in other ways. In some cases, workers as young as age forty are considered to be "old" and complain that their experience and skills are no longer valued. Age-discrimination lawsuits are increasingly common in the United States.[13] Such discrimination also operates in Britain, where 44 percent of older managers say they have experienced age discrimination.[14] On the other hand, small businesses in particular tend to value older workers for their experience, stability, and low turnover. Research is consistent with these preferences and also shows lower avoidable absences.[15] Finally, to the extent age is linked to experience or job tenure, there is a positive relationship between seniority and performance. More experienced workers tend to have low absence rates and relatively low turnover.

ABLE-BODIEDNESS

Even though recent studies report that disabled workers do their jobs as well, or better than, nondisabled workers, nearly three quarters of severely disabled persons are reported to be unemployed. Almost 80 percent of those with disabilities say they want to work.[16] Once again, the expected shortage of traditional workers is predicted to lead to a reexamination of hiring policies. More firms are expected to give serious consideration to hiring disabled workers, particularly given that the cost of accommodating these workers has been shown to be low.[17]

RACIAL AND ETHNIC GROUPS

Consistent with some current literature, we use the term *racial and ethnic groups* to reflect the broad spectrum of employees of differing ethnicities or races who make up an ever-increasing portion of the new workforce.[18] Of particular significance in the American workplace is diversity reflected in an increasing proportion of African Americans, Asian Americans, and Hispanic Americans.[19] Projections by the Bureau of Labor Statistics estimate that they will constitute 27 percent of the workforce by the year 2005. The Hudson Institute extends this projection to 32 percent by the year 2020.[20] The potential for stereotypes and discrimination to adversely affect career opportunities and progress for members of these and other minority groups must be recognized.

Even though employment decisions based on demographic differences are allowable under Title VII if they can be justified as bona fide occupational qualifications reasonable to normal business operations, race cannot be one of these. Case law has shown that these qualifications are always extremely difficult to justify.[21] In any event the flight attendant job is a case in point. When the airlines failed to show why men could not perform flight attendant duties as well as females, gender restrictions on hiring were lifted.

Before leaving this section on demographic differences, it is important to reiterate:

- Demographic variables are important to consider in order to respect and best deal with the needs or concerns of people of different genders, ethnic backgrounds, ages, and so forth.
- However, these differences are too easily linked with stereotypes, which must be avoided.
- Demography is not a good indicator in seeking good individual-job fits. Rather aptitude/ability, personality, and values and attitudes are what count.

APTITUDE AND ABILITY

Given the previous discussion, let's consider aptitude and ability. **Aptitude** represents a person's capability of learning something, whereas **ability** reflects a person's existing capacity to perform the various tasks needed for a given job and includes both relevant knowledge and skills.[22] In other words, aptitudes are potential abilities, whereas abilities are the knowledge and skills that an individual currently possesses.

Aptitudes and abilities are important considerations for a manager when initially hiring or selecting candidates for a job. We are all acquainted with various tests used to measure mental aptitudes and abilities. Some of these provide an overall intelligence quotient (IQ) score (e.g., the Stanford-Binet IQ Test). Others provide measures of more specific competencies that are required of people entering various educational programs or career fields. You have probably taken the ACT or SAT college entrance tests. Such tests are designed to facilitate the screening and selection of applicants for educational programs or jobs. In addition to mental aptitudes and abilities, some jobs, such as firefighters and police, require tests for physical abilities. Muscular strength and cardiovascular endurance are two of many physical ability dimensions.[23]

For legal purposes, demonstrated evidence must be presented that those scoring more favorably on the tests will tend to be more successful in their educational program, career field, or job performance than those with lower scores. In other words, there must be a fit between specific aptitudes and abilities and job requirements. If you want to be a surgeon, for instance, and cannot demonstrate good hand-eye coordination, there will not be a good ability-job fit. Such a fit is so important that it is a core concept in Chapter 7 on managing human resources.

PERSONALITY

In addition to demographics and aptitude and ability, a third important individual attribute is personality. The term **personality** represents the overall profile or combination of characteristics that capture the unique nature of a person as that person reacts and interacts with others. As an example, think of a person who was the billionaire founder of a fast-growing, high-tech computer company by the time he was 30; who in his senior year in high school had turned selling newspapers into enough of a business to buy a BMW; who told his management team that his daughter's first words were "Daddy kill-IBM, Gateway, Compaq;" who learned from production mistakes and brought in senior managers to help his firm; and who is so private he seldom talks about himself: In other words, think of Michael Dell, the founder of Dell Computer, and his personality.[24]

Personality combines a set of physical and mental characteristics that reflect how a person looks, thinks, acts, and feels. Sometimes attempts are made to measure personality with questionnaires or special tests. Frequently, personality can be implied from behavior alone, such as by the actions of Michael Dell. Either way, personality is an important individual characteristic for managers to understand. An understanding of personality contributes to an understanding of organizational behavior in that we expect a predictable interplay between an individual's personality and his or her tendency to behave in certain ways.

PERSONALITY DETERMINANTS AND DEVELOPMENT

Just what determines personality? Is personality inherited or genetically determined, or is it formed by experience? You may have heard someone say something like, "She acts like her mother." Similarly, someone may argue that "Bobby is the way he is because of the way he was raised." These two arguments illustrate the nature/nurture controversy: Is personality determined by heredity, that is, by genetic endowment, or by one's environment? As Figure 4.1 shows, these two forces actually operate in combination. Heredity consists of those factors that are determined at conception, including physical characteristics, gender, and personality factors. Environment consists of cultural, social, and situational factors.

The impact of heredity on personality continues to be the source of considerable debate. Perhaps the most general conclusion we can draw is that heredity sets the limits on just how much personality characteristics can be developed; environment determines development within these limits. For instance, a person could be born with a tendency toward authoritarianism, and that tendency could be reinforced in an authoritarian work environment. These limits appear to vary from one characteristic to the next and across all characteristics there is about a 50-50 heredity-environment split.[25]

As we show throughout this book, *cultural values and norms* play a substantial role in the development of an individual's personality and behaviors. Contrast the individualism of U.S. culture with the collectivism of Mexican culture, for example.[26] Social factors reflect such things as family life, religion, and the many kinds of formal and informal groups in which people participate throughout their lives—friendship groups, athletic groups, as well as formal workgroups. Finally, the demands of differing *situational factors* emphasize or constrain different aspects of an individual's personality. For example, in class you are likely to rein in your high spirits and other related behaviors encouraged by your personality. However, at a sporting event, you may be jumping up, cheering, and loudly criticizing the referees.

The **developmental approaches** of Chris Argyris, Daniel Levinson, and Gail Sheehy systematically examine the ways personality develops across time. Argyris notes that people develop along a continuum of dimensions from immaturity to maturity as shown in Figure 4.2. He believes that many organizations treat mature adults as if they were still immature and this creates many problems in terms of bringing out the best in employees. Levinson and Sheehy maintain that an individual's personality unfolds in a series of stages across time. Sheehy's model, for example, talks about three stages—ages 18–30, 30–45, and 45–85+. Each of these has a crucial impact on the worker's employment and career, as we show in Chapter 7. The implications are that personalities develop over time and require different managerial responses. Thus, needs and other personality aspects of people initially entering an organization change sharply as they move through different stages or toward increased maturity.[27]

FIGURE 4.1	HEREDITY AND ENVIRONMENTAL LINKAGE WITH PERSONALITY

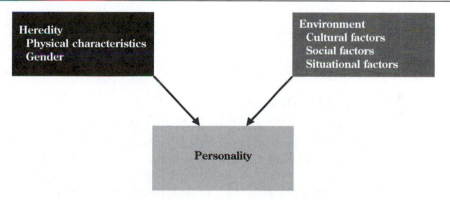

Heredity
  Physical characteristics
  Gender

Environment
  Cultural factors
  Social factors
  Situational factors

Personality

FIGURE 4.2	ARGYRIS'S MATURITY—IMMATURITY CONTINUUM

From Immaturity	To Maturity
Passivity	Activity
Dependence	Independence
Limited behavior	Diverse behavior
Shallow interests	Deep interests
Short time perspective	Long time perspective
Subordinate position	Superordinate position
Little self-awareness	Much self-awareness

PERSONALITY TRAITS AND CLASSIFICATIONS

Numerous lists of personality traits—enduring characteristics describing an individual's behavior—have been developed, many of which have been used in OB research and can be looked at in different ways. First, recent research has examined people using extensive lists of personality dimensions and distilled them into the "Big Five":[28]

- *Extraversion*—outgoing, sociable, assertive
- *Agreeableness*—good-natured, trusting, cooperative
- *Conscientiousness*—responsible, dependable, persistent
- *Emotional stability*—unworried, secure, relaxed
- *Openness to experience*—imaginative, curious, broad-minded

Standardized personality tests determine how positively or negatively an individual scores on each of these dimensions. For instance, a person scoring high on openness to experience tends to ask lots of questions and to think in new and unusual ways. You can consider a person's individual personality profile across the five dimensions. In terms of job performance, research has shown that conscientiousness predicts job performance across five occupational groups of professions—engineers, police, managers, sales, and skilled and semiskilled employees. Predictability of the other dimensions depends on the occupational group. For instance, not surprisingly, extraversion predicts performance for sales and managerial positions.

A second approach to looking at OB personality traits is to divide them into social traits, personal conception traits, and emotional adjustment traits, and then to consider how those categories come together dynamically.[29]

SOCIAL TRAITS

Social traits are surface-level traits that reflect the way a person appears to others when interacting in various social settings. Problem-solving style, based on the work of Carl Jung, a noted psychologist, is one measure representing social traits.[30] It reflects the way a person goes about gathering and evaluating information in solving problems and making decisions.

Information gathering involves getting and organizing data for use. Styles of information gathering vary from sensation to intuitive. *Sensation-type individuals* prefer routine and order and emphasize well-defined details in gathering information; they would rather work with known facts than look for possibilities. By contrast, *intuitive-type individuals* prefer the "big picture." They like solving new problems, dislike routine, and would rather look for possibilities than work with facts.

The second component of problem solving, *evaluation*, involves making judgments about how to deal with information once it has been collected. Styles of information evaluation vary from an emphasis on feeling to an emphasis on thinking. *Feeling-type individuals* are oriented toward conformity and try to accommodate themselves to other people. They try to avoid problems that may result in disagreements. *Thinking-type individuals* use reason and intellect to deal with problems and downplay emotions.

When these two dimensions (information gathering and evaluation) are combined, four basic problem-solving styles result: sensation-feeling (SF), intuitive-feeling (IF), sensation-thinking (ST), and intuitive-thinking (IT), together with summary descriptions, as shown in Figure 4.3.

Research indicates that there is a fit between the styles of individuals and the kinds of decisions they prefer. For example, STs (sensation-thinkers) prefer analytical strategies—those that emphasize detail and method. IFs (intuitive-feelers) prefer intuitive strategies—those that emphasize an overall pattern and fit. Not surprisingly, mixed styles (sensation-feelers or intuitive-thinkers) select both analytical and intuitive strategies. Other findings also indicate that thinkers tend to have higher motivation than do feelers and that individuals who emphasize sensations tend to have higher job satisfaction than do intuitives. These and other findings suggest a number of basic differences among different problem-solving styles, emphasizing the importance of fitting such styles with a task's information processing and evaluation requirements.[31]

Problem-solving styles are most frequently measured by the (typically 100-item) *Myers-Briggs Type Indicator (MBTI),* which asks individuals how they usually act or feel in specific situations. Firms such as Apple, AT&T, and Exxon, as well as hospitals, educational institutions, and military organizations, have used the Myers-Briggs for various aspects of management development.[32]

FIGURE 4.3   **FOUR PROBLEM-SOLVING STYLE SUMMARIES**

S

Sensation-*Feeling*	Sensation-*Thinking*
Interpersonal	**Technical detail-oriented**
Specific human detail	**Logical analysis of hard data**
Friendly, sympathetic	**Precise, orderly**
Open communication	**Careful about rules and procedures**
Respond to people now	**Dependable, responsible**
Good at:	*Good at*:
Empathizing	**Observing, ordering**
Cooperating	**Filing, recalling**
Goal: **To be helpful**	*Goal*: **Do it correctly**
Illustrated by: **Anita Rudick, CEO Body Shop International (International Cosmetics Organization)**	*Illustrated by*: **Enita Nordeck, President Unity Forest Products (a small and growing builder's supply firm)**

F ← → T

Intuitive-*Feeling*	Intuitive-*Thinking*
Insightful, mystical	**Speculative**
Idealistic, personal	**Emphasize understanding**
Creative, original	**Synthesize, interpret**
Global ideas oriented to people	**Logic-oriented ideas**
Human potential	**Objective, impersonal, idealistic**
Good at:	*Good at*:
Imagining	**Discovery, inquiry**
New combinations	**Problem solving**
Goal: **To make things beautiful**	*Goal*: **To think things through**
Illustrated by: **Herb Kelleher, former CEO, Southwest Airlines (a fast-growing, large, regional airline)**	*Illustrated by*: **Paul Allaire, former CEO, Xerox Corporation (a huge multi-national, recently innovatively reorganized)**

I

PERSONAL CONCEPTION TRAITS

The *personal conception traits* represent the way individuals tend to think about their social and physical setting, as well as their major beliefs and personal orientation concerning a range of issues.

Locus of Control   The extent to which a person feels able to control his or her own life is concerned with a person's internal-external orientation and is measured by Rotter's locus of control instrument.[33] People have personal conceptions about whether events are controlled primarily by themselves, which indicates an internal orientation, or by outside forces, such as their social and physical environment, which indicates an external orientation. Internals, or persons with an internal locus of control, believe that they control their own fate or destiny. In contrast, externals, or persons with an external locus of control, believe that much of what happens to them is beyond their control and is determined by environmental forces.

In general, externals are more extraverted in their interpersonal relationships and are more oriented toward the world around them. Internals tend to be more introverted and are more oriented toward their own feelings and ideas. Figure 4.4 suggests that internals tend to do better on tasks requiring complex information processing and learning, as well as initiative. Many managerial and professional jobs have these kinds of requirements.

FIGURE 4.4	SOME WAYS IN WHICH INTERNALS DIFFER FROM EXTERNALS

Information processing	Internals make more attempts to acquire information, are less satisfied with the amount of information they possess, and are better at utilizing information.
Job satisfaction	Internals are generally more satisfied, less alienated, less rootless, and there is a stronger job satisfaction/ performance relationship for them.
Performance	Internals perform better on learning and problem-solving tasks, when performance leads to valued rewards.
Self-control, risk, and anxiety	Internals exhibit greater self-control, are more cautious, engage in less risky behavior, and are less anxious.
Motivation, expectancies, and results	Internals display greater work motivation, see a stronger relationship between what they do and what happens to them, expect that working hard leads to good performance, feel more control over their time.
Response to others	Internals are more independent, more reliant on their own judgment, and less susceptible to the influence of others; they are more likely to accept information on its merit.

Authoritarianism/Dogmatism   Both "authoritarianism" and "dogmatism" deal with the rigidity of a person's beliefs. A person high in **authoritarianism** tends to adhere rigidly to conventional values and to obey recognized authority. This person is concerned with toughness and power and opposes the use of subjective feelings. An individual high in **dogmatism** sees the world as a threatening place. This person regards legitimate authority as absolute and accepts or rejects others according to how much they agree with accepted authority. Superiors who possess these latter traits tend to be rigid and closed. At the same time, dogmatic subordinates tend to want certainty imposed upon them.[34]

From an ethical standpoint, we can expect highly authoritarian individuals to present a special problem because they are so susceptible to authority that in their eagerness to comply they may behave unethically.[35] For example, we might speculate that many of the Nazis who were involved in war crimes during World War II were high in authoritarianism or dogmatism; they believed so strongly in authority that they followed their unethical orders without question.

Machiavellianism   The third personal conceptions dimension is Machiavellianism, which owes its origins to Niccolo Machiavelli. The very name of this sixteenth-century author evokes visions of a master of guile, deceit, and opportunism in interpersonal relations. Machiavelli earned his place in history by writing *The Prince,* a nobleman's guide to the acquisition and use of power.[36] The subject of Machiavelli's book is manipulation as the basic means of gaining and keeping control of others. From its pages emerges the personality profile of a Machiavellian—someone who views and manipulates others purely for personal gain.

Psychologists have developed a series of instruments called Mach scales to measure a person's Machiavellian orientation.[37] A high-Mach personality is someone who tends to behave in ways consistent with Machiavelli's basic principles. Such individuals approach situations logically and thoughtfully and are even capable of lying to achieve personal goals. They are rarely swayed by loyalty, friendships, past promises, or the opinions of others, and they are skilled at influencing others.

Research using the Mach scales provides insight into the way high and low Machs may be expected to behave in various situations. A person with a "cool" and "detached" high-Mach personality can be expected to take control and try to exploit loosely structured environmental situations but will perform in a perfunctory, even detached, manner in highly structured situations. Low Machs tend to accept direction imposed by others in loosely structured situations; they work hard to do well in highly structured ones. For example, we might expect that, where the situation permitted, a high Mach would do or say whatever it took to get his or her way. In contrast, a low Mach would tend to be much more strongly guided by ethical considerations and would be less likely to lie or cheat or to get away with lying or cheating.

Self-Monitoring   A final personal conceptions trait of special importance to managers is self-monitoring. **Self-monitoring** reflects a person's ability to adjust his or her behavior to external, situational (environmental) factors.[38]

High self-monitoring individuals are sensitive to external cues and tend to behave differently in different situations. Like high Machs, high self-monitors can present a very different appearance from their true self. In contrast, low self-monitors, like their low-Mach counterparts, aren't able to disguise their behaviors—"what you see is what you get." There is also evidence that high self-monitors are closely attuned to the behavior of others and conform more readily than do low self-monitors.[39] Thus, they appear flexible and may be especially good at responding to the kinds of situational contingencies emphasized throughout this book. For example, high self-monitors should be especially good at changing their leadership behavior to fit subordinates with high or low experience, tasks with high or low structure, and so on.

EMOTIONAL ADJUSTMENT TRAITS

The **emotional adjustment traits** measure how much an individual experiences emotional distress or displays unacceptable acts. Often the person's health is affected. Although numerous such traits are cited in the literature, a frequently encountered one especially important for OB is the Type A/Type B orientation.

Type A and Type B Orientation To get a feel for this orientation, take the following quiz and then read on.[40] Circle the number that best characterizes you on each of the following pairs of characteristics.

Casual about appointments	1 2 3 4 5 6 7 8	Never late
Not competitive	1 2 3 4 5 6 7 8	Very competitive
Never feel rushed	1 2 3 4 5 6 7 8	Always feel rushed
Take one thing at a time	1 2 3 4 5 6 7 8	Try to do many things
Do things slowly	1 2 3 4 5 6 7 8	Do things fast
Express my feelings	1 2 3 4 5 6 7 8	Hold in my feelings
Many outside interests	1 2 3 4 5 6 7 8	Few outside interests

Total your points for the seven items in the quiz. Multiply this total by 3 to arrive at a final score. Use this total to locate your Type A/Type B orientation on the following list.

Final Points	**A/B Orientation**
Below 90	B
90–99	B+
100–105	A-
106–119	A
120 or more	A+

Individuals with a **Type A orientation** are characterized by impatience, desire for achievement, and perfectionism. In contrast, those with **Type B orientations** are characterized as more easygoing and less competitive in relation to daily events.[41]

Type A people tend to work fast and to be abrupt, uncomfortable, irritable, and aggressive. Such tendencies indicate "obsessive" behavior, a fairly widespread—but not always helpful—trait among managers. Many managers are hard-driving, detail-oriented people who have high performance standards and thrive on routine. But when such work obsessions are carried to the extreme, they may lead to greater concerns for details than for results, resistance to change, overzealous control of subordinates, and various kinds of interpersonal difficulties, which may even include threats and physical violence. In contrast, Type B managers tend to be much more laid back and patient in their dealings with co-workers and subordinates.

PERSONALITY AND SELF-CONCEPT

Collectively, the ways in which an individual integrates and organizes the previously discussed categories and the traits they contain are referred to as **personality dynamics.** It is this category that makes personality more than just the sum of the separate traits. A key personality dynamic in your study of OB is the self-concept.

We can describe the **self-concept** as the view individuals have of themselves as physical, social, and spiritual or moral beings.[42] It is a way of recognizing oneself as a distinct human being. A person's self-concept is greatly influenced by his or her culture. For example, Americans tend to disclose much more about themselves than do the English; that is, an American's self-concept is more assertive and talkative.[43]

Two related—and crucial—aspects of the self-concept are self-esteem and self-efficacy. *Self-esteem* is a belief about one's own worth based on an overall self-evaluation.[44] People high in self-esteem see themselves as capable, worthwhile, and acceptable and tend to have few doubts about themselves. The opposite is true of a person low in self-esteem. Some OB research suggests that, whereas high self-esteem generally can boost performance and human resource maintenance, when under pressure, people with high self-esteem may become boastful and act egotistically. They also may be overconfident at times and fail to obtain important information.[45]

Self-efficacy, sometimes called the "effectance motive," is a more specific version of self-esteem; it is an individual's belief about the likelihood of successfully completing a specific task. You could be high in self-esteem, yet have a feeling of low self-efficacy about performing a certain task, such as public speaking.

VALUES AND ATTITUDES

Joining demographic and personality characteristics as important individual difference characteristics are values and attitudes.

VALUES

Values can be defined as broad preferences concerning appropriate courses of action or outcomes. As such, values reflect a person's sense of right and wrong or what "ought" to be.[46] "Equal rights for all" and "People should be treated with respect and dignity" are representative of values. Values tend to influence attitudes and behavior. For example, if you value equal rights for all and you go to work for an organization that treats its managers much better than it does its workers, you may form the attitude that the company is an unfair place to work; consequently, you may not produce well or may perhaps leave the company. It's likely that if the company had had a more equalitarian policy, your attitude and behaviors would have been more positive.

Sources and Types of Values   Parents, friends, teachers, and external reference groups can all influence individual values. Indeed, peoples' values develop as a product of the learning and experience they encounter in the cultural setting in which they live. As learning and experiences differ from one person to another, value differences result. Such differences are likely to be deep seated and difficult (though not impossible) to change; many have their roots in early childhood and the way a person has been raised.[47]

The noted psychologist Milton Rokeach has developed a well-known set of values classified into two broad categories.[48] **Terminal values** reflect a person's preferences concerning the "ends" to be achieved; they are the goals individuals would like to achieve during their lifetime. Rokeach divides values into 18 terminal values and 18 instrumental values, as summarized in Figure 4.5. **Instrumental values** reflect the "means" for achieving desired ends. They represent how you might go about achieving your important end states, depending on the relative importance you attached to the instrumental values.

Illustrative research shows, not surprisingly, that both terminal and instrumental values differ by group (for example, executives, activist workers, and union members).[49] These preference differences can encourage conflict or agreement when different groups have to deal with each other.

Another frequently used classification of human values has been developed by psychologist Gordon Allport and his associates. These values fall into six major types:[50]

- *Theoretical*—interest in the discovery of truth through reasoning and systematic thinking.

- *Economic*—interest in usefulness and practicality, including the accumulation of wealth.

FIGURE 4.5   **ROKEACH VALUE SURVEY**

Terminal Values	Instrumental Values
A comfortable life (and prosperous)	Ambitious (hardworking)
An exciting life (stimulating)	Broad-minded (open-minded)
A sense of accomplishment (lasting contribution)	Capable (competent, effective)
A world at peace (free of war and conflict)	Cheerful (lighthearted, joyful)
A world of beauty (beauty of nature and the arts)	Clean (neat, tidy)
Equality (brotherhood, equal opportunity)	Courageous (standing up for beliefs)
Family security (taking care of loved ones)	Forgiving (willing to pardon)
Freedom (independence, free choice)	Helpful (working for others' welfare)
Happiness (contentedness)	Honest (sincere, truthful)
Inner harmony (freedom from inner conflict)	Imaginative (creative, daring)
Mature love (sexual and spiritual intimacy)	Independent (self-sufficient, self-reliant)
National security (attack protection)	Intellectual (intelligent, reflective)
Pleasure (leisurely, enjoyable life)	Logical (rational, consistent)
Salvation (saved, eternal life)	Loving (affectionate, tender)
Self-respect (self-esteem)	Obedient (dutiful, respectful)
Social recognition (admiration, respect)	Polite (courteous, well-mannered)
True friendship (close companionship)	Responsible (reliable, dependable)
Wisdom (mature understanding of life)	Self-controlled (self-disciplined)

- *Aesthetic*—interest in beauty, form, and artistic harmony.
- *Social*—interest in people and love as a human relationship.
- *Political*—interest in gaining power and influencing other people.
- *Religious*—interest in unity and in understanding the cosmos as a whole.

Once again, groups differ in the way they rank order the importance of these values, as shown in the following.[51]

- *Ministers*—religious, social, aesthetic, political, theoretical, economic.
- *Purchasing Executive*—economic, theoretical, political, religious, aesthetic, social.
- *Industrial Scientists*—theoretical, political, economic, aesthetic, religious, social.

The previous value classifications have had a major impact on the values literature, but they were not specifically designed for people in a work setting. A more recent values schema, developed by Maglino and associates, is aimed at people in the workplace:[52]

- *Achievement*—getting things done and working hard to accomplish difficult things in life.
- *Helping and Concern for Others*—being concerned with other people and helping others.
- *Honesty*—telling the truth and doing what you feel is right.
- *Fairness*—being impartial and doing what is fair for all concerned.

These four values have been shown to be especially important in the workplace; thus, the framework should be particularly relevant for studying values in OB.

In particular, values can be influential through **value congruence,** which occurs when individuals express positive feelings upon encountering others who exhibit values similar to their own. When values differ, or are *incongruent,* conflicts over such things as goals and the means to achieve them may result. The Maglino et al. value schema was used to examine value congruence between leaders and followers. The researchers found greater follower satisfaction with the leader when there was such congruence in terms of achievement, helping, honesty, and fairness values.[53]

Patterns and Trends in Values   We should also be aware of applied research and insightful analyses of values trends over time. Daniel Yankelovich, for example, is known for his informative public opinion polls among North American workers, and William Fox has prepared a carefully reasoned book analyzing values trends.[54] Both Yankelovich and Fox note movements away from earlier values, with Fox emphasizing a decline in such shared values as duty, honesty, responsibility, and the like, while Yankelovich notes a movement away from valuing economic incentives, organizational loyalty, and work-related identity. The movement is toward valuing meaningful work, pursuit of leisure, and personal identity and self-fulfillment. Yankelovich believes that the modern manager must be able to recognize value differences and trends among people at work. For example, he reports finding higher productivity among younger workers who are employed in jobs that match their values and/or who are supervised by managers who share their values, reinforcing the concept of value congruence.

In a nationwide sample, managers and human-resource professionals were asked to identify the work-related values they believed to be most important to individuals in the workforce, both now and in the near future.[55] The nine most popular values named were: recognition for competence and accomplishments; respect and dignity; personal choice and freedom; involvement at work; pride in one's work; lifestyle quality; financial security; self-development; and health and wellness. These values are especially important for managers because they indicate some key concerns of the new workforce. Even though each individual worker places his or her own importance on these values, and even though the United States today has by far the most diverse workforce in its history, this overall characterization is a good place for managers to start when dealing with workers in the new workplace. It is important to note, however, that, although values are individual preferences, many tend to be shared within cultures and organizations.

ATTITUDES

Attitudes are influenced by values and are acquired from the same sources as values: friends, teachers, parents, and role models. Attitudes focus on specific people or objects, whereas values have a more general focus and are more stable than attitudes. "Employees should be allowed to participate" is a value; your positive or negative feeling about your job because of the participation it allows is an attitude. Formally defined, an **attitude** is a predisposition to respond in a positive or negative way to someone or something in one's environment. For example, when you say that you "like" or "dislike" someone or something, you are expressing an attitude. It's important to remember that an attitude, like a value, is a hypothetical construct; that is, one never sees, touches, or actually isolates an attitude. Rather, attitudes are *inferred* from the things people say, informally or in formal opinion polls or through their behavior.

Figure 4.6 shows attitudes as accompanied by antecedents and results.[56] The beliefs and values antecedents in the figure form the **cognitive component** of an attitude: the beliefs, opinions, knowledge, or information a person possesses. **Beliefs** represent ideas about someone or something and the conclusions people draw about them; they convey a sense of "what is" to an individual. "My job lacks responsibility" is a belief shown in the figure. Note that the beliefs may or may not be accurate. "Responsibility is important" is a corresponding aspect of the cognitive component, which reflects an underlying value.

The **affective component** of an attitude is a specific feeling regarding the personal impact of the antecedents. This is the actual attitude itself, such as "I don't like my job." The

---

FIGURE 4.6 | **A WORK-RELATED EXAMPLE OF THE THREE COMPONENTS OF ATTITUDES**

ANTECEDENTS		ATTITUDE		RESULT
Beliefs and values	— create —	Feelings	that influence →	Intended behavior
"My job lacks responsibility." "Job responsibility is important."		"I don't like my job."		"I'm going to quit my job."

behavioral component is an intention to behave in a certain way based on your specific feelings or attitudes. This intended behavior is a result of an attitude and is a predisposition to act in a specific way, such as "I'm going to quit my job."

Attitudes and Behavior   You should recognize that the link between attitudes and behavior is tentative. An attitude results in *intended* behavior; this intention may or may not be carried out in a given circumstance.

In general, the more specific attitudes and behaviors are, the stronger the relationship. For example, say you are a French-Canadian webmaster and you are asked about your satisfaction with your supervisor's treatment of French-Canadian webmasters. You also indicate the strength of your intent to look for another webmaster job in a similar kind of organization within the next six months. Here, both the attitude and the behavior are specifically stated (they refer to French-Canadian webmasters, and they identify a given kind of organization over a specific time period). Thus, we would expect to find a relatively strong relationship between these attitudes and how aggressively you actually start looking for another webmaster job.

It is also important that a good deal of freedom be available to carry out the intent. In the example just given, the freedom to follow through would be sharply restricted if the demand for webmasters dropped substantially.

Finally, the attitude and behavior linkage tends to be stronger when the person in question has had experience with the stated attitude. For example, assuming you are a business administration or management major, the relationship between your course attitude and/or your intent to drop the course and your later behavior of actually doing so would probably be stronger in your present OB course than in the first week of your enrollment in an advanced course in nuclear fission.[57]

Even though attitudes do not always predict behavior, the link between attitudes and potential or intended behavior is important for managers to understand. Think about your work experiences or conversations with other people about their work. It is not uncommon to hear concerns expressed about someone's "bad attitude." These concerns typically reflect displeasure with the behavioral consequences with which the poor attitude is associated. Unfavorable attitudes in the form of low job satisfaction can result in costly labor turnover, absenteeism, tardiness, and even impaired physical or mental health. One of the manager's responsibilities, therefore, is to recognize attitudes and to understand both their antecedents and their potential implications.

Attitudes and Cognitive Consistency   Leon Festinger, a noted social psychologist, uses the term **cognitive dissonance** to describe a state of inconsistency between an individual's attitudes and his or her behavior.[58] Let's assume that you have the attitude that recycling is good for the economy but you don't recycle. Festinger predicts that such an inconsistency results in discomfort and a desire to reduce or eliminate it by (1) changing the underlying attitude, (2) changing future behavior, or (3) developing new ways of explaining or rationalizing the inconsistency.

Two factors that influence which of the above choices tend to be made are the degree of control a person thinks he or she has over the situation and the magnitude of the rewards involved. In terms of control, if your boss won't let you recycle office trash, you would be less likely to change your attitude than if you voluntarily chose not to recycle. You might instead choose the rationalization option. In terms of rewards, if they are high enough, rewards tend to reduce your feeling of inconsistency: If I'm rewarded even though I don't recycle, the lack of recycling must not be so bad after all.

MANAGING DIVERSITY AND INDIVIDUAL DIFFERENCES

Dealing with diversity and individual differences has to be included among the most important issues challenging all managers in the quest for high performance and organizational competitiveness. This is true not only in the United States but also in Canada, European Union countries, and several countries in Asia.[59] Only the details differ.

So how do managers deal with all this? To convey the flavor of what some of the more progressive employers have done in managing diversity, let's now consider Boston-based Harvard Pilgrim Health Care (HPHC). Barbara Stern is the vice president of diversity.[60] She argues that what has traditionally been a "soft" issue is now becoming a business necessity in terms of better serving customers, understanding markets, and obtaining full benefit from staff talents. Each year, HPHC attempts to increase its diversity in terms of the proportion of women and racial minorities by 0.5 percent, which allows for continuous improvement. Such improvement raised the proportion of minority new hires from 14 to 28 percent over four years, and the total minority employees went from 16 to 21 percent over the same period.

To ensure that diversity was more than just a fad, a corporate diversity council was established. This council set up specific actions to serve as the initial focus of the diversity efforts. The council determined it needed a vice presidential-level person to oversee the effort. The council's goals were: (1) to create accountability for measuring diversity (tie meeting of diversity goals into salaries of the organization's top 85 managers); (2) to provide a custom-made education program; (3) to develop an explicit code of conduct and communication with a zero-tolerance policy (for example, the code spells out inappropriate behavior such as racist jokes and creates appropriate expectations and behavior standards); (4) to commit to creating diverse candidate pools for all managerial hiring and promotion decisions (traditional closed networks that were once used are no longer appropriate); and (5) to use cultural audits, surveys, focus groups, and broad networking groups to assess diversity.

HPHC also includes seven questions in a carefully phrased opinion survey. Questions such as how employees feel they are valued; what they feel their career opportunities are; and how well the organization supports work-life balance, are asked. HPHC uses improvements in these areas as partial indicators of successful diversity.

The organization also includes the Health Triangle—a networking group of more than 200 gay and lesbian employees—and the Disability Council to help the company keep abreast of issues relevant to each group of employees. These groups also have helped to attract additional customers.

Stern, the VP, argues that simplicity and clarity are keys in diversity communication. She states that one should be able to communicate the information in 10 minutes and make it easy to understand; represent the data in a variety of ways; report on progress; and keep people at all levels informed about the progress. The Effective Manager 4.2 provides an example and illustrates insights suitable for diversity programs in general.

THE EFFECTIVE MANAGER 4.2

DIVERSITY CHECKUP REPORT

The Checkup Report used at Harvard Pilgrim Health Care combines interviews, internal and external data, and research results in the following areas:

- Recruitment in candidates of color
- Community demographic changes
- Women in leadership
- Attraction and retention of gays and lesbians
- Able-bodiedness among employees
- Flexible work arrangements
- Non-English-speaking customers
- White men
- Customer service

The following factors, encompassing and moving beyond those of HPHC, have been obtained from in-depth interviews and focus groups—they are important in tracking diversity programs: demographics, organizational culture, accountability, productivity, growth and profitability, benchmarking against the "best" programs, and measurement of the program.[61] Additionally, the Society for Human Resource Management (SHRM) has developed a survey instrument for focusing on a bottom-line analysis of diversity programs.[62]

Some firms, such as Microsoft, have moved far toward measurement and computerization of key diversity measures. Three Microsoft employees, Stutz, Massengale, and Gordon, developed the SMG Index acronym. It provides a separate bottom-line figure, encompassing both Microsoft's women and minorities; it allows managers to analyze goals and accomplishments for both affirmative action and diversity. The lower the SMG Index (zero is best), the lower the percentage of hires, promotions, and/or retentions needed to correct group disparities. The Index is compared across groups and time.[63]

CHAPTER 4 SUMMARY

What is workforce diversity, and why is it important?

- Workforce diversity is the mix of gender, race and ethnicity, age, and able-bodiedness in the workforce.
- Workforces in the United States, Canada, and Europe are becoming more diverse, and valuing and managing such diversity is becoming increasingly more important to enhance organizational competitiveness and provide individual development.

What are demographic differences among individuals, and why are they important?

- Demographic differences are background characteristics that help shape what a person has become.

- Gender, age, race and ethnicity, and able-bodiedness are particularly important demographic characteristics.
- The use of demographic differences in employment is covered by a series of federal, state/provincial, and local laws outlawing discrimination.
- Demographic differences can be the basis for inappropriate stereotyping that can influence workplace decisions and behaviors.

What are aptitude and ability differences among individuals, and why are they important?

- Aptitude is a person's capability of learning something.
- Ability is a person's existing capacity to perform the various tasks needed for a given job.
- Aptitudes are potential abilities.
- Both mental and physical aptitudes and abilities are used in matching individuals to organizations and jobs.

What are personality determinants and differences among individuals, and why are they important?

- Personality captures the overall profile or combination of characteristics that represent the unique nature of an individual as that individual interacts with others.
- Personality is determined by both heredity and environment; across all personality characteristics, the mix of heredity and environment is about 50–50.
- The Big Five personality framework consists of extraversion, agreeableness, conscientiousness, emotional stability, and openness to experience.
- A useful personality framework consists of social traits, personal conceptions, emotional adjustment, and personality dynamics, where each category represents one or more personality dimensions.
- Personality characteristics are important because of their predictable interplay with an individual's behavior. Along with demographics and aptitude/ability differences, personality characteristics must be matched to organizations and jobs.

What are value and attitude differences among individuals, and why are they important?

- Values are broad preferences concerning courses of action or outcomes.
- Rokeach divides 18 values into terminal values (preferences concerning ends) and instrumental values (preferences concerning means).
- Allport and his associates identify six value categories, ranging from theoretical to religious.
- Meglino and his associates classify values into achievement, helping and concern for others, honesty, and fairness.
- There have been societal changes in value patterns away from economic and organizational loyalty and toward meaningful work and self-fulfillment.

- Attitudes are a predisposition to respond positively or negatively to someone or something in one's environment; they are influenced by values but are more specific.
- Individuals desire consistency between their attitudes and their behaviors.
- Values and attitudes are important because they indicate predispositions toward behaviors.
- Along with demographics, aptitude/ability, and personality differences, values and attitudes need to be matched to organizations and jobs.

What does managing diversity and individual differences involve, and why is it important?

- Managing diversity and individual differences involves striving for a match between the firm, specific jobs, and the people recruited, hired, and developed, while recognizing an increasingly diverse workforce.
- Affirmative action; ethical considerations; local, national, and global competitive pressures; and a projected change in the nature of the workforce provide increasing workforce diversity.
- Once a match between organizational and job requirements and individual characteristics is obtained, it is necessary to manage the increasing diversity in the workforce.
- Firms now use a wide variety of practices in managing workforce diversity; for example: interactive networks, recruitment, education, development, promotion, pay, and assessment.

5

Perception and Attribution

Study Questions

Perceptions and attributions influence an individual's interpretation of his or her environment. As you read Chapter 5, keep in mind these key questions.

- What is the perceptual process?
- What are common perceptual distortions?
- How can the perceptual process be managed?
- What is attribution theory?

In Pikeville, Kentucky, there is a Hillbilly Days festival developed as a touch of self parody to change peoples' perceptions of the rapidly emerging Appalacia area.[1] Such stereotyped perceptions and accompanying attributions are a part of the overall perceptual and attributional processes that are critical components of OB and are the topics of this chapter.

THE PERCEPTUAL PROCESS

A spectacular completed pass during the 1982 National Football Conference championship game helped propel Joe Montana, former San Francisco 49er quarterback, into the legendary status he enjoys today. The reverse effect apparently occurred for Danny White, Dallas Cowboys' quarterback. He fumbled in the final minute of the same game and never obtained the status of his predecessor, Roger Staubach, even though White took the Cowboys to the championship game three years in a row.[2]

This example illustrates the notion of **perception,** the process by which people select, organize, interpret, retrieve, and respond to information from the world around them.[3] This information is gathered from the five senses of sight, hearing, touch, taste, and smell. As Montana, White, and Staubach can attest, perception and reality are not necessarily the same thing. The perceptions or responses of any two people are also not necessarily identical, even when they are describing the same event.

Through perception, people process information inputs into responses involving feelings and action. Perception is a way of forming impressions about oneself, other people, and daily life experiences. It also serves as a screen or filter through which information passes before it has an effect on people. The quality or accuracy of a person's perceptions, therefore, has a major impact on his or her responses to a given situation.

Perceptual responses are also likely to vary between managers and subordinates. Consider Figure 5.1, which depicts contrasting perceptions of a performance appraisal between managers and subordinates. Rather substantial differences exist in the two sets of perceptions; the responses can be significant. In this case, managers who perceive that they already give adequate attention to past performance, career development, and supervisory help are unlikely to give greater emphasis to these points in future performance appraisal interviews. In contrast, their subordinates are likely to experience continued frustration because they perceive that these subjects are not being given sufficient attention.

FACTORS INFLUENCING THE PERCEPTUAL PROCESS

The factors that contribute to perceptual differences and the perceptual process among people at work are summarized in Figure 5.2 and include characteristics of the *perceiver,* the *setting,* and the *perceived.*

The Perceiver   A person's past experiences, needs or motives, personality, and values and attitudes may all influence the perceptual process. A person with a strong achievement need tends to perceive a situation in terms of that need. If you see doing well in class as a way to help meet your achievement need, for example, you will tend to emphasize that aspect when considering various classes. By the same token, a person with a negative attitude toward unions may look for antagonisms even when local union officials

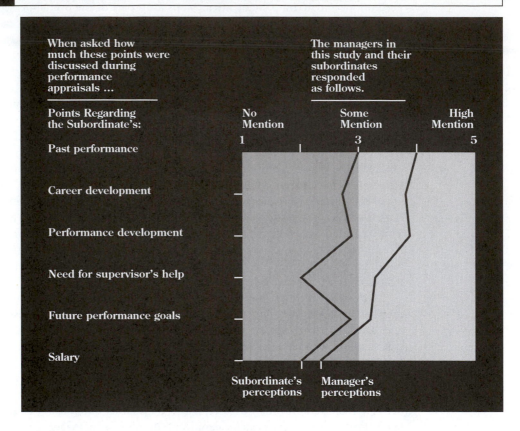

make routine visits to the organization. These and other perceiver factors influence the various aspects of the perceptual process.

The Setting The physical, social, and organizational context of the perceptual setting can also influence the perceptual process. Kim Jeffrey, the recently appointed CEO of Nestle's Perrier, was perceived by his subordinates as a frightening figure when he gave vent to his temper and had occasional confrontations with them. In the previous setting, before he was promoted, Jeffrey's flare-ups have been tolerable; now they caused intimidation, so his subordinates feared to express their opinions and recommendations. Fortunately, after he received feedback about this problem, he was able to change his subordinates' perceptions in the new setting.[4]

The Perceived Characteristics of the perceived person, object, or event, such as contrast, intensity, figure–ground separation, size, motion, and repetition or novelty, are also important in the perceptual process. For example, one mainframe computer among six PCs or one man among six women will be perceived differently than one of six mainframe computers or one of six men—where there is less contrast. Intensity can vary in terms of brightness, color, depth, sound, and the like. A bright red sports car stands out from a

FIGURE 5.2	**FACTORS INFLUENCING THE PERCEPTUAL PROCESS**

Perceiver
**Experience
Needs or Motives
Values
Attitudes**

Setting
**Physical
Social
Organizational**

Perceived
**Contrast
Figure–Ground Separation
Intensity
Size
Motion
Repetition/Novelty**

FIGURE 5.3	**FIGURE-GROUND SEPARATION**

group of gray sedans; whispering or shouting stands out from ordinary conversation. The concept is known as figure–ground separation, and it depends on which image is perceived as the background and which as the figure. For an illustration, look at Figure 5.3. What do you see? Faces or a vase?

In the matter of size, very small or very large people tend to be perceived differently and more readily than average-sized people. Similarly, in terms of motion, moving objects are perceived differently from stationary objects. And, of course, advertisers hope that ad repetition or frequency will positively influence peoples' perception of a product. Television advertising blitzes for new models of personal computers are a case in point. Finally, the novelty of a situation affects its perception. A purple-haired teenager is perceived differently from a blond or a brunette, for example.

STAGES OF THE PERCEPTUAL PROCESS

So far we have discussed key factors influencing the perceptual process. Now we'll look at the stages involved in processing the information that ultimately determines a person's perception and reaction, as shown in Figure 5.4. The information-processing stages are divided into information attention and selection; organization of information; information interpretation; and information retrieval.

Attention and Selection Our senses are constantly bombarded with so much information that if we don't screen it, we quickly become incapacitated with information overload. *Selective screening* lets in only a tiny proportion of all of the information available. Some of the selectivity comes from controlled processing— consciously deciding what information to pay attention to and what to ignore. In this case, the perceivers are aware that they are processing information. Think about the last time you were at a noisy restaurant and screened out all the sounds but those of the person with whom you were talking.

In contrast to controlled processing, screening can also take place without the perceiver's conscious awareness. For example, you may drive a car without consciously thinking about the process of driving; you may be thinking about a problem you are having with your course work instead. In driving the car, you are affected by information from the world around you, such as traffic lights and other cars, but you don't pay conscious attention to that information. Such selectivity of attention and automatic information processing works well most of the time when you drive, but if a nonroutine event occurs, such as

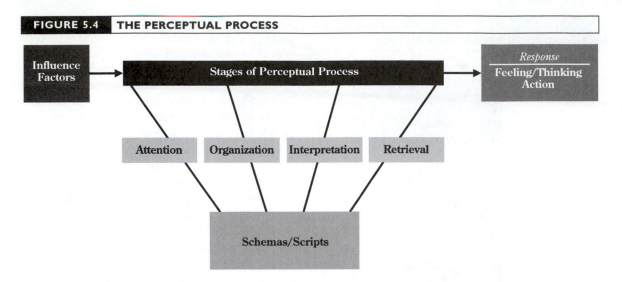

FIGURE 5.4   THE PERCEPTUAL PROCESS

an animal darting into the road, you may have an accident unless you quickly shift to controlled processing.

Organization   Even though selective screening takes place in the attention stage, it is still necessary to find ways to organize the information efficiently. **Schemas** help us do this. Schemas are cognitive frameworks that represent organized knowledge about a given concept or stimulus developed through experience.[5] A self schema contains information about a person's own appearance, behavior, and personality. For instance, a person with a decisiveness schema tends to perceive himself or herself in terms of that aspect, especially in circumstances calling for leadership.

Person schemas refer to the way individuals sort others into categories, such as types or groups, in terms of similar perceived features. The term *prototype,* or *stereotype,* is often used to represent these categories; it is an abstract set of features commonly associated with members of that category. Once the prototype is formed, it is stored in long-term memory; it is retrieved when it is needed for a comparison of how well a person matches the prototype's features. For instance, you may have a "good worker" prototype in mind, which includes hard work, intelligence, punctuality, articulateness, and decisiveness; that prototype is used as a measure against which to compare a given worker. Stereotypes, as discussed in Chapter 4, may be regarded as prototypes based on such demographic characteristics as gender, age, able-bodiedness, and racial and ethnic groups. In the chapter opener, for example, we are told that the term *hillbilly* conjured up a stereotype based on numerous demographic and behavioral characteristics. The Festival was a communitywide attempt to change that stereotype.

A *script schema* is defined as a knowledge framework that describes the appropriate sequence of events in a given situation.[6] For example, an experienced manager would use a script schema to think about the appropriate steps involved in running a meeting. Finally, *person-in-situation schemas* combine schemas built around persons (self and person schemas) and events (script schemas).[7] Thus, a manager might organize his or her perceived information in a meeting around a decisiveness schema for both himself or herself and a key participant in the meeting. Here, a script schema would provide the steps and their sequence in the meeting; the manager would push through the steps decisively and would call on the selected participants periodically throughout the meeting to respond decisively. Note that, although this approach might facilitate organization of important information, the perceptions of those attending might not be completely accurate because decisiveness of the person-in-situation schema did not allow the attendees enough time for open discussion.

As you can see in Figure 5.4, schemas are not important just in the organization stage; they also affect other stages in the perception process. Furthermore, schemas rely heavily on automatic processing to free people up to use controlled processing as necessary. Finally, as we will show, the perceptual factors described earlier, as well as the distortions, to be discussed shortly, influence schemas in various ways.

Interpretation   Once your attention has been drawn to certain stimuli and you have grouped or organized this information, the next step is to uncover the reasons behind the actions. That is, even if your attention is called to the same information and you organize it in the same way your friend does, you may interpret it differently or make different attributions about the reasons behind what you have perceived. For example, as a manager, you might attribute compliments from a friendly subordinate to his being an eager worker, whereas your friend might interpret the behavior as insincere flattery.

Retrieval   So far, we have discussed the stages of the perceptual process as if they all occurred at the same time. However, to do so ignores the important component of memory. Each of the previous stages forms part of that memory and contributes to the stimuli or information stored there. The information stored in our memory must be retrieved if it is to be used. This leads us to the retrieval stage of the perceptual process summarized in Figure 5.4.

All of us at times can't retrieve information stored in our memory. More commonly, our memory decays, so that only some of the information is retrieved. Schemas play an important role in this area. They make it difficult for people to remember things not included in them. For example, based on your prototype about the traits comprising a "high performing employee" (hard work, punctuality, intelligence, articulateness, and decisiveness), you may overestimate these traits and underestimate others when you are evaluating the performance of a subordinate whom you generally consider good. Thus, you may overestimate the person's decisiveness since it is a key part of your high performance prototype.

Indeed, people are as likely to recall nonexistent traits as they are to recall those that are really there. Furthermore, once formed, prototypes may be difficult to change and tend to last a long time.[8] Obviously, this distortion can cause major problems in terms of performance appraisals and promotions, not to mention numerous other interactions on and off the job. By the same token, such prototypes allow you to "chunk" information and reduce overload. Thus, prototypes are a double-edged sword.

RESPONSE TO THE PERCEPTUAL PROCESS

Throughout this chapter, we have shown how the perceptual process influences numerous OB responses. Figure 5.4 classifies such responses into thoughts and feelings and actions. For example, in countries such as Mexico, bosses routinely greet their secretaries with a kiss, and that is expected behavior. In contrast, in this country your thoughts and feelings might be quite different about such behavior. You might very well perceive this as a form of sexual harassment. As you cover the other OB topics in the book, you also should be alert to the importance of perceptual responses covering thoughts, feelings, and actions.

COMMON PERCEPTUAL DISTORTIONS

Figure 5.5 shows some common kinds of distortions that can make the perceptual process inaccurate and affect the response. These are stereotypes and prototypes, halo effects, selective perception, projection, contrast effects, and self-fulfilling prophecy.

STEREOTYPES OR PROTOTYPES

Earlier, when discussing person schemas, we described stereotypes, or prototypes, as useful ways of combining information in order to deal with information overload. At the same time, we pointed out how stereotypes can cause inaccuracies in retrieving information, along with some further problems. In particular, stereotypes obscure individual differences; that is, they can prevent managers from getting to know people as individuals and from accurately assessing their needs, preferences, and abilities. We compared these stereotypes with research results and showed the errors that can occur when stereotypes are relied on for decision making. Nevertheless, stereotypes continue to exist at the board of directors level in organizations. A recent survey from 133 *Fortune* 500 firms showed that female directors were favored for membership on only the relatively peripheral public affairs committee in these organizations. Males were favored for membership on the more important compensation, executive, or finance committee, even when the females were equally or more experienced than their male counterparts.[9]

Here, we reiterate our previous message: both managers and employees need to be sensitive to stereotypes; they also must attempt to overcome them and recognize that an increasingly diverse workforce can be a truly competitive advantage, as we showed in Chapter 4.

FIGURE 5.5 DISTORTIONS OCCURRING IN PERCEPTUAL PROCESS STAGES

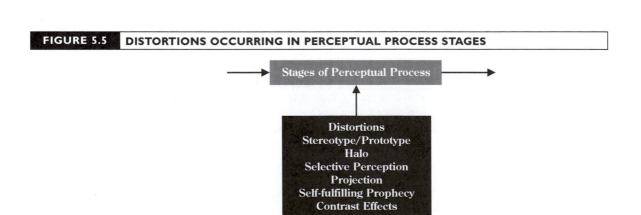

HALO EFFECTS

A **halo effect** occurs when one attribute of a person or situation is used to develop an overall impression of the individual or situation. Like stereotypes, these distortions are more likely to occur in the organization stage of perception. Halo effects are common in our everyday lives. When meeting a new person, for example, a pleasant smile can lead to a positive first impression of an overall "warm" and "honest" person. The result of a halo effect is the same as that associated with a stereotype, however: individual differences are obscured.

Halo effects are particularly important in the performance appraisal process because they can influence a manager's evaluations of subordinates' work performance. For example, people with good attendance records tend to be viewed as intelligent and responsible; those with poor attendance records are considered poor performers. Such conclusions may or may not be valid. It is the manager's job to try to get true impressions rather than allowing halo effects to result in biased and erroneous evaluations.

SELECTIVE PERCEPTION

Selective perception is the tendency to single out those aspects of a situation, person, or object that are consistent with one's needs, values, or attitudes. Its strongest impact occurs in the attention stage of the perceptual process. This perceptual distortion is identified in a classic research study involving executives in a manufacturing company.[10] When asked to identify the key problem in a comprehensive strategic management case, each executive selected problems consistent with his or her functional area work assignments. For example, most marketing executives viewed the key problem area as sales, whereas production people tended to see the problem as one of production and organization. These differing viewpoints would affect how the executive would approach the problem; they might also create difficulties once these people tried to work together to improve things.

More recently, 121 middle- and upper-lever managers attending an executive development program expressed broader views in conjunction with an emphasis on their own function. For example, a chief financial officer indicated an awareness of the importance of manufacturing, and an assistant marketing manager recognized the importance of accounting and finance along with each of their own functions.[11] Thus, this more current research demonstrated very little perceptual selectivity. The researchers were not, however, able to state definitively what accounted for the differing results.

These results suggest that selective perception is more important at some times than at others. Managers should be aware of this characteristic and test whether or not situations, events, or individuals are being selectively perceived. The easiest way to do this is to gather additional opinions from other people. When these opinions contradict a manager's own, an effort should be made to check the original impression.

PROJECTION

Projection is the assignment of one's personal attributes to other individuals; it is especially likely to occur in the interpretation stage of perception. A classic projection error is illustrated by managers who assume that the needs of their subordinates and their own coincide. Suppose, for example, that you enjoy responsibility and achievement in your work. Suppose, too, that you are the newly appointed manager of a group whose jobs seem dull and routine. You may move quickly to expand these jobs to help the workers achieve increased satisfaction from more challenging tasks because you want them to experience things that you, personally, value in work. But this may not be a good decision. If you project your needs onto the subordinates, individual differences are lost. Instead of designing the subordinates' jobs to fit their needs best, you have designed their jobs to fit your needs. The problem is that the subordinates may be quite satisfied and productive doing jobs that seem dull and routine to you. Projection can be controlled through a high degree of self-awareness and empathy—the ability to view a situation as others see it.

CONTRAST EFFECTS

Earlier, when discussing the perceived, we mentioned how a red sports car would stand out from others because of its contrast. Here, we show the perceptual distortion that can occur when, say, a person gives a talk following a strong speaker or is interviewed for a job following a series of mediocre applicants. We can expect a **contrast effect** to occur when an individual's characteristics are contrasted with those of others recently encountered who rank higher or lower on the same characteristics. Clearly, both managers and employees need to be aware of the possible perceptual distortion the contrast effect may create in many work settings.

SELF-FULFILLING PROPHECY

A final perceptual distortion that we consider is the **self-fulfilling prophecy**—the tendency to create or find in another situation or individual that which you expected to find in the first place. Self-fulfilling prophecy is sometimes referred to as the "Pygmalion effect," named for a mythical Greek sculptor who created a statue of his ideal mate and then made her come to life.[12] His prophecy came true! Through self-fulfilling prophecy, you also may create in the work situation that which you expect to find.

Self-fulfilling prophecy can have both positive and negative results for you as a manager. Suppose you assume that your subordinates prefer to satisfy most of their needs outside the work setting and want only minimal involvement with their jobs. Consequently, you are likely to provide simple, highly structured jobs designed to require little involvement. Can you predict what response the subordinates would have to this situation? Their most likely response would be to show the lack of commitment you assumed they would have in the first place. Thus, your initial expectations are confirmed as a self-fulfilling prophecy.

Self-fulfilling prophecy can have a positive side, however (see The Effective Manager 5.1). Students introduced to their teachers as "intellectual bloomers" do better on achievement tests than do their counterparts who lack such a positive introduction. A particularly interesting example of the self-fulfilling prophecy is that of Israeli tank crews. One set of tank commanders was told that according to test data some members of their assigned crews had exceptional abilities but others were only average. In reality, the crew members were assigned randomly, so that the two test groups were equal in ability. Later, the commanders reported that the so-called exceptional crew members performed better than the "average" members. As the study revealed, however, the commanders had paid more attention to and praised the crew members for whom they had the higher expectancies.[13] The

---

THE EFFECTIVE MANAGER 5.1
CREATING POSITIVE SELF-FULFILLING PROPHECIES FOR EMPLOYEES

- Create a warmer interpersonal climate between your subordinates and you.
- Give more performance feedback to subordinates—make it as positive as possible, given their actual performance.
- Spend more time helping subordinates learn job skills.
- Provide more opportunities for subordinates to ask questions.

---

self-fulfilling effects in these cases argue strongly for managers to adopt positive and optimistic approaches to people at work.

MANAGING THE PERCEPTUAL PROCESS

To be successful, managers must understand the perceptual process, the stages involved, and the impact the perceptual process can have on their own and others' responses. They must also be aware of what roles the perceiver, the setting, and the perceived have in the perceptual process. Particularly important with regard to the perceived is the concept of impression management—for both managers and others.

IMPRESSION MANAGEMENT

Impression management is a person's systematic attempt to behave in ways that will create and maintain desired impressions in the eyes of others. First impressions are especially important and influence how people respond to one another. Impression management is influenced by such activities as associating with the "right people," doing favors to gain approval, flattering others to make oneself look better, taking credit for a favorable event, apologizing for a negative event while seeking a pardon, agreeing with the opinions of others, downplaying the severity of a negative event, and doing favors for others.[14] Successful managers learn how to use these activities to enhance their own images, and they are sensitive to their use by their subordinates and others in their organizations. In this context job titles are particularly important.

DISTORTION MANAGEMENT

During the attention and selection stage, managers should be alert to balancing automatic and controlled information processing. Most of their responsibilities, such as performance assessment and clear communication, will involve controlled processing, which will take away from other job responsibilities. Along with more controlled processing, managers need to be concerned about increasing the frequency of observations and about getting representative information rather than simply responding to the most recent information about a subordinate or a production order, for instance. Some organizations, including 911 systems, have responded to the need for representative and more accurate information by utilizing current technology. In addition, managers should not fail to seek out disconfirming information that will help provide a balance to their typical perception of information.

The various kinds of schemas and prototypes and stereotypes are particularly important at the information organizing stage. Managers should strive to broaden their schemas or should even replace them with more accurate or complete ones.

At the interpretation stage, managers need to be especially attuned to the impact of attribution on information; we discuss this concept further in the section on managing the attributional process later in the chapter. At the retrieval stage, managers should be sensitive to the fallibility of memory. They should recognize the tendency to overly rely on schemas, especially prototypes or stereotypes that may bias information stored and retrieved.

Throughout the entire perception process managers should be sensitive to the information distortions caused by halo effects, selective perception, projection, contrast effects, and self-fulfilling prophecy, in addition to the distortions of stereotypes and prototypes.

ATTRIBUTION THEORY

Earlier in the chapter we mentioned attribution theory in the context of perceptual interpretation. **Attribution theory** aids in this interpretation by focusing on how people attempt to (1) understand the causes of a certain event, (2) assess responsibility for the outcomes of the event, and (3) evaluate the personal qualities of the people involved in the event.[15] In applying attribution theory, we are especially concerned with whether one's behavior has been internally or externally caused. Internal causes are believed to be under an individual's control—you believe Jake's performance is poor because he is lazy. External causes are seen as outside a person—you believe Kellie's performance is poor because her machine is old.

Attributions can have far-reaching effects. For example, over their lifetimes, obese women don't accumulate as much net worth as slender women. Even after controlling for such things as health and marital status, women pay a heavy economic penalty for fat. However, the same is not true for obese men. Attributions concerning fat men are ones of wealth and success, whereas attributions concerning fat women are that they "let themselves go." For obese women, internal attributional causes seem to be operating to their detriment.[16]

According to attribution theory, three factors influence this internal or external determination: distinctiveness, consensus, and consistency. *Distinctiveness* considers how consistent a person's behavior is across different situations. If Jake's performance is low, regardless of the machine on which he is working, we tend to give the poor performance an internal attribution; if the poor performance is unusual, we tend to assign an external cause to explain it.

Consensus takes into account how likely all those facing a similar situation are to respond in the same way. If all the people using machinery like Kellie's have poor performance, we tend to give her performance an external attribution. If other employees do not perform poorly, we attribute internal causation to her performance.

Consistency concerns whether an individual responds the same way across time. If Jake has a batch of low-performance figures, we tend to give the poor performance an internal attribution. In contrast, if Jake's low performance is an isolated incident, we attribute it to an external cause.

ATTRIBUTION ERRORS

In addition to these three influences, two errors have an impact on internal versus external determination—the *fundamental attribution error* and the *self-serving bias*.[17] Figure 5.6 provides data from a group of health-care managers. When supervisors were asked to identify, or attribute, causes of poor performance among their subordinates, the supervisors more often chose the individual's internal deficiencies—lack of ability and effort—rather than external deficiencies in the situation—lack of support. This demonstrates a **fundamental attribution error**—the tendency to underestimate the influence of situational factors and to overestimate the influence of personal factors in evaluating someone else's behavior. When asked to identify causes of their own poor performance, however, the supervisors overwhelmingly cited lack of support—an external, or situational, deficiency. This indicates a **self-serving bias**—the tendency to deny personal responsibility for performance problems but to accept personal responsibility for performance success.

To summarize, we tend to overemphasize other people's internal personal factors in their behavior and to underemphasize external factors in other people's behavior. In contrast, we tend to attribute our own success to our own internal factors and to attribute our failure to external factors.

The managerial implications of attribution theory can be traced back to the fact that perceptions influence responses. For example, a manager who feels that subordinates are not performing well and perceives the reason to be an internal lack of effort is likely to respond with attempts to "motivate" the subordinates to work harder; the possibility of changing external, situational factors that may remove job constraints and provide better organizational support may be largely ignored. This oversight could sacrifice major performance gains. Interestingly, because of the self-serving bias, when they evaluated their own behavior, the supervisors in the earlier study indicated that their performance would benefit from having better support. Thus, the supervisors' own abilities or willingness to work hard were not felt to be at issue.

ATTRIBUTIONS ACROSS CULTURES

Research on the self-serving bias and fundamental attribution error has been done in cultures outside the United States with unexpected results.[18] In Korea, for example, the self-serving bias was found to be negative; that is, Korean managers attribute work-group failure to themselves—"I was not a capable leader"—rather than to external causes. In India, the fundamental attribution error overemphasizes external rather than internal

FIGURE 5.6 **HEALTH-CARE MANAGERS' ATTRIBUTIONS OF CAUSES FOR POOR PERFORMANCE**

Cause of Poor Performance by Their Subordinates	Most Frequent Attribution	Cause of Poor Performance by Themselves
7	Lack of *ability*	1
12	Lack of *effort*	1
5	Lack of *support*	23

causes for failure. Still another interesting cultural twist on the self-serving bias and funda-mental attribution error is suggested by an example of a Ghanian woman who was the only female sea captain in the fleet. The difficulty of her becoming a captain is reinforced by Africans' tendency to attribute negative consequences—driving away fish and angering mermaids into creating squalls—to women but apparently not to men. Why these various differences occurred is not clear, but differing cultural values appear to play a role. Finally, there is some evidence that U.S. females may be less likely to emphasize the self-serving bias than males.[19]

Certain cultures, such as the United States, tend to overemphasize internal causes and underemphasize external causes. Such overemphasis may result in negative attributions toward employees. These negative attributions, in turn, can lead to disciplinary actions, negative performance evaluations, transfers to other departments, and overreliance on training, rather than focusing on such external causes as lack of workplace support.[20] Employees, too, take their cues from managerial misattributions and, through negative self-fulfilling prophecies, may reinforce managers' original misattributions. Employees and managers alike (see The Effective Manager 5.2) can be taught attributional realignment to help deal with such misattributions.[21]

CHAPTER 5 SUMMARY

What is the perceptual process?

- Individuals use the perceptual process to pay attention to and to select, organize, interpret, and retrieve information from the world around them.
- The perceptual process involves the perceiver, the setting, and the perceived.
- Responses to the perceptual process involve thinking and feeling and action classifications.

What are common perceptual distortions?

- Stereotypes or prototypes.
- Halo effects.
- Selective perception.

THE EFFECTIVE MANAGER 5.2

KEYS IN MANAGING PERCEPTIONS AND ATTRIBUTIONS

- Be self-aware.
- Seek a wide range of differing information.
- Try to see a situation as others would.
- Be aware of different kinds of schemas.
- Be aware of perceptual distortions.
- Be aware of self and other impression management.
- Be aware of attribution theory implications.

- Projection.
- Contrast effects.
- Expectancy.

How can the perceptual process be managed?

Managing the perceptual process involves:

- Impression management of self and others.
- Managing the information attention and selection stages.
- Managing the information organizing stage.
- Managing the information interpretation stage.
- Managing the information storage and retrieval stage.
- Being sensitive to effects of the common perceptual distortions.

What is attribution theory?

- Attribution theory involves emphasis on the interpretation stage of the perceptual process and consideration of whether individuals' behaviors result primarily from external causes or from causes internal to the individuals.
- Three factors influence an external or internal causal attribution—distinctiveness, consensus, and consistency.
- Two errors influencing an external or internal causal attribution are fundamental attribution error and self-serving bias.
- Attributions can be managed by recognizing a typical overemphasis on internal causes of behavior and an underemphasis on external causes.
- An overemphasis on internal causes tends to lead to assignment of failure to employees with accompanying disciplinary actions, negative performance evaluations, and the like.
- An underemphasis on external causes tends to lead to lack of workplace support.

CHAPTER 6

Motivation and Reinforcement

Today's workplace is more globally competitive than ever. Its long-term success rests squarely on the motivation and behavior of the individuals who are a part of it.

WHAT IS MOTIVATION?

If asked to identify a major concern or problem at work, a manager is very likely to cite a "motivational" need to do something that will encourage people to work harder to do "what I want." Formally defined, **motivation** refers to the individual forces that account for the direction, level, and persistence of a person's effort expended at work. *Direction* refers to an individual's choice when presented with a number of possible alternatives (e.g., whether to exert effort toward product quality or toward product quantity). *Level* refers to the amount of effort a person puts forth (e.g., a lot or a little). *Persistence* refers to the length of time a person sticks with a given action (e.g., to try to achieve product quality and give up when it is found difficult to attain).

REINFORCEMENT, CONTENT, AND PROCESS THEORIES

The theories of motivation can be divided into three broad categories.[1] **Reinforcement theories** emphasize the means through which the process of controlling an individual's behavior by manipulating its consequences takes place. They focus on the observable rather than what is inside an employee's head. Thus, reinforcement views place a premium on observing individuals to see which work-related outcomes are highly valued. By altering when, where, how, and why some types of rewards are given, the manager can change the apparent motivation of employees by providing a systematic set of consequences to shape behavior. **Content theories** focus primarily on individual needs—the physiological or psychological deficiencies that we feel a compulsion to reduce or eliminate. These theories suggest that the manager's job is to create a work environment that responds positively to individual needs. They help to explain how poor performance, undesirable behaviors, low satisfaction, and the like can be caused by "blocked" needs or needs that are not satisfied on the job. **Process theories** focus on the thought or cognitive processes that take place within the minds of people and that influence their behavior. Whereas a content approach may identify job security as an important need for an individual, a process approach probes further to identify why the person behaves in particular ways relative to available rewards and work opportunities. Although each type of theory contributes to our understanding of motivation, none offers a complete explanation. Ultimately, we use the insights of three sets of theories to offer an integrated view of motivational dynamics that should be useful in any work setting.[2]

MOTIVATION ACROSS CULTURES

Before we examine the motivation theories in detail, an important caveat is in order. Motivation is a key concern in firms across the globe. However, North American theories (and these are the only ones discussed in this chapter) are subject to cultural limitations.[3] The determinants of motivation and the best ways to deal with it are likely to vary considerably across Asia, South America, Eastern Europe, and Africa. As we pointed out in Chapter 3, individual values and attitudes—both important aspects of motivation—have strong cultural foundations. What proves "motivational" as a reward in one culture, for example, might not work in another. We should be sensitive to these issues and avoid being parochial or ethnocentric by assuming that people in all cultures are motivated by the same things in the same ways.[4]

REINFORCEMENT

In OB, reinforcement has a very specific meaning that has its origin in some classic studies in psychology.[5] **Reinforcement** is the administration of a consequence as a result of a behavior. Managing reinforcement properly can change the direction, level, and persistence of an individual's behavior. To understand this idea, we need to review some of the concepts on conditioning and reinforcement you learned in your basic psychology course. We will then move on to applications.

CLASSICAL AND OPERANT CONDITIONING

Recall that Ivan Pavlov studied classical conditioning. **Classical conditioning** is a form of learning through association that involves the manipulation of stimuli to influence behavior. The Russian psychologist "taught" dogs to salivate at the sound of a bell by ringing the bell when feeding the dogs. The sight of the food naturally caused the dogs to salivate. Eventually, the dogs "learned" to associate the bell ringing with the presentation of meat and to salivate at the ringing of the bell alone. Such "learning" through association is so common in organizations that it is often ignored until it causes considerable confusion. Take a look at Figure 6.1. The key is to understand a stimulus and a conditioned stimulus. A **stimulus** is something that incites action and draws forth a response (the meat for the

| FIGURE 6.1 | DIFFERENCES BETWEEN CLASSICAL AND OPERANT CONDITIONING APPROACHES FOR A BOSS AND SUBORDINATE |

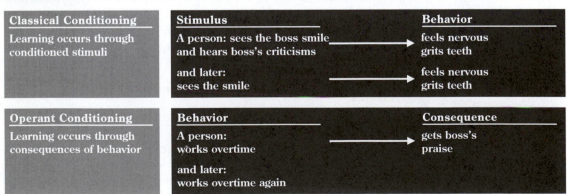

Classical Conditioning	Stimulus	Behavior
Learning occurs through conditioned stimuli	A person: sees the boss smile and hears boss's criticisms	feels nervous grits teeth
	and later: sees the smile	feels nervous grits teeth

Operant Conditioning	Behavior	Consequence
Learning occurs through consequences of behavior	A person: works overtime	gets boss's praise
	and later: works overtime again	

dogs). The trick is to associate one neutral potential stimulus (the bell ringing) with another initial stimulus that already affects behavior (the meat). The once-neutral stimulus is called a *conditioned stimulus* when it affects behavior in the same way as the initial stimulus. In Figure 6.1, the boss's smiling becomes a conditioned stimulus because of its linkage to his criticisms.

Operant conditioning, popularized by B. F. Skinner, is an extension of the classical case to much more practical affairs.[6] It includes more than just a stimulus and a response behavior. **Operant conditioning** is the process of controlling behavior by manipulating its consequences. Classical and operant conditioning differ in two important ways. First, control in operant conditioning is via manipulation of consequences. Second, operant conditioning calls for examining antecedents, behavior, and consequences. The *antecedent* is the condition leading up to or "cueing" behavior. For example, in Figure 6.1, an agreement between the boss and the employee to work overtime as needed is an antecedent. If the employee works overtime, this would be the *behavior* while the *consequence* would be the boss's praise.

If a boss wants a behavior to be repeated, such as working overtime, she must manipulate the consequences. The basis for manipulating consequences is E. L. Thorndike's law of effect.[7] The **law of effect** is simple but powerful: behavior that results in a pleasant outcome is likely to be repeated while behavior that results in an unpleasant outcome is not likely to be repeated. The implications of this law are rather straightforward. If, as a supervisor, you want more of a behavior, you must make the consequences for the individual positive.

Note that the emphasis is on consequences that can be manipulated rather than on consequences inherent in the behavior itself. OB research often emphasizes specific types of rewards that are considered by the reinforcement perspective to influence individual behavior. *Extrinsic rewards* are positively valued work outcomes that are given to the individual by some other person. They are important external reinforcers or environmental consequences that can substantially influence a person's work behaviors through the law of effect. Figure 6.2 presents a sample of extrinsic rewards that managers can allocate to their subordinates.[8] Some of these rewards are contrived, or planned, rewards that have direct costs and budgetary implications. Examples are pay increases and cash bonuses. A second category includes natural rewards that have no cost other than the manager's personal time and efforts. Examples are verbal praise and recognition in the workplace.

FIGURE 6.2   A SAMPLE OF EXTRINSIC REWARDS ALLOCATED BY MANAGERS

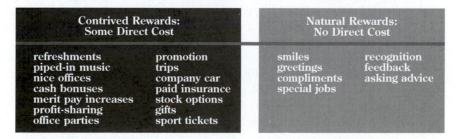

Contrived Rewards: Some Direct Cost		Natural Rewards: No Direct Cost	
refreshments	promotion	smiles	recognition
piped-in music	trips	greetings	feedback
nice offices	company car	compliments	asking advice
cash bonuses	paid insurance	special jobs	
merit pay increases	stock options		
profit-sharing	gifts		
office parties	sport tickets		

REINFORCEMENT STRATEGIES

We now bring the notions of classical conditioning, operant conditioning, reinforcement, and extrinsic rewards together to show how the direction, level, and persistence of individual behavior can be changed. This combination is called "OB Mod" after its longer title of **organizational behavior modification. OB Mod** is the systematic reinforcement of desirable work behavior and the nonreinforcement or punishment of unwanted work behavior. OB Mod includes four basic reinforcement strategies: positive reinforcement, negative reinforcement (or avoidance), punishment, and extinction.[9]

Positive Reinforcement B. F. Skinner and his followers advocate **positive reinforcement**—the administration of positive consequences that tend to increase the likelihood of repeating the desirable behavior in similar settings. For example, a Texas Instruments manager nods to a subordinate to express approval after she makes a useful comment during a sales meeting. Obviously, the boss wants more useful comments. Later, the subordinate makes another useful comment, just as the boss hoped she would.

To begin using a strategy of positive reinforcement, we need to be aware that positive reinforcers and rewards are not necessarily the same. Recognition, for example, is both a reward and a potential positive reinforcer. Recognition becomes a positive reinforcer only if a person's performance later improves. Sometimes, rewards turn out not to be positive reinforcers. For example, a supervisor at Boeing might praise a subordinate in front of other group members for finding errors in a report. If the group members then give the worker the silent treatment, however, the worker may stop looking for errors in the future. In this case, the supervisor's "reward" does not serve as a positive reinforcer.

To have maximum reinforcement value, a reward must be delivered only if the desired behavior is exhibited. That is, the reward must be contingent on the desired behavior. This principle is known as the **law of contingent reinforcement.** In the previous Texas Instruments example, the supervisor's praise was contingent on the subordinate's making constructive comments. Finally, the reward must be given as soon as possible after the desired behavior. This is known as the **law of immediate reinforcement.**[10] If the TI boss waited for the annual performance review to praise the subordinate for providing constructive comments, the law of immediate reinforcement would be violated.

Now that we have presented the general concepts, it is time to address two important issues of implementation. First, what do you do if the behavior approximates what you want but is not exactly on target? Second, is it necessary to provide reinforcement each and every time? These are issues of shaping and scheduling, respectively.

Shaping If the desired behavior is specific in nature and is difficult to achieve, a pattern of positive reinforcement, called shaping, can be used. **Shaping** is the creation of a new behavior by the positive reinforcement of successive approximations leading to the desired behavior. For example, new machine operators in the Ford Motor casting operation in Ohio must learn a complex series of tasks in pouring molten metal into the casting in order to avoid gaps, overfills, or cracks.[11] The molds are filled in a three-step process, with each step progressively more difficult than its predecessor. Astute master craftspersons first show neophytes how to pour the first step and give praise based on what they did right. As the apprentices gain experience, they are given praise only when all of the elements of the first step are completed successfully. Once the apprentices have mastered the first step, they progress to the second. Reinforcement is given only when the entire first step and an aspect of the second step are completed successfully. Over time, apprentices learn all three steps and are given contingent positive rewards immediately for a complete casting that has no cracks or gaps. In this way, behavior is shaped gradually rather than changed all at once.

Scheduling Positive Reinforcement   Positive reinforcement can be given according to either continuous or intermittent schedules. **Continuous reinforcement** administers a reward each time a desired behavior occurs. **Intermittent reinforcement** rewards behavior only periodically. These alternatives are important because the two schedules may have very different impacts on behavior. In general, continuous reinforcement elicits a desired behavior more quickly than does intermittent reinforcement. Thus, in the initial training of the apprentice casters, continuous reinforcement would be important. At the same time, continuous reinforcement is more costly in the consumption of rewards and is more easily extinguished when reinforcement is no longer present. In contrast, behavior acquired under intermittent reinforcement lasts longer upon the discontinuance of reinforcement than does behavior acquired under continuous reinforcement. In other words, it is more resistant to extinction. Thus, as the apprentices master an aspect of the pouring, the schedule is switched from continuous to intermittent reinforcement.

As shown in Figure 6.3, intermittent reinforcement can be given according to fixed or variable schedules. *Variable schedules* typically result in more consistent patterns of desired behavior than do fixed reinforcement schedules. *Fixed interval schedules* provide rewards at the first appearance of a behavior after a given time has elapsed. *Fixed ratio schedules* result in a

FIGURE 6.3	FOUR TYPES OF INTERMITTENT REINFORCEMENT SCHEDULES

	Interval	Ratio
Fixed	**Fixed interval** Reinforcer given after a given time Weekly or monthly paychecks Regularly scheduled exams	**Fixed ratio** Reinforcer given after a given number of behavior occurrences Piece rate pay Commissioned salespeople; certain amount is given for each dollar of sales
Variable	**Variable interval** Reinforcer given at random times Occasional praise by boss on unscheduled visits Unspecified number of pop quizzes to students	**Variable ratio** Reinforcer given after a random number of behavior occurrences Random quality checks with praise for zero defects Commissioned salespeople; a varying number of calls is required to obtain a given sale
	Time based	**Behavior occurrence based**

reward each time a certain number of the behaviors have occurred. A *variable interval schedule* rewards behavior at random times, while a *variable ratio schedule* rewards behavior after a random number of occurrences. For example, as the apprentices perfect their technique for a stage of pouring castings, the astute masters switch to a variable ratio reinforcement.

Let's look at an example from Drankenfeld Colors, Washington, Pennsylvania, with 250 employees. The absentee rate of these employees was very low, and in a recent year 44 percent of the employees had perfect attendance records. The firm wanted to use positive reinforcement to showcase perfect attendance, even though attendance was already so positive. Consequently, it gave monetary awards of $50 for perfect attendance at 6 and 12 months, with a $25 bonus for a full year of perfect attendance. In addition, the firm entered employees with perfect attendance into a sweepstakes drawing at special award banquets. The winners received an all-expense-paid trip for two to a resort. Perfect attendance increased from 44 percent to 62 percent in the program's first year.[12]

Let's also consider what kind of reinforcement scheduling was used in this program. A strong argument can be made that a fixed ratio schedule was used, in conjunction with a variable ratio schedule. The first schedule rewarded attendance behaviors occurring within 6 months and 12 months, or the specific number of workday attendance behaviors occurring within these periods. Thus, for each period during which a perfect number of attendance days occurred, a person received an award—a fixed ratio schedule one.

The second schedule focuses on eligibility for the drawing. It is a variable ratio one because a random number of perfect attendance days must pass before a specific employee receives a trip. Maintaining perfect attendance to qualify for the drawing is similar to playing a slot machine. In this variable ratio system, players keep putting coins in the machines because they don't have any idea when they will hit the jackpot.[13] Lotteries similar to Drankenfeld's have been used by firms as different as new car dealerships and New York Life Insurance.[14]

Negative Reinforcement (Avoidance)   A second reinforcement strategy used in OB Mod is **negative reinforcement** or avoidance—the withdrawal of negative consequences, which tends to increase the likelihood of repeating the desirable behavior in similar settings. For example, a manager at McDonald's regularly nags a worker about his poor performance and then stops nagging when the worker does not fall behind one day. We need to focus on two aspects here: the negative consequences followed by the withdrawal of these consequences when desirable behavior occurs. The term negative reinforcement comes from this withdrawal of the negative consequences. This strategy is also sometimes called avoidance because its intent is for the person to avoid the negative consequence by performing the desired behavior. For instance, we stop at a red light to avoid a traffic ticket, or a worker who prefers the day shift is allowed to return to that shift if she performs well on the night shift.

Punishment   A third OB Mod strategy is punishment. Unlike positive reinforcement and negative reinforcement, punishment is not intended to encourage positive behavior but to discourage negative behavior. Formally defined, **punishment** is the administration of negative consequences or the withdrawal of positive consequences that tend to reduce the likelihood of repeating the behavior in similar settings. The first type of punishment is illustrated by a Burger King manager who assigns a tardy worker to an unpleasant job, such as cleaning the restrooms. An example of withdrawing positive consequences is a Burger King manager who docks the employee's pay when she is tardy.

Some scholarly work illustrates the importance of punishment by showing that punishment administered for poor performance leads to enhanced performance without a significant effect on satisfaction. However, punishment seen by the workers as arbitrary and capricious leads to very low satisfaction, as well as low performance.[15] Thus, punishment can be handled poorly, or it can be handled well. Of course, the manager's challenge is to know when to use this strategy and how to use it correctly.

Finally, punishment may be offset by positive reinforcement received from another source. It is possible for a worker to be reinforced by peers at the same time that the worker is receiving punishment from the manager. Sometimes the positive value of such peer support is so great that the individual chooses to put up with the punishment. Thus, the undesirable behavior continues. As many times as an experienced worker may be verbally reprimanded by a supervisor for playing jokes on new employees, for example, the "grins" offered by other workers may well justify continuation of the jokes in the future.

Does all of this mean that punishment should never be administered? Of course not. The important things to remember are to administer punishment selectively and then to do it right.

Extinction   The final OB Mod reinforcement strategy is **extinction**—the withdrawal of the reinforcing consequences for a given behavior. For example, Jack is often late for work, and his co-workers cover for him (positive reinforcement). The manager instructs Jack's co-workers to stop covering for him, withdrawing the reinforcing consequences. The manager has deliberately used extinction to get rid of an undesirable behavior. This strategy decreases the frequency of or weakens the behavior. The behavior is not "unlearned"; it simply is not exhibited. Since the behavior is no longer reinforced, it will reappear if reinforced again. Whereas positive reinforcement seeks to establish and maintain desirable work behavior, extinction is intended to weaken and eliminate undesirable behavior.

Summary of Reinforcement Strategies   Figure 6.4 summarizes and illustrates the use of each OB Mod strategy. They are all designed to direct work behavior toward practices desired by management. Both positive and negative reinforcement are used to strengthen the desirable behavior of improving work quality when it occurs. Punishment is used to weaken the undesirable behavior of high error rate and involves either administering negative consequences or withdrawing positive consequences. Similarly, extinction is used deliberately to weaken the undesirable high error rate behavior when it occurs. Note also, however, that extinction is used inadvertently to weaken the desirable low error rate behavior. Finally, these strategies may be used in combination as well as independently.

REINFORCEMENT PERSPECTIVES: USAGE AND ETHICAL ISSUES

The effective use of reinforcement strategies can help manage human behavior at work. Testimony to this effect is found in the application of these strategies in many large firms, such as General Electric and BFGoodrich, and even in small firms, such as Mid-America Building Maintenance. Mid-America, a janitorial services firm in Wichita, Kansas, provides

FIGURE 6.4	APPLYING REINFORCEMENT STRATEGIES

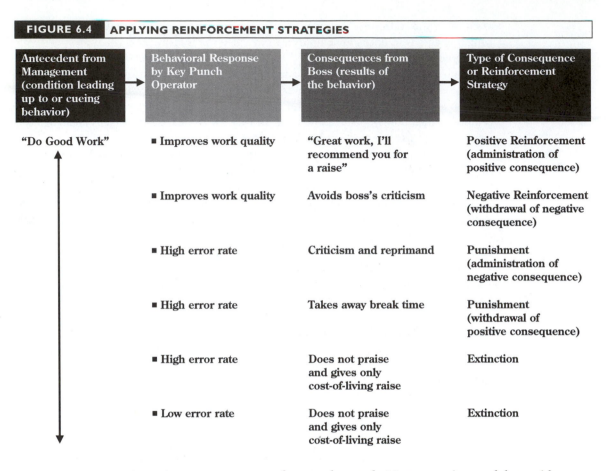

Antecedent from Management (condition leading up to or cueing behavior)	Behavioral Response by Key Punch Operator	Consequences from Boss (results of the behavior)	Type of Consequence or Reinforcement Strategy
"Do Good Work"	■ Improves work quality	"Great work, I'll recommend you for a raise"	Positive Reinforcement (administration of positive consequence)
	■ Improves work quality	Avoids boss's criticism	Negative Reinforcement (withdrawal of negative consequence)
	■ High error rate	Criticism and reprimand	Punishment (administration of negative consequence)
	■ High error rate	Takes away break time	Punishment (withdrawal of positive consequence)
	■ High error rate	Does not praise and gives only cost-of-living raise	Extinction
	■ Low error rate	Does not praise and gives only cost-of-living raise	Extinction

an incentive program to employees who work 90 consecutive workdays without an absence.[16] Reinforcement strategies are also supported by the growing number of consulting firms that specialize in reinforcement techniques.

Managerial use of these approaches is not without criticism, however. For example, some reports on the "success" of specific programs involve isolated cases that have been analyzed without the benefit of scientific research designs. It is hard to conclude definitively whether the observed results were caused by reinforcement dynamics. In fact, one critic argues that the improved performance may well have occurred only because of the goal setting involved—that is, because specific performance goals were clarified, and workers were individually held accountable for their accomplishment.[17]

Another major criticism rests with the potential value dilemmas associated with using reinforcement to influence human behavior at work. For example, some critics maintain that the systematic use of reinforcement strategies leads to a demeaning and dehumanizing view of people that stunts human growth and development.[18] A related criticism is that managers abuse the power of their position and knowledge by exerting external control over individual behavior. Advocates of the reinforcement approach attack the problem head on: they agree that behavior modification involves the control of behavior, but they also argue that behavior control is an irrevocable part of every manager's job. The real question is how to ensure that any manipulation is done in a positive and constructive fashion.[19]

CONTENT THEORIES OF MOTIVATION

Content theories, as noted earlier, suggest that motivation results from the individual's attempts to satisfy needs. Four of the better known content theories have been proposed by Abraham Maslow, Clayton Alderfer, David McClelland, and Frederick Herzberg. Each of these scholars offers a slightly different view of the needs individuals may bring with them to work.

HIERARCHY OF NEEDS THEORY

Abraham Maslow's **hierarchy of needs theory,** as shown in Figure 6.5, identifies five distinct levels of individual needs: from self-actualization and esteem, at the top, to social, safety, and physiological at the bottom.[20] Maslow assumes that some needs are more important than others and must be satisfied before the other needs can serve as motivators. For example, physiological needs must be satisfied before safety needs are activated, safety needs must be satisfied before social needs are activated, and so on.

Maslow's view is quite popular in U.S. firms because it appears easily implemented. Unfortunately, however, research evidence fails to support the existence of a precise five-step hierarchy of needs. The needs more likely operate in a flexible hierarchy. Some research

FIGURE 6.5   HIGHER ORDER AND LOWER ORDER NEEDS IN MASLOW'S HIERARCHY OF NEEDS

HIGHER ORDER NEEDS

Self-Actualization
Highest need level; need to fulfill oneself; to grow and use abilities to fullest and most creative extent.

Esteem
Need for esteem of others; respect, prestige, recognition, need for self-esteem, personal sense of competence, mastery.

LOWER ORDER NEEDS

Social
Need for love, affection, sense of belongingness in one's relationships with other persons.

Safety
Need for security, protection, and stability in the physical and interpersonal events of day-to-day life.

Physiological
Most basic of all human needs; need for biological maintenance; need for food, water, and sustenance.

suggests that **higher order needs** (esteem and self-actualization) tend to become more important than **lower order needs** (psychological, safety, and social) as individuals move up the corporate ladder.[21] Other studies report that needs vary according to a person's career stage, the size of the organization, and even geographical location.[22] There is also no consistent evidence that the satisfaction of a need at one level decreases its importance and increases the importance of the next higher need.[23] Finally, when the hierarchy of needs is examined across cultures, values such as those discussed in Chapter 2 become important. For instance, social needs tend to dominate in more collectivist societies, such as Mexico and Pakistan.[24]

ERG THEORY

Clayton Alderfer's **ERG theory** is also based on needs but differs from Maslow's theory in three basic respects.[25] First, the theory collapses Maslow's five need categories into three: **existence needs**—desire for physiological and material well-being; **relatedness needs**—desire for satisfying interpersonal relationships; and **growth needs**—desire for continued personal growth and development. Second, whereas Maslow's theory argues that individuals progress up the "needs" hierarchy, ERG theory emphasizes a unique *frustration-regression* component. An already satisfied lower level need can become activated when a higher level need cannot be satisfied. Thus, if a person is continually frustrated in his or her attempts to satisfy growth needs, relatedness needs can again surface as key motivators. Third, unlike Maslow's theory, ERG theory contends that more than one need may be activated at the same time.

Even though more research is needed to shed more light on its validity, the supporting evidence on ERG theory is encouraging.[26] In particular, the theory's allowance for regression back to lower level needs is a valuable contribution to our thinking. It may help to explain why in some settings, for example, workers' complaints focus on wages, benefits, and working conditions—things relating to existence needs. Although these needs are important, their importance may be exaggerated because the workers' jobs cannot otherwise satisfy relatedness and growth needs. ERG theory thus offers a more flexible approach to understanding human needs than does Maslow's strict hierarchy.

ACQUIRED NEEDS THEORY

In the late 1940s, psychologist David I. McClelland and his co-workers began experimenting with the Thematic Apperception Test (TAT) as a way of measuring human needs.[27] The TAT is a projective technique that asks people to view pictures and write stories about what they see. In one case, McClelland showed three executives a photograph of a man sitting down and looking at family photos arranged on his work desk. One executive wrote of an engineer who was daydreaming about a family outing scheduled for the next day. Another described a designer who had picked up an idea for a new gadget from remarks made by his family. The third described an engineer who was intently working on a bridge-stress problem that he seemed sure to solve because of his confident look.[28] McClelland identified three themes in these TAT stories, with each corresponding to an underlying need that he believes is important for understanding individual behavior. These needs are (1) **need for achievement (nAch)**—the desire to do something better or more efficiently, to solve problems, or to master complex tasks; (2) **need for affiliation (nAff)**—the desire to establish and maintain friendly and warm relations with others; and (3) **need for power (nPower)**—the desire to control others, to influence their behavior, or to be responsible for others.

McClelland posits that these three needs are acquired over time, as a result of life experiences. He encourages managers to learn how to identify the presence of nAch, nAff, and nPower in themselves and in others and to be able to create work environments that are responsive to the respective need profiles.

The theory is particularly useful because each need can be linked with a set of work preferences. A high-need achiever will prefer individual responsibilities, challenging goals, and performance feedback. A high-need affiliator is drawn to interpersonal relationships and opportunities for communication. The high need-for-power type seeks influence over others and likes attention and recognition. If these needs are truly acquired, it may be possible to acquaint people with the need profiles required to succeed in various types of jobs. For instance, McClelland found that the combination of a moderate to high need for power and a lower need for affiliation is linked with senior executive success. High nPower creates the willingness to have influence or impact on others; lower nAff allows the manager to make difficult decisions without undue worry over being disliked.[29]

Research lends considerable insight into nAch in particular and includes some especially interesting applications in developing nations. For example, McClelland trained businesspeople in Kakinda, India, to think, talk, and act like high achievers by having them write stories about achievement and participate in a business game that encouraged achievement. The businesspeople also met with successful entrepreneurs and learned how to set challenging goals for their own businesses. Over a two-year period following these activities, the participants from the Kakinda study engaged in activities that created twice as many new jobs as those who hadn't received the training.[30]

TWO-FACTOR THEORY

Frederick Herzberg took a different approach to examining motivation. He simply asked workers to report the times they felt exceptionally good about their jobs and the times they felt exceptionally bad about them.[31] As shown in Figure 6.6, Herzberg and his associates noted that the respondents identified somewhat different things when they felt good or bad about their jobs. From this study they developed the **two-factor theory,** also known as the motivator-hygiene theory, which portrays different factors as primary causes of job satisfaction and job dissatisfaction.

According to this theory, **hygiene factors** are sources of job dissatisfaction. These factors are associated with the job context or work setting; that is, they relate more to the environment in which people work than to the nature of the work itself. Among the hygiene factors shown on the left in Figure 6.6 perhaps the most surprising is salary. Herzberg found that low salary makes people dissatisfied, but that paying them more does not necessarily satisfy or motivate them. In the two-factor theory, job satisfaction and job dissatisfaction are totally separate dimensions. Therefore, improving a hygiene factor, such as working conditions, will not make people satisfied with their work; it will only prevent them from being dissatisfied.

To improve job satisfaction, the theory directs attention to an entirely different set of factors—the **motivator factors** shown on the right in Figure 6.6. These factors are related to job context—what people actually do in their work. Adding these satisfiers or motivators to

FIGURE 6.6	SOURCES OF DISSATISFACTION AND SATISFACTION IN HERZBERG'S TWO-FACTOR THEORY

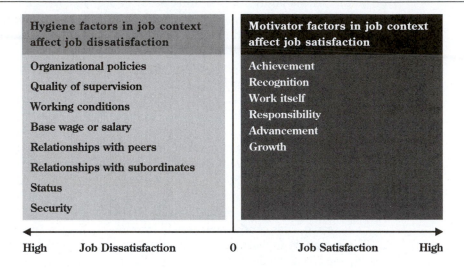

Hygiene factors in job context affect job dissatisfaction	Motivator factors in job context affect job satisfaction
Organizational policies	Achievement
Quality of supervision	Recognition
Working conditions	Work itself
Base wage or salary	Responsibility
Relationships with peers	Advancement
Relationships with subordinates	Growth
Status	
Security	

← High   Job Dissatisfaction   0   Job Satisfaction   High →

people's jobs is Herzberg's link to performance. These factors include sense of achievement, recognition, and responsibility.

According to Herzberg, when these opportunities are not available, low job satisfaction causes a lack of motivation and performance suffers. He suggests the technique of job enrichment as a way of building satisfiers into job content. This topic is given special attention in Chapter 8. For now, the notion is well summarized in this statement by Herzberg: "If you want people to do a good job, give them a good job to do."[32]

OB scholars continue to debate the merits of the two-factor theory and its applications.[33] Many are unable to confirm the theory. Many criticize it as being method bound. This is a serious criticism, for the scientific approach requires that theories be verifiable under different research methods. Furthermore, this theory, just like the other content theories, fails to account for individual differences, to link motivation and needs to both satisfaction and performance, or to consider cultural and professional differences.[34]

The content theories remain popular in management circles because of their simplicity and the direct apparent linkage from needs to behavior. At the same time, none of the theories links needs directly to motivated behavior desired by the manager. Rather, managers just misinterpret the theories and often inappropriately assume that they know the needs of their subordinates. Thus, we advise extreme care in simplistic application of content theories. We will return to these theories when we incorporate satisfaction into the discussion of motivation.

PROCESS THEORIES

The various content theories emphasize the "what" aspects of motivation. That is, they tend to look for ways to improve motivation by dealing with activated or deprived needs. They do not delve formally into the thought processes through which people choose one action over another in the workplace. *Process theories* focus on thought processes. Although there are many process theories, we will concentrate on equity and expectancy theory.

EQUITY THEORY

Equity theory is based on the phenomenon of social comparison and is best applied to the workplace through the writing of J. Stacy Adams.[35] Adams argues that when people gauge the fairness of their work outcomes relative to others, any perceived inequity is a motivating state of mind. Perceived inequity occurs when someone believes that the rewards received for their work contributions compare unfavorably to the rewards other people appear to have received for their work. When such perceived inequity exists, the theory states that people will be motivated to act in ways that remove the discomfort and restore a sense of felt equity.

Felt negative inequity exists when an individual feels that he or she has received relatively less than others have in proportion to work inputs. *Felt positive inequity* exists when an individual feels that he or she has received relatively more than others have. When either feeling exists, the individual will likely engage in one or more of the following behaviors to restore a sense of equity.

- Change work inputs (e.g., reduce performance efforts).
- Change the outcomes (rewards) received (e.g., ask for a raise).
- Leave the situation (e.g., quit).
- Change the comparison points (e.g., compare self to a different co-worker).
- Psychologically distort the comparisons (e.g., rationalize that the inequity is only temporary and will be resolved in the future).
- Take actions to change the inputs or outputs of the comparison person (e.g., get a co-worker to accept more work).

The equity comparison intervenes between the allocation of rewards and the ultimate impact on the recipients. What may seem fair and equitable to a group leader, for example, might be perceived as unfair and inequitable by a team member after comparisons are made with other teammates. Furthermore, such feelings of inequity are determined solely by the individual's interpretation of the situation. It is not the reward-giver's intentions that count, but it is how the recipient perceives the reward that will determine actual motivational outcomes. The Effective Manager 6.1 offers ideas for coping with equity comparisons.

THE EFFECTIVE MANAGER 6.1
STEPS FOR MANAGING THE EQUITY PROCESS

- Recognize that equity comparisons are inevitable in the workplace.
- Anticipate felt negative inequities when rewards are given.
- Communicate clear evaluations of any rewards given.
- Communicate an appraisal of performance on which reward is based.
- Communicate comparison points appropriate in the situation.

Research indicates that people who feel they are overpaid (perceived positive inequity) increase the quantity or quality of their work, whereas those who feel they are underpaid (perceived negative inequity) decrease the quantity or quality of their work.[36] The research is most conclusive with respect to felt negative inequity. It appears that people are less comfortable when they are underrewarded than when they are overrewarded. Such results, however, are particularly tied to individualistic cultures in which self-interests tend to govern social comparisons. In more collectivist cultures, such as those of many Asian countries, the concern often runs more for equality than equity. This allows for solidarity with the group and helps to maintain harmony in social relationships.[37]

EXPECTANCY THEORY

Victor Vroom's **expectancy theory** posits that motivation is a result of a rational calculation.[38] A person is motivated to the degree that he or she believes that (1) effort will yield acceptable performance, (2) performance will be rewarded, and (3) the value of the rewards is highly positive. The interactive combination of all three influences motivation. (See Figure 6.7.) Thus, some key concepts are defined in terms of probabilities.

- The probability assigned by an individual that work effort will be followed by a given level of achieved task performance is called **expectancy.** Expectancy would equal 0 if the person felt it were impossible to achieve the given performance level; it would equal 1 if a person were 100 percent certain that the performance could be achieved.

- **Instrumentality** is the probability assigned by the individual that a given level of achieved task performance will lead to various work outcomes. Instrumentality also varies from 0 to 1.*

- **Valence** is the value attached by the individual to various work outcomes. Valences form a scale from -1 (very undesirable outcome) to +1 (very desirable outcome). Vroom posits that motivation *(M)*, expectancy *(E)*, instrumentality *(I)*, and valence *(V)* are related to one another by the equation: $M = (E) \times (I) \times (V)$.

* Strictly speaking, Vroom's treatment of instrumentality would allow it to vary from -1 to +1. We use the probability definition here and the 0 to +1 range for pedagogical purposes; it is consistent with the instrumentality notion.

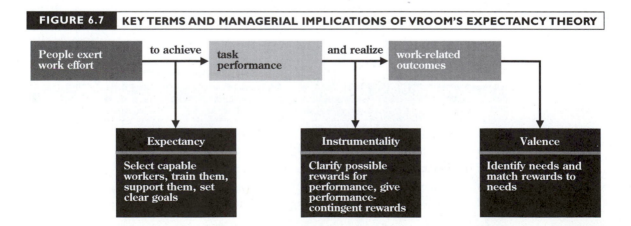

FIGURE 6.7   KEY TERMS AND MANAGERIAL IMPLICATIONS OF VROOM'S EXPECTANCY THEORY

This multiplier effect means that the motivational appeal of a given work path is sharply reduced whenever any one or more of these factors approaches the value of zero. Conversely, for a given reward to have a high and positive motivational impact as a work outcome, the expectancy, instrumentality, and valence associated with the reward all must be high and positive.

Suppose that a manager is wondering whether or not the prospect of earning a merit raise will be motivational to an employee. Expectancy theory predicts that motivation to work hard to earn the merit pay will be low if *expectancy* is low—a person feels that he or she cannot achieve the necessary performance level. Motivation will also be low if *instrumentality* is low—the person is not confident a high level of task performance will result in a high merit pay raise. Motivation will also be low if *valence* is low—the person places little value on a merit pay increase. And motivation will be low if any combination of these exists. Thus, the multiplier effect requires managers to act to maximize expectancy, instrumentality, and valence when seeking to create high levels of work motivation. A zero at any location on the right side of the expectancy equation will result in zero motivation.

Expectancy logic argues that a manager must try to intervene actively in work situations to maximize work expectancies, instrumentalities, and valences that support organizational objectives.[39] To influence expectancies, managers should select people with proper abilities, train them well, support them with needed resources, and identify clear performance goals. To influence instrumentality, managers should clarify performance-reward relationships and confirm these relationships when rewards are actually given for performance accomplishments. To influence valences, managers should identify the needs that are important to each individual and then try to adjust available rewards to match these needs.

A great deal of research on expectancy theory has been conducted, and review articles are available.[40] Although the theory has received substantial support, specific details, such as the operation of the multiplier effect, remain subject to some question. One of the more popular modifications of Vroom's original version of the theory distinguishes between work outcomes for calculating valence.[41] Researchers have separated **extrinsic rewards**—positively valued work outcomes given to the individual by some other person—from intrinsic rewards (see The Effective Manager 6.2). **Intrinsic rewards** are positively valued work outcomes that the individual receives directly as a result of task performance. A feeling of achievement after accomplishing a particularly challenging task is an example.

Expectancy theory does not specify exactly which rewards will motivate particular groups of workers. In this sense, the theory allows for the fact that the rewards and their

---

THE EFFECTIVE MANAGER 6.2

WORK GUIDELINES FOR ALLOCATING EXTRINSIC REWARDS

1. Clearly define the desired behaviors.
2. Maintain an inventory of rewards that have the potential to serve as positive reinforcers.
3. Recognize individual differences in the rewards that will have positive value for each person.
4. Let each person know exactly what must be done to receive a desirable reward. Set clear target antecedents and give performance feedback.
5. Allocate rewards contingently and immediately upon the appearance of the desired behaviors.
6. Allocate rewards wisely in terms of scheduling the delivery of positive reinforcement.

link with performance are likely to be seen as quite different in different cultures. It helps to explain some apparently counterintuitive findings. For example, a pay raise motivated one group of Mexican workers to work fewer hours. They wanted a certain amount of money in order to enjoy things other than work rather than just more money. A Japanese sales representative's promotion to manager of a U.S. company adversely affected his performance. His superiors did not realize that the promotion embarrassed him and distanced him from his colleagues.[42]

INTEGRATING THE MOTIVATION THEORIES

The previously discussed reinforcement, content, and process motivational approaches deal with one or more aspects of rewards, needs, cognitions, satisfaction, and performance. We have tended to treat each of these separately and they may be used that way or mixed and matched, as the occasion demands and in whichever way you are comfortable in using them. Now, however, we treat the linkage between satisfaction and performance to help integrate all the views we have discussed.

JOB SATISFACTION

Formally defined, **job satisfaction** is the degree to which individuals feel positively or negatively about their jobs. It is an attitude or emotional response to one's tasks, as well as to the physical and social conditions of the workplace. At first glance, and from the perspective of Herzberg's two-factor theory, some aspects of job satisfaction should be motivational and lead to positive employment relationships and high levels of individual job performance. But as we will discuss, the issues are more complicated than this conclusion suggests.

On a daily basis, managers must be able to infer the job satisfaction of others by careful observation and interpretation of what they say and do while going about their jobs. Sometimes, it is also useful to examine more formally the levels of job satisfaction among groups of workers, especially through formal interviews or questionnaires. Increasingly, other methods are being used as well, such as focus groups and computer-based attitude surveys.[43]

Among the many available job satisfaction questionnaires that have been used over the years, two popular ones are the Minnesota Satisfaction Questionnaire (MSQ) and the Job Descriptive Index (JDI).[44] Both address aspects of satisfaction with which good managers should be concerned for the people reporting to them. For example, the MSQ measures satisfaction with working conditions, chances for advancement, freedom to use one's own judgment, praise for doing a good job, and feelings of accomplishment, among others. The five facets of job satisfaction measured by the JDI are:

- *The work itself*—responsibility, interest, and growth.
- *Quality of supervision*—technical help and social support.
- *Relationships with co-workers*—social harmony and respect.
- *Promotion opportunities*—chances for further advancement.
- *Pay*—adequacy of pay and perceived equity vis-à-vis others.

JOB SATISFACTION, RETENTION, AND PERFORMANCE

The importance of job satisfaction can be viewed in the context of two decisions people make about their work. The first is the decision to belong—that is, to join and remain a member of an organization. The second is the decision to perform—that is, to work hard in pursuit of high levels of task performance. Not everyone who belongs to an organization performs up to expectations.

The decision to belong concerns an individual's attendance and longevity at work. In this sense, job satisfaction influences *absenteeism,* or the failure of people to attend work. In general, workers who are satisfied with the job itself have more regular attendance and are less likely to be absent for unexplained reasons than are dissatisfied workers. Job satisfaction can also affect turnover, or decisions by people to terminate their employment. Simply put, dissatisfied workers are more likely than satisfied workers to quit their jobs.[45]

What is the relationship between job satisfaction and performance? There is considerable debate on this issue, with three alternative points of view evident: (1) satisfaction causes performance, (2) performance causes satisfaction, and (3) rewards cause both performance and satisfaction.[46]

Argument: Satisfaction Causes Performance   If job satisfaction causes high levels of performance, the message to managers is quite simple: to increase employees' work performance, make them happy. Research, however, indicates that no simple and direct link exists between individual job satisfaction at one point in time and work performance at a later point. This conclusion is widely recognized among OB scholars, even though some evidence suggests that the relationship holds better for professional or higher level employees than for nonprofessionals or those at lower job levels. Job satisfaction alone is not a consistent predictor of individual work performance.

Argument: Performance Causes Satisfaction   If high levels of performance cause job satisfaction, the message to managers is quite different. Rather than focusing first on peoples' job satisfaction, attention should be given to helping people achieve high performance; job satisfaction would be expected to follow. Research indicates an empirical relationship between individual performance measured at a certain time period and later job satisfaction. A basic model of this relationship, based on the work of Edward E. Lawler and Lyman Porter, maintains that performance accomplishment leads to rewards that, in turn, lead to satisfaction.[47] In this model rewards are intervening variables; that is, they "link" performance with later satisfaction. In addition, a moderator variable—perceived equity of rewards—further affects the relationship. The moderator indicates that performance will lead to satisfaction only if rewards are perceived as equitable. If an individual feels that his or her performance is unfairly rewarded, the performance-causes-satisfaction will not hold.

Argument: Rewards Cause Both Satisfaction and Performance   This final argument in the job satisfaction–performance controversy is the most compelling. It suggests that a proper allocation of rewards can positively influence both performance and satisfaction. The key word in the previous sentence is *proper.* Research indicates that people who receive high rewards report higher job satisfaction. But research also indicates that performance-contingent rewards influence a person's work performance. In this case, the size and value of the reward vary in proportion to the level of one's performance accomplishment. Large rewards are given for high performance; small or no rewards are given for low performance. And whereas giving a low performer only small rewards initially may lead to dissatisfaction, the expectation is that the individual will make efforts to improve performance in order to obtain greater rewards in the future.

The point is that managers should consider satisfaction and performance as two separate but interrelated work results that are affected by the allocation of rewards. Whereas job satisfaction alone is not a good predictor of work performance, well-managed rewards can have a positive influence on both satisfaction and performance.

INTEGRATED MODEL OF MOTIVATION

Figure 6.8 outlines the integrated view. Note that the figure has much in common with Vroom's expectancy theory and the Porter-Lawler framework, both process theories, just discussed.[48] In the figure, job performance and satisfaction are separate, but potentially interdependent, work results. Performance is influenced most directly by individual attributes of the kind treated in Chapter 4, such as ability and experience, organizational support such as resources and technology, and work effort—the point at which an individual's level of motivation comes directly to bear. Individual motivation directly determines work effort, and the key to motivation is the ability to create a work setting that positively responds to individual needs and goals. Whether or not a work setting proves motivational for a given individual depends on the availability of rewards and their perceived value. Note also the importance of contingent rewards, reflecting the law of contingent reinforcement. Recall also the importance of immediacy in rewarding.

The content theories enter the model as the guide to understanding individual attributes and identifying the needs that give motivational value to the possible rewards. When the individual experiences intrinsic rewards for work performance, motivation will be directly and positively affected. Motivation can also occur when job satisfactions result from either extrinsic or intrinsic rewards that are felt to be equitably allocated. When felt negative inequity results, satisfaction will be low and motivation will be reduced. Recall that equity comparison is a key process theory aspect.

With this discussion of reinforcement, content, and process theories, you should have a better understanding of motivation. Although it will always be difficult to motivate

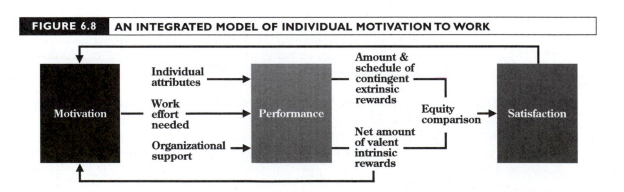

FIGURE 6.8   AN INTEGRATED MODEL OF INDIVIDUAL MOTIVATION TO WORK

employees, the knowledge in this chapter should help you reach toward higher performance and satisfaction. Finally, the integrating model rests on cultural assumptions, so that the meaning of the concepts may be culturally specific. The importance of various intrinsic and extrinsic rewards may well differ across cultures, as may the aspects of performance that are highly valued.

CHAPTER 6 SUMMARY

What is motivation to work?

- Motivation is an internal force that accounts for the level, direction, and persistence of effort expended at work.
- Reinforcement theories emphasize the means through which the process of controlling an individual's behavior by manipulating its consequences takes place. They focus on observable aspects rather than what is inside an employee's head.
- Content theories, including the work of Maslow, Alderfer, McClelland, and Herzberg, focus on locating individual needs that influence behavior in the workplace.
- Process theories, such as equity and expectancy theory, examine the thought processes that affect decisions about alternative courses of action by people at work.

What are reinforcement theories, and how are they linked to motivation?

- The foundation of reinforcement is the law of effect, which states that behavior will be repeated or extinguished depending on whether the consequences are positive or negative.
- Positive reinforcement is the administration of positive consequences that tend to increase the likelihood of a person's repeating a behavior in similar settings.
- Positive reinforcement should be contingent and immediate, and it can be scheduled continuously or intermittently, depending on resources and desired outcomes.
- Negative reinforcement (avoidance) is used to encourage desirable behavior through the withdrawal of negative consequences for previously undesirable behavior.
- Punishment is the administration of negative consequences or the withdrawal of positive consequences, which tends to reduce the likelihood of repeating an undesirable behavior in similar settings.
- Extinction is the withdrawal of reinforcing consequences for a given behavior.

What do the content theories suggest about individual needs and motivation?

- Maslow's hierarchy of needs theory views human needs as activated in a five-step hierarchy ranging from (lowest) physiological, safety, social, esteem, to self-actualization (highest).
- Alderfer's ERG theory collapses the five needs into three: existence, relatedness, and growth; it maintains that more than one need can be activated at a time.

- McClelland's acquired needs theory focuses on the needs for achievement, affiliation, and power, and it views needs as developed over time through experience and training.
- Herzberg's two-factor theory links job satisfaction to motivator factors, such as responsibility and challenge, associated with job content.
- Herzberg's two-factor theory links job dissatisfaction to hygiene factors, such as pay and working conditions, associated with job context.

What do the process theories suggest about individual motivation?

- Equity theory points out that social comparisons take place when people receive rewards and that any felt inequity will motivate them to try to restore a sense of perceived equity.
- When felt inequity is negative, that is, when the individual feels unfairly treated, he or she may decide to work less hard in the future or to quit a job.
- Vroom's expectancy theory describes motivation as a function of an individual's beliefs concerning effort-performance relationships (expectancy), work-outcome relationships (instrumentality), and the desirability of various work outcomes (valence).
- Expectancy theory states that Motivation = Expectancy × Instrumentality × Valence, and argues that managers should make each factor positive in order to ensure high levels of motivation.

How can satisfaction and its linkage with performance help tie together insights of the motivational theories into an integrated motivational model?

- Job satisfaction is a work attitude that reflects the degree to which people feel positively or negatively about a job and its various facets.
- Common aspects of job satisfaction relate to pay, working conditions, quality of supervision, co-workers, and the task itself.
- Job satisfaction is empirically related to employee turnover and absenteeism.
- The relationship between job satisfaction and performance is more controversial; current thinking focuses on how rewards influence both satisfaction and performance.
- Reinforcement views emphasize contingent rewards as well as the speed of the rewards.
- The content theories help identify important needs and determine what a person values by way of rewards.
- The equity theory suggests that any rewards must be perceived as equitable in the social context of the workplace.
- Although motivation predicts work efforts, individual performance also depends on job-relevant abilities and organizational support.

Human Resource Management Systems

Study Questions

Management of human resources and employee rewards are increasingly important in the new workplace. As you read Chapter 7, keep in mind the following key questions.

- What are the essentials of human resource strategy and practice?
- What is training and career planning and development?
- What is performance appraisal?
- What are rewards and reward systems?
- How does one manage pay as an extrinsic reward?
- How does one manage intrinsic rewards?

In this chapter, we focus on human resource management systems and rewards. We include human resource strategic planning, staffing, training, career planning and development, performance appraisal, and rewards.

HUMAN RESOURCE STRATEGY AND PRACTICE

Human resource (HR) strategic planning is the process of providing capable and motivated people to carry out the organization's mission and strategy. A key part of this process is the *staffing function,* which involves the recruitment of employees—generating applicants; selection—making hiring decisions for each applicant; and socialization—orienting new hires to the organization.[1] This function is a critical part of an organization's job requirements—the employee characteristics match emphasized so strongly in Chapter 4. Once an HR staffing strategy is in place, managers must continue to assess current HR needs to make sure the organization continues to retain people to meet its strategic objectives.[2]

JOB ANALYSIS

Staffing begins with an understanding of the positions or jobs for which individuals are needed in the organization. **Job analysis** provides this information; it is the process and procedures used to collect and classify information about tasks the organization needs to complete.[3] Job analysis assists in the understanding of job activities required in a work process and helps define jobs, their interrelationships, and the demographic, aptitude and ability, and personality characteristics needed to do these jobs. The results can be applied to job descriptions, job evaluation and classification, training and career development, performance appraisal, and other HR aspects. Information concerned with the job itself is laid out in the job description. The job description typically contains such information as job duties and responsibilities, equipment and materials used, working conditions and hazards, supervision, work schedules, standards of performance, and relationships to other jobs.[4]

The worker characteristics of job analysis needed to meet the job requirements and specified in the job description are laid out in a job specification. For example, a safety supervisor must have a knowledge of safety regulations. The job requirements and minimum qualifications make up the job specification part of the job analysis.

In addition to other important contributions, the job content and relative importance of different job duties and responsibilities included in job analysis help organizations deal with legal requirements. Such information is useful in defending actions from legal challenges that allege discrimination or unfairness. The generic defense against a charge of discrimination is that the contested decision (hiring, providing a pay raise, termination) was made for job-related reasons, such as provided by job analysis. For example, a firefighter may be required to carry a 150-pound person from a burning building. Job analysis can help a city defend itself against sex discrimination if it can show the relevance of this requirement with a job analysis.[5]

RECRUITMENT

Once job analysis provides the necessary job requirements and employee characteristics, qualified people need to be drawn in to apply for various positions. **Recruitment** is the process of attracting the best qualified individuals to apply for a given job.[6]

It typically involves (1) advertisement of a position vacancy, (2) preliminary contact with potential job candidates, and (3) preliminary screening to obtain a pool of candidates. These practices are an example of external recruitment or of attracting individuals from outside the organization. External recruitment involves such sources as general advertisements, often in newspapers, trade journals, or via external Internet; word-of-mouth suggestions from current employees; use of employment agencies; and applicant walk-ins. By contrast, internal recruitment is a process for attracting job applicants from those currently working for the firm. Posting vacant positions on bulletin boards, in internal memos, and over intranets are frequently used ways to recruit internally.

Most firms tend to use a mix of external and internal recruitment. Some organizations, notably the United States armed forces, rely heavily on external recruitment for entry-level positions and then fill higher level positions entirely from internal promotions. Both approaches have advantages. Internal recruitment is encouraging to current employees, and external recruitment tends to bring in "new blood" and fresh ideas to the firm.

Traditionally, firms have attempted to "sell" their organization and jobs to build up the applicant pool. More recently, an approach called a **realistic job preview,** is increasingly being used. In a realistic job preview, applicants are provided with an objective description of the prospective organization and job. Such descriptions have been found to reduce turnover and to better prepare new hires to cope with their jobs.[7]

SELECTION

Once an applicant pool has been recruited, the selection aspect of staffing comes into play. **Selection** involves the series of steps from initial applicant screening to final hiring of the new employee. The selection process involves completing application materials, conducting an interview, completing any necessary tests, doing a background investigation, and deciding to hire or not to hire.

Application Materials   These materials may involve a traditional application form requesting various aspects of background and experience. These forms may be in traditional hard copy or on the Internet. Sometimes resumes (brief summaries of one's background and qualifications) are used in lieu of, or in addition to, other materials. Sometimes tests are included as part of the application materials.

Employment Interviews   Many of you have experienced employment interviews at one time or another. Interviews are almost invariably used in the selection process (see The Effective Manager 7.1), although they are prone to the kinds of perceptual distortions discussed in Chapter 5, as well as other problems. Nevertheless, they are a mainstay of the selection process, perhaps because they can serve as public relations tools for the organization. At their best, interviews provide rough ideas concerning fit with the job and organization.[8]

THE EFFECTIVE MANAGER 7.1

STEPS TO EMPHASIZE IN CONDUCTING HIRING INTERVIEWS

- Prepare yourself—check applicant's resume and prepare agenda.
- Initially put applicant at ease—use smalltalk.
- Guard against stereotypes—emphasize applicant as individual.
- Emphasize results-oriented questions—not only what applicant has done but results of these actions.
- Allow for pauses to gather thoughts.
- Bring interview to a natural close.

Tests   Tests may be administered either before or after the interview. They include cognitive aptitude or ability and personality tests and, increasingly, tests for drug use. Intelligence tests are the most common examples of cognitive tests. Other examples are clerical and mechanical tests. Personality tests evaluate the kinds of personality characteristics discussed in Chapter 4. For example, the California Personality Inventory measures such characteristics as dominance, sociability, and flexibility. Again, whatever kind of test is used must be validated against job requirements so that the organization is not guilty of discrimination.

Performance tests take many forms but often ask candidates to perform tasks that are identical to or at least closely related to what will be required on the job. As technology has become more important, performance tests involving computer skills have become more frequent. Also, a battery of tests often is used to explore a range of job behaviors.

For managerial jobs in particular, but increasingly for other jobs as well, assessment centers are often used. *Assessment centers* provide a firm with a comprehensive view of a candidate by evaluating the candidate's performance across many situations. Such assessments typically involve one to four days of various tests, simulations, role plays, and interviews, all based on dimensions the person occupying the job will need to demonstrate. AT&T has used assessment centers for many years, with considerable effectiveness, spending as much as $1,500 per employee in the process.[9] IBM and the FBI are also among the more than 2,000 organizations that use assessment centers for managerial selection and promotion.[10]

Background Investigation   Background investigation is yet another step that can be used either early or late in the selection process. Companies providing background audits say requests for their services have jumped sharply in the wake of the World Trade Center disaster. Hospitals, retailers, and firms that own private jets have had special interest. Two-thirds of employers check on potential hires. Basic level checks often include a Social Security trace, employment history, educational records, criminal records, and driving records.

Typically, a background investigation also involves reference checks. Generally, letters of reference tend to be positively biased and so are not highly related to job performance.[11] Moreover, unless the references, either written or provided over the phone, are very carefully worded, they can lead to lawsuits. References should only disclose information about the job duties the individual in question has been performing. Any personal descriptions should involve only information that can be objectively verified.

Decision to Hire   Based on the previous steps, the organization may choose to make the hiring decision and present a formal job offer. The offer may be made by the potential employee's future boss or by a group of people. At this point, a physical examination may be required if it is shown to be relevant for job performance. For some jobs, negotiations concerning salary or other benefits may occur.

SOCIALIZATION

Once hiring is completed, **socialization** is the final step in the staffing process. It involves orienting new employees to the firm and specifically to the work units in which they will be working. At this stage, the new employee is familiarized with the firm's policies and procedures and begins to get a feel for the organization's culture. Orientation can be conducted formally or informally, or it may involve a combination of the two. In complex positions, orientation may take place over an extended period of time. Socialization can help with the job requirements–employee characteristics match by helping to fill in gaps.

TRAINING AND CAREER DEVELOPMENT

After an employee is selected, it is important that he or she undergo training and long-term career planning and development.

TRAINING

Training is a set of activities that provides the opportunity to acquire and improve job-related skills.[12] In addition to initial training, training to improve skills is important and might cover such areas as computer skills, diversity, sexual harassment, and implementation of new systems or technology.

Training can be on the job, off the job, or both. *On-the-job training (OJT)* involves job instruction while performing the job in the actual workplace. Internships, apprenticeships, and job rotation are common forms of OJT. Internships are an opportunity for students to gain real-world experience. They are often offered in the summer and may or may not be paid. *Apprenticeships* involve learning a trade from an experienced worker. They are quite common in Europe and relatively uncommon in the United States.

Related coaching or mentoring programs for managerial and professional jobs are quite common in the United States, however. *Job rotation* provides a broad range of experience in different kinds of jobs in a firm. It is often used as part of management training programs where future managers may spend from a few weeks to much longer in activities such as information processing, computer software, or computer sales. The total program could last up to one or two years, with varying amounts of mentoring.

Off-the-job training commonly involves lectures, videos, and simulations. E-training is becoming more popular. It includes such developments as classes or information modules delivered via computer or the Internet that may be completed at any time or place, and group workshops offered through "virtual classroom" distance learning technology. Lectures convey specific information and work well for problem-solving and technical skills. Videos are particularly good for demonstrating various skills. Simulations, such as experiential exercises, business games, and various computer-based exercises, are particularly useful for teaching interpersonal, leadership, strategic management, and other complex skills such as those required of police officers.

A Canadian airline used a comprehensive combination of on- and off-the-job training to deal with the impact of five mergers and to cope with an extremely dynamic environment. The training was done worldwide and was conducted in combination with American Airlines. Numerous Canadian/U.S. cultural differences had to be worked through in the process.[13]

CAREER PLANNING AND DEVELOPMENT

In addition to employee training for short-term jobs, both the employee and the organization need to be concerned about longer term **career planning and development,** whereby individuals work with their managers and/or HR experts on career issues.[14]

Figure 7.1 offers a basic framework for formal career planning. The five steps in the framework begin with personal assessment and then progress through analysis of opportunities, selection of career objectives, and implementation of strategies, until the final step: evaluation of results. The process is recycled as necessary to allow for constructive revision of the career plan over time. Success in each of these steps entails a good deal of self-awareness and frank assessment. Thus, a successful career begins with sufficient insight to make good decisions about matching personal needs and capabilities with job opportunities over time. The manager's responsibility concerning career planning is twofold: first, planning and managing a personal career; second, assisting subordinates in assuming responsibility for their career planning and development.

Thoughts about careers take on a special relevance in the new workplace. We live and work in a time when the implications of constant change pressure us to continually review and reassess our career progress. Businesses are becoming smaller, employing fewer people, and moving beyond traditional organizational forms. Thus, there is increasing emphasis on horizontal and cross-functional relationships. Technical workers are becoming so important that they are being treated almost like high-level managers in terms of perquisites and rewards. The nature of "work" is changing and will be less bound by "9 to 5" traditions. Continuous learning will be required, and training and electronic education marketplaces will become more and more important.

In this setting, the old notions of a career based within a single organization that takes responsibility for a person's career development are becoming increasingly obsolete. In his book, *The Age of Unreason,* British scholar and consultant Charles Handy argues forcefully

FIGURE 7.1	FIVE STEPS IN FORMAL CAREER PLANNING

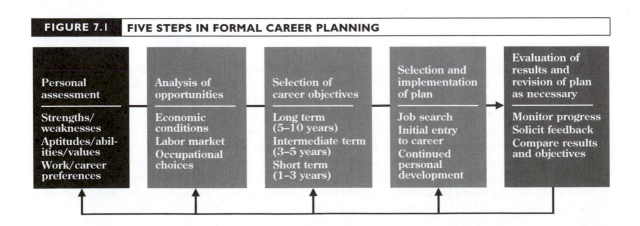

that each of us must take charge of our own careers and prepare for inevitable uncertainties and changes by building a "portfolio" of skills.[15] This portfolio needs continuous development: each new job assignment must be well selected and rigorously pursued as a learning opportunity.

Initial Entry to a Career   The full implications of the new workplace become apparent at the point of initial entry to a career. Choosing a job and a work organization are difficult decisions; our jobs inevitably exert a lot of influence over our lives. Whenever a job change is considered, the best advice is to know yourself and to learn as much as possible about the new job and the organization. This helps to ensure the best person-job-organization match. By working hard to examine personal needs, goals, and capabilities and to gather relevant information, share viewpoints, and otherwise make the recruitment process as realistic as possible, you can help start a new job on the best possible note.

When considering a new job or a possible job change, a "balance sheet" analysis of possible "gains" and "losses" is important. Ask at least two questions. First: What are my potential gains and losses? Things to consider in answering this question include salary and fringe benefits, work hours and schedules, travel requirements, use and development of skills and competencies, and opportunities for challenging new job assignments. Second: What are the potential gains and losses for significant others? Here, you should consider income available to meet family responsibilities, time available to be with family and friends, impacts of a geographical move on family and friends, and implications of work stress for nonwork life.

Adult Life Cycle and Career Stages   Chapter 4 showed that as people mature they pass through an adult life cycle with many different problems and prospects. As a manager, it is especially important to recognize the effects of this cycle on the people with whom you work. Recall that the earlier-mentioned life cycle stages popularized by Gail Sheehy were: provisional adulthood (ages 18–30), first adulthood (ages 30–45), and second adulthood (ages 45–85+).[16] These are only approximate ages, and there are transitional periods in moving from one stage to the next.

Given the age of change in which we live, the stages and transitions are also much less predictable than in earlier years. Where once a person had one or two careers and a single spouse, now there also can be numerous careers and either no spouse or more than one spouse. In the provisional adult period, people may move back with their parents, stretch out their education, and try many jobs, for example. And where once people retired at age 65, now it is becoming increasingly common to start yet another career at that age.

It is useful to link the adult life cycle literature and the **career stages** literature. For those who still follow a traditional career path, we can think of it in terms of: entry and establishment—roughly comparable to the provisional adulthood stage; advancement—the first adulthood stage; and maintenance, withdrawal, and retirement—the second adulthood stage.

Entry and establishment involve on-the-job development of relevant skills and abilities. Individuals also undergo organizational and professional socialization mentioned earlier. At the same time, progressive organizations engage actively in mentoring new employees.

In the advancement stage, the individual seeks growth and increased responsibility. There may be advancement through internal career paths or external career paths, outside the organization.

During the maintenance, withdrawal, and retirement stage of second adulthood individuals may experience continued growth of accomplishments or may encounter career stability. Many people encounter a **career plateau**—they find themselves in a position where they are unlikely to advance to a higher level of responsibility.

At some point during the maintenance career stage, individuals consider withdrawal and ultimate retirement. Now, some prolong this stage well into the second adulthood life cycle stage. Others start planning for an orderly retirement at age 65 or so.

Of course, as we have said, the traditional route above is no longer typical. People may very well have many jobs and more than one career and choose not to retire until they can no longer work. All of these changes reinforce the difficulty of managers building and maintaining commitment to the job and organization and provide many OB challenges.

PERFORMANCE APPRAISAL

Yet another key HR management function, performance appraisal, helps both the manager and subordinate maintain the organization–job–employee characteristics match. Formally defined, **performance appraisal** is a process of systematically evaluating performance and providing feedback on which performance adjustments can be made.[17] If the desired level of performance exceeds actual levels, a performance variance requiring special attention exists. For example, if you have a sales quota of twenty CD-ROM drives per month—the desired performance—and you sell only two CD-ROM drives per month—your actual performance—your performance variance of eighteen CD-ROMS will require the attention of the sales manager. The performance appraisal process should be based on the job analysis mentioned earlier. The job description, describing organizational job requirements, and the job specification, describing individual worker characteristics, provide the core.

PURPOSES OF PERFORMANCE APPRAISAL

Any performance appraisal system is central to an organization's human-resource management activities. Performance appraisals are intended to:

- Define the specific job criteria against which performance will be measured.
- Measure past job performance accurately.
- Justify the rewards given to individuals and/or groups, thereby discriminating between high and low performance.
- Define the development experiences the ratee needs to enhance performance in the current job and to prepare for future responsibilities.

These four functions describe two general purposes served by good performance appraisal systems: evaluation, and feedback and development. From an evaluative perspective, performance appraisal lets people know where they stand relative to objectives and standards. As such, the performance appraisal is an input to decisions that allocate rewards and otherwise administer the organization's personnel functions. From a counseling perspective, performance appraisal facilitates implementing decisions relating to planning for and gaining commitment to the continued training and personal development of subordinates.

Evaluative Decisions   Evaluative decisions are concerned with such issues as promotions, transfers, terminations, and salary increases. When these decisions are made on the basis of performance criteria, as opposed to some other basis, such as seniority, a performance appraisal system is necessary.

Performance appraisal information is also useful for making selection and placement decisions. In this case, performance results are matched against individual characteristics to determine which of these characteristics are most closely related to performance. For example, management checks various individual characteristics, such as education, mathematical ability, verbal ability, mechanical ability, and achievement motivation, to see how closely they are related to performance.

Individuals who score well on those characteristics found to be closely tied to performance for a given job are considered for that position. In addition, if specific aspects of a ratee's performance are found to be inadequate, the performance appraisal process may lead to remedial training. Finally, appraisals form the basis of any performance-contingent reward system (i.e., any system that ties rewards, such as pay, to an individual's or group's performance).

Feedback and Development Decisions   Performance appraisals also can be used to let ratees know where they stand in terms of the organization's expectations and performance objectives. Performance appraisal feedback should involve a detailed discussion of the ratee's job-related strengths and weaknesses. This feedback can then be used for developmental purposes. In terms of the expectancy motivation approach discussed in Chapter 6, feedback can help clarify the ratees' sense of both instrumentality—it can help them better understand what kinds of rewards they will receive if they perform well—and expectancy—it lets them know what actions they need to take to reach that level of performance. Performance appraisal feedback also can be used as a basis for individual coaching or training by the manager to help a subordinate overcome performance deficiencies. Surveys typically indicate that around two-thirds of the sampled firms use performance appraisals for developmental purposes.

WHO DOES THE PERFORMANCE APPRAISAL?

Performance appraisals traditionally have been conducted by an individual's immediate superior,[18] the presumption being that since the immediate superior is responsible for the subordinate's performance, the superior should do the appraisal. In many cases, however, others may be able to better perform at least some aspects of the appraisal. For example, peers are closest to the action, and their appraisals can be especially valuable when they are obtained from several peers. Immediate subordinates also can provide insightful evaluations as long as the ratings remain anonymous.

To obtain as much appraisal information as possible, as many as one-quarter of U.S. organizations are now using not only the evaluations of bosses, peers, and subordinates, but also self-ratings, customer ratings, and others with whom the ratee deals outside the immediate work unit. Such a comprehensive approach is called **360-degree evaluation.** The number of appraisals typically ranges from five to ten per person under evaluation. Firms such as Alcoa and UPS now use 360-degree evaluations. They are made to order for the new, flatter, team-oriented organizations emphasizing total quality or high performance management, whereby input from many sources is crucial. Computer technology can now facilitate the collection and analysis of some or all of these 360-degree evaluations.[19]

One example involves the use of self- and superior ratings in an innovative way. The subordinate rates himself or herself on the importance of a given job function to the subordinate's performance and on how well the subordinate thinks he or she is performing the function. The supervisor performs a similar evaluation of the employee. A computer program then highlights those areas on which there is the most disagreement. Only the associate gets the printout and may choose to discuss these areas with the supervisor. Both the timing and the specific content of such a meeting are at the discretion of the subordinate.[20]

PERFORMANCE APPRAISAL DIMENSIONS AND STANDARDS

In addition to performance outcomes, the behaviors or activities that result in these outcomes are frequently important to performance appraisal as well.

Output Measures   A number of production and sales jobs provide ready measures of *work output.* For example, a final-stage assembler may have a goal of fifteen completed computer monitors per hour. The number of monitors is easily measurable, and the organization can set standards concerning how many computer monitors should be completed per hour. Here, the performance dimension of interest is a quantitative one: fifteen completed computer monitors per hour. However, the organization also may introduce a *quality* dimension. The individual may be evaluated in terms not only of the number of monitors per hour but also the number of units that pass a *quality control inspection* per hour. Now, both quantity and quality are important, and the individual cannot trade one for the other. Assembling twenty monitors per hour will not do if only ten pass inspection, nor will having a larger proportion of monitors pass inspection if only ten monitors are assembled per hour.

In addition, management may be interested in other performance dimensions, such as downtime of the equipment used for assembling. In this case, the assembler would be evaluated in terms of quantity and quality of assembly output and equipment downtime. Management could thereby not only ensure that a desirable product is being assembled at a desirable rate but that the employee is careful with the equipment as well.

Activity Measures   In the preceding example, the output measures were straightforward, as was the measure of equipment downtime. Often, however, output measures may be a function of group efforts; or they may be extremely difficult to measure; or they may take so long to accomplish that they can't be readily determined for a given individual during a given time period. For example, it may be very difficult to determine the output of a research scientist attempting to advance new knowledge. In such a case, activity or behavioral measures may be called for, rather than output measures. The research scientist may be appraised in terms of his or her approach to problems, his or her interactions with other scientists, and the like.

Activity measures are typically obtained from the evaluator's observation and rating. In contrast, output measures are often obtained directly from written records or documents, such as production records. The difficulty of obtaining output measures may be one reason for using activity measures. Activity measures are also typically more useful for employee feedback and development than are output measures alone. For example, a salesperson may sell twenty insurance policies a month when the quota is twenty five. However, activities such as number of sales calls per day or number of community volunteer events attended per week (where some potential clients are likely to be found) can provide more specific information than simply the percentage of monthly quota output measures. Where jobs lend themselves to systematic analysis, important activities can be inferred from the job analysis.

PERFORMANCE APPRAISAL METHODS

Performance appraisal methods can be divided into two general categories: comparative methods and absolute methods.[21]

Comparative methods of performance appraisal seek to identify one's relative standing among those being rated, that is, comparative methods can establish that Bill is better than Mary, who is better than Leslie, who is better than Tom on a performance dimension. Comparative methods can indicate that one person is better than another on a given dimension, but not *how much better*. These methods also fail to indicate whether the person receiving the better rating is "good enough" in an absolute sense. It may well be that Bill is merely the best of a bad lot. Three comparative performance appraisal methods are (1) ranking, (2) paired comparison, and (3) forced distribution.

In contrast, absolute methods of performance appraisal specify precise measurement standards. For example, tardiness might be evaluated on a scale ranging from "never tardy" to "always tardy." Four of the more common absolute rating procedures are (1) graphic rating scales, (2) critical incident diary, (3) behaviorally anchored rating scales, and (4) management by objectives. The comparative methods are less likely than absolute measures to be used in more collectivist-oriented cultures because of their emphasis on the collectivity.

Ranking **Ranking** is the simplest of all the comparative techniques. It consists of merely rank ordering each individual from best to worst on each performance dimension being considered. For example, in evaluating work quality, I compare Smith, Jones, and Brown. I then rank Brown number 1, Smith number 2, and Jones number 3. The ranking method, though relatively simple to use, can become burdensome when there are many people to consider.

Paired Comparison In a **paired comparison** method, each person is directly compared with every other person being rated. The frequency of endorsement across all pairs determines one's final ranking. Every possible paired comparison within a group of ratees is considered, as shown below (italics indicate the person rated better in each pair):

Bill vs. Mary	*Mary* vs. Leslie	*Leslie* vs. Tom
Bill vs. Leslie	*Mary* vs. Tom	
Bill vs. Tom		

Number of times Bill is better   = 3
Number of times Mary is better   = 2
Number of times Leslie is better = 1
Number of times Tom is better   = 0

The best performer in this example is Bill, followed by Mary, then Leslie, and, last of all, Tom. When there are many people to compare, the paired comparison approach can be even more tedious than the ranking method.

Forced Distribution   **Forced distribution** uses a small number of performance categories, such as "very good," "good," "adequate," "poor," and "very poor." Each rater is instructed to rate a specific proportion of employees in each of these categories. For example, 10 percent of employees must be rated very good; 20 percent must be rated good, and so on. This method *forces* the rater to use all of the categories and to avoid rating everyone as outstanding, poor, average, or the like. It can be a problem if most of the people are truly superior performers or if most of the people perform about the same.

Graphic Rating Scales   Graphic rating scales list a variety of dimensions that are thought to be related to high performance outcomes in a given job and that the individual is accordingly expected to exhibit, such as cooperation, initiative, and attendance. The scales allow the manager to assign the individual scores on each dimension. An example is shown in Figure 7.2. These ratings are sometimes given point values and combined into numerical ratings of performance.

| FIGURE 7.2 | SIXTH-MONTH PERFORMANCE REVIEWS FOR BURROUGHS AND WATSON |

Employee: _Jayne Burroughs_   Supervisor: _Dr. Cutter_
Department: _Pathology_   Date: _11-28-02_

Work Quantity		Work Quality		Cooperation	
1. Far below average	—	1. Far below average	—	1. Far below average	—
2. Below average	✓	2. Below average	—	2. Below average	✓
3. Average	—	3. Average	✓	3. Average	—
4. Above average	—	4. Above average	—	4. Above average	—
5. Far above average	—	5. Far above average	—	5. Far above average	—

Employee: _John Watson_   Supervisor: _Dr. Cutter_
Department: _Pathology_   Date: _12-24-02_

Work Quantity		Work Quality		Cooperation	
1. Far below average	—	1. Far below average	—	1. Far below average	—
2. Below average	—	2. Below average	—	2. Below average	—
3. Average	✓	3. Average	—	3. Average	—
4. Above average	—	4. Above average	✓	4. Above average	—
5. Far above average	—	5. Far above average	—	5. Far above average	✓

The primary appeal of graphic rating scales is their ease of use. In addition they are efficient in the use of time and other resources, and they can be applied to a wide range of jobs. Unfortunately, because of generality, they may not be linked to job analysis or to other specific aspects of a given job. This difficulty can be dealt with by ensuring that only relevant dimensions of work based on sound job analysis procedures are rated. However, there is a tradeoff: the more the scales are linked to job analyses, the less general they are when comparing people on different jobs.

Critical Incident Diary   Supervisors may use **critical incident diaries** to record incidents of each subordinate's behavior that led to either unusual success or failure in a given performance aspect. These incidents are typically recorded in a diary-type log that is kept daily or weekly under predesignated dimensions. In a sales job, for example, following up sales calls and communicating necessary customer information might be two of the dimensions recorded in a critical incident diary. Descriptive paragraphs can then be used to summarize each salesperson's performance for each dimension as it is observed.

This approach is excellent for employee development and feedback. Since the method consists of qualitative statements rather than quantitative information, however, it is difficult to use for evaluative decisions. To provide for such information, the critical incident technique is sometimes combined with one of the other methods.

Behaviorally Anchored Rating Scales   The **behaviorally anchored rating scales (BARS)** is a performance appraisal approach that has received increasing attention. The procedure for developing this type of scale starts with the careful collection of descriptions of observable job behaviors. These descriptions are typically provided by managers and personnel specialists and include both superior and inferior performance. Once a large sample of behavioral descriptions is collected, each behavior is evaluated to determine the extent to which it describes good versus bad performance. The final step is to develop a rating scale in which the anchors are specific critical behaviors, each reflecting a different degree of performance effectiveness. An example of a BARS is shown in Figure 7.3 for a retail department manager. Note the specificity of the behaviors and the scale values for each. Similar behaviorally anchored scales would be developed for other dimensions of the job.

As you can see, the BARS approach is detailed and complex. It requires lots of time and effort to develop. But the BARS also provides specific behaviors that are useful for counseling and feedback, combined with quantitative scales that are useful for evaluative comparative purposes. Initial results of the use of BARS suggested that they were less susceptible to common rating errors than were more traditional scales. More recent evidence suggests that the scales may not be as superior as originally thought, especially if an equivalent amount of developmental effort is put into other types of measures.[22] A somewhat simpler variation of behaviorally anchored scales is the *Behavioral Observation Scale (BOS),* which uses a five-point frequency scale (ranging from almost always to almost never) for each separate statement of behavior.

Management by Objectives   Of all the appraisal methods available, **management by objectives (MBO)** is linked most directly to means-ends chains and goal setting, as discussed in Chapter 8.[23] When an MBO system is used, subordinates work with their supervisor to establish specific task-related objectives that fall within their domains and serve as

| FIGURE 7.3 | EXAMPLE OF A BEHAVIORALLY ANCHORED RATING SCALE DIMENSION |

Supervising Sales Personnel

Gives sales personnel a clear idea of their job duties and responsibilities; exercises tact and consideration in working with subordinates; handles work scheduling efficiently and equitably; supplements formal training with his or her own "coaching"; keeps informed of what the salespeople are doing on the job; and follows company policy in agreements with subordinates.

Effective 9   Could be expected to conduct full day's sales clinic with two new sales personnel and thereby develop them into top salespeople in the department.

8   Could be expected to give his or her sales personnel confidence and strong sense of responsibility by delegating many important tasks.

7   Could be expected never to fail to conduct weekly training meetings with his or her people at a scheduled hour and to convey to them exactly what is expected.

6   Could be expected to exhibit courtesy and respect toward his or her sales personnel.

5   Could be expected to remind sales personnel to wait on customers instead of conversing with one another.

4   Could be expected to be rather critical of store standards in front of his or her own people, thereby risking their development of poor attitudes.

3   Could be expected to tell an individual to come in anyway even though he or she called in to say he or she was ill.

2   Could be expected to go back on a promise to an individual who he or she had told could transfer back into previous department if he or she did not like the new one.

Ineffective 1   Could be expected to make promises to an individual about his or her salary being based on department sales even when he or she knew such a practice was against company policy.

means to help accomplish the supervisor's higher level objectives. Each set of objectives is worked out between a supervisor and a subordinate for a given time period. The establishment of objectives is similar to a job analysis, except that it is directed toward a particular individual in his or her job rather than toward a particular job type alone. The increased discretion of the MBO approach means that each specific person is likely to have a custom-tailored set of work goals while still working within the action context of organizational means-ends chains.

MBO is the most individualized of all the appraisal systems and tends to work well for counseling if the objectives go beyond simply desired outputs and focus on important activities as well. In comparing one employee with another, a key concern is the ease or difficulty of achieving the goals. If one person has an easier set of objectives to meet than another, then comparisons are unfair. Since MBO tends to rely less heavily on ratings than do other appraisal systems, rating errors are less likely to be a problem.

MEASUREMENT ERRORS IN PERFORMANCE APPRAISAL

To be meaningful, an appraisal system must be both *reliable*—provide consistent results each time it is used—and *valid*—actually measure people on relevant job content. A number of measurement errors can threaten the reliability or validity of performance appraisals.[24] Note the strong tie between these errors and Chapter 5, covering perception and attribution.

Halo Errors   A **halo error** results when one person rates another person on several different dimensions and gives a similar rating for each dimension. For example, a sales representative considered to be a "go-getter" and thus rated high on "dynamism" also would be rated high on dependability, tact, and whatever other performance dimensions were used. The rater fails to discriminate between the person's strong and weak points; a "halo" carries over from one dimension to the next. This effect can create a problem when each performance dimension is considered an important and relatively independent aspect of the job. A variation is the *single criterion error,* in which only one of several important performance aspects is considered at all.

Leniency/Strictness Errors   Just as some professors are known as "easy A's," some managers tend to give relatively high ratings to virtually everyone under their supervision. This is known as a **leniency error.** Sometimes the opposite occurs; some raters tend to give everyone a low rating. This is called a **strictness error.** The problem in both instances is the inadequate discrimination between good and poor performers. Leniency is likely to be a problem when peers assess one another, especially if they are asked to provide feedback to each other, because it is easier to discuss high ratings than low ones.

Central Tendency Errors   **Central tendency errors** occur when managers lump everyone together around the "average," or middle, category. This tendency gives the impression that there are no very good or very poor performers on the dimensions being rated. No true performance discrimination is made. Both leniency and central tendency errors are examples of raters who exhibit **low differentiation errors.** These raters simply restrict themselves to only a small part of the rating scale.

Recency Errors   A different kind of error, known as a **recency error,** occurs when a rater allows recent events to influence a performance rating over earlier events. Take, for example, the case of an employee who is usually on time but shows up one hour late for work the day before his or her performance rating. The employee is rated low on "promptness" because the one incident of tardiness overshadows his or her usual promptness.

Personal Bias Errors   Raters sometimes allow specific biases to enter into performance evaluations. When this happens, **personal bias errors** occur. For example, a rater may intentionally give higher ratings to white employees than to nonwhite employees. In this case, the performance appraisal reflects a racial bias. Bias toward members of other demographic categories, such as age, gender, and disability, also can occur, based on stereotypes the rater may have. Such bias appears to have been widespread at Monarch Paper Company, when a former vice president was demoted to a warehouse-maintenance job for not accepting an early retirement offer. A federal jury judged the firm guilty of age bias.[25] This example shows that raters must reflect carefully on their personal biases and guard against their interference with performance-based ratings of subordinates.

Cultural Bias Errors   Managers must be aware of the cultural backgrounds that they bring with them to the task of performance appraisal. They should be careful to avoid criticizing employees for cultural differences described in Chapter 3, such as time orientation or ideas of appropriate power distance, unless these differences adversely affect performance on a regular basis.

IMPROVING PERFORMANCE APPRAISALS

As is true of most other issues in organizational behavior, managers must recognize certain tradeoffs in setting up and implementing any performance appraisal system. In addition to the pros and cons already mentioned for each method, some specific issues to keep in mind in order to reduce errors and improve appraisals include the following:[26]

1. Train raters so that they understand the evaluation process rationale and can recognize the sources of measurement error.

2. Make sure that raters observe ratees on an ongoing, regular basis and that they do not try to limit all their evaluations to the formally designated evaluation period, for instance, every six months or every year.

3. Do not have the rater rate too many ratees. The ability to identify performance differences drops, and fatigue sets in when the evaluation of large numbers of people is involved.

4. Make sure that the performance dimensions and standards are stated clearly and that the standards are as noncontaminating and nondeficient as possible.

5. Avoid terms such as *average* because different evaluators tend to react differently to the terms.

Remember that appraisal systems cannot be used to discriminate against employees on the basis of age, gender, race, ethnicity, and so on. To help provide a legally defensible system in terms of governing legislation, the following recommendations are useful.[27]

- Appraisal must be based on an analysis of job requirements as reflected in performance standards.

- Appraisal is appropriate only where performance standards are clearly understood by employees.

- Clearly defined individual dimensions should be used rather than global measures.

- Dimensions should be behaviorally based and supported by observable evidence.

- If rating scales are used, abstract trait names, such as "loyalty," should be avoided unless they can be defined in terms of observable behaviors.

- Rating scale anchors should be brief and logically consistent.

- The system must be validated and psychometrically sound, as must the ratings given by individual evaluators.

- An appeal mechanism must be in place in the event the evaluator and the ratee disagree.

Technological advances now provide various PC programs designed to facilitate the rating process. Specifically, these allow for easier and more comprehensive scale construction, faster feedback, and the additional flexibility called for in today's new workplace.[28]

GROUP EVALUATION

As indicated earlier, the growing trend is toward group or team performance evaluations. Such an evaluation is consistent with self-managed teams and high performance organizations. Frequently, this emphasis is accompanied by a group-based compensation system such as discussed later in this chapter. Traditional individually oriented appraisal systems are no longer appropriate and need to be replaced with a group system such as suggested in The Effective Manager 7.2.

REWARDS AND REWARD SYSTEMS

In addition to staffing, training, career planning and development, and performance appraisal, another key aspect of HR management is the design and implementation of reward systems. These reward systems emphasize a mix of extrinsic and intrinsic rewards. As we noted in Chapter 6, *extrinsic rewards* are positively valued work outcomes that are given to an individual, or group by some other person or source in the work setting. In contrast, *intrinsic rewards* are positively valued work outcomes that the individual receives directly as a result of task performance; they do not require the participation of another person or source. A feeling of achievement after accomplishing a particularly challenging task is an example of an intrinsic reward. Managing intrinsic work rewards presents the additional challenge of designing a work setting so that employees can, in effect, reward themselves for a job well done. Managers can also provide a variety of extrinsic rewards, as described in Chapter 6. Many, such as sincere praise for a job well done, or symbolic tokens of accomplishment such as "employee-of-the-month" awards, involve low cost to the company. That is the topic of Chapter 8. In the remainder of this chapter, we emphasize the management of pay as an extrinsic reward.

PAY AS AN EXTRINSIC REWARD

Pay is an especially complex extrinsic reward. It can help organizations attract and retain highly capable workers, and it can help satisfy and motivate these workers to work hard to achieve high performance. But if there is dissatisfaction with the salary, pay can also lead to strikes, grievances, absenteeism, turnover, and sometimes even poor physical and mental health.

Edward Lawler, a management expert, has contributed greatly to our understanding of pay as an extrinsic reward. His research generally concludes that, for pay to serve as a source of work motivation, high levels of job performance must be viewed as the path through which high pay can be achieved.[29] **Merit pay** is defined as a compensation system that bases an individual's salary or wage increase on a measure of the person's

---

THE EFFECTIVE MANAGER 7.2

SUGGESTIONS FOR A GROUP PERFORMANCE EVALUATION SYSTEM

- Link the team's results to organizational goals.
- Start with the team's customers and the team work process needed to satisfy those needs:.
  - ❑ Customer requirements
  - ❑ Delivery and quality
  - ❑ Waste and cycle time
- Evaluate team and each individual member's performance.
- Train the team to develop its own measures.

performance accomplishments during a specified time period. That is, merit pay is an attempt to make pay contingent upon performance.

Although research supports the logic and theoretical benefits of merit pay, it also indicates that the implementation of merit pay plans is not as universal or as easy as we might expect. In fact, surveys over the past thirty years have found that as many as 80 percent of respondents felt that they were not rewarded for a job well done.[30] An effective merit pay system is one approach to dealing with this problem.

To work well, a merit pay plan should be based on realistic and accurate measures of individual work performance and create a belief among employees that the way to achieve high pay is to perform at high levels. In addition, merit pay should clearly discriminate between high and low performers in the amount of pay reward received. Finally, managers should avoid confusing "merit" aspects of a pay increase with "cost-of-living" adjustments.

CREATIVE PAY PRACTICES

Merit pay plans are just one attempt to enhance the positive value of pay as a work reward. But some argue that merit pay plans are not consistent with the demands of today's organizations, for they fail to recognize the high degree of task interdependence among employees, as illustrated particularly in high performance management organizations. Also, as we argued earlier, HR management strategies should be consistent with overall organization strategies. For example, the pay system of a firm with an emphasis on highly skilled individuals in short supply should emphasize employee retention rather than performance.[31]

With these points in mind, let us examine a variety of creative pay practices. These practices are becoming more common in organizations with increasingly diverse workforces and increased emphasis on TQM or similar setups.[32] They include skill-based pay, gain-sharing plans, profit-sharing plans, employee stock ownership plans, lump-sum pay increases, and flexible benefit plans.

Skill-Based Pay   **Skill-based pay** rewards people for acquiring and developing job-relevant skills. Pay systems of this sort pay people for the mix and depth of skills they possess, not for the particular job assignment they hold. An example is the cross-functional team approach at Monsanto-Benevia where each team member has developed quality, safety, administrator, maintenance, coaching, and team leader skills. In most cases, these skills involve high-tech, automated equipment. Workers are paid for this "breadth" of capability and their willingness to use any of the skills needed by the company.

Skill-based pay is one of the fastest growing pay innovations in the United States. Among the better known firms using this plan is Polaroid.[33] Besides flexibility, some advantages of skill-based pay are employee cross-training—workers learn to do one another's job; fewer supervisors—workers can provide more of these functions themselves; and more individual control over compensation—workers know in advance what is required to receive a pay raise. One disadvantage is possible higher pay and training costs that are not offset by greater productivity. Another is that of deciding on appropriate monetary values for each skill.[34]

Gain-Sharing Plans   Cash bonuses, or extra pay for performance above standards or expectations, have been common practice in the compensation of managers and executives for a long time. Top managers in some industries earn annual bonuses of 50 percent or more of their base salaries. Attempts to extend such opportunities to all employees are growing in number and importance today. One popular plan is **gain sharing,** which links pay and performance by giving workers the opportunity to share in productivity gains through enhanced earnings.

The Scanlon Plan is probably the oldest and best known gain-sharing plan. Others you may have heard about are the Lincoln Electric Plan, the Rucker Plan™ or IMPROSHARE™. Gain-sharing plans possess some similarities to profit-sharing plans, but they are not the same. Typically, profit-sharing plans grant individuals or workgroups a specified portion of any economic profits earned by an organization as a whole. Gain-sharing plans involve a specific measurement of productivity combined with a calculation of a bonus designed to offer workers a mutual share of any increase in total organizational productivity.

The intended benefits of gain-sharing plans include increased worker motivation because of the pay-for-performance incentives, and a greater sense of personal responsibility for making performance contributions to the organization. Because they can be highly participative in nature, gain-sharing plans also may encourage cooperation and teamwork in the workplace. Although more remains to be learned about gain sharing, the plans are receiving increasing attention from organizations.[35]

Profit-Sharing Plans **Profit-sharing plans** possess some similarities to gain-sharing plans, but they are not identical. Profit-sharing plans reward employees based on the entire organization's performance. Unlike gain sharing, profit-sharing plans do not attempt to reward employees for productivity gains, and they reflect things, such as economic conditions, over which employees have no control. At the same time, gain-sharing plans generally use a "hard productivity" measure, while profit-sharing plans do not.

Profit sharing also tends to use a mechanistic formula for profit allocation and does not utilize employee participation. Most often, profit-sharing plans fund employee retirement and thus are considered benefits and not incentives.[36]

Employee Stock Ownership Plans (ESOPs) Like profit sharing, **ESOPs** are based on the total organization's performance—but measured in terms of stock price. The stock may be given to employees, or employees may purchase it at a price below market value. Organizations often use ESOPs as a low-cost retirement benefit for employees because they are nontaxable to the organization until the employees redeem the stock. Of course, like all stock investments, ESOPs involve risk.[37]

Lump-Sum Pay Increases While most pay plans distribute increases as part of a regular pay check, an interesting alternative is the **lump-sum increase** program, by which individuals can elect to receive an increase in one or more lump-sum payments. The full increase may be taken at the beginning of the year and used for some valued purpose, for example, a down payment on a car or a sizable deposit in a savings account. Or a person may elect to take one-half of the raise early and get the rest at the start of the winter holiday season. In either case, the individual should be more motivated because of the larger doses or because it is attached to something highly valued.

A related, but more controversial, development in this area is the lump-sum payment, which differs from the lump-sum increase. The lump-sum payment is an attempt by employers to hold labor costs in line while still giving workers more money, if corporate earnings allow. It involves giving workers a one-time lump-sum payment, often based on a gain-sharing formula, instead of a yearly percentage wage or salary increase. In this way, a person's base pay remains fixed, whereas overall monetary compensation varies according to the bonus added to this figure by the annual lump-sum payment. American labor unions typically are resistant to this approach since base pay does not increase and management determines the size of the bonus. However, surveys generally show that around two-thirds of the respondents have favorable reactions and think that the plans have a positive effect on performance.[38]

Flexible Benefit Plans   An employee's total compensation package includes not only direct pay but also any fringe benefits that are paid by the organization. These fringe benefits often add an equivalent of 10 to 40 percent to a person's salary. It is argued that organizations need to allow for individual differences when developing such benefit programs. Otherwise, the motivational value of this indirect form of pay incentive is lost. One approach is to let individuals choose their total pay package by selecting benefits, up to a certain dollar amount, from a range of options made available by the organization. These **flexible benefit plans** allow workers to select benefits according to needs. A single worker, for example, may prefer quite a different combination of insurance and retirement contributions than would a married person.[39]

CHAPTER 7 SUMMARY

What are the essentials of human resource strategy and practice?

- HR planning is the process of providing capable and motivated people to carry out the organization's mission and strategy.
- HR staffing involves job analysis, attracting individuals through recruitment, selecting those best qualified through screening and hiring, and socializing employees through initial orientation and follow-up over time.

What is training and career planning and development?

- Training is a set of activities that provides the opportunity to acquire and improve job-related skills.
- On-the-job training involves job instruction in the workplace and commonly utilizes internships, apprenticeships, and job rotation.
- Off-the-job training takes place off the job and commonly involves lectures, videos, and simulations.
- Career planning and development involves working with managers and HR experts on careers and involves the following: a five-stage planning framework; personal responsibilities for developing of a portfolio of skills to keep one marketable at any time; a balance sheet approach to evaluating each career opportunity; and recognition of the relationship between life and career stages and transitions.

What is performance appraisal?

- Performance appraisal involves systematically evaluating performance and providing feedback on which performance adjustments can be made.

- Performance appraisals serve the two general purposes of evaluation and feedback and development.

- Performance appraisals traditionally are done by an individual's immediate superior but are moving toward 360-degree evaluations involving the full circle of contacts a person may have in job performance.

- Performance appraisals use either or both output measures and activity measures.

- Performance appraisal methods involve comparative methods and absolute methods.

- There are at least half-a-dozen rater errors important in performance appraisal.

- There are six steps that can be used to reduce errors and improve performance appraisals.

- Group performance evaluation systems are being increasingly used.

What are rewards and reward systems?

- Rewards are another key aspect of HR management and involve the design and implementation of positively valued work outcomes.

- Reward systems emphasize a mix of extrinsic and intrinsic rewards.

How does one manage pay as an extrinsic reward?

- Pay as an extrinsic reward involves merit pay and creative pay practices.

- Creative pay practices include skill-based pay, gain-sharing plans, lump-sum pay increases, and flexible benefit plans.

How does one manage intrinsic rewards?

- Managing intrinsic rewards involves the challenge of designing a work setting so that employees can, in effect, reward themselves for a job well done.

8

High Performance Job Designs

Study Questions

Chapter 8 introduces the essentials of job design, goal setting, and work scheduling as important strategies for developing high performance work settings. As you read the chapter, keep in mind these key questions.

- What are the alternative job design approaches?
- What are the keys to designing motivating jobs?
- How does technology influence job design?
- How can goal setting improve performance?
- What alternative work arrangements are used today?

Workers at California-based Peet's Coffee and Tea take pride in being known as "Peetniks." The firm's unique culture caters to part-timers, paying them relatively well, and allowing full benefits to those who work at least 21 hours a week. Peetniks enjoy flexible hours, and the firm promotes from within.

One has to wonder. Could Peet's formula for high performance be brewed in other workplaces?[1] The kind of opportunities part-timers find at Peet's are altogether too rare; the implications extend as well into the work lives of full-time employees. Just talk to your family and friends. There are too many people still working today in jobs that do not provide substantial opportunities for personal growth, creative contribution, and job satisfaction. A student of ours, for example, passed along this comment that he had once heard: "Even the best day at work can never be as good as the worst day of golf."

This chapter on high performance job designs takes a more positive view, indeed, an ethical and socially responsible one. Our point is that jobs can and should be designed for both high performance and individual satisfaction. When a job is properly designed, when the tasks are clear, when the goals are challenging but attainable, and when the work schedules respect individual needs, both outcomes are possible. High performance and satisfaction can become the standards of the new workplace instead of exceptions to the rule.

JOB DESIGN APPROACHES

Through the process of **job design,** managers plan and specify job tasks and the work arrangements through which they are accomplished. Figure 8.1 shows how alternative job-design approaches differ in the way required tasks are defined and in the amount of intrinsic motivation provided for the worker. The "best" job design is always one that meets organizational requirements for high performance, offers a good fit with individual skills and needs, and provides opportunities for job satisfaction.

FIGURE 8.1	A CONTINUUM OF JOB-DESIGN STRATEGIES

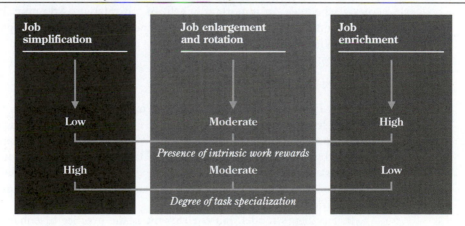

Job simplification	Job enlargement and rotation	Job enrichment
Low	Moderate	High

Presence of intrinsic work rewards

High	Moderate	Low

Degree of task specialization

SCIENTIFIC MANAGEMENT

The history of scholarly interest in job design can be traced in part to Frederick Taylor's work with *scientific management* in the early 1900s.[2] Taylor and his contemporaries sought to increase people's efficiency at work. Their approach was to study a job carefully, break it into its smallest components, establish exact time and motion requirements for each task to be done, and then train workers to do these tasks in the same way over and over again. These early efforts were forerunners of current industrial engineering approaches to job design that emphasize efficiency. Such approaches attempt to determine the best processes, methods, work-flow layouts, output standards, and person-machine interfaces for various jobs.

Today the term **job simplification** is used to describe the approach of standardizing work procedures and employing people in clearly defined and highly specialized tasks. The machine-paced automobile assembly line is a classic example of this job-design strategy. Why is it used? Typically, the answer is to increase operating efficiency by reducing the number of skills required to do a job, being able to hire low-cost labor, keeping the needs for job training to a minimum, and emphasizing the accomplishment of repetitive tasks. However, the very nature of such jobs creates potential disadvantages as well. These include loss of efficiency in the face of lower quality, high rates of absenteeism and turnover, and demand for higher wages to compensate for unappealing jobs.

JOB ENLARGEMENT AND JOB ROTATION

In job simplification the number or variety of different tasks performed is limited. Although this makes the tasks easier to master, the repetitiveness can reduce motivation. Thus, a second set of job-design approaches has been created to add breadth to the variety of tasks performed. **Job enlargement** increases task variety by combining into one job two or more tasks that were previously assigned to separate workers. Sometimes called *horizontal loading,* this approach increases *job breadth* by having the worker perform more and different tasks, but all at the same level of responsibility and challenge. **Job rotation,** another horizontal loading approach, increases task variety by periodically shifting workers among jobs involving different tasks. Again, the responsibility level of the tasks stays the same. The rotation can be arranged according to almost any time schedule, such as hourly, daily, or weekly schedules. An important benefit of job rotation is training. It allows workers to become more familiar with different tasks and increases the flexibility with which they can be moved from one job to another.

JOB ENRICHMENT

Frederick Herzberg's two-factor theory of motivation (described in Chapter 6) suggests that high levels of motivation should not be expected from jobs designed on the basis of simplification, enlargement, or rotation.[3] "Why," asks Herzberg, "should a worker become motivated when one or more 'meaningless' tasks are added to previously existing ones or when work assignments are rotated among equally 'meaningless' tasks?" Instead of pursuing one of these job-design strategies, therefore, Herzberg recommends an alternative approach he calls "job enrichment."

In Herzberg's model, **job enrichment** is the practice of enhancing job content by building into it more motivating factors such as responsibility, achievement, recognition, and personal growth. This job-design strategy differs markedly from strategies previously discussed in that it adds to job content planning and evaluating duties that would otherwise be reserved for managers. These content changes (see The Effective Manager 8.1) involve what Herzberg calls *vertical loading* to increase *job depth*. Enriched jobs, he states, help to satisfy the higher-order needs that people bring with them to work and will therefore increase their motivation to achieve high levels of job performance.

Despite the inherent appeal of Herzberg's ideas, two common questions raise words of caution. *Is job enrichment expensive?* Job enrichment can be very costly, particularly when it requires major changes in work flows, facilities, or technology. *Will workers demand higher pay when moving into enriched jobs?* Herzberg argues that if employees are being paid a truly competitive wage or salary, then the intrinsic rewards of performing enriched tasks will be adequate compensation. Other researchers are more skeptical, advising that pay must be carefully considered.[4]

DESIGNING JOBS TO INCREASE MOTIVATION

OB scholars have been reluctant to recommend job enrichment as a universal solution to all job performance and satisfaction problems. The prior questions raise cost and pay concerns. Also, individual differences must be considered in answering the additional question: "Is job enrichment for everyone?" A diagnostic approach developed by Richard Hackman and Greg Oldham offers a broader and contingency-based framework for job design to increase motivation.[5] This model opens up many opportunities to individualize job designs.

JOB CHARACTERISTICS MODEL

Figure 8.2 presents the **job characteristics model.** It identifies five core job characteristics that are particularly important to job designs. The higher a job scores on each characteristic, the more it is considered to be enriched. The core job characteristics are:

- *Skill variety*—the degree to which a job includes a variety of different activities and involves the use of a number of different skills and talents.

THE EFFECTIVE MANAGER 8.1

JOB ENRICHMENT ADVICE FROM FREDERICK HERZBERG

- Allow workers to plan.
- Allow workers to control.
- Maximize job freedom.
- Increase task difficulty.
- Help workers become task experts.
- Provide performance feedback.
- Increase performance accountability.
- Provide complete units of work.

- *Task identity*—the degree to which the job requires completion of a "whole" and identifiable piece of work, one that involves doing a job from beginning to end with a visible outcome.

- *Task significance*—the degree to which the job is important and involves a meaningful contribution to the organization or society in general.

- *Autonomy*—the degree to which the job gives the employee substantial freedom, independence, and discretion in scheduling the work and determining the procedures used in carrying it out.

- *Job feedback*—the degree to which carrying out the work activities provides direct and clear information to the employee regarding how well the job has been done.

For those who use this model in an actual work situation, Hackman and Oldham recommend determining the current status of each job on each core characteristic.[6] These characteristics can then be changed systematically to enrich the job and increase its motivational potential. Hackman and his colleagues have developed an instrument called the Job Diagnostic Survey (JDS) for such an assessment (see the end-of-book experiential exercise, "Job Design"). Scores on the JDS are then combined to create a **motivating potential score,** which indicates the degree to which the job is capable of motivating people.

$$\text{MPS} = \frac{\text{Skill variety} + \text{Task identity} + \text{Task significance}}{3} \times \text{Autonomy} \times \text{Feedback}$$

A job's MPS can be raised by combining tasks to create larger jobs, opening feedback channels to enable workers to know how well they are doing, establishing client relationships to

---

FIGURE 8.2   JOB-DESIGN IMPLICATIONS OF JOB CHARACTERISTICS THEORY

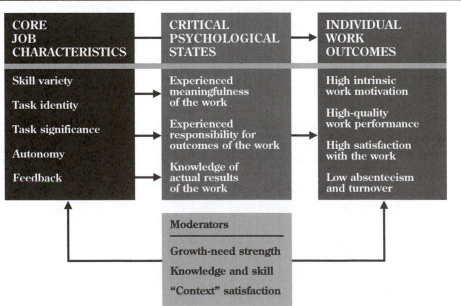

experience such feedback directly from customers, and employing vertical loading to create more planning and controlling responsibilities. When the core characteristics are enriched in these ways and the MPS for a job is raised as high as possible, they can be expected to positively influence three critical psychological states for the individual: (1) experienced meaningfulness in the work; (2) experienced responsibility for the outcomes of the work; and (3) knowledge of actual results of the work activities. The positive psychological states, in turn, can be expected to create more positive work outcomes in respect to individual motivation, performance, and satisfaction.

Individual Difference Moderators   The job characteristics model recognizes that the five core job characteristics do not affect all people in the same way. Rather than Herzberg's implication that enriched jobs should be good for everyone, this approach allows for individual differences. It accepts the idea that jobs should be designed to arrive at the best match of core characteristics and individual needs and talents. Specifically, the model suggests that enriched jobs will lead to positive outcomes only for those persons who are a good match for them. When the fit between the person and an enriched job is poor, positive outcomes are less likely and problems may well result.

Figure 8.2 highlights three individual difference moderators that can influence individual preferences in how their jobs are designed. The first moderator is *growth-need strength*—the degree to which a person desires the opportunity for self-direction, learning, and personal accomplishment at work. It is similar to Abraham Maslow's esteem and self-actualization needs and Alderfer's growth needs, as discussed in Chapter 6. When applied here, the expectation is that people with high growth-need strengths at work will respond positively to enriched jobs, whereas people low in growth-need strengths will find enriched jobs a source of anxiety. The second moderator is *knowledge and skill*. People whose capabilities fit the demands of enriched jobs are predicted to feel good about them and perform well. Those who are inadequate or who feel inadequate in this regard are likely to experience difficulties. The third moderator is *context satisfaction,* or the extent to which an employee is satisfied with aspects of the work setting such as salary levels, quality of supervision, relationships with co-workers, and working conditions. In general, people more satisfied with job context are more likely than dissatisfied ones to support and do well with job enrichment.

Research Results   Considerable research has been done on the job characteristics model in a variety of work settings, including banks, dentist offices, corrections departments, telephone companies, and manufacturing firms, as well as in government agencies. Experts generally agree that the model and its diagnostic approach are useful, but not yet perfect, guides to job design.[7] On the average, job characteristics do affect performance but not nearly as much as they do satisfaction. The research also emphasizes the importance of growth-need strength as a moderator of the job design–job performance/job satisfaction relationships. Positive job characteristics affect performance more strongly for high-growth need than low-growth need individuals. The relationship is about the same with job satisfaction. It is also clear that job enrichment can fail when job requirements are increased beyond the level of individual capabilities or interests. Finally, employee perceptions of job characteristics often differ from measures taken by managers and consultants. These perceptions are important and must be considered. After all, they will largely determine whether the workers view a job as high or low in the core characteristics, and consequently will affect work outcomes.

SOCIAL INFORMATION PROCESSING

Gerald Salancik and Jeffrey Pfeffer question whether or not jobs have stable and objective characteristics to which individuals respond predictably and consistently.[8] Instead, they view job design from the perspective of **social information processing theory.** This theory argues that individual needs, task perceptions, and reactions are a result of socially constructed realities. Social information in organizations influences the way people perceive their jobs and respond to them. The same holds true, for example, in the classroom. Suppose that several of your friends tell you that the instructor for a course is bad, the content is boring, and the requirements involve too much work. You may then think that the critical characteristics of the class are the instructor, the content, and the workload, and that they are all bad. All of this may substantially influence the way you perceive your instructor and the course and the way you deal with the class—regardless of the actual characteristics.

Research on social information processing indicates that both social information and core characteristics are important. Although social information processing influences task perceptions and attitudes, the job characteristics discussed earlier are also important. Indeed, how someone perceives job characteristics is likely to be influenced by both the objective characteristics themselves and the social information present in the workplace.

MANAGERIAL AND GLOBAL IMPLICATIONS

A question-and-answer approach can again be used to summarize final points and implications worth remembering about job enrichment. *Should everyone's job be enriched?* The answer is clearly "No." The logic of individual differences suggests that not everyone will want an enriched job. Individuals most likely to have positive reactions to job enrichment are those who need achievement, who hold middle-class working values, or who are seeking higher-order growth-need satisfaction at work. Job enrichment also appears to be most advantageous when the job context is positive and when workers have the abilities needed to do the enriched job. Furthermore, costs, technological constraints, and workgroup or union opposition may make it difficult to enrich some jobs.[9] *Can job enrichment apply to groups?* The answer is "Yes." The application of job-design strategies at the group level is growing in many types of settings. In Part 3 we discuss creative workgroup designs, including cross-functional work teams and self-managing teams.

A final question extends the job enrichment context globally. *What is the impact of culture on job enrichment?* The answer is: "Substantial." Research conducted in Belgium, Israel, Japan, The Netherlands, the United States, and Germany found unique aspects of what constitutes work in each country.[10] Work was seen as a social requirement most strongly in Belgium and Japan and least so in Germany. Work was regarded as something done for money in all countries but Belgium. In most cases, however, work was regarded as having both an economic and a societal contribution component. These results, as well as differences in such national culture dimensions as power distance and individualism, reinforce a contingency approach to job enrichment, and further suggest that cultural differences should be given consideration in job design.

TECHNOLOGY AND JOB DESIGN

The concept of **sociotechnical systems** is used in organizational behavior to indicate the importance of integrating people and technology to create high performance work systems.[11] As computers and information technologies continue to dominate the modern workplace, this concept is essential in new developments in job designs.

AUTOMATION AND ROBOTICS

As mentioned earlier, highly simplified jobs often cause problems because they offer little intrinsic motivation for the worker. Such tasks have been defined so narrowly that they lack challenge and lead to boredom when someone has to repeat them over and over again. Given the high technology now available, one way to tackle this problem is through complete **automation** where a machine is used to do the work previously accomplished by a human. This approach increasingly involves the use of robots, which are becoming ever more versatile and reliable. Also, robot prices are falling as the cost of human labor rises. Japan presently leads the world in robot use; the United States lags behind, but its robot use is growing rapidly. In a modern automobile manufacturing plant, robots can do most of the welding work and can be programmed to perform many different tasks. Computers control the assembly line, adjusting production to fit schedules for different models and options.

FLEXIBLE MANUFACTURING SYSTEMS

In **flexible manufacturing systems,** adaptive computer-based technologies and integrated job designs are used to shift work easily and quickly among alternative products. This approach is increasingly common, for example, in companies supporting the automobile industry with machined metal products, such as cylinder heads and gear boxes. A cellular manufacturing system, for example, might contain a number of automated production machines that cut, shape, drill, and fasten together various metal components. The machines can be quickly changed from manufacturing one product to another. Workers in flexible manufacturing cells perform few routine assembly-line tasks. Rather, they ensure that the operations are handled correctly, and they deal with the changeover from one product configuration to another. They develop expertise across a wide range of functions and the jobs are rich in potential for enriched core job characteristics.

ELECTRONIC OFFICES

Electronic office technology was the key when U.S. Healthcare, a large, private practice–based health maintenance organization (HMO), became interested in improving the quality of its health-care services. The company installed large electronic bulletin boards that monitored progress toward a range of performance goals, put in robots to deliver the paper mail, and emphasized e-mail and computerized answering services. Essentially, the company tried to automate as many tasks as possible to free people for more challenging work. Similarly, Mutual Benefit Life completely reorganized the way it serviced insurance application forms—once handled by as many as nineteen people across five departments.

Mutual created a new case manager position responsible for processing applications from their inception until policies were issued. Accompanying this radical change in job design were powerful PC-based workstations designed to assist decision making and connected to a variety of automated subsystems on a mainframe.[12]

Continuing developments in electronic offices offer job enrichment possibilities for those workers equipped to handle the technology. But those jobs can be stressful and difficult for those who do not have the necessary education or skills. One survey showed that even in highly developed countries like those in Europe, 54 percent of workers possessed inadequate skills to operate a computer; the proportion was about one-third in the United States.[13] People who work continuously with computers are also beginning to experience physical ailments associated with repetitive keyboarding and mouse movements. Clearly, the high technologies of the new workplace must be carefully integrated with the human factor.

WORKFLOW AND PROCESS REENGINEERING

Another approach for improving job designs and performance is based on the concept of **process reengineering**—the analysis, streamlining, and reconfiguration of actions and tasks required to reach a work goal.[14] The process design approach systematically breaks processes down into their specific components and subtasks, analyzes each for relevance and simplicity, and then does everything possible to reconfigure the process to eliminate wasted time, effort, and resources. A classic example might be the various steps required to gain approval for a purchase order to buy a new computer. The process reengineering approach looks at every step in the process, from searching for items and vendors to obtaining bids, completing necessary forms, securing required signatures and approvals, actually placing the order, and so on to the point at which the new computer arrives, is checked in, is placed into an equipment inventory, and then is finally delivered to the workplace. In all this, one simple question drives the reengineering approach: What is necessary and what else can be eliminated?

GOAL SETTING AND JOB DESIGN

Goals are important aspects of any job design. Without proper goals, employees may suffer a direction problem. Some years ago, for example, a Minnesota Vikings' defensive end gathered up an opponent's fumble. Then, with obvious effort and delight, he ran the ball into the wrong end zone. Clearly, the athlete did not lack motivation. Unfortunately, however, he failed to channel his energies toward the right goal. Similar problems are found in many work settings. They can be eliminated, or at least reduced, by the proper setting and clarification of task goals.

GOAL-SETTING THEORY

Goals play an important part in high performance work environments. **Goal setting** is the process of developing, negotiating, and formalizing the targets or objectives that a person is responsible for accomplishing.[15] Over a number of years, Edwin Locke and his associates have developed a comprehensive framework linking goals to performance as shown in

Figure 8.3. The model uses elements of expectancy theory from Chapter 6 to help clarify the implications of goal setting for performance while taking into account certain moderating conditions, such as ability and task complexity.

GOAL-SETTING GUIDELINES

Research on goal setting is now quite extensive. Indeed, more research has been done on goal setting than on any other theory related to work motivation.[16] Nearly 400 studies have been conducted in several countries, including Australia, England, Germany, Japan, and the United States.[17] The basic precepts of goal-setting theory remain a most important source of advice for managing human behavior in the work setting.

Managerially speaking, the implications of the Locke and Latham model and related goal-setting research can be summarized as follows.[18] First, *difficult goals are more likely to lead to higher performance than are less difficult ones.* However, if the goals are seen as too difficult or impossible, the relationship with performance no longer holds. For example, you will likely perform better as a financial services agent if you have a goal of selling six annuities a week than if you have a goal of three. However, if your goal is fifteen annuities a week, you may consider that as impossible to achieve, and your performance may well be lower than what it would be with a more realistic goal.

Second, *specific goals are more likely to lead to higher performance than are no goals or vague or very general ones.* All too often people work with very general goals such as the encouragement to "do your best." Research indicates that more specific goals, such as selling six computers a day, are much more motivational than a simple "do your best" goal.

Third, *task feedback, or knowledge of results, is likely to motivate people toward higher performance by encouraging the setting of higher performance goals.* Feedback lets people know where they stand and whether they are on course or off course in their efforts. For example, think about how eager you are to find out how well you did on an examination.

FIGURE 8.3	**ESSENTIALS OF THE LOCKE AND LATHAM GOAL-SETTING FRAMEWORK**

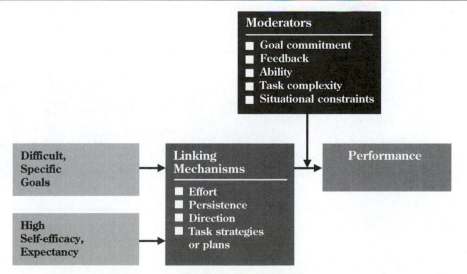

Fourth, *goals are most likely to lead to higher performance when people have the abilities and the feelings of self-efficacy required to accomplish them.* The individual must be able to accomplish the goals and feel confident in those abilities. To take the financial services example again, you may be able to do what's required to sell six annuities a week and feel confident that you can. If your goal is fifteen, however, you may believe that your abilities are insufficient to the task and thus lack the confidence to work hard enough to accomplish it.

Fifth, *goals are most likely to motivate people toward higher performance when they are accepted and there is commitment to them.* Participating in the goal-setting process helps build such acceptance and commitment. It helps create "ownership" of the goals. However, Locke and Latham report that goals assigned by someone else can be equally effective. The assigners are likely to be authority figures, and that can have an impact. The assignment also implies that the subordinate can actually reach the goal. Moreover, assigned goals often are a challenge and help define the standards people use to attain self-satisfaction with their performance. According to Locke and Latham, assigned goals most often lead to poor performance when they are curtly or inadequately explained.

GOAL SETTING AND MBO

When we speak of goal setting and its potential to influence individual performance at work, the concept of *management by objectives (MBO)* immediately comes to mind. The essence of MBO is a process of joint goal setting between a supervisor and a subordinate.[19] It involves managers working with their subordinates to establish performance goals and plans that are consistent with higher level work unit and organizational objectives. When this process is followed throughout an organization, MBO helps clarify the hierarchy of objectives as a series of well-defined means-end chains.

Figure 8.4 shows a comprehensive view of MBO. The concept is consistent with the notion of goal setting and its associated principles discussed above. Notice how joint supervisor-subordinate discussions are designed to extend participation from the point of

---

FIGURE 8.4   HOW THE MANAGEMENT BY OBJECTIVES PROCESS WORKS

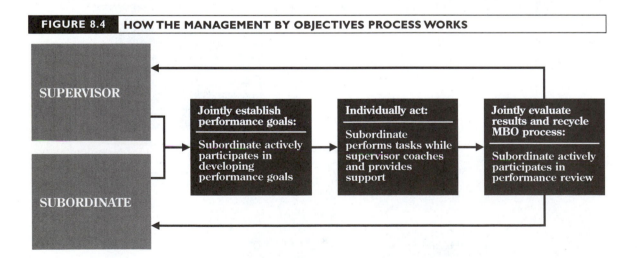

SUPERVISOR

SUBORDINATE

Jointly establish
performance goals:

Subordinate actively
participates in
developing
performance goals

Individually act:

Subordinate
performs tasks while
supervisor coaches
and provides
support

Jointly evaluate
results and recycle
MBO process:

Subordinate actively
participates in
performance review

establishing initial goals to the point of evaluating results in terms of goal attainment. In addition to these goal-setting steps, a successful MBO system calls for careful implementation. Not only must workers have the freedom to carry out the required tasks, managers should be prepared to actively support their efforts to achieve the agreed-upon goals.

Although a fair amount of research based on case studies of MBO success is available, few rigorously controlled studies have been done. What there is reports mixed results.[20] In general, and as an application of goal-setting theory, MBO has much to offer. But it is by no means easy to start and keep going. Many firms have started and dropped the approach because of difficulties experienced early on. Among the specific problems it creates are too much paperwork documenting goals and accomplishments and too much emphasis on goal-oriented rewards and punishments, top-down goals, goals that are easily stated in objective terms, and individual instead of group goals. MBO also may need to be implemented organizationwide if it is to work well.

ALTERNATIVE WORK ARRANGEMENTS

Alternative ways of scheduling time are becoming increasingly common in the workplace. These arrangements are essentially reshaping the traditional 40-hour week, 9-to-5 schedules where work is done on the premises. Virtually all such plans are designed to influence employee satisfaction and to help employees balance the demands of their work and nonwork lives.[21] They are becoming more and more important in fast-changing societies where demands for "work-life balance" and more "family-friendly" employers are growing ever more apparent. For example, dual-career families with children, part-time students, older workers (retired or near retirement age), and single parents are all candidates for alternative work arrangements.

COMPRESSED WORK WEEKS

A **compressed work week** is any scheduling of work that allows a full-time job to be completed in fewer than the standard five days. The most common form of compressed work week is the "4/40" or 40 hours of work accomplished in four 10-hour days.

This approach has many possible benefits. For the worker added time off is a major feature of this schedule. The individual often appreciates increased leisure time, three-day weekends, free weekdays to pursue personal business, and lower commuting costs. The organization can benefit, too, in terms of lower employee absenteeism, and improved recruiting of new employees. But, there are also potential disadvantages. Individuals can experience increased fatigue from the extended workday and family adjustment problems. The organization can experience work scheduling problems and customer complaints because of breaks in work coverage. Some organizations may face occasional union opposition and laws requiring payment of overtime for work exceeding eight hours of individual labor in any one day. Overall reactions to compressed work weeks are likely to be most favorable for employees allowed to participate in the decision to adopt the new work week, who have their jobs enriched as a result of the new schedule, and who have strong higher-order needs in Maslow's hierarchy.[22]

FLEXIBLE WORKING HOURS

Another innovative work schedule, **flexible working hours** or flextime, gives individuals a daily choice in the timing of their work commitments. One such schedule requires employees to work four hours of "core" time but leaves them free to choose their remaining four hours of work from among flexible time blocks. One person, for example, may start early and leave early, whereas another may start later and leave later. This flexible work schedule is becoming increasingly popular and is a valuable alternative for structuring work to accommodate individual interests and needs.

Flextime increases individual autonomy in work scheduling and offers many opportunities and benefits (see The Effective Manager 8.2). It is a way for dual-career couples to handle children's schedules as well as their own; it is a way to meet the demands of caring for elderly parents or ill family members; it is even a way to better attend to such personal affairs as medical and dental appointments, home emergencies, banking needs, and so on. Proponents of this scheduling strategy argue that the discretion it allows workers in scheduling their own hours of work encourages them to develop positive attitudes and to increase commitment to the organization. Flextime programs are growing in American workplaces. An Aetna manager, commenting on the firm's flexible working hours program, said: "We're not doing flexible work scheduling to be nice, but because it makes business sense."[23]

JOB SHARING

In **job sharing,** one full-time job is assigned to two or more persons who then divide the work according to agreed-upon hours. Often, each person works half a day, but job sharing can also be done on a weekly or monthly basis. Although it is practiced by only a relatively small percentage of employers, human-resource experts believe that job sharing is a valuable alternative work arrangement.[24]

Organizations benefit from job sharing when they can attract talented people who would otherwise be unable to work. An example is the qualified teacher who also is a parent. This person may be able to work only half a day. Through job sharing, two such persons can be employed to teach one class. Some job sharers report less burnout and claim that they feel recharged each time they report for work. The tricky part of this arrangement is finding two people who will work well with each other. When middle managers Sue

---

THE EFFECTIVE MANAGER 8.2

FLEXTIME BENEFITS

For organizations:
- Less absenteeism, tardiness, turnover
- More commitment
- Higher performance

For workers:
- Shorter commuting time
- More leisure time
- More job satisfaction
- Greater sense of responsibility

Mannix and Charlotte Schutzman worked together at Bell Atlantic, for example, they faithfully coordinated each other's absences with Schutzman working Mondays, Tuesdays, and Wednesday mornings and Mannix working the rest of the work week.[25]

Job sharing should not be confused with a more controversial arrangement called *work sharing.* This occurs when workers agree to cut back on the number of hours they work in order to protect against layoffs. Workers may agree to voluntarily reduce 20 percent of hours worked and pay received, rather than have the employer cut 20 percent of the workforce during difficult economic times. Legal restrictions prohibit this practice in some settings.

WORK AT HOME AND THE VIRTUAL OFFICE

High technology is influencing yet another alternative work arrangement that is becoming increasingly visible in many employment sectors ranging from higher education to government and from manufacturing to services. **Telecommuting** describes work done at home or in a remote location via use of computers and advanced telecommunications linkages with a central office or other employment locations. At IBM, Canada, an arrangement called *flexiplace* means working most of the time from a home office and coming into IBM corporate offices only for special meetings. In a practice known as *hoteling,* temporary offices are reserved for these workers during the times they visit the main office. [26]

The notion of telecommuting is more and more associated with the *virtual office,* where the individual works literally "from the road" and while traveling from place-to-place or customer-to-customer by car or airplane. In all cases, the worker remains linked electronically with the home office.[27] The number of workers who are telecommuting is growing daily with organizations like AT&T and Cisco Systems reporting that over 50 percent of their workers telecommute at least part of the time.[28]

Telecommuting offers the individual the potential advantages of flexibility, the comforts of home, and choice of locations consistent with one's lifestyle. In terms of advantages to the organization, this alternative often produces cost savings and efficiency as well as employee satisfaction. On the negative side, telecommuters sometimes complain of isolation from co-workers, decreased identification with the work team, and technical difficulties with the computer linkages essential to their work arrangement. Yet overall, the practice continues to grow, with more organizations now offering special training in the *virtual management* of telecommuters.

PART-TIME WORK

Part-time work has become an increasingly prominent and controversial work arrangement. In **temporary part-time work** an employee is classified as "temporary" and works less than the standard 40-hour work week. In **permanent part-time work** the person is considered a "permanent" member of the workforce but contributes fewer hours than the standard, typically 40-hour work week. In the chapter opening example of Peet's Coffee and Tea, many of the loyal and satisfied Peetniks fall into this category. By working at least 21 hours a week, they are considered permanent and gain access to important benefits otherwise denied to the temporary part-time workers.[29]

Usually, temporary part-timers are easily released and hired as needs dictate. Accordingly, many organizations use part-time work to hold down labor costs and to help smooth out peaks and valleys in the business cycle. Employers also may use part-time work to better manage what may be called "retention quality." These workers are highly skilled individuals committed to their careers who want to continue to develop professionally but who can only work part time. Part-time nurses, among others, fall in this category.[30]

The part-time work schedule can be a benefit to people who want to supplement other jobs or who want something less than a full work week for a variety of personal reasons. For someone who is holding two jobs, including at least one part time, the added burdens can be stressful and may affect performance in either one or both work settings. Furthermore, part-timers often fail to qualify for fringe benefits, such as health care, life insurance, and pensions, and they may be paid less than their full-time counterparts. Nevertheless, part-time work schedules are of growing practical importance because of the organizational advantages they offer.

CHAPTER 8 SUMMARY

What are the alternative job design approaches?

- Job design is the creation of tasks and work settings for specific jobs.
- Job design by scientific management or job simplification standardizes work and employs people in clearly defined and specialized tasks.
- Job enlargement increases task variety by combining two or more tasks previously assigned to separate workers.
- Job rotation increases task variety by periodically rotating workers among jobs involving different tasks.
- Job enrichment builds bigger and more responsible jobs by adding planning and evaluating duties.

What are the keys to designing motivating jobs?

- Job characteristics theory offers a diagnostic approach to job enrichment based on the analysis of five core job characteristics: skill variety, task identity, task significance, autonomy, and feedback.
- Job characteristics theory does not assume that everyone wants an enriched job; it indicates that job enrichment will be more successful for persons with high-growth needs, requisite job skills, and context satisfaction.
- The social information processing theory points out that information from co-workers and others in the workplace influences a worker's perceptions and responses to a job.
- Not everyone's job should be enriched; job enrichment can be done for groups as well as individuals; cultural factors may influence job enrichment success.

How does technology influence job design?

- Well-planned sociotechnical systems integrate people and technology for high performance.

- Robotics and complete automation are increasingly used to replace people to perform jobs that are highly simplified and repetitive.

- Workers in flexible manufacturing cells utilize the latest technology to produce high-quality products with short cycle times.

- The nature of office work is being changed by computer workstation technologies, networks, and various forms of electronic communication.

- Workflow and business process reengineering analyzes all steps in work sequences to streamline activities and tasks, save costs, and improve performance.

How can goal setting improve job performance?

- Goal setting is the process of developing, negotiating, and formalizing performance targets or objectives.

- Research supports predictions that the most motivational goals are challenging and specific, allow for feedback on results, and create commitment and acceptance.

- The motivational impact of goals may be affected by individual difference moderators such as ability and self-efficacy.

- Management by objectives is a process of joint goal setting between a supervisor and worker.

- The management by objectives process is a good action framework for applying goal-setting theory on an organizationwide basis.

What alternative work arrangements are used today?

- Today's complex society is giving rise to a number of alternative work arrangements designed to balance the personal demands on workers with job responsibilities and opportunities.

- The compressed work week allows a full-time work week to be completed in under five days, typically offering four 10-hour days of work and three days free.

- Flexible working hours allow employees some daily choice in timing between work and nonwork activities.

- Job sharing occurs when two or more people divide one full-time job according to agreements among themselves and the employer.

- Telecommuting involves work at home or at a remote location while communicating with the home office as needed via computer and related technologies.

- Part-time work requires less than a 40-hour work week and can be done on a schedule classifying the worker as temporary or permanent.

CHAPTER 9

The Nature of Groups

Study Questions

Groups can be important sources of performance, creativity, and enthusiasm for organizations. This chapter introduces you to the basic attributes of groups as they are found in today's progressive organizations. As you read Chapter 9, keep in mind these study questions.

- What is the nature of groups in organizations?
- What are the stages of group development?
- What are the foundations of group effectiveness?
- What are group and intergroup dynamics?
- How do groups make decisions?

The new workplace places great value on change and adaptation. Organizations are continually under pressure to find new ways of operating in the quest for higher productivity, total quality and service, customer satisfaction, and better quality of working life. Among the many trends and developments we perceive today, none is more important than the attempts being made to tap the full potential of groups more creatively as critical organizational resources.

The team that created Apple's original Macintosh computer was really "hot." The brainchild of Apple's cofounder Steve Jobs, it was composed of high-achieving members who were excited and turned on to their highly challenging task. They worked all hours and at an unrelenting pace. The result was a benchmark computer produced in record time.

There is no doubt that an organization's success depends in significant part on the performance of its internal networks of formal and informal groups. They are focal points as organizations seek the advantages of smaller size, flatter structures, cross-functional integration, and more flexible operations. To meet competitive demands in challenging environments, the best organizations mobilize groups and teams in many capacities in the quest to reach their full potential as high performance systems.

More recently at Apple, Jobs built another team charged with reinvigorating the company. This was the team "at the top," including sales, hardware, software, services, inventory, and legal gurus. Together they brought about major changes in such areas as human resources, manufacturing, and marketing, and created the first iMac.[1]

GROUPS IN ORGANIZATIONS

A **group** is a collection of two or more people who work with one another regularly to achieve common goals. In a true group, members (1) are mutually dependent on one another to achieve common goals and (2) interact regularly with one another to pursue those goals over a sustained period of time.[2] Groups are important resources that are good for both organizations and their members. They help organizations to accomplish important tasks. They also help to maintain a high-quality workforce by satisfying needs of their members. Consultant and management scholar Harold J. Leavitt is a well-known advocate for the power and usefulness of groups.[3] He describes "hot groups" as ones that thrive in conditions of crisis and competition and whose creativity and innovativeness generate extraordinary returns.[4] The original MacIntosh team featured in the chapter opener was a hot group; in many ways, Apple's current top management team is one, too.

WHAT IS AN EFFECTIVE GROUP?

An **effective group** is one that achieves high levels of task performance, member satisfaction and team viability. With regard to *task performance,* an effective group achieves its performance goals—in the standard sense of quantity, quality, and timeliness of work results. For a formal workgroup, such as a manufacturing team, this may mean meeting daily production targets. For a temporary group, such as a new policy task force, this may involve meeting a deadline for submitting a new organizational policy to the company president. With regard to *member satisfaction,* an effective group is one whose members believe that their participation and experiences are positive and meet important personal needs. They are satisfied with their tasks, accomplishments, and interpersonal relationships. With regard to *team viability,* the members of an effective group are sufficiently satisfied to continue working well together on an ongoing basis and/or to look forward to working together again at some future point in time. Such a group has all-important long-term performance potential.

UNIQUE CONTRIBUTIONS OF GROUPS

Effective groups help organizations accomplish important tasks. In particular, they offer the potential for **synergy**—the creation of a whole that is greater than the sum of its parts. When synergy occurs, groups accomplish more than the total of their members' individual capabilities. Group synergy is necessary for organizations to become competitive and achieve long-term high performance in today's dynamic times.

The Effective Manager 9.1 lists several benefits that groups can bring to organizations. In three specific situations, groups often have performance advantages over individuals acting alone.[5] First, when there is no clear "expert" in a particular task or problem, groups seem to make better judgments than does the average individual alone. Second, when problem solving can be handled by a division of labor and the sharing of information, groups are typically more successful than individuals. Third, because of their tendencies to make riskier decisions, groups can be more creative and innovative than individuals.

Groups are important settings where people learn from one another and share job skills and knowledge. The learning environment and the pool of experience within a group can be used to solve difficult and unique problems. This is especially helpful to newcomers who often need help in their jobs. When group members support and help each other in acquiring and improving job competencies, they may even make up for deficiencies in organizational training systems.

Groups are able to satisfy the needs of members. They offer opportunities for social interaction and can provide individuals with a sense of security in available work assistance and technical advice. They can provide emotional support in times of special crisis or pressure, and allow for ego involvement in group goals and activities.

At the same time that they have enormous performance potential, however, groups can also have problems. One concern is **social loafing,** also known as the *Ringlemann effect.* It is the tendency of people to work less hard in a group than they would individually.[6] Max Ringlemann, a German psychologist, pinpointed the phenomenon by asking people to pull on a rope as hard as they could, first alone and then in a group.[7] He found

---

THE EFFECTIVE MANAGER 9.1

HOW GROUPS CAN HELP ORGANIZATIONS

- Groups are good for people.
- Groups can improve creativity.
- Groups can make better decisions.
- Groups can increase commitments to action.
- Groups help control their members.
- Groups help offset large organization size.

that average productivity dropped as more people joined the rope-pulling task. He suggested two reasons why people may not work as hard in groups as they would individually: (1) their individual contribution is less noticeable in the context of the group, and (2) they prefer to see others carry the workload. Some ways for dealing with social loafing or trying to prevent it from occurring include:

- Define member roles and tasks to maximize individual interests.
- Link individual rewards to performance contributions to the group.
- Raise accountability by identifying individuals' performance contributions to the group.

Another issue in group work is **social facilitation**—the tendency for one's behavior to be influenced by the presence of others in a group or social setting.[8] In general, *social facilitation theory* indicates that working in the presence of others creates an emotional arousal or excitement that stimulates behavior and therefore affects performance. Arousal tends to work positively when one is proficient with the task. Here, the excitement leads to extra effort at doing something that already comes quite naturally. An example is the play of a world-class athlete in front of an enthusiastic "hometown" crowd. On the other hand, the effect of social facilitation can be negative when the task is not well learned. You may know this best in the context of public speaking. When asked to speak in front of a class or larger audience, you may well stumble as you try hard in public to talk about an unfamiliar topic.

FORMAL GROUPS

There are many ways in the new workplace for groups to be used to great advantage. A **formal group** is officially designated to serve a specific organizational purpose. An example is the work unit headed by a manager and consisting of one or more direct reports. The organization creates such a group to perform a specific task, which typically involves the use of resources to create a product such as a report, decision, service, or commodity. The head of a formal group is responsible for the group's performance accomplishments, but all members contribute the required work. Also, the head of the group plays a key "linking-pin" role that ties it horizontally and vertically with the rest of the organization.[9]

Formal groups may be permanent or temporary. *Permanent workgroups,* or *command groups* in the vertical structure, often appear on organization charts as departments (e.g., market research department), divisions (e.g., consumer products division), or teams (e.g., product-assembly team). Such groups can vary in size from very small departments or teams of just a few people to large divisions employing a hundred or more people. As permanent workgroups, they are each officially created to perform a specific function on an ongoing basis. They continue to exist until a decision is made to change or reconfigure the organization for some reason.

In contrast, *temporary workgroups* are *task groups* specifically created to solve a problem or perform a defined task. They often disband once the assigned purpose or task has been accomplished.[10] Examples are the many temporary committees and task forces that are important components of any organization. Indeed, today's organizations tend to make more use of *cross-functional teams* or *task forces* for special problem-solving efforts. The president of a company, for example, might convene a task force to examine the possibility of implementing flexible work hours for nonmanagerial employees. Usually, such temporary groups appoint chairpersons or heads who are held accountable for results, much as is the manager of a work unit. Another common form is the *project team* that is formed, often cross-functionally, to complete a specific task with a well-defined end point. Examples include installing a new e-mail system and introducing a new product modification.

Information technology is bringing a new type of group into the workplace. This is the **virtual group,** a group whose members convene and work together electronically via networked computers. In this electronic age, virtual groups are increasingly common in organizations. Facilitated by ever-advancing team-oriented software, or groupware, members of virtual groups can do the same things as members of face-to-face groups. They can share information, make decisions, and complete tasks. The important role of virtual groups or teams in the high performance workplace is discussed in the next chapter.

INFORMAL GROUPS

Informal groups emerge without being officially designated by the organization. They form spontaneously through personal relationships or special interests, not by any specific organizational endorsement. *Friendship groups* for example, consist of persons with natural affinities for one another. They tend to work together, sit together, take breaks together, and even do things together outside of the workplace. *Interest groups* consist of persons who share common interests. These may be job-related interests, such as an intense desire to learn more about computers, or nonwork interests, such as community service, sports, or religion.

Informal groups often help people get their jobs done. Through their network of interpersonal relationships, they have the potential to speed up the work flow as people assist each other in ways that formal lines of authority fail to provide. They also help individuals satisfy needs that are thwarted or otherwise left unmet in a formal group. In these and related ways, informal groups can provide their members with social satisfactions, security, and a sense of belonging.

STAGES OF GROUP DEVELOPMENT

Whether one is part of a formal work unit, a temporary task force, or a virtual team, the group itself passes through a series of life cycle stages.[11] Depending on the stage the group has reached, the leader and members can face very different challenges. Figure 9.1 describes five stages of group development: (1) forming, (2) storming, (3) norming, (4) performing, and (5) adjourning.[12]

FORMING STAGE

In the *forming stage* of group development, a primary concern is the initial entry of members to a group. During this stage, individuals ask a number of questions as they begin to identify with other group members and with the group itself. Their concerns may include: "What can the group offer me?" "What will I be asked to contribute?" "Can my needs be met at the same time I contribute to the group?" Members are interested in getting to know each other and discovering what is considered acceptable behavior, in determining the real task of the group, and in defining group rules.

FIGURE 9.1	FIVE STAGES OF GROUP DEVELOPMENT

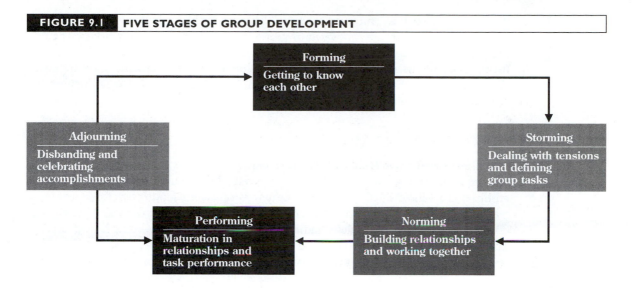

STORMING STAGE

The *storming stage* of group development is a period of high emotionality and tension among the group members. During this stage, hostility and infighting may occur, and the group typically experiences many changes. Coalitions or cliques may form as individuals compete to impose their preferences on the group and to achieve a desired status position. Outside demands, including premature expectations for performance results, may create uncomfortable pressures. In the process, membership expectations tend to be clarified, and attention shifts toward obstacles standing in the way of group goals. Individuals begin to understand one another's interpersonal styles, and efforts are made to find ways to accomplish group goals while also satisfying individual needs.

NORMING STAGE

The *norming stage* of group development, sometimes called initial integration, is the point at which the group really begins to come together as a coordinated unit. The turmoil of the storming stage gives way to a precarious balancing of forces. With the pleasures of a new sense of harmony, group members will strive to maintain positive balance. Holding the group together may become more important to some than successfully working on the group's tasks. Minority viewpoints, deviations from group directions, and criticisms may be discouraged as group members experience a preliminary sense of closeness. Some members may mistakenly perceive this stage as one of ultimate maturity. In fact, a premature sense of accomplishment at this point needs to be carefully managed as a "stepping stone" to the next higher level of group development.

PERFORMING STAGE

The *performing stage* of group development, sometimes called total integration, marks the emergence of a mature, organized, and well-functioning group. The group is now able to deal with complex tasks and handle internal disagreements in creative ways. The structure is stable, and members are motivated by group goals and are generally satisfied. The primary challenges are continued efforts to improve relationships and performance. Group members should be able to adapt successfully as opportunities and demands change over time. A group that has achieved the level of total integration typically scores high on the criteria of group maturity shown in Figure 9.2.

ADJOURNING STAGE

A well-integrated group is able to disband, if required, when its work is accomplished. The *adjourning stage* of group development is especially important for the many temporary groups that are increasingly common in the new workplace, including task forces, committees, project teams and the like. Members of these groups must be able to convene quickly, do their jobs on a tight schedule, and then adjourn—often to reconvene later if needed. Their willingness to disband when the job is done and to work well together in future responsibilities, group or otherwise, is an important long-run test of group success.

FOUNDATIONS OF GROUP EFFECTIVENESS

To achieve and maintain high levels of group effectiveness, any manager or leader must understand the way groups operate as organizational resources. The systems model in Figure 9.3 shows how groups, like organizations, pursue effectiveness by interacting with their environments to transform resource inputs into product outputs.[13] The inputs are

FIGURE 9.2	TEN CRITERIA FOR MEASURING THE MATURITY OF A GROUP

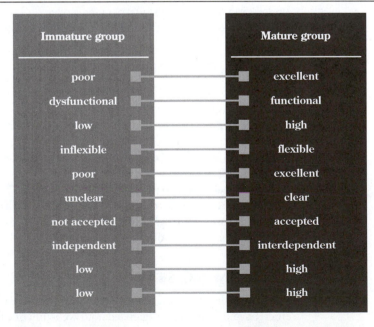

	Immature group	Mature group
1. Feedback mechanisms	poor	excellent
2. Decision-making methods	dysfunctional	functional
3. Group loyalty/cohesion	low	high
4. Operating procedures	inflexible	flexible
5. Use of member resources	poor	excellent
6. Communications	unclear	clear
7. Goals	not accepted	accepted
8. Authority relations	independent	interdependent
9. Participation in leadership	low	high
10. Acceptance of minority views	low	high

| FIGURE 9.3 | **THE WORKGROUP AS AN OPEN SYSTEM TRANSFORMING RESOURCE INPUTS INTO PRODUCT OUTPUTS** |

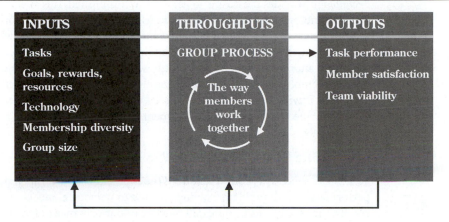

the initial "givens" in any group situation. They are the foundations for all subsequent action. As a general rule-of-thumb, the stronger the input foundations the better the chances for long-term group effectiveness. Key group inputs include the nature of the task, goals, rewards, resources, technology, membership diversity, and group size.

TASKS

The tasks they are asked to perform can place different demands on groups, with varying implications for group effectiveness. The *technical demands* of a group's task include its routineness, difficulty, and information requirements. The *social demands* of a task involve relationships, ego involvement, controversies over ends and means, and the like. Tasks that are complex in technical demands require unique solutions and more information processing; those that are complex in social demands involve difficulties reaching agreement on goals or methods for accomplishing them. Naturally, group effectiveness is harder to achieve when the task is highly complex.[14] To master complexity, group members must apply and distribute their efforts broadly and actively cooperate to achieve desired results. When their efforts are successful at mastering complex tasks, however, group members tend to experience high levels of satisfaction with the group and its accomplishments.

GOALS, REWARDS, AND RESOURCES

Appropriate goals, well-designed reward systems, and adequate resources are all essential to support long-term performance accomplishments. A group's performance, just like individual performance, can suffer when goals are unclear, insufficiently challenging, or arbitrarily imposed. It can also suffer if goals and rewards are focused too much on individual-level instead of group-level accomplishments. And it can suffer if adequate budgets, the right facilities, good work methods and procedures, and the best technologies are not available. By contrast, having the right goals, rewards, and resources can be a strong launching pad for group success.

TECHNOLOGY

Technology provides the means to get work accomplished. It is always necessary to have the right technology available for the task at hand. The nature of the workflow technology can also influence the way group members interact with one another while performing their tasks. It is one thing to be part of a group that crafts products to specific customer requests; it is quite another to be part of a group whose members staff one section of a machine-paced assembly line. The former technology permits greater interaction among group members. It will probably create a closer knit group with a stronger sense of identity than the one formed around one small segment of an assembly line.

MEMBERSHIP CHARACTERISTICS

To achieve success, a group must have the right skills and competencies available for task performance and problem solving. Although talents alone cannot guarantee desired results, they establish an important baseline of performance potential. It is difficult to overcome the performance limits that result when the input competencies are insufficient to the task at hand.

In *homogeneous groups* where members are very similar to one another, members may find it very easy to work together. But they may still suffer performance limitations if their collective skills, experiences, and perspectives are not a good match for complex tasks. In *heterogeneous groups* whose members vary in age, gender, race, ethnicity, experience, culture, and the like, a wide pool of talent and viewpoints is available for problem-solving. But this diversity may create difficulties as members try to define problems, share information, and handle interpersonal conflicts. These difficulties may be quite pronounced in the short run or early stages of group development. Once members learn how to work together, however, research confirms that diversity can be turned into enhanced performance potential.[15]

Researchers identify what is called the **diversity-consensus dilemma.** This is the tendency for increasing diversity among group members to make it harder for group members to work together, even though the diversity itself expands the skills and perspectives available for problem solving.[16] The challenge to group effectiveness in a culturally mixed multinational team, for example, is to take advantage of the diversity without suffering process disadvantages.[17]

The blend of personalities is also important in a group or team. The **FIRO-B theory** (with "FIRO" standing for fundamental interpersonal orientation) identifies differences in how people relate to one another in groups based on their needs to express and receive feelings of inclusion, control, and affection.[18] Developed by William Schutz, the theory suggests that groups whose members have compatible needs are likely to be more effective than groups whose members are more incompatible. Symptoms of incompatibilities in a group include withdrawn members, open hostilities, struggles over control, and domination of the group by a few members. Schutz states the management implications of the FIRO-B theory this way: "If at the outset we can choose a group of people who can work together harmoniously, we shall go far toward avoiding situations where a group's efforts are wasted in interpersonal conflicts."[19]

Another source of diversity in group membership is *status*—a person's relative rank, prestige, or standing in a group. Status within a group can be based on any number of factors, including age, work seniority, occupation, education, performance, or standing in other groups. **Status congruence** occurs when a person's position within the group is equivalent in status to positions held outside of the group. Problems are to be expected when status incongruence is present. In high-power distance cultures such as Malaysia, for example, the chair of a committee is expected to be the highest-ranking member of the group. When present, such status congruity helps members feel comfortable in proceeding with their work. If the senior member is not appointed to head the committee, members are likely to feel uncomfortable and have difficulty working as a group. Similar problems might occur, for example, when a young college graduate is appointed to chair a project group composed of senior and more experienced workers.

GROUP SIZE

The size of a group, as measured by the number of its members, can have an impact on group effectiveness. As a group becomes larger, more people are available to divide up the work and accomplish needed tasks. This can boost performance and member satisfaction, but only up to a point. As a group continues to grow in size, communication and coordination problems often set in. Satisfaction may dip, and turnover, absenteeism, and social loafing may increase. Even logistical matters, such as finding time and locations for meetings, become more difficult for larger groups and can hurt performance.[20]

A good size for problem-solving groups is between five and seven members. A group with fewer than five may be too small to adequately share responsibilities. With more than seven, individuals may find it harder to participate and offer ideas. Larger groups are also more prone to possible domination by aggressive members and have tendencies to split into coalitions or subgroups.[21] Groups with an odd number of members find it easier to use majority voting rules to resolve disagreements. When speed is required, this form of conflict management is useful, and odd-numbered groups may be preferred. But when careful deliberations are required and the emphasis is more on consensus, such as in jury duty or very complex problem solving, even-numbered groups may be more effective unless an irreconcilable deadlock occurs.[22]

GROUP AND INTERGROUP DYNAMICS

The effectiveness of any group as an open system (depicted in Figure 9.3) requires more than the correct inputs. It always depends also on how well members work together to utilize these inputs to produce the desired outputs. When we speak about people "working together" in groups, we are dealing with issues of **group dynamics**—the forces operating in groups that affect the way members relate to and work with one another. In the open systems model, group dynamics are the *processes* through which inputs are transformed into outputs.

WHAT GOES ON WITHIN GROUPS

George Homans described a classic model of group dynamics involving two sets of behaviors—required and emergent. In a workgroup, *required behaviors* are those formally defined and expected by the organization.[23] For example, they may include such behaviors as punctuality, customer respect, and assistance to co-workers. *Emergent behaviors* are those that group members display in addition to what the organization asks of them. They derive not from outside expectations but from personal initiative. *Emergent behaviors* often include things that people do beyond formal job requirements and that help get the job done in the best ways possible. Rarely can required behaviors be specified so perfectly that they meet all the demands that arise in a work situation. This makes emergent behaviors essential. An example might be someone taking the time to send an e-mail to an absent member to keep her informed about what happened during a group meeting. The concept of empowerment, often discussed in this book as essential to the high performance workplace, relies strongly on unlocking this positive aspect of emergent behaviors.

Homans' model of group dynamics also describes member relationships in terms of activities, interactions, and sentiments, all of which have their required and emergent forms. *Activities* are the things people do or the actions they take in groups while working on tasks. *Interactions* are interpersonal communications and contacts. *Sentiments* are the feelings, attitudes, beliefs, or values held by group members.

WHAT GOES ON BETWEEN GROUPS

The term **intergroup dynamics** refers to the dynamics that take place between two or more groups. Organizations ideally operate as cooperative systems in which the various components support one another. In the real world, however, competition and intergroup problems often develop within an organization and have mixed consequences. On the negative side—such as when manufacturing and sales units don't get along, intergroup dynamics may divert energies as members focus more on their animosities toward the other group than on the performance of important tasks.[24] On the positive side, competition among groups can stimulate them to work harder, become more focused on key tasks, develop more internal loyalty and satisfaction, or achieve a higher level of creativity in problem solving. Japanese companies, for example, often use competitive themes to motivate their organizationwide workforces. At Sony, it has been said that the slogan "BMW" stands for "Beat Matsushita Whatsoever."[25]

Organizations and their managers go to great lengths to avoid the negative and achieve the positive aspects of intergroup dynamics. Groups engaged in destructive competition, for example, can be refocused on a common enemy or a common goal. Direct negotiations can be held among the groups, and members can be trained to work more cooperatively. It is important to avoid win-lose reward systems in which one group must lose something in order for the other to gain. Rewards can be refocused on contributions to the total organization and on how much groups help one another. Also, cooperation tends to increase as interaction between groups increases.

DECISION MAKING IN GROUPS

One of the most important activities in any group is *decision making*—discussed in detail in Chapter 17 as the process of choosing among alternative courses of action. Obviously, the quality and timeliness of decisions made and the processes through which they are arrived at can have an important impact on group effectiveness.

HOW GROUPS MAKE DECISIONS

Edgar Schein, a noted scholar and consultant, has worked extensively with groups to analyze and improve their decision-making processes.[26] He observes that groups may make decisions through any of the following six methods: lack of response, authority rule, minority rule, majority rule, consensus, or unanimity.

In *decision by lack of response,* one idea after another is suggested without any discussion taking place. When the group finally accepts an idea, all others have been bypassed and discarded by simple lack of response rather than by critical evaluation. In *decision by authority rule,* the chairperson, manager, or leader makes a decision for the group. This can be done with or without discussion and is very time efficient. Whether the decision is a good one or a bad one depends on whether the authority figure has the necessary information and on how well other group members accept this approach. In *decision by minority rule,* two or three people are able to dominate or "railroad" the group into making a decision to which they agree. This is often done by providing a suggestion and then forcing quick agreement by challenging the group with such statements as: "Does anyone object?… No? Well, let's go ahead then."

One of the most common ways groups make decisions, especially when early signs of disagreement set in, is *decision by majority rule.* Formal voting may take place or members may be polled to find the majority viewpoint. This method parallels the democratic political system and is often used without awareness of its potential problems. The very process of voting can create coalitions. That is, some people will be "winners," and others will be "losers" when the final vote is tallied. Those in the minority—the "losers," may feel left out or discarded without having had a fair say. As a result, they may be less enthusiastic about implementing the decision of the "winners." Lingering resentments may impair group effectiveness in the future.

Another alternative is *decision by consensus.* Formally defined, **consensus** is a state of affairs whereby discussion leads to one alternative being favored by most members and the other members agreeing to support it. When a consensus is reached, even those who may have opposed the chosen course of action know that they have been listened to and have had a fair chance to influence the outcome. Consensus, as suggested by the guidelines in The Effective Manager 9.2, does not require unanimity. What it does require is the opportunity for any dissenting members to feel they have been able to speak, and that their voices have been heard.[27]

THE EFFECTIVE MANAGER 9.2
GUIDELINES FOR GROUP CONSENSUS

1. Don't argue blindly; consider others' reactions to your points.
2. Don't change your mind just to reach quick agreement.
3. Avoid conflict reduction by voting, coin tossing, and bargaining.
4. Try to involve everyone in the decision process.
5. Allow disagreements to surface so that information and opinions can be deliberated.
6. Don't focus on winning versus losing; seek alternatives acceptable to all.
7. Discuss assumptions, listen carefully, and encourage participation by everyone.

A *decision by unanimity* may be the ideal state of affairs. Here, all group members agree totally on the course of action to be taken. This is a "logically perfect" group decision method that is extremely difficult to attain in actual practice. One reason that groups sometimes turn to authority decisions, majority voting, or even minority decisions is the difficulty of managing the group process to achieve consensus or unanimity.[28]

ASSETS AND LIABILITIES OF GROUP DECISION MAKING

The best groups don't limit themselves to just one decision-making method, using it over and over again regardless of circumstances. Instead, they operate in contingency fashion by changing decision methods to best fit the problem and situation at hand. Indeed, an important leadership skill is helping a group choose the "right" decision method—one providing for a timely and quality decision to which the members are highly committed.

The choice among decision methods should be made with a full awareness of both the potential assets and liabilities of group decision making. For example, the *potential advantages of group decision making* include:[29]

1. *Information*—more knowledge and expertise is applied to solve the problem.
2. *Alternatives*—a greater number of alternatives are examined, avoiding tunnel vision.
3. *Understanding and acceptance*—the final decision is better understood and accepted by all group members.
4. *Commitment*—there is more commitment among all group members to make the final decision work.

We also know that groups can experience problems when they are making decisions. The *potential disadvantages of group decision making* include:[30]

1. *Social pressure to conform*—individuals may feel compelled to go along with the apparent wishes of the group.
2. *Minority domination*—the group's decision may be forced or "railroaded" by one individual or a small coalition.
3. *Time demands*—with more people involved in the dialogue and discussion, group decisions usually take longer to make than individual decisions.

GROUPTHINK

An important potential problem in group decision making, identified by social psychologist Irving Janis, is **groupthink**—the tendency of members in highly cohesive groups to lose their critical evaluative capabilities.[31] Janis believes that, because highly cohesive groups demand conformity, their members tend to become unwilling to criticize one another's ideas and suggestions. Desires to hold the group together and to avoid unpleasant disagreements lead to an overemphasis on agreement and an underemphasis on critical discussion. The possible result is a poor decision. Janis suggests that groupthink played a role in the lack of preparedness of U.S. forces at Pearl Harbor in World War II. It has also been linked to U.S. decision making during the Vietnam War and to the space shuttle *Challenger* disaster.

Group leaders and members should be alert to the symptoms of groupthink and quick to take any necessary action to prevent its occurrence.[32] The Effective Manager 9.3 identifies steps that can be taken to avoid groupthink. Among them, for example, President Kennedy

> **THE EFFECTIVE MANAGER 9.3**
> **HOW TO AVOID GROUPTHINK**
>
> - Assign the role of critical evaluator to each group member.
> - Have the leader avoid seeming partial to one course of action.
> - Create subgroups to work on the same problem.
> - Have group members discuss issues with outsiders and report back.
> - Invite outside experts to observe and react to group processes.
> - Assign someone to be a "devil's advocate" at each meeting.
> - Write alternative scenarios for the intentions of competing groups.
> - Hold "second-chance" meetings after consensus is apparently achieved.

chose to absent himself from certain strategy discussions by his cabinet during the Cuban Missile crisis. Reportedly, this facilitated discussion and helped to improve decision making as the crisis was successfully resolved.

HOW TO IMPROVE GROUP DECISION MAKING

In order to take full advantage of the group as a decision-making resource, care must be taken to manage group dynamics to balance individual contributions and group operations.[33] A particular concern is with the process losses that often occur in free-flowing meetings, such as a committee deliberation or a staff meeting on a specific problem. In these settings the risk of social pressures to conform, domination, time pressures, and even highly emotional debates may detract from the purpose at hand. They are also settings in which special group decision techniques may be used to advantage.[34]

Brainstorming   In **brainstorming,** group members actively generate as many ideas and alternatives as possible, and they do so relatively quickly and without inhibitions. Four rules typically govern the brainstorming process. First, *all criticism is ruled out.* No one is allowed to judge or evaluate any ideas until the idea-generation process has been completed. Second, *"free-wheeling" is welcomed.* The emphasis is on creativity and imagination; the wilder or more radical the ideas, the better. Third, *quantity is wanted.* The emphasis is also on the number of ideas; the greater the number, the more likely a superior idea will appear. Fourth, *"piggy-backing" is good.* Everyone is encouraged to suggest how others' ideas can be turned into new ideas or how two or more ideas can be joined into still another new idea. Typical results include enthusiasm, involvement, and a free flow of ideas useful in creative problem solving.

Nominal Group Technique   In any group, there will be times when the opinions of members differ so much that antagonistic arguments will develop during free-wheeling discussions. At other times the group will be so large that open discussion and brainstorming are awkward to manage. In such cases, a form of structured group decision making called the **nominal group technique** may be helpful.[35] It puts people in small groups of six to seven members and asks everyone to respond individually and in writing to a "nominal question" such as: "What should be done to improve the effectiveness of this work team?" Everyone is encouraged to list as many alternatives or ideas as they can. Next, participants read aloud their responses to the nominal question in round-robin fashion. The recorder writes each response on large newsprint as it is offered. No criticism is allowed. The recorder asks for any questions that may clarify items on the newsprint. This is again done in round-robin fashion, and no evaluation is allowed. The goal is simply to make sure that everyone present fully understands each response. A structured voting procedure is then used to prioritize responses to the nominal question. The nominal group procedure allows ideas to be evaluated without risking the inhibitions, hostilities, and distortions that may occur in an open meeting.

Delphi Technique   A third group decision approach, the **Delphi technique,** was developed by the Rand Corporation for use in situations where group members are unable to meet face to face. In this procedure, a series of questionnaires are distributed to a panel of decision makers, who submit initial responses to a decision coordinator. The coordinator summarizes the solutions and sends the summary back to the panel members, along with a follow-up questionnaire. Panel members again send in their responses, and the process is repeated until a consensus is reached and a clear decision emerges.

Computer-Mediated Decision Making   Today's information and computer technologies enable group decision making to take place across great distances with the help of group decision support systems. The growing use of *electronic brainstorming* is one example of the trend toward virtual meetings. Assisted by special software, participants use personal computers to enter ideas at will, either through simultaneous interaction or over a period of time. The software compiles and disseminates the results. Both the nominal group and Delphi techniques also lend themselves to computer mediation. Electronic approaches to group decision making can offer several advantages, including the benefits of anonymity, greater number of ideas generated, efficiency of recording and storing for later use, and ability to handle large groups with geographically dispersed members.[36]

CHAPTER 9 SUMMARY

What is the nature of groups in organizations?

- A group is a collection of people who interact with one another regularly to attain common goals.
- Groups can help organizations by helping their members to improve task performance and experience more satisfaction from their work.
- One way to view organizations is as interlocking networks of groups, whose managers serve as leaders in one group and subordinates in another.
- Synergy occurs when groups are able to accomplish more than their members could by acting individually.
- Formal groups are designated by the organization to serve an official purpose; examples are work units, task forces, and committees; informal groups are unofficial and emerge spontaneously because of special interests.

What are the stages of group development?

- Groups pass through various stages in their life cycles, and each stage poses somewhat distinct management problems.

- In the forming stage, groups have problems managing individual entry.
- In the storming stage, groups have problems managing expectations and status.
- In the norming or initial integration stage, groups have problems managing member relations and task efforts.
- In the performing or total integration stage, groups have problems managing continuous improvement and self-renewal.
- In the adjourning stage, groups have problems managing task completion and the process of disbanding.

What are the foundations of group effectiveness?

- An effective group is one that achieves high levels of task accomplishment and member satisfaction, and achieves viability to perform successfully over the long term.
- As open systems, groups must interact successfully with their environments to obtain resources that are transformed into outputs.
- Group input factors establish the core foundations for effectiveness, and include: goals, rewards, resources, technology, the task, membership characteristics, and group size, among other possibilities.

What are group and intergroup dynamics?

- Group dynamics are the way members work together to utilize inputs; they are another foundation of group effectiveness.
- Group dynamics are based on the interactions, activities, and sentiments of group members, and on the required and emergent ways in which members work together.
- Intergroup dynamics are the forces that operate between two or more groups.
- Although groups in organizations ideally cooperate with one another, they often become involved in dysfunctional conflicts and competition.
- The disadvantages of intergroup competition can be reduced through management strategies to direct, train, and reinforce groups to pursue cooperative instead of purely competitive actions.

How do groups make decisions?

- Groups can make decisions by lack of response, authority rule, minority rule, majority rule, consensus, and unanimity.
- The potential assets to more group decision making include having more information available and generating more understanding and commitment.
- The potential liabilities to more group decision making include social pressures to conform and greater time requirements.
- "Groupthink" is the tendency of some groups to lose critical evaluative capabilities.
- Techniques for improving creativity in group decision making include brainstorming, nominal group technique, and the Delphi method, including computer applications.

10

Teamwork and High Performance Teams

"Who needs a boss?" once read the headline of a provocative *Fortune* magazine article. "Not the employees who work in self-managed teams," answers the first paragraph.[1] Since then the shift of focus from individual jobs to teams and teamwork is one of the most notable ways in which work is changing today.[2] In many situations teams and teamwork are considered major, even essential, keys to productivity and quality of working life improvements. But putting team concepts to work is a major challenge for people used to more traditional ways of working. As more and more jobs are turned over to teams, special problems relating to group and intergroup dynamics may occur. It is not enough for visionary entrepreneurs, leaders, and managers to recognize the value of teams and implement creative workgroup designs. They must also carefully nurture and support people and relationships if the groups are to become confident and enduring high performance teams.

HIGH PERFORMANCE TEAMS

When we think of the word "teams," a variety of popular sporting teams usually comes to mind. Workgroups can also be considered as teams to the extent that they meet the demands of this definition. A **team** is a small group of people with complementary skills, who work actively together to achieve a common purpose for which they hold themselves collectively accountable.[3]

Teams are one of the major forces behind today's revolutionary changes in organizations. Management scholar Jay Conger calls the team-based organization the management system of the future, the business world's response to the need for speed in an ever more competitive environment.[4] He cites the example of an American jet engine manufacturer that switched to cross-functional teams instead of traditional functional work units. The firm cut the time required to design and produce new engines by 50 percent. Conger says: "Cross-functional teams are speed machines."[5] Clearly, we need to know more about such teams and the processes of teamwork in organizations.

TYPES OF TEAMS

A major challenge in any organization is to turn formal groups, as discussed in Chapter 9, into true high performance teams in any of the following settings.[6] First, there are *teams that recommend things*. Established to study specific problems and recommend solutions to them, these teams typically work with a target completion date and disband once their purpose has been fulfilled. They are temporary groups including task forces, ad-hoc committees, project teams, and the like. Members of these teams must be able to learn quickly how to work well together, accomplish the assigned task, and make good action recommendations for follow-up work by other people.

Second, there are *teams that run things*. Such management teams consist of people with the formal responsibility for leading other groups. These teams may exist at all levels of responsibility, from the individual work unit composed of a team leader and team members to the top management team composed of a CEO and other senior executives. Teams can add value to work processes at any level and offer special opportunities for dealing with complex problems and uncertain situations. Key issues addressed by top management teams, for example, include identifying overall organizational purposes, goals, and values, crafting strategies, and persuading others to support them.[7]

Third, there are *teams that make or do things.* These are functional groups and work units that perform ongoing tasks, such as marketing or manufacturing. Members of these teams must have good long-term working relationships with one another, solid operating systems, an the external support needed to achieve effectiveness over a sustained period of time. They also need energy to keep up the pace and meet the day-to-day challenges of sustained high performance.

THE NATURE OF TEAMWORK

All teams need members who believe in team goals and are motivated to work with others actively to accomplish important tasks—whether those tasks involve recommending things, making or doing things, or running things. Indeed, an essential criterion of a true team is that the members feel "collectively accountable" for what they accomplish.[8]

This sense of collective accountability sets the stage for real **teamwork,** with team members actively working together in such a way that all their respective skills are well utilized to achieve a common purpose.[9] A commitment to teamwork is found in the willingness of every member to "listen and respond constructively to views expressed by others, give others the benefit of the doubt, provide support, and recognize the interests and achievements of others."[10] Teamwork of this type is the central foundation of any high performance team. But developing teamwork is a challenging leadership task, regardless of the setting. It takes a lot more work to build a well-functioning team than to simply assign members to the same group and then expect them to do a great job.[11] See, for example, The Effective Manager 10.1.

High performance teams have special characteristics that allow them to excel at teamwork and achieve special performance advantages. First, *high performance teams have strong core values* that help guide their attitudes and behaviors in directions consistent with the team's purpose. Such values act as an internal control system for a group or team that can substitute for outside direction and supervisory attention. Second, *high performance teams turn a general sense of purpose into specific performance objectives.* Whereas a shared sense

---

THE EFFECTIVE MANAGER 10.1

HOW TO CREATE A HIGH-PERFORMING TEAM

- Communicate high performance standards.
- Set the tone in the first team meeting.
- Create a sense of urgency.
- Make sure members have the right skills.
- Establish clear rules for team behavior.
- As a leader, model expected behaviors.
- Find ways to create early "successes."
- Continually introduce new information.
- Have members spend time together
- Give positive feedback.
- Reward high performance.

---

of purpose gives general direction to a team, commitment to specific performance results makes this purpose truly meaningful. Specific objectives—such as reducing the time of getting the product to market by half—provide a clear focus for solving problems and resolving conflicts. They also set standards for measuring results and obtaining performance feedback. And, they help group members understand the need for "collective" versus purely individual efforts. Third, members of *high performance teams have the right mix of skills,* including technical skills, problem-solving and decision-making skills, and interpersonal skills. Finally, *high performance teams possess creativity.* In the new workplace, teams must use their creativity to assist organizations in continuous improvement of operations and in continuous development of new products, services, and markets.

DIVERSITY AND TEAM PERFORMANCE

In order to create and maintain high performance teams, all of the various elements of group effectiveness discussed in Chapter 9 must be addressed and successfully managed. As an important input to group and team dynamics, membership diversity carries special significance in today's workplace.[12] When team members are homogeneous, that is, when members are alike in respect to such things as age, gender, race, experience, ethnicity, and culture, there are certain potential benefits for group dynamics. It will probably be easy for members to quickly build social relationships and begin the interactions needed to work harmoniously together. On the other hand, a homogeneous membership may limit the group in terms of ideas, viewpoints, and creativity. Teams that are diverse in terms of members' demography, experiences, and cultures, by contrast, have a rich pool of information, talent, and varied perspectives that can help improve problem solving and increase creativity. These assets are especially valuable to teams working on complex and very demanding tasks.

Research indicates that diversity among team members may create performance difficulties early in the team's life or stage of development. This happens when interpersonal stresses and conflicts relating to diversity slow down group processes such as relationship building, problem definition, and information sharing.[13] Even though diverse teams may struggle in the short run to resolve these issues, however, they are likely to develop enhanced long-run performance potential once things are worked out.[14] Although it may take a bit more time and effort to create teamwork from foundations of diversity, longer-term gains in creativity and performance can make it all worthwhile. Teamwork rich in diversity is one of the great advantages of high performance organizations.

TEAM BUILDING

Teamwork doesn't always happen naturally in a group. It is something that team members and leaders must work hard to achieve. In the sports world, for example, coaches and managers focus on teamwork when building new teams at the start of each season. And as you are aware, even experienced teams often run into problems as a season progresses. Members slack off or become disgruntled; some have performance "slumps"; some are traded to other teams. Even world-champion teams have losing streaks, and the most talented players can lose motivation at times, quibble among themselves, and end up contributing little to team success. When these things happen, the owners, managers, and players are apt to examine their problems, take corrective action to rebuild the team, and restore the teamwork needed to achieve high performance results.[15]

Workgroups and teams have similar difficulties. When newly formed, they must master challenges in the early stages of group development. Even when they are mature, most work teams encounter problems of insufficient teamwork at different points in time. When difficulties occur, or as a means of preventing them from occurring, a systematic process of **team building** can help. This is a sequence of planned activities designed to gather and analyze data on the functioning of a group and to initiate changes designed to improve teamwork and increase group effectiveness.[16]

HOW TEAM BUILDING WORKS

The action steps and continuous improvement theme highlighted in Figure 10.1 are typical of most team-building approaches. The process begins when someone notices that a problem exists or may develop with team effectiveness. Members then work together to gather data relating to the problem, analyze these data, plan for improvements, and implement the action plans. The entire team-building process is highly collaborative. Everyone is expected to participate actively as group operations are evaluated and decisions are made on what needs to be done to improve the team's functioning in the future. This process can and should become an ongoing part of any team's work agenda. It is an approach to continuous improvement that can be very beneficial to long-term effectiveness.

Team-building is participatory, and it is data based. Whether the data are gathered by questionnaire, interview, nominal group meeting, or other creative methods, the goal is to get good answers to such questions as: "How well are we doing in terms of task accomplishment?"… "How satisfied are we as individual members with the group and the way

---

FIGURE 10.1   **THE TEAM-BUILDING PROCESS**

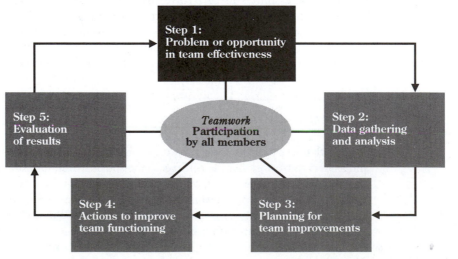

it operates?" There are a variety of ways for such questions to be asked and answered in a collaborative and motivating manner.

APPROACHES TO TEAM BUILDING

In the *formal retreat approach,* team building takes place during an off-site "retreat." During this retreat, which may last from one to several days, group members work intensively on a variety of assessment and planning tasks. They are initiated by a review of team functioning using data gathered through survey, interviews, or other means. Formal retreats are often held with the assistance of a consultant, who is either hired from the outside or made available from in-house staff. Team-building retreats offer opportunities for intense and concentrated efforts to examine group accomplishments and operations.

Not all team building is done in a formal retreat format or with the assistance of outside consultants. In a *continuous improvement approach,* the manager, team leader, or group members themselves take responsibility for regularly engaging in the team-building process. This method can be as simple as periodic meetings that implement the team-building steps; it can also include self-managed formal retreats. In all cases, the team members commit themselves to monitoring group development and accomplishments continuously and making the day-to-day changes needed to ensure team effectiveness. Such continuous improvement of teamwork is essential to the total quality and total service management themes so important to organizations today.

The *outdoor experience approach* is an increasingly popular team-building activity that may be done on its own or in combination with other approaches. It places group members in a variety of physically challenging situations that must be mastered through teamwork, not individual work. By having to work together in the face of difficult obstacles, team members are supposed to experience increased self-confidence, more respect for others' capabilities, and a greater commitment to teamwork. A popular sponsor of team building through outdoor experience is the Outward Bound Leadership School, but many others exist. For a group that has never done team building before, outdoor experience can be an exciting way to begin; for groups familiar with team building, it can be a way of further enriching the experience.

IMPROVING TEAM PROCESSES

Like many changes in the new workplace, the increased emphasis on teams and teamwork is a major challenge for people used to more traditional ways of working. As more and more jobs are turned over to teams and as more and more traditional supervisors are asked to function as team leaders, special problems relating to team processes may arise. As teams become more integral to organizations, multiple and shifting memberships can cause complications. Team leaders and members alike must be prepared to deal positively with such issues as introducing new members, handling disagreements on goals and responsibilities, resolving delays and disputes when making decisions, and reducing friction and interpersonal conflicts. Given the complex nature of group dynamics, team building in a sense is never done. Something is always happening that creates the need for further leadership efforts to help improve team processes.

NEW MEMBER PROBLEMS

Special difficulties are likely to occur when members first get together in a new group or work team, or when new members join an existing one. Problems arise as new members try to understand what is expected of them while dealing with the anxiety and discomfort of a new social setting. New members, for example, may worry about: *Participation*—"Will I be allowed to participate?" *Goals*—"Do I share the same goals as others?" *Control*—"Will I be able to influence what takes place?" *Relationships*—"How close do people get?" *Processes*—"Are conflicts likely to be upsetting?"

Edgar Schein points out that people may try to cope with individual entry problems in self-serving ways that may hinder group operations.[17] He identifies three behavior profiles that are common in such situations. The *tough battler* is frustrated by a lack of identity in the new group and may act aggressively or reject authority. This person wants answers to the question: "Who am I in this group?" The *friendly helper* is insecure, suffering uncertainties of intimacy and control. This person may show extraordinary support for others, behave in a dependent way, and seek alliances in subgroups or cliques. The friendly helper needs to know whether she or he will be liked. The *objective thinker* is anxious about how personal needs will be met in the group. This person may act in a passive, reflective, and even single-minded manner while struggling with the fit between individual goals and group directions.

TASK AND MAINTENANCE LEADERSHIP

Research in social psychology suggests that the achievement of sustained high performance by groups requires that both "task needs" and "maintenance needs" be met.[18] Although anyone formally appointed as group leader should help fulfill these needs, all members should also contribute. This responsibility for **distributed leadership** in group dynamics is an important requirement of any high performance team.[19]

Figure 10.2 describes group **task activities** as the various things members do that directly contribute to the performance of important group tasks. They include initiating discussion, sharing information, asking information of others, clarifying something that has been said, and summarizing the status of a deliberation. If these task activities are not adequate, the group will have difficulty accomplishing its objectives. In an effective group, members contribute important task activities as needed and as building blocks for performance success.

Maintenance activities support the group's social and interpersonal relationships. They help the group stay intact and healthy as an ongoing social system. A member contributes

FIGURE 10.2	TASK AND MAINTENANCE LEADERSHIP IN GROUP TEAM DYNAMICS

Leading by Task Contributions
- Offering ideas
- Clarifying suggestions
- Giving information
- Seeking information
- Summarizing discussion

How to lead groups and teams

Leading by Maintenance Contributions
- Encouraging others
- Reconciling differences
- Expressing standards
- Offering agreement
- Inviting participation

maintenance leadership, for example, by encouraging the participation of others, trying to harmonize differences of opinion, praising the contributions of others, and agreeing to go along with a popular course of action. When maintenance leadership is poor, members become dissatisfied with one another and their group membership. This sets the stage for conflicts that can drain energies otherwise needed for task performance. In an effective group, maintenance activities help sustain the relationships needed for group members to work well together over time.

In addition to helping meet a group's task and maintenance needs, group members share the additional responsibility of avoiding *disruptive behaviors*—behaviors that harm the group process. Full participation in distributed leadership means taking individual responsibility for avoiding the following types of behaviors, and helping others do the same:

1. Being overly aggressive toward other members.
2. Withdrawing and refusing to cooperate with others.
3. Horsing around when there is work to be done.
4. Using the group as a forum for self-confession.
5. Talking too much about irrelevant matters.
6. Trying to compete for attention and recognition.

ROLES AND ROLE DYNAMICS

In groups and teams, new and old members alike need to know what others expect of them and what they can expect from others. A **role** is a set of expectations associated with a job or position on a team. When roles are unclear or conflictive, performance problems can occur. Groups and work teams sometimes experience problems that are caused by difficulties in defining and managing the roles of members.

Role ambiguity occurs when a person is uncertain about his or her role. To do any job well, people need to know what is expected of them. In new group or team situations, role ambiguities may create problems as members find that their work efforts are wasted or unappreciated by others. Even on mature groups and teams, the failure of members to share expectations and listen to one another may at times create a similar lack of understanding. Being asked to do too much or too little can also create problems. **Role overload** occurs when too much is expected and the individual feels overwhelmed with work. **Role underload** occurs when too little is expected and the individual feels underutilized. Any group benefits from clear and realistic expectations regarding the contributions of each member.

Role conflict occurs when a person is unable to meet the expectations of others. The individual understands what needs to be done but for some reason cannot comply. The resulting tension can reduce job satisfaction and affect both work performance and relationships with other group members. There are four common forms of role conflict. (1) *Intrasender role conflict* occurs when the same person sends conflicting expectations. (2) *Intersender role conflict* occurs when different people send conflicting and mutually exclusive expectations. (3) *Person role conflict* occurs when one's personal values and needs come into conflict with role expectations. (4) *Interrole conflict* occurs when the expectations of two or more roles held by the same individual become incompatible, such as the conflict between work and family demands.

One way of managing role dynamics in any group or work setting is by role negotiation. This is a process through which individuals negotiate to clarify the role expectations each holds for the other. Sample results from an actual role negotiation are shown in Figure 10.3. Note the "give and take" between negotiators.

POSITIVE NORMS

The **norms** of a group or team represent ideas or beliefs about how members are expected to behave. They can be considered as "rules" or "standards" of conduct.[20] Norms help clarify the expectations associated with a person's membership in a group. They allow members to structure their own behavior and to predict what others will do. They help members gain a common sense of direction, and they reinforce a desired group or team culture. When someone violates a group norm, other members typically respond in ways that are aimed at enforcing the norm. These responses may include direct criticisms, reprimands, expulsion, and social ostracism.

Managers, task force heads, committee chairs, and team leaders should help their groups adopt positive norms that support organizational goals (see The Effective Manager 10.2). A key norm in any setting is the *performance norm,* that conveys expectations about how hard group members should work. Other norms are important too. In order for a task force or a committee to operate effectively, for example, norms regarding attendance at meetings, punctuality, preparedness, criticism, and social behaviors are needed. Groups also commonly have norms regarding how to deal with supervisors, colleagues, and customers, as well as norms establishing guidelines for honesty and ethical behaviors. Norms are often evident in the everyday conversations of people at work. The following examples show the types of norms that operate with positive and negative implications for groups and organizations.[21]

- *Organizational and personal pride norms*—"It's a tradition around here for people to stand up for the company when others criticize it unfairly" (positive); "In our company, they are always trying to take advantage of us" (negative).

FIGURE 10.3 **A SAMPLE ROLE NEGOTIATIONS AGREEMENT**

ROLE NEGOTIATIONS

Issue Diagnosis Form
Messages from: Jim
            to: Diane

If you were to do the following, it would help me to increase my performance:
- Be more receptive to my suggestions for improvement
- Provide help when new software is installed
- Work harder to support my staffing request
- Stop asking for so many detailed progress reports
- Keep providing full information in our weekly meetings
- Keep being available when I need to talk with you

- *High-achievement norms*—"On our team, people always try to work hard" (positive); "There's no point in trying harder on our team, nobody else does" (negative).

- *Support and helpfulness norms*—"People on this committee are good listeners and actively seek out the ideas and opinions of others" (positive); "On this committee it's dog-eat-dog and save your own skin" (negative).

- *Improvement and change norms*—"In our department people are always looking for better ways of doing things" (positive); "Around here, people hang on to the old ways even after they have outlived their usefulness" (negative).

TEAM COHESIVENESS

The **cohesiveness** of a group or team is the degree to which members are attracted to and motivated to remain part of it.[22] Persons in a highly cohesive group value their membership and strive to maintain positive relationships with other group members. In this sense, cohesive groups and teams are good for their members. In contrast to less cohesive groups, members of highly cohesive ones tend to be more energetic when working on group activities, less likely to be absent, and more likely to be happy about performance success and sad about failures. Cohesive groups generally have low turnover and satisfy a broad range of individual needs, often providing a source of loyalty, security, and esteem for their members.

Cohesiveness tends to be high when group members are similar in age, attitudes, needs, and backgrounds. It also tends to be high in groups of small size, where members respect one another's competencies, agree on common goals, and work on interdependent tasks. Cohesiveness tends to increase when groups are physically isolated from others and when they experience performance success or crisis.

Conformity to Norms   Even though cohesive groups are good for their members, they may or may not be good for the organization. This will depend on the match of cohesiveness with performance norms. Figure 10.4 shows the performance implications of a basic *rule of conformity in group dynamics:* the more cohesive the group, the greater the conformity of members to group norms.

When the performance norms are positive in a highly cohesive workgroup or team, the resulting conformity to the norm should have a positive effect on task performance as well as member satisfaction. This is a "best-case" situation for everyone. When the performance norms are negative in a highly cohesive group, however, the same power of conformity creates

FIGURE 10.4	HOW COHESIVENESS AND CONFORMITY TO NORMS AFFECT GROUP PERFORMANCE

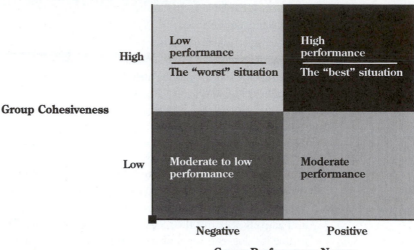

a "worst-case" situation for the organization. Although team members are highly motivated to support group norms, the organization suffers from poor performance results. In between these two extremes are mixed-case situations in which a lack of cohesion fails to rally strong conformity to the norm. With its strength reduced, the outcome of the norm is somewhat unpredictable and performance will most likely fall on the moderate or low side.

Influencing Cohesiveness   Team leaders and managers must be aware of the steps they can take to build cohesiveness, such as in a group that has positive norms but suffers from low cohesiveness. They must also be ready to deal with situations when cohesiveness adds to the problems of negative and hard-to-change performance norms. Figure 10.5 shows how group cohesiveness can be increased or decreased by making changes in group goals, membership composition, interactions, size, rewards, competition, location, and duration.

TEAMS AND THE HIGH PERFORMANCE WORKPLACE

When it was time to re-engineer its order-to-delivery process to eliminate an uncompetitive and costly 26-day cycle time, Hewlett-Packard turned to a team. In just nine months they slashed the time to eight days, improved service, and cut costs. How did they do it? Team leader Julie Anderson says: "We took things away: no supervisors, no hierarchy, no titles, no job descriptions ... the idea was to create a sense of personal ownership." Says a team member: "...no individual is going to have the best idea, that's not the way it works— the best ideas come from the collective intelligence of the team."[23]

Just like this example from Hewlett-Packard, organizations everywhere in the new workplace are finding creative ways of using teams to solve problems and make changes to

FIGURE 10.5	WAYS TO INCREASE AND DECREASE GROUP COHESIVENESS

	TARGETS	
How to Decrease Cohesion		**How to Increase Cohesion**
Create disagreement	Goals	Get agreement
Increase heterogeneity	Membership	Increase homogeneity
Restrict within team	Interactions	Enhance within team
Make team bigger	Size	Make team smaller
Focus within team	Competition	Focus on other teams
Reward individual results	Rewards	Reward team results
Open up to other teams	Location	Isolate from other teams
Disband the team	Duration	Keep team together

improve performance. The catchwords of these new approaches to teamwork are empowerment, participation, and involvement, and the setting is increasingly described as an organization that looks and acts much more "lateral" or "horizontal" than vertical.[24]

PROBLEM-SOLVING TEAMS

One way organizations can use teams is in creative problem solving. The term **employee involvement team** applies to a wide variety of teams whose members meet regularly to collectively examine important workplace issues. They discuss ways to enhance quality, better satisfy customers, raise productivity, and improve the quality of work life. In this way, employee involvement teams mobilize the full extent of workers' know-how and gain the commitment needed to fully implement solutions.

A special type of employee involvement group is the **quality circle,** or QC for short. It is a small group of persons who meet periodically (e.g., an hour or so, once a week) to discuss and develop solutions for problems relating to quality, productivity, or cost.[25] QCs are popular in organizations around the world, but cannot be seen as panaceas for all of an organization's ills. To be successful, members of QCs should receive special training in group dynamics, information gathering, and problem analysis techniques. Leaders of quality circles should also be trained in participation and team building. Any solutions to problems should be jointly pursued by QC members and organizational management. QCs work best in organizations that place a clear emphasis on quality in their mission and goals, promote a culture that supports participation and empowerment, encourage trust and willingness to share important information, and develop a "team spirit."

CROSS-FUNCTIONAL TEAMS

In today's organizations, teams are essential components in the achievement of more horizontal integration and better lateral relations. The **cross-functional team,** consisting of members representing different functional departments or work units, plays an important role in this regard. Traditionally, many organizations have suffered from what is often called the **functional silos problem.** This problem occurs when members of functional units stay focused on matters internal to the function and minimize their interactions with members of other functions. In this sense, the functional departments or work units create artificial boundaries or "silos" that discourage rather than encourage more integrative thinking and active coordination with other parts of the organization.

The new emphasis on team-based organizations, discussed in Chapter 11, is designed to help break down this problem and improve lateral communication.[26] Members of cross-functional teams can solve problems with a positive combination of functional expertise and integrative or total systems thinking. They do so with the great advantages of better information and more speed. Boeing, for example, used this concept to great advantage in designing and bringing to market the 777 passenger jet.[27] A complex network of cross-functional teams brought together design engineers, mechanics, pilots, suppliers, and even customers to manage the "design/build" processes.

VIRTUAL TEAMS

Until recently, teamwork was confined in concept and practice to those circumstances in which members could meet face-to-face. Now, the advent of new technologies and sophisticated computer programs known as groupware have changed all that. **Virtual teams,** introduced in the last chapter as ones whose members meet at least part of the time electronically and with computer support, are a fact of life.[28] The real world of work in businesses and other organizations today involves a variety of electronic communications that allow people to work together through computer mediation, and often separated by vast geographical space. *Groupware* in a variety of popular forms easily allows for virtual meetings and group decision making in a variety of situations.[29] This is further supported by advancements in conferencing and collaboration, including audio, data, and videoconferencing alternatives.[30]

Virtual teams offer a number of potential advantages. They bring cost-effectiveness and speed to teamwork where members are unable to meet easily face-to-face. They also bring the power of the computer to bear on typical team needs for information processing and decision making. When the computer is the "go-between" among virtual team members, however, group dynamics can be different from those of face-to-face settings.[31] Although technology makes communication possible among people separated by great distance, the team members may have very little, if any, direct "personal" contact. Virtual teams may suffer from less social rapport and less direct interaction among members. Whereas computer mediation may have an advantage of focusing interaction and decision making on facts and objective information rather than emotional considerations, it also may increase risks as group decisions are made in a limited social context.

Just as with any form of teamwork, virtual teams rely on the efforts and contributions of their members as well as organizational support to achieve effectiveness. Teamwork in any form always takes work. The same stages of development, the same input considerations, and same process requirements are likely to apply in a virtual team as with any team. Where possible, the advantages of face-to-face and virtual teamwork should be combined for maximum benefit. The computer technology should also be appropriate and team members should be well trained in using it.

SELF-MANAGING TEAMS

A high-involvement workgroup design that is increasingly well-established today is known as the **self-managing team.** These are small groups empowered to make the decisions needed to manage themselves on a day-to-day basis.[32] Although there are different variations of this theme, Figure 10.6 shows that members of a true self-managing work team make decisions on scheduling work, allocating tasks, training for job skills, evaluating performance, selecting new team members, and controlling quality of work. Members are collectively held accountable for the team's overall performance results.

How Self-Managing Teams Work   Self-managing teams, also called self-directed teams or empowered teams, are permanent and formal elements in the organizational structure. They replace the traditional workgroup headed by a supervisor. What differentiates self-managing teams from the more traditional workgroup is that the team members assume duties otherwise performed by a manager or first-line supervisor. The team members, not a supervisor, perform and are collectively accountable for such activities as planning and work scheduling, performance evaluation, and quality control.

A self-managing team should probably include between five and fifteen members. The teams must be large enough to provide a good mix of skills and resources, but small enough to function efficiently. Members must have substantial discretion in determining work pace and in distributing tasks. This is made possible, in part, by **multiskilling,** whereby team

---

FIGURE 10.6   **ORGANIZATIONAL AND MANAGEMENT IMPLICATIONS OF SELF-MANAGING TEAMS**

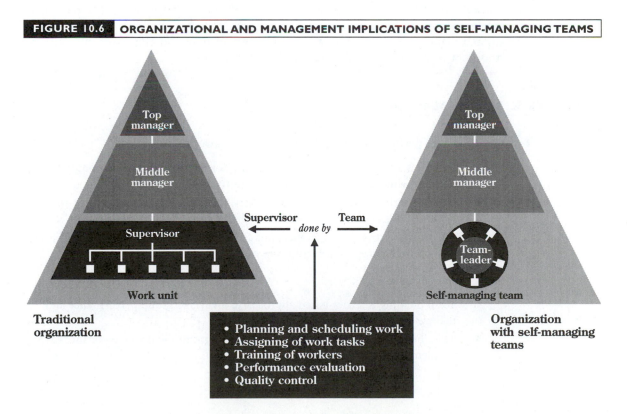

members are trained in performing more than one job on the team. In self-managing teams, each person is expected to perform many different jobs—even all of the team's jobs, as needed. The more skills someone masters, the higher the base pay. Team members themselves conduct the job training and certify one another as having mastered the required skills.

Operational Implications of Self-Managing Teams   The expected benefits of self-managing teams include productivity and quality improvements, production flexibility and faster response to technological change, reduced absenteeism and turnover, and improved work attitudes and quality of work life. But these results are not guaranteed. Like all organizational changes, the shift to self-managing teams can encounter difficulties. Structural changes in job classifications and management levels will have consequent implications for supervisors and others used to more traditional ways. Simply put, with a self-managing team you don't need the formal first-line supervisor anymore. The possible extent of this change is shown in Figure 10.6, where the first level of supervisory management in the traditional organization has been eliminated and replaced by self-managing teams. Note also that the supervisor's tasks are reallocated to the team.

For persons used to more traditional work, the new team-based work arrangements can be challenging. Managers must learn to deal with teams rather than individual workers; for any supervisors displaced by self-managing teams, the implications are even more personal and threatening. Given this situation, a question must be asked: *Should all organizations operate with self-managing teams?* The best answer is "No." Self-managing teams are probably not right for all organizations, work situations, and people. They have great potential, but they also require a proper setting and support. At a minimum, the essence of any self-managing team—high involvement, participation, and empowerment, must be consistent with the values and culture of the organization.

Chapter 10 Summary

What is a high performance team...and what is teamwork?

- A team is a small group of people working together to achieve a common purpose for which they hold themselves collectively accountable.
- High performance teams have core values, clear performance objectives, the right mix of skills, and creativity.
- Teamwork occurs when members of a team work together so that their skills are well utilized to accomplish common goals.

What is team building?

- Team building is a data-based approach to analyzing group performance and taking steps to improve it in the future.
- Team building is participative and engages all group members in collaborative problem solving and action.

What can be done to improve team processes?

- Individual entry problems are common when new teams are formed and when new members join existing teams.

- Task leadership involves initiating and summarizing, making direct contributions to the group's task agenda; maintenance leadership involves gatekeeping and encouraging, helping to support the social fabric of the group over time.

- Role difficulties occur when expectations for group members are unclear, overwhelming, underwhelming, or conflicting.

- Norms, as rules or standards for what is considered appropriate behavior by group members, can have a significant impact on group processes and outcomes.

- Members of highly cohesive groups value their membership and are very loyal to the group; they also tend to conform to group norms.

How do teams contribute to the high performance workplace?

- An employee involvement team is one whose members meet regularly to address important work-related problems and opportunities.

- Members of a quality circle, a popular type of employee involvement group, meet regularly to deal with issues of quality improvement in work processes.

- Self-managing teams are small workgroups that operate with empowerment and essentially manage themselves on a day-to-day basis.

- Members of self-managing teams typically plan, complete, and evaluate their own work, train and evaluate one another in job tasks, and share tasks and responsibilities.

- Self-managing teams have structural and management implications for organizations because they largely eliminate the first-line supervisors.

11

Basic Attributes of Organizations

Study Questions

The basic attributes of organizations create the setting for individual and group action in the workplace. This setting may both liberate and constrain individuals as they pursue their careers. As you read Chapter 11, keep in mind these study questions.

- What is strategy?
- What types of contributions do organizations make, and what types of goals do they adopt?
- What is the formal structure of the organization, and what is meant by the term *division of labor*?
- How is vertical specialization used to allocate formal authority within the organization?
- How does an organization control the actions of its members?
- What different patterns of horizontal specialization can be used in the organization?
- Which personal and impersonal coordination techniques should the organization use?
- What are bureaucracies and what are the common types?

In Chapter 1 we said that organizations are collections of people working together to achieve common goals. Now we want to be much more specific about the goals of organizations and how firms can use the basic attributes of organizations to reach toward accomplishment. In this chapter we provide you with a working knowledge of strategy and its link to goals, the types of goals organizations select, and the ways firms organize managers and departments to reach goals.[1] While the bulk of this chapter deals with the basic attributes of organizations, many once-successful firms have floundered simply because their managers ignored such basics.[2]

STRATEGY AND THE BASIC ATTRIBUTES OF ORGANIZATIONS

Strategy is the process of positioning the organization in the competitive environment and implementing actions to compete successfully. It is a pattern in a stream of decisions.[3] Choosing the types of contributions the firm intends to make to its larger society, precisely whom it will serve, and exactly what it will provide to others are a conventional way firms begin to make the pattern of decisions and corresponding implementations that define its strategy. The strategy process is ongoing. It should involve individuals at all levels of the firm to ensure that there is a recognizable, consistent pattern—yielding a superior capability over rivals—up and down the firm and across all of its activities. This recognizable pattern can be unique to a firm and involves many facets. In the following sections we will show how choices concerning the goals of the firm and the way it organizes to accomplish these goals are an important part of the overall positioning of the organization.

STRATEGY, CONTRIBUTIONS, AND GOALS

There are no more important choices than establishing goals for the firm. No firm can be all things to all people. By selecting goals, firms also define who they are and what they will try to become. From these elementary choices executives can work with subordinates to develop ways of accomplishing the chosen targets.

The notion that organizations have goals is very familiar to us simply because our world is one of organizations. Most of us are born, go to school, work, and retire in organizations. Without organizations and their limited, goal-directed behavior, modern societies would simply cease to function. We would need to revert to older forms of social organization based on royalty, clans, and tribes. Organizational goals are so pervasive we rarely give them more than passing notice. Jim Adamany of First Community Financial knows the goals of his firm. He knows the type of social contribution it makes, whom it serves, and the myriad ways of improving its performance. He is aware that his organization's goals are multifaceted and conflict with one another. He is also aware that corporate goals are common to individuals within the firm only to the extent that an individual's interests can be partially served by the organization. And he understands that the pattern of goals selected and emphasized can help to motivate members and gain support from outsiders.

SOCIETAL CONTRIBUTIONS OF ORGANIZATIONS

Organizations do not operate in a social vacuum but reflect the needs and desires of the societies in which they operate. **Societal goals** reflect an organization's intended contributions to the broader society.[4] Organizations normally serve a specific societal function or an enduring need of the society. Astute top-level managers build on the professed societal contribution of the organization by relating specific organizational tasks and activities to higher purposes. **Mission statements**—written statements of organizational purpose—may include these corporate ideas of service to the society. Weaving a mission statement together with an emphasis on implementation to provide direction and motivation is an executive order of the first magnitude. A good mission statement says whom the firm will serve and how it will go about accomplishing its societal purpose.[5] A mission statement is often the first visible outcome in developing a strategy. It may be several paragraphs long or as simple as that of Stericycle's.

A sense of mission in a political party may be linked to generating and allocating power for the betterment of citizens. Universities profess to both develop and disseminate knowledge. Churches intend to instill values and protect the spiritual well-being of all. Courts are expected to integrate the interests and activities of citizens. Finally, business firms are expected to provide economic sustenance and material well-being to society.

By claiming to provide specific types of societal contributions, an organization can make legitimate claims over resources, individuals, markets, and products. For instance, would you not want more money to work for a tobacco firm than a health food store? Tobacco firms are also very heavily taxed and under increasing pressure for regulation simply because their societal contribution is highly questionable.

Organizations that can more effectively translate the positive character of their societal contribution into a favorable image have an advantage over firms that neglect this sense of purpose. More astute executives who link their firm to a desirable mission can lay claim to important motivational tools that are based on a shared sense of noble purpose.

PRIMARY BENEFICIARIES

Organizations need to refine their societal contributions in order to target their efforts toward a particular group.[6] In the United States, for example, it is generally expected that the primary beneficiary of business firms is the stockholder. Interestingly, in Japan employees are much more important, and stockholders are considered as important as banks and other financial institutions.

Although each organization may have a primary beneficiary, its mission statement may also recognize the interests of many other parties. Thus, business mission statements often include service to customers, the organization's obligations to employees, and its intention to support the community.

STRATEGY AND OUTPUT GOALS

Firms need to consider how they will accomplish their missions. This refinement can begin with a very clear statement of which business they are in.[7] This statement can form the basis for long-term planning and may help prevent huge organizations from diverting too many resources to peripheral areas. For some corporations, answering the question of which business they are in may yield a more detailed statement concerning their products and services. These product and service goals provide an important basis for judging the firm. **Output goals** define the type of business an organization is in and provide some substance to the more general aspects of mission statements. For instance, First Community Federal's output goals would center around loans and factoring to small businesses.

SYSTEMS GOALS AND ORGANIZATIONAL SURVIVAL

Fewer than 10 percent of the businesses founded in a typical year can be expected to survive to their twentieth birthday.[8] The survival rate for public organizations is not much better. Even in organizations for which survival is not an immediate problem, managers seek specific types of conditions within their firms that minimize the risk of demise and promote survival. These conditions are positively stated as systems goals.

Systems goals are concerned with the conditions within the organization that are expected to increase the organization's survival potential. The list of systems goals is almost endless, since each manager and researcher links today's conditions to tomorrow's existence in a different way. For many organizations, however, the list includes growth, productivity, stability, harmony, flexibility, prestige, and human-resource maintenance. In some businesses, analysts consider market share and current profitability important systems goals. Other recent studies suggest that innovation and quality are also considered important.[9] In a very practical sense, systems goals represent short-term organizational characteristics that higher level managers wish to promote. Systems goals must often be balanced against one another. For instance, a productivity and efficiency drive, if taken too far, may reduce the flexibility of an organization.

Different parts of the organization are often asked to pursue different types of systems goals. For example, higher level managers may expect to see their production operations strive for efficiency while pressing for innovation from their R&D lab and promoting stability in their financial affairs. In the case of First Community Federal, Jim Adamany recognizes the tension between the marketing groups and their desire for loan and factoring volume and the other groups' concern with the quality of these loans and factoring agreements.

The relative importance of different systems goals can vary substantially across various types of organizations. Although we may expect the University of British Columbia or the University of New South Wales to emphasize prestige and innovation, few expect such businesses as Pepsi or AT&T to subordinate growth and profitability to prestige.

Systems goals are important to firms because they provide a road map that helps them link together various units of their organization to assure survival. Well-defined systems goals are practical and easy to understand; they focus the manager's attention on what needs to be done. Accurately stated systems goals also offer managers flexibility in devising ways to meet important targets. They can be used to balance the demands, constraints, and opportunities facing the firm. In addition, they can form a basis for dividing the work of the firm—a basis for developing a formal structure.

STRATEGY, FORMAL STRUCTURES, AND THE DIVISION OF LABOR

Since the work of Alfred Chandler in the 1960s, OB scholars have known that successful organizations develop a structure consistent with the pattern of goals established by senior management.[10] That is, decisions regarding what to accomplish must be matched with decisions on an appropriate way of organizing to reach these goals. The formal structure shows the planned configuration of positions, job duties, and the lines of authority among different parts of the enterprise. The configuration selected provides the organization with specific strengths to reach toward some goals more than others. Traditionally, the formal structure of the firm has also been called the *division of labor.* Some still use this terminology to isolate decisions concerning formal structure from choices regarding the division of markets and/or technology. We will deal with environmental and technology issues in the next chapter after discussing the structure as a foundation for managerial action. Here we emphasize that the formal structure outlines the jobs to be done, the person(s) (in terms of position) who are to perform specific activities, and the ways the total tasks of the organization are to be accomplished. In other words, the formal structure is the skeleton of the firm.

Organization charts are diagrams that depict the formal structures of organizations. A typical chart shows the various positions, the position holders, and the lines of authority that link them to one another. Figure 11.1 presents a partial organization chart for a large university. The total chart allows university employees to locate their positions in the structure and to identify the lines of authority linking them with others in the organization. For instance, in this figure, the treasurer reports to the vice president of administration, who, in turn, reports to the president of the university.

VERTICAL SPECIALIZATION

In larger organizations, there is a clear separation of authority and duties by hierarchical rank. This separation represents **vertical specialization,** a hierarchical division of labor that distributes formal authority and establishes where and how critical decisions are to be made. This division creates a hierarchy of authority—an arrangement of work positions in order of increasing authority.

| FIGURE 11.1 | A PARTIAL ORGANIZATION CHART FOR A STATE UNIVERSITY |

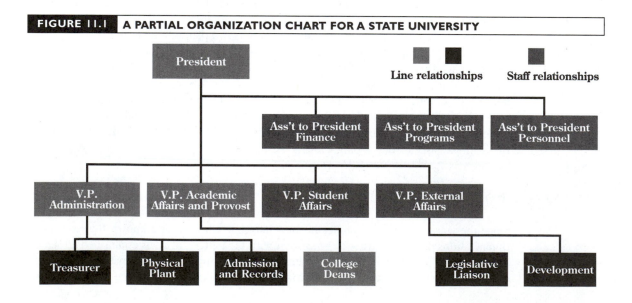

In the United States, the distribution of formal authority is evident in the responsibilities typical of managers. Top managers or senior executives plan the overall strategy of the organization and plot its long-term future.[11] They also act as final judges for internal disputes and certify promotions, reorganizations, and the like.

Middle managers guide the daily operations of the organization, help formulate policy, and translate top-management decisions into more specific guidelines for action. Lower level managers supervise the actions of subordinates to ensure implementation of the strategies authorized by top management and compliance with the related policies established by middle management. Managers in Japan often have different responsibilities than their counterparts in the typical U.S. firm. Japanese top managers do not develop and decide the overall strategy of the firm. Instead, they manage a process involving middle managers. The process involves extensive dialogue about actions the firm needs to take. Lower level managers are also expected to act as advocates for the ideas and suggestions of their subordinates. The strategy of the firm emerges from dialogue and discussion, and implementation proceeds according to the ideas and suggestions of lower managers and nonmanagers.

In many European firms, the senior managers are highly trained in the core of their business. For example, it is not unusual for the head of a manufacturing firm to have a Ph.D. in engineering. Thus, many European executives become more centrally involved in plotting the technical future of their firm. In contrast, few U.S. or Japanese executives have the necessary technical background to tackle this responsibility. Despite the differences in managerial responsibilities across Japan, Europe, and North America, all organizations have vertical specialization.

CHAIN OF COMMAND AND THE SPAN OF CONTROL

Executives, managers, and supervisors are hierarchically connected through the *chain of command*—a listing of who reports to whom up and down the firm. Individuals are expected to follow their supervisor's decisions in the areas of responsibility outlined in the organization chart. Traditional management theory suggests that each individual should have one boss and each unit one leader. Under the circumstances, there is a "unity of command." Unity of command is considered necessary to avoid confusion, to assign accountability to specific individuals, and to provide clear channels of communication up and down the organization. Under traditional management, with unity of command, the number of individuals a manager can supervise directly is obviously limited.

The number of individuals reporting to a supervisor is called the **span of control.** Narrower spans of control are expected when tasks are complex, when subordinates are inexperienced or poorly trained, or when tasks call for team effort. Unfortunately, narrow spans of control yield many organizational levels. The excessive number of levels is not only expensive, but it also makes the organization unresponsive to necessary change. Communications in such firms often become less effective because they are successively screened and modified so that subtle but important changes get ignored. Furthermore, with many levels, managers are removed from the action and become isolated.

New information technologies, discussed in the next chapter, now allow organizations to broaden the span of control, flatten their formal structures, and still maintain control of complex operations.[12] At Nucor, for instance, senior managers pioneered the development of "minimills" for making steel and developed what they call "lean" management. At the same time, management has expanded the span of control with extensive employee education and training backed by sophisticated information systems. The result: Nucor has four levels of management from the bottom to the top.

LINE AND STAFF UNITS

A very useful way to examine the vertical division of labor is to separate line and staff units. **Line units** and personnel conduct the major business of the organization. The production and marketing functions are two examples. In contrast, **staff units** and personnel assist the line units by providing specialized expertise and services, such as accounting and public relations. For example, the vice president of administration in a university (Figure 11.1) heads a staff unit, as does the vice president of student affairs. All academic departments are line units since they constitute the basic production function of the university.

Two useful distinctions are often made in firms. One distinction is the nature of the relationship of a unit in the chain of command. A staff department, such as the office of the V.P for External Affairs in Figure 11.1, may be divided into subordinate units, such as Legislative Liaison and Development (again see Figure 11.1). Although all units reporting to a higher level staff unit are considered staff from an organizational perspective, some subordinate staff units are charged with conducting the major business of the higher unit—they have a line relationship up the chain of command. In Figure 11.1 both Legislative Liaison and Development are staff units with a line relationship to the unit immediately above them in the chain of command—the V.P. for External Affairs. Why the apparent confusion? It is a matter of history with the notion of line and staff originally coming from the military with its emphasis on command. In a military sense the V.P. for External Affairs is the commander of this staff effort—the individual responsible for this activity and the one held accountable.

A second useful distinction to be made for both line and staff units concerns the amount and types of contacts each maintains with outsiders to the organization. Some units are mainly internal in orientation; others are more external in focus. In general, internal line units (e.g., production) focus on transforming raw materials and information into products and services, whereas external line units (e.g., marketing) focus on maintaining linkages to suppliers, distributors, and customers. Internal staff units (e.g., accounting) assist the line units in performing their function. Normally, they specialize in specific technical or financial areas. External staff units (e.g., public relations) also assist the line units, but the focus of their actions is on linking the firm to its environment and buffering internal operations. To recapitulate, the Legislative Liaison unit is external staff with a line relationship to the office of the V.P. for External Affairs.

CONFIGURING STAFF AND INFORMATION SYSTEMS FOR IMPLEMENTATION

Staff, particularly internal staff, contribute indirectly to corporate goals by using their specialized knowledge and talents. Traditionally, someone needed to keep the books, hire and train the personnel, and conduct the research and development. Figure 11.2 shows how the placement of staff alters the appearance of the firm. Staff units can be assigned predominantly to senior, middle, or lower level managers. When staff is assigned predominantly to

| FIGURE 11.2 | HOW THE PLACEMENT OF STAFF ALTERS THE LOOK OF AN ORGANIZATION |

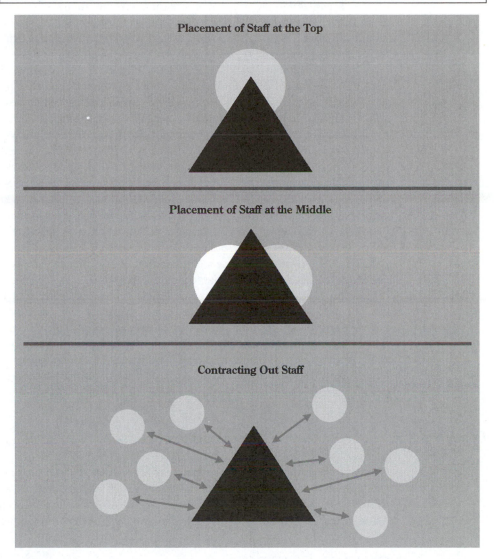

senior management, the capability of senior management to develop alternatives and make decisions is expanded. When staff is at the top, senior executives can directly develop information and alternatives and check on the implementation of their decisions. Here, the degree of vertical specialization in the firm is comparatively lower because senior managers plan, decide, and control via their centralized staff. With new information technologies, fewer and fewer firms are placing most staff at the top. They are replacing internal staff with information systems and placing talented individuals further down the hierarchy. For instance, executives at Owens-Illinois have shifted staff from top management to middle management. When staff are moved to the middle of the organization, middle managers now have the specialized help necessary to expand their role.

Many firms are also beginning to ask whether certain staff should be a permanent part of the organization at all. Some are outsourcing many of their staff functions. Manufacturing firms are spinning off much of their accounting, personnel, and public relations activities to small, specialized firms.[13] Outsourcing by large firms has been a boon for smaller corporations. Figure 11.2 illustrates the use of staff via "contracting out."

One of the foremost trends in management involves using information technology to streamline operations and reduce staff in order to lower costs and raise productivity.[14] One way to facilitate these actions is to provide line managers and employees with information and managerial techniques designed to expand on their analytical and decision-making capabilities—that is, to replace internal staff. For instance, those studying financial management recognize the importance of financial planning models (in detecting problems), financial decision aids, such as capital budgeting models and discounted cash-flow analyses (for selecting among alternatives), and budgets (to monitor progress and ensure that managers stay within financial limits). With computer programs, each of these is now accessible to all levels of management and is no longer restricted to financial staff.[15]

Although a great variety of managerial techniques have been available to managers for decades, only with the widespread use of computers have the costs of these techniques been reduced. Most organizations use a combination of line and staff units, alliances with specialized providers, plus managerial techniques to specialize the division of labor vertically (e.g., to distribute formal authority). The most appropriate pattern of vertical specialization depends on the environment of the organization, its size, its technology, and its goals. For instance, as organizations grow, vertical specialization typically increases just to keep up with the volume of work. We will return to this theme in the next chapter and pay special attention to information technology and its role in changing organizations. For now, let us turn our attention to those issues relating to control of the organization simply because the issue of control should not be separated from the division of labor.

CONTROL

Control is the set of mechanisms used to keep action or outputs within predetermined limits. Control deals with setting standards, measuring results versus standards, and instituting corrective action. Although all organizations need controls, just a few controls may go a long way. Astute managers need to be aware of the danger of too much control in the organization.

OUTPUT CONTROLS

Earlier in this chapter, we suggested that systems goals could be used as a road map to tie together the various units of the organization toward achieving a practical objective. Developing targets or standards, measuring results against these targets, and taking corrective action are all steps involved in developing output controls.[16] **Output controls** focus on desired targets and allow managers to use their own methods to reach defined targets. Most modern organizations use output controls as part of an overall method of managing by exception.

Output controls are popular because they promote flexibility and creativity as well as facilitate dialogue concerning corrective action. Reliance on outcome controls separates what is to be accomplished from how it is to be accomplished. Thus, the discussion of goals is separated from the dialogue concerning methods. This separation can facilitate the movement of power down the organization, as senior managers are reassured that individuals at all levels will be working toward the goals senior management believes are important, even as lower level managers innovate and introduce new ways to accomplish these goals.

PROCESS CONTROLS

Few organizations run on outcome controls alone. Once a solution to a problem is found and successfully implemented, managers do not want the problem to recur, so they institute process controls. **Process controls** attempt to specify the manner in which tasks are accomplished. There are many types of process controls, but three groups have received considerable attention: (1) policies, procedures, and rules; (2) formalization and standardization; and (3) total quality management controls.

Policies, Procedures, and Rules   Most organizations implement a variety of policies, procedures, and rules to help specify how goals are to be accomplished. Usually, we think of a *policy* as a guideline for action that outlines important objectives and broadly indicates how an activity is to be performed. A policy allows for individual discretion and minor adjustments without direct clearance by a higher level manager. *Procedures* indicate the best method for performing a task, show which aspects of a task are the most important, or outline how an individual is to be rewarded.

Many firms link *rules and procedures*. Rules are more specific, rigid, and impersonal than policies. They typically describe in detail how a task or a series of tasks is to be performed, or they indicate what cannot be done. They are designed to apply to all individuals, under specified conditions. For example, most car dealers have detailed instruction manuals for repairing a new car under warranty, and they must follow very strict procedures to obtain reimbursement from the manufacturer for warranty work.

Rules, procedures, and policies are often employed as substitutes for direct managerial supervision. Under the guidance of written rules and procedures, the organization can specifically direct the activities of many individuals. It can ensure virtually identical treatment across even distant work locations. For example, a McDonald's hamburger and fries taste much the same whether they are purchased in Hong Kong, Indianapolis, London, or Toronto simply because the ingredients and the cooking methods follow written rules and procedures.

Formalization and Standardization   **Formalization** refers to the written documentation of rules, procedures, and policies to guide behavior and decision making. Beyond substituting for direct management supervision, formalization is often used to simplify jobs. Written instructions allow individuals with less training to perform comparatively sophisticated tasks. Written procedures may also be available to ensure that a proper sequence of tasks is executed, even if this sequence is performed only occasionally.

Most organizations have developed additional methods for dealing with recurring problems or situations. **Standardization** is the degree to which the range of allowable actions in a job or series of jobs is limited. It involves the creation of guidelines so that similar work activities are repeatedly performed in a similar fashion. Such standardized methods may come from years of experience in dealing with typical situations, or they may come from outside training. For instance, if you are late in paying your credit card, the bank will automatically send you a notification and start an internal process of monitoring your account.

Total Quality Management The process controls discussed so far—policies, procedures, rules, formalization, and standardization—represent the lessons of experience within an organization. That is, managers institute these process controls based on past experience typically one at a time. Often there is no overall philosophy for using control to improve the overall operations of the company. Another way to institute process controls is to establish a total quality management process within the firm.

The late W. Edwards Deming is the modern-day founder of the total quality management movement.[17] When Deming's ideas were not generally accepted in the United States, he found an audience in Japan. Thus, to some managers, Deming's ideas appear in the form of the best Japanese business practices.

The heart of Deming's approach is to institute a process approach to continual improvement based on statistical analyses of the firm's operations. Around this core idea, Deming built a series of fourteen points for managers to implement. As you look at these points, note the emphasis on both managers and employees working together using statistical controls to continually improve. Deming's fourteen points are:

1. Create a consistency of purpose in the company to
   a. innovate.
   b. put resources into research and education.
   c. put resources into maintaining equipment and new production aids.
2. Learn a new philosophy of quality to improve every system.
3. Require statistical evidence of process control and eliminate financial controls on production.
4. Require statistical evidence of control in purchasing parts; this will mean dealing with fewer suppliers.
5. Use statistical methods to isolate the sources of trouble.
6. Institute modern on-the-job training.
7. Improve supervision to develop inspired leaders.
8. Drive out fear and instill learning.
9. Break down barriers between departments.
10. Eliminate numerical goals and slogans.
11. Constantly revamp work methods.
12. Institute massive training programs for employees in statistical methods.
13. Retrain people in new skills.
14. Create a structure that will push, every day, on the above thirteen points.

All levels of management are to be involved in the quality program. Managers are to improve supervision, train employees, retrain employees in new skills, and create a structure that pushes the quality program. Where the properties of the firm's outcomes are well defined, as in most manufacturing operations, Deming's system and emphasis on quality appears to work well when it is implemented in conjunction with empowerment and participative management.

ALLOCATING FORMAL AUTHORITY: CENTRALIZATION AND DECENTRALIZATION

Different firms use very different mixes of vertical specialization, output controls, process controls, and managerial techniques to allocate the authority or discretion to act.[18] The farther up the hierarchy of authority the discretion to spend money, to hire people, and to make similar decisions is moved, the greater the degree of **centralization.** The more such decisions are delegated, or moved down the hierarchy of authority, the greater the degree of **decentralization.** Greater centralization is often adopted when the firm faces a single major threat to its survival. Thus, it is little wonder that armies tend to be centralized and that firms facing bankruptcy increase centralization.

Generally speaking, greater decentralization provides higher subordinate satisfaction and a quicker response to a diverse series of unrelated problems. Decentralization also assists in the on-the-job training of subordinates for higher level positions. Decentralization is now a popular approach in many industries. For instance, Union Carbide is pushing responsibility down the chain of command, as are General Motors, Fifth-Third Bank, and Hewlett-Packard. In each case, the senior managers hope to improve both performance quality and organizational responsiveness. Closely related to decentralization is the notion of participation. Many people want to be involved in making decisions that affect their work. Participation results when a manager delegates some authority for such decision making to subordinates in order to include them in the choice process. Employees may want a say both in what the unit objectives should be and in how they may be achieved.[19]

Firms such as Intel Corporation, Eli Lilly, Dow Chemical, Ford Motor Company, and Hoffman-LaRoche have also experimented by moving decisions down the chain of command and increasing participation. These firms found that just cutting the number of organizational levels was insufficient. They also needed to alter their controls toward quality, to stress constant improvement, and to change other basic features of the organization. As these firms have increased participation they have emphasized the importance of ethical decision making.

HORIZONTAL SPECIALIZATION

Vertical specialization and control are only half the picture. Managers must also divide the total task into separate duties and group similar people and resources together.[20] **Horizontal specialization** is a division of labor that establishes specific work units or groups within an organization; it is often referred to as the process of departmentation. There are a variety of pure forms of departmentation.

DEPARTMENTATION BY FUNCTION

Grouping individuals by skill, knowledge, and action yields a pattern of **functional departmentation.** Recall Figure 11.1 shows the partial organization chart for a large university in which each department has a technical specialty. Marketing, finance, production, and personnel are important functions in business. In many small firms, this functional pattern dominates. Even large firms use this pattern in technically demanding areas. Figure 11.3

summarizes the advantages of the functional pattern. With all these advantages, it is not surprising that the functional form is extremely popular. It is used in most organizations, particularly toward the bottom of the hierarchy. Functional specialization also has some disadvantages, which are summarized in Figure 11.3. Organizations that rely heavily on functional specialization may expect the following tendencies to emerge over time: an emphasis on quality from a technical standpoint, rigidity to change, and difficulty in coordinating the actions of different functional areas.

DEPARTMENTATION BY DIVISION

Divisional departmentation groups individuals and resources by products, territories, services, clients, or legal entities.[21] Figure 11.4 shows a divisional pattern of organization grouped around products, regions, and customers for three divisions of a conglomerate. This pattern is often used to meet diverse external threats and opportunities. As shown in Figure 11.4, the major advantages of the divisional pattern are its flexibility in meeting external demands, spotting external changes, integrating of specialized individuals deep within the organization, and focusing on the delivery of specific products to specific customers. Among its disadvantages are duplication of effort by function, the tendency for divisional goals to be placed above corporate interests, and conflict among divisions. It is also not the structure most desired for training individuals in technical areas, and firms relying on this pattern may fall behind competitors with a functional pattern.

Many larger, geographically dispersed organizations that sell to national and international markets may rely on departmentation by geography. The savings in time, effort, and travel can be substantial, and each territory can adjust to regional differences. Organizations that rely on a few major customers may organize their people and resources by client. Here, the idea is to focus attention on the needs of the individual customer.[22] To the extent that customer needs are unique, departmentation by customer can also reduce confusion and increase synergy. Organizations expanding internationally may also form divisions to meet the demands of complex host country ownership requirements. For example, NEC, Sony, Nissan, and many other Japanese corporations have developed U.S. divisional subsidiaries to service their customers in the U.S. market. Some huge Europe-based corporations such as

---

FIGURE 11.3 | **MAJOR ADVANTAGES AND DISADVANTAGES OF FUNCTIONAL SPECIALIZATION**

Major Advantages and Disadvantages of Functional Specialization

Advantages	Disadvantages
1. Yields very clear task assignments, consistent with an individual's training.	1. May reinforce the narrow training of individuals.
2. Individuals within a department can easily build on one another's knowledge, training, and experience.	2. May yield narrow, boring, and routine jobs.
3. Provides an excellent training ground for new managers.	3. Communication across technical areas is complex and difficult.
4. It is easy to explain.	4. "Top management overload" with too much attention to cross-functional problems.
5. Takes advantage of employee technical quality.	5. Individuals may look up the organizational hierarchy for direction and reinforcement rather than focus attention on products, services, or clients.

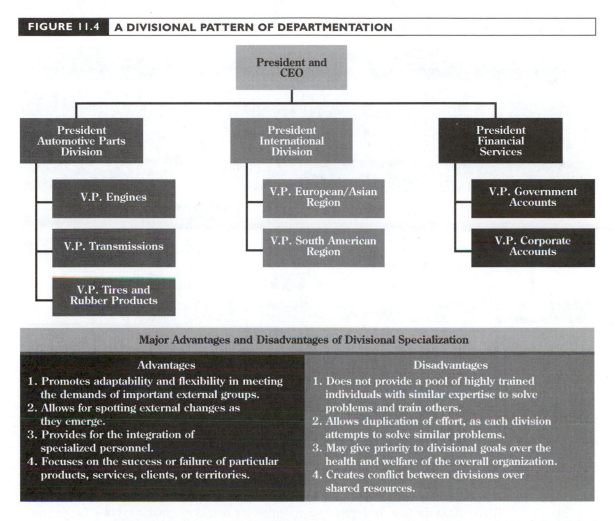

FIGURE 11.4   A DIVISIONAL PATTERN OF DEPARTMENTATION

Major Advantages and Disadvantages of Divisional Specialization

Advantages	Disadvantages
1. Promotes adaptability and flexibility in meeting the demands of important external groups.	1. Does not provide a pool of highly trained individuals with similar expertise to solve problems and train others.
2. Allows for spotting external changes as they emerge.	2. Allows duplication of effort, as each division attempts to solve similar problems.
3. Provides for the integration of specialized personnel.	3. May give priority to divisional goals over the health and welfare of the overall organization.
4. Focuses on the success or failure of particular products, services, clients, or territories.	4. Creates conflict between divisions over shared resources.

Philips and Nestlé have also adopted a divisional structure in their expansion to the United States. Similarly, most of the internationalized U.S.-based firms, such as IBM, GE, and DuPont, have incorporated the divisional structure as part of their internalization programs.

DEPARTMENTATION BY MATRIX

Originally from the aerospace industry, a third unique form of departmentation was developed and is now becoming more popular; it is now called **matrix departmentation**.[23] In aerospace efforts, projects are technically very complex, involving hundreds of subcontractors located throughout the world. Precise integration and control are needed across many sophisticated functional specialties and corporations. This is often more than a functional or divisional structure can provide, for many firms do not want to trade the responsiveness of the divisional form for the technical emphasis provided by the functional form. Thus, matrix departmentation uses both the functional and divisional forms simultaneously. Figure 11.5 shows the basic matrix arrangement for an

FIGURE 11.5	A MATRIX PATTERN OF DEPARTMENTATION IN AN AEROSPACE DIVISION

Major Advantages and Disadvantages of a Matrix	
Advantages	**Disadvantages**
1. Combines strengths of both functional and divisional departmentation. 2. Blends technical and market emphasis. 3. Provides a series of managers able to converse with both technical and marketing personnel.	1. Very expensive. 2. Unity of command is lost (individuals have more than one supervisor). 3. Authority and responsibilities of managers may overlap, causing conflicts and gaps in effort across units and inconsistencies in priorities. 4. It is difficult to explain to employees.

aerospace program. Note the functional departments on one side and the project efforts on the other. Workers and supervisors in the middle of the matrix have two bosses—one functional and one project.

The major advantages and disadvantages of the matrix form of departmentation are also summarized in Figure 11.5. The key disadvantage of the matrix method is the loss of unity of command. Individuals can be unsure as to what their jobs are, whom they report to for specific activities, and how various managers are to administer the effort. It can also be a very expensive method because it relies on individual managers to coordinate efforts deep within the firm. In Figure 11.5, note that the number of managers in a matrix structure almost doubles compared to either a functional or a divisional structure. Despite these limitations, the matrix structure provides a balance between functional and divisional concerns. Many problems can be resolved at the working level, where the balance among technical, cost, customer, and organizational concerns can be dealt with.

The matrix structure is ideally suited for Pacific Northwest Labs (PNL). PNL is one of the Department of Energy's laboratories for researching new and improved ways to develop energy and clean up the mess from decades of producing nuclear material for bombs. Technical specialists are housed in functional departments while project managers draw talent from these groups to work on a myriad of new energy and cleanup projects. Some projects may last a few weeks and involve only a handful of technicians while other larger projects may last several years. As the large projects evolve, the project manager can shift the composition of the team to reflect the type of specialized human resources needed at any given stage in a project.

Many organizations also use elements of the matrix structure without officially using the term *matrix*. For example, special project teams, coordinating committees, and task forces can be the beginnings of a matrix. Yet, these temporary structures can be used within a predominantly functional or divisional form and without upsetting the unity of command or hiring additional managers.

MIXED FORMS OF DEPARTMENTATION

Which form of departmentation should be used? As the matrix concept suggests, it is possible to departmentalize by two different methods at the same time. Actually, organizations often use a mixture of departmentation forms. It is often desirable to divide the effort (group people and resources) by two methods at the same time in order to balance the advantages and disadvantages of each. In the next chapter we will discuss several mixed forms. These mixed forms help firms use their division of labor to capitalize on environmental opportunities, capture the benefits of larger size, and realize the potential of new technologies in pursuit of its strategy.

COORDINATION

Whatever is divided up horizontally must also be integrated.[24] **Coordination** is the set of mechanisms that an organization uses to link the actions of their units into a consistent pattern. Much of the coordination within a unit is handled by its manager. Smaller organizations may rely on their management hierarchy to provide the necessary consistency and integration. As the organization grows, however, managers become overloaded. The organization then needs to develop more efficient and effective ways of linking work units to one another.

PERSONAL METHODS OF COORDINATION

Personal methods of coordination produce synergy by promoting dialogue, discussion, innovation, creativity, and learning, both within and across organizational units. Personal methods allow the organization to address the particular needs of distinct units and individuals simultaneously. There are a wide variety of personal methods of coordination.[25] Perhaps the most popular is direct contact between and among organizational members. As new information technologies have moved into practice, the potential for developing and maintaining effective contact networks has expanded. For example, many executives use e-mail, Lotus Notes, and other computer-based links to supplement direct personal communication. Direct personal contact is also associated with the ever-present "grapevine." Although the grapevine is notoriously inaccurate in its role as the corporate rumor mill, it is often both accurate enough and quick enough that managers cannot ignore it. Instead, managers need to work with and supplement the rumor mill with accurate information.

Managers are also often assigned to numerous committees to improve coordination across departments. Even though committees are generally expensive and have a very poor reputation, they can become an effective personal mechanism for mutual adjustment across unit heads. Committees can be effective in communicating complex qualitative information and in helping managers whose units must work together to adjust schedules, workloads, and work assignments to increase productivity. As more organizations develop flatter structures with greater delegation, they are finding that task forces can be quite useful. Whereas committees tend to be long lasting, task forces are typically formed with a more limited agenda. Individuals from different parts of the organization are assembled into a task force to identify and solve problems that cut across different departments.

No magic is involved in selecting the appropriate mix of personal coordination methods and tailoring them to the individual skills, abilities, and experience of subordinates. Managers need to know the individuals involved, their preferences, and the accepted approaches in different organizational units. Different personal methods can be tailored to match different individuals (see The Effective Manager 11.1). Personal methods are only one important part of coordination. The manager may also establish a series of impersonal mechanisms.

IMPERSONAL METHODS OF COORDINATION

Impersonal methods of coordination produce synergy by stressing consistency and standardization so that individual pieces fit together. Impersonal coordination methods are often refinements and extensions of process controls with an emphasis on formalization and standardization. Most larger organizations have written policies and procedures, such as schedules, budgets, and plans that are designed to mesh the operations of several units into a whole by providing predictability and consistency.

The most highly developed form of impersonal coordination comes with the adoption of a matrix form of departmentation. As noted earlier, this form of departmentation is expressly designed to coordinate the efforts of diverse functional units. Although a few organizations rely exclusively on a matrix structure, many firms are using cross-functional task forces. These task forces are replacing specialized staff units that once dealt mainly with ensuring coordination.

The final example of impersonal coordination mechanisms is undergoing radical change in many modern organizations. Originally, management information systems were developed and designed so that senior managers could coordinate and control the operations of diverse subordinate units. These systems were intended to be computerized substitutes for schedules, budgets, and the like. In some firms, the management information system still operates as a combined process control and impersonal coordination mechanism. In the hands of astute managers, the management information system becomes an electronic network, linking individuals throughout the organization. Using decentralized communication systems, supplemented with the phone, fax machine, and e-mail, a once centrally controlled system becomes a supplement to personal coordination.

The fundamental change ongoing in most larger organizations is the realization of the potential offered by information technologies. This fundamental change is so important and so pervasive that it is altering the way firms put together their specialization of labor,

---

THE EFFECTIVE MANAGER 11.1
ADJUSTING COORDINATION EFFORTS

The astute manager should recognize some individuals and/or units:

1. Have their own views of how best to move toward organizational goals.
2. Emphasize immediate problems and quick solutions; others stress underlying problems and longer-term solutions.
3. Have their own unique vocabulary and standard way of communicating.
4. Have pronounced preferences for formality or informality.

control, and coordination. This will be shown in the next chapter. For now it is important to understand basic combinations of specialization control and coordination.

BUREAUCRACY

In the developed world, most firms are bureaucracies. In OB this term has a very special meaning, beyond its negative connotation (see The Effective Manager 11.2). The famous German sociologist Max Weber suggested that organizations would thrive if they became **bureaucracies** by emphasizing legal authority, logic, and order.[26] Bureaucracies rely on a division of labor, hierarchical control, promotion by merit with career opportunities for employees, and administration by rule. He argued that the rational and logical idea of bureaucracy was superior to building the firm on the basis of charisma or cultural tradition. The "charismatic" ideal-type organization was overreliant on the talents of one individual and would likely fail when the leader left. Too much reliance on cultural traditions blocked innovation, stifled efficiency, and was often unfair. Since the bureaucracy prizes efficiency, order, and logic, Weber hoped that it could also be fair to employees and provide more freedom for individual expression than is allowed when tradition dominates. Although far from perfect, Weber predicted that the bureaucracy, or some variation of this ideal form, would dominate modern society. And it has. While charismatic leadership and cultural traditions are still important today, it is the rational, legal, and efficiency aspects of the firm that characterize modern corporations.

TYPES OF BUREAUCRACIES

The notion of a bureaucracy has evolved over time. Figure 11.6 illustrates three popular basic types of bureaucracies: the mechanistic, the organic, and the divisionalized approaches. And it shows how some huge corporations are collections of very different firms called conglomerates. Each is a different mix of the basic elements discussed in this chapter, and each mix yields firms with a slightly different blend of capabilities and natural tendencies.

The Mechanistic Type The **mechanistic type** emphasizes vertical specialization and control.[27] Organizations of this type stress rules, policies, and procedures; specify techniques for decision making; and emphasize developing well-documented control systems backed by a strong middle management and supported by a centralized staff. There is often extensive use of the functional pattern of departmentation throughout the firm. Henry Mintzberg uses the term *machine bureaucracy* to describe an organization that is entirely structured in this manner.[28]

The mechanistic design results in a management emphasis on routine for efficiency. Until the implementation of new information systems, most large-scale firms in basic industries were machine bureaucracies. Included in this long list were all the auto firms, banks, insurance companies, steel mills, large retail establishments, and government offices. Efficiency was achieved through extensive vertical and horizontal specialization tied together with elaborate controls and informal coordination mechanisms.

There are, however, limits to the benefits of specialization backed by rigid controls. Employees do not like rigid designs, and so motivation becomes a problem. Unions further solidify narrow job descriptions by demanding fixed work rules and regulations to protect

FIGURE 11.6   DIFFERENT BASIC OVERALL BUREAUCRATIC PATTERNS

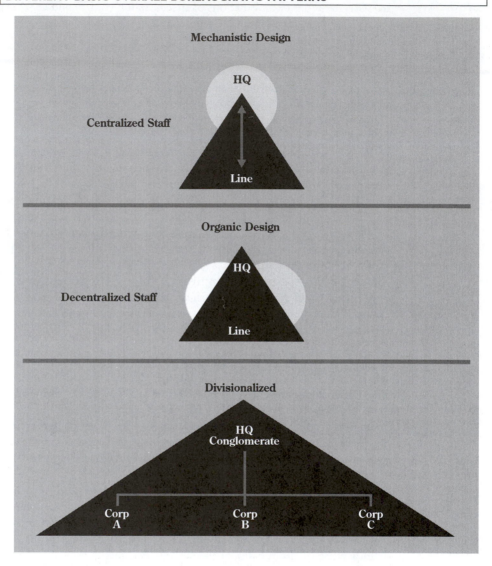

employees from the extensive vertical controls. Key employees may leave. In short, using a machine bureaucracy can hinder an organization's capacity to adjust to subtle external changes or new technologies. You are already familiar with this tendency toward stagnation—your high school was probably a machine bureaucracy with the assistant principal as the chief enforcement officer.

The Organic Type   The **organic type** is much less vertically oriented than its mechanistic counterpart; it emphasizes horizontal specialization. Procedures are minimal, and those that do exist are not as formalized. The organization relies on the judgments of experts and personal means of coordination. When controls are used, they tend to back up professional socialization, training, and individual reinforcement. Staff units tend to be placed toward the middle of the organization. Because this is a popular design in professional firms, Mintzberg calls it a professional bureaucracy.[29]

Your university is probably a professional bureaucracy that looks like a broad, flat pyramid with a large bulge in the center for the professional staff. Power in this ideal type rests with knowledge. Furthermore, the elaborate staff historically helped the line managers and often had very little formal power, other than to block action. Control is enhanced by the standardization of professional skills and the adoption of professional routines, standards, and procedures. Other examples of organic types include most hospitals, libraries, and social service agencies.

Although not as efficient as the machine bureaucracy, the professional bureaucracy is better for problem solving and for serving individual customer needs. Since lateral relations and coordination are emphasized, centralized direction by senior management is less intense. Thus, this type is good at detecting external changes and adjusting to new technologies, but at the sacrifice of responding to central management direction.[30]

Hybrid Types   Many very large firms found that neither the mechanistic nor the organic approach was suitable for all their operations. Adopting a machine bureaucracy would overload senior management and yield too many levels of management. Yet, adopting an organic type would mean losing control and becoming too inefficient. Senior managers may opt for one of a number of hybrid types.

Two hybrid types we have already introduced. One is an extension of the divisional pattern of departmentation, so that different divisions can be more or less organic or mechanistic. Here the divisions may be treated as separate businesses, even though they share a similar mission and output and systems goals.[31]

A second hybrid is the true conglomerate. A **conglomerate** is a single corporation that contains a number of unrelated businesses. On the surface, these firms look like divisionalized firms, but when the various businesses of the divisions are unrelated, the term conglomerate is applied.[32] For instance, General Electric is a conglomerate that has divisions in quite unrelated businesses and industries, ranging from producing light bulbs, to designing and servicing nuclear reactors, to building jet engines, to operating the National Broadcasting Company. RJR-Nabisco was created through a series of financial maneuvers that brought together a food company and a tobacco firm. Many state and federal entities are also, by necessity, conglomerates. For instance, a state governor is the chief executive officer of those units concerned with higher education, welfare, prisons, highway construction and maintenance, police, and the like.

The conglomerate type also simultaneously illustrates two important points that will be the highlight of the next chapter. (1) All structures are combinations of the basic elements. (2) There is no one best structure—it all depends on a number of factors such as the size of the firm, its environment, its technology, and, of course, its strategy.

CHAPTER 11 SUMMARY

What is strategy?

- Strategy is a process.
- Strategy is positioning the organization in the competitive environment.

- Strategy is implementing actions.
- Strategy is a pattern in a stream of actions.

What types of contributions do organizations make, and what types of goals do they adopt?

- Organizations make specific contributions to society.
- Firms often concentrate on primary beneficiaries and specify output goals (specific products and services).
- A societal contribution focused on a primary beneficiary may be represented in the firm's mission statement.
- Corporations have systems goals to show the conditions managers believe will yield survival and success.

What is the formal structure of the organization, and what is meant by the term *division of labor*?

- The formal structure defines the intended configuration of positions, job duties, and lines of authority among different parts of the enterprise.
- The formal structure is also known as the firm's division of labor.

How is vertical specialization used to allocate formal authority within the organization?

- Vertical specialization is the hierarchical division of labor that specifies where formal authority is located.
- Typically, a chain of command exists to link lower level workers with senior managers.
- The distinction between line and staff units also indicates how authority is distributed, with line units conducting the major business of the firm and staff providing support.
- Managerial techniques, such as decision support and expert computer systems, are used to expand the analytical reach and decision-making capacity of managers to minimize staff.

How does an organization control the actions of its members?

- Control is the set of mechanisms the organization uses to keep action or outputs within predetermined levels.
- Output controls focus on desired targets and allow managers to use their own methods for reaching these targets.
- Process controls specify the manner in which tasks are to be accomplished through (1) policies, rules, and procedures; (2) formalization and standardization; and (3) total quality management processes.
- Firms are learning that decentralization often provides substantial benefits.

What different patterns of horizontal specialization can be used in the organization?

- Horizontal specialization is the division of labor that results in various work units and departments in the organization.
- Three main types or patterns of departmentation are observed: functional, divisional, and matrix. Each pattern has a mix of advantages and disadvantages.
- Organizations may successfully use any type, or a mixture, as long as the strengths of the structure match the needs of the organization.

Which personal and impersonal coordination techniques should the organization use?

- Coordination is the set of mechanisms an organization uses to link the actions of separate units into a consistent pattern.
- Personal methods of coordination produce synergy by promoting dialogue, discussion, innovation, creativity, and learning.
- Impersonal methods of control produce synergy by stressing consistency and standardization so that individual pieces fit together.

What are bureaucracies and what are the common types?

- The bureaucracy is an ideal form based on legal authority, logic, and order that provides superior efficiency and effectiveness.
- Mechanistic, organic, and hybrids are common types of bureaucracies.
- Hybrid types include the divisionalized firm and the conglomerate. No one type is always superior to the others.

CHAPTER 12

Strategic Competency and Organizational Design

Study Questions

As you read Chapter 12, keep in mind these study questions.

- What is the co-evolution view of strategy and what is its linkage to organizational design?
- What is organizational design, and how do the designs of small and large firms differ?
- How does the operations and information technology of the firm influence its organizational design?
- What is the relationship between environmental conditions and organizational design?
- What is organizational learning?
- How are organizational learning cycles helpful in understanding organizational behavior?

Compare the description of IBM's research labs to a manufacturing operation such as a Ford assembly plant. We all recognize that a Ford assembly plant and an IBM research lab are quite different, but they also have something in common. Auto assembly plants are organized to emphasize routine, efficient production, while the IBM research lab is loose, experimental, and devoted to innovation. Yet, both must also use the most recent and competitive information technologies. For the auto plant it is an information system that supports just-in-time delivery of components.[1] For IBM it is a comprehensive information system to promote learning. In this chapter we will discuss how managers mutually adjust strategy, the internal capabilities of their firms for strategic implementation, and the organizational design of the firm to reach toward their goals. We will also show how drastically the competitive environment has changed and how new organizational design options are allowing firms to refine their strategies and continually improve their operations.

STRATEGY AND ORGANIZATIONAL DESIGN

TWO ASPECTS OF STRATEGY

It is important to reiterate and extend the dualistic notion of strategy noted in the previous chapter.[2] Strategy is a positioning of the firm in its environment to provide it with the capability to succeed, and strategy is also a pattern in the stream of decisions. In Chapter 11 we emphasized goals and the basic aspects of structure as important elements in this positioning and in the pattern. Now it is time to emphasize that what the firm intends to do must be backed up by capabilities for implementation in a setting that facilitates success. Once, executives were told that firms had available a limited number of economically determined generic strategies which were built upon the foundations of such factors as efficiency and innovation. If the firm wanted efficiency it should adopt the machine bureaucracy (many levels of management backed with extensive controls replete with written procedures). If it wanted innovation, it should adopt a more organic form (fewer levels of management with an emphasis on coordination). Today the world of corporations is much more complex and executives have found much more sophisticated ways of competing.

Today many senior executives are emphasizing the skills and abilities that their firms need not only to compete but also to remain agile and dynamic in a rapidly changing world. The structural configuration or organizational design of the firm should not only facilitate the types of accomplishment desired by senior management, but also allow for individuals to experiment, grow, and develop competencies so that the strategy of the firm can evolve. Over time, the firm may develop specific administrative and technical skills as middle and lower-level managers institute minor adjustments to solve specific problems. As they learn, so can their firms if the individual learning of employees can be transferred across and up the organization's hierarchy. As the skills of employees and managers develop, they may be recognized by senior management and become a foundation for revisions in the overall strategy of the firm.

Just as employees and managers are changing, the world in which we operate also changes. There are new technologies; there are new administrative systems available from the information revolution. Competitors are also innovating and presenting new challenges. And, of course, customers want new products and services and lower prices. Thus, the position of the firm in its environment must change. It must develop new capabilities to respond to these changes even as it seeks to alter some of these developments.

STRATEGY AND CO-EVOLUTION

With astute senior management the firm can co-evolve. That is, the firm can adjust to external changes even as it shapes some of the challenges facing it. Co-evolution is a process. One aspect of this process is repositioning the firm in its setting as the setting itself changes, the firm's scale of operations expands, and its technology shifts. Senior management can guide the process of positioning and repositioning in the environment. However, senior management can help shape some of these influences as well, particularly the capabilities of organizational members and the ability of the firm's administrative and technical systems. Shaping these influences is the other aspect of co-evolution.

Successful firms must adjust to the ever-changing competitive world as they develop internal capabilities to match their intentions and shape their competitive landscape. All the while, successful firms also need to build upon and refine their unique experience and specific competencies. These competencies include the technology used to produce goods and services, the individuals in the firm, and the administrative support systems, particularly the firm's information technology.

IBM, once known as *big blue,* was a button-down, white-shirt, blue-tie-and-black-shoe, second-to-market imitator with the bulk of its business centered on mainframe computers. As the introduction suggests, IBM is now on the move in an entirely different way. Via innovation it is now a major hub in e-commerce and is on the cutting edge as an integrator across systems, equipment, and service. To remain successful IBM will continue to rely upon the willingness of employees to take chances, refine their skills, and work together creatively.

ORGANIZATIONAL DESIGN AS PART OF A RECOGNIZABLE PATTERN IN DECISIONS AND IMPLEMENTATION

Obviously, this co-evolution stuff is complex and challenging. Fortunately, firms have developed successful patterns for co-evolution. That is, there are successful consistent and recognizable decisions and implementations that bring clarity out of the complexity. One aspect of this consistency for effective co-evolution is organizational design.

Organizational design is the process of choosing and implementing a structural configuration.[3] The choice of an appropriate organizational design is contingent upon several factors, including the size of the firm, its operations and information technology, its environment, and the strategy it selects for growth and survival. For example, IBM's senior management has selected a form of organization for each component of IBM that matches that component's contribution to the whole. The overall organizational design matches the technical challenges facing IBM, allows it to adjust to new development, and helps it shape its competitive landscape. Above all, the design promotes the development of individual skills and abilities. To understand how firms develop a successful pattern, in this chapter we show how firms can use their organizational design to both respond to their scope of operations, technology, and environment, and shape their competitive landscape.

ORGANIZATIONAL DESIGN AND SIZE

For many reasons, large organizations cannot be just bigger versions of their smaller counterparts. As the number of individuals in a firm increases arithmetically, the number of possible interconnections among them increases geometrically. In other words, the direct interpersonal contact among all members in a large organization must be managed. The design of small firms is directly influenced by its core operations technology, whereas larger firms have many core operations technologies in a wide variety of much more specialized units. In short, larger organizations are often more complex than smaller firms. While all larger firms are bureaucracies, smaller firms need not be. In larger firms, additional complexity calls for a more sophisticated organizational design.

THE SIMPLE DESIGN FOR SMALLER UNITS AND FIRMS

The **simple design** is a configuration involving one or two ways of specializing individuals and units. That is, vertical specialization and control typically emphasize levels of supervision without elaborate formal mechanisms (e.g., rule books, policy manuals), and the majority of the control resides in the manager. Thus, the simple design tends to minimize the bureaucratic aspects and rest more heavily on the leadership of the manager.

The simple design pattern is appropriate for many small firms, such as family businesses, retail stores, and small manufacturing firms.[4] The strengths of the simple design are simplicity, flexibility, and responsiveness to the desires of a central manager—in many cases, the owner. Because a simple design relies heavily on the manager's personal leadership, however, this configuration is only as effective as is the senior manager.

OPERATIONS TECHNOLOGY AND ORGANIZATIONAL DESIGN

Although the design for an organization should reflect its size, it must also be adjusted to fit technological opportunities and requirements.[5] That is, successful organizations are said to arrange their internal structures to meet the dictates of their dominant "technologies" or workflows and, more recently, information technology opportunities.[6] **Operations technology** is the combination of resources, knowledge, and techniques that creates a product or service output for an organization.[7] **Information technology** is the combination of machines, artifacts, procedures, and systems used to gather, store, analyze, and disseminate information for translating it into knowledge.[8]

For over 30 years, researchers in OB have charted the links between operations technology and organizational design. For operations technology, two common classifications have received considerable attention: Thompson's and Woodward's classifications.

THOMPSON'S VIEW OF TECHNOLOGY

James D. Thompson classified technologies based on the degree to which the technology could be specified and the degree of interdependence among the work activities with categories called intensive, mediating, and long linked.[9] Under *intensive technology,* there is uncertainty as to how to produce desired outcomes. A group of specialists must be brought together interactively to use a variety of techniques to solve problems. Examples are found in a hospital emergency room or a research and development laboratory. Coordination and knowledge exchange are of critical importance with this kind of technology.

Mediating technology links parties that want to become interdependent. For example, banks link creditors and depositors and store money and information to facilitate such exchanges. Whereas all depositors and creditors are indirectly interdependent, the reliance is pooled through the bank. The degree of coordination among the individual tasks with pooled technology is substantially reduced, and information management becomes more important than coordinated knowledge application.

Under *long-linked technology,* also called mass production or industrial technology, the way to produce the desired outcomes is known. The task is broken down into a number of sequential steps. A classic example is the automobile assembly line. Control is critical, and coordination is restricted to making the sequential linkages work in harmony.

WOODWARD'S VIEW OF TECHNOLOGY

Joan Woodward also divides technology into three categories: small-batch, mass production, and continuous-process manufacturing.[10] In units of *small-batch production,* a variety of custom products are tailor-made to fit customer specifications, such as tailor-made suits. The machinery and equipment used are generally not very elaborate, but considerable craftsmanship is often needed. In *mass production,* the organization produces one or a few products through an assembly-line system. The work of one group is highly dependent on that of another; the equipment is typically sophisticated; and the workers are given very detailed instructions. Automobiles and refrigerators are produced in this way. Organizations using *continuous-process technology* produce a few products using considerable automation. Classic examples are automated chemical plants and oil refineries. Millennium Chemicals' operations are a good example of what Woodward called continuous-process manufacturing. As the ethics module suggests, innovative firms such as Millennium Chemicals are infusing ethics into day-to-day operations and making ethics a part of a recognizable pattern we have called *strategy.*

From her studies, Woodward concluded that the combination of structure and technology was critical to the success of the organizations. When technology and organizational design were properly matched, a firm was more successful. Specifically, successful small-batch and continuous-process plants had flexible structures with small workgroups at the bottom; more rigidly structured plants were less successful. In contrast, successful mass production operations were rigidly structured and had large workgroups at the bottom. Since Woodward's studies, this technological imperative has been supported by various other investigations. Yet, today we recognize that operations technology is just one factor involved in the success of an organization.[11]

WHERE OPERATIONS TECHNOLOGY DOMINATES: THE ADHOCRACY

The influence of operations technology is most clearly seen in small organizations and in specific departments within large ones. In some instances, managers and employees simply do not know the appropriate way to service a client or to produce a particular product. This is the extreme of Thompson's intensive type of technology, and it may be found in some small-batch processes where a team of individuals must develop a unique product for a particular client.

Mintzberg suggests that at these technological extremes, the "adhocracy" may be an appropriate design.[12] An **adhocracy** is characterized by few rules, policies, and procedures; substantial decentralization; shared decision making among members; extreme horizontal specialization (as each member of the unit may be a distinct specialist); few levels of management; and virtually no formal controls.

The adhocracy is particularly useful when an aspect of the firm's operations technology presents two sticky problems: (1) the tasks facing the firm vary considerably and provide many exceptions, as in a hospital, or (2) problems are difficult to define and resolve.[13] The adhocracy places a premium on professionalism and coordination in problem solving.[14] Large firms may use temporary task forces, form special committees, and even contract consulting firms to provide the creative problem identification and problem solving that the adhocracy promotes. For instance, Microsoft creates new autonomous departments to encourage talented employees to develop new software programs. Allied Chemical and 3M also set up quasi-autonomous groups to work through new ideas.

INFORMATION TECHNOLOGY AND ORGANIZATIONAL DESIGN

Today, information technology (IT), the Web, and the computer are virtually inseparable.[15] Some even suggest that IT only refers to computer-based systems used in the management of the enterprise.[16] Certainly, the computer and extensions of the personal computer are a major force in most corporations. However, substantial collateral advances have also been made in telecommunication options. Furthermore, advances in the computer as a machine are much less profound than how information technology is transforming how firms manage.

It is important to understand just what IT does from an organizational standpoint—not from the view of the PC user.[17] From an organizational standpoint IT can be used, among other things, as (1) a partial substitute for some operations, as well as some process controls and impersonal methods of coordination, (2) a capability for transforming information to knowledge for learning, and (3) a strategic capability.

INFORMATION TECHNOLOGY AS A SUBSTITUTE

Old bureaucracies prospered and dominated other forms, in part, because they provided more efficient production through specialization and their approach to dealing with information. Where the organization used mediating technology or long-linked technology, the machine bureaucracy ran rampant. In these firms rules, policies, and procedures, as well as many other process controls, could be rigidly enforced based on very scant information.[18] Such was the case for the post office: postal clerks even had rules telling them how to hold their hands when sorting mail.

In many organizations, the initial implementation of IT would displace the most routine, highly specified, and repetitive jobs.[19] The clerical tasks in bookkeeping, writing checks for payroll, and keeping track of sales were some of the first targets of computerization. Here

IT was often initiated in the form of a large centralized mainframe computer. For instance, mainframe computers were still the major business for IBM well into the 1990s. Initial implementation did not alter the fundamental character or design of the organization. To continue the example of the post office, initial computerization focused mainly on replacing the hand tracking of mail. Then IT was infused into automated reading machines to help sort mail. This called for implementation of the ZIP code.

A second wave of substitution replaced process controls and informal coordination mechanisms. Rules, policies, and procedures could be replaced with a decision support system (DSS). In the case of a DSS, repetitive routine choices could be programmed into a computer-based system. For instance, if you applied for a credit card, a computer program would check your credit history and other financial information. If your application passed several preset tests, you would be issued a credit card. If your application failed any of the tests, it would either be rejected or sent to an individual for further analysis.

The second wave of implementation brought some marginal changes in organizational design. Specifically, the firm often needed fewer levels of management and fewer internal staff. A small number of firms also recognized that they could outsource some internal staff operations. For instance, in many firms independent organizations actually do all of their employee payroll.

The emphasis on direct substitution was still the norm in many organizations well into the 1990s, and in smaller firms it continues today. This is much as one would expect with the implementation of a new-to-the-world technology. It takes decades to move from the lab to full implementation, and the first applications are often in the form of substitutes for existing solutions. For instance, autos were once just substitutes for the horse and buggy. Both computer technology and the auto took about twenty years to enter the mass market. However, IT, just as the auto, has transformed our society because it added new capability.

INFORMATION TECHNOLOGY AS A CAPABILITY FOR LEARNING

IT has also long been recognized for its potential to add capability.[20] For over 20 years, scholars have talked of using IT to improve the efficiency, speed of responsiveness, and effectiveness of operations. Married to machines, IT became advanced manufacturing technology when computer-aided design (CAD) was combined with computer-aided manufacturing (CAM) to yield the automated manufacturing cell. More complex decision support systems have provided middle and lower level managers programs to aid in analyzing complex problems rather than just ratify routine choices. Computer-generated reports now give even senior executives the opportunity to track the individual sales performance of the lowliest salesperson.

Now instead of substituting for existing operations, or process controls, IT provides individuals deep within the organization the information they need to plan, make choices, coordinate with others, and control their own operations.

Although simple substitution could proceed one application at a time, the real impact of adding IT capability could not come until it was broadly available to nearly everyone.[21] To use the auto analogy again, the real impact of the auto was felt only after Henry Ford sold hundreds of thousands of his Model T and new roads were constructed. For IT to have a similar impact on organizational design, the seamless use of computerized information across the organization was needed. The extremely powerful mainframe of the 1970s and 1980s was not up to the task simply because the information individuals required to do their jobs more quickly and better was often unique to them. They now needed a common technology with the capability for uniqueness. And nearly everyone would have to have it and use it in cooperation with others.

Enter WINTEL—that is, Microsoft Windows in combination with an Intel microprocessing chip. This combination provided a relatively cheap, easy-to-use personal computer with an almost standardized technology that could be individually tailored at a comparatively modest cost. WINTEL was the PC equivalent of the tin lizzie—Henry Ford's Model T designed for the masses.

With the adoption of WINTEL, three important changes occurred. First, IT applications for tasks found across many organizations were quickly developed and received broad acceptance. Thus, the era of the spreadsheet and the word processing program began and displaced the old mainframes. Individuals could develop and transfer information to others with some assurance that the other party could read their output and duplicate their processes. Second, WINTEL expanded to incorporate existing telecommunications systems such as the Internet.[22] Thus, the era of connectivity also emerged. Married to parallel developments in telecommunications, a whole world of electronic commerce, teleconferencing—with combinations of data, pictures, and sound—and cell phones emerged. Third, IT was transformed from a substitute to a mechanism for learning.[23] For example, we now ask you to learn from the Internet connections and Web exercises at the end of each chapter.

Collectively, the impact of IT organizational design was and remains profound. The changes can often occur from the bottom up. New IT systems empower individuals, expanding their jobs and making them both interesting and challenging. The emphasis on narrowly defined jobs replete with process controls imposed by middle management can be transformed to broadly envisioned, interesting jobs based on IT-embedded processes with output controls. A new series of coordination devices based on IT can displace the memo and the coordinating department as firms constitute temporary teams and task forces using "virtual meetings"—meetings via e-mail to solve cross-departmental problems.[24] The whole world of staff units has changed as bureaucratic professionals have adjusted to the new world of IT. And many middle managers replete with their staff assistants are no longer needed.

For the production segments of firms using long-linked technology such as in auto assembly plants and canneries, IT can be linked to total quality management (TQM) programs and be embedded in the machinery. Data on operations can be transformed into knowledge of operations and used to systematically improve quality and efficiency. This also has meant that firms have had to rethink their view of employees as brainless robots. To make TQM work with IT all employees must plan, do, and control. As we discussed when we talked about job enrichment and job design in Chapter 8, combining IT and TQM with empowerment and participation is fundamental for success. For instance, in the mid-1990s two computer equipment manufacturers embarked on improvement programs combining IT and TQM. One manufacturer imposed the program on all employees. There was some initial success, but ultimately this program failed. The second combined the IT-TQM program with extensive empowerment and participation. Although implementation was slower, today the combination has produced a constantly improving learning environment.[25]

INFORMATION TECHNOLOGY AS A STRATEGIC CAPABILITY

Just as the automobile spawned the mobile society and led to the development of a plethora of auto-related businesses, IT has spawned a whole new series of corporations called e-businesses. It is also transforming aging bricks-and-mortar firms as they incorporate a new type of capability.

IT AND E-BUSINESS

E-business is here to stay.[26] Whether it is business to business (B2B) or business to consumers (B2C), there is a whole new set of dot-com firms with information technology at the core of their operations. One of the more flamboyant entrants to the B2C world is the now-familiar Amazon.com. Opened in 1995 to sell books directly to customers via the Internet, it rapidly expanded to toys and games, health and beauty products, computers and video games, as well as cameras and photography. It is now a virtual general store. After over six years of losses, Amazon.com posted a modest profit in 2002. It is most interesting to examine the transformation in the design of this firm to illustrate the notion of co-evolution presented in the introduction. Initially, it was organized as a simple structure. As it grew, it became more complex by adding divisions devoted to each of its separate product areas. To remain flexible and promote growth in both the volume of operations and the capabilities of employees, it did not develop an extensive bureaucracy. There are still very few levels of management. It built separate organizational components based on product categories (divisional structure, as described in Chapter 11) with minimal rules, policies, and procedures. In other words, the organizational design it adopted appeared relatively conventional. What was not conventional was the use of IT for learning about customers and the use of IT for coordinating and tracking operations. Although their Web site was not the most technically advanced, you could easily order the book you wanted, track the delivery, and feel confident it would arrive as promised. This use of IT was also adopted by others such as Barnes and Noble. Amazon.com changed the competitive landscape.

In comparison to Amazon.com, many other new dot-com firms adopted a variation of the adhocracy as their design pattern. The thinking was that e-business was fundamentally different from the old bricks-and-mortar operations. Thus, an entirely new structural configuration was needed to accommodate the development of new e-products and services. The managers of these firms forgot two important liabilities of the adhocracy as they grew. First, there are limits on the size of an effective adhocracy. Second, the actual delivery of their products and services did not require continual innovation but rested more on responsiveness to clients and maintaining efficiency. The design did not deliver what they needed. In common terms they had great Web sites, but they were grossly inefficient.

IT AS A STRATEGIC CAPABILITY
FOR THE BRICKS-AND-MORTAR FIRMS

IT as a strategic capability is now changing many traditional bricks-and-mortar firms. Perhaps IT's most profound effect can be seen in firms that rely on a mediating technology; banks, finance companies, dating services, and employment agencies are some examples. The job of the firm, as we know, is to facilitate exchange by matching types of individuals. In the case of banks, individuals who want to borrow are matched with those who want to lend by placing individual interests into categories. So those who have a savings account are put in a category of precisely that type of savings account and are pooled with others. IT can revolutionize the categorization process that underlies the matching by helping to create much more sophisticated categories and link these categories in novel ways. For example, IT lies behind the multibillion-dollar secondary market for home mortgages. Until recent years, a bank or savings and loan (S&L) provided the funds for the mortgage from its depositors and would hold the mortgage until it was paid off. You would apply to a local bank or S&L for a mortgage. If they granted you a mortgage, you would pay the bank or the S&L that sold it to you. Much the same was the case for student loans. Now with IT, the bank or S&L can sell the mortgage to others, and normally does, so that it can recoup new funds to sell additional mortgages. It may even sell the right to "service" the loan so that you no longer send your money to the originating bank but to someone else. This change in information technology now allows all types of financial institutions to participate in lending money for mortgages. The job of the old banker or S&L manager has fundamentally changed. Now you can get a mortgage, a credit card, or use the ATM machine without ever contacting an individual.

Some financial firms could not exist without IT, which has become the basis for whole new industries. For instance, IT is the foundation for multitrillion-dollar markets in international finance in which new exotic products are available which were nonexistent twenty years ago. For example, in the 1980s few existing financial managers or regulatory agencies had the understanding of IT to develop effective controls for the global derivatives markets. However, a small handful of individuals in Connecticut working for a firm called Long-Term Capital Management used sophisticated IT systems to bet several billion dollars on the interest spread between different kinds of bonds. Although they made several hundred million dollars in the mid-1990s, in 1998 their losses threatened the whole U.S. financial system to the point that the Federal Reserve (a quasigovernment agency) had to orchestrate a rescue. Of course, IT has not developed in a vacuum, and its effective implementation often rests on others adopting common IT standards and operations. Just because IT presents a potential capability does not automatically mean the firm should adopt it or change its design to facilitate its use. The appropriate design also rests on external factors and the strategy of the firm. We turn to these issues now.

ENVIRONMENT AND ORGANIZATIONAL DESIGN

An effective organizational design also reflects powerful external forces as well as size and technological factors. Organizations, as open systems, need to receive inputs from the environment and in turn to sell outputs to their environment. Therefore, understanding the environment is important.[27]

The *general environment* is the set of cultural, economic, legal-political, and educational conditions found in the areas in which the organization operates. Much of Chapter 3 on international concerns dealt with the influences of the general environment, and throughout this book we have shown examples of globalization. The owners, suppliers, distributors, government agencies, and competitors with which an organization must interact to grow and survive constitute its *specific environment*. A firm typically has much more choice in the composition of its specific environment than its general environment. Although it is often convenient to separate the general and specific environmental influences on the firm, managers need to recognize the combined impact of both. Choosing some businesses, for instance, means entering global competition with advanced technologies.

ENVIRONMENTAL COMPLEXITY

A basic concern that must be addressed in analyzing the environment of the organization is its complexity. A more complex environment provides an organization with more opportunities and more problems. **Environmental complexity** refers to the magnitude of the problems and opportunities in the organization's environment, as evidenced by three main factors: the degree of richness, the degree of interdependence, and the degree of uncertainty stemming from both the general and the specific environment.

Environmental Richness Overall, the environment is richer when the economy is growing, when individuals are improving their education, and when those on whom the organization relies are prospering. For businesses, a richer environment means that economic conditions are improving, customers are spending more money, and suppliers (especially banks) are willing to invest in the organization's future. In a rich environment, more organizations survive, even if they have poorly functioning organizational designs. A richer environment is also filled with more opportunities and dynamism—the potential for change. The organizational design must allow the company to recognize these opportunities and capitalize on them.

The opposite of richness is decline. For business firms, a general recession is a good example of a leaner environment. Whereas corporate reactions vary, it is instructive to examine typical responses to decline.

In the United States, firms have traditionally reacted to decline first by issuing layoffs to nonsupervisory workers and then by moving up the organizational ladder as the environment becomes leaner. As global competition has increased and new IT options have become more widely available, firms have also started to alter their organizational designs by cutting staff units and the number of organizational levels. This downsizing, though traumatic, can be minimized.

Many European firms find it very difficult to cut full-time employees legally when the economy deteriorates. In sustained periods of decline, many firms have therefore turned to national governments for help. Much like U.S.-based firms, European-based firms view changes in organizational design as a last but increasingly necessary resort as they must now compete globally.

Environmental Interdependence The link between external interdependence and organizational design is often subtle and indirect. The organization may coopt powerful outsiders by including them. For instance, many large corporations have financial representatives from banks and insurance companies on their boards of directors. The organization may also adjust its overall design strategy to absorb or buffer the demands of a more powerful external element. Perhaps the most common adjustment is the development of a centralized staff department to handle an important external group. For instance, few large U.S. corporations lack some type of governmental relations group at the top. Where service to a few large customers is considered critical, the organization's departmentation is likely to switch from a functional to a divisionalized form.[28]

Uncertainty and Volatility   Environmental uncertainty and volatility can be particularly damaging to large bureaucracies. In times of change, investments quickly become outmoded, and internal operations no longer work as expected. The obvious organizational design response to uncertainty and volatility is to opt for a more organic form. At the extremes, movement toward an adhocracy may be important. However, these pressures may run counter to those that come from large size and operations technology. In these cases, it may be too hard or too time consuming for some organizations to make the design adjustments. Thus, the organization may continue to struggle while adjusting its design just a little bit at a time.

USING ALLIANCES WHERE ENVIRONMENTAL FACTORS DOMINATE

In high-tech areas and businesses dominated by IT, such as robotics, semiconductors, advanced materials (ceramics and carbon fibers), and advanced information systems, a single company often does not have all the knowledge necessary to bring new products to the market. Often, the firms with the knowledge are not even in the same country. The organizational design must therefore go beyond the boundaries of the organization into **interfirm alliances**—announced cooperative agreements or joint ventures between two independent firms. Often, these agreements involve corporations that are headquartered in different nations.[29]

Alliances are quite common in such high-technology industries. In these international alliances high-tech firms seek not only to develop technology but to ensure that their solutions become standardized across regions of the world. Corning is one high-tech firm that uses alliances extensively.

Firms may also develop alliances to explore potentials for future collaboration. One of the largest and potentially most influential strategic alliances is the cooperation between West Germany's Daimler-Chrysler and Japan's Mitsubishi. The two companies agreed to share technology and to develop joint ventures, market-based cooperations, or high-tech consortia, as the need arises. Yet some alliances to share technology date to the turn of the twentieth century.

In more developed industries, interfirm alliances are also quite popular, but they are often known by other names. In Europe, for example, they are called *informal combines* or *cartels*. Competitors work cooperatively to share the market in order to decrease uncertainty and improve favorability for all. Except in rare cases, these arrangements are often illegal in the United States.

In Japan, the network of relationships among well-established firms in many industries is called a *keiretsu*. There are two common forms. The first is a bank-centered keiretsu, in which firms are linked to one another directly through cross ownership and historical ties to one bank. The Mitsubishi group is a good example. In the second type, a vertical keiretsu, a key manufacturer is at the hub of a network of supplier firms or distributor firms. The manufacturer typically has both long-term supply contracts with members and cross-ownership ties. These arrangements help isolate Japanese firms from stockholders and provide a mechanism for sharing and developing technology. Toyota is an example of a firm at the center of a vertical keiretsu.

The network organization is beginning to evolve in the United States as well. Here, the central firm specializes in a core activity, such as design and assembly, and works with a comparatively small number of participating suppliers on a long-term basis for both component development and manufacturing efficiency. Nike is a leader in the development of these relationships.

More extreme variations of this network design are also emerging to meet apparently conflicting environmental, size, and technological demands simultaneously. Firms are spinning off staff functions to reduce their overall size and take advantage of new IT options. With these new environmental challenges and technological opportunities, firms must choose and not just react blindly.

Strategic Competency Through Learning

Throughout this chapter we have emphasized co-evolution. The firm must not only adapt to its size, technology, and environment, but must also shape these forces. In the introduction we stressed the development of individuals and their skills. In the OB literature the development of individual skills and capabilities organizationwide is discussed under the topic of *organizational learning*. Organizational learning is the key to successful co-evolution. **Organizational learning** is the process of knowledge acquisition, information distribution, information interpretation, and organizational retention in adapting successfully to changing circumstances.[30] In simpler terms, organizational learning involves the adjustment of the organization's and individual's actions based on its experience and that of others. The challenge is doing to learn and learning to do.

KNOWLEDGE ACQUISITION

Firms obtain information in a variety of ways and at different rates during their histories. Perhaps the most important information is obtained from sources outside the firm at the time of its founding. During the firm's initial years, its managers copy, or mimic, what they believe are the successful practices of others.[31] As they mature, however, firms can also acquire knowledge through experience and systematic search.

Mimicry Mimicry is important to the new firm because (1) it provides workable, if not ideal, solutions to many problems; (2) it reduces the number of decisions that need to be analyzed separately, allowing managers to concentrate on more critical issues; and (3) it establishes legitimacy or acceptance by employees, suppliers, and customers and narrows the choices calling for detailed explanation.

One of the key factors involved in examining mimicry is the extent to which managers attempt to isolate cause-effect relationships. Simply copying others without attempting to understand the issues involved often leads to failure. The literature is filled with examples of firms that have tried to implement quality circles, empowerment, and decentralization simply because others have used them successfully. Too many firms have abandoned these techniques because managers failed to understand why and under what conditions they worked for other firms. When mimicking others, managers need to adjust for the unique circumstances of their corporation.

Experience   A primary way to acquire knowledge is through experience. All organizations and managers can learn in this manner. Besides learning by doing, managers can also systematically embark on structured programs to capture the lessons to be learned from failure and success. For instance, a well-designed research and development program allows managers to learn as much through failure as through success.

Learning by doing in an intelligent way is at the heart of many Japanese corporations, with their emphasis on statistical quality control, quality circles, and other such practices. Many firms have discovered that numerous small improvements can cumulatively add up to a major improvement in both quality and efficiency. The major problem with emphasizing learning by doing is the inability to forecast precisely what will change and how it will change. Managers need to believe that improvements can be made, listen to suggestions, and actually implement the changes. It is much more difficult to do than to say, however.

Vicarious Learning   Vicarious learning involves capturing the lessons of others' experiences. At the individual level, managers are building on individualized "social learning" and using it to help transform their potential for organizational improvement.

Individual Social Learning   *Social learning* is learning that is achieved through the reciprocal interactions among people, behavior, and environment. Figure 12.1 illustrates and elaborates on this individualized view of learning drawn from the work of Albert Bandura.[32] According to the figure, the individual uses modeling or vicarious learning to acquire behavior by observing and imitating others. The person then attempts to acquire these behaviors by modeling them through practice. In a work situation, the model may be a manager or co-worker who demonstrates desired behaviors. Mentors or senior workers who befriend younger and more inexperienced protégés can also be important models.

FIGURE 12.1 SOCIAL LEARNING MODEL

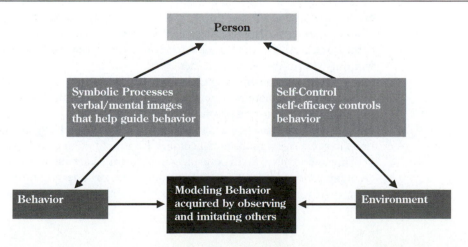

Indeed, some have argued that a shortage of mentors for women in management is a major constraint to their progression up the career ladder.[33]

The symbolic processes depicted in Figure 12.1 are also important in social learning. Words and symbols used by managers and others in the workplace can help communicate values, beliefs, and goals and thus serve as guides to the individual's behavior. For example, a "thumbs up" or a symbol from the boss lets you know your behavior is appropriate. At the same time, the person's self-control is important in influencing his or her own behavior. *Self-efficacy*—the person's belief that he or she can perform adequately in a situation—is an important part of such self-control. People with self-efficacy believe that they have the necessary ability for a given job; that they are capable of the effort required; and that no outside events will hinder them from attaining their desired performance level.[34] In contrast, people with low self-efficacy believe that no matter how hard they try, they cannot manage their environment well enough to be successful. For example, if you feel self-efficacious as a student, a low grade on one test is likely to encourage you to study harder, talk to the instructor, or do other things to enable you to do well the next time. In contrast, a person low in self-efficacy would probably drop the course or give up studying. Of course, even people who are high in self-efficacy do not control their environment entirely.

Much of the learning in corporations is less systematic than that depicted in Figure 12.1. Some firms have learned that the process of searching for new information may not always be structured or planned in conjunction with an identified problem or opportunity. Managers may embark upon learning in less systematic ways, including scanning, grafting, and contracting out.

Scanning involves looking outside the firm and bringing back useful solutions. At times, these solutions may be applied to recognized problems. More often, these solutions float around management until they are needed to solve a problem.[35] Astute managers can contribute to organizational learning by scanning external sources, such as competitors, suppliers, industry consultants, customers, and leading firms. For instance, by reverse engineering the competitor's products (developing the engineering drawings and specifications from the existing product), an organization can quickly match all standard product features. By systematically exploring the proposed developments from suppliers, a firm may become a lead user and be among the first to capitalize on the developments of suppliers. **Grafting** is the process of acquiring individuals, units, or firms to bring in useful knowledge. Almost all firms seek to hire experienced individuals from other firms simply because experienced individuals may bring with them a whole new series of solutions. For instance, at Dayton-Hudson senior management hired a new vice president for one of its department stores from a leading competitor, Nordstrom's. Dayton-Hudson wanted to know the winning ways of this industry leader.

The critical problem in grafting is much the same as that in scanning: obtaining the knowledge is not enough; it must be translated into action. A key problem with grafting one unit onto an existing organization is discussed in Chapter 13, on organizational culture. That is, there may be a clash of cultures, and instead of getting new solutions, both units may experience substantial conflict. Contracting out or outsourcing is the reverse of grafting and involves asking outsiders to perform a particular function. Whereas virtually all organizations contract out and outsource, the key question for managers is often what to keep. As we have already noted, firms often outsource peripheral or staff functions.

INFORMATION DISTRIBUTION

Once information is obtained, managers must establish mechanisms to distribute relevant information to the individuals who may need it. A primary challenge in larger firms is to locate quickly who has the appropriate information and who needs specific types of information. A partial solution is the development of disbursed IT networks that connect related organizational units.

Although data collection is helpful, it is not enough. Data are not information; the information must be interpreted.

INFORMATION INTERPRETATION

Information within organizations is a collective understanding of the firm's goals and of how the data relate to one of the firm's stated or unstated objectives within the current setting. Unfortunately, the process of developing multiple interpretations is often thwarted by a number of common problems.[36]

Self-Serving Interpretations   Among managers, the ability to interpret events, conditions, and history to their own advantage is almost universal. Managers and employees alike often see what they have seen in the past or see what they want to see. Rarely do they see what is or can be.

Managerial Scripts   A *managerial script* is a series of well-known routines for problem identification and alternative generation and analysis common to managers within a firm.[37] Different organizations have different scripts, often based on what has worked in the past. In a way, the script is a ritual that reflects what the "memory banks" of the corporation hold. Managers become bound by what they have seen. The danger is that they may not be open to what actually is occurring. They may be unable to unlearn.

The script may be elaborate enough to provide an apparently well-tested series of solutions based on the firm's experience. Larger, older firms are rarely structured for learning; rather, they are structured for efficiency. That is, the organizational design emphasizes repetition, volume processing, and routine. In order to learn, the organization needs to be able to unlearn, switch routines to obtain information quickly, and provide various interpretations of events rather than just tap into external archives.[38]

Few managers question a successful script. Consequently, they start solving today's problems with yesterday's solutions. Managers have been trained, both in the classroom and on the job, to initiate corrective action within the historically shared view of the world. That is, managers often initiate small, incremental improvements based on existing solutions instead of creating new approaches to identify the underlying problems.

Common Myths   An **organizational myth** is a commonly held cause-effect relationship or assertion that cannot be empirically supported.[39] Even though myths cannot be substantiated, both managers and workers may base their interpretations of problems and opportunities on the potentially faulty views. Three common myths often block the development of multiple interpretations.

The first common myth is the presumption that *there is a single organizational truth.* This myth is often expressed as, "Although others may be biased, I am able to define problems and develop solutions objectively." We are all subject to bias in varying degrees and in varying ways. The more complex the issue, the stronger the likelihood of many different supportable interpretations.

A second common myth is the *presumption of competence.* Managers at all levels are subject to believing that their part of the firm is okay and just needs minor improvements in implementation. As we have documented throughout this book, such is rarely the case. We are in the middle of a managerial revolution in which all managers need to reassess their general approach to managing organizational behavior.

A third common myth is the *denial of tradeoffs.* Most managers believe that their group, unit, or firm can avoid making undesirable tradeoffs and simultaneously please nearly every constituency. Whereas the denial of trade-offs is common, it can be a dangerous myth in some firms. For instance, when complex, dangerous technologies are involved, safe operations may come at some sacrifice to efficiency. Yet, some firms claim that "an efficient operation is a safe one" and aggressively move to improve efficiency. Although managers are stressing efficiency, they may fail to work on improving safety. The result may be a serious accident.[40]

INFORMATIONAL RETENTION

Organizations contain a variety of mechanisms that can be used to retain useful information.[41] Seven important mechanisms are: individuals, culture, transformation procedures, formal structures, ecology, external archives, and internal information technologies.

Individuals are the most important storehouses of information for organizations. Organizations that retain a large and comparatively stable group of experienced individuals are expected to have a higher capacity to acquire, retain, and retrieve information. Collectively, the organizational *culture* is an important repository of the shared experiences of corporate members. The culture often maintains the organizational memory via rich, vivid, and meaningful stories that outlive those who experienced the event.

Documents, rule books, written procedures, and even standard but unwritten methods of operation are all *transformation mechanisms* used to store accumulated information. In cases where operations are extremely complex but rarely needed, written sources of information are often invaluable. Pacific Gas and Electric, for example, maintains an extensive library for its Diablo Canyon nuclear power plant. In the library, one can find the complete engineering drawings for the whole plant as well as the changes made since the plant opened, together with a step-by-step plan for almost every possible accident scenario.

The organization's *formal structure* and the positions in an organization are less obvious but equally important mechanisms for storing information. When an aircraft lands on the deck of a U.S. Navy aircraft carrier, there are typically dozens of individuals on the deck, apparently watching the aircraft land. Each person on the deck is there for a specific purpose. Each can often trace his or her position to a specific accident that would not have occurred had some individual originally been assigned that position.

Physical structures (or *ecology,* in the language of learning theorists) are potentially important but often neglected mechanisms used to store information. For example, a traditional way of ordering parts and subcomponents in a factory is known as the "two-bin" system. One bin is always kept in reserve. Once an individual opens the reserve bin, he or she automatically orders replacements. In this way, the plant never runs out of components.

External archives can be tapped to provide valuable information on most larger organizations. Former employees, stock market analysts, suppliers, distributors, and the media can be important sources of valuable information. These external archives are important because they may provide a view of events quite different from that held in the organization.

Finally, the IT system of the organization, its *internal information technology,* can provide a powerful and individually tailored mechanism for storing information. All too often, however, managers are not using their IT systems strategically and are not tapping into them as mechanisms for retention.

STRATEGIC ORGANIZATIONAL LEARNING CYCLES

Throughout the beginning of this century a common headline running in the business press was: "Major Corporation Downsizes." Whether the corporation was AT&T, General Motors, or IBM, the message appeared to be the same: major U.S.-based corporations were in trouble. They were finally adjusting to a new competitive reality—on the backs of their workers and managers. As we have noted in this chapter, today the message from these firms is quite different. All are emphasizing competency via individual development and empowerment to learn and to make the needed incremental changes and decisions along the way. All are trying to avoid the past mistakes where they engaged in massive attempts to redirect themselves when it was apparent to all that change was overdue (see The Effective Manager 12.1). Some recent work on learning cycles helps explain why many organizations apparently fail to learn, while others appear to improve rapidly.[42]

DEFICIT CYCLES

A **deficit cycle** is a pattern of deteriorating performance that is followed by even further deterioration. Firms that are continually downsizing, such as Boeing Aircraft, are examples of firms in a deficit cycle. The same problems keep reoccurring, and the firm fails to develop adequate mechanisms for learning. The firm often has problems in one or more phases of the learning process. The past inability to adjust yields more problems and fewer resources available to solve the next wave of problems, and the firm continues to deteriorate.

THE EFFECTIVE MANAGER 12.1
AVOIDING MORE PROBLEMS WITH DOWNSIZING

When downsizing, firms should keep in mind that they must:

1. Accurately identify the causes of the decline.
2. Avoid grandiose attempts to reverse past history.
3. Avoid the tendency to increase centralization and rigidity and to reduce participation.
4. Target cuts and retrain employees wherever possible.
5. Keep employees informed to alleviate fear.
6. Systematically work to rebuild morale and emphasize more participation.

Major factors associated with deficit cycles are still being uncovered, but three are obvious from current research.[43] One is *organizational inertia*. It is very difficult to change organizations, and the larger the organization, the more inertia it often has. A second is *hubris*. Too few senior executives are willing to challenge their own actions or those of their firms because they see a history of success. They fail to recognize that yesterday's successful innovations are today's outmoded practices. A third is the issue of *detachment*. Executives often believe they can manage far-flung, diverse operations through analysis of reports and financial records. They lose touch and fail to make the needed unique and special adaptations required of all firms. One consultant has made millions advising executives to focus on improvement and to practice management by walking around the office to avoid detachment.

BENEFIT CYCLES

Inertia, hubris, and detachment are common maladies, but they are not the automatic fate of all corporations. Firms can successfully co-evolve. As we have repeatedly demonstrated, managers are trying to reinvent their firms each and every day. They hope to initiate a **benefit cycle**—a pattern of successful adjustment followed by further improvements. Microsoft is an example of a firm experiencing a benefit cycle. In this cycle, the same problems do not keep reoccurring as the firm develops adequate mechanisms for learning. The firm has few major difficulties with the learning process, and managers continually attempt to improve knowledge acquisition, information distribution, information interpretation, and organizational memory.

Organizations that successfully co-evolve can ride the benefit cycle. Inertia can work for managers if they do not become overconfident and if they can stay directly involved with the key operations of the firm and if they accurately forecast changes in the environment and technology.

CHAPTER 12 SUMMARY

What is the co-evolution view of strategy and what is its linkage to organizational design?

- Firms need to adjust to their environments and contexts as well as to influence them.
- The capabilities of organizational members are critical in both reacting to and molding the firm's environment, size, and technology.
- Strategy and organizational design are interrelated. The organization's design must support the strategy if the firm is to be successful.

What is organizational design, and how do the designs of small and large firms differ?

- Organizational design is the process of choosing and implementing a structural configuration for an organization.
- Smaller firms often adopt a simple structure, whereas larger firms often adopt a bureaucratic form.

How does the operations and information technology of the firm influence its organizational design?

- Operations technology and organizational design are interrelated.
- In highly intensive and small-batch technologies, organizational designs may tend toward the adhocracy, a very decentralized form of operation.
- Information technology and organizational design can be interrelated.
- IT provides an opportunity to change the design by substitution, for learning, and to capture strategic advantages.

What is the relationship between environmental conditions and organizational design?

- Environmental and organizational design are interrelated.
- In analyzing environments, both the general (background conditions) and specific (key actors and organizations) environments are important.
- The more complex the environment, the greater the demands on the organization, and firms should respond with more complex designs, such as the use of interfirm alliances.

What is organizational learning?

- Organizational learning is the process of knowledge acquisition, information distribution, information interpretation, and organizational memory used to adapt successfully to changing circumstances.

How are organizational learning cycles helpful in understanding organizational behavior?

- Organizational learning cycles help us understand how some organizations continually decline while others appear to be rising stars.

13

High Performance Organizational Cultures

Study Questions

The not-so-hidden advantage of many leading high performance organizations is their corporate culture. As you read Chapter 13, keep in mind these questions.

- What is organizational culture?
- What are the observable aspects of organizational culture?
- How do values and assumptions influence organizational cultures?
- How can the organizational culture be "managed," "nurtured," and "guided"?
- How can the process of organizational development enhance organizational culture?

For many firms, the hidden strength is its culture as formed by employees and partially shaped by management.[1] Where there is an emphasis by management on such values as quality, innovation, and long-term value over the drive toward short-term performance, firms are building high performance cultures that stand for something.[2] Employees need to believe that their efforts and those of their firm stand for something worth preserving. Something beyond the individual efforts. In this chapter we will deal with a very important aspect of that something—the culture inside the firm.

THE CONCEPT OF ORGANIZATIONAL CULTURE

Organizational or corporate culture is the system of shared actions, values, and beliefs that develops within an organization and guides the behavior of its members.[3] In the business setting, this system is often referred to as the *corporate culture*. Just as no two individual personalities are the same, no two organizational cultures are identical. Most significantly, management scholars and consultants increasingly believe that cultural differences can have a major impact on the performance of organizations and the quality of work life experienced by their members.

FUNCTIONS AND COMPONENTS OF ORGANIZATIONAL CULTURE

Through their collective experience, members of an organization solve two extremely important survival issues.[4] The first is the question of external adaptation: What precisely needs to be accomplished, and how can it be done? The second is the question of internal integration: How do members resolve the daily problems associated with living and working together?

External Adaptation **External adaptation** involves reaching goals and dealing with outsiders. The issues concerned are tasks to be accomplished, methods used to achieve the goals, and methods of coping with success and failure.

Through their shared experiences, members may develop common views that help guide their day-to-day activities. Organizational members need to know the real mission of the organization, not just the pronouncements to key constituencies, such as stockholders. Members will naturally develop an understanding of how they contribute to the mission via interaction. This view may emphasize the importance of human resources, the role of employees as cogs in a machine, or a cost to be reduced.

Closely related to the organization's mission and view of its contribution are the questions of responsibility, goals, and methods. For instance, at 3M, employees believe that it is their responsibility to innovate and contribute creatively. They see these responsibilities reflected in achieving the goal of developing new and improved products and processes.

Each collection of individuals in an organization also tends to (1) separate more important from less important external forces; (2) develop ways to measure their accomplishments; and (3) create explanations for why goals are not always met. At Dell, the direct retailer of computers, managers, for example, have moved away from judging their progress against specific targets to estimating the degree to which they are moving a development process forward. Instead of blaming a poor economy or upper level managers for the firm's failure to reach a goal, Dell managers have set hard goals that are difficult to reach and have redoubled their efforts to improve participation and commitment.[5]

The final issues in external adaptation deal with two important, but often neglected, aspects of coping with external reality. First, individuals need to develop acceptable ways of telling outsiders just how good they really are. At 3M, for example, employees talk about the quality of their products and the many new, useful products they have brought to the market. Second, individuals must collectively know when to admit defeat. At 3M, the answer is easy for new projects: at the beginning of the development process, members establish "drop" points at which to quit the development effort and redirect it.[6]

In sum, external adaptation involves answering important instrumental or goal-related questions concerning coping with reality: What is the real mission? How do we contribute? What are our goals? How do we reach our goals? What external forces are important? How do we measure results? What do we do if specific targets are not met? How do we tell others how good we are? When do we quit?

Internal integration   The corporate culture also provides answers to the problems of internal integration. **Internal integration** deals with the creation of a collective identity and with finding ways of matching methods of working and living together.

The process of internal integration often begins with the establishment of a unique identity; that is, each collection of individuals and each subculture within the organization develops some type of unique definition of itself. Through dialogue and interaction, members begin to characterize their world. They may see it as malleable or fixed, filled with opportunity or threatening. Real progress toward innovation can begin when group members collectively believe that they can change important parts of the world around them and that what appears to be a threat is actually an opportunity for change.[7]

Three important aspects of working together are (1) deciding who is a member and who is not; (2) developing an informal understanding of acceptable and unacceptable behavior; and (3) separating friends from enemies. Effective total quality management holds that subgroups in the organization need to view their immediate supervisors as members of the group who are expected to represent them to friendly higher managers.

To work together effectively, individuals need to decide collectively how to allocate power, status, and authority. They need to establish a shared understanding of who will get rewards and sanctions for specific types of actions. Too often, managers fail to recognize these important aspects of internal integration. For example, a manager may fail to explain the basis for a promotion and to show why this reward, the status associated with it, and the power given to the newly promoted individual are consistent with commonly shared beliefs.

Collections of individuals need to work out acceptable ways to communicate and to develop guidelines for friendships. Although these aspects of internal integration may appear esoteric, they are vital. To function effectively as a team, individuals must recognize that some members will be closer than others; friendships are inevitable. However, the basis for friendships can be inappropriately restricted. At the U.S. Department of Interior, for example, recent budget cuts may have had a beneficial effect. At one time, the political appointees could be found eating together in their own executive dining room. Now, all employees eat at the Interior Department lunchroom, and even the political appointees are making new friends with the career civil servants.

In sum, internal integration involves answers to important questions associated with living together. What is our unique identity? How do we view the world? Who is a member?

How do we allocate power, status, and authority? How do we communicate? What is the basis for friendship? Answering these questions is important to organizational members because the organization is more than a place to work; it is a place where individuals spend much of their adult life.[8]

DOMINANT CULTURE, SUBCULTURES, AND COUNTERCULTURES

Smaller firms often have a single dominant culture with a unitary set of shared actions, values, and beliefs. Most larger organizations contain several subcultures as well as one or more countercultures.[9] **Subcultures** are groups of individuals with a unique pattern of values and philosophy that is not inconsistent with the organization's dominant values and philosophy.[10] Interestingly, strong subcultures are often found in high performance task forces, teams, and special project groups in organizations. The culture emerges to bind individuals working intensely together to accomplish a specific task. For example, there are strong subcultures of stress engineers and liaison engineers in the Boeing Renton plant. These highly specialized groups must solve knotty technical issues to ensure that Boeing planes are safe. Though distinct, these groups of engineers share in the dominant values of Boeing.

In contrast, **countercultures** have a pattern of values and a philosophy that reject the surrounding culture.[11] When Stephen Jobs reentered Apple computer as its interim CEO, he quickly formed a counterculture within Apple. Over the next 18 months, numerous clashes occurred as the followers of the old CEO (Gil Amelio) fought to maintain their place. Jobs won and Apple won. His counterculture became dominant.

Within an organization, mergers and acquisitions may produce countercultures. Employers and managers of an acquired firm may hold values and assumptions that are quite inconsistent with those of the acquiring firm. This is known as the "clash of corporate cultures."[12]

Importing Subcultures Every large organization imports potentially important subcultural groupings when it hires employees from the larger society. In North America, for instance, subcultures and countercultures may naturally form based on ethnic, racial, gender, generational, or locational similarities. In Japanese organizations, subcultures often form based on the date of graduation from a university, gender, or geographic location. In European firms, ethnicity and language play an important part in developing subcultures, as does gender. In many less developed nations, language, education, religion, or family social status are often grounds for forming societally popular subcultures and countercultures. As more firms globalize and use mergers and acquisitions to expand, often they must cope with both importing subcultures and the clash of corporate cultures. For instance, when Daimler Benz said it was merging with Chrysler Corporation it was billed as a merger of equals. The new combined firm would have a global reach. The corporate culture clash came quickly, however, when Chrysler managers and employees realized that Daimler executives would control the new combination and forge it around the German partner.

The difficulty with importing groupings from the larger societies lies in the relevance these subgroups have to the organization as a whole. At the one extreme, senior managers can merely accept these divisions and work within the confines of the larger culture. There are three primary difficulties with this approach. First, subordinated groups, such as members of a specific religion or ethnic group, are likely to form into a counterculture and to work more diligently to change their status than to better the firm. Second, the firm may find it extremely difficult to cope with broader cultural changes. For instance, in the United States the expected treatment of women, ethnic minorities, and the disabled has changed dramatically over the last 20 years. Firms that merely accept old customs and prejudices have experienced a greater loss of key personnel and increased communication difficulties, as well as greater interpersonal conflict, than have their more progressive counterparts. Third, firms that accept and build on natural divisions from the larger culture may find it extremely difficult to develop sound international operations. For example, many Japanese firms have had substantial difficulty adjusting to the equal treatment of women in their U.S. operations.[13]

Valuing Cultural Diversity   Managers can work to eradicate all naturally occurring subcultures and countercultures. Firms are groping to develop what Taylor Cox calls the multicultural organization. The multicultural organization is a firm that values diversity but systematically works to block the transfer of societally based subcultures into the fabric of the organization.[14] Because Cox focuses on some problems unique to the United States, his prescription for change may not apply to organizations located in other countries with much more homogeneous populations.

Cox suggests a five-step program for developing the multicultural organization. First, the organization should develop pluralism with the objective of multibased socialization. To accomplish this objective, members of different naturally occurring groups need to school one another to increase knowledge and information and to eliminate stereotyping. Second, the firm should fully integrate its structure so that there is no direct relationship between a naturally occurring group and any particular job—for instance, there are no distinct male or female jobs. Third, the firm must integrate the informal networks by eliminating barriers and increasing participation. That is, it must break down existing societally based informal groups. Fourth, the organization should break the linkage between naturally occurring group identity and the identity of the firm. In other words, the firm should not be just for the young, old, men, women, and so on. Fifth, the organization must actively work to eliminate interpersonal conflict based on either the group identity or the natural backlash of the largest societally based grouping.

The key problems associated with fully implementing Cox's program are separating the firm from the larger culture in which it must operate and eliminating some societally based groupings that are relevant for achieving the firm's goals. For instance, the U.S. military is barred from fully implementing Cox's recommendations simply because it is not currently legal to put women into all combat roles. The issue of generational groupings provides another example. Implementing Cox's recommendations would call for 20-year-olds to be represented proportionally in the senior management ranks; most corporations want and need the judgment honed by experience. However, astute senior managers are recognizing that they may be out of touch with younger employees. For example, Robert Hausman, chairman of Coventry Industries of Boca Raton, Florida, routinely meets young employees once a month over pizza.[15]

LEVELS OF CULTURAL ANALYSIS

Three important levels of cultural analysis in organizations are: observable culture, shared values, and common assumptions.[16] These levels may be envisioned as layers. The deeper one gets, the more difficult it is to discover the culture.

The first level concerns *observable culture,* or "the way we do things around here." These are the methods the group has developed and teaches to new members. The observable culture includes the unique stories, ceremonies, and corporate rituals that make up the history of a successful workgroup.

The second level of analysis recognizes that *shared values* can play a critical part in linking people together and can provide a powerful motivational mechanism for members of the culture. Many consultants suggest that organizations should develop a "dominant and coherent set of shared values."[17] The term *shared* in cultural analysis implies that the group is a whole. Every member may not agree with the shared values, but they have all been exposed to them and have often been told they are important. At Hewlett-Packard, for example, "quality" is part of everyone's vocabulary. The firm was founded on the belief that everyone could make a creative contribution to developing quality products.

At the deepest level of cultural analysis are common assumptions, or the taken-for-granted truths that collections of corporate members share as a result of their joint experience. It is often extremely difficult to isolate these patterns, but doing so helps explain why culture invades every aspect of organizational life.

OBSERVABLE ASPECTS OF ORGANIZATIONAL CULTURE

Important parts of an organization's culture emerge from the collective experience of its members. These emergent aspects of the culture help make it unique and may well provide a competitive advantage for the organization. Some of these aspects may be directly observed in day-to-day practices. Others may have to be discovered—for example, by asking members to tell stories of important incidents in the history of the organization. We often learn about the unique aspects of the organizational culture through descriptions of specific events.[18] By observing employee actions, listening to stories, and asking members to interpret what is going on, one can begin to understand the organization's culture.

STORIES, RITES, RITUALS, AND SYMBOLS

Organizations are rich with stories of winners and losers, successes and failures. Perhaps one of the most important stories concerns the founding of the organization. The founding story often contains the lessons learned from the heroic efforts of an embattled entrepreneur, whose vision may still guide the firm. The story of the founding may be so embellished that it becomes a **saga**—a heroic account of accomplishments.[19] Sagas are important because they are used to tell new members the real mission of the organization, how the organization operates, and how individuals can fit into the company. Rarely is the founding story totally accurate, and it often glosses over some of the more negative aspects of the founders.

If you have job experience, you may well have heard stories concerning the following questions: How will the boss react to a mistake? Can someone move from the bottom to the top of the company? What will get me fired? These are common story topics in many organizations.[20] Often, the stories provide valuable hidden information about who is more equal than others, whether jobs are secure, and how things are really controlled. In essence, the stories begin to suggest how organizational members view the world and live together. Some of the most obvious aspects of organizational culture are rites and rituals. **Rites** are standardized and recurring activities that are used at special times to influence the behaviors and understanding of organizational members; **rituals** are systems of rites. It is common, for example, for Japanese workers and managers to start their workdays together with group exercises and singing of the "company song." Separately, the exercises and song are rites. Together, they form part of a ritual. In other settings, such as the Mary Kay Cosmetics company, scheduled ceremonies reminiscent of the Miss America pageant (a ritual) are used regularly to spotlight positive work achievements and reinforce high performance expectations with awards, including gold and diamond pins and fur stoles.

Rituals and rites may be unique to particular groups within the organization. Subcultures often arise from the type of technology deployed by the unit, the specific function being performed, and the specific collection of specialists in the unit. The boundaries of the subculture may well be maintained by a unique language. Often, the language of a subculture, and its rituals and rites, emerge from the group as a form of jargon. In some cases, the special language starts to move outside the firm and begins to enter the larger society. For instance, an ad for a Hewlett-Packard hand-held computer read: "All the features you need are built right in, MS-DOS, Lotus 1-2-3…and a 512 K RAM version of the HP 95LX." Not everyone found this a user-friendly ad, but it did appeal to knowledgeable individuals.[21]

Another observable aspect of corporate culture centers on the symbols found in organizations. A **cultural symbol** is any object, act, or event that serves to transmit cultural meaning. Good examples are the corporate uniforms worn by UPS and Federal Express delivery personnel. Although many such symbols are quite visible, their importance and meaning may not be.

CULTURAL RULES AND ROLES

Organizational culture often specifies when various types of actions are appropriate and where individual members stand in the social system. These cultural rules and roles are part of the normative controls of the organization and emerge from its daily routines.[22] For instance, the timing, presentation, and methods of communicating authoritative directives are often quite specific to each organization. In one firm, meetings may be forums for dialogue and discussion, where managers set agendas and then let others offer new ideas, critically examine alternatives, and fully participate. In another firm, the "rules" may be quite different: the manager goes into the meeting with fixed expectations. Any new ideas, critical examinations, and the like are expected to be worked out in private before the meeting takes place. The meeting is a forum for letting others know what is being done and for passing out orders on what to do in the future.

THE EVOLUTION OF SHARED MEANINGS FROM OBSERVABLE CULTURE

What you see as an outside observer may not be what organizational members see. You may see a crane operator moving wreckage from an 18-acre pile of rubble into a waiting truck. Further up the worksite one sees steel workers cutting beams while police seem to stand around talking to a few firemen. If you ask what these individuals are doing, however, you get a whole different picture. They are not just hauling away the remnants of the twin towers at the World Trade Center complex. They are rebuilding America. These workers have infused a larger shared meaning—or sense of broader purpose—into their tasks. Through interaction with one another, and as reinforced by the rest of their organizations and the larger society, their work has deeper meaning. In this deeper sense, organizational culture is a "shared" set of meanings and perceptions. In most corporations these shared meanings and perceptions may not be as dramatic as those shared at Ground Zero, yet in most firms employees create and learn a deeper aspect of their culture.[23]

VALUES AND ORGANIZATIONAL CULTURE

To describe more fully the culture of an organization, it is necessary to go deeper than the observable aspects. To many researchers and managers, shared common values lie at the very heart of organizational culture. Shared values help turn routine activities into valuable, important actions, tie the corporation to the important values of society, and may provide a very distinctive source of competitive advantage. In organizations, what works for one person is often taught to new members as the correct way to think and feel. Important values are then attributed to these solutions to everyday problems. By linking values and actions, the organization taps into some of the strongest and deepest realms of the individual. The tasks a person performs are given not only meaning but value: what one does is not only workable but correct, right, and important.

Some successful organizations share some common cultural characteristics.[24] Organizations with "strong cultures" possess a broadly and deeply shared value system. Unique, shared values can provide a strong corporate identity, enhance collective commitment, provide a stable social system, and reduce the need for formal and bureaucratic controls. A strong culture can be a double-edged sword, however. A strong culture and value system can reinforce a singular view of the organization and its environment. If dramatic changes are needed, it may be very difficult to change the organization. General Motors may have a "strong" culture, for example, but the firm faces enormous difficulty in its attempts to adapt its ways to a dynamic and highly competitive environment.

In many corporate cultures, one finds a series of common assumptions known to most everyone in the corporation: "We are different." "We are better at...." "We have unrecognized talents." Cisco Systems provides an excellent example. Senior managers often share common assumptions, such as, "We are good stewards." "We are competent managers." "We are practical innovators." Like values, such assumptions become reflected in the organizational culture.

The Effective Manager 13.1 discusses assumptions and other elements of a strong organizational culture.

ORGANIZATIONAL MYTHS

In many firms, the management philosophy is supported by a series of organizational myths. **Organizational myths** are unproven and often unstated beliefs that are accepted uncritically. In a study of safety in nuclear power plants, senior managers were asked whether they felt there was a tradeoff between safeness and efficiency. The response was clear: a safe plant is an efficient plant. Yet, most of these executives had seen data showing that measures of safeness and efficiency were quite independent. To admit there was a tradeoff raised the issue of making choices between efficiency and safety. All wanted to believe that to do one was to promote the other.[25]

THE EFFECTIVE MANAGER 13.1

ELEMENTS OF STRONG CORPORATE CULTURES

- A widely shared real understanding of what the firm stands for, often embodied in slogans
- A concern for individuals over rules, policies, procedures, and adherence to job duties
- A recognition of heroes whose actions illustrate the company's shared philosophy and concerns
- A belief in ritual and ceremony as important to members and to building a common identity
- A well-understood sense of the informal rules and expectations so that employees and managers understand what is expected of them
- A belief that what employees and managers do is important and that it is important to share information and ideas

---

Whereas some may scoff at these organizational myths and want to see rational, hard-nosed analysis replace mythology, each firm needs a series of managerial myths.[26] Myths allow executives to redefine impossible problems into more manageable components. Myths can facilitate experimentation and creativity, and they allow managers to govern. For instance, senior executives are not just decision makers or rational allocators of resources. All organization members hope these individuals will also be fair, just, and compassionate.

NATIONAL CULTURE INFLUENCES

Widely held common assumptions may often be traced to the larger culture of the corporation's host society.[27] The difference between Sony's corporate emphasis on group achievements and Zenith's emphasis on individual engineering excellence, for example, can be traced to the Japanese emphasis on collective action versus the U.S. emphasis on individualism.

National cultural values may also become embedded in the expectations of important organizational constituencies and in generally accepted solutions to problems. When moving across national cultures, managers need to be sensitive to national cultural differences so that their actions do not violate common assumptions in the underlying national culture. In Japan and Western Europe, for example, executives are expected to work cooperatively with government officials on an informal basis. Informal business-government relations that are perfectly acceptable in these countries are considered influence peddling in the United States.

Inappropriate actions that violate common assumptions drawn from national culture can have an important impact on performance and may alienate organizational members, even if managers have the best intentions. To improve morale at General Electric's new French subsidiary, Chi. Generale de Radiologie, American managers invited all the European managers to a "get acquainted" meeting near Paris. The Americans gave out colorful T-shirts with the GE slogan, "Go for One," a typical maneuver in many American training programs. The French resented the T-shirts. One outspoken individual said, "It was like Hitler was back, forcing us to wear uniforms. It was humiliating."

MANAGING ORGANIZATIONAL CULTURE

The culture should be considered as critical as structure and strategy in establishing the organizational foundations of high performance. Good managers are able to reinforce and support an existing strong culture; good managers are also able to help build resilient cultures in situations where they are absent. For instance, CEO Mike Walsh of Union Pacific has brought a new and fresh approach to the firm with what *Fortune* magazine called an "introverted corporate culture." Cultural changes under Walsh's leadership included the empowerment of managers at all levels. A typical response: "We were so elated the company was willing to give new authority that we wanted it to work."

MANAGEMENT PHILOSOPHY AND STRATEGY

Perhaps the first step in managing an organizational culture is for management to recognize its own subculture. This is often referred to in the OB literature under the term management philosophy. A **management philosophy** links key goal-related strategic issues with key collaboration issues and comes up with a series of general ways by which the firm will manage its affairs.[28] A well-developed management philosophy is important because it links strategy to a more basic understanding of how the firm is to operate. Specifically, it (1) establishes generally understood boundaries for all members of the firm; (2) provides a consistent way of approaching new and novel situations; and (3) helps hold individuals together by assuring them of a known path toward success. Cisco systems has a clearly identified management philosophy linking the strategic concerns of growth, profitability, and customer service with observable aspects of culture and selected desired underlying values. For instance, Sue Bostrom heads Cisco's Internet Business Solutions Group. She emphasizes the link between strategy and culture in three important elements of Cisco's management philosophy. These three aspects emphasize: (1) empowering employees to generate the best ideas quickly and to implement them successfully, (2) hiring the best people because it's the ideas and intellectual assets of these colleagues that drive success, and (3) developing and disseminating information to compete in the world of ideas. While elements of a management philosophy may be formally documented in a corporate plan or statement of business philosophy, it is the well-understood fundamentals these written documents signify that form the heart of a well-developed management philosophy. In the case of Sue Bostrom, her unit in Cisco is not waiting on the competition, building bricks-and-mortar monuments, or developing elaborate bureaucratic procedures. Her unit's philosophy is clear, and it forms a basis for managing the shared actions and values that emerge in her group.

Two broad strategies for managing the corporate culture have received considerable attention in the OB literature. One strategy calls for managers to help modify observable culture, shared values, and common assumptions directly. A second strategy involves the use of organizational development techniques to modify specific elements of the culture.

BUILDING, REINFORCING, AND CHANGING CULTURE

Managers can modify the visible aspects of culture, such as the language, stories, rites, rituals, and sagas. They can change the lessons to be drawn from common stories and even encourage individuals to see the reality they see. Because of their positions, senior managers can interpret situations in new ways and can adjust the meanings attached to important corporate events. They can create new rites and rituals. This takes time and enormous energy, but the long-run benefits can also be great.

Top managers, in particular, can set the tone for a culture and for cultural change. Managers at Aetna Life and Casualty Insurance built on its humanistic traditions to provide basic skills to highly motivated but underqualified individuals. Even in the highly cost-competitive steel industry, Chairperson F. Kenneth Iverson of Nucor built on basic entrepreneurial values in U.S. society to reduce the number of management levels by half. And at Procter & Gamble, Richard Nicolosi evoked the shared values for greater participation in decision making dramatically to improve creativity and innovation.

Each of these examples illustrates how managers can help foster a culture that provides answers to important questions concerning external adaptation and internal integration. Recent work on the linkages among corporate culture and financial performance reaffirms the importance of an emphasis on helping employees adjust to the environment. It also suggests that this emphasis alone is not sufficient. Neither is an emphasis solely on stockholders or customers associated with long-term economic performance. Instead, managers must work to emphasize all three issues simultaneously. This emphasis on customers, stockholders, and employees comes at a cost of emphasizing management. Large offices, multimillion-dollar salaries, golden parachutes (protections for executives if the firm is bought by others), as well as the executive plane, dining room, and country club are out.

Early research on culture and culture change often emphasized direct attempts to alter the values and assumptions of individuals by resocializing them—that is, trying to change their hearts so that their minds and actions would follow.[29] The goal was to establish a clear, consistent organizationwide consensus. More recent work suggests that this unified approach of working through values may not be either possible or desirable.

Trying to change people's values from the top down without also changing how the organization operates and recognizing the importance of individuals does not work very well. Take another look at the example of Cisco Systems. Here managers realize that keeping a dynamic, change-oriented culture is a mix of managerial actions, decisions about technology, and initiatives from all employees. The values are not set and imposed from someone on high. The shared values emerge, and they are not identical across all of Cisco's operating sites. For instance, subtle but important differences emerge across their operations in Silicon Valley, the North Carolina operation, and the Australian setting.

It is also a mistake for managers to attempt to revitalize an organization by dictating major changes and ignoring shared values. Although things may change a bit on the surface, a deeper look often shows whole departments resisting change and many key people unwilling to learn new ways. Such responses may indicate that the managers responsible are insensitive to the effects of their proposed changes on shared values. They fail to ask whether the changes are contrary to the important values of participants within the firm, a challenge to historically important corporatewide assumptions, and inconsistent with important common assumptions derived from the national culture, outside the firm. Note the example of Stephen Jobs at Apple earlier in this chapter. He did not make all the changes. Rather, he worked with others to make changes in strategy, structure, products, and marketing and to build on deep-seated common assumptions that long-term employees shared. The Effective Manager 13.2 provides some key characteristics managers should foster in Internet companies.

CONTINUOUS CULTURAL DEVELOPMENT

To keep the culture fresh and competitive, the challenge today is to engage in a process of continuous self-assessment and planned change in order to stay abreast of problems and opportunities in a complex and demanding environment. **Organizational development (OD)** is a

THE EFFECTIVE MANAGER 13.2

FOSTERING AN EFFECTIVE INTERNET CULTURE

To cope with the constant rapid changes in e-business, some recommend developing an Internet culture. Key distinguishing characteristics of such a culture include:

- Embracing open communication in all forms and in all possible media
- Emphasizing constant learning and individual development
- Stressing leadership that reinforces courage and risk-taking

---

comprehensive approach to planned change that is designed to improve the overall effectiveness of organizations. Formally defined, OD is the application of behavioral science knowledge in a long-range effort to improve an organization's ability to cope with change in its external environment and to increase its internal problem-solving capabilities.[30]

Organizational development is used to improve performance in organizations of many types, sizes, and settings. It includes a set of tools with which any manager who is concerned about achieving and maintaining high levels of productivity will want to be familiar. Because of its comprehensive nature and scientific foundations, OD was frequently implemented with the aid of an external consultant. As OD techniques have been combined with a better understanding of organizational culture, its basic concepts can and should be used routinely by all managers.

ORGANIZATIONAL DEVELOPMENT PROCESSES AND APPLICATIONS

Organizational development provides a set of well-proven methods for developing and changing what cultural analyses call *external adaptation* and *internal integration*. Importantly, OD seeks to achieve change in such a way that the organization's members become more active and confident in taking similar steps to maintain the culture and longer-run organizational effectiveness. A large part of any OD program's success in this regard rests with its assumptions, values, and action research foundations.

UNDERLYING ASSUMPTIONS OF OD

The organizational development foundations for achieving change are rooted in underlying assumptions about individuals, groups, and organizations. At the individual level, OD is guided by principles that reflect an underlying respect for people and their capabilities. It assumes that individual needs for growth and development are most likely to be satisfied in a supportive and challenging work environment. It also assumes that most people are capable of taking responsibility for their own actions and of making positive contributions to organizational performance.

At the *group level*, OD is guided by principles that reflect a belief that groups can be good for both people and organizations. It assumes that groups help their members satisfy important individual needs and can also be helpful in supporting organizational objectives. And it assumes that effective groups can be created by people working in collaboration to meet individual and organizational needs.

At the *organizational level,* OD is guided by principles that show a respect for the complexity of an organization as a system of interdependent parts. It assumes that changes in one part of the organization will affect other parts as well. And it assumes that organizational structures and jobs can be designed to meet the needs of individuals and groups as well as those of the organization.

SHARED VALUES AND PRINCIPLES UNDERLYING OD

Organizational development offers a systematic approach to planned change in organizations which addresses two main goals: outcome goals (mainly issues of external adaptation) and process goals (mainly issues of internal integration). Outcome goals include achieving improvements in task performance by improving external adaptation capabilities. In OD, these goals focus on what is actually accomplished through individual and group efforts. Process goals include achieving improvements in such things as communication, interaction, and decision making among an organization's members. These goals focus on how well people work together, and they stress improving internal integration.

In pursuit of these goals, OD is intended to help organizations and their members by (1) creating an open problem-solving climate throughout an organization, (2) supplementing formal authority with that of knowledge and competence, (3) moving decision making to points where relevant information is available, (4) building trust and maximizing collaboration among individuals and groups, (5) increasing the sense of organizational "ownership" among members, and (6) allowing people to exercise self-direction and self-control at work.[31] Thus, using OD implicitly involves these values. That is, organization development is designed to improve the contributions of individual members in achieving the organizational goals, and it seeks to do so in ways that respect the organization's members as mature adults who need and deserve high-quality experiences in their working lives.

ACTION RESEARCH FOUNDATIONS OF OD

Organizational development practitioners refer to **action research** as the process of systematically collecting data on an organization, feeding it back to the members for action planning, and evaluating results by collecting and reflecting on more data after the planned actions have been taken. This is a data-based and collaborative approach to problem solving and organizational assessment. When used in the OD process, action research helps identify action directions that may enhance an organization's effectiveness. In a typical action-research sequence depicted in Figure 13.1, the sequence is initiated when someone senses a performance gap and decides to analyze the situation systematically for the problems and opportunities it represents. The process continues through the following steps: data gathering, data feedback, data analysis, and action planning. It continues to the point at which action is taken and results are evaluated. The evaluation or reassessment stage may or may not generate another performance gap. If it does, the action-research cycle begins anew.

Figure 13.2 identifies one set of frameworks that can assist OD practitioners in accomplishing the required diagnoses. These foundations apply the open systems framework and OB concepts with which you are already familiar from earlier parts of this book. At the organizational level, the figure indicates that effectiveness must be understood with respect to forces in the external environment and major organizational aspects, such as strategy, technology, structure, culture, and management systems. At the group level,

FIGURE 13.1 | **AN ACTION-RESEARCH MODEL FOR ORGANIZATIONAL DEVELOPMENT**

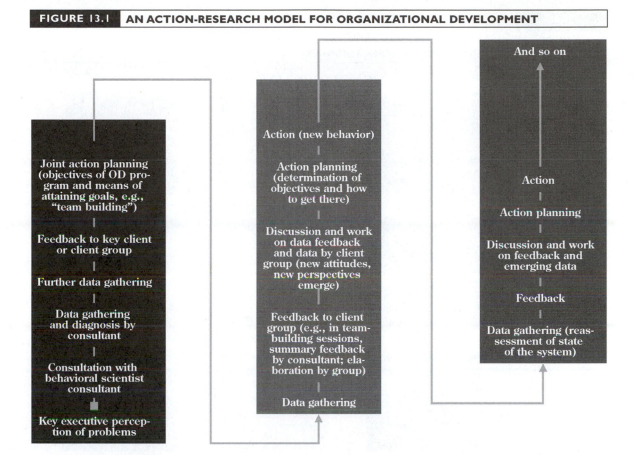

effectiveness is viewed in a context of forces in the internal environment of the organization and major group aspects, such as tasks, membership, norms, cohesiveness, and group processes. At the individual level, effectiveness is considered in relationship to the internal environment of the workgroup and individual aspects, such as tasks, goals, needs, and interpersonal relationships.

ORGANIZATIONAL DEVELOPMENT INTERVENTIONS

The action research process should engage members of an organization in activities designed to accomplish the required diagnoses and to develop and implement plans for constructive change. Action research, data collection, and the diagnostic foundations should come together through the choice and use of OD "interventions." **Organizational development interventions** are activities initiated by the consultant to facilitate planned change and to assist the client system in developing its own problem-solving capabilities. With less formality, many of these techniques are also now being used by managers to help understand and improve their own operations. Major OD interventions can be categorized with respect to their major impact at the organizational, group, and individual levels of action.[32]

FIGURE 13.2	DIAGNOSTIC FOUNDATIONS OF ORGANIZATIONAL DEVELOPMENT AND OD TECHNIQUES: CONCERNS FOR INDIVIDUAL, GROUP, AND ORGANIZATIONAL EFFECTIVENESS

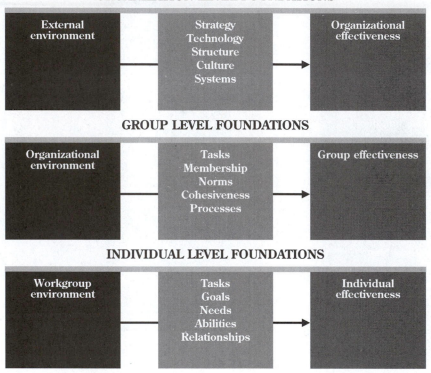

ORGANIZATION LEVEL FOUNDATIONS

GROUP LEVEL FOUNDATIONS

INDIVIDUAL LEVEL FOUNDATIONS

Organizationwide Interventions   An effective organization is one that achieves its major performance objectives while maintaining a high quality of work life for its members. OD interventions designed for systemwide application include the following.

Survey feedback begins with the collection of data via questionnaire responses from organization members, or a representative sample of such responses. The data are then presented, or fed back, to the members. They subsequently engage in a collaborative process to interpret the data and to develop action plans in response.

Confrontation meetings are designed to help determine quickly how an organization may be improved and to take initial actions to better the situation.[33] The intervention involves a one-day meeting conducted by an OD facilitator for a representative sample of organizational members, including top management. In a structured format, the consultant asks participants to make individual lists of what they feel can be done to improve things. Then, through a series of small-group work sessions and sharing of results, these ideas are refined into a tentative set of actions that top management then endorses for immediate implementation. The major trick here is to get senior managers to propose changing their part of the firm. Confrontation meetings fail if all the proposed changes call for adjustments by subordinates without any alterations by the top managers.

Structural redesign involves realigning the structure of the organization or major sub-systems to improve performance. It includes examining the best fit between structure, technology, and environment. In today's highly dynamic environments, in light of the increasing involvement of organizations in international operations and with rapid changes in information technology, a structure can easily grow out of date. Thus, structural redesign is an important OD intervention that can be used to help maintain the best fit between organizational structures and situational demands.

Collateral organization is designed to make creative problem solving possible by pulling a representative set of members out of the formal organization structure to engage in periodic small-group problem-solving sessions.[34] These collateral, or "parallel," structures are temporary and exist only to supplement the activities of the formal structure.

Group and Intergroup Interventions   OD interventions at the group level are designed to improve group effectiveness. The major interventions at this level are team building, process consultation, and intergroup team building.

Team building involves a manager or consultant engaging the members of a group in a series of activities designed to help them examine how the group functions and how it may function better. Like survey feedback at the organizational level, team building involves some form of data collection and feedback. The key elements, however, are a collaborative assessment of the data by all members of the group and the achievement of consensus regarding what may be done to improve group effectiveness. Team building is often done at "retreats" or off-site meetings, where group members spend two to three days working intensely together on this reflection-analysis-planning process.

Process consultation involves structured activities that are facilitated by an OD practitioner and is designed to improve group functioning. Process consultation has a more specific focus than does team building, however: its attention is directed toward the key "processes" through which members of a group work with one another. The process consultant is concerned with helping a group function better on such things as norms, cohesiveness, decision-making methods, communication, conflict, and task and maintenance activities.

Intergroup team building is a special form of team building. It is designed to help two or more groups improve their working relationships with one another and, it is hoped, to experience improved group effectiveness as a result. Here, the OD practitioner engages the groups or their representatives in activities that increase awareness of how each group perceives the other. Given this understanding, collaborative problem solving can improve coordination between the groups and encourage more mutual support of one another as important components in the total organization.

Individual Interventions   Task performance and job satisfaction are important concerns with respect to improving individual effectiveness in the workplace. OD interventions at this level of attention range from those that address personal issues to those that deal more with specific job and career considerations. Individual-level OD interventions include the following.

Role negotiation is a means of clarifying what individuals expect to give and receive of one another in their working relationship. Because roles and personnel change over time, role negotiation can be an important way to maintain task understandings among individuals in an organization. This kind of understanding is quite easily accomplished by helping people who work together clarify what they need from one another to do their jobs well.

Job redesign is the process of creating long-term congruence between individual goals and organizational career opportunities. A good example is the Hackman and Oldham diagnostic approach to job enrichment discussed in Chapter 8.[35] Recall that this approach involves (1) analyzing the core characteristics of a job or group of jobs, (2) analyzing the needs and capabilities of workers in those jobs, and (3) taking action to adjust the core job characteristics either to enrich or to simplify the jobs to best match individual preferences.

Career planning takes the form of structured opportunities for individuals to work with their managers or staff experts from the personnel or human resources department on career issues. They may map career goals, assess personal development needs, and actively plan short-term and long-term career moves. Increasingly, career planning is becoming a major part of the support that highly progressive organizations provide for their members.

OD and the Continuous Evolution   Today, a new wave of successful high-tech firms exemplifies the use of organizational development assumptions, values, and techniques without using the term OD. It is not that such firms as Herman Miller or Starbucks are trying to force change on their employees. Rather, the managers in these systems take a very practical approach to managing culture. They realize that both external adaptation and internal integration are important for a variety of subcultures within their firms. They use OD intervention techniques to improve both. They do not dictate values or set common assumptions in isolation but with their fellow employees. They are working with others to help nurture and guide the continual evolution of organizational culture from day to day.

CHAPTER 13 SUMMARY

What is organizational culture?

- Organizational or corporate culture is the system of shared actions, values, and beliefs that develops within an organization and guides the behavior of its members.
- Corporate culture can assist in responding to both external adaptation and internal integration issues.
- Most organizations contain a variety of subcultures, and a few have countercultures that can become the source of potentially harmful conflicts.
- Organizational cultures may be analyzed in terms of observable actions, shared values, and common assumptions (the taken-for-granted truths).

What are the observable aspects of organizational culture?

- Observable aspects of culture include the stories, rites, rituals, and symbols that are shared by organization members.

- Cultural rules and roles specify when various types of actions are appropriate and where individual members stand in the social system.

- Shared meanings and understandings help everyone know how to act and expect others to act in various circumstances.

How do values and assumptions influence organizational cultures?

- Common assumptions are the taken-for-granted truths that are shared by collections of corporate members.

- Some organizations express these truths in a management philosophy that links key goal-related issues with key collaboration issues into a series of general ways in which the firm will manage its affairs.

How can the organizational culture be "managed," "nurtured," and "guided"?

- The management philosophy is supported by a series of corporate myths.

- Executives may manage many aspects of the observable culture directly.

- Nurturing shared values among the membership is a major challenge for executives.

- Adjusting actions to common understandings limits the decision scope of even the CEO.

How can the process of organizational development enhance organizational culture?

- All managers may use organizational development (OD) techniques in their attempts to manage, nurture, and guide cultural change.

- OD is a special application of knowledge gained from behavioral science to create a comprehensive effort to improve organizational effectiveness.

- OD has both outcome goals, with respect to improved task accomplishments, and process goals, with respect to improvements in the way organization members work together.

- With a strong commitment to collaborative efforts and human values, OD utilizes basic behavioral science principles with respect to individuals, groups, and organizations.

- Organizationwide interventions include survey feedback, confrontation meetings, structural redesign, and collateral organization.

- Group and intergroup interventions include team building, process consultation, and intergroup team building.

- Individual interventions include sensitivity training, role negotiation, job redesign, and career planning.

High Performance Leadership

Study Questions

As you read Chapter 14, keep in mind these key questions.

- What is leadership, and how does it differ from management?
- What are the trait or behavioral leadership perspectives?
- What are the situational or contingency leadership approaches?
- How does attribution theory relate to leadership?
- What are the new leadership perspectives and why are they especially important in high performance organizations?

For many, the essence of leadership is the vision to seize the day and make a difference. Although most people probably agree that leadership makes a difference, some argue that it isn't important. For them, leaders are so bound by constraints that they just don't have much impact. Some also see leadership as so mystical that they can't define it but know it when they see it. In this chapter, we address these views and more in examining how leadership fits in organizations in general, and especially high performance organizations.

LEADERSHIP AND MANAGEMENT

In the chapters in Part 1, we talked about managers and management functions, roles, activities, and skills. The question to ask now is how are leaders and leadership linked to all this?

Currently, controversy has arisen over whether leaders are different from managers or whether management is different from leadership and, if so, how. One way of making these differentiations is to argue that the role of *management* is to promote stability or to enable the organization to run smoothly, whereas the role of *leadership* is to promote adaptive or useful changes.[1] Persons in managerial positions could be involved with both management and leadership activities, or they could emphasize one activity at the expense of the other. Both management and leadership are needed, however, and if managers don't assume responsibility for both, then they should ensure that someone else handles the neglected activity.

For our purpose, we treat **leadership** as a special case of interpersonal influence that gets an individual or group to do what the leader or manager wants done. The broader influence notions, of which leadership is a part, are dealt with in Chapter 15. Leadership appears in two forms: (1) *formal leadership,* which is exerted by persons appointed to or elected to positions of formal authority in organizations; and (2) *informal leadership,* which is exerted by persons who become influential because they have special skills that meet the resource needs of others. Although both types are important in organizations, this chapter will emphasize formal leadership.

The leadership literature is vast—10,000 or so studies at last count—and consists of numerous approaches.[2] We have grouped these into: trait and behavioral theory perspectives; situational or contingency perspectives; attributional leadership perspectives; and "new leadership" perspectives—including charismatic approaches, transformational approaches, and leadership of self-directing work teams. These new leadership theories are especially important for high performance organizations. Within each of these perspectives are several models. While each of these models may be useful to you in a given work setting, we invite you to mix and match them as necessary in your setting, just as we earlier did with the motivational models in Chapter 6. This is a trial-and-error process but it is a good way to bring together the contributions from each model in a combination that meets your needs as a manager.

TRAIT AND BEHAVIORAL THEORIES PERSPECTIVES

TRAIT THEORIES

Trait perspectives assume that traits play a central role in differentiating between leaders and nonleaders (leaders must have the "right stuff")[3] or in predicting leader or organizational outcomes. The *great person–trait approach* reflects this leader and nonleader difference and is the earliest approach in studying leadership, having been introduced more than a century ago. What traits differentiated "great persons" from the masses? (For example, How did Catherine the Great differ from her subjects?)[4] Later studies examined both leader/nonleader differences and trait predictions of outcomes. For various reasons, including inadequate theorizing and trait measurement, the studies were not successful enough to provide consistent findings.

More recent work has yielded more promising results. A number of traits have been identified that help identify important leadership strengths (see Figure 14.1). As it turns out, most of these traits also tend to predict leadership outcomes.[5]

Leaders tend to be energetic and to operate on an even keel. They crave power not as an end in itself but as a means to achieving a vision or desired goals. Leaders also are very ambitious and have a high need for achievement. At the same time, they have to be emotionally mature enough to recognize their own strengths and weaknesses, and they are oriented toward self-improvement. Furthermore, to be trusted they must have integrity; without trust, they cannot hope to maintain the loyalty of their followers. Leaders also must not be easily discouraged. They need to stick to a chosen course of action and to push toward goal accomplishment. At the same time, they must be cognitively sharp enough to deal well with the large amount of information they receive. However, they do not need to be brilliant; they just need to show above-average intelligence. In addition, leaders must have a good understanding of their social setting. Finally, they must possess lots of specific knowledge concerning their industry, firm, and job.

BEHAVIORAL THEORIES

Like the trait perspective covered above, the **behavioral perspective** assumes that leadership is central to performance and other outcomes. In this case, however, instead of dealing with underlying traits, behaviors are considered. Two classic research programs—at the University of Michigan and Ohio State University—provide useful insights into leadership behaviors.

FIGURE 14.1   TRAITS WITH POSITIVE IMPLICATIONS FOR SUCCESSFUL LEADERSHIP

Energy and adjustment or stress tolerance: Physical vitality and emotional resilience.

Prosocial power motivation: A high need for power exercised primarily for the benefit of others.

Achievement orientation: Need for achievement, desire to excel, drive to success, willingness to assume responsibility, concern for task objectives.

Emotional maturity: Well adjusted, does not suffer from severe psychological disorders.

Self-confidence: General confidence in self and in the ability to perform the job of a leader.

Integrity: Behavior consistent with espoused values; honest, ethical, trustworthy.

Perseverance or tenacity: Ability to overcome obstacles; strength of will.

Cognitive ability, intelligence, social intelligence: Ability to gather, integrate, and interpret information; intelligence; understanding of social setting.

Task-relevant knowledge: Knowledge about the company, industry, and technical aspects.

Flexibility: Ability to respond appropriately to changes in the setting.

Michigan Studies   In the late 1940s, researchers at the University of Michigan introduced a research program on leadership behavior. They sought to identify the leadership pattern that results in effective performance. From interviews of high- and low-performing groups in different organizations, the researchers derived two basic forms of leader behaviors: employee centered and production centered. Employee-centered supervisors are those who place strong emphasis on their subordinates' welfare. In contrast, production-centered supervisors are more concerned with getting the work done. In general, employee-centered supervisors were found to have more productive workgroups than did the production-centered supervisors.[6]

These behaviors may be viewed on a continuum, with employee-centered supervisors at one end and production-centered supervisors at the other. Sometimes, the more general terms *human relations oriented* and *task oriented* are used to describe these alternative leader behaviors.

Ohio State Studies   At about the same time as the Michigan studies, an important leadership research program was started at Ohio State University. A questionnaire was administered in both industrial and military settings to measure subordinates' perceptions of their superiors' leadership behavior. The researchers identified two dimensions similar to those found in the Michigan studies: **consideration** and **initiating structure**.[7] A highly considerate leader is sensitive to people's feelings and, much like the employee-centered leader, tries to make things pleasant for his or her followers. In contrast, a leader high in initiating structure is more concerned with defining task requirements and other aspects of the work agenda; he or she might be seen as similar to a production-centered supervisor. These dimensions are related to what people sometimes refer to as socioemotional and task leadership, respectively.

At first, the Ohio State researchers believed that a leader high on consideration, or socioemotional warmth, would have more highly satisfied or better performing subordinates. Later results indicated that leaders should be high on both consideration and initiating structure behaviors, however. This dual emphasis is reflected in the leadership grid approach.

The Leadership Grid   Robert Blake and Jane Mouton have developed the Leadership Grid approach, based on extensions of the Ohio State dimensions. Results are plotted on a nine-position grid that places concern for production on the horizontal axis and concern for people on the vertical axis, where 1 is minimum concern and 9 is maximum concern. As an example, those with a 1/9 concern for production/concern for people are termed "country club management." They do not emphasize task accomplishment and stress the attitudes, feelings, and social needs of people.

Similarly, leaders with a 1/1, style, low concern for both production and people, are termed "impoverished," while a 5/5 style is labeled "middle of the road." A 9/1 leader, high on task and low on people, has a "task management" style. Finally, a 9/9 leader, high on both dimensions, is considered to have a "team management" style, ideal in Blake and Mouton's framework.

Graen's Leader–Member Exchange Theory   Another perspective that emphasizes the centrality of leadership on outcomes is Graen's Leader–Member Exchange (LMX) approach. However, in contrast to the perspectives just described, which emphasize the influence of the leader's behavior on follower outcomes, LMX theory focuses on the quality of the working relationship between leaders and followers. The LMX 7 scale assesses the degree to which leaders and followers have mutual respect for each other's capabilities, feel a deepening sense of mutual trust, and have a strong sense of obligation to one another. Taken together, these dimensions determine the extent to which followers will be part of the leader's "in group" or "out group."[8]

In-group followers tend to function as assistants, lieutenants, or advisers and to have higher-quality personalized exchanges with the leader than do out-group followers. The out-group followers tend to emphasize more formalized job requirements, and a relatively low level of mutual influence exists between leaders and out-group followers. The more personalized in-group exchanges typically involve a leader's emphasis on assignments to interesting tasks, delegation of important responsibilities, information sharing, and participation in the leader's decisions, as well as special benefits, such as personal support and approval and favorable work schedules.

Research suggests that high-quality LMX is associated with increased follower satisfaction and productivity, decreased turnover, increased salaries, and faster promotion rates. These findings are encouraging, and the approach continues to receive increasing emphasis in the literature. Of course, many questions remain, such as: What happens in the event of too much disparity in the treatment of in-group and out-group members? Will out-group members become resentful and sabotage team efforts? In addition, more needs to be learned about how the in-group/out-group exchange starts in the first place and how these relations change over time.[9]

Cross-Cultural Implications   It is important to consider how well the kinds of behavioral dimensions discussed earlier transfer internationally. Some work in the United States, Britain, Hong Kong, and Japan shows that the behaviors must be carried out in different ways in alternative cultures. For instance, British leaders are seen as considerate if they show subordinates how to use equipment, whereas in Japan the highly considerate leader helps subordinates with personal problems.[10] Similarly, LMX theory has been shown to operate in Japan.[11]

SITUATIONAL CONTINGENCY THEORIES

The trait and behavioral perspectives assume that leadership, by itself, would have a strong impact on outcomes. Another development in leadership thinking recognized, however, that leader traits and behaviors can act in conjunction with *situational contingencies*—other important aspects of the leadership situation—to predict outcomes.

House and Aditya argue that the effects of traits are enhanced by their relevance to the leader's situational contingencies.[12] For example, achievement motivation should be most effective for challenging tasks that require initiative and require assumption of personal responsibility for success. Leader flexibility should be most predictive in unstable environments or when leaders lead different people over time. Prosocial power motivation is likely to be most important in complex organizations where decision implementation requires lots of persuasion and social influence. "Strong" or "weak" situations also make a difference. An example of a strong situation is a highly formal organization with lots of rules, procedures, and so forth. Here, traits will have less impact than in a weaker, more unstructured situation (e.g., I can't show my dynamism as much when the organization restricts me). Traits sometimes have a direct relationship to outcomes or to leaders versus nonleaders. They may also make themselves felt by influencing leader behaviors (e.g., a leader high in energy engages in directive, take-charge behaviors).[13]

FIEDLER'S LEADERSHIP CONTINGENCY THEORY

Fred Fiedler's work began the situational contingency era in the mid-1960s.[14] His theory holds that group effectiveness depends on an appropriate match between a leader's style (essentially a trait measure) and the demands of the situation. Specifically, Fiedler considers **situational control**—the extent to which a leader can determine what his or her group is going to do, as well as the outcomes of the group's actions and decisions.

Fiedler uses an instrument called the **least preferred co-worker (LPC)** scale to measure a person's leadership style. Respondents are asked to describe the person with whom they have been able to work least well—their least preferred co-worker, or LPC—using a series of adjectives such as the following two:

Unfriendly	__	__	__	__	__	__	__	__	Friendly
	1	2	3	4	5	6	7	8	
Pleasant	__	__	__	__	__	__	__	__	Unpleasant
	1	2	3	4	5	6	7	8	

Fiedler argues that high-LPC leaders (those describing their LPC very positively) have a relationship-motivated style, whereas low-LPC leaders have a task-motivated style. He considers this task or relationship motivation to be a trait that leads to either directive or nondirective behavior, depending on the amount of situational control that the leader has. Here, a task-motivated leader tends to be nondirective in high- and low-control situations and directive in those in between. A relationship-motivated leader tends to be the opposite.

Figure 14.2 shows the task-motivated leader as having greater group effectiveness under high and low situational control, and the relationship-motivated leader as having a more effective group under moderate situational control. The figure also shows that Fiedler measures the range of control with the following three variables arranged in the situational combinations indicated:

- *Leader-member relations* (good/poor)—membership support for the leader.
- *Task structure* (high/low)—spelling out the leader's task goals, procedures, and guidelines in the group.
- *Position power* (strong/weak)—the leader's task expertise and reward or punishment authority.

Consider an experienced and well-trained supervisor of a group manufacturing a part for a personal computer. The leader is highly supported by his group members and can grant raises and make hiring and firing decisions. This supervisor has very high situational control and is operating in situation 1 in Figure 14.2. Those leaders operating in situations 2 and 3 would have high situational control, though lower than our production supervisor. For these high-control situations, a task-oriented leader behaving directively would have the most effective group.

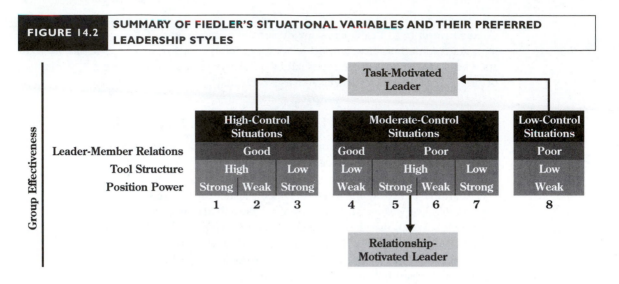

FIGURE 14.2 SUMMARY OF FIEDLER'S SITUATIONAL VARIABLES AND THEIR PREFERRED LEADERSHIP STYLES

Now consider the chair of a student council committee of volunteers (the chair's position power is weak) who are unhappy about this person being the chair and who have the low-structured task of organizing a Parents' Day program to improve university-parent relations. This low-control situation 8 calls for a task-motivated leader who needs to behave directively to keep the group together and focus on the ambiguous task; in fact, the situation demands it. Finally, consider a well-liked academic department chair with tenured faculty. This is a situation 4 moderate-control situation with good leader-member relations, low task structure, and weak position power, calling for a relationship-motivated leader. The leader should emphasize nondirective and considerate relationships with the faculty.

Fiedler's Cognitive Resource Theory   Fiedler recently moved beyond his contingency theory by developing the cognitive resource theory.[15] Cognitive resources are abilities or competencies. According to this approach, whether a leader should use directive or nondirective behavior depends on the following situational contingencies: (1) the leader's or subordinate group members' ability or competency, (2) stress, (3) experience, and (4) group support of the leader. Basically, cognitive resource theory is most useful because it directs us to leader or subordinate group-member ability, an aspect not typically considered in other leadership approaches.

The theory views directiveness as most helpful for performance when the leader is competent, relaxed, and supported. In this case, the group is ready, and directiveness is the clearest means of communication. When the leader feels stressed, he or she is diverted. In this case, experience is more important than ability. If support is low, then the group is less receptive, and the leader has less impact. Group-member ability becomes most important when the leader is nondirective and receives strong support from group members. If support is weak, then task difficulty or other factors have more impact than do either the leader or the subordinates.

Evaluation and Application   The roots of Fiedler's contingency approach date back to the 1960s and have elicited both positive and negative reactions. The biggest controversy concerns exactly what Fiedler's LPC instrument measures. Some question Fiedler's behavioral interpretation, whereby the specific behaviors of high- and low-LPC leaders change, depending on the amount of situational control. Furthermore, the approach makes the most accurate predictions in situations I and VIII and IV and V; results are less consistent in the other situations.[16] Tests of cognitive resource theory have shown mixed results.[17]

In terms of application, Fiedler has developed **leader match training,** which Sears, Roebuck and other organizations have used. Leaders are trained to diagnose the situation to match their high and low LPC scores with situational control, as measured by leader-member relations, task structure, and leader position power, following the general ideas shown in Figure 14.2. In cases with no match, the training shows how each of these situational control variables can be changed to obtain a match. Alternatively, another way of getting a match is through leader selection or placement based on LPC scores.[18] For example, a high-LPC leader would be selected for a position with high situational control, as in our earlier example of the manufacturing supervisor. As in the case of Fiedler's contingency theory, a number of studies have been designed to test leader match. Although they are not uniformly supportive, more than a dozen such tests have found increases in group effectiveness following the training.[19]

We conclude that although there are still unanswered questions concerning Fiedler's contingency theory, especially concerning the meaning of LPC, the theory and the leader match program have relatively strong support.[20] The approach and training program are also especially useful in encouraging situational contingency thinking.

HOUSE'S PATH-GOAL THEORY OF LEADERSHIP

Another well-known approach to situational contingencies is one developed by Robert House based on the earlier work of others.[21] This theory has its roots in the expectancy model of motivation discussed in Chapter 6. The term **path-goal** is used because of its emphasis on how a leader influences subordinates' perceptions of both work goals and personal goals and the links, or paths, found between these two sets of goals.

The theory assumes that a leader's key function is to adjust his or her behaviors to complement situational contingencies, such as those found in the work setting. House argues that when the leader is able to compensate for things lacking in the setting, subordinates are likely to be satisfied with the leader. For example, the leader could help remove job ambiguity or show how good performance could lead to more pay. Performance should improve as the paths by which (1) effort leads to performance—expectancy—and (2) performance leads to valued rewards—instrumentality—become clarified.

House's approach is summarized in Figure 14.3. The figure shows four types of leader behavior—directive, supportive, achievement oriented, and participative—and two categories of situational contingency variables—subordinate attributes and work-setting attributes. The leader behaviors are adjusted to complement the situational contingency variables in order to influence subordinate satisfaction, acceptance of the leader, and motivation for task performance.

Directive leadership has to do with spelling out the what and how of subordinates' tasks; it is much like the initiating structure mentioned earlier. **Supportive leadership** focuses on subordinate needs and well-being and promoting a friendly work climate; it is similar to consideration. **Achievement-oriented leadership** emphasizes setting challenging goals, stressing excellence in performance, and showing confidence in the group members'

FIGURE 14.3	SUMMARY OF MAJOR PATH-GOAL RELATIONSHIPS IN HOUSE'S LEADERSHIP APPROACH

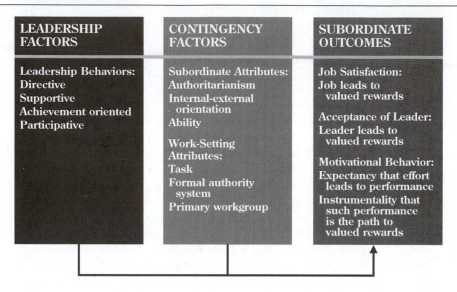

LEADERSHIP FACTORS	CONTINGENCY FACTORS	SUBORDINATE OUTCOMES
Leadership Behaviors: Directive Supportive Achievement oriented Participative	Subordinate Attributes: Authoritarianism Internal-external orientation Ability Work-Setting Attributes: Task Formal authority system Primary workgroup	Job Satisfaction: Job leads to valued rewards Acceptance of Leader: Leader leads to valued rewards Motivational Behavior: Expectancy that effort leads to performance Instrumentality that such performance is the path to valued rewards

ability to achieve high standards of performance. **Participative leadership** focuses on consulting with subordinates and seeking and taking their suggestions into account before making decisions.

Important subordinate characteristics are *authoritarianism* (close-mindedness, rigidity), *internal-external orientation* (e.g., locus of control), and *ability.* The key work-setting factors are the nature of the subordinates' tasks (task structure), the *formal authority system,* and the *primary workgroup.*

Predictions from Path-Goal Theory   **Directive leadership** is predicted to have a positive impact on subordinates when the task is ambiguous; it is predicted to have just the opposite effect for clear tasks. In addition, the theory predicts that when ambiguous tasks are being performed by highly authoritarian and close-minded subordinates, even more directive leadership is called for.

Supportive leadership is predicted to increase the satisfaction of subordinates who work on highly repetitive tasks or on tasks considered to be unpleasant, stressful, or frustrating; the leader's supportive behavior helps compensate for these adverse conditions. For example, many would consider traditional assembly-line auto worker jobs to be highly repetitive, perhaps even unpleasant and frustrating. A supportive supervisor could help make these jobs more pleasant. Achievement-oriented leadership is predicted to encourage subordinates to strive for higher performance standards and to have more confidence in their ability to meet challenging goals. For subordinates in ambiguous, nonrepetitive jobs, achievement-oriented leadership should increase their expectancies that effort leads to desired performance.

Participative leadership is predicted to promote satisfaction on nonrepetitive tasks that allow for the ego involvement of subordinates. For example, on a challenging research project, participation allows employees to feel good about dealing with the challenge of the project on their own. On repetitive tasks, open-minded or nonauthoritarian subordinates will also be satisfied with a participative leader. On a task where employees screw nuts on bolts hour after hour, for example, those who are nonauthoritarian will appreciate having a leader who allows them to get involved in ways that may help break the monotony.

Evaluation and Application   House's path-goal approach has now been with us for thirty years or so. Early work provided some support for the theory in general and for the particular predictions discussed earlier.[22] However, current assessments by well-known scholars have pointed out that many aspects have not been tested adequately, and there is very little recent research concerning the theory.[23] House himself recently revised and extended path-goal theory into the Theory of Work Unit Leadership. It's beyond our scope to discuss details of this new theory, but as a base, the new theory expands the list of leader behaviors beyond those in path-goal theory, including aspects of both traditional and new leadership.[24] It remains to be seen how much research it will generate.

In terms of application, there is enough support for original path-goal theory to suggest two possibilities. First, training could be used to change leadership behavior to fit the situational contingencies. Second, the leader could be taught to diagnose the situation and to learn how to try to change the contingencies, as in leader match.

Hersey and Blanchard's Situational Leadership Model   Like other situational contingency approaches, the situational leadership model developed by Paul Hersey and Kenneth Blanchard posits that there is no single best way to lead.[25] Hersey and Blanchard focus on the situational contingency of maturity, or "readiness," of followers, in particular. Readiness is the extent to which people have the ability and willingness to accomplish a specific task. Hersey and Blanchard argue that "situational" leadership requires adjusting the leader's emphasis on task behaviors, for instance, giving guidance and direction, and relationship behaviors, for example, providing socioemotional support, according to the readiness of followers to perform their tasks. Figure 14.4 identifies four leadership styles: delegating, participating, selling, and telling. Each emphasizes a different combination of task and relationship behaviors by the leader. The figure also suggests the following situational matches as the best choice of leadership style for followers at each of four readiness levels.

- A *"telling" style (S1) is best for low follower readiness (R1)*. The direction provided by this style defines roles for people who are unable and unwilling to take responsibility themselves; it eliminates any insecurity about the task that must be done.

- A *"selling" style (S2) is best for low to moderate follower readiness (R2)*. This style offers both task direction and support for people who are unable but willing to take task responsibility; it involves combining a directive approach with explanation and reinforcement in order to maintain enthusiasm.

- A *"participating" style (S3) is best for moderate to high follower readiness (R3)*. Able but unwilling followers require supportive behavior in order to increase their motivation; by allowing followers to share in decision making, this style helps enhance the desire to perform a task.

- A *"delegating" style (S4) is best for high readiness (R4)*. This style provides little in terms of direction and support for the task at hand; it allows able and willing followers to take responsibility for what needs to be done.

FIGURE 14.4 HERSEY AND BLANCHARD MODEL OF SITUATIONAL LEADERSHIP

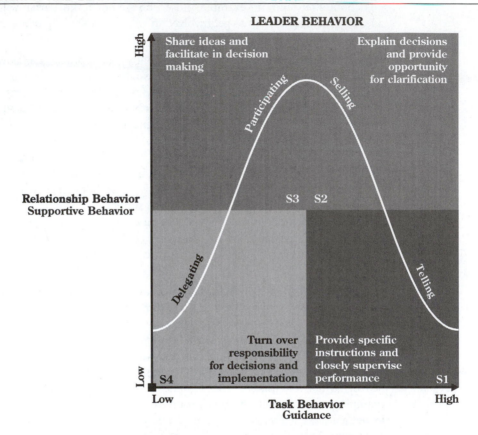

This situational leadership approach requires the leader to develop the capability to diagnose the demands of situations and then to choose and implement the appropriate leadership response. The model gives specific attention to followers and their feelings about the task at hand and suggests that an effective leader focus especially on emerging changes in the level of readiness of the people involved in the work.

In spite of its considerable history and incorporation into training programs by a large number of firms, the situational leadership approach has only recently begun to receive systematic research attention.[26]

SUBSTITUTES FOR LEADERSHIP

In contrast to the previous traditional leadership approaches, the substitutes for leadership theory argues that sometimes hierarchical leadership makes essentially no difference. John Jermier and others contend that certain individual, job, and organizational variables can either serve as substitutes for leadership or neutralize a leader's impact on subordinates.[27] Some examples of these variables are shown in Figure 14.5.

Substitutes for Leadership make a leader's influence either unnecessary or redundant in that they replace a leader's influence. For example, in Figure 14.5, it will be unnecessary and perhaps not even possible for a leader to provide the kind of task-oriented direction already available from an experienced, talented, and well-trained subordinate. In contrast, neutralizers prevent a leader from behaving in a certain way or nullify the effects of a leader's actions. If a leader has little formal authority or is physically separated, for example, his or her leadership may be nullified even though task supportiveness may still be needed.

Some research comparing Mexican and U.S. workers, as well as workers in Japan, suggest both similarities and differences between various substitutes in the countries examined. More generally, a review of seventeen studies in the United States as well as other countries found mixed results for the substitutes theory. Among other things, the authors argued that the kinds of characteristics and leader behaviors should be broadened and that the approach appeared to be especially important for high performance work teams.[28] With regard to these work teams, for example, in place of a hierarchical leader specifying standards and ways of achieving goals (task-oriented behaviors), the team might set its own standards and substitute those for the leader's.

FIGURE 14.5   **SOME EXAMPLE LEADERSHIP SUBSTITUTES AND NEUTRALIZERS**

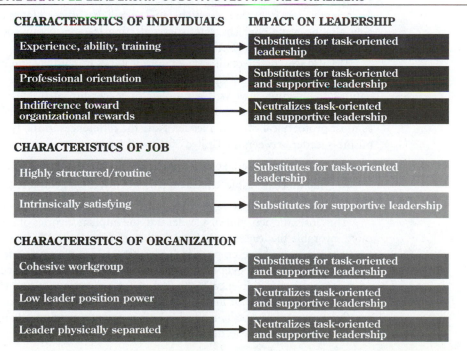

CHARACTERISTICS OF INDIVIDUALS   **IMPACT ON LEADERSHIP**

Experience, ability, training	→	Substitutes for task-oriented leadership
Professional orientation	→	Substitutes for task-oriented and supportive leadership
Indifference toward organizational rewards	→	Neutralizes task-oriented and supportive leadership

CHARACTERISTICS OF JOB

| Highly structured/routine | → | Substitutes for task-oriented leadership |
| Intrinsically satisfying | → | Substitutes for supportive leadership |

CHARACTERISTICS OF ORGANIZATION

Cohesive workgroup	→	Substitutes for task-oriented and supportive leadership
Low leader position power	→	Neutralizes task-oriented and supportive leadership
Leader physically separated	→	Neutralizes task-oriented and supportive leadership

ATTRIBUTION THEORY AND LEADERSHIP

The traditional leadership theories discussed so far have all assumed that leadership and its substantive effects can be identified and measured objectively. This is not always the case, however. Attribution theory addresses this very point—that of individuals trying to understand causes, to assess responsibilities, and to evaluate personal qualities, as all of these are involved with certain events. Attribution theory is particularly important in understanding leadership.

For openers, think about a workgroup or student group that you see as performing really well. Now assume that you are asked to describe the leader on one of the leadership scales discussed earlier in the chapter. If you are like many others, the group's high performance probably encouraged you to describe the leader favorably; in other words, you attributed good things to the leader based on the group's performance. Similarly, leaders themselves make attributions about subordinate performance and react differently depending on those attributions. For example, if leaders attribute an employee's poor performance to lack of effort, they may issue a reprimand, whereas if they attribute the poor performance to an external factor, such as work overload, they will probably try to fix the problem. A great deal of evidence supports these attributional views of subordinates and leaders.[29]

LEADERSHIP PROTOTYPES

There is also evidence that people have a mental picture of what makes a "good leader" or ways in which "real leaders" would act in a given situation. The view that people have an image in their minds of what a model leader should look like is sometimes called a **leadership prototype**.[30] These implicit theories or prototypes usually consist of a mix of specific and more general characteristics. For example, a prototype of a bank president would differ in many ways from that of a high-ranking military officer. However, there would probably also be some core characteristics reflecting leaders in our society in general—for example, integrity and self-efficacy.

We also would expect differences in prototypes by country and by national culture.[31] As an example of such country differences, a study asked people from eight different nations to describe how well a number of leadership attributes previously identified described their image of a business leader. In each country, five attributes were identified as most prototypical of such a leader. Note the differences in the prototype of the typical business leader between the United States and Japan.

- **U.S.:** determined, goal-oriented, verbally skilled, industrious, persistent.
- **Japan:** responsible, educated, trustworthy, intelligent, disciplined.

Similar differences exist across other countries, although there is some overlap as well.

The closer the behavior of a leader is to the implicit theories of his or her followers, the more favorable the leader's relations and key outcomes tend to be.[32] Both of the attributional treatments above emphasize leadership as something that is largely symbolic or resides in the eye of the beholder. This general notion has also carried over to a related set of research directions. Ironically, the first of these directions argues that leadership makes little or no real difference in organizational effectiveness. The second tends to attribute greatly exaggerated importance to leadership and ultimately leads us into charisma and other aspects of the new leadership.

EXAGGERATION OF THE LEADERSHIP DIFFERENCE

Jeffrey Pfeffer has looked at what happens when leaders at the top of the organization are changed. Pfeffer is among those contending that even CEOs of large corporations have little leadership impact on profits and effectiveness compared to environmental and industry forces, such as cutbacks in the federal defense budget. Furthermore, these leaders are typically accountable to so many groups of people for the resources they use that their leadership impact is greatly constrained. Pfeffer argues that in light of such forces and constraints, much of the impact a top leader does have is symbolic; leaders and others develop explanations to legitimize the actions they take.[33]

This symbolic treatment of leadership occurs particularly when performance is either extremely high or extremely low or when the situation is such that many people could have been responsible for the performance. James Meindl and his colleagues call this phenomenon the **romance of leadership,** whereby people attribute romantic, almost magical, qualities to leadership.[34] Consider the firing of a baseball manager or football coach whose team doesn't perform well. Neither the owner nor anyone else is really sure why this occurred. But the owner can't fire all the players, so a new team manager is brought in to symbolize "a change in leadership" that is "sure to turn the team around."

FROM TRADITIONAL TO NEW LEADERSHIP PERSPECTIVES

The focus on leadership attributions and symbolic aspects moves us away from traditional leadership and into the new leadership. The **new leadership** emphasizes charismatic and transformational leadership approaches and various aspects of vision related to them, and we extend the term to include leadership of self-directing work teams. The new leadership is considered especially important in changing and transforming individuals and organizations with a commitment to high performance.[35]

CHARISMATIC APPROACHES

Robert House and his associates have done a lot of work recently based on extensions of an earlier charismatic theory House developed. (Do not confuse this with House's path-goal theory or its extension, discussed earlier in the chapter.)[36] Of special interest is the fact that House's theory uses both trait and behavior combinations.

House's **charismatic leaders** are leaders who, by force of their personal abilities, are capable of having a profound and extraordinary effect on followers. These leaders are high in need for power and have high feelings of self-efficacy and conviction in the moral rightness of their beliefs. That is, the need for power motivates these people to want to be leaders. This need is then reinforced by their conviction of the moral rightness of their beliefs. The feeling of self-efficacy, in turn, makes these people feel that they are capable of being leaders. These traits then influence such charismatic behaviors as role modeling, image building, articulating goals (focusing on simple and dramatic goals), emphasizing high expectations, showing confidence, and arousing follower motives.

Some of the more interesting and important work based on aspects of House's charismatic theory involves a study of U.S. presidents.[37] The research showed that behavioral charisma was substantially related to presidential performance and that the kind of personality traits in House's theory, along with response to crisis, among other things, predicted behavioral charisma for the sample of presidents. Related presidential work by others also shows that voters who saw Bill Clinton as charismatic followed through by voting for him.[38]

House and his colleagues summarize other work that partially supports the theory. Some of the more interesting related work has shown that negative, or "dark-side," charismatic leaders emphasize personalized power—focus on themselves—whereas positive, or "bright-side," charismatics emphasize socialized power that tends to empower their followers. This helps explain differences between such dark-side leaders as Adolf Hitler and David Koresh, and a bright-side Martin Luther King, Jr.[39]

Jay Conger and Rabindra Kanungo have developed a three-stage charismatic leadership model.[40] In the initial stage, the leader critically evaluates the status quo. Deficiencies in the status quo lead to formulations of future goals. Before developing these goals, the leader assesses available resources and constraints that stand in the way of the goals. The leader also assesses follower abilities, needs, and satisfaction levels. In the second stage, the leader formulates and articulates the goals along with an idealized future vision. Here the leader emphasizes articulation and impression management skills. Then in the third stage, the leader shows how these goals and the vision can be achieved. The leader emphasizes innovative and unusual means to achieve the vision. Martin Luther King, Jr. illustrated these three stages in his nonviolent civil rights approach, where he changed race relations in this country.

Conger and Kanungo have argued that if leaders use behaviors such as vision articulation, environmental sensitivity, and unconventional behavior, rather than maintaining the status quo, followers will attribute charismatic leadership to them. Such leaders are also seen as behaving quite differently from those labeled "noncharismatic."[41]

Finally, an especially important question about charismatic leadership is whether it is described in the same way for close-up or at-a-distance leaders. Boas Shamir recently examined this issue in Israel.[42] He found that descriptions of distant charismatics, for instance, former Israeli prime minister Golda Meir, and close-up charismatics, for instance, a specific teacher, were generally more different than they were similar. Figure 14.6 shows the high points of his findings. Clearly, leaders with whom followers have close contact and those with whom they seldom, if ever, have direct contact are both described as charismatic but possess quite different traits and behaviors.

TRANSFORMATIONAL VERSUS TRANSACTIONAL APPROACHES

Building on notions originated by James MacGregor Burns, as well as ideas from House's work, Bernard Bass has developed an approach that focuses on both transformational and transactional leadership.[43]

Transactional leadership involves leader-follower exchanges necessary for achieving routine performance agreed upon between leaders and followers. These exchanges involve four dimensions as shown in The Effective Manager 14.1.

Transformational leadership goes beyond this routine accomplishment, however. For Bass, **transformational leadership** occurs when leaders broaden and elevate their follower's interests, when they generate awareness and acceptance of the group's purposes and

| FIGURE 14.6 | DESCRIPTIONS OF CHARACTERISTICS OF DISTANT AND CLOSE-UP CHARISMATICS |

Distant Charismatics Should Demonstrate

- Persistence
- Rhetorical skills
- Courage
- Emphasizing social courage (expressing opinions, not conforming to pressure)
- Ideological orientation

Close-up Charismatics Should Demonstrate

- Sociability
- Expertise
- Humor
- Dynamism, activity
- Physical appearance
- Intelligence
- Setting high standards
- Originality

Both Distant and Close-up Charismatics Should Demonstrate

- Self-confidence
- Honesty
- Authoritativeness
- Sacrifice

mission, and when they stir their followers to look beyond their own self-interests for the good of others.

Dimensions of Transformational Leadership   Transformational leadership has four dimensions: charisma, inspiration, intellectual stimulation, and individualized considera- tion. *Charisma* provides vision and a sense of mission, and it instills pride, along with fol- lower respect and trust. For example, Steve Jobs, who founded Apple Computer, showed charisma by emphasizing the importance of creating the Macintosh as a radical new com- puter. Inspiration communicates high expectations, uses symbols to focus efforts, and expresses important purposes in simple ways. For example, in the movie *Patton*, George C. Scott stood on a stage in front of his troops with a wall-sized American flag in the back- ground and ivory-handled revolvers in holsters at his side. *Intellectual stimulation* promotes intelligence, rationality, and careful problem solving. For instance, your boss encourages you to look at a very difficult problem in a new way. *Individualized consideration* provides personal attention, treats each employee individually, and coaches and advises. For exam- ple, your boss drops by and makes remarks reinforcing your worth as a person.

| THE EFFECTIVE MANAGER 14.1 |
| FOUR DIMENSIONS OF TRANSACTIONAL LEADERSHIP |

- Contingent rewards: Providing various kinds of rewards in exchange for mutually agreed upon goal accomplishment
- Active management by exception: Watching for deviations from rules and standards and tak- ing corrective action
- Passive management by exception: Intervening only if standards are not met
- Laissez-faire: Abdicating responsibilities and avoiding decisions

Bass concludes that transformational leadership is likely to be strongest at the top-management level, where there is the greatest opportunity for proposing and communicating a vision. However, it is not *restricted* to the top level; it is found throughout the organization. Furthermore, transformational leadership operates *in combination with* transactional leadership. Transactional leadership is similar to most of the traditional leadership approaches mentioned earlier. Leaders need both transformational and transactional leadership in order to be successful, just as they need both leadership and management.[44]

Evaluation and Application   Reviews have summarized a large number of studies using Bass's approach. These reviews report significant favorable relationships between Bass's leadership dimensions and various aspects of performance and satisfaction, as well as extra effort, burnout and stress, and predispositions to act as innovation champions on the part of followers. The strongest relationships tend to be associated with charisma or inspirational leadership, although, in most cases, the other dimensions are also important. These findings are consistent with those reported elsewhere.[45] They broaden leadership outcomes beyond those cited in traditional leadership studies.

LEADERSHIP IN HIGH PERFORMANCE WORK TEAMS

An extension of the earlier new leadership approaches is that of leadership in self-directing work teams. As mentioned previously, such teams are particularly important in high performance organizations, and the workers in them lead the teams themselves.[46] The question then is, do they have a leader from outside? The answer is yes, but what the leader does is quite different from what a traditional supervisor does. Indeed, even the title is different—a widely used one is "coordinator," although "facilitator" is not uncommon.

Among the key leadership behaviors by coordinators are those in Figure 14.7. These behaviors focus on coordinator encouragements, and the team activities show the specific actions involved in meeting the coordinator's expectations. Even if team members do carry out the team activities encouraged by the coordinator, how much difference does it make? One study showed that perceived coordinator encouragement of the team self-leadership activities was positively related to coordinator effectiveness. Another study showed that coordinator leader behavior predicted positive team performance and various aspects of satisfaction.[47] So these leader behaviors do seem to be important.

Take another look at the figure. Notice that while these behaviors are important, they focus on self-leadership activities. They do not examine other leadership functions such as managing resources and boundary spanning with other units. In other words, they emphasize the social system and not the technical system. Indeed, Manz and Sims[48] suggest that the coordinator, outside the group, has the fundamental responsibility to get the team to lead itself and thus emphasizes various team self-leadership behaviors. In contrast, these authors argue that the team leader within the team serves as an additional member who facilitates the team's organizing itself, coordinating job assignments and making sure resources are available. A second set of authors points out that even though coordinator self-leadership encouragement was related to team effectiveness and satisfaction, the relationship probably would

| FIGURE 14.7 | SAMPLE LEADER BEHAVIORS FOR HIGH PERFORMANCE WORK TEAMS |

COORDINATOR BEHAVIOR

ACTIVITIES INVOLVED IN COORDINATOR TEAM ENCOURAGEMENTS*

Encourages rehearsal
Work team goes over an activity and "thinks it through" before actually performing the activity

- Go over activity
- Practice new task
- Go over new task
- Think about how to do a job

Encourages self-goal setting
Work team sets performance goals

- Define team goals
- Define own goals
- Establish task goals
- Set team performance goals

Encourages self-criticism
Work team self-critical of low team performance

- Be critical of ourselves
- Be tough on ourselves
- Be self-critical
- Be critical when we do poorly

Encourages self-reinforcement
Work team self-reinforcing of high team performance

- Praise each other
- Feel positive about ourselves
- Praise each other for a good job
- Feel good about ourselves

Encourages self-expectation
Work team has high expectations for team performance

- Think we can do very well
- Expect high performance
- Expect a lot from ourselves

Encourages self-observation/evaluation
Work team monitors, is aware of, and evaluates levels of performance

- Be aware of performance level
- Know how our performance stands
- Judge how well we are performing

*These activities were specifically described in a questionnaire, and some of the questions were designed to be very similar to increase the reliability of the questionnaire.

have been much stronger if these other kinds of leadership dimensions had been included, in addition to the self-leadership ones.[49]

An example is the Brookhaven facility of Delphi Packard Electric Systems, the world's leading supplier of automotive power and signal distribution systems. It uses self-led work teams and has team leaders responsible for ten tasks from conducting meetings to training team leader replacements.

To conclude, note two other considerations. First, these self-leadership activities from the team members themselves can be considered a partial substitute for hierarchical leadership, even though the coordinator encourages them. For example, members praise each other rather than looking to the coordinator for praise. As we have shown previously, such behaviors are becoming increasingly important in high performance organizations.

Second, although these behaviors provide a lot of participation from team members, they do not appear to be particularly charismatic. They should work best when combined with the kinds of resource and coordination behaviors mentioned above and when reinforced by new leadership from bright-side leaders higher up in the organization.

SOME NEW LEADERSHIP ISSUES

We now examine some charismatic, transformational, and visionary new leadership issues. First, *Can people be trained in new leadership?* According to research in this area, the answer is yes. Bass and his colleagues have put a lot of work into such training efforts. For example, they have created a workshop where leaders are given initial feedback on their scores on Bass's measures. The leaders then devise improvement programs to strengthen their weaknesses and work with the trainers to develop their leadership skills. Bass and Bass and Avolio report findings that demonstrate the beneficial effects of this training. They also report team training and programs tailored to individual firms' needs.[50] Similarly, Conger and Kanungo propose training to develop the kinds of behaviors summarized in their model as suggested in The Effective Manager 14.2.[51]

Approaches with special emphasis on vision often emphasize training. Kouzas and Posner report results of a week-long training program at AT&T. The program involved training leaders on five dimensions oriented around developing, communicating, and reinforcing a shared vision. According to Kouzas and Posner, leaders showed an average 15 percent increase in these visionary behaviors ten months after participating in the program.[52] Similarly, Sashkin has developed a leadership approach that emphasizes various aspects of vision and organizational culture change. Sashkin discusses a number of ways to train leaders to be more visionary and to enhance the culture change.[53] All of the new leadership training programs involve a heavy hands-on workshop emphasis so that leaders do more than just read about vision.

A second issue involves the question: *Is new leadership always good?* As we pointed out earlier, dark-side charismatics, such as Adolf Hitler, can have negative effects on the population of followers. Similarly, new leadership is not always needed. Sometimes emphasis on a vision diverts energy from more important day-to-day activities. It is also important to note that new leadership by itself is not sufficient. New leadership needs to be used in conjunction with traditional leadership. Finally, new leadership is important not only at the top. A number of experts argue that it applies at all levels of organizational leadership.

THE EFFECTIVE MANAGER 14.2
FIVE CHARISMATIC SKILLS

- Sensitivity to most appropriate contexts for charisma—Emphasis on critical evaluation and problem detection
- Visioning—Emphasis on creative thinking to learn and think about profound change
- Communication—Working with oral and written linguistic aspects
- Impression management—Emphasis on modeling, appearance, body language, and verbal skills
- Empowering—Emphasis on communicating high performance expectations, improving participation in decision making, loosening up bureaucratic constraints, setting meaningful goals, and establishing appropriate reward systems

---

Chapter 14 Summary

What is leadership, and how does it differ from management?

- Leadership is a special case of interpersonal influence that gets an individual or group to do what the leader wants done.
- Leadership and management differ in that management is designed to promote stability or to make the organization run smoothly, whereas the role of leadership is to promote adaptive change.

What are the trait or behavioral leadership perspectives?

- Trait, or great person, approaches argue that leader traits have a major impact on differentiating between leaders and nonleaders and predicting leadership outcomes.
- Traits are considered relatively innate and hard to change.
- Similar to trait approaches, behavioral theories argue that leader behaviors have a major impact on outcomes.
- The Michigan, Ohio State, and Graen's Leader–Member Exchange (LMX) approaches are particularly important leader behavior theories.
- Leader behavior theories are especially suitable for leadership training.

What are the situational or contingency leadership approaches?

- Leader situational contingency approaches argue that leadership, in combination with various situational contingency variables, can have a major impact on outcomes.
- The effects of traits are enhanced to the extent of their relevance to the situational contingencies faced by the leader.
- Strong or weak situational contingencies influence the impact of leadership traits.
- Fiedler's contingency theory, House's path–goal theory, Hersey and Blanchard's situational leadership theory, and Kerr and Jermier's substitutes for leadership theory are particularly important, specific situational contingency approaches.
- Sometimes, as in the case of the substitutes for leadership approach, the role of the situational contingencies replaces that of leadership so that leadership has little or no impact in itself.

How does attribution theory relate to leadership?

- Attribution theory extends traditional leadership approaches by recognizing that substantive effects cannot always be objectively identified and measured.
- Leaders form attributions about why their employees perform well or poorly and respond accordingly.
- Leaders and followers often infer that there is good leadership when their group performs well.

- Leaders and followers often have in mind a good leader prototype, compare the leader against such a prototype, and conclude that the closer the fit the better the leadership.

- Some contend that leadership makes no real difference and is largely symbolic; others, following the "romance of leadership" notion, embrace this symbolic emphasis and attribute almost magical qualities to leadership.

What are the new leadership perspectives and why are they especially important in high performance organizations?

- The new leadership consists of charismatic, transformation, and visionary leadership, and leadership of self-directing work teams.

- Charismatic, transformational, and visionary attributions help move followers to achieve goals that transcend their own self-interests and help transform the organization.

- Particularly important new leadership approaches are Bass's transformational theory and House's and Conger and Kanungo's charismatic theories.

- Transformational approaches are broader than charismatic ones and often include charisma as one of their dimensions.

- Leadership in self-leading teams, particularly involved in high performing organizations, changes the external leadership role by making it a facilitative one to encourage team members to lead themselves.

- Behaviors of team coordinators are assumed to work best when reinforced by leaders who provide empowerment and stress various aspects of the new leadership.

- The new leadership, in general, is important because it goes beyond traditional leadership in facilitating change in the increasingly fast-moving and high performance workplace.

Study Questions

Analysis of power and politics is crucial to understanding the roles of individuals in organizations. As you read Chapter 15 keep in mind these study questions.

- What is power?
- How do managers acquire the power needed for leadership?
- What is empowerment, and how can managers empower others?
- What are organizational politics?
- How do organizational politics affect managers and management?
- Can the firm use politics strategically?

Individuals rarely join a corporation simply to work for the organization's stated goals. They join for their own reasons to meet their own goals. As individuals vie for their own interests in a hierarchical setting, analyses of power and politics are a key to understanding the behavior of individuals within organizations. Such is the case even with the high tech firms such as Microsoft.[1] Yet, managers find there are never enough resources, either money, people, time, or authority to get things done. They see a power gap.[2] As discussed throughout this chapter, power and politics have two sides. On the one hand, power and politics represent the seamy side of management, since organizations are not democracies composed of individuals with equal influence. On the other hand, power and politics are important organizational tools that managers must use to get the job done. In effective organizations, power is delicately developed, nurtured, and managed by astute individuals. Politics is always infused into the organization. Yet it is possible to isolate many instances where individual and organizational interests are compatible. The astute manager knows how to find these opportunities.[3]

POWER

In OB, **power** is defined as the ability to get someone to do something you want done or the ability to make things happen in the way you want them to. In Chapter 14, we examined leadership as a key power mechanism to make things happen. Now it is time to discusses other ways. The essence of power is control over the behavior of others.[4] While power is the force you use to make things happen in an intended way, **influence** is what you have when you exercise power, and it is expressed by others' behavioral response to your exercise of power. Managers derive power from both organizational and individual sources. These sources are called *position power* and *personal power,* respectively.[5]

POSITION POWER

Six popular bases of power in the modern firm are available to a manager solely as a result of his or her position in the organization: reward, coercive, legitimate, process, information, and representative power.

   Reward power is the extent to which a manager can use extrinsic and intrinsic rewards to control other people. Examples of such rewards include money, promotions, compliments, or enriched jobs. Although all managers have some access to rewards, success in accessing and utilizing rewards to achieve influence varies according to the skills of the manager.

   Power can also be founded on punishment instead of reward. For example, a manager may threaten to withhold a pay raise, or to transfer, demote, or even recommend the firing of a subordinate who does not act as desired. Such **coercive power** is the extent to which a manager can deny desired rewards or administer punishments to control other people. The availability of coercive power also varies from one organization and manager to another. The presence of unions and organizational policies on employee treatment can weaken this power base considerably.

   The third base of "position" power is **legitimate power,** or formal hierarchical authority. It stems from the extent to which a manager can use subordinates' internalized values or beliefs that the "boss" has a "right of command" to control their behavior. For example, the boss may have the formal authority to approve or deny such employee requests as job transfers, equipment purchases, personal time off, or overtime work. Legitimate power represents a special kind of power a manager has because subordinates believe it is legitimate for a person occupying the managerial position as their boss to have the right to command. If this legitimacy is lost, authority will not be accepted by subordinates.

Process power is the control over methods of production and analysis. The source of this power is the placing of the individual in a position to influence how inputs are transformed into outputs for the firm, a department in the firm, or even a small group. Firms often establish process specialists who work with managers to insure that production is accomplished efficiently and effectively. Closely related to this is control of the analytical processes used to make choices. For example, many organizations have individuals with specialties in financial analysis. They may review proposals from other parts of the firm for investments. Their power derives not from the calculation itself, but from the assignment to determine the analytical procedures used to judge the proposals. Process power may be separated from legitimate hierarchical power simply because of the complexity of the firm's operations. A manager may have the formal hierarchical authority to decide, but may be required to use the analytical schemes of others and/or to consult on effective implementation with process specialists. As you can tell, the issue of position power can get quite complex very quickly in sophisticated operations. This leads us to another related aspect of position power—the role of the access to and control of information.

Information power is the access to and/or the control of information. It is one of the most important aspects of legitimacy. The "right to know" and use information can be, and often is, conferred on a position holder. Thus, information power may complement legitimate hierarchical power. Information power may also be granted to specialists and managers who are in the middle of the information systems of the firm. For example, the chief information officer of the firm may not only control all the computers, but may also have access to almost any information desired. Managers jealously guard the formal "right to know," because it means they are in a position to influence events, not merely react to them. For example, most chief executive officers believe they have the right to know about everything in "their" firm. Deeper in the organization, managers often protect information from others under the notion that outsiders would not understand it. For instance, engineering drawings are not typically allowed outside of engineering. In other instances information is to be protected from outsiders. Marketing plans may be labeled "top secret." In most instances the nominal reason for controlling information is to protect the firm. The real reason is often to allow information holders to increase their power.

Representative power is the formal right conferred by the firm to speak as a representative for a potentially important group composed of individuals across departments or outside the firm. In most complex organizations there are a wide variety of different constituencies that may have an important impact on their firm's operations and/or its success. Many of the constituencies are outside the firm. They include such groups as investors, customers, alliance partners, and, of course, unions. Astute executives often hire individuals to act as representatives of and to these constituencies to ensure that their influence is felt, but does not dominate. So, for instance, investor relations managers are expected to deal with the mundane inquiries of small investors, anticipate the questions of financial analysts, and represent the sentiment of investors to senior management. To continue the example, the investor relations manager may be asked to anticipate the questions of investors, and guide the type of responses senior management may make. The influence of the investor relations manager is in part based on the assignment to represent the interests of this important group.

Finally, it is important to stress the unstated underpinning of legitimacy in most organizations. This is an implicit moral and technical order. As we will note later in this chapter, from the crib to the school to work to retirement, individuals in our society are taught to obey "higher authority." In U.S. firms, "higher authority" means those close to the top of the corporate pyramid. In other societies, "higher authority" does not have a bureaucratic or organizational reference but consists of those with moral authority such as tribal chiefs, religious leaders, and the like. In firms, the legitimacy of those at the top increasingly derives from their positions as representatives for various constituencies. This is a technical or instrumental role. Many senior executives also evoke ethics and social causes in their role as authority figures.

PERSONAL POWER

Personal power resides in the individual and is independent of that individual's position. Personal power is important in many well-managed firms. Three bases of personal power are expertise, rational persuasion, and reference.

Expert power is the ability to control another person's behavior through the possession of knowledge, experience, or judgment that the other person does not have but needs. A subordinate obeys a supervisor possessing expert power because the boss ordinarily knows more about what is to be done or how it is to be done than does the subordinate. Expert power is relative, not absolute.

Rational persuasion is the ability to control another's behavior because through the individual's efforts, the person accepts the desirability of an offered goal and a reasonable way of achieving it. Much of what a supervisor does day to day involves rational persuasion up, down, and across the organization.

Rational persuasion involves both explaining the desirability of expected outcomes and showing how specific actions will achieve these outcomes.

Referent power is the ability to control another's behavior because the person wants to identify with the power source. In this case, a subordinate obeys the boss because he or she wants to behave, perceive, or believe as the boss does. This obedience may occur, for example, because the subordinate likes the boss personally and therefore tries to do things the way the boss wants them done. In a sense, the subordinate attempts to avoid doing anything that would interfere with the pleasing boss-subordinate relationship. A person's referent power can be enhanced when the individual taps into the moral order or shows a clearer long-term path to a morally desirable end. In common language, individuals with the ability to tap into these more esoteric aspects of corporate life have "charisma" and "the vision thing." Followership is not based on what the subordinate will get for specific actions or specific levels of performance, but on what the individual represents—a path toward a loftier future.

ACQUIRING AND USING POWER AND INFLUENCE

A considerable portion of any manager's time is directed toward what is called *power-oriented behavior*. Power-oriented behavior is action directed primarily at developing or using relationships in which other people are to some degree willing to defer to one's wishes.[6] Figure 15.1 shows three basic dimensions of power and influence with which a manager will become

FIGURE 15.1	THREE DIMENSIONS OF MANAGERIAL POWER AND INFLUENCE

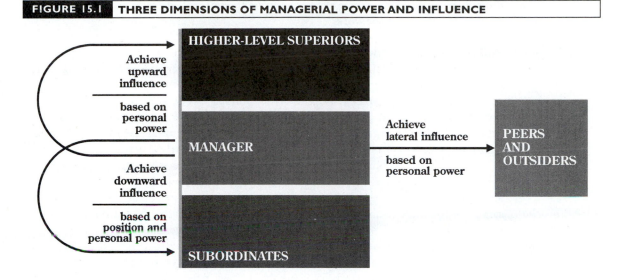

involved in this regard: downward, upward, and lateral. Also shown in the figure are some preliminary ideas for achieving success along each of these dimensions.

The effective manager is one who succeeds in building and maintaining high levels of both position and personal power over time. Only then is sufficient power of the right types available when the manager needs to exercise influence on downward, lateral, and upward dimensions.

Building Position Power   Position power can be enhanced when managers are able to demonstrate to others that their work units are highly relevant to organizational goals and are able to respond to urgent organizational needs. To increase centrality and criticality in the organization, managers may seek to acquire a more central role in the workflow by having information filtered through them, making at least part of their job responsibilities unique, expanding their network of communication contacts, and occupying an office convenient to main traffic flows.

Managers may also attempt to increase the relevance of their tasks and those of their unit to the organization. There are many ways to do this. Executives may attempt to become an internal coordinator within the firm or external representative. They may suggest their subordinates take on these roles, particularly when the firm is downsizing. When the firm is in a dynamic setting of changing technology, the executive may also move to provide unique services and information to other units. This is particularly effective if the executive moves his unit into becoming involved with decisions central to the organization's top-priority goals. To expand their position, managers may also delegate routine activities, expand the task variety and novelty for subordinates, initiate new ideas, and get involved in new projects. We will have more to say about this matter when discussing empowerment.

There are also ways managers attempt to build influence that may or may not have a positive effect on the organization. Managers may attempt to define tasks so that they are difficult to evaluate, such as by creating an ambiguous job description or developing a unique language for their work.

Building Personal Power   Personal power arises from the personal characteristics of the manager rather than from the location and other characteristics of his or her position in the organization's hierarchy of authority.

Three personal characteristics, expertise, political savvy, and likability, have special potential for enhancing personal power in an organization. The most obvious is *building expertise.* Additional expertise may be gained by advanced training and education, participation in professional associations, and involvement in the early stages of projects.

A somewhat less obvious way to increase personal power is to learn *political savvy*— better ways to negotiate, persuade individuals, and understand the goals and means they are most willing to accept. The novice believes that most individuals are very much the same, see the same goals, and will accept much the same paths toward these goals. The more astute individual recognizes important individual differences.

A manager's reference power is increased by characteristics that enhance his or her *likability* and create personal attraction in relationships with other people. These include pleasant personality characteristics, agreeable behavior patterns, and attractive personal appearance. The demonstration of sincere hard work on behalf of task performance can also increase personal power by enhancing both expertise and reference. A person who is perceived to try hard may be expected to know more about the job and thus be sought out for advice. A person who tries hard is also likely to be respected for the attempt and may even be depended on by others to maintain that effort.

Combined Building of Position and Personal Power   From a purely analytical standpoint, most sources of power can be traced to position power or personal power. However, many of the influential actions and behaviors are combinations of position and personal power.

Most managers attempt to increase the visibility of their job performance by (1) expanding the number of contacts they have with senior people, (2) making oral presentations of written work, (3) participating in problem-solving task forces, (4) sending out notices of accomplishment, and (5) generally seeking additional opportunities to increase personal name recognition. Most managers also recognize that, between superiors and subordinates, access to or control over information is an important element. A boss may appear to expand his or her expert power over a subordinate by not allowing the individual access to critical information. Although the denial may appear to enhance the boss's expert power, it may reduce the subordinate's effectiveness. In a similar manner a supervisor may also control access to key organizational decision makers. An individual's ability to contact key persons informally can offset some of this disadvantage. Furthermore, astute senior executives routinely develop "back channels" to lower-level individuals deep within the firm to offset the tendency of bosses to control information and access.

Expert power is often relational and embedded within the organizational context. Many important decisions are made outside formal channels and are substantially influenced by key individuals with the requisite knowledge. By developing and using coalitions and networks, an individual may build on his or her expert power. Through coalitions and networks, an individual may alter the flow of information and the context for analysis. By developing coalitions and networks, executives also expand their access to information and their opportunities for participation.

Executives also attempt to control, or at least influence, decision premises. A decision premise is a basis for defining the problem and for selecting among alternatives. By defining a problem in a manner that fits the executive's expertise, it is natural for that executive to be in charge of solving it. Thus, the executive subtly shifts his or her position power.

Executives who want to increase their power often make their goals and needs clear and bargain effectively to show that their preferred goals and needs are best. They do not show their power base directly but instead provide clear "rational persuasion" for their preferences. So the astute executive does not threaten or attempt to evoke sanctions to build power. Instead, he or she combines personal power with the position of the unit to enhance total power. As illustrated in The Effective Manager 15.1, it is important for the aspiring manager to build trust. As the organizational context changes, different personal sources of power may become more important alone and in combination with the individual's position power. So there is an art to building power.

TURNING POWER INTO RELATIONAL INFLUENCE

Using position and personal power well to achieve the desired influence over other people is a challenge for most managers. Practically speaking, there are many useful ways of exercising relational influence. The most common strategies involve the following:[7]

- *Reason*   Using facts and data to support a logical argument.
- *Friendliness*   Using flattery, goodwill, and favorable impressions.
- *Coalition*   Using relationships with other people for support.
- *Bargaining*   Using the exchange of benefits as a basis for negotiation.
- *Assertiveness*   Using a direct and forceful personal approach.
- *Higher authority* Gaining higher-level support for one's requests.
- *Sanctions*   Using organizationally derived rewards and punishments.

Research on these strategies suggests that reason is the most popular strategy overall.[8] In addition, friendliness, assertiveness, bargaining, and higher authority are used more frequently to influence subordinates than to influence supervisors. This pattern of influence attempts is consistent with our earlier contention that downward influence generally includes mobilization of both position and personal power sources, whereas upward influence is more likely to draw on personal power.

THE EFFECTIVE MANAGER 15.1

DEVELOPING TRUST

One key to ethically developing power is to build trust. To build trust a manager should, at a minimum:

- Always honor implied and explicit social contracts
- Seek to prevent, avoid, and rectify harm to others
- Respect the unique needs of others

Little research is available on the subject of upward influence in organizations. This is unfortunate, since truly effective managers are able to influence their bosses as well as their subordinates. One study reports that both supervisors and subordinates view reason, or the logical presentation of ideas, as the most frequently used strategy of upward influence.[9] When queried on reasons for success and failure, however, the viewpoints of the two groups show both similarities and differences. The perceived causes of success in upward influence are similar for both supervisors and subordinates and involve the favorable content of the influence attempt, a favorable manner of its presentation, and the competence of the subordinate.[10] The two groups disagree on the causes of failure, however. Subordinates attribute failure in upward influence to the close-mindedness of the supervisor, unfavorable content of the influence attempt, and unfavorable interpersonal relationships with the supervisor. In contrast, supervisors attribute failure to the unfavorable content of the attempt, the unfavorable manner in which it was presented, and the subordinate's lack of competence.

POWER, FORMAL AUTHORITY, AND OBEDIENCE

As we have shown, power is the potential to control the behavior of others, and formal authority is the potential to exert such control through the legitimacy of a managerial position. Yet, we also know that people who seem to have power don't always get their way. Why do some people obey directives and others do not? More specifically, why should subordinates respond to a manager's authority, or "right to command," in the first place? Furthermore, given that subordinates are willing to obey, what determines the limits of obedience?

The Milgram Experiments   The mythology of American independence and unbridled individualism is so strong we need to spend some time explaining how most of us are really quite obedient. So we turn to the seminal studies of Stanley Milgram on obedience.[11] Milgram designed experiments to determine the extent to which people obey the commands of an authority figure, even if they believe they are endangering the life of another person. Subjects, ranging in age from twenty to fifty and representing a diverse set of occupations (engineers, salespeople, schoolteachers, laborers, and others), were paid a nominal fee for participation in the project.

The subjects were falsely told that the purpose of the study was to determine the effects of punishment on learning. The subjects were to be the "teachers." The "learner" was a confederate of Milgram's, who was strapped to a chair in an adjoining room with an electrode attached to his wrist. The "experimenter," another confederate of Milgram's, was dressed in a gray laboratory coat. Appearing impassive and somewhat stern, the experimenter instructed the "teacher" to read a series of word pairs to the "learner" and then to reread the first word along with four other terms. The learner was supposed to indicate which of the four terms was in the original pair by pressing a switch that caused a light to flash on a response panel in front of the teacher.

The teacher was instructed to administer a shock to the learner each time a wrong answer was given. This shock was to be increased one level of intensity each time the learner made a mistake. The teacher controlled switches that ostensibly administered shocks ranging from 15 to 450 volts. In reality, there was no electric current in the apparatus, but the learners purposely "erred" often and responded to each level of "shock" in progressively distressing ways. If a "teacher" (subject) proved unwilling to administer a shock, the experimenter used the following sequential prods to get him or her to perform as requested. (1) "Please continue" or "Please go on"; (2) "The experiment requires that you continue"; (3) "It is absolutely essential that you continue"; and (4) "You have no choice, you must go on." Only when the "teacher" refused to go on after the fourth prod would the experiment be stopped. When would you expect the "teachers" to refuse to go on?

Milgram asked some of his students and colleagues the same question. Most felt that few, if any, of the subjects would go beyond the "very strong shock" level. Actually, twenty-six subjects (65 percent) continued to the end of the experiment and shocked the "learners" to the maximum. None stopped before 300 volts, the point at which the learner pounded on the wall. The remaining fourteen subjects refused to obey the experimenter at various intermediate points.

Most people are surprised by these results, as was Milgram. The question is why other people would have a tendency to accept or comply with authoritative commands under such extreme conditions. Milgram conducted further experiments to try to answer this question. The subjects' tendencies toward compliance were somewhat reduced (1) when experimentation took place in a rundown office (rather than a university lab), (2) when the victim was closer, (3) when the experimenter was farther away, and (4) when the subject could observe other subjects. However, the level of compliance was still much higher than most of us would expect. In short, there is the tendency for individuals to comply and be obedient—to switch off and merely do exactly what they are told to do.

Obedience and the Acceptance of Authority   Direct defiance within organizational settings is quite rare, as is the individual who institutes new and different ways to get the job done. If the tendency to follow instructions is great and defiance is rare, then why do so many organizations appear to drift into apparent chaos?

The answer to this question can be found in work by the famous management writer Chester Barnard.[12] Barnard's argument focused on the "consent of the governed" rather than on the rights derived from ownership. He argued that subordinates accepted or followed a directive from the boss only under special circumstances.

All four of these circumstances must be met: (1) the subordinate can and must understand the directive; (2) the subordinate must feel mentally and physically capable of carrying out the directive; (3) the subordinate must believe that the directive is not inconsistent with the purpose of the organization; and (4) the subordinate must believe that the directive is not inconsistent with his or her personal interests.

These four conditions are very carefully stated. For instance, to accept and follow an order, the subordinate does not need to understand how the proposed action will help the organization. He or she only needs to believe that the requested action is not inconsistent with the purpose of the firm. The astute manager will not take these guidelines for granted. In giving directives, the astute manager recognizes that the acceptance of the request is not assured.

Obedience and the Zone of Indifference   Most people seek a balance between what they put into an organization (contributions) and what they get from an organization in return (inducements). Within the boundaries of the psychological contract, therefore, employees will agree to do many things in and for the organization because they think they should. In exchange for certain inducements, subordinates recognize the authority of the organization and its managers to direct their behavior in certain ways.

Based on his acceptance view of authority, Chester Barnard calls this area in which directions are obeyed the "zone of indifference."[13]

A **zone of indifference** is the range of authoritative requests to which a subordinate is willing to respond without subjecting the directives to critical evaluation or judgment. Directives falling within the zone are obeyed. Requests or orders falling outside the zone of indifference are not considered legitimate under terms of the psychological contract. Such "extraordinary" directives may or may not be obeyed. This link between the zone of indifference and the psychological contract is shown in Figure 15.2.

The zone of indifference is not fixed. There may be times when a boss would like a subordinate to do things falling outside the zone. In this case, the manager must enlarge the zone to accommodate additional behaviors. In these attempts, a manager most likely will have to use more incentives than pure position power. In some instances, no power base may be capable of accomplishing the desired result. Consider your own zone of indifference and tendency to obey. When will you say "No" to your boss? When should you be willing to say "No"? At times, the situation may involve ethical dilemmas, where you may be asked to do things that are illegal, unethical, or both.

Research on ethical managerial behavior shows that supervisors can become sources of pressure for subordinates to do such things as support incorrect viewpoints, sign false documents, overlook the supervisor's wrongdoing, and do business with the supervisor's friends.[14] Most of us will occasionally face such ethical dilemmas during our careers. For now, we must simply remember that saying "No" or "refusing to keep quiet" can be difficult and potentially costly.

FIGURE 15.2 | **HYPOTHETICAL PSYCHOLOGICAL CONTRACT FOR A SECRETARY**

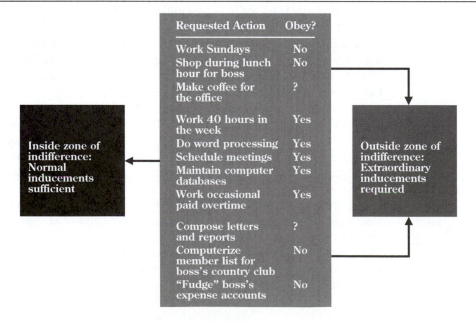

Requested Action	Obey?
Work Sundays	No
Shop during lunch hour for boss	No
Make coffee for the office	?
Work 40 hours in the week	Yes
Do word processing	Yes
Schedule meetings	Yes
Maintain computer databases	Yes
Work occasional paid overtime	Yes
Compose letters and reports	?
Computerize member list for boss's country club	No
"Fudge" boss's expense accounts	No

Inside zone of indifference: Normal inducements sufficient

Outside zone of indifference: Extraordinary inducements required

EMPOWERMENT

Empowerment is the process by which managers help others to acquire and use the power needed to make decisions affecting themselves and their work. More than ever before, managers in progressive organizations are expected to be good at (and highly comfortable with) empowering the people with whom they work. Rather than considering power to be something to be held only at higher levels in the traditional "pyramid" of organizations, this view considers power to be something that can be shared by everyone working in flatter and more collegial structures.

The concept of empowerment is part of the sweeping change being witnessed in today's corporations. Corporate staff is being cut back; layers of management are being eliminated; the number of employees is being reduced as the volume of work increases. What is left is a leaner and trimmer organization staffed by fewer managers who must share more power as they go about their daily tasks. Indeed, empowerment is a key foundation of the increasingly popular self-managing work teams and other creative worker involvement groups.

THE POWER KEYS TO EMPOWERMENT

One of the bases for empowerment is a radically different view of power itself. So far, our discussion has focused on power that is exerted over other individuals. In this traditional view, power is relational in terms of individuals. In contrast, the concept of empowerment emphasizes the ability to make things happen. Power is still relational, but in terms of problems and opportunities, not individuals. Cutting through all the corporate rhetoric on empowerment is quite difficult, since the term has become quite fashionable in management circles. Each individual empowerment attempt needs to be examined in light of how power in the organization will be changed.

Changing Position Power   When an organization attempts to move power down the hierarchy, it must also alter the existing pattern of position power. Changing this pattern raises some important questions. Can "empowered" individuals give rewards and sanctions based on task accomplishment? Has their new right to act been legitimized with formal authority? All too often, attempts at empowerment disrupt well-established patterns of position power and threaten middle and lower level managers. As one supervisor said, "All this empowerment stuff sounds great for top management. They don't have to run around trying to get the necessary clearances to implement the suggestions from my group. They never gave me the authority to make the changes, only the new job of asking for permission."

Expanding the Zone of Indifference   When embarking on an empowerment program, management needs to recognize the current zone of indifference and systematically move to expand it. All too often, management assumes that its directive for empowerment will be followed; management may fail to show precisely how empowerment will benefit the individuals involved, however.

POWER AS AN EXPANDING PIE

Along with empowerment, employees need to be trained to expand their power and their new influence potential. This is the most difficult task for managers and a difficult challenge for employees, for it often changes the dynamic between supervisors and subordinates. The key is to change the concept of power within the organization from a view that stresses power over others to one that emphasizes the use of power to get things done. Under the new definition of power, all employees can be more powerful.

A clearer definition of roles and responsibilities may help managers empower others. For instance, senior managers may choose to concentrate on long-term, large-scale adjustments to a variety of challenging and strategic forces in the external environment. If top management tends to concentrate on the long term and downplay quarterly mileposts, others throughout the organization must be ready and willing to make critical operating decisions to maintain current profitability. By providing opportunities for creative problem solving coupled with the discretion to act, real empowerment increases the total power available in an organization. In other words, the top levels don't have to give up power in order for the lower levels to gain it. Note that senior managers must give up the illusion of control—the false belief that they can direct the actions of employees five or six levels of management below them.

The same basic arguments hold true in any manager-subordinate relationship. Empowerment means that all managers need to emphasize different ways of exercising influence. Appeals to higher authority and sanctions need to be replaced by appeals to reason. Friendliness must replace coercion, and bargaining must replace orders for compliance.

Given the all too familiar history of an emphasis on coercion and compliance within firms, special support may be needed for individuals so that they become comfortable in developing their own power over events and activities. What executives fear, and all too often find, is that employees passively resist empowerment by seeking directives they can obey or reject. The fault lies with the executives and the middle managers who need to rethink what they mean by power and rethink their use of traditional position and personal power sources. The key is to lead, not push; reward, not sanction; build, not destroy; and expand, not shrink. To expand the zone of indifference also calls for expanding the inducements for thinking and acting, not just for obeying.

ORGANIZATIONAL POLITICS

Any study of power and influence inevitably leads to the subject of "politics." For many, this word may conjure up thoughts of illicit deals, favors, and special personal relationships. Perhaps this image of shrewd, often dishonest, practices of obtaining one's way is reinforced by Machiavelli's classic fifteenth-century work *The Prince,* which outlines how to obtain and hold power via political action. It is important, however, to adopt a perspective that allows politics in organizations to function in a much broader capacity.[15]

THE TWO TRADITIONS OF ORGANIZATIONAL POLITICS

There are two quite different traditions in the analysis of organizational politics. One tradition builds on Machiavelli's philosophy and *defines politics in terms of self-interest and the use of nonsanctioned means.* In this tradition, **organizational politics** may be formally defined as the management of influence to obtain ends not sanctioned by the organization or to obtain sanctioned ends through nonsanctioned influence means.[16] Managers are often considered political when they seek their own goals or use means that are not currently authorized by the organization or that push legal limits. Where there is uncertainty or ambiguity, it is often extremely difficult to tell whether a manager is being political in this self-serving sense.[17] For instance, was John Meriwether a great innovator when he established Long-Term Capital Management (LTCM) as a hedge fund to bet on interest rate spreads?[18] At one time, the firm included two Nobel laureates and some twenty-five Ph.D.s. Or was he the consummate insider when he got the U.S. Federal Reserve to orchestrate a bailout when it looked like he would either go broke or lose control to a rich investor? Or as often happens in the world of corporate politics, could both of these statements be partially true?

The second tradition *treats politics as a necessary function resulting from differences in the self-interests of individuals.* Here, organizational politics is viewed as the art of creative compromise among competing interests. In the case of John Meriwether and LTCM, when it went bankrupt the country's financial leaders were concerned that it could cause a panic in the markets and so hurt everyone. So the Federal Reserve stepped in. That Meriwether did not lose everything was merely a byproduct of saving the whole financial system. In a heterogeneous society, individuals will disagree as to whose self-interests are most valuable and whose concerns should therefore be bounded by collective interests. Politics arise because individuals need to develop compromises, avoid confrontation, and live together. The same holds true in organizations, where individuals join, work, and stay together because their self-interests are served. Furthermore, it is important to remember that the goals of the organization and the acceptable means are established by organizationally powerful individuals in negotiation with others. Thus, organizational politics is also the use of power to develop socially acceptable ends and means that balance individual and collective interests.

THE DOUBLE-EDGED SWORD OF ORGANIZATIONAL POLITICS

The two different traditions of organizational politics are reflected in the ways executives describe their effects on managers and their organizations. In one survey, some 53 percent of those interviewed indicated that organizational politics enhanced the achievement of organizational goals and survival.[19] Yet, some 44 percent suggested that it distracted individuals from organizational goals. In this same survey, 60 percent of respondents suggested that organizational politics was good for career advancement; 39 percent reported that it led to a loss of power, position, and credibility. As shown in The Effective Manager 15.2, political skill has been linked to lower executive stress.

THE EFFECTIVE MANAGER 15.2

POLITICAL SKILL AS AN ANTIDOTE FOR STRESS

Ever wonder why executives under tremendous daily stress don't burn out? Some argue it is their political skill that saves them. Which specific political skills? Think of these:

- The ability to use practical intelligence (as opposed to analytical or creative intelligence)
- The ability to be calculating and shrewd about social connections
- The ability to inspire trust and confidence
- The ability to deal with individuals having a wide variety of backgrounds, styles, and personalities

Organizational politics is not automatically good or bad. It can serve a number of important functions, including overcoming personnel inadequacies, coping with change, and substituting for formal authority.

Even in the best managed firms, mismatches arise among managers who are learning, burned out, lacking in needed training and skills, overqualified, or lacking the resources needed to accomplish their assigned duties. Organizational politics provides a mechanism for circumventing these inadequacies and getting the job done. Organizational politics can facilitate adaptation to changes in the environment and technology of an organization.

Organizational politics can help identify such problems and move ambitious, problem-solving managers into the breach. It is quicker than restructuring. It allows the firm to meet unanticipated problems with people and resources quickly, before small headaches become major problems. Finally, when a person's formal authority breaks down or fails to apply to a particular situation, political actions can be used to prevent a loss of influence. Managers may use political behavior to maintain operations and to achieve task continuity in circumstances where the failure of formal authority may otherwise cause problems.

ORGANIZATIONAL POLITICS AND SELF-PROTECTION

Whereas organizational politics may be helpful to the organization as a whole, it is probably more commonly known and better understood in terms of self-protection.[20] Whether or not management likes it, all employees recognize that in any organization they must watch out for themselves first. In too many organizations, if the employee doesn't protect himself or herself, no one else will.

Individuals can employ three common strategies to protect themselves. They can (1) avoid action and risk taking, (2) redirect accountability and responsibility, or (3) defend their turf.

Avoidance   *Avoidance* is quite common in controversial areas where the employee must risk being wrong or where actions may yield a sanction. Perhaps the most common reaction is to "work to the rules." That is, employees are protected when they adhere strictly to all the rules, policies, and procedures or do not allow deviations or exceptions. Perhaps one of the most frustrating but effective techniques is to "play dumb." We all do this at some time or another. When was the last time you said, "Officer, I didn't know the speed limit was 35. I couldn't have been going 52."

Although working to the rules and playing dumb are common techniques, experienced employees often practice somewhat more subtle techniques of self-protection. These include depersonalization and stalling. Depersonalization involves treating individuals, such as customers, clients, or subordinates, as numbers, things, or objects. Senior managers don't fire long-term employees; the organization is merely "downsized" or "delayered." Routine stalling involves slowing down the pace of work to expand the task so that the individuals look as if they are working hard. With creative stalling, the employees may spend the time supporting the organization's ideology, position, or program and delaying implementation.

Redirecting Responsibility   Politically sensitive individuals will always protect themselves from accepting blame for the negative consequences of their actions. Again, a variety of well-worn techniques may be used for *redirecting responsibility*. "Passing the buck" is a common method employees and managers use. The trick here is to define the task in such a way that it becomes someone else's formal responsibility. The ingenious ways individuals can redefine an issue to avoid action and transfer responsibility are often amazing.

Both employees and managers may avoid responsibility by *buffing,* or *rigorous documentation.* Here, individuals take action only when all the paperwork is in place and it is clear that they are merely following procedure. Closely related to rigorous documentation is the "blind memo," which explains an objection to an action implemented by the individual. Here, the required action is taken, but the blind memo is prepared should the action come into question. Politicians are particularly good at this technique. They will meet with a lobbyist and then send a memo to the files confirming the meeting. Any relationship between what was discussed in the meeting and the memo is accidental.

As the last example suggests, a convenient method some managers use to avoid responsibility is merely to *rewrite history.* If a program is successful, the manager claims to have been an early supporter. If a program fails, the manager was the one who expressed serious reservations in the first place. Whereas a memo in the files is often nice to have to show one's early support or objections, some executives don't bother with such niceties. They merely start a meeting by recapping what has happened in such a way that makes them look good.

For the really devious, there are three other techniques for redirecting responsibility. One technique is to blame the problem on someone or some group that has difficulty defending themselves. Fired employees, outsiders, and opponents are often targets of such scapegoating. Closely related to scapegoating is blaming the problem on uncontrollable events. The really astute manager goes far beyond the old "the-dog-ate-my-homework" routine. A perennial favorite is, "Given the unexpected severe decline in the overall economy, firm profitability was only somewhat below reasonable expectations." Meaning, the firm lost a bundle.

Should these techniques fail, there is always another possibility: facing apparent defeat, the manager can escalate commitment to a losing cause of action. That is, when all appears lost, assert your confidence in the original action, blame the problems on not spending enough money to implement the plan fully, and embark on actions that call for increased effort. The hope is that you will be promoted or retired by the time the negative consequences are recognized.

Defending Turf   Defending turf is a time-honored tradition in most large organizations. As noted earlier in the chapter, managers seeking to improve their power attempt to expand the jobs their groups perform. Defending turf also results from the coalitional nature of organizations. That is, the organization may be seen as a collection of competing interests held by various departments and groups. As each group attempts to expand its influence, it starts to encroach on the activities of other groups. Turf protection can be seen more easily in the following analysis of political action and the manager.

POLITICAL ACTION AND THE MANAGER

Managers may gain a better understanding of political behavior by placing themselves in the positions of other persons involved in critical decisions or events. Each action and decision can be seen as having benefits for and costs to all parties concerned. Where the costs exceed the benefits, the manager may act to protect his or her position.

Figure 15.3 shows a sample payoff table for two managers, Lee and Leslie, in a problem situation involving a decision as to whether or not to allocate resources to a special project. If both managers authorize the resources, the project gets completed on time, and their company keeps a valuable client. Unfortunately, if they do this, both Lee and Leslie overspend their budgets. Taken on its own, a budget overrun would be bad for the managers' performance records. Assume that the overruns are acceptable only if the client is kept. Thus, if both managers act, both they and the company win, as depicted in the upper left block of the figure. Obviously, this is the most desirable outcome for all parties concerned.

Assume that Leslie acts, but Lee does not. In this case, the company loses the client, Leslie overspends the budget in a futile effort, but Lee ends up within budget. While the company and Leslie lose, Lee wins. This scenario is illustrated in the lower-left block of the figure. The upper-right block shows the reverse situation, where Lee acts but Leslie does not. In this case, Leslie wins, while the company and Lee lose. Finally, if both Lee and Leslie fail to act, each stays within the budget and therefore gains, but the company loses the client.

The company clearly wants both Lee and Leslie to act. But will they? Would you take the risk of overspending the budget, knowing that your colleague may refuse? The question of trust is critical here, but building trust among co-managers and other workers takes time and can be difficult. The involvement of higher-level managers may be needed to set the stage better. Yet, in many organizations both Lee and Leslie would fail to act because the "climate" or "culture" too often encourages people to maximize their self-interest at minimal risks.

FIGURE 15.3	**POLITICAL PAYOFF MATRIX FOR THE ALLOCATION OF RESOURCES ON A SAMPLE PROJECT**

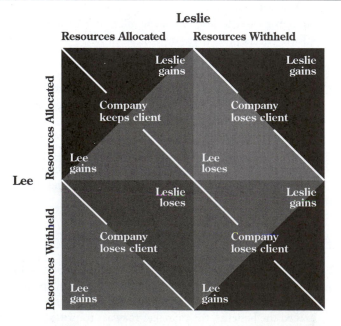

POLITICAL ACTION AND SUBUNIT POWER

Political action links managers more formally to one another as representatives of their work units. Five of the more typical lateral, intergroup relations in which you may engage as a manager are workflow, service, advisory, auditing, and approval.[21] Workflow linkages involve contacts with units that precede or follow in a sequential production chain. Service ties involve contacts with units established to help with problems. For instance, an assembly-line manager may develop a service link by asking the maintenance manager to fix an important piece of equipment on a priority basis. In contrast, advisory connections involve formal staff units having special expertise, such as a manager seeking the advice of the personnel department on evaluating subordinates. Auditing linkages involve units that have the right to evaluate the actions of others after action has been taken, whereas approval linkages involve units whose approval must be obtained before action may be taken.

To be effective in political action, managers should understand the politics of subunit relations. Line units are typically more powerful than are staff groups, and units toward the top of the hierarchy are often more powerful than are those toward the bottom. In general, units gain power as more of their relations with others are of the approval and auditing types. Workflow relations are more powerful than are advisory associations, and both are more powerful than are service relations.

POLITICAL ACTION IN THE CHIEF EXECUTIVE SUITE

From descriptions of the 1890s' robber barons such as Jay Gould to the actions of Microsoft's Bill Gates, Americans have been fascinated with the politics of the chief executive suite. An analytical view of executive suite dynamics may lift some of the mystery behind the political veil at the top levels in organizations.

Resource Dependencies Executive behavior can sometimes be explained in terms of resource dependencies—the firm's need for resources that are controlled by others.[22] Essentially, the resource dependence of an organization increases as (1) needed resources become more scarce, (2) outsiders have more control over needed resources, and (3) there are fewer substitutes for a particular type of resource controlled by a limited number of outsiders. Thus, one political role of the chief executive is to develop workable compromises among the competing resource dependencies facing the organization—compromises that enhance the executive's power. To create such compromises, executives need to diagnose the relative power of outsiders and to craft strategies that respond differently to various external resource suppliers.

For larger organizations, many strategies may center on altering the firm's degree of resource dependence. Through mergers and acquisitions, a firm may bring key resources within its control. By changing the "rules of the game," a firm may also find protection from particularly powerful outsiders. In the late 1990s, for instance, Netscape was seeking relief from the onslaught of Microsoft by appealing to the U.S. government. Markets may also be protected by trade barriers, or labor unions may be put in check by "right to work" laws. Yet, there are limits on the ability of even our largest and most powerful organizations to control all important external contingencies.

International competition has narrowed the range of options for chief executives; they can no longer ignore the rest of the world. Some may need to redefine fundamentally how they expect to conduct business. For instance, once U.S. firms could go it alone without the assistance of foreign corporations. Now, chief executives are increasingly leading them in the direction of more joint ventures and strategic alliances with foreign partners from around the globe. Such "combinations" provide access to scarce resources and technologies among partners, as well as new markets and shared production costs.

On the seamier side, there is a new wrinkle in the discussion of resource dependencies—executive pay. Traditionally, U.S. CEOs made about 30 times the pay of the average worker. This was similar to CEO pay scales in Europe and Japan.[23] Today many U.S. CEOs are making 3,000 times the average pay of workers. How did they get so rich? CEOs may tie themselves to the short-term interests of powerful stockholders. Their pay may be directly linked to short-term stock price increases, even though CEOs are most often expected to focus on the long-term health of the firm. When a CEO downsizes, embarks on a merger campaign, or cuts such benefits as worker health care, short-term profits may jump dramatically and lift the stock price. Although the long-term health of the firm may be put in jeopardy, few U.S. CEOs seem able to resist the temptation. It is little wonder that there is renewed interest in how U.S. firms are governed.

Politics and Corporate Strategy   While much of the strategy literature has been preoccupied with the economic and organizational aspects of strategy, there is growing awareness of the importance of political strategy. Three aspects have received considerable recent attention. First is the absence of a political strategy in some corporations, mainly Silicon Valley and software firms. It can be argued, for example, that Microsoft's antitrust problems were in part due to an unwillingness of Gates and Ballmer to consider the political ramifications of their attempts to block competitors by coercing computer manufacturers. In contrast, consider the approach of John Chambers, CEO of Cisco Systems. Cisco has over 80 percent of the high-speed server market, clearly almost a monopolistic position. He met with U.S. Justice Department officials to preempt government action. He assured regulators his firm was not acting like Microsoft. It just had the patents and a superior technology.[24] In general, U.S. firms are admonished to reject passive reaction to government policy or even passive anticipation. Instead they are advised to engage in the public political process.[25]

A second aspect of a corporate political strategy is turning the government from a regulator against the industry to a protector. Immediately after the events of 9/11, a wounded airline industry collectively sought government help with an immediate financial bailout in the billions of dollars.[26] On a more routine basis, U.S. steel companies have sought protection from foreign competition for over 40 years. Here, the industry's largest firms dominated the politics surrounding trade protection. They sought and generally received protection when U.S. demand was weakest. They used a variety of tactics ranging from political contributions to information campaigns to establish an agenda favoring their position.[27]

Of course, a third and most critical aspect of a corporate political strategy is when and how to get involved in the public policy processes. There are no easy answers. Smaller firms with less governmental regulation of their industry may be willing to take a so-called transactional approach. They become involved on specific issues with specific public policy officials who deal with a given issue. Larger firms in more regulated settings should not wait for the agenda to be formed. Instead they should be more relationally oriented. That is, they should monitor the environment, help shape emerging issues, and build solid relationships with a broad spectrum of policymakers. While firms may do this alone, most seek allies and build coalitions of firms to shape and guide the process of issue development.

As our economy continues to globalize and firms move across national boundaries, the development and implementation of an effective political strategy has become both more important and more difficult. For example, U.S. regulators were willing to allow General Electric to buy a firm called Honeywell. Unfortunately for General Electric, European Union representatives were not, and the proposed merger fell through. While Microsoft has apparently resolved its U.S. antitrust problems, the European Union has yet to rule.

Organizational Governance   **Organizational governance** refers to the pattern of authority, influence, and acceptable managerial behavior established at the top of the organization. This system establishes what is important, how issues will be defined, who should and should not be involved in key choices, and the boundaries for acceptable implementation.

Students of organizational governance suggest that a "dominant coalition" comprised of powerful organizational actors is a key to understanding a firm's governance.[28] Although one expects many top officers within the organization to be members of this coalition, the dominant coalition occasionally includes outsiders with access to key resources. Thus, analysis of organizational governance builds on the resource dependence perspective by highlighting the effective control of key resources by members of a dominant coalition.

This view of the executive suite recognizes that the daily practice of organizational governance is the development and resolution of issues. Through the governance system, the dominant coalition attempts to define reality. By accepting or rejecting proposals from subordinates, by directing questions toward the interests of powerful outsiders, and by selecting individuals who appear to espouse particular values and qualities, the pattern of governance is slowly established within the organization. Furthermore, this pattern rests, at least in part, on very political foundations.

While organizational governance was an internal and a rather private matter in the past, it is now becoming more public and openly controversial. Some argue that senior managers don't represent shareholder interests well enough. Others are concerned that they give too little attention to broader constituencies.

It has been estimated that the *Fortune* 500 corporations have cut some eight million positions over the last fifteen years of downsizing.[29] Managers and employees of these firms once felt confident that the management philosophy of their firm included their interests. In the new millennium, only a few employees seem to share this confidence. For instance, Boeing announced record production, near-record profits, and a merger with McDonnell-Douglas at the same time that it eliminated some 20,000 engineers from its home Seattle operations. After the tragedy of 9/11, it announced another round of cuts expected to be 30,000. Boeing eliminated almost all of the engineers hired in the last four years. As one critic caustically noted, "They ate their young to get executive bonuses." Obviously, Boeing is not a high performance organization even though it expresses a concern for ethics.

Organizational Governance and Ethics   Public concerns about U.S. corporations, especially those organizations with high-risk technologies such as chemical processing, medical technology, and integrated oil refineries, appear on the rise. For instance, Dow-Corning's survival is questionable because it has been accused of selling breast implants that cause immune system problems. Dow-Corning cites the lack of scientific evidence linking their product with such problems, but jury after jury is awarding damages to women who have had Dow-Corning implants and immune system problems. Without doubt juries are holding Dow-Corning management accountable.

Imbalanced organizational governance by some U.S. corporations may limit their ability to manage global operations effectively. Although U.S. senior managers may blame such externalities as unfavorable trade laws for their inability to compete in Japan or other Asian competitors, their critics suggest that it's just a lack of global operating savvy that limits the corporations these managers are supposed to be leading. Organizational governance is too closely tied to the short-term interests of stockholders and the pay of the CEO.

On a more positive note, there are bright spots suggesting that the governance of U.S. firms is extending well beyond the limited interests of the owners to include employees and into communities.

Cavanagh, Moberg, and Velasquez argue that organizational governance should have an ethical base.[30] They suggest that from the CEO to the lowest employee, a person's behavior must satisfy the following criteria to be considered ethical. First, the behavior must result in optimizing the satisfaction of people both inside and outside the organization to produce the greatest good for the greatest number of people. Second, the behavior must respect the rights of all affected parties, including the human rights of free consent, free speech, freedom of conscience, privacy, and due process. Third, the behavior must respect the rules of justice by treating people equitably and fairly, as opposed to arbitrarily.

There may be times when a behavior is unable to fulfill these criteria but can still be considered ethical in the given situation. This special case must satisfy the criterion of overwhelming factors, in which the special nature of the situation results in (1) conflicts among criteria (e.g., a behavior results in some good and some bad being done), (2) conflicts within criteria (e.g., a behavior uses questionable means to achieve a positive end), or (3) incapacity to employ the criteria (e.g., a person's behavior is based on inaccurate or incomplete information).

Choosing to be ethical often involves considerable personal sacrifice, and, at all corporate levels, it involves avoiding common rationalizations. CEOs and employees alike may justify unethical actions by suggesting that (1) the behavior is not really illegal and so could be moral; (2) the action appears to be in the firm's best interests; (3) the action is unlikely ever to be detected; and (4) it appears that the action demonstrates loyalty to the boss, the firm, or short-term stockholder interests. Whereas these rationalizations may appear compelling at the moment of action, each deserves close scrutiny if the firm's organizational governance system is to avoid falling into being dominated by the more unsavory side of organizational politics.

CHAPTER 15 SUMMARY

What is power?

- Power is the ability to get someone else to do what you want him or her to do.
- Power vested in managerial positions derives from three sources: rewards, punishments, and legitimacy (formal authority).

How do managers acquire the power needed for leadership?

- Formal authority is based on the manager's position in the hierarchy of authority, whereas personal power is based on one's expertise and referent capabilities.
- Managers can pursue various ways of acquiring both position and personal power.
- They can also become skilled at using various tactics, such as reason, friendliness, ingratiation, and bargaining, to influence superiors, peers, and subordinates.
- People may have a tendency to obey directives coming from others who appear powerful and authoritative.
- The zone of indifference defines the boundaries within which people in organizations let others influence their behavior.
- Ultimately, power and authority work only if the individual "accepts" them.

What is empowerment, and how can managers empower others?

- Empowerment is the process through which managers help others acquire and use the power needed to make decisions that affect themselves and their work.
- Empowerment emphasizes power as the ability to get things done rather than the ability to get others to do what you want.
- Clear delegation of authority, integrated planning, and the involvement of senior management are all important to implementing empowerment.

What are organizational politics?

- Organizational politics are inevitable.
- Politics involves the use of power to obtain ends not officially sanctioned and the use of power to find ways of balancing individual and collective interests in otherwise difficult circumstances.

How do organizational politics affect managers and management?

- For the manager, politics often occurs in decision situations where the interests of another manager or individual must be reconciled with one's own.
- For managers, politics also involves subunits that jockey for power and advantageous positions vis-à-vis one another.
- For chief executives, politics come into play as resource dependencies with external environmental elements must be strategically managed.
- Politics can also be used strategically.
- Organizational governance is the pattern of authority, influence, and acceptable managerial behavior established at the top of the organization.
- CEOs and managers can develop an ethical organizational governance system that is free from rationalizations.

CHAPTER 16

Information and Communication

Study Questions

Chapter 16 examines the process of communication, with special attention to its interpersonal and organizational challenges as well as the opportunities of new developments in information technology. As you read this chapter, keep in mind these questions.

- What is the nature of the communication process?
- What are the essentials of interpersonal communication?
- What barriers interfere with effective communication?
- What is organizational communication?
- What forces influence communication in the high performance workplace?

Everyone knows that "communication" is vital to an organization. But it takes hard work and true commitment to create an information-rich environment that fosters creativity, motivation, and high performance. This is especially true in a technology-intense age where speed is of utmost importance to organizations and where Microsoft's chairman Bill Gates says: "Only managers who master the digital universe will gain competitive advantage."[1]

Using information and technology for the high performance advantage requires an extraordinary willingness to open up communication linkages and opportunities among people in organizations, and between them and their customers. It also requires a culture of trust throughout the organization, a culture that encourages a free flow of ideas and suggestions up and down the hierarchy, as well as among peers and colleagues. In a recent survey by the American Management Association, however, respondents gave their managers only a 63 percent success rating in respect to "communicating information and direction." Respondents in another sample rated their managers' skills in "listening and asking questions" at only an average 3.36 on a five-point scale.[2] Obviously, there is a lot yet to be accomplished in respect to managerial and workplace communication!

THE NATURE OF COMMUNICATION

Have you ever stopped to consider just how great an impact information technology has had on our communication practices? One can safely estimate that today there will be more than a billion voice-mail messages exchanged, 3.4 trillion e-mails will be sent in a year, over 100 million Internet users will come online in a year, and Internet traffic will double as fast as every 100 days.[3] The figures are amazing, and the implications are clear. Appetites for information are growing by leaps and bounds, and the future of organizations is increasingly linked to their abilities to harness information and information technology for competitive advantage. At the center of all this stands the great demands and opportunities of the process we know as "communication."

THE COMMUNICATION PROCESS

It is useful to think of **communication** as a process of sending and receiving messages with attached meanings. The key elements in the communication process are illustrated in Figure 16.1. They include a *source,* who encodes an intended meaning into a message, and a *receiver,* who decodes the message into a perceived meaning. The receiver may or may not give feedback to the source. Although this process may appear to be very elementary, it is not quite as simple as it looks. **Noise** is the term used to describe any disturbance that disrupts it and interferes with the transference of messages within the communication process.

The information source is a person or group trying to communicate with someone else. The source seeks to communicate, in part, to change the attitudes, knowledge, or behavior of the receiver. A team leader, for example, may want to communicate with a division manager in order to explain why the team needs more time or resources to finish an assigned project. This involves *encoding*—the process of translating an idea or thought into a message consisting of verbal, written, or nonverbal symbols (such as gestures), or some combination of them. Messages are transmitted through various **communication channels,** such as face-to-face meetings, electronic mail and other forms, written letters or

| FIGURE 16.1 | THE COMMUNICATION PROCESS AND POSSIBLE SOURCES OF "NOISE" |

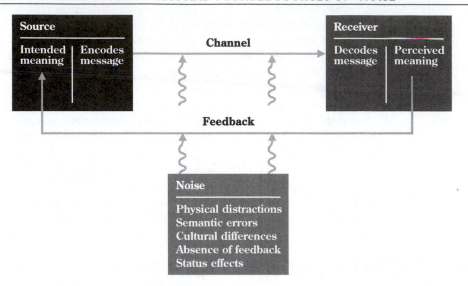

memorandums, and telephone communications or voice-mail, among others. The choice of channel can have an important impact on the communication process. Some people are better at using certain channels over others, and some messages are better handled by specific channels. In the case of the team leader communicating with the division manager, for example, it can make quite a difference whether the message is sent face to face, in a written memo, by voice-mail, or by e-mail.

The communication process is not completed just because a message is sent. The receiver is the individual or group of individuals to whom a message is directed. In order for meaning to be assigned to any received message, its contents must be interpreted through *decoding*. This process of translation is complicated by many factors, including the knowledge and experience of the receiver and his or her relationship with the sender. A message may also be interpreted with the added influence of other points of view, such as those offered by friends, co-workers, or organizational superiors. Ultimately, the decoding may result in the receiver interpreting a message in a way that is different from that originally intended by the source.

FEEDBACK AND COMMUNICATION

Most receivers are well aware of the potential gap between the intended message of the source and the perceived meaning assigned to it by the recipient. One way in which these gaps are identified is through **feedback,** the process through which the receiver communicates with the sender by returning another message. The exchange of information through feedback can be very helpful in improving the communication process, and the popular advice to always "keep the feedback channels open" is good to remember.

In practice, giving "feedback" is often associated with one or more persons communicating an evaluation of what another person has said or done. The practice of **360-degree feedback,** in which not just a supervisor, but also one's peers, co-workers, and direct reports provide feedback on performance, was introduced in Chapter 7. This is an increasingly popular approach to performance reviews that adds further challenge to feedback processes. Like any feedback situation, all parties must engage in the 360-degree feedback situation carefully and with interpersonal skill.[4]

There is an art to giving feedback so that the receiver accepts it and uses it constructively (see The Effective Manager 16.1). Words that are intended to be polite and helpful can easily end up being perceived as unpleasant and even hostile. This risk is particularly evident in the performance appraisal process. A manager or team leader must be able to do more than just complete a written appraisal to document another person's performance for the record. To serve the person's developmental needs, feedback regarding the results of the appraisal—both the praise and the criticism, must be well communicated.

ESSENTIALS OF INTERPERSONAL COMMUNICATION

Organizations today are information rich. They are also increasingly "high-tech." But, we always need to remember that people still drive the system. And if people are to work together well and commit their mutual talents and energies to create high performance organizations, they must excel at interpersonal communication.

EFFECTIVE AND EFFICIENT COMMUNICATION

When people communicate with one another, at least two important things are at issue. One is the accuracy of the communication—an issue of effectiveness; the other is its cost—an issue of efficiency.

Effective communication occurs when the intended meaning of the source and the perceived meaning of the receiver are virtually the same. Although this should be the goal in any communication, it is not always achieved. Even now, we worry about whether or not you are interpreting these written words exactly as we intend. Our confidence would be higher if we were face to face in class together and you could ask clarifying questions. Opportunities to offer feedback and ask questions are important ways of increasing the effectiveness of communication.

Efficient communication occurs at minimum cost in terms of resources expended. Time, for example, is an important resource. Picture your instructor taking the time to communicate individually with each student in your class about the course subject matter.

THE EFFECTIVE MANAGER 16.1

HOW TO GIVE CONSTRUCTIVE FEEDBACK

- Give directly and in a spirit of mutual trust.
- Be specific, not general; use clear examples.
- Give when receiver is most ready to accept.
- Be accurate; check validity with others.
- Focus on things the receiver can control.
- Limit how much receiver gets at one time.

It would be virtually impossible to do so. Even if it were possible, it would be very costly in terms of time. People at work often choose not to visit one another personally to communicate messages. Instead, they rely on the efficiency of written memos, posted bulletins, group meetings, e-mail, or voice-mail.

As efficient as these forms of communication may be, they are not always effective. A change in policy posted by efficient e-mail may save time for the sender, but it may not achieve the desired interpretations and responses. Similarly, an effective communication may not be efficient. For a business manager to visit each employee and explain a new change in procedures may guarantee that everyone understands the change, but it may also be prohibitively expensive in terms of the required time expenditure.

NONVERBAL COMMUNICATION

We all know that people communicate in ways other than the spoken or written word. Indeed, **nonverbal communication** that takes place through facial expressions, body position, eye contact, and other physical gestures is important both to understand and master. It is basically the act of speaking without using words. *Kinesics,* the study of gestures and body postures, has achieved a rightful place in communication theory and research.[5] The nonverbal side to communication can often hold the key to what someone is really thinking or meaning. It can also affect the impressions we make on others. Interviewers, for example, tend to respond more favorably to job candidates whose nonverbal cues, such as eye contact and erect posture, are positive than to those displaying negative nonverbal cues, such as looking down or slouching. The art of impression management during interviews and in other situations requires careful attention to both verbal and nonverbal aspects of communication, including one's dress, timeliness, and demeanor.

Nonverbal communication can also take place through the physical arrangement of space, such as that found in various office layouts. *Proxemics,* the study of the way space is utilized, is important to communication.[6] Figure 16.2 shows three different office arrangements and the messages they may communicate to visitors. Check the diagrams against the

---

FIGURE 16.2 FURNITURE PLACEMENT AND NONVERBAL COMMUNICATION IN THE OFFICE

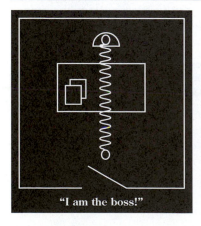
"I am the boss!"

"I am the boss, but let's talk."

"Forget I'm the boss, let's talk."

furniture arrangement in your office or that of your instructor or a person with whom you are familiar. What are you/they saying to visitors by the choice of furniture placement?[7]

ACTIVE LISTENING

The ability to listen well is a distinct asset to anyone whose job involves a large proportion of time spent "communicating" with other people. After all, there are always two sides to the communication process: (1) sending a message, or "telling," and (2) receiving a message, or "listening." Unfortunately, too many people emphasize the telling and neglect the listening.[8]

Everyone in the new workplace should develop good skills in **active listening**—the ability to help the source of a message say what he or she really means. The concept comes from the work of counselors and therapists, who are trained to help people express themselves and talk about things that are important to them.[9] Take a moment to more thoroughly consider the guidelines for active listening shown in The Effective Manager 16.2. Then read the conversations below. One involves active listening on the part of the branch manager; the other does not. How would you feel as the group leader in each case?[10]

Example 1

Group leader: Hey, Sal, I don't get this work order. We can't handle this today. What do they think we are?

Branch manager: But that's the order. So get it out as soon as you can. We're under terrific pressure this week.

Group leader: Don't they know we're behind schedule already because of that software problem?

Branch manager: Look, I don't decide what goes on upstairs. I just have to see that the work gets out, and that's what I'm going to do.

Group leader: The team won't like this.

Branch manager: That's something you'll have to work out with them, not me.

Example 2

Group leader: Hey, Kelley, I don't get this work order. We can't handle this today. What do they think we are?

Branch manager: Sounds like you're pretty sore about it.

Group leader: I sure am. We're just about getting back to schedule while fighting that software breakdown. Now this comes along.

Branch manager: As if you didn't have enough work to do?

Group leader: Right, I don't know how to tell the team about this. They're under a real strain today. Seems like everything we do around here is rush, rush, rush.

Branch manager: I guess you feel like it's unfair to load anything more on them.

Group leader: Well, yes. But I know there must be plenty of pressure on everybody up the line. If that's the way it is, I'll get the word to them.

Branch manager: Thanks. If you'll give it a try, I'll do my best to hold with the schedule in the future.

The branch manager in Example 2 possesses active listening skills. She responded to the group leader's communication in a way that increased the flow of information. The manager learned more about the situation. The group leader felt better after having been able to really say what she thought, and after being heard!

COMMUNICATION BARRIERS

It is important to understand six sources of noise that are common to most interpersonal exchanges: physical distractions, semantic problems, mixed messages, cultural differences, absence of feedback, and status effects. They were shown earlier in Figure 16.1 as potential threats to the communication process.

PHYSICAL DISTRACTIONS

Any number of physical distractions can interfere with the effectiveness of a communication attempt. Some of these distractions are evident in the following conversation between an employee, George, and his manager.[11]

> Okay, George, let's hear your problem (phone rings, boss picks it up, promises to deliver the report, "just as soon as I can get it done"). Uh, now, where were we—oh, you're having a problem with marketing. They (the manager's secretary brings in some papers that need immediate signatures; he scribbles his name and the secretary leaves)…you say they're not cooperative? I tell you what, George, why don't you (phone rings again, lunch partner drops by)…uh, take a stab at handling it yourself. I've got to go now.

Besides what may have been poor intentions in the first place, George's manager allowed physical distractions to create information overload. As a result, the communication with George suffered. This mistake can be eliminated by setting priorities and planning. If George has something to say, his manager should set aside adequate time for the meeting. In addition, interruptions such as telephone calls, drop-in visitors, and the like, should be prevented. At a minimum, George's manager could start by closing the door to the office and instructing his secretary not to disturb them.

SEMANTIC PROBLEMS

Semantic barriers to communication involve a poor choice or use of words and mixed messages. The following illustrations of the "bafflegab" that once tried to pass as actual "executive communication" are a case in point.[12]

A. "We solicit any recommendations that you wish to make, and you may be assured that any such recommendations will be given our careful consideration."

B. "Consumer elements are continuing to stress the fundamental necessity of a stabilization of the price structure at a lower level than exists at the present time."

One has to wonder why these messages weren't stated more simply as: (A) "Send us your recommendations. They will be carefully considered," and (B) "Consumers want lower prices." When in doubt regarding the clarity of your written or spoken messages, the popular **KISS principle** of communication is always worth remembering: "Keep it short and simple."

MIXED MESSAGES

Mixed messages occur when a person's words communicate one thing while actions or "body language" communicate another. They are important to spot since nonverbals can add important insight into what is really being said in face-to-face communication.[13] For instance, someone may voice a cautious "Yes" during a business meeting at the same time that her facial expression shows stress and she begins to lean back in her chair. The body language in this case may suggest the existence of important reservations, even though the words indicate agreement.

CULTURAL DIFFERENCES

People must always exercise caution when they are involved in cross-cultural communication—whether between persons of different geographical or ethnic groupings within one country, or between persons of different national cultures. A common problem is *ethnocentrism,* first defined in Chapter 3 as the tendency to believe one's culture and its values are superior to those of others. It is often accompanied by an unwillingness to try to understand alternative points of view and to take the values they represent seriously. This mindset can easily create communication problems among people of diverse backgrounds.

The difficulties with cross-cultural communication are perhaps most obvious in respect to language differences. Advertising messages, for example, may work well in one country but encounter difficulty when translated into the language of another. Problems accompanied the introduction of Ford's European model, the "Ka," in Japan. (In Japanese, *Ka* means mosquito.) Gestures may also be used quite differently in the various cultures of the world. For example, crossed legs in the United Kingdom are quite acceptable, but are rude in Saudi Arabia if the sole of the foot is directed toward someone. Pointing at someone to get their attention may be acceptable in Canada, but in Asia it is considered inappropriate.[14]

International business experts advise that one of the best ways to gain understanding of cultural differences is to learn at least some of the language of the country that one is dealing with. Although the prospect of learning another language may sound daunting, The Effective Manager 16.3 points out that it can be well worth the effort.[15]

ABSENCE OF FEEDBACK

One-way communication flows from sender to receiver only, as in the case of a written memo or a voice-mail message. There is no direct and immediate feedback from the

---

THE EFFECTIVE MANAGER 16.3

WHY BUILD FOREIGN LANGUAGE SKILLS?

- Increase your self-confidence as a traveler.
- Show respect to local hosts.
- Build relationships with locals.
- Earn the trust and respect of locals.
- Gain insights into local culture.
- Prepare for emergencies.
- Find greater pleasure in day-to-day interactions.
- Experience less frustration with local ways.

---

recipient. Two-way communication, by contrast, goes from sender to receiver and back again. It is characterized by the normal interactive conversations in our daily experiences. Research indicates that two-way communication is more accurate and effective than is one-way communication, even though it is also more costly and time consuming. Because of their efficiency, however, one-way forms of communication—memos, letters, e-mail, voice-mail, and the like are frequently used in work settings. One-way messages are easy for the sender but often frustrating for the receiver, who may be left unsure of just what the sender means or wants done.

STATUS EFFECTS

Status differences in organizations create potential communication barriers between persons of higher and lower ranks. On the one hand, given the authority of their positions, managers may be inclined to do a lot of "telling" but not much "listening." On the other hand, we know that communication is frequently biased when flowing upward in organizational hierarchies.[16] Subordinates may *filter* information and tell their superiors only what they think the boss wants to hear. Whether the reason is a fear of retribution for bringing bad news, an unwillingness to identify personal mistakes, or just a general desire to please, the result is the same: The higher level decision maker may end up taking the wrong actions because of biased and inaccurate information supplied from below. This is sometimes called the **MUM effect** in reference to tendencies to sometimes keep "mum" from a desire to be polite and a reluctance to transmit bad news.[17]

To avoid such problems, managers and group leaders must develop trust in their working relationships with subordinates and team members, and take advantage of all opportunities for face-to-face communications. *Management by wandering around,* or **MBWA** for short, is now popularly acclaimed as one way to achieve this trust.[18] It simply means getting out of the office and talking to people regularly as they do their jobs. Managers who spend time walking around can greatly reduce the perceived "distance" between themselves and their subordinates. It helps to create an atmosphere of open and free-flowing communication between the ranks. As a result, more and better information is available for decision making, and the relevance of decisions to the needs of operating workers increases.

ORGANIZATIONAL COMMUNICATION

Communication among members of an organization, as well as between them and external customers, suppliers, distributors, alliance partners, and a host of outsiders, provides vital information for the enterprise. **Organizational communication** is the specific process through which information moves and is exchanged throughout an organization.[19] Information flows through both formal and informal structures, and it flows downward, upward, and laterally.

Today, more than ever before, computer technology plays a major role in how information is shared and utilized in organizations. Research in the area of *channel richness*, the capacity of a channel to convey information effectively, lends insight into how various channel alternatives may be used depending on the type of message to be conveyed. In general, the richest channels are face to face. Next are telephone, electronic characteristics, e-mail, written memos and letters. The leanest channels are posted notices and bulletins. When messages get more complex and open ended, richer channels are necessary to achieve effective communication; leaner channels work well for more routine and straightforward messages, such as announcing the location of a previously scheduled meeting.

FORMAL AND INFORMAL CHANNELS

Information flows in organizations through both formal and informal channels of communication. **Formal channels** follow the chain of command established by an organization's hierarchy of authority. For example, an organization chart indicates the proper routing for official messages passing from one level or part of the hierarchy to another. Because formal channels are recognized as authoritative, it is typical for communication of policies, procedures, and other official announcements to adhere to them. On the other hand, much "networking" takes place through the use of **informal channels** that do not adhere to the organization's hierarchy of authority.[20] They coexist with the formal channels but frequently diverge from them by skipping levels in the hierarchy or cutting across vertical chains of command. Informal channels help to create open communications in organizations and ensure that the right people are in contact with one another.[21]

One familiar informal channel is the **grapevine** or network of friendships and acquaintances through which rumors and other unofficial information are passed from person to person. Grapevines have the advantage of being able to transmit information quickly and efficiently. Grapevines also help fulfill the needs of people involved in them. Being part of a grapevine can provide a sense of security from "being in the know" when important things are going on. It also provides social satisfaction as information is exchanged interpersonally. The primary disadvantage of grapevines occurs when they transmit incorrect or untimely information. Rumors can be very dysfunctional, to both people and organizations. One of the best ways to avoid them is to make sure that key persons in a grapevine get the right information to begin with.

COMMUNICATION FLOWS AND DIRECTIONS

As shown in Figure 16.3, *downward communication* follows the chain of command top to bottom. One of its major functions is to achieve influence through information. Lower-level personnel need to know what higher levels are doing and to be regularly reminded of key policies, strategies, objectives, and technical developments. Of special importance is feedback and information on performance results. Sharing such information helps minimize the spread of rumors and inaccuracies regarding higher-level intentions. It also helps create a sense of security and involvement among receivers, who feel they know the whole story. Unfortunately, a lack of adequate downward communication is often cited as a management failure. On the issue of corporate downsizing, for example, one sample showed that 64 percent of employees did not believe what management said, 61 percent felt uninformed about company plans, and 54 percent complained that decisions were not well explained.[22]

The flow of messages from lower to higher levels is *upward communication*. As shown in Figure 16.3, it serves several purposes. Upward communication keeps higher levels informed about what lower level workers are doing, what their problems are, what suggestions they have for improvements, and how they feel about the organization and their jobs. But, status effects can potentially interfere with the effectiveness of upward communication.

The importance of *lateral communication* in the new workplace has been a recurrent theme in this book. Today's customer-sensitive organizations need timely and accurate feedback and product information. To serve customer needs they must get the right information—and get it fast enough—into the hands of workers. Furthermore, inside the organization, people must be willing and able to communicate across departmental or functional

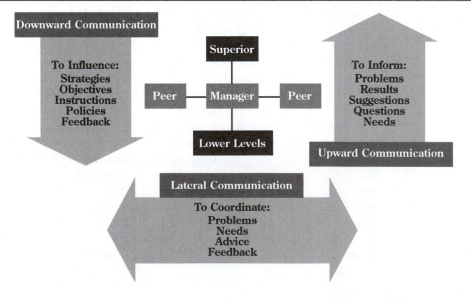

FIGURE 16.3   DIRECTIONS FOR INFORMATION FLOWS IN ORGANIZATIONS

boundaries and to listen to one another's needs as "internal customers." New organization designs are emphasizing lateral communication in the form of cross-departmental committees, teams, or task forces and the matrix organization. Among the developments is growing attention to *organizational ecology*—the study of how building design may influence communication and productivity by improving lateral communications.

COMMUNICATION NETWORKS

Figure 16.4 depicts three interaction patterns and communication networks that are common within organizations.[23] Having the right interaction pattern and communication network can make a big difference in the way groups function and in the performance results they achieve.

Some work arrangements involve *interacting groups* whose members work closely together on tasks and in which close coordination of activities takes place. Information flows to everyone. This interaction pattern results in a **decentralized communication network** in which all group members communicate directly and share information with one another. Sometimes these are also referred to as all-channel or star communication networks.[24] They work best for complex and nonroutine tasks. They also tend to create high levels of member satisfaction.

Other work arrangements involve *coacting groups* whose members work on tasks independently, while linked through some form of central coordination. The required work is

---

FIGURE 16.4 | **INTERACTION PATTERNS AND COMMUNICATION NETWORKS FOUND IN GROUPS**

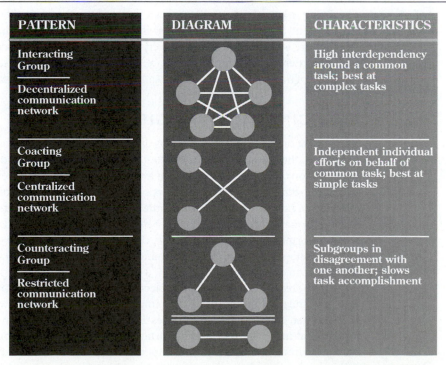

PATTERN	DIAGRAM	CHARACTERISTICS
Interacting Group Decentralized communication network		High interdependency around a common task; best at complex tasks
Coacting Group Centralized communication network		Independent individual efforts on behalf of common task; best at simple tasks
Counteracting Group Restricted communication network		Subgroups in disagreement with one another; slows task accomplishment

divided up and then largely completed by individuals working alone. Each individual's activities are coordinated and results pooled by a central control point. Information flows to a central person and is redistributed. This creates a **centralized communication network,** with the central person serving as the "hub." Sometimes these are called wheel or chain communication networks. They work best when tasks are easily routinized or subdivided. In these groups, it is usually the central or "hub" person who experiences this satisfaction. After all, he or she alone is most involved in all aspects of group information processing.

Counteracting groups exist when subgroups disagree on some aspect of workplace operations. The subgroups may experience issue-specific disagreements—such as a temporary debate over the best means to achieve a goal, or the disagreements may be of longer-term duration—such as labor–management disputes. In either case, the resulting interaction pattern involves a **restricted communication network** in which polarized subgroups contest one another's positions and maintain sometimes antagonistic relations. As would be expected, communication between the groups is often limited and biased. Problems of destructive competition in intergroup dynamics are likely under such circumstances.

COMMUNICATION AND THE HIGH PERFORMANCE WORKPLACE

One of the greatest changes in organizations and in everyday life in recent years has been the great explosion in new communication technologies. We have moved from the world of the telephone, mail, photocopying, and face-to-face meetings into one of voice-mail, e-mail, facsimile transmission, computer-mediated conferencing, and use of the Internet and intranets. The ability to participate effectively in all forms of the electronic office and communications environment is well established as an essential career skill. The increasing importance of e-commerce is also transforming the very nature of business in modern society.[25] Given the pace and extensiveness of these dynamics, everyone must keep themselves up to date with the full range of information technologies and emerging issues in organizational communication.

CHANGING TECHNOLOGIES

The impact of the new technologies is discussed throughout this book with respect to job design and the growth of telecommuting, organizational design and the growth of network organizations, and teamwork and the availability of software for electronic meetings and decision making, among many other applications. Advances in information technology are allowing organizations to (1) distribute information much faster than before; (2) make more information available than ever before; (3) allow broader and more immediate access to this information; (4) encourage participation in the sharing and use of information; and (5) integrate systems and functions, and use information to link with environments in unprecedented ways.

The potential disadvantages of electronic communications must also be recognized. To begin, the technologies are largely impersonal; people interact with machines, not with one another. Electronics also removes nonverbal communications from the situation—aspects that may otherwise add important context to an interaction. In addition, the electronic medium can influence the emotional aspects of communication. Some argue, for example, that it is far easier to be blunt, overly critical, and insensitive when conveying messages electronically rather than face-to-face. The term "flaming" is sometimes used to describe rudeness in electronic communication. In this sense, the use of computer mediation may make people less inhibited and more impatient in what they say.

Another risk of the new communication technologies is information overload. In some cases, too much information may find its way into the communication networks and e-mail systems and basically overload the systems—both organizational and individual. Individual users may have difficulty sorting the useful from the trivial and may become impatient while doing so. Even the IT giant Intel experiences e-mail problems. Employees at the firm reportedly handle 3+ million e-mail messages a day; some individuals handle as many as 300 in a day. Says one: "We're so wrapped up in sending e-mail to each other, we don't have time to be dealing with the outside." Intel offers training in e-mail processing as a way of helping employees gain the advantages and avoid the disadvantages of electronic messaging. The Effective Manager 16.4 lists several suggested guidelines.[26]

In all this, one point remains undeniable: new communication technologies will continue to keep changing the nature of work and of office work in particular. The once-conventional office is fast giving way to new forms such as telecommuting and the use of electronic networks. Workers in the future will benefit as new technologies allow them to spend more time out of the traditional office and more time working with customers on terms that best fit individual needs.

COMPLEX SOCIAL CONTEXT

There are any number of issues affecting communication in the complex social context of organizations today. Of continuing interest, for example, is the study of *male and female communication styles.* In her book *Talking 9 to 5,* Deborah Tannen argues that men and women learn or are socialized into different styles and as a result often end up having difficulties communicating with one another.[27] She sees women more oriented toward relationship building in communication, for example, while men are more prone to seek status through communications.[28] Because people tend to surround themselves with those whose communication styles fit with their own, a further implication is that either women or men may dominate communications in situations where they are in the majority.[29]

More and more people are asking a question related to the prior discussion: "Are women better communicators than men?" A study by the consulting firm Lawrence A. Pfaff and Associates suggests they may well be.[30] The survey shows that supervisors rank women managers higher than men managers on communication, approachability, evaluations, and

---

THE EFFECTIVE MANAGER 16.4

HOW TO STREAMLINE YOUR E-MAIL

- Read items once.
- Take action immediately to answer, move to folders, or delete.
- Regularly purge folders of outdated messages.
- Send group mail and use "reply to all" only when really necessary.
- Get off distribution lists that don't offer value to your work.
- Send short messages in the subject line, avoiding a full-text message.
- Put large files on Web sites, instead of sending as attachments.

empowering others; the subordinates also rank women higher on these same items. A possible explanation is that early socialization and training better prepare women for the skills involved in communication and may make them more sensitive in interpersonal relationships. In contrast, men may be more socialized in ways that cause communication problems—such as aggression, competitiveness, and individualism.[31] In considering such possibilities, however, it is important to avoid gender stereotyping and to focus instead on the point of ultimate importance—how communication in organizations can be made most effective.[32]

Among the controversies in organizational communication today is the issue of *privacy*. An example is eavesdropping by employers on employee use of electronic messaging in corporate facilities. A study by the American Management Association found that electronic monitoring of employee performance increased over 45 percent in a year's time. You may be surprised to learn that the most frequently reported things bosses watch are: number of telephone calls and time spent on telephone calls (39 percent), e-mail messages (27 percent), computer files (21 percent), telephone conversations (11 percent), and voice-mail messages (6 percent).[33]

Progressive organizations are developing internal policies regarding the privacy of employee communications, and the issue is gaining attention from legislators. A state law in Illinois now makes it legal for bosses to listen in on employees' telephone calls. But the law leaves the boundaries of appropriateness unclear. Such eavesdropping is common in some service areas such as airlines reservations, where union concerns are sometimes expressed in the context of "Big brother is watching you!" The privacy issue is likely to remain controversial as communication technologies continue to make it easier for employers to electronically monitor the performance and communications of their workers.

Our society also struggles with the *political correctness* of communications in the workplace. The vocabulary of work is changing, and people are ever more on guard not to let their choice of words offend another individual or group. We now hear references to "people of color," the "physically challenged," and "seniors"; not too long ago these references may have been different, and they may be different again in the future. Organizations are taking notice of this issue and are offering more training to their members to help eliminate in any communications possible overtones of intolerance and insensitivity.

Chapter 16 Summary

What is the nature of the communication process?

- Communication is the process of sending and receiving messages with attached meanings.
- The communication process involves encoding an intended meaning into a message, sending the message through a channel, and receiving and decoding the message into perceived meaning.
- Noise is anything that interferes with the communication process.
- Feedback is a return message from the original recipient back to the sender.
- To be constructive, feedback must be direct, specific, and given at an appropriate time.

What are the essentials of interpersonal communication?

- Communication is effective when both sender and receiver interpret a message in the same way.

- Communication is efficient when messages are transferred at a low cost.

- Nonverbal communication occurs through facial expressions, body position, eye contact, and other physical gestures.

- Active listening encourages a free and complete flow of communication from the sender to the receiver; it is nonjudgmental and encouraging.

- Communication in organizations uses a variety of formal and informal channels; the richness of the channel, or its capacity to convey information, must be adequate for the message.

What barriers interfere with effective communication?

- The possible barriers to communication include physical distractions, semantic problems, and cultural differences.

- Mixed messages that give confused or conflicting verbal and nonverbal cues may interfere with communications.

- The absence of feedback can make it difficult to know whether or not an intended message has been accurately received.

- Status effects in organizations may result in restricted and filtered information exchanges between subordinates and their superiors.

What is organizational communication?

- Organizational communication is the specific process through which information moves and is exchanged within an organization.

- Organizations depend on complex flows of information, upward, downward, and laterally, to operate effectively.

- Groups in organizations work with different interaction patterns and use different communication networks.

- Interacting groups with decentralized networks tend to perform well on complex tasks; coacting groups with centralized networks may do well at simple tasks.

- Restricted communication networks are common in counteracting groups involving subgroup disagreements.

What forces influence communication in the high performance workplace?

- As new electronic communication technologies change the workplace, they bring many advantages of rapid and greater information processing capability.

- These same technologies have the potential to bring disadvantages in the form of a loss of emotion and personality in the communication process.

- Researchers are interested in possible differences in communication styles among men and women and in the relative effectiveness of these styles for conditions in the new workplace.

- Current controversies in organizational communication also include both issues of privacy and political correctness in workplace communications.

17

Decision Making

Study Questions

Chapter 17 examines the many aspects of decision making in organizations. As you read the chapter, keep in mind these key questions.

- How are decisions made in organizations?
- What are the useful decision-making models?
- How do intuition, judgment, and creativity affect decision making?
- How can the decision-making process be managed?
- How do technology, culture, and ethics influence decision making?

An organization's success depends, in large part, on the day-to-day decisions made by its members. The quality of these decisions influences both the long-term performance of an organization and its day-to-day "character"—in the eyes of employees, customers, and society at large. Today's challenging environments also demand ever more rigor and creativity in the decision-making process. New products, new manufacturing, and new service processes all come from ideas. Organizations must provide for decision making that encourages the free flow of new ideas and supports the efforts of people who want to make their ideas work. And just as with organizations themselves, the success of our individual careers depends on the quality of the decisions we make regarding our jobs and employment situations.[1]

DECISION-MAKING PROCESS

Formally defined, **decision making** is the process of choosing a course of action for dealing with a problem or opportunity.[2] The five basic steps involved in systematic decision making are:

1. Recognize and define the problem or opportunity.
2. Identify and analyze alternative courses of action, and estimate their effects on the problem or opportunity.
3. Choose a preferred course of action.
4. Implement the preferred course of action.
5. Evaluate the results and follow up as necessary.

We must also recognize that in settings where substantial change and many new technologies prevail, this step-by-step approach may not be followed. Occasionally, a nontraditional sequence works and yields superior performance over the traditional view. We also think it is important to consider the ethical consequences of decision making. To understand when and where to use the traditional or novel decision techniques calls for a further understanding of decision environments and the types of decisions to be made.

DECISION ENVIRONMENTS

Problem-solving decisions in organizations are typically made under three different conditions or environments: certainty, risk, and uncertainty.[3] **Certain environments** exist when information is sufficient to predict the results of each alternative in advance of implementation. When a person invests money in a savings account, for example, absolute certainty exists about the interest that will be earned on that money in a given period of time. Certainty is an ideal condition for managerial problem solving and decision making. The challenge is to simply develop an alternative offering a near ideal solution. Unfortunately, certainty is the exception instead of the rule in decision environments.

Risk environments exist when decision makers lack complete certainty regarding the outcomes of various courses of action, but they are aware of the probabilities associated with their occurrence. A *probability,* in turn, is the degree of likelihood of an event's occurrence. Probabilities can be assigned through objective statistical procedures or through personal intuition. For instance, managers can make statistical estimates of quality rejects in production runs, or a senior production manager can make similar estimates based on past experience. Risk is a common decision environment in today's organizations.

Uncertain environments exist when managers have so little information on hand that they cannot even assign probabilities to various alternatives and their possible outcomes. This is the most difficult of the three decision environments. Uncertainty forces decision makers to rely heavily on individual and group creativity to succeed in problem solving. It requires unique, novel, and often totally innovative alternatives to existing patterns of behavior. Responses to uncertainty are often heavily influenced by intuition, educated guesses, and hunches. Furthermore, an uncertain decision environment may also be characterized as a rapidly changing organizational setting in terms of (a) external conditions, (b) the information technology requirements called for to analyze and make decisions, and (c) the personnel influencing problem and choice definitions. This has been called an **organized anarchy,** a firm or division in a firm in a transition characterized by very rapid change and lack of a legitimate hierarchy and collegiality. Although this was once a very unique setting, many high-tech firms and those with expanding global operations share many of the characteristics of an organized anarchy.

KPMG, one of the world's largest and most prestigious consulting firms, has a large practice in what they call enterprise risk management to help firms identify risks and manage them.[4] They go far beyond the traditional risk mitigation notion of using controls to limit the exposure of a firm. They systematically ask managers to separately identify: (1) strategic risks (threats to overall business success); (2) operational risks (threats inherent in the technologies used to reach business success); and (3) reputation risks (threats to a brand or to the firm's reputation). While they also note the importance of threats from regulatory sources, they pay special attention to financial threats, challenges to information systems, and new initiatives from competitors, in addition to change in the competitive setting (e.g., recession, disasters). They want firms to focus on critical risks, develop a strategy for dealing with these critical risks, and define specific responsibilities for dealing with the identified risks. They coach executives to know their risk tolerances and move toward viewing risks in the context of the firm's strategy. This allows leaders to recognize the risk environment in which they operate and incorporate this into their decision-making process. Further, by a systematic process, firms can more clearly identify which aspects of their environment and operations are risky and which are truly uncertain.

TYPES OF DECISIONS

The many routine and nonroutine problems in the modern workplace call for different types of decisions. Routine problems arise on a regular basis and can be addressed through standard responses, called **programmed decisions.** These decisions simply implement solutions that have already been determined by past experience as appropriate for the problem at hand. Examples of programmed decisions are reordering inventory automatically when stock falls below a predetermined level and issuing a written reprimand to someone who violates a certain personnel procedure.

Routine operations are at the heart of many corporations and they are finding that when they or their customers face programmed decisions, they can utilize new Web-based technologies to get speedier and better decisions.

Nonroutine problems are unique and new, having never been encountered before. Because standard responses are not available, these circumstances call for creative problem solving. These **nonprogrammed decisions** are specifically crafted or tailored to the situation at hand. Higher level managers generally spend a greater proportion of their decision-making time on nonroutine problems. An example is a senior marketing manager who has to respond to the introduction of a new product by a foreign competitor. Although past experience may help deal with this competitive threat, the immediate decision requires a creative solution based on the unique characteristics of the present market situation.

For firms in or characterized by "organized anarchy," we also suggest there is a third class of decisions called associative choices. **Associative choices** are decisions that can be loosely linked to nagging continual problems but that were not specifically developed to solve the problem. Given the chaotic nature of the setting, the necessity to take action as opposed to waiting, and the ability of employees to make nearly any "decision" work, a stream of associative choices may be used to improve the setting, even though the problems are not solved.

DECISION-MAKING MODELS

The field of organizational behavior historically emphasizes two alternative approaches to decision making—classical and behavioral (see Figure 17.1).[5] **Classical decision theory** models view the manager as acting in a world of complete certainty. **Behavioral decision theory** models accept the notion of bounded rationality and suggest that people act only in terms of what they perceive about a given situation.

CLASSICAL AND BEHAVIORAL DECISION THEORY

Ideally, the manager faces a clearly defined problem, knows all possible action alternatives and their consequences, and then chooses the alternative that offers the best, or "optimum," solution to the problem. This optimizing style is an ideal way to make decisions.

| **FIGURE 17.1** | **DECISION MAKING VIEWED FROM THE CLASSICAL AND BEHAVIORAL PERSPECTIVES** |

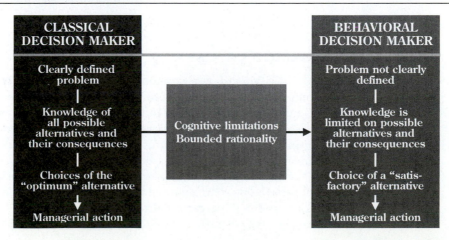

This classical approach is normative and prescriptive, and is often used as a model for how managers should make decisions.

Behavioral scientists are cautious about applying classical decision theory to many decision situations. They recognize that the human mind is a wonderful creation, capable of infinite achievements. But they also recognize that human beings have *cognitive limitations* that restrict their information-processing capabilities. Information deficiencies and overload compromise the ability of decision makers to achieve complete certainty and otherwise operate according to the classical model. Human decision makers also operate with *bounded rationality.*[6] Bounded rationality is a short-hand term suggesting that, while individuals are reasoned and logical, humans have their limits. Individuals interpret and make sense of things within the context of their personal situation. They engage in decision making "within the box" of a simplified view of a more complex reality. This makes it difficult to realize the ideal of classical decision making. As a result, the classical model does not give a full and accurate description of how most decisions are made in organizations.[7]

Classical decision theory does not appear to fit today's chaotic world of globalizing high-tech organizations, yet it would be a mistake to dismiss it and the types of progress that can be made with classical models. Classical models can be used toward the bottom of many firms. For instance, even the most high-tech firm faces many clearly defined problems with known alternatives where firms have already selected an optimal solution. That a firm's managers don't know the answer may make it appear nonclassical when, in fact, it should not be.

As noted above, *behavioral decision theory* models accept the notion of bounded rationality and suggest that people act only in terms of what they perceive about a given situation. Because these perceptions are frequently imperfect, most organizational decision making does not take place in a world of complete certainty. Rather, the behavioral decision maker is viewed as acting most often under uncertain conditions and with limited information. Organizational decision makers face problems that are often ambiguous, and they have only partial knowledge of the available action alternatives and their consequences. This leads to a phenomenon which Herbert Simon has described as **satisficing**— decision makers choose the first alternative that appears to give an acceptable or a satisfactory resolution of the problem. As Simon states: "Most human decision making, whether individual or organizational, is concerned with the discovery and selection of satisfactory alternatives; only in exceptional cases is it concerned with the discovery and selection of optimal decisions."[8]

THE GARBAGE CAN MODEL

A third view of decision making stems from the so-called **garbage can model.**[9] In this view, the main components of the choice process—problems, solutions, participants, and choice situations—are all mixed up together in the "garbage can" of the organization. In many organizations where the setting is stable and the technology is well known and fixed, tradition, strategy, and the administrative structure help order the contents of the garbage can. Specific problems can be matched to specific solutions, an orderly process can be maintained, and the behavioral view of decision making may be appropriate.

But when the setting is dynamic, the technology is changing, demands are conflicting or the goals are unclear, things can get mixed up. More action than thinking can take place. Solutions emerge as "potential capabilities"—capabilities independent of problems or opportunities. Solutions often emerge not to solve specific problems but as lessons learned from the experience of other organizations. These new solution/capabilities may be in the form of new employees, new technical experts, consultants, or reports on best practices. Many solutions might well be implemented even if they cannot be tied to a specific problem. Solutions may also be implemented when no other solution has solved a persistent, chronic problem. Although implemented solutions change the organization, they are unlikely to solve specific problems.

The garbage can model highlights an important feature of decision making in many large organizations. Choice making and implementation may be done by quite different individuals. Often, the job of subordinates is to make the decisions of senior managers work. They must interpret the intentions of their bosses as well as solve local problems. Implementation becomes an opportunity to instill many changes related to the choice of more senior executives. So what is chosen gets implemented along with many other changes. The link between choice and implementation may become even weaker when senior managers are vague or do not vigorously follow up on implementation. The net result from those actually implementing the decision is the appearance that what was chosen does not exactly match what is implemented.

There is a final aspect of the garbage can view. Many problems go unsolved. That is, all organizations have chronic, persistent deficiencies that never seem to get much better. In a garbage can view, this is because decision makers cannot agree to match these problems with solutions, make a choice, and implement it on a timely and consistent basis; nor do they know how to resolve chronic problems. It is only when a problem and a solution "bump into one another" under a decision maker willing to implement a choice that problems, solutions, and choice come together as expected under other views. Thus, one key job challenge for the astute manager is to make the appropriate linkages among problems and solutions.

DECISION-MAKING REALITIES

All three of these models highlight specific features of the complex choice processes managers must engage in as professionals. A key difference between a manager's ability to make an optimum decision in the classical style and the manager's tendency to make a satisfying decision in the behavioral style is the availability of information. The organizational realities of bounded rationality and cognitive limitations affect the way people define problems, identify action alternatives, and choose preferred courses of action. By necessity, most decision making in organizations involves more than the linear and step-by-step rational choice that models often suggest. The process may not be as chaotic as the garbage can models; yet it is often not as rational as even a behavioral view suggests. In real organizations, decisions must be made under risk and uncertainty. Decisions must be made to solve nonroutine problems. And decisions must be made under the pressures of time and information limitations. Finally, we hope decisions will be made on an ethical foundation.

INTUITION, JUDGMENT, AND CREATIVITY

Choices always bear the unique imprint of the individuals who make them, the politics within the organization, and the challenges facing its decision makers. In reality, intuition, judgment, and creativity are as critical as understanding how decisions can be made.

A key element in decision making under risk and uncertainty is intuition. **Intuition** is the ability to know or recognize quickly and readily the possibilities of a given situation.[10] Intuition adds elements of personality and spontaneity to decision making. As a result, it offers potential for creativity and innovation.

In an earlier time, scholars carried on a vigorous debate regarding how managers should plan and make decisions.[11] On one side of the issue were those who believed that planning could be accomplished in a systematic step-by-step fashion. On the other side were those who believed that the very nature of managerial work made this hard to achieve in actual practice. We now know that managers favor verbal communication. Thus, they are more likely to gather data and to make decisions in a relational or interactive way than in a systematic step-by-step fashion.[12] Managers often deal with impressions. Thus, they are more likely to synthesize than to analyze data as they search for the "big picture" in order to redefine problems and link problems with a variety of solutions. Managers work fast, do a variety of things, and are frequently interrupted. Thus, they do not have a lot of quiet time alone to think, plan, or make decisions systematically (see The Effective Manager 17.1).

Are managers correct when they favor the more intuitive and less systematic approach? The more chaotic environments and technologies of many of today's organizations press for this emphasis on intuition. Unfortunately, many business firms are better at implementing the common solutions of others than uniquely solving their problems. Since managers do work in chaotic settings, this reality should be accepted and decision makers should be confident in using their intuitive skills. However, they should combine analytical and intuitive approaches to create new and novel solutions to complex problems.

JUDGMENTAL HEURISTICS

Judgment, or the use of one's intellect, is important in all aspects of decision making. When we question the ethics of a decision, for example, we are questioning the "judgment" of the person making it. Research shows that people are prone to mistakes using biases that often interfere with the quality of decision making.[13] These can be traced to the use of **heuristics**—simplifying strategies or "rules of thumb" used to make decisions. Heuristics serve a useful purpose in making it easier to deal with uncertainty and limited information in problem situations. But they can also lead to systematic errors that affect the quality, and perhaps

---

THE EFFECTIVE MANAGER 17.1

WAYS TO IMPROVE INTUITION

Relaxation Techniques

- Drop the problem for a while.
- Spend some quiet time by yourself.
- Try to clear your mind.

Mental Exercises

- Use images to guide your thinking.
- Let ideas run freely without a specific goal.

the ethical implications, of any decisions made. It is helpful to understand the common judgmental heuristics of availability, representativeness, and anchoring and adjustment.[14]

The **availability heuristic** involves assessing a current event based in past occurrences that are easily available in one's memory. An example is the product development specialist who bases a decision not to launch a new product on her recent failure with another product offering. In this case, the existence of a past product failure has negatively, and perhaps inappropriately, biased the decision maker's judgment of how to best handle the new product.

The **representativeness heuristic** involves assessing the likelihood that an event will occur based on its similarity to one's stereotypes of similar occurrences. An example is the team leader who selects a new member not because of any special qualities of the person, but only because the individual comes from a department known to have produced high performers in the past. In this case, it is the individual's current place of employment—and not his or her job qualifications—that is the basis for the selection decision.

The **anchoring and adjustment heuristic** involves assessing an event by taking an initial value from historical precedent or an outside source, and then incrementally adjusting this value to make a current assessment. An example is the executive who makes salary increase recommendations for key personnel by simply adjusting their current base salaries by a percentage amount. In this case, the existing base salary becomes an "anchor" that drives subsequent salary increases. In some situations this anchor may be inappropriate, such as the case of an individual whose market value has become substantially higher than is reflected by the base salary plus increment.

In addition to using the common judgmental heuristics, decision makers are also prone to more general biases in decision making. One bias is the **confirmation trap,** whereby the decision maker seeks confirmation for what is already thought to be true and neglects opportunities to acknowledge or find disconfirming information. A form of selective perception, this bias involves seeking only those cues in a situation that support a pre-existing opinion. A second bias is the **hindsight trap,** whereby the decision maker overestimates the degree to which he or she could have predicted an event that has already taken place. One risk of hindsight is that it may foster feelings of inadequacy or insecurity in dealing with future decision situations.

CREATIVITY FACTORS

Creativity in decision making involves the development of unique and novel responses to problems and opportunities. In a dynamic environment full of nonroutine problems, creativity in crafting decisions often determines how well people and organizations do in response to complex challenges.[15]

In Part 3 of this book, we examined the group as an important resource for improving creativity in decision making. Indeed, making good use of such traditional techniques as brainstorming, nominal groups, and the Delphi method can greatly expand the creative potential of people and organizations. The addition of new computer-based group meeting and decision-making techniques extends this great potential even further.

Creative thinking may unfold in a series of five stages. First is *preparation.*[16] Here people engage in the active learning and day-to-day sensing required to deal successfully with complex environments. The second stage is *concentration,* whereby actual problems are defined and framed so that alternatives can be considered for dealing with them. In the third stage, *incubation,* people look at the problems in diverse ways that permit the consideration of unusual alternatives, avoiding tendencies toward purely linear and systematic problem solving. The fourth stage is *illumination,* in which people respond to flashes of insight and recognize when all pieces to the puzzle suddenly fit into place. The fifth and final stage is *certification,* which proceeds with logical analysis to confirm that good problem-solving decisions have really been made.[17]

All of these stages of creativity need support and encouragement in the organizational environment. However, creative thinking in decision making can be limited by a number of factors. Judgmental heuristics like those just reviewed can limit the search for alternatives. When attractive options are left unconsidered, creativity can be limited. Cultural and environmental blocks can also limit creativity. This occurs when people are discouraged from considering alternatives viewed as inappropriate by cultural standards or inconsistent with prevailing norms.

MANAGING THE DECISION-MAKING PROCESS

As suggested by our discussion of creativity, people working at all levels, in all areas, and in all types and sizes of organizations are not supposed to simply make decisions. They must make good decisions—the right decisions in the right way at the right time.[18] Managing the decision-making process involves choices itself. Critical choices include which "problems" to work on, who to involve and how to involve them, as well as when to quit.

CHOOSING PROBLEMS TO ADDRESS

Most people are too busy and have too many valuable things to do with their time to personally make the decisions on every problem or opportunity that comes their way. The effective manager and team leader knows when to delegate decisions to others, how to set priorities, and when to abstain from acting altogether. When faced with the dilemma of whether or not to deal with a specific problem, asking and answering the following questions can sometimes help.[19]

Is the problem easy to deal with? Small and less significant problems should not get the same time and attention as bigger ones. Even if a mistake is made, the cost of decision error on small problems is also small. *Might the problem resolve itself?* Putting problems in rank order leaves the less significant for last. Surprisingly, many of these less important problems resolve themselves or are solved by others before you get to them. One less problem to solve leaves decision-making time and energy for other uses. *Is this my decision to make?* Many problems can be handled by other persons. They should be delegated to people who are best prepared to deal with them; ideally, they should be delegated to people whose work they most affect. Finally, *is this a solvable problem within the context of the organization?* The astute decision maker recognizes the difference between problems that realistically can be solved and those that are simply not solvable for all practical purposes.

Paul Nutt, a leading authority on decision making in corporations, argues that half the decisions in organizations fail.[20] Why? The decision tactics managers most often use are those most prone to failure. Managers take too many short cuts. Too often, they merely copy the choices of others and try to sell these to subordinates. While such copying appears practical and pragmatic, it fails to recognize unanticipated difficulties and delays. No two firms are alike and subtle adjustments are typically needed to copy another's solution. Subordinates may believe the manager is just imposing his or her clout—not working for the best interests of all. Related to the overemphasis on immediate action is the tendency for managers to emphasize problems and solutions. The tactics related to success are underutilized. Managers need to focus on the outcomes they want, rather than the problems they see. Above all, managers need to use participation more. Let's take a closer look.

DECIDING WHO SHOULD PARTICIPATE

A mistake commonly made by many new managers and team leaders is presuming that they must solve every problem by making every decision themselves.[21] In practice, good organizational decisions are made by individuals acting alone, by individuals consulting with others, and by groups of people working together.

When individual decisions, also called **authority decisions,** are made, the manager or team leader uses information that he or she possesses and decides what to do without involving others. This decision method often reflects the prerogatives of a person's position of formal authority in the organization. For instance, in deciding a rotation for lunch hours in a retail store, the manager may post a schedule. In **consultative decisions,** by contrast, inputs on the problem are solicited from other persons. Based on this information and its interpretation, the decision maker arrives at a final choice. To continue the example, the manager may tell subordinates that a lunch schedule is needed and ask them when they would like to schedule their lunch and why before making the decision. In other cases, true **group decisions** can be made by both consulting with others and allowing them to help make the final choice. To complete the example, the manager may hold a meeting to get everyone's agreement on a lunch schedule or a system for deciding how to make the schedule.

Victor Vroom, Phillip Yetton, and Arthur Jago have developed a framework for helping managers choose which of these decision-making methods is most appropriate for various problem situations.[22] (See Figure 17.2.) The central proposition in their model is that the decision-making method used should always be appropriate to the problem being solved. The challenge is to know when and how to implement each of the possible methods as the situation demands. They further clarify individual, consultative, and group decision options as follows.

- **AI** *(first variant on the authority decision):* The manager solves the problem or makes the decision alone, using information available at that time.

- **AII** *(second variant on the authority decision):* The manager obtains the necessary information from subordinate(s) or other group members and then decides on the problem solution. The manager may or may not tell subordinates what the problem is before obtaining the information from them. The subordinates provide the necessary information but do not generate or evaluate alternatives.

- **CI** *(first variant on the consultative decision):* The manager shares the problem with relevant subordinates or other group members individually, getting their ideas and suggestions without bringing them together as a group. The manager then makes a decision that may or may not reflect the subordinates' input.

FIGURE 17.2	SELECTING ALTERNATIVE DECISION-MAKING METHODS: THE VROOM AND JAGO DECISION PROCESS FLOWCHART

Problem Attributes		Manager's Questions
QR	Quality requirement	How important is the technical quality of this decision?
CR	Commitment requirement	How important is subordinate commitment to the decision?
LI	Leader's information	Do you have sufficient information to make a high-quality decision?
ST	Problem structure	Is the problem well structured?
CP	Commitment probability	If you were to make the decision by yourself, is it reasonably certain that your subordinate(s) would be committed to the decision?
GC	Goal congruence	Do subordinates share the organizational goals to be attained in solving this problem?
CO	Subordinate conflict	Is conflict among subordinates over preferred solutions likely?
SI	Subordinate information	Do subordinates have sufficient information to make a high-quality decision?

Decision Methods

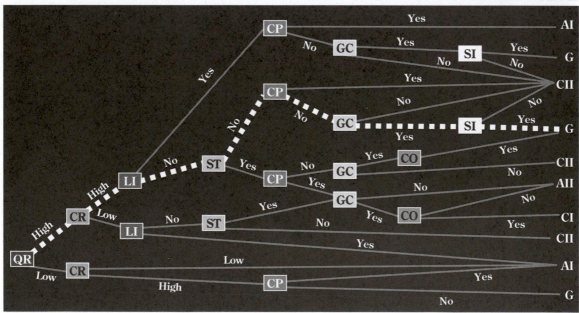

State the Problem

- **CII** *(second variant on the consultative decision):* The manager shares the problem with subordinates or other group members, collectively obtaining their ideas and suggestions. The manager then makes a decision that may or may not reflect the subordinates' input.

- **G** *(the group or consensus decision):* The manager shares the problem with the subordinates as a total group and engages the group in consensus seeking to arrive at a final decision.

In the most recent version of this decision-making framework, Vroom and Jago use the flowchart shown in Figure 17.2 to help managers analyze problem situations and choose the most appropriate decision-making methods. Key issues involve the quality requirements of a decision, the availability and location of the relevant information, the commitments needed to fully implement the decision, and the amount of time available. Although this model appears complex and cumbersome, its underlying logic offers a useful decision-making discipline. Try it by working through Figure 17.2 for an organizational problem with which you are familiar. The analysis forces you to recognize how time, quality requirements, information availability, and subordinate acceptance issues can affect decision outcomes. It also reminds you that all of the decision methods are important and useful. The key to effectively managing participation in decision making is first knowing when to use each decision method and then knowing how to implement each of them well.

KNOWING WHEN TO QUIT— ELIMINATING ESCALATING COMMITMENTS

The organization's natural desire to continue on a selected course of action reinforces some natural tendencies among decision makers.[23] Once the agonizing process of making a choice is apparently completed, executives make public commitments to implementation, and implementation begins, managers are often reluctant to change their minds and admit a mistake. Instead of backing off, the tendency is to press on to victory. This is called **escalating commitment**—continuation and renewed efforts on a previously chosen course of action, even though it is not working. Escalating commitment is reflected in the popular adage, "If at first you don't succeed, try, try, again."

In beginning Finance courses, students learn about the fallacy of sunk costs. Money committed and spent is gone. The decision to continue is just that—a decision. It needs to be based on what investment is needed and the returns on that investment. This is one of the most difficult aspects of decision making to convey to executives simply because so many of these executives rose to their positions by turning apparently losing courses of action into winners.[24] The tendency to escalate commitments often outweighs the willingness to disengage from them. Decision makers may rationalize negative feedback as a temporary condition, protect their egos by not admitting that the original decision was a mistake, or characterize any negative results as a "learning experience" that can be overcome with added future effort.[25]

The self-discipline required to admit mistakes and change direction, however, is sometimes difficult to achieve. Escalating commitments are a form of decision entrapment that leads people to do things that the facts of a situation do not justify. We should be proactive in spotting "failures" and more open to reversing decisions or dropping plans that do not appear to be working.[26] But again, this is easier said than done. Good decision makers know when to call it quits. They are willing to reverse previous decisions and stop investing time and other resources in unsuccessful courses of action. As the late W. C. Fields is said to have muttered, "If at first you don't succeed, try, try, again. Then quit."

Technology, Culture, and Ethics in Decision Making

In today's environments, the problems facing organizational decision makers seem to get ever more complex. For example, consider the following workplace trends.[27]

- Business units are becoming smaller in size: they are doing more outsourcing and employing fewer full-time workers.
- New, more flexible, and adaptable organizational forms are replacing the traditional pyramid structures.
- Multifunctional understanding is increasingly important as organizations emphasize lateral coordination.
- Workers with both technical knowledge and team skills are becoming increasingly sought after.
- The nature of "work" is in flux as jobs change fast, require continuous learning, and are less bound by the "9-to-5" tradition.

Each of these trends is changing by whom, when, where, and how decision making is accomplished. We face difficult stresses and strains as the quest for higher and higher productivity challenges the needs, talents, and opportunities of people at work. Complexities in the decision-making process include issues of information technology, culture, and ethics.

INFORMATION TECHNOLOGY AND DECISION MAKING

As we have discussed throughout this book, today's organizations are becoming ever-more sophisticated in applying information technologies. Eventually, developments in the field of **artificial intelligence (AI),** the study of how computers can be programmed to think like the human brain, will allow computers to displace many decision makers.[28] Nobel Laureate and decision scientist Herbert Simon is convinced that computers will someday be more intelligent than humans.

Already, the applications of AI to organizational decision making are significant. We have access to decision-making support from expert systems that reason like human experts and follow "either-or" rules to make deductions. For example, if you call an advertised 800 number to apply for a home equity loan, you will not get a human but a computer program to take all the necessary information and provide confirmation of a loan. On the factory floor, decision support systems schedule machines and people for maximum production efficiencies.

In the very near future, fuzzy logic that reasons beyond either-or choices and neural networks that reason inductively by simulating the brain's parallel processing capabilities will become operational realities to move beyond simple programmed decisions. Uses for such systems may be found everywhere from hospitals where they will check on medical diagnoses to investment houses where they will analyze potential investment portfolios to a wide and growing variety of other settings.[29]

Computer support for group decision making, including developments with the Internet and with intranets, has broken the decision-making meeting out of the confines of face-to-face interactions. With the software now available, problems can be defined and decisions can be made through virtual teamwork by people in geographically dispersed locations. We know that group decision software can be especially useful for generating ideas, such as in electronic brainstorming, and for improving the time efficiency of decisions. People working under electronically mediated conditions tend to stay focused on tasks and avoid the interpersonal conflicts and other problems common in face-to-face deliberations. On the negative side, decisions made by "electronic groups" carry some risks of being impersonal and perhaps less compelling in terms of commitments to implementation and follow-through. There is evidence, moreover, that use of computer technology for decision making is better accepted by today's college students than by persons who are already advanced in their organizational careers.[30]

What new information technology will not do is deal with the issues raised by the garbage can model. The information technologies promise a more orderly world where the process of choosing conforms more to the traditional models with an extension of the normal boundaries of rationality. For us, what is still on the information technology horizon are the most important decisions that come before the classical and standard approaches. These are predecision choices that are heavily influenced by cultural factors and ethics.

CULTURAL FACTORS AND DECISION MAKING

Fons Trompenaars notes that culture is "the way in which a group of people solves problems."[31] It is only reasonable to expect that as cultures vary so too will choices concerning what is to be solved and how. For example, there are historical cultural preferences for solving problems. The approach favored in this chapter emphasizes the North American view stressing decisiveness, speed, and individual selection of alternatives. This view speaks more to choice and less to implementation. Yet, the garbage can view suggests that implementation can proceed almost separately from other aspects of decision making.

Other cultures place less emphasis on individual choice than on developing implementations that work. They start with what is workable and better rather than with the classical and behavioral comparison of current conditions with some ideal.[32] If a change can improve the current situation, even if it is not apparently directed toward a problem identified by senior management, subordinate managers may work together to implement it. And then senior management may be informed of the success of the change. To emphasize the importance of smooth implementation over grand decision making, corporations may adopt systems similar to the Japanese ringi system where lower-levels indicate their written approval of proposals prior to formal implementation. Written approval is an issue not of whether the change should be done but whether it is feasible for the group to implement.[33]

The more important role of culture in decision making concerns not how problems are solved but which concerns are elevated to the status of problems solvable within the firm. For instance, the very fact that a procedure is old may make it more suspect in the United States than in France.[34] Far too many of our views may be dictated by Western bureaucratic thinking.[35] Not all cultures are as pluralistic, bluntly competitive, or impersonal as that of the United States. In other parts of the world, personal loyalties may drive decisions, and preserving harmony may be considered more important than achieving a bit more efficiency. In short, problems may be more person centered and socially defined than bureaucratically proscribed.

ETHICAL ISSUES AND DECISION MAKING

The subject of ethical behavior in the workplace cannot be overemphasized, and it is worth reviewing once again the framework for ethical decision making first introduced in Chapter 1. An *ethical dilemma* was defined as a situation in which a person must decide whether or not to do something that, although personally or organizationally beneficial, may be considered unethical and perhaps illegal. Often, ethical dilemmas are associated with risk and uncertainty, and with nonroutine problem situations. Just how decisions are handled under these circumstances, ones that will inevitably appear during your career, may well be the ultimate test of your personal ethical framework.

An Effective Manager feature in Chapter 1 introduced a useful decision-making checklist for resolving ethical dilemmas. Before any decision is made, the checklist tests the preliminary decision with stiff questions.[36] First, it would have you ask: "Is my action legal? Is it right? Is it beneficial?" Second, it would have you ask: "How would I feel if my family found out about this? How would I feel if my decision were printed in the local newspaper?" Only after these questions are asked and satisfactorily answered, does the model suggest you should take action. As a manager you also have the responsibility to integrate ethical decision making into your part of the firm. Check The Effective Manager 17.2 for some help.

When it comes to the ethics of decision making, the criteria individuals use to define problems and the values that underlie these criteria must be considered.[37] Moral conduct is involved in choosing problems, deciding who should be involved, estimating the impacts of alternatives, and selecting an alternative for implementation.

Moral conduct does not arise from after-the-fact embarrassment. As Fineman suggests, "If people are unable to anticipate shame or guilt before they act in particular ways, then moral codes are invalid.... Decisions may involve lying, deceit, fraud, evasion of negligence—disapproved of in many cultures. But ethical monitoring and control go beyond just the pragmatics of harm."[38] In other words, when you are the decision maker, decision making is not just a choice process followed by implementation for the good of the organization. It involves your values and your morality whether or not you think it should. Thus, effective implemented choices need to not only solve a problem or capitalize on choices but also match your values and help others. It is little wonder, then, that decision making will likely be the biggest challenge of your organizational career.

THE EFFECTIVE MANAGER 17.2

SUGGESTIONS FOR INTEGRATING ETHICAL DECISION MAKING INTO A FIRM

Infusing ethics into decision making is difficult. Several scholars recommend the following:

- Develop a code of ethics and follow it.
- Establish procedures for reporting violations.
- Involve employees in identifying ethical issues.
- Monitor ethical performance.
- Reward ethical behavior.
- Publicize efforts.

CHAPTER 17 SUMMARY

How are decisions made in organizations?

- Decision making is a process of identifying problems and opportunities and choosing among alternative courses of action for dealing successfully with them.
- Organizational decisions are often made in risky and uncertain environments, where situations are ambiguous and information is limited.
- Routine and repetitive problems can be dealt with through programmed decisions; nonroutine or novel problems require nonprogrammed decisions that are crafted to fit the situation at hand.

What are the useful decision-making models?

- According to classical decision theory, optimum decisions are made after carefully analyzing all possible alternatives and their known consequences.
- According to behavioral decision theory, most organizational decisions are made with limited information and by satisficing—choosing the first acceptable or satisfactory solutions to problems.
- According to the garbage can model, the main components of the choice process—problems, solutions, participants, choice situations—are all mixed up together in the garbage can of the organization.

How do intuition, judgment, and creativity affect decision making?

- Intuition is the ability to recognize quickly the action possibilities for resolving a problem situation.
- Both systematic decision making and intuitive decision making are important in today's complex work environments.
- The use of judgmental heuristics, or simplifying rules of thumb, is common in decision making but can lead to biased results.
- Common heuristics include availability decisions based on recent events; representativeness decisions based on similar events; and anchoring and adjustment decisions based on historical precedents.
- Creativity in finding unique and novel solutions to problems can be enhanced through both individual and group problem-solving strategies.

How can the decision-making process be managed?

- Good managers know that not every problem requires an immediate decision; they also know how and when to delegate decision-making responsibilities.
- A common mistake is for a manager or team leader to make all decisions alone; instead, a full range of individual, consultative, and group decision-making methods should be utilized.
- The Vroom-Yetton-Jago model offers a way of matching problems with appropriate decision methods, based on quality requirements, information availability, and time constraints.

- Tendencies toward escalating commitment, continuing previously chosen courses of action even when they are not working, should be recognized in work settings.

How do technology, culture, and ethics influence decision making?

- Technological developments are continuing to change the nature of organizational decision making.
- Culture counts; differences in culture alter by whom, how, when, and why decisions are made.
- Ethics is involved in each stage of the decision-making process, and effective decision making includes individual moral criteria and values.

Study Questions

This chapter introduces you to conflict and negotiation as key processes of organizational behavior that can have a substantial impact on the performance and satisfaction of people at work. As you read Chapter 18, keep in mind these study questions.

- What is conflict?
- How can conflict be managed successfully?
- What is negotiation?
- What are the different strategies involved in negotiation?

When Whitney Johns Martin couldn't get sufficient investment capital to expand her consulting firm for small and midsized businesses, she took matters into her own hands. She founded a venture capital fund, Capital Across America, specifically to serve women-owned businesses. Most of the venture capital funds that Martin dealt with were managed by men, who seemed more comfortable dealing with men. Martin believes that women often underestimate themselves and consequently don't ask for enough money during negotiations to accomplish their business goals. Men, by contrast, "shoot for the moon," and ask for more than they typically need. But, she says, women have a great capacity to develop extensive networks and relationships—with customers, suppliers, and others. These are great resources that can be rallied to help a business succeed.[1]

The daily work of people in organizations is intensely based on communication and interpersonal relationships. Managers must therefore have the interpersonal skills to work well with others in order to implement action agendas in situations that are often complicated and stressful.[2] The exchange of information in the workplace is typically purposeful and intentionally persuasive, as was the case of Whitney Johns Martin and her quest for venture business capital. At the same time, communication in interpersonal relationships frequently opens the door for differences and disagreements that can create difficulties. Success in today's high performance organizations increasingly requires a good understanding of the fundamentals of conflict and negotiation.

CONFLICT

Conflict occurs whenever disagreements exist in a social situation over issues of substance or whenever emotional antagonisms create frictions between individuals or groups.[3] Managers and team leaders can spend considerable time dealing with conflict, including conflicts in which the manager or leader is directly involved as one of the principal actors.[4] In other situations, the manager or leader may act as a mediator, or third party, whose job it is to resolve conflicts between other people. In all cases, a manager and team leader must be comfortable with the interpersonal conflict. This includes being able to recognize situations that have the potential for conflict and to deal with these situations in ways that will best serve the needs of both the organization and the people involved.[5]

TYPES OF CONFLICT

Conflict as it is experienced in the daily workplace involves at least two basic forms. **Substantive conflict** is a fundamental disagreement over ends or goals to be pursued and the means for their accomplishment.[6] A dispute with one's boss over a plan of action to be followed, such as the marketing strategy for a new product, is an example of substantive conflict. When people work together day in and day out, it is only normal that different viewpoints on a variety of substantive workplace issues will arise. At times people will disagree over such things as group and organizational goals, the allocation of resources, the distribution of rewards, policies and procedures, and task assignments. Dealing with such conflicts successfully is an everyday challenge for most managers.

By contrast, **emotional conflict** involves interpersonal difficulties that arise over feelings of anger, mistrust, dislike, fear, resentment, and the like.[7] This conflict is commonly known as a "clash of personalities." Emotional conflicts can drain the energies of people and distract them from important work priorities. They can emerge from a wide variety of settings and are common among co-workers as well as in superior-subordinate relationships. The latter form of emotional conflict is perhaps the most upsetting organizational conflict for any person to experience. Unfortunately, competitive pressures in today's business environment and the resulting emphasis on downsizing and restructuring have created more situations in which the decisions of a "tough" boss can create emotional conflict.

LEVELS OF CONFLICT

When dealing personally with conflicts in the workplace, the relevant question becomes: "How well prepared are you to encounter and deal successfully with conflicts of various types?" People at work may encounter conflict at the intra-personal level (conflict within the individual), the interpersonal level (individual-to-individual conflict), the intergroup level, or the interorganizational level.

Some conflicts that affect behavior in organizations involve the individual alone. These **intrapersonal conflicts** often involve actual or perceived pressures from incompatible goals or expectations of the following types: *Approach-approach conflict* occurs when a person must choose between two positive and equally attractive alternatives. An example is having to choose between a valued promotion in the organization or a desirable new job with another firm. *Avoidance-avoidance conflict* occurs when a person must choose between two negative and equally unattractive alternatives. An example is being asked either to accept a job transfer to another town in an undesirable location or to have one's employment with an organization terminated. *Approach-avoidance conflict* occurs when a person must decide to do something that has both positive and negative consequences. An example is being offered a higher paying job whose responsibilities entail unwanted demands on one's personal time.

Interpersonal conflict occurs between two or more individuals who are in opposition to one another. It may be substantive or emotional or both. Two persons debating each other aggressively on the merits of hiring a job applicant is an example of a substantive interpersonal conflict. Two persons continually in disagreement over each other's choice of work attire is an example of an emotional interpersonal conflict.

Intergroup conflict that occurs among members of different teams or groups can also have substantive and/or emotional underpinnings. Intergroup conflict is quite common in organizations, and it can make the coordination and integration of task activities very difficult.[8] The classic example is conflict among functional groups or departments, such as marketing and manufacturing, in organizations. The growing use of cross-functional teams and task forces is one way of trying to minimize such conflicts and promote more creative and efficient operations.

Interorganizational conflict is most commonly thought of in terms of the competition and rivalry that characterizes firms operating in the same markets. A good example is the continuing battle between U.S. businesses and their global rivals. But interorganizational conflict is a much broader issue than that represented by market competition alone. Consider, for example, disagreements between unions and the organizations employing their members; between government regulatory agencies and the organizations subject to their surveillance; between organizations and those who supply them with raw materials.

FUNCTIONAL AND DYSFUNCTIONAL CONFLICTS

Conflict in organizations can be upsetting both to the individuals directly involved and to others affected by its occurrence. It can be quite uncomfortable, for example, to work in an environment in which two co-workers are continually hostile toward each other. In OB, however, the two sides to conflict shown in Figure 18.1 are recognized—the functional or constructive side, and the dysfunctional or destructive side.

Functional conflict, alternatively called *constructive conflict,* results in positive benefits to individuals, the group, or the organization. On the positive side, conflict can bring important problems to the surface so that they can be addressed. It can cause decisions to be considered carefully and perhaps reconsidered to ensure that the right path of action is being followed. It can increase the amount of information used for decision making. And it can offer opportunities for creativity that can improve individual, team, or organizational performance. Indeed, an effective manager is able to stimulate constructive conflict in situations in which satisfaction with the status quo inhibits needed change and development.

Dysfunctional conflict, or *destructive conflict,* works to the individual's, group's, or organization's disadvantage. It diverts energies, hurts group cohesion, promotes interpersonal hostilities, and overall creates a negative environment for workers. This occurs, for example, when two employees are unable to work together because of interpersonal differences (a destructive emotional conflict) or when the members of a committee fail to act because they cannot agree on group goals (a destructive substantive conflict). Destructive conflicts of these types can decrease work productivity and job satisfaction and contribute to absenteeism and job turnover. Managers must be alert to destructive conflicts and be quick to take action to prevent or eliminate them or at least minimize their disadvantages.

FIGURE 18.1	THE TWO FACES OF CONFLICT: FUNCTIONAL CONFLICT AND DYSFUNCTIONAL CONFLICT

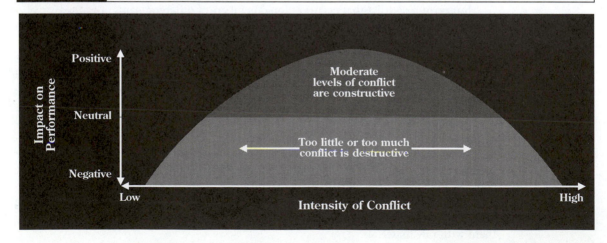

CULTURE AND CONFLICT

Society today shows many signs of wear and tear in social relationships. We experience difficulties born of racial tensions, homophobia, gender gaps, and more. All trace in some way to tensions among people who are different in some ways from one another. They are also a reminder that culture and cultural differences must be considered for their conflict potential.

Among the popular dimensions of culture discussed in Chapter 3, for example, substantial differences may be noted in time orientation. When persons from short-term cultures such as the United States try to work with persons from long-term cultures such as Japan, the likelihood of conflict developing is high. The same holds true when individualists work with collectivists and when persons from high-power distance work with those from low-power distance cultures.[9] In each case, individuals who are not able to recognize and respect the impact of culture on behavior may contribute to the emergence of dysfunctional situations. On the other hand, by approaching a cross-cultural work situation with sensitivity and respect, one can find ways to work together without great difficulty and even with the advantages that constructive conflict may offer.

MANAGING CONFLICT

Conflict can be addressed in many ways, but the important goal is to achieve or set the stage for true **conflict resolution**—a situation in which the underlying reasons for a given destructive conflict are eliminated. The process begins with a good understanding of causes and recognition of the stage to which conflict has developed.

STAGES OF CONFLICT

Most conflicts develop in stages, as shown in Figure 18.2. Managers should recognize that unresolved prior conflicts help set the stage for future conflicts of the same or related sort. Rather than try to deny the existence of conflict or settle on a temporary resolution, it is always best to deal with important conflicts so that they are completely resolved.[10] *Conflict antecedents* establish the conditions from which conflicts are likely to develop. When the antecedent conditions become the basis for substantive or emotional differences between people or groups, the stage of *perceived conflict* exists. Of course, this perception may be held by only one of the conflicting parties. It is important to distinguish between perceived and *felt conflict*. When conflict is felt, it is experienced as tension that motivates the person to take action to reduce feelings of discomfort. For conflict to be resolved, all parties should both perceive it and feel the need to do something about it.

When conflict is expressed openly in behavior, it is said to be manifest. A state of *manifest conflict* may be resolved by removing or correcting its antecedents. It can also be suppressed. With suppression, no change in antecedent conditions occurs; the manifest conflict behaviors are controlled. For example, one or both parties may choose to ignore the conflict in their dealings with one another. *Suppression* is a superficial and often temporary form of conflict resolution. Indeed, we have already noted that unresolved and suppressed conflict fall into this category. Both may continue to fester and cause future conflicts over similar issues. For the short run, however, they may represent the best a manager can achieve until antecedent conditions can be changed.

FIGURE 18.2	**THE STAGES OF CONFLICT**

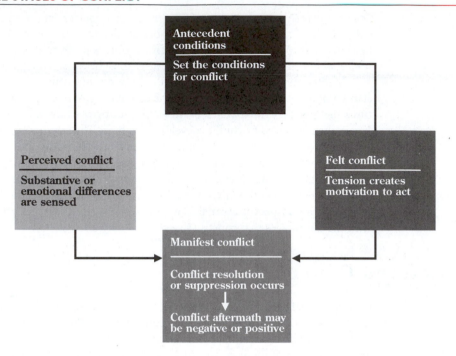

Unresolved substantive conflicts can result in sustained emotional discomfort and escalate into dysfunctional emotional conflict between individuals. In contrast, truly resolved conflicts may establish conditions that reduce the potential for future conflicts or make it easier to deal with them. Thus, any manager should be sensitive to the influence of *conflict aftermath* on future conflict episodes.

CAUSES OF CONFLICT

The process of dealing successfully with conflict begins with a recognition of several types of conflict situations. *Vertical conflict* occurs between hierarchical levels. It commonly involves supervisor-subordinate disagreements over resources, goals, deadlines, or performance results. *Horizontal conflict* occurs between persons or groups at the same hierarchical level. These disputes commonly involve goal incompatibilities, resource scarcities, or purely interpersonal factors. A common variation of horizontal conflict is *line-staff conflict*. It often involves disagreements over who has authority and control over certain matters such as personnel selection and termination practices.

Also common to work situations are *role conflicts* that occur when the communication of task expectations proves inadequate or upsetting. As discussed in respect to teamwork in Chapter 9, this often involves unclear communication of work expectations, excessive expectations in the form of job overloads, insufficient expectations in the form of job underloads, and incompatibilities among expectations from different sources.

Workflow interdependencies are breeding grounds for conflicts. Disputes and open disagreements may erupt among people and units who are required to cooperate to meet challenging goals.[11] When interdependence is high—that is, when a person or group must rely on ask contributions from one or more others to achieve its goals—conflicts often occur. You will notice this, for example, in a fast-food restaurant, when the people serving the food have to wait too long for it to be delivered from the cooks. Conflict also escalates when individuals or groups lack adequate task direction or goals. *Domain ambiguities* involve misunderstandings over such things as customer jurisdiction or scope of authority. Conflict is likely when individuals or groups are placed in ambiguous situations where it is difficult for them to understand just who is responsible for what.

Actual or perceived *resource scarcity* can foster destructive competition. When resources are scarce, working relationships are likely to suffer. This is especially true in organizations that are experiencing downsizing or financial difficulties. As cutbacks occur, various individuals or groups try to position themselves to gain or retain maximum shares of the shrinking resource pool. They are also likely to try to resist resource redistribution, or to employ countermeasures to defend their resources from redistribution to others.

Finally, *power or value asymmetries* in work relationships can create conflict. They exist when interdependent people or groups differ substantially from one another in status and influence or in values. Conflict resulting from asymmetry is prone to occur, for example, when a lower-power person needs the help of a high-power person, who does not respond; when people who hold dramatically different values are forced to work together on a task; or when a high-status person is required to interact with and perhaps be dependent on someone of lower status.

INDIRECT CONFLICT MANAGEMENT APPROACHES

Indirect conflict management approaches share the common ground of avoiding direct dealings with personalities. They include reduced interdependence, appeals to common goals, hierarchical referral, and alterations in the use of mythology and scripts.

Reduced Interdependence   When workflow conflicts exist, managers can adjust the level of interdependency among units or individuals.[12] One simple option is *decoupling,* or taking action to eliminate or reduce the required contact between conflict parties. In some cases, the units' tasks can be adjusted to reduce the number of required points of coordination. The conflicting units can then be separated from one another, and each can be provided separate access to valued resources. Although decoupling may reduce conflict, it may also result in duplication and a poor allocation of valued resources.

Buffering is another approach that can be used when the inputs of one group are the outputs of another group. The classic buffering technique is to build an inventory, or buffer, between the two groups so that any output slowdown or excess is absorbed by the inventory and does not directly pressure the target group. Although it reduces conflict, this technique is increasingly out of favor because it increases inventory costs. This consequence is contrary to the elements of just-in-time delivery, which is now valued in operations management.

Conflict management can be facilitated by assigning people to serve as formal *linking pins* between groups that are prone to conflict.[13] Persons in linking-pin roles, such as project liaison, are expected to understand the operations, members, needs, and norms of their host group. They are supposed to use this knowledge to help their group work better with other groups in order to accomplish mutual tasks. Though expensive, this technique is often used when different specialized groups, such as engineering and sales, must closely coordinate their efforts on complex and long-term projects.

Appeals to Common Goals An *appeal to common goals* can focus the attention of potentially conflicting parties on one mutually desirable conclusion. By elevating the potential dispute to a common framework wherein the parties recognize their mutual interdependence in achieving common goals, petty disputes can be put in perspective. However, this can be difficult to achieve when prior performance is poor and individuals or groups disagree over how to improve performance. In this negative situation, the manager needs to remember the attributional tendency of individuals to blame poor performance on others or on external conditions. In this case, conflict resolution begins by making sure that the parties take personal responsibility for improving the situation.

Hierarchical Referral *Hierarchical referral* makes use of the chain of command for conflict resolution. Here, problems are simply referred up the hierarchy for more senior managers to reconcile. Whereas hierarchical referral can be definitive in a given case, it also has limitations. If conflict is severe and recurring, the continual use of hierarchical referral may not result in true conflict resolution. Managers removed from day-to-day affairs may fail to diagnose the real causes of a conflict, and conflict resolution may be superficial. Busy managers may tend to consider most conflicts as results of poor interpersonal relations and may act quickly to replace a person with a perceived "personality" problem.[14]

Altering Scripts and Myths In some situations, conflict is superficially managed by *scripts,* or behavioral routines that become part of the organization's culture.[15] The scripts become rituals that allow the conflicting parties to vent their frustrations and to recognize that they are mutually dependent on one another via the larger corporation. An example is a monthly meeting of "department heads," held presumably for purposes of coordination and problem solving but that actually becomes just a polite forum for superficial agreement.[16] Managers in such cases know their scripts and accept the difficulty of truly resolving any major conflicts. By sticking with the script, expressing only low-key disagreement and then quickly acting as if everything has been resolved, for instance, the managers publicly act as if problems are being addressed. Such scripts can be altered to allow and encourage active confrontation of issues and disagreements.

DIRECT CONFLICT MANAGEMENT APPROACHES

Figure 18.3 describes the five approaches to conflict management from the perspective of their relative emphasis on cooperativeness and assertiveness in the relationship. Consultants and academics generally agree that true conflict resolution can occur only when the underlying substantive and emotional reasons for the conflict are identified and dealt with through a solution that allows all conflicting parties to "win."[17] (See The Effective Manager 18.1.) This important issue of "Who wins?" can be addressed from the perspective of each conflicting party.

Lose-Lose Conflict *Lose-lose conflict* occurs when nobody really gets what he or she wants. The underlying reasons for the conflict remain unaffected and a similar conflict is likely to occur in the future. Lose-lose conflicts often result when there is little or no

| **FIGURE 18.3** | **FIVE WAYS TO MANAGE CONFLICT** |

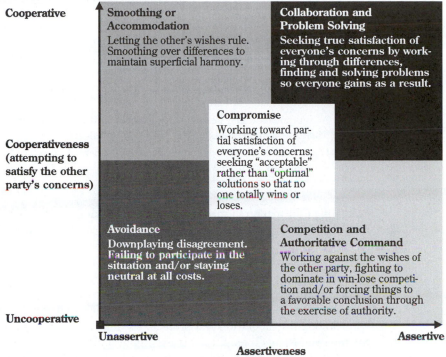

Cooperative

Smoothing or Accommodation
Letting the other's wishes rule. Smoothing over differences to maintain superficial harmony.

Collaboration and Problem Solving
Seeking true satisfaction of everyone's concerns by working through differences, finding and solving problems so everyone gains as a result.

Cooperativeness (attempting to satisfy the other party's concerns)

Compromise
Working toward partial satisfaction of everyone's concerns; seeking "acceptable" rather than "optimal" solutions so that no one totally wins or loses.

Avoidance
Downplaying disagreement. Failing to participate in the situation and/or staying neutral at all costs.

Competition and Authoritative Command
Working against the wishes of the other party, fighting to dominate in win-lose competition and/or forcing things to a favorable conclusion through the exercise of authority.

Uncooperative

Unassertive   **Assertive**

Assertiveness
(attempting to satisfy one's own concerns)

assertiveness and conflict management takes these forms. **Avoidance** is an extreme form of inattention; everyone simply pretends that the conflict does not really exist and hopes that it will go away. **Accommodation,** or **smoothing** as it is sometimes called, involves playing down differences among the conflicting parties and highlighting similarities and areas of agreement. This peaceful coexistence ignores the real essence of a given conflict and often creates frustration and resentment. **Compromise** occurs when each party gives up something of value to the other. As a result of no one getting its full desires, the antecedent conditions for future conflicts are established.

Win-Lose Conflict   In *win-lose conflict,* one party achieves its desires at the expense and to the exclusion of the other party's desires. This is a high-assertiveness and low-cooperativeness situation. It may result from outright **competition** in which a victory is achieved through force, superior skill, or domination by one party. It may also occur as a result of **authoritative command,** whereby a formal authority simply dictates a solution and specifies what is gained and what is lost by whom. Win-lose strategies fail to address the root causes of the conflict and tend to suppress the desires of at least one of the conflicting parties. As a result, future conflicts over the same issues are likely to occur.

Win-Win Conflict   *Win-win conflict* is achieved by a blend of both high cooperativeness and high assertiveness.[18] **Collaboration** or **problem solving** involves a recognition by all conflicting parties that something is wrong and needs attention. It stresses gathering and

THE EFFECTIVE MANAGER 18.1

WHEN TO USE CONFLICT MANAGEMENT STYLES

- Collaboration and problem solving is preferred to gain true conflict resolution when time and cost permit.

- Avoidance may be used when an issue is trivial or more important issues are pressing, or when people need to cool down temporarily and regain perspective.

- Authoritative command may be used when quick and decisive action is vital or when unpopular actions must be taken.

- Accommodation may be used when issues are more important to others than to yourself or when you want to build "credits" for use in later issues.

- Compromise may be used for temporary settlements to complex issues to arrive at expedient solutions when time is limited.

evaluating information in solving disputes and making choices. Win-win conditions eliminate the reasons for continuing or resurrecting the conflict since nothing has been avoided or suppressed. All relevant issues are raised and openly discussed. The ultimate test for a win-win solution is whether or not the conflicting parties see that the solution (1) achieves each other's goals, (2) is acceptable to both parties, and (3) establishes a process whereby all parties involved see a responsibility to be open and honest about facts and feelings. When success is achieved, true conflict resolution has occurred.

Although collaboration and problem solving are generally favored, one limitation is the time and energy it requires. It is also important to realize that both parties to the conflict need to be assertive and cooperative in order to develop a win-win joint solution. Finally, collaboration and problem solving may not be feasible if the firm's dominant culture does not place a value on cooperation.[19]

NEGOTIATION

Talk about conflict! Picture yourself trying to make a decision in the following situation: You have ordered a new state-of-the-art notebook computer for a staff member in your department. At about the same time another department ordered a different brand. Your boss indicates that only one brand will be ordered. Of course, you believe the one chosen by your department is the best.

WHAT IS NEGOTIATION?

This is just a sample of the many situations that involve managers and others in **negotiation**—the process of making joint decisions when the parties involved have different preferences.[20] Negotiation has special significance in work settings, where disagreements are likely to arise over such diverse matters as wage rates, task objectives, performance evaluations, job assignments, work schedules, work locations, and more.

NEGOTIATION GOALS AND OUTCOMES

In negotiation two important goals must be considered: substance and relationship goals. *Substance goals* deal with outcomes that relate to the "content" issues under negotiation.

The dollar amount of a wage agreement in a collective bargaining situation is one example. *Relationship goals* deal with outcomes that relate to how well people involved in the negotiation and any constituencies they may represent are able to work with one another once the process is concluded. An example is the ability of union members and management representatives to work together effectively after a contract dispute has been settled.

Unfortunately, many negotiations result in damaged relationships because the negotiating parties become preoccupied with substance goals and self-interests. In contrast, *effective negotiation* occurs when substance issues are resolved and working relationships are maintained or even improved. It results in overlapping interests and joint decisions that are "for the better" of all parties. Three criteria for effective negotiation are described in The Effective Manager 18.2.

ETHICAL ASPECTS OF NEGOTIATION

To maintain good working relationships in negotiations, managers and other involved parties should strive for high ethical standards. This goal may be side-tracked by an overemphasis on self-interests. The motivation to behave ethically in negotiations is put to the test by each party's desire to "get more" than the other from the negotiation, and/or with a belief that there are insufficient resources to satisfy all parties.[21] After the heat of negotiations dies down, the parties involved often try to rationalize or explain away questionable ethics as unavoidable, harmless, or justified. Such after-the-fact rationalizations may be offset by long-run negative consequences, such as not being able to achieve one's wishes again the next time. At the very least, the unethical party may be the target of revenge tactics by those who were disadvantaged. Furthermore, once some people have behaved unethically in one situation, they may become entrapped by such behavior and prone to display it again in the future.[22]

ORGANIZATIONAL SETTINGS FOR NEGOTIATION

Managers and team leaders should be prepared to participate in at least four major action settings for negotiations. In *two-party negotiation* the manager negotiates directly with one other person. In *group negotiation* the manager is part of a team or group whose members are negotiating to arrive at a common decision. In *intergroup negotiation* the manager is part of a group that is negotiating with another group to arrive at a decision regarding a problem or situation affecting both. And in *constituency negotiation* the manager is involved in negotiation with other persons, with each party representing a broader constituency. A common example of constituency negotiation involves representatives of management and labor negotiating a collective bargaining agreement.

THE EFFECTIVE MANAGER 18.2

CRITERIA OF AN EFFECTIVE NEGOTIATION

1. *Quality*—The negotiation results offer a "quality" agreement that is wise and satisfactory to all sides.
2. *Harmony*—The negotiation is "harmonious" and fosters rather than inhibits good interpersonal relations.
3. *Efficiency*—The negotiation is "efficient" and no more time consuming or costly than absolutely necessary.

CULTURE AND NEGOTIATION

The existence of cultural differences in time orientation, individualism-collectivism, and power distance can have a substantial impact on negotiation. For example, when American businesses try to negotiate quickly with Chinese counterparts, they often do so with the goal of getting definitive agreements that will govern a working relationship. Culture isn't always on their side. A typical Chinese approach to negotiation might move much more slowly, require the development of good interpersonal relationships prior to reaching any agreement, display reluctance to commit everything to writing, and anticipate that any agreement reached will be subject to modification as future circumstances may require. All this is quite the opposite of the typical expectations of negotiators used to the individualist and short-term American culture.

NEGOTIATION STRATEGIES

Managers and other workers frequently negotiate with one another over access to scarce organizational resources. These resources may be money, time, people, facilities, equipment, and so on. In all such cases, the general approach to or strategy for the negotiation can have a major influence on its outcomes. In **distributive negotiation,** the focus is on "positions" staked out or declared by conflicting parties. Each party is trying to claim certain portions of the available "pie." In **integrative negotiation,** sometimes called *principled negotiation,* the focus is on the "merits" of the issues. Everyone involved tries to enlarge the available pie rather than stake claims to certain portions of it.[23] (See the Effective Manager 18.2.)

DISTRIBUTIVE NEGOTIATION

In distributive bargaining approaches, the participants would each ask the question: "Who is going to get this resource?" This question, and the way in which it frames subsequent behavior, will have a major impact on the negotiation process and outcomes. A case of distributive negotiation usually unfolds in one of two directions, neither of which yields optimal results. *"Hard" distributive negotiation* takes place when each party holds out to get its own way. This leads to competition, whereby each party seeks dominance over the other and tries to maximize self-interests. The hard approach may lead to a win-lose outcome in which one party dominates and gains. Or it can lead to an impasse.

"Soft" distributive negotiation, by contrast, takes place when one party is willing to make concessions to the other to get things over with. In this case, one party tries to find ways to meet the other's desires. A soft approach leads to accommodation in which one party gives in to the other, or to compromise in which each party gives up something of value in order to reach agreement. In either case at least some latent dissatisfaction is likely to develop. Even when the soft approach results in compromise (e.g., splitting the difference between the initial positions equally), dissatisfaction may exist since each party is still deprived of what it originally wanted.

Figure 18.4 introduces the case of the graduating senior negotiating a job offer with a corporate recruiter.[24] The example illustrates the basic elements of classic two-party negotiation in distributive contexts. To begin, look at the situation from the graduate's

FIGURE 18.4 | **AN EXAMPLE OF THE BARGAINING ZONE IN CLASSIC TWO-PARTY NEGOTIATION**

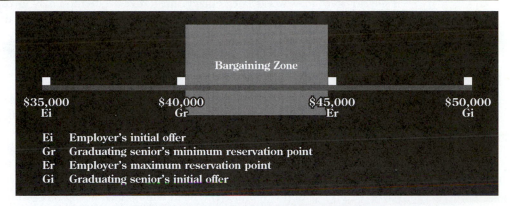

perspective. She has told the recruiter that she would like a salary of $50,000; this is her initial offer. But she also has in mind a minimum reservation point of $40,000—the lowest salary that she will accept for this job. Thus, she communicates a salary request of $50,000 but is willing to accept one as low as $40,000. The situation is somewhat reversed from the recruiter's perspective. His initial offer to the graduate is $35,000, and his maximum reservation point is $45,000; this is the most he is prepared to pay.

The **bargaining zone** is defined as the range between one party's minimum reservation point and the other party's maximum reservation point. In Figure 18.4, the bargaining zone is $45,000–50,000. This is a positive bargaining zone since the reservation points of the two parties overlap. Whenever a positive bargaining zone exists, bargaining has room to unfold. Had the graduate's minimum reservation point been greater than the recruiter's maximum reservation point (for example, $47,000), no room would have existed for bargaining. Classic two-party bargaining always involves the delicate tasks of first discovering the respective reservation points (one's own and the other's) and then working toward an agreement that lies somewhere within the resulting bargaining zone and is acceptable to each party.

INTEGRATIVE NEGOTIATION

In the integrative approach to negotiation, participants would ask: "How can the resource best be utilized?" Notice that this question is very different from the one described for distributive negotiation. It is much less confrontational, and it permits a broader range of alternatives to be considered in the process. From the outset there is much more of a "win-win" orientation.

At one extreme, integrative negotiation may involve selective avoidance, in which both parties realize that there are more important things on which to focus their time and attention. The time, energy, and effort needed to negotiate may not be worth the rewards. Compromise can also play a role in the integrative approach, but it must have an enduring basis. This is most likely to occur when the compromise involves each party giving up something of perceived lesser personal value to gain something of greater value. For instance, in the classic two-party bargaining case over salary, both the graduate and the recruiter could expand the negotiation to include the starting date of the job. Since it will be a year before the candidate's first vacation, she may be willing to take a little less money if she can start a few weeks later. Finally, integrative negotiation may involve true collaboration. In this case, the negotiating parties engage in problem solving to arrive at a mutual agreement that maximizes benefits to each.

HOW TO GAIN INTEGRATIVE AGREEMENTS

Underlying the integrative or principled approach is negotiation based on the merits of the situation. The foundations for gaining truly integrative agreements rest in supportive attitudes, constructive behaviors, and good information.[25]

Attitudinal Foundations   There are three attitudinal foundations of integrative agreements. First, each party must approach the negotiation with a *willingness to trust* the other party. This is a reason why ethics and maintaining relationships are so important in negotiations. Second, each party must convey a *willingness to share information* with the other party. Without shared information, effective problem solving is unlikely to occur. Third, each party must show a *willingness to ask concrete questions* of the other party. This further facilitates information sharing.

Behavioral Foundations   During a negotiation, all behavior is important for both its actual impact and the impressions it leaves behind. Accordingly, the following behavioral foundations of integrative agreements must be carefully considered and included in any negotiator's repertoire of skills and capabilities:

- The ability to separate the people from the problem to avoid allowing emotional considerations to affect the negotiation.
- The ability to focus on interests rather than positions.
- The ability to avoid making premature judgments.
- The ability to keep the acts of alternative creation separate from their evaluation.
- The ability to judge possible agreements on an objective set of criteria or standards.

Information Foundations   The information foundations of integrative agreements are substantial. They involve each party becoming familiar with the BATNA, or "best alternative to a negotiated agreement." That is, each party must know what he or she will do if an agreement can't be reached. This requires that both negotiating parties identify and understand their personal interests in the situation. They must know what is really important to them in the case at hand, and they must come to understand the relative importance of the other party's interests. As difficult as it may seem, each party must achieve an understanding of what the other party values, even to the point of determining its BATNA.

COMMON NEGOTIATION PITFALLS

The negotiation process is admittedly complex on cultural and many other grounds. It is further characterized by all the possible confusions of sometimes volatile interpersonal and group dynamics. Accordingly, negotiators need to guard against some common negotiation pitfalls.[26]

First is the tendency in negotiation to stake out your position based on the assumption that in order to gain your way, something must be subtracted from the other party's way. This *myth of the fixed pie* is a purely distributive approach to negotiation. The whole concept of integrative negotiation is based on the premise that the pie can sometimes be expanded or utilized to the maximum advantage of all parties, not just one.

Second, because parties to negotiations often begin by stating extreme demands, the possibility of *escalating commitment* is high. That is, once demands have been stated, people become committed to them and are reluctant to back down. Concerns for protecting one's ego and saving face may lead to nonrational escalation of conflict. Self-discipline is needed to spot this tendency in one's own behavior as well as in others.

Third, negotiators often develop *overconfidence* that their positions are the only correct ones. This can lead them to ignore the other party's needs. In some cases, negotiators completely fail to see merits in the other party's position—merits that an outside observer would be sure to spot. Such overconfidence makes it harder to reach a positive common agreement.

Fourth, *communication* problems can cause difficulties during a negotiation. It has been said that "negotiation is the process of communicating back and forth for the purpose of reaching a joint decision."[27] This process can break down because of a *telling problem*—the parties don't really talk to one another, at least not in the sense of making themselves truly understood. It can also be damaged by a *hearing problem*—the parties are unable or unwilling to listen well enough to understand what each other is saying. Indeed, positive negotiation is most likely when each party engages in active listening and frequently asks questions to clarify what the other is saying. Each party occasionally needs to "stand in the other party's shoes" and to view the situation from their perspective.[28]

THIRD-PARTY ROLES IN NEGOTIATION

Negotiation may sometimes be accomplished through the intervention of third parties, such as when stalemates occur and matters appear unresolvable under current circumstances. In **arbitration,** such as the salary arbitration now common in professional sports, this third party acts as the "judge" and has the power to issue a decision that is binding on all parties. This ruling takes place after the arbitrator listens to the positions advanced by the parties involved in a dispute. In **mediation,** a neutral third party tries to engage the parties in a negotiated solution through persuasion and rational argument. This is a common approach in labor-management negotiations, where trained mediators acceptable to each side are called in to help resolve bargaining impasses. Unlike an arbitrator, the mediator is not able to dictate a solution.

CHAPTER 18 SUMMARY

What is conflict?

- Conflict appears in a social situation as any disagreement over issues of substance or emotional antagonisms that create friction between individuals or groups.
- Conflict can be either emotional (based on personal feelings) or substantive (based on work goals).

- When kept within tolerable limits, conflict can be a source of creativity and performance enhancement; it becomes destructive when these limits are exceeded.
- Conflict situations in organizations occur in vertical and lateral working relations and in line-staff relations.
- Most typically, conflict develops through a series of stages, beginning with antecedent conditions and progressing into manifest conflict.
- Unresolved prior conflicts set the stage for future conflicts of a similar nature.

How can conflict be managed successfully?

- Indirect forms of conflict management include appeals to common goals, hierarchical referral, organizational redesign, and the use of mythology and scripts.
- Direct conflict management proceeds with different combinations of assertiveness and cooperativeness by conflicting parties.
- Win-win conflict resolution is preferred; it is achieved through collaboration and problem solving.
- Win-lose conflict resolution should be avoided; it is associated with competition and authoritative command.

What is negotiation?

- Negotiation occurs whenever two or more people with different preferences must make joint decisions.
- Managers may find themselves involved in various types of negotiation situations, including two-party, group, intergroup, and constituency negotiation.
- Effective negotiation occurs when issues of substance are resolved and human relationships are maintained, or even improved, in the process.
- Ethical conduct is important to successful negotiations.

What are the different strategies involved in negotiation?

- In distributive negotiation, the focus of each party is on staking out positions in the attempt to claim desired portions of a "fixed pie."
- In integrative negotiation, sometimes called principled negotiation, the focus is on determining the merits of the issues and finding ways to satisfy one another's needs.
- The success of the strategies depends on avoiding common negotiating pitfalls and building good communications.

Change, Innovation, and Stress

Study Questions

This chapter addresses the important issues of change, innovation, and stress as they relate to developments in the modern workplace. As you read Chapter 19, keep in mind these questions.

- What is organizational change?
- What change strategies are used in organizations?
- What can be done about resistance to change?
- How do organizations innovate?
- How does stress affect people at work?

A recent *Harvard Business Review* article opens with this sentence: "The new economy has ushered in great business opportunities—and great turmoil.[1] Not since the Industrial Revolution have the stakes of dealing with change been so high." The terms "turmoil" and "turbulence" are now often used to describe the current environment of business and management. The global economy is full of problems and opportunities, and is constantly springing new surprises on even the most experienced business executives. Standing at the heart of any successful response to the challenges of change are the people who make organizations work. This is what makes the insights of organizational behavior so essential to change leadership.

As the environment changes, organizations must change too—not just in the quest for customers in highly competitive markets, but also in the quest for the best in employee talents. Flexibility, competency, and commitment are rules of the day. People in the new workplace must be comfortable dealing with adaptation and continuous change. Amid the calls for greater productivity, willingness to learn from the successes of others, total quality, and continuous improvement, everyone is being called upon to achieve success while pursuing change and innovation and experiencing inevitable stress. In the words of management consultant Tom Peters: "The turbulent marketplace demands that we make innovation a way of life for everyone. We must learn—individually and as organizations—to welcome change and innovation as vigorously as we have fought it in the past."[2]

CHANGE IN ORGANIZATIONS

"Change" is the watchword of the day for many, if not most, organizations. Some of this change may be described as *radical change,* or frame-breaking change.[3] This is **transformational change,** which results in a major overhaul of the organization or its component systems. Organizations experiencing transformational change undergo significant shifts in basic characteristic features, including the overall purpose/mission, underlying values and beliefs, and supporting strategies and structures.[4] In today's business environments, transformational changes are often initiated by a critical event, such as a new CEO, a new ownership brought about by merger or takeover, or a dramatic failure in operating results. When it occurs in the life cycle of an organization, such radical change is intense and all-encompassing.

Another common form of organizational change is *incremental change,* or frame-bending change. This type of change, being part of an organization's natural evolution, is frequent and less traumatic. Typical changes of this type include the introduction of new products, new technologies, and new systems and processes. Although the nature of the organization remains relatively the same, incremental change builds on the existing ways of operating to enhance or extend them in new directions. The capability of improving continuously through incremental change is an important asset in today's demanding environments.

The success of both radical and incremental change in organizations depends in part on **change agents** who lead and support the change processes. These are individuals and groups who take responsibility for changing the existing behavior patterns of another person or social system. Although change agents sometimes are hired as consultants from outside the organization, any manager or leader in today's dynamic times is expected to act in a change agent capacity. Indeed, this responsibility is increasingly defined even more specifically as essential to the leadership role. Simply put, being an effective change agent means being a great "change leader."

PLANNED AND UNPLANNED CHANGE

Not all change in organizations is the result of a change agent's direction. **Unplanned changes** occur spontaneously or randomly. They may be disruptive, such as a wildcat strike that ends in a plant closure, or beneficial, such as an interpersonal conflict that results in a new procedure designed to smooth the flow of work between two departments. When the forces of unplanned change begin to appear, the appropriate goal is to act quickly to minimize any negative consequences and maximize any possible benefits. In many cases, unplanned changes can be turned into good advantage.

In contrast, **planned change** is the result of specific efforts by a change agent. It is a direct response to someone's perception of a *performance gap*—a discrepancy between the desired and actual state of affairs. Performance gaps may represent problems to be resolved or opportunities to be explored. Most planned changes may be regarded as efforts intended to deal with performance gaps in ways that benefit an organization and its members. The processes of continuous improvement require constant vigilance to spot performance gaps—both problems and opportunities—and to take action to resolve them.

ORGANIZATIONAL FORCES AND TARGETS FOR CHANGE

The forces for change driving organizations of all types and sizes are ever present in and around today's dynamic work settings. They are found in the *organization-environment relationship,* with mergers, strategic alliances, and divestitures among the examples of organizational attempts to redefine their relationships with challenging social and political environments. They are found in the *organizational life cycle,* with changes in culture and structure among the examples of how organizations must adapt as they evolve from birth through growth and toward maturity. They are found in the *political nature of organizations,* with changes in internal control structures, including benefits and reward systems, that attempt to deal with shifting political currents.

Planned change based on any of these forces can be internally directed toward a wide variety of organizational components, most of which have already been discussed in this book. As shown in Figure 19.1, these targets include organizational purpose, strategy, structure, and people, as well as objectives, culture, tasks, and technology. When considering these targets, however, it must be recognized that they are highly intertwined in the workplace. Changes in any one are likely to require or involve changes in others. For example, a change in the basic *tasks*—what it is that people do—is almost inevitably accompanied by a change in *technology*—the way in which tasks are accomplished. Changes in tasks and technology usually require alterations in structures, including changes in the patterns of authority and communication, as well as in the roles of workers. These technological and structural changes can, in turn, necessitate changes in the knowledge, skills, and behaviors of *people*—the members of the organization.[5] In all cases, of course, tendencies to accept easy-to-implement, but questionable, "quick fixes" to problems should be avoided.

PHASES OF PLANNED CHANGE

Researchers suggest that the failure rate of organizational change attempts is as high as 70 percent.[6] The challenges of transformational change are especially large, as The Effective

| FIGURE 19.1 | ORGANIZATIONAL TARGETS FOR PLANNED CHANGE |

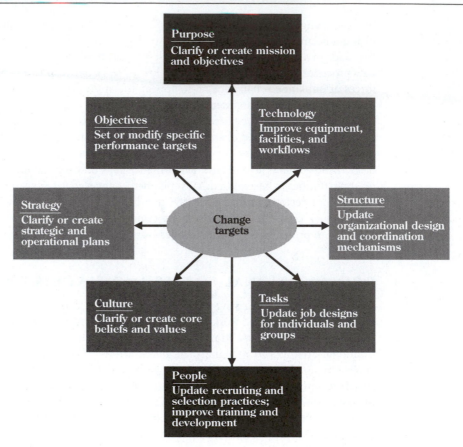

Manager 19.1 suggests.[7] One way to approach the task of improving the success rate of change initiatives is by understanding the underlying processes of social change in organizations. Psychologist Kurt Lewin recommends that any change effort be viewed in three phases—unfreezing, changing, and refreezing, all of which must be well handled for a change to be successful.[8] He also suggests that we may become easily preoccupied with the changing phase and neglect the importance of the unfreezing and refreezing stages.

Unfreezing In Lewin's model, **unfreezing** is the managerial responsibility of preparing a situation for change. It involves disconfirming existing attitudes and behaviors to create a felt need for something new. Unfreezing is facilitated by environmental pressures, declining performance, recognition of a problem, or awareness that someone else has found a better way, among other things. Many changes are never tried or they fail simply because situations are not properly unfrozen to begin with.

Large systems seem particularly susceptible to what is sometimes called the *boiled frog phenomenon*.[9] This refers to the notion that a live frog will immediately jump out when placed in a pan of hot water. When placed in cold water that is then heated very slowly,

THE EFFECTIVE MANAGER 19.1

WHY TRANSFORMATIONAL EFFORTS FAIL

1. No sense of urgency
2. No powerful guiding coalition
3. No competing vision
4. Failure to communicate the vision
5. Failure to empower others to act
6. Failure to celebrate short-term wins
7. Failure to build on accomplishments
8. Failure to institutionalize results

however, the frog will stay in the water until the water boils the frog to death. Organizations, too, can fall victim to similar circumstances. When managers fail to monitor their environments, recognize the important trends, or sense the need to change, their organizations may slowly suffer and lose their competitive edge. Although the signals that change may be needed are available, they aren't noticed or given any special attention—until it is too late. In contrast, the best organizations are led by people who are always on the alert and understand the importance of "unfreezing" in the change process.

Changing   The **changing** stage involves taking action to modify a situation by changing things, such as the people, tasks, structure, or technology of the organization. Lewin believes that many change agents are prone to an activity trap. They bypass the unfreezing stage and start changing things prematurely or too quickly. Although their intentions may be correct, the situation has not been properly prepared for change. This often leads to failure. Changing something is difficult enough in any situation, let alone having to do so without the proper foundations.

Refreezing   The final stage in the planned change process is **refreezing.** Designed to maintain the momentum of a change and eventually institutionalize it as part of the normal routine, refreezing secures the full benefits of long-lasting change. Refreezing involves positively reinforcing desired outcomes and providing extra support when difficulties are encountered. It involves evaluating progress and results, and assessing the costs and benefits of the change. And it allows for modifications to be made in the change to increase its success over time. When all of this is not done and refreezing is neglected, changes are often abandoned after a short time or incompletely implemented.

PLANNED CHANGE STRATEGIES

Managers and other change agents use various means for mobilizing power, exerting influence over others, and getting people to support planned change efforts. As described in Figure 19.2, each of these strategies builds from the various bases of social power discussed in Chapter 15. Note in particular that each power source has somewhat different implications for the planned change process.[10]

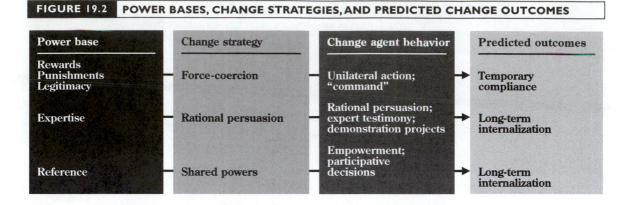

FIGURE 19.2 POWER BASES, CHANGE STRATEGIES, AND PREDICTED CHANGE OUTCOMES

Power base	Change strategy	Change agent behavior	Predicted outcomes
Rewards Punishments Legitimacy	Force-coercion	Unilateral action; "command"	Temporary compliance
Expertise	Rational persuasion	Rational persuasion; expert testimony; demonstration projects	Long-term internalization
Reference	Shared powers	Empowerment; participative decisions	Long-term internalization

FORCE-COERCION

A **force-coercion strategy** uses legitimacy, rewards, or punishments as primary inducements to change. That is, the change agent acts unilaterally to "command" change through the formal authority of his or her position, to induce change via an offer of special rewards, or to bring about change via threats of punishment. People respond to this strategy mainly out of the fear of being punished if they do not comply with a change directive or out of the desire to gain a reward if they do. Compliance is usually temporary and continues only as long as the change agent and his or her legitimate authority are visible, or as long as the opportunities for rewards and punishments remain obvious.

Your actions as a change agent using the force-coercion strategy might match the following profile.

> You believe that people who run things are basically motivated by self-interest and by what the situation offers in terms of potential personal gains or losses. Since you feel that people change only in response to such motives, you try to find out where their vested interests lie and then put the pressure on. If you have formal authority, you use it. If not, you resort to whatever possible rewards and punishments you have access to and do not hesitate to threaten others with these weapons. Once you find a weakness, you exploit it and are always wise to work "politically" by building supporting alliances wherever possible.[11]

RATIONAL PERSUASION

Change agents using a **rational persuasion strategy** attempt to bring about change through the use of special knowledge, empirical support, or rational arguments. This strategy assumes that rational people will be guided by reason and self-interest in deciding whether or not to support a change. Expert power is mobilized to convince others that the change will leave them better off than before. It is sometimes referred to as an *empirical-rational strategy* of planned change. When successful, this strategy results in a longer lasting, more naturalized change than does force-coercion.

As a change agent taking the rational persuasion approach to a change situation, you might behave as follows.

> You believe that people are inherently rational and are guided by reason in their actions and decision making. Once a specific course of action is demonstrated to be in a person's self-interest, you assume that reason and rationality will cause the person to adopt it. Thus, you approach change with the objective of communicating—through information and facts—the essential "desirability" of change from the perspective of the person whose behavior you seek to influence. If this logic is effectively communicated, you are sure of the person's adopting the proposed change.[12]

SHARED POWER

A **shared-power strategy** actively and sincerely involves the people who will be affected by a change in planning and making key decisions relating to this change. Sometimes called a *normative-reeducative approach,* this strategy tries to develop directions and support for change through involvement and empowerment. It builds essential foundations, such as personal values, group norms, and shared goals, so that support for a proposed change emerges naturally. Managers using normative-reeducative approaches draw upon the power of personal reference and also share power by allowing others to participate in planning and implementing the change. Given this high level of involvement, the strategy is likely to result in a longer lasting and internalized change.

As a change agent who shares power and adopts a normative-reeducative approach to change, you are likely to fit this profile:

> You believe that people have complex motivations. You feel that people behave as they do as a result of sociocultural norms and commitments to these norms. You also recognize that changes in these orientations involve changes in attitudes, values, skills, and significant relationships, not just changes in knowledge, information, or intellectual rationales for action and practice. Thus, when seeking to change others, you are sensitive to the supporting or inhibiting effects of group pressures and norms. In working with people, you try to find out their side of things and to identify their feelings and expectations.[13]

RESISTANCE TO CHANGE

In organizations, **resistance to change** is any attitude or behavior that indicates unwillingness to make or support a desired change. Change agents often view any such resistance as something that must be "overcome" in order for change to be successful. This is not always the case, however. It is helpful to view resistance to change as feedback that the change agent can use to facilitate gaining change objectives.[14] The essence of this constructive approach to resistance is to recognize that when people resist change, they are defending something important and that appears threatened by the change attempt.

WHY PEOPLE RESIST CHANGE

People have many reasons to resist change. The Effective Manager 19.2 identifies fear of the unknown, insecurity, lack of a felt need to change, threat to vested interests, contrasting interpretations, and lack of resources, among other possibilities. A work team's members, for example, may resist the introduction of advanced workstation computers because they have never used the operating system and are apprehensive. They may wonder whether the new computers will eventually be used as justification for "getting rid" of some of them; or they may believe that they have been doing their jobs just fine and do not need the new computers to improve things. These and other viewpoints often create resistance to even the best and most well-intended planned changes.

Resistance to the Change Itself   Sometimes a change agent experiences resistance to the change itself. People may reject a change because they believe it is not worth their time, effort, or attention. To minimize resistance in such cases, the change agent should make sure that everyone who may be affected by a change knows specifically how it satisfies the following criteria.[15]

- *Benefit*—The change should have a clear relative advantage for the people being asked to change; it should be perceived as "a better way."
- *Compatibility*—The change should be as compatible as possible with the existing values and experiences of the people being asked to change.
- *Complexity*—The change should be no more complex than necessary; it must be as easy as possible for people to understand and use.
- *Triability*—The change should be something that people can try on a step-by-step basis and make adjustments as things progress.

Resistance to the Change Strategy   Change agents must also be prepared to deal with resistance to the change strategy. Someone who attempts to bring about change via force-coercion, for example, may create resistance among individuals who resent management by "command" or the use of threatened punishment. People may resist a rational

---

THE EFFECTIVE MANAGER 19.2

EIGHT REASONS FOR RESISTING CHANGE

1. Fear of the unknown
2. Lack of good information
3. Fear for loss of security
4. No reasons to change
5. Fear for loss of power
6. Lack of resources
7. Bad timing
8. Habit

persuasion strategy in which the data are suspect or the expertise of advocates is not clear. They may resist a shared-power strategy that appears manipulative and insincere.

Resistance to the Change Agent   Resistance to the change agent is directed at the person implementing the change and often involves personality and other differences. Change agents who are isolated and aloof from other persons in the change situation, who appear self-serving, or who have a high emotional involvement in the changes are especially prone to such problems. Research also indicates that change agents who differ from other persons in the change situation on such dimensions as age, education, and socioeconomic factors may encounter greater resistance to change.[16]

HOW TO DEAL WITH RESISTANCE

An informed change agent has many options available for dealing positively with resistance to change, in any of its forms.[17] The first approach is through *education and communication.* The objective is to educate people about a change before it is implemented and to help them understand the logic of the change. Education and communication seem to work best when resistance is based on inaccurate or incomplete information. A second way is the use of *participation and involvement.* With the goal of allowing others to help design and implement the changes, this approach asks people to contribute ideas and advice or to work on task forces or committees that may be leading the change. This is especially useful when the change agent does not have all the information needed to successfully handle a problem situation.

Facilitation and support involves providing assistance—both emotional and material—for people experiencing the hardships of change. A manager using this approach actively listens to problems and complaints, provides training in the new ways, and helps others to overcome performance pressures. Facilitation and support is highly recommended when people are frustrated by work constraints and difficulties encountered in the change process. A *negotiation and agreement* approach offers incentives to actual or potential change resistors. Tradeoffs are arranged to provide special benefits in exchange for assurances that the change will not be blocked. It is most useful when dealing with a person or group that will lose something of value as a result of the planned change.

Manipulation and cooptation makes use of covert attempts to influence others, selectively providing information and consciously structuring events so that the desired change occurs. In some cases, leaders of the resistance may be "bought off" with special side deals to gain their support. Manipulation and cooptation are common when other tactics do not work or are too expensive. Finally, *explicit or implicit coercion* employs the force of authority to get people to accept change. Often, resistors are threatened with a variety of undesirable consequences if they do not go along as planned. This may be done, for example, in crisis situations when speed is of the essence.

Figure 19.3 summarizes additional insights into how and when each of these methods may be used to deal with resistance to change. Regardless of the chosen strategy, it is always best to remember that the presence of resistance typically suggests that something can be done to achieve a better fit among the change, the situation, and the people affected. A good change agent deals with resistance to change by listening to feedback and acting accordingly.

FIGURE 19.3	METHODS FOR DEALING WITH RESISTANCE TO CHANGE

Method →	Use when →	Advantages →	Disadvantages
Education & communication	People lack information or have inaccurate information	Creates willingness to help with the change	Can be very time consuming
Participation & involvement	Other people have important information and/or power to resist	Adds information to change planning; builds commitment to the change	Can be very time consuming
Facilitation & support	Resistance traces to resource or adjustment problems	Satisfies directly specific resource or adjustment needs	Can be time consuming; can be expensive
Negotiation & agreement	A person or group will "lose" something because of the change	Helps avoid major resistance	Can be expensive; can cause others to seek similar "deals"
Manipulation & cooptation	Other methods don't work or are too expensive	Can be quick and inexpensive	Can create future problems if people sense manipulation
Explicit & implicit coercion	Speed is important and change agent has power	Quick; overpowers resistance	Risky if people get "mad"

INNOVATION IN ORGANIZATIONS

The best organizations don't stagnate; they innovate.[18] And they are able to innovate on an ongoing basis—they value and expect "innovation," and it becomes a normal part of everyday operations. **Innovation** is the process of creating new ideas and putting them into practice.[19] It is the means by which creative ideas find their way into everyday practices, ideally practices that contribute to improved customer service or organizational productivity. **Product innovations** result in the introduction of new or improved goods or services to better meet customer needs. **Process innovations** result in the introduction of new and better work methods and operations.

THE INNOVATION PROCESS

The basic steps in a typical process of organizational innovation are shown in Figure 19.4. They include:

1. *Idea creation*—to create an idea through spontaneous creativity, ingenuity, and information processing.
2. *Initial experimentation*—to establish the idea's potential value and application.
3. *Feasibility determination*—to identify anticipated costs and benefits.
4. *Final application*—to produce and market a new product or service, or to implement a new approach to operations.

The innovation process is not complete until final application has been achieved. A new idea—even a great one—is not enough. In any organization, the idea must pass

| FIGURE 19.4 | THE INNOVATION PROCESS: A CASE OF NEW PRODUCT DEVELOPMENT |

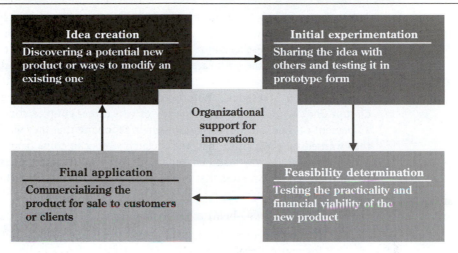

through all stages of innovation and reach the point of final application before its value can be realized.

FEATURES OF INNOVATIVE ORGANIZATIONS

The new workplace is placing great demands on organizations and their members to be continuously innovative. When we examine the characteristics of high-performing and innovative organizations, we observe certain common features. Highly innovative organizations have *strategies and cultures* that are built around a commitment to innovation. This includes tolerance for mistakes and respect for well-intentioned ideas that just do not work. Highly innovative organizations have *structures* that support innovation. They emphasize creativity through teamwork and cross-functional integration. They also utilize decentralization and empowerment to overcome the limitations of great size. In highly innovative organizations, *staffing* is done with a clear commitment to innovation. Special attention is given to critical innovation roles of idea generators, information gatekeepers, product champions, and project leaders. Finally, innovative organizations benefit from *top-management support*. Senior managers provide good examples for others, eliminate obstacles to innovation, and try to get things done that make innovation easier. Former Johnson & Johnson CEO James Burke, for example, once said, "I try to give people the feeling that it's okay to fail," while Quad Graphics founder Harry V. Quadrucci practiced what has been dubbed "management by walking away." The implication in both approaches is that employees know what needs to be done, and management's job is to trust and help them to do their best.[20]

DYNAMICS OF STRESS

The processes of change and innovation often create new and increased pressures on the people involved. **Stress** must be understood as a state of tension experienced by individuals facing extraordinary demands, constraints, or opportunities.[21]

SOURCES OF STRESS

Any look toward your career future in today's dynamic times must include an awareness that stress is something you, as well as others, are sure to encounter.[22] **Stressors** are the wide variety of things that cause stress for individuals. Some stressors can be traced directly to what people experience in the workplace, whereas others derive from nonwork and personal factors.

Work-Related Stressors Without doubt work can be stressful, and job demands can disrupt one's work-life balance. A study of two-career couples, for example, found some 43 percent of men and 34 percent of women reporting that they worked more hours than they wanted to.[23] We know that work-related stress can come from many sources—from excessively high or low task demands, role conflicts or ambiguities, poor interpersonal relations, or career progress that is either too slow or too fast. A list of common stressors includes the following:

- *Task demands*—being asked to do too much or being asked to do too little.
- *Role ambiguities*—not knowing what one is expected to do or how work performance is evaluated.
- *Role conflicts*—feeling unable to satisfy multiple, possibly conflicting, performance expectations.
- *Ethical dilemmas*—being asked to do things that violate the law or personal values.
- *Interpersonal problems*—experiencing bad relationships or working with others who do not get along.
- *Career developments*—moving too fast and feeling stretched; moving too slowly and feeling plateaued.
- *Physical setting*—being bothered by noise, lack of privacy, pollution, or other unpleasant working conditions.

Nonwork and Personal Stressors A less obvious, though important, source of stress for people at work is the "spillover" effect from forces in their nonwork lives. Family events (e.g., the birth of a new child), economic difficulties (e.g., the sudden loss of a big investment), and personal affairs (e.g., a separation or divorce) can all be extremely stressful. Since it is often difficult to completely separate work and nonwork lives, stress of this nonwork sort can affect the way people feel and behave on the job as well as away from it.

Another set of stressors includes personal factors, such as individual needs, capabilities, and personality. Stress can reach a destructive state more quickly, for example, when experienced by highly emotional people or by those with low self-esteem. People who perceive a good fit between job requirements and personal skills seem to have a higher tolerance for stress than do those who feel less competent as a result of a person-job mismatch.[24] Basic aspects of personality are also important. The achievement orientation, impatience, and perfectionism of individuals with Type A personalities, for example, often create stress for them in work settings that others find relatively stress-free.[25]

STRESS AND PERFORMANCE

Stress isn't always negative as an influence on our lives. It has two faces—one positive and one negative.[26] **Constructive stress,** or *eustress,* acts in a positive way. Moderate levels of stress by prompting increased work effort, stimulating creativity, and encouraging greater diligence. You may know such stress as the tension that causes you to study hard before exams, pay attention, and complete assignments on time in a difficult class. **Destructive stress,** or *distress,* is dysfunctional for both the individual and the organization. Too much stress can overload and break down a person's physical and mental systems resulting in absenteeism, turnover, errors, accidents, dissatisfaction, reduced performance, unethical behavior, and even illness. Stanford scholar and consultant Jeffrey Pfeffer, for example, criticizes organizations that suffer from such excessive practices for creating *toxic workplaces.*[27] A toxic company implicitly says to its employees: "We're going to put you in an environment where you have to work in a style and at a pace that is not sustainable. We want you to come in here and burn yourself out. Then you can leave."[28]

STRESS AND HEALTH

As is well known, stress can impact a person's health. It is a potential source of both anxiety and frustration, which can harm the body's physiological and psychological well-being over time.[29] Health problems associated with stress include heart attack, stroke, hypertension, migraine headache, ulcers, substance abuse, overeating, depression, and muscle aches. As noted in The Effective Manager 19.3, managers and team leaders should be alert to signs of excessive stress in themselves and their co-workers. Key symptoms to look for are changes from normal patterns—changes from regular attendance to absenteeism, from punctuality to tardiness, from diligent work to careless work, from a positive attitude to a negative attitude, from openness to change to resistance to change, or from cooperation to hostility.

STRESS MANAGEMENT

Stress prevention is the best first-line strategy in the battle against stress. It involves taking action to keep stress from reaching destructive levels in the first place. Personal and nonwork stressors must be recognized so that action can be taken to prevent them from adverse impact. Persons with Type A personalities, for example, may exercise self-discipline; supervisors of Type A employees may try to model a lower key, more relaxed approach to work. Family problems may be partially relieved by a change of work schedule; the anxiety caused by pressing family concerns may be reduced by simply knowing that your supervisor understands.

Once stress has reached a destructive point, special techniques of **stress management** can be implemented. This process begins with the recognition of stress symptoms and continues

---

THE EFFECTIVE MANAGER 19.3

SIGNS OF EXCESSIVE STRESS

- Change in eating habits
- Change in alcohol consumption or smoking
- Unhealthy feelings—aches and pains, upset stomach
- Restlessness, inability to concentrate, sleeping problems
- Tense, uptight, fidgety, nervous feelings
- Disoriented, overwhelmed, depressed, irritable feelings

with actions to maintain a positive performance edge. The term **wellness** is increasingly used these days. Personal wellness involves the pursuit of one's physical and mental potential through a personal health promotion program. The concept recognizes individual responsibility to enhance and maintain wellness through a disciplined approach to physical and mental health. It requires attention to such factors as smoking, weight, diet, alcohol use, and physical fitness. Organizations can benefit from commitments to support personal wellness. A University of Michigan study indicates that firms have saved up to $600 per year per employee by helping them to cut the risk of significant health problems.[30] Arnold Coleman, CEO of Healthy Outlook Worldwide, a health fitness consulting firm, states: "If I can save companies 5 to 20 percent a year in medical costs, they'll listen. In the end you have a well company and that's where the word 'wellness' comes from."[31]

Organizations that build positive work environments and make significant investments in their employees are best positioned to realize the benefits of their full talents and work potential. As Pfeffer says: "All that separates you from your competitors are the skills, knowledge, commitment, and abilities of the people who work for you. Organizations that treat people right will get high returns...."[32] That, in essence, is what the study of organizational behavior is all about.

Chapter 19 Summary

What is organizational change?

- Planned change takes place because change agents, individuals and groups, make it happen to resolve performance problems or realize performance opportunities.
- Transformational change radically shifts fundamental aspects of organizations such as purpose and mission, beliefs and values, strategies, and structures.
- Organizational targets for planned change include purpose, strategy, culture, structure, people, tasks, and technology.
- The planned change process requires attention to the three phases—unfreezing, changing, and refreezing.

What change strategies are used in organizations?

- Change strategies are the means change agents use to bring about desired change in people and systems.
- Force-coercion change strategies use position power to bring about change through direct command or through rewards and punishments.
- Rational persuasion change strategies use logical arguments and appeals to knowledge and facts to convince people to change.
- Shared-power change strategies involve other persons in planning and implementing change.

What can be done about resistance to change?

- Resistance to change should be expected and not feared; it is a source of feedback that can be used to improve a change effort.

- People usually resist change because they are defending something of value; they may focus their resistance on the change itself, the change strategy, or the change agent as a person.

- Strategies for dealing with resistance to change include education and communication, participation and involvement, facilitation and support, negotiation and agreement, manipulation and cooptation, and explicit or implicit coercion.

How do organizations innovate?

- Innovation is the process of creating new ideas and then implementing them in practical applications.

- Product innovations result in improved goods or services; process innovations result in improved work methods and operations.

- Steps in the innovation process normally include idea generation, initial experimentation, feasibility determination, and final application.

- Common features of highly innovative organizations include supportive strategies, cultures, structures, staffing, and senior leadership.

How does stress affect people at work?

- Stress emerges when people experience tensions caused by extraordinary demands, constraints, or opportunities in their jobs.

- Work-related stressors arise from such things as excessive task demands, interpersonal problems, unclear roles, ethical dilemmas, and career disappointments.

- Nonwork stress can spill over to affect people at work; nonwork stressors may be traced to family situations, economic difficulties, and personal problems.

- Personal stressors derive from personality type, needs, and values, and can influence how stressful different situations become for different people.

- Stress can be managed by prevention—such as making adjustments in work and nonwork factors; it can also be dealt with through personal wellness—taking steps to maintain a healthy body and mind capable of better withstanding stressful situations.

Supplementary Module: Research Foundations of Organizational Behavior

While we realize you are most interested in applications, we hope you will take a minute to examine some of the foundations for the theory and research that should underlie applications. Almost anyone who can write well has some commentary about OB. Many are quick to make recommendations for immediate application. Many apparently successful executives without any specialized training seem willing to write about OB and give their advice. There are also many consulting firms willing to give managers helpful hints in exchange for large fees. In the babble you may find it difficult to decide what to believe and what to dismiss. As an educated individual you should be willing to ask some fundamental questions before you attempt to make improvements based on the mere suggestions of others.

OB is an applied social science that combines basic theory and applications. If you are an engineer, you apply basic physics. You know the laws of physics. You know that applications inconsistent with the laws of physics will fail. As an engineer you will not normally get involved in researching physics or writing about it. Physics is an ancient academic discipline with very specialized theories, language, and standards of proof. For example, there is no perpetual motion machine, even though many have bought variations of it. Well, OB is not physics and management is not the application of a well-developed academic discipline. There are no "laws" of OB. There are many theories.

THEORY IN OB

Throughout this book we have discussed many theories. In a very broad sense a theory is simply a story of what to look for, how the things you are looking at are related, and why the pieces do or do not fit together into some meaningful tale. The purpose of a theory is to explain and predict. The better the theory, the better the explanation and prediction. More formally stated, a **theory** is a set of systematically interrelated concepts and hypotheses that are advanced to explain and predict phenomena.[1]

In OB, some scholars also incorporate an applications aspect. That is, a good theory also can be applied with confidence. John Miner is one of those who has outlined some bases for judging theory in OB.[2] These include:

1.   It should aid in understanding, permit prediction, and facilitate influence.
2.   There would be clear boundaries for application.
3.   It should direct efforts toward important, high-priority items.
4.   It should produce generalizable results beyond a single setting.
5.   It should be tested using clearly defined concepts and operational measures.
6.   It should be both internally consistent and consistent with studies derived from it.
7.   It should be stated in understandable terms.

Now that is a very tall order for any theory and we know of no theory in OB that passes muster on all accounts. Clearly some are better than others. Some theories are pretty good at explanation but lousy at prediction, while others do a reasonable job of prediction but do not facilitate influence. For example, if circumstances are highly similar, predicting an individual will repeat a behavior is a sound bet. Unfortunately, this prediction is rarely supported by a theory explaining why the individual acted in a given manner in the first place. As a manager, even if you know that an individual will repeat a behavior, you also need to know how to change it. And so it goes.

The bottom line is that theory and research go together. The theory tells one what to look for and the research tells what was found. What was found also tells us what to look for again. It is important to realize that we may not see what we do not conceptualize. But it is equally important to note that for an acceptable theory others must understand, see, and verify what we see and understand. Among OB researchers, this process of seeing, understanding, and verifying is generally accomplished through the scientific method.

THE SCIENTIFIC METHOD

A key part of OB research foundations is the **scientific method,** which involves four steps. First, a *research question* or *problem* is specified. Then one or more *hypotheses* or explanations of what the research parties expect to find are formulated. These may come from many sources, including previous experience and careful review of the literature covering the problem area. The next step is the creation of a *research design*—an overall plan or strategy for conducting the research to test the hypothesis(es). Finally, *data gathering, analysis,* and *interpretation* are carried out.[3]

THE VOCABULARY OF RESEARCH

The previous discussion conveyed a quick summary of the scientific method. It's important to go beyond that summation and further develop a number of aspects of the scientific method. Before doing that, we consider the vocabulary of research. Knowing that vocabulary can help you feel comfortable with several terms used in OB research as well as help in our later discussion.[4]

Variable   A **variable** is a measure used to describe a real-world phenomenon. For example, a researcher may count the number of parts produced by workers in a week's time as a measure of the workers' individual productivity.

Hypothesis   Building on our earlier use of the term, we can define a **hypothesis** as a tentative explanation about the relationship between two or more variables. For example, OB researchers have hypothesized that an increase in supervisory participation will increase productivity. Hypotheses are "predictive" statements. Once supported through empirical research, a hypothesis can be a source of direct action implications. Confirmation of the above hypothesis would lead to the following implication: If you want to increase individual productivity in a work unit, increase the level of supervisory participation.

Dependent Variable   The **dependent variable** is the event or occurrence expressed in a hypothesis that indicates what the researcher is interested in explaining. In the previous example, individual performance was the dependent variable of interest. OB researchers often try to determine what factors appear to predict increases in performance.

Independent Variable   An **independent variable** is the event or occurrence that is presumed by a hypothesis to affect one or more other events or occurrences as dependent variables. In the example of individual performance, supervisory participation is the independent variable.

Intervening Variable   An **intervening variable** is an event or occurrence that provides the linkage through which an independent variable is presumed to affect a dependent variable. It has been hypothesized, for instance, that participative supervisory practices (independent variable) improve worker satisfaction (intervening variable) and therefore increase performance (dependent variable).

Moderator Variable   A **moderator variable** is an event or occurrence that, when systematically varied, changes the relationship between an independent variable and a dependent variable. The relationship between these two variables differs depending on the level, for instance, high/low, young/old, male/female, of the moderator variable. To illustrate, consider again the previous example of the individual performance hypothesis that participative supervision leads to increased productivity. It may well be that this relationship holds true only when the employees feel that their participation is real and legitimate—a moderator variable. Likewise, it may be that participative supervision leads to increased performance for Canadian workers but not those from Brazil—here, the country is a moderator variable.

Validity   **Validity** is concerned with the degree of confidence one can have in the results of a research study. It is focused on limiting research errors so that results are accurate and usable.[5] There are two key types of validity: internal and external. *Internal validity* is the degree to which the results of a study can be relied upon to be correct. It is strongest when alternative interpretations of the study's findings can be ruled out.[6] To illustrate, if performance improves with more participative supervisory practices, these results have a higher degree of internal validity if we can rule out the effects of differences in old and new machines.

External validity is the degree to which the study's results can be generalized across the entire population of people, settings, and other similar conditions.[7] We cannot have external validity unless we first have internal validity; that is, we must have confidence that the results are caused by what the study says they are before we can generalize to a broader context.

Reliability **Reliability** is the consistency and stability of a score from a measurement scale. There must be reliability for there to be validity or accuracy. Think of shooting at a bull's-eye. If the shots land all over the target, there is neither reliability (consistency) nor validity (accuracy). If the shots are clustered close together but outside the outer ring of the target, they are reliable but not valid. If they are grouped together within the bull's-eye, they are both reliable and valid.[8]

Causality **Causality** is the assumption that change in the independent variable caused change in the dependent variable. This assumption is very difficult to prove in OB research. Three types of evidence are necessary to demonstrate causality: (1) the variables must show a linkage or association; (2) one variable must precede the other in time; and (3) there must be an absence of other causal factors.[9] For example, say we note that participation and performance increase together—there is an association. If we can then show that an increase in participation has preceded an increase in performance and that other factors, such as new machinery, haven't been responsible for the increased performance, we can say that participation probably has caused performance.

RESEARCH DESIGNS

As noted earlier, a **research design** is an overall plan or strategy for conducting the research to test the hypothesis(es). Four of the most popular research designs are laboratory experiments, field experiments, case studies, and field surveys.[10]

LABORATORY EXPERIMENTS

Laboratory experiments are conducted in an artificial setting in which the researcher intervenes and manipulates one or more independent variables in a highly controlled situation. Although there is a high degree of control, which, in turn, encourages internal validity, since these studies are done in an artificial setting, they may suffer from a lack of external validity.

To illustrate, assume we are interested in the impact of three different incentive systems on employee absenteeism: (1) a lottery with a monetary reward; (2) a lottery with a compensatory time off reward; and (3) a lottery with a large prize, such as a car. The researcher randomly selects individuals in an organization to come to an office to take part in the study. This randomization is important because it means that variables that are not measured are randomly distributed across the subjects so that unknown variables shouldn't be causing whatever is found. However, it often is not possible to obtain subjects randomly in organizations since they may be needed elsewhere by management.

The researcher is next able to select randomly each worker to one of the three incentive systems, as well as a control group with no incentive system. The employees report to work in their new work stations under highly artificial but controlled conditions, and their absenteeism is measured both at the beginning and end of the experiment. Statistical comparisons are made across each group, considering before and after measures.

Ultimately, the researcher develops hypotheses about the effects of each of the lottery treatments on absenteeism. Given support for these hypotheses, the researcher could feel with a high degree of confidence that a given incentive condition caused less absenteeism than did the others since randomized subjects, pre- and post-test measures, and a comparison with a control group were used. However, since the work stations were artificial and the lottery conditions were highly simplified to provide control, external validity could be questioned. Ideally, the researcher would conduct a follow-up study with another design to check for external validity.

FIELD EXPERIMENTS

Field experiments are research studies that are conducted in a realistic setting. Here, the researcher intervenes and manipulates one or more independent variables and controls the situation as carefully as the situation permits.

Applying the same research question as before, the researcher obtains management permission to assign one incentive treatment to each of three similar organizational departments, similar in terms of the various characteristics of people. A fourth control department keeps the current payment plan. The rest of the experiment is similar to the laboratory study except that the lottery treatments are more realistic but also less controlled. Also, it may be particularly difficult to obtain random assignment in this case since it may disrupt day-to-day work schedules, etc. When random assignment is not possible, the other manipulations may still be possible. An experimental research design without any randomization is called a *quasi-experimental design* and does not control for unmeasured variables as well as a randomized design.

CASE STUDIES

Case studies are in-depth analyses of one or a small number of settings. Case studies often are used when little is known about a phenomenon and the researcher wants to examine relevant concepts intensely and thoroughly. They can sometimes be used to help develop theory that can then be tested with one of the other research designs. Returning to the participation and performance example, one might look at one or more organizations and intensely study organizational success or failure in designing or implementing participation. You might look for differences in how employees and managers define participation. This information could provide insights to be investigated further with additional case studies or other research designs.

A major strength of case studies is their realism and the richness of data and insights they can provide. Some disadvantages are their lack of control by the researcher, the difficulty of interpreting the results because of their richness, and the large amount of time and cost that may be involved.

FIELD SURVEYS

Field surveys typically depend on the use of some form of questionnaire for the primary purpose of describing and/or predicting some phenomenon. Typically, they utilize a sample drawn from some large population. A key objective of field surveys is to look for relationships between or among variables. Two major advantages are their ability to examine and describe large populations quickly and inexpensively and their flexibility. They can be used to do many kinds of OB research, such as testing hypotheses and theories and evaluating programs. Field surveys assume that the researcher has enough knowledge of the problem area to know the kinds of questions to ask; sometimes, earlier case studies help provide this knowledge.

A key disadvantage of field surveys is the lack of control. The researcher does not manipulate variables; even such things as who completes the surveys and their timing may not be under the researcher's control. Another disadvantage is the lack of depth of the standardized responses; thus, sometimes the data obtained are superficial.

DATA GATHERING, ANALYSIS, AND INTERPRETATION

Once the research design has been established, we are ready for data gathering, analysis, and interpretation—the final step in the scientific method. Four common OB data-gathering approaches are interviews, observation, questionnaires, and nonreactive measures.[11]

INTERVIEWS

Interviews involve face-to-face, telephone, or computer-assisted interactions to ask respondents questions of interest. Structured interviews ask the respondents the same questions in the same sequence. Unstructured interviews are more spontaneous and do not require the same format. Often a mixture of structured and unstructured formats is used. Interviews allow for in-depth responses and probing. They are generally time consuming, however, and require increasing amounts of training and skill, depending on their depth and amount of structure.

OBSERVATION

Observation involves watching an event, object, or person and recording what is seen. Sometimes, the observer is separate from the participants and events and functions as an outside researcher. In other cases, the observer participates in the events as a member of a work unit. In the latter case, observations are summarized in some kind of diary or log. Sometimes, the observer is hidden and records observations behind one-way glass or by using hidden cameras and the like.

Two advantages of observation are that (1) behavior is observed as it occurs rather than being obtained by asking people after the fact, and (2) the observer can often obtain data that subjects can't or won't provide themselves. A couple of disadvantages are cost and the possible fallibility of observers who sometimes do not provide complete and accurate data.

QUESTIONNAIRES

Questionnaires ask respondents for their opinions, attitudes, perceptions, and/or descriptions of work-related matters. They usually are based on previously developed instruments. Typically, a respondent completes the questionnaire and returns it to the researcher. Questions may be open ended, or they may be structured with true-false or multiple-choice responses.

Advantages of questionnaires include the relatively low cost and the fact that the anonymity that often accompanies them may lead to more open and truthful responses. Some disadvantages are the low response rates, which may threaten the generalizability of the results, and the lack of depth of the responses.

NONREACTIVE MEASURES

Nonreactive measures are used to obtain data without disturbing the setting being studied. Sometimes, these are termed *unobtrusive measures* since they are designed not to intrude in a research situation. Nonreactive measures can focus on such things as physical traces, archives, and hidden observation. A kind of physical trace occurred when John Fry at 3M distributed test batches of Post-It Notes to 3M employees and discovered that they were using them at higher rates than 3M's leading adhesive product, Scotch Tape.[12] Archives are records that an organization keeps as a part of its day-to-day activities, for example, minutes or daily production counts.

A major advantage of nonreactive measures is that they don't disturb the research setting and so avoid the reaction of a respondent to a researcher. One possible disadvantage is their indirectness; incorrect inferences may be drawn from nonreactive measures. They work best in combination with more direct measures.

DATA ANALYSIS AND INTERPRETATION

Once the data have been gathered, they need to be *analyzed*. The most common means of analysis involves some kind of statistical approach, ranging from simple counting and categorizing to sophisticated multivariate statistical techniques.[13] It's beyond our scope to discuss this area beyond simply emphasizing its importance. However, various statistical tests often are used to examine support for hypotheses, to check for the reliability of various data-gathering approaches, and to provide information on causality and many other aspects of analysis.

After systematic analysis has been performed, the researcher *interprets* the results and prepares a report.[14] Sometimes, the report is used in-house by management; other times, the results are reported at various conferences and published in journals. Ultimately, many of the results in the OB area appear in textbooks like this one.

ETHICAL CONSIDERATIONS IN RESEARCH

Given our emphasis on ethical considerations throughout this book, it is appropriate to end our discussion of OB research with a look at its ethical considerations. These ethical considerations involve rights of four broad parties involved in research in general and in OB research in particular: society, subjects, clients, and researchers.[15]

In terms of *societal rights*—those of the broadest of the parties involved in OB research—three key areas exist: the right to be informed, the right to expect objective results, and the right to privacy or to be left alone. Subjects of research also have rights: the right to choose (to participate or not), to safety, and to be informed. The rights of the client involve two primary concerns: the right to expect high-quality research and the right of confidentiality. Finally, two rights of the researcher stand out: the right to expect ethical client behavior and the right to expect ethical subject behavior.

All of these rights need to be communicated and adhered to by all parties. Indeed, various organizations conducting research are increasingly endorsing codes of ethics to codify such rights. Two particular organizations that have codes of ethics for research covering OB and related areas are the American Psychological Association and the Academy of Management.

Notes

CHAPTER 1

1. See Jeffrey Pfeffer, *The Human Equation: Building Profits by Putting People First* (Boston: Harvard Business School Press, 1998) and Charles O'Reilly III and Jeffrey Pfeffer, *Hidden Value: How Great Companies Achieve Extraordinary Results with Ordinary People* (Boston: Harvard Business School Press, 2000).
2. John Huey, "Managing in the Midst of Chaos," *Fortune* (April 5, 1993), pp. 38–48. See also Tom Peters, *Thriving on Chaos* (New York: Knopf, 1991); Jay R. Galbraith, Edward E. Lawler III, and Associates, *Organizing for the Future: The New Logic for Managing Organizations* (San Francisco: Jossey-Bass, 1993); William H. Davidow and Michael S. Malone, *The Virtual Corporation: Structuring and Revitalizing the Corporation of the 21st Century* (New York: Harper Business, 1993); Charles Handy, *The Age of Unreason* (Boston: Harvard Business School Press, 1990) and *The Age of Paradox* (Boston: Harvard Business School Press, 1994). Peter Drucker. *Managing in a Time of Great Change* (New York: Truman Talley, 1995) and *Management Challenges for the 21st Century* (New York: Harper, 1999).
3. See Daniel H. Pink, "Free Agent Nation," *Fast Company* (December 1997), pp. 131ff; and Tom Peters, "The Brand Called You," *Fast Company* (August/September 1997).
4. Robert B. Reich, "The Company of the Future," *Fast Company* (November 1998), p. 124ff.
5. Based on Jay A. Conger, *Winning 'em Over: A New Model for Managing in the Age of Persuasion* (New York: Simon & Schuster, 1998), pp. 180–181; Stewart D. Friedman, Perry Christensen, and Jessica DeGroot, "Work and Life: The End of the Zero-Sum Game, *Harvard Business Review* (November/December 1998): 119–129; and C. Argyris, "Empowerment: The Emperor's New Clothes," *Harvard Business Review:* (May/June 1998): 98–105.
6. The foundation report on diversity in the American workplace is *Workforce 2000: Work and Workers in the 21st Century* (Indianapolis: Hudson Institute, 1987). For comprehensive discussions, see Martin M. Chemers, Stuart Oskamp, and Mark A. Costanzo, *Diversity in Organizations: New Perspectives for a Changing Workplace* (Beverly Hills, CA: Sage, 1995); and Robert T. Golembiewski, *Managing Diversity in Organizations* (Tuscaloosa, AL: University of Alabama Press, 1995).
7. See R. Roosevelt Thomas, Jr. with Marjorie I. Woodruff, *Building a House for Diversity* (New York: AMACOM, 1999); R. Roosevelt Thomas, "From Affirmative Action to Affirming Diversity," *Harvard Business Review* (March/April 1990): 107–117; and *Beyond Race and Gender: Unleashing the Power of Your Total Workforce by Managing Diversity* (New York: AMACOM, 1992).
8. For discussions of the glass ceiling effect see Ann M. Morrison, Randall P. White, and Ellen Van Velso, *Breaking the Glass Ceiling* (Reading, MA: Addison-Wesley, 1987); Anne E. Weiss, *The Glass Ceiling: A Look at Women in the Workforce* (New York: Twenty First Century, 1999); Debra E. Myerson and Joyce K. Fletcher, "A Modest Manifesto for Shattering the Glass Ceiling," *Harvard Business Review* (January/February 2000).
9. David A. Thomas and Suzy Wetlaufer, "A Question of Color: A Debate on Race in the U.S. Workplace," *Harvard Business Review* (September/October 1997): 118–132.
10. *Business Week* (August 6, 2001), p. 22; "Change at the Top," *Wall Street Journal* (March 9, 1999), p. B12; *The 2000 Catalyst Census of Women Corporate Officers and Top Earners* (New York: Catalyst 2000). For a look at corporate best practices, see Catalyst, *Advancing Women in Business: The Catalyst Guide* (San Francisco: Jossey-Bass, 1998).
11. James G. March, *The Pursuit of Organizational Intelligence* (Malden, MA: Blackwell, 1999).
12. See Peter Senge, *The Fifth Discipline* (New York: Harper, 1990); D. A. Garvin, "Building a Learning Organization," *Harvard Business Review* (November/December 1991): 78–91; Chris Argyris, *On Organizational Learning*, 2nd ed. (Malden, MA: Blackwell, 1999).
13. See Jay W. Lorsch ed., *Handbook of Organizational Behavior* (Englewood Cliffs, NJ: Prentice Hall, 1987), for a general overview.
14. Geert Hofstede, "Cultural Constraints in Management Theories," *Academy of Management Executive*, 7 (1993): 81–94.
15. For more on mission statements see Patricia Jones and Larry Kahaner, *Say It and Live It: The 50 Corporate Mission Statements That Hit the Mark* (New York: Currency/Doubleday, 1995) and John Graham and Wendy Havlick, *Mission Statements: A Guide to the Corporate and Nonprofit Sectors* (New York: Garland Publishers, 1995).
16. James C. Collins and Jerry I. Porras, "Building Your Company's Vision," *Harvard Business Review* (September/October 1996): 65–77.

17. America West Airlines corporate Web site: www.america west.com.

18. Reich, op. cit. (1998).

19. See Michael E. Porter. *Competitive Strategy: Techniques for Analyzing Industries and Competitors* (New York: Free Press, 1980) and *Competitive Advantage: Creating and Sustaining Superior Performance* (New York: Free Press, 1986); Gary Hamel and C. K. Prahalad, "Strategic Intent," *Harvard Business Review* (May/June 1989): 63–76; and Richard A. D'Aveni, *Hyper Competition: Managing the Dynamics of Strategic Maneuvering* (New York: Free Press, 1994).

20. Quote from Jeffrey Pfeffer, *The Human Equation: Building Profits by Putting People First* (Boston: Harvard Business School Press, 1998).

21. See Dave Ulrich, "Intellectual Capital = Competence × Commitment," *Harvard Business Review* (Winter 1998): 15–26.

22. "What Makes a Company Great?" *Fortune* (October 26, 1998), p. 218.

23. See Brian Dumaine, "The New Non-Manager Managers," *Fortune* (February 22, 1993), pp. 80–84; and Walter Kiechel III, "How We Will Work in the Year 2000," *Fortune* (May 17, 1993), p. 38.

24. The review is from Henry Mintzberg, *The Nature of Managerial Work* (New York: Harper & Row, 1973). For related and further developments, see Morgan W. McCall, Jr., Ann M. Morrison, and Robert L. Hannan, *Studies of Managerial Work: Results and Methods, Technical Report No. 9* (Greensboro, NC: Center for Creative Leadership, 1978); John P. Kotter, *The General Managers* (New York: Free Press, 1982); Fred Luthans, Stuart Rosenkrantz, and Harry Hennessey, "What Do Successful Managers Really Do?" *Journal of Applied Behavioral Science* 21, No. 2 (1985): 255–270; Robert E. Kaplan, *The Warp and Woof of the General Manager's Job, Technical Report No. 27* (Greensboro, NC: Center for Creative Leadership, 1986); and Fred Luthans, Richard M. Hodgetts, and Stuart A. Rosenkrantz, *Real Managers* (New York: HarperCollins, 1988).

25. John R. Schermerhorn, Jr., *Management*, 7th ed. update (New York: Wiley, 2003).

26. Mintzberg, op. cit. (1973). See also Henry Mintzberg, *Mintzberg on Management* (New York: Free Press, 1989) and "Rounding Out the Manager's Job," *Sloan Management Review* (Fall 1994): 11–26.

27. Kotter, op. cit., (1982); John P. Kotter, "What Effective General Managers Really Do," *Harvard Business Review*, 60 (November/December 1982): 161. See Kaplan, op. cit., 1984.

28. Herminia Ibarra, "Managerial Networks," Teaching Note: #9–495–039, Harvard Business School Publishing, Boston, MA.

29. Robert L. Katz, "Skills of an Effective Administrator, *Harvard Business Review*, 52 (September/October 1974): 94. See also Richard E. Boyatzis, *The Competent Manager: A Model for Effective Performance* (New York: Wiley, 1982).

30. Daniel Goleman, *Emotional Intelligence* (New York: Bantam, 1995) and *Working with Emotional Intelligence* (New York: Bantam, 1998). See also his articles "What Makes a Leader," *Harvard Business Review* (November/December 1998): 93–102, and "Leadership that Makes a Difference," *Harvard Business Review* (March/April 2000): 79–90, quote from p. 80.

31. A good overview is available in Linda K. Trevino and Katherine J. Nelson, *Managing Business Ethics,* 2nd ed. (New York: Wiley, 1999).

32. See Blair Sheppard, Roy J. Lewicki, and John Minton, *Organizational Justice: The Search for Fairness in the Workplace* (New York: Lexington Books, 1992); and Jerald Greenberg, *The Quest for Justice on the Job: Essays and Experiments* (Thousand Oaks, CA: Sage Publications, 1995); Robert Folger and Russell Cropanzano, *Organizational Justice and Human Resource Management* (Thousand Oaks, CA: Sage, 1998); Mary A. Konovsky, "Understanding Procedural Justice and its Impact on Business Organizations," *Journal of Management,* 26 (2000): 489–511.

33. Interactional justice is described by Robert J. Bies, "The Predicament of Injustice: The Management of Moral Outrage," in L. L. Cummings & B. M. Staw (eds.), *Research in Organizational Behavior,* Vol. 9 (Greenwich, CT: JAI Press, 1987), pp. 289–319. The example is from Carol T. Kulik and Robert L. Holbrook, "Demographics in Service Encounters: Effects of Racial and Gender Congruence on Perceived Fairness," *Social Justice Research* (in press).

34. See Steven N. Brenner and Earl A. Mollander, "Is the Ethics of Business Changing?" *Harvard Business Review,* 55 (January/February 1977): 50–57; Saul W. Gellerman, "Why 'Good Managers Make Bad Ethical Choices," *Harvard Business Review,* 64 (July/August 1986): 85–90; Barbara Ley Toffler, *Tough Choices: Managers Talk Ethics* (New York: John Wiley, 1986); Justin G. Longnecker, Joseph A. McKinney, and Carlos W. Moore, "The Generation Gap in Business Ethics," *Business Horizons,* 32 (September/October 1989): 9–14; John B. Cullen, Vart Victor, and Carroll Stephens, "An Ethical Weather Report: Assessing the Organization's Ethical Climate," *Organizational Dynamics* (Winter 1990): 50–62; Dawn Blalock, "Study Shows Many Execs Are Quick to Write Off Ethics," *Wall Street Journal* (March 26, 1996), p. C1.

35. Based on Gellerman, op. cit., 1986.

36. A classic book is Archie B. Carroll, *Business and Society: Managing Corporate Social Performance* (Boston: Little Brown, 1981).

37. For research on whistleblowers, see Paula M. Miceli and Janet P. Near, *Blowing the Whistle* (New York: Lexington, 1992).

38. A vast amount of material on the Enron and Andersen debacles is available in the press, with the *Wall Street Journal, Business Week, Fortune,* and others, reporting and documenting the story.

39. Douglas McGregor, *The Human Side of Enterprise* (New York: McGraw-Hill, 1960).

40. David A. Nadler and Edward E. Lawler III, "Quality of Work Life: Perspectives and Directions," *Organizational Dynamics* 11 (1983): 22–36; the discussion of QWL, in Thomas G. Cummings and Edgar F. Huse, *Organizational Development and Change* (St. Paul, MN: West, 1990); and Stewart D. Friedman, Perry Christensen, and Jessica DeGroot, "Work and Life: The End of the Zero-Sum Game," *Harvard Business Review* (November–December 1998): 119–129.

41. Pfeffer, *The Human Equation: Building Profits by Putting People First,* op. cit., p. 292.

CHAPTER 2

1. This discussion comes from Course Notes for Management 5371, *Managing Organizational Behavior and Organizational Design,* prepared by Barry A. Macy, Texas Tech University, Fall 2001.

2. Personal Communication with Barry A. Macy, March 5, 1999.

3. "What Makes a Company Great?" *Fortune* (October 26, 1998), p. 218.

4. See Thomas A. Stewart, "Planning a Career Without Managers," *Fortune* (March 20, 1995), pp. 72–80.

5. Workplace Visions (September/October 1998), p. 2.

6. Lester Thurow, *Head to Head: The Coming Economic Battle among Japan, Europe, and America* (New York: Morrow, 1992) and Barry A. Macy, *Successful Strategic Change* (San Francisco: Barrett-Koehler, in preparation).

7. Nina Munk, "The New Organization Man," *Fortune* (March 16, 1998), pp. 63–64.

8. Thurow.

9. See, for example, Jay R. Galbraith, Edward E. Lawler III, and Associates, *Organizing for the Future: The New Logic for Managing Organizations* (San Francisco: Jossey-Bass, 1993); and Peter Drucker, *Managing in a Time of Great Change* (New York: Truman Talley, 1995).

10. Michael Hammer and James Champy, *Reengineering the Corporation* (New York: Harper Collins, 1993).

11. See Gary Hammel and Jeff Sampler, "The e-Corporation," *Fortune* (December 7, 1998), pp. 79–90; and David Kirkpatrick, "The E-Ware War," *Fortune* (December 7, 1998), pp. 115–117.

12. William H. Davidow and Michael S. Malone, *The Virtual Corporation: Structuring and Revitalizing the Corporation of the 21st Century* (New York: Harper Business, 1993). Also, Andrew Kupfer, "Alone Together: Will Being Wired Set Us Free?" *Fortune* (March 20, 1995), pp. 94–104.

13. See Daniel H. Pink, "Free Agent Nation," *Fast Company* (December, 1997), pp. 131ff; and Tom Peters, "The Brand Called You," *Fast Company* (August/September 1997).

14. Charles Handy, *The Age of Unreason* (Boston: Harvard Business School Press, 1990). See also his later book, *The Age of Paradox* (Boston: Harvard Business School Press, 1994).

15. Jeffrey Pfeffer, *The Human Equation: Building Profits by Putting People First* (Boston: Harvard Business School Press, 1998).

16. See Dave Ulrich, "Intellectual Capital = Competence × Commitment," *Harvard Business Review* (Winter 1998), pp.15–26.

17. Bradley L. Kirksman, Kevin B. Lowe, and Dianne P. Young, "The Challenge in High Performance Work Organizations," *Journal of Leadership Studies,* Vol. 5, No. 2 (Spring 1998): 3–15.

18. Kirksman, Lowe, and Young, p. 5.

19. See Kirksman, Lowe, and Young, ibid., for a discussion of this point, and Kirksman, Lowe, and Young, *High Performance Work Organizations* (Greensboro, NC: Center for Creative Leadership, 1999), for a more detailed treatment of high performance organizations.

20. Kirksman, Lowe, and Young (1998); Course Notes for Barry Macy, Management 5371, Texas Tech University (Fall 2001).

21. Kirksman, Lowe, and Young (1998), pp. 5, 6.

22. Ibid., p. 5.

23. C. B. Gibson and B. L. Kirksman, "Our Past, Present and Future in Teams: The Role of the Human Resources Professional in Managing Team Performance," in A. L. Kraut and A. K. Korman (eds.), *Changing Concepts and Practices for Human Resources Management: Contributions from Industrial Organizational Psychology* (San Francisco: Jossey-Bass, in press).

24. P. S. Goodman, R. Devadas, and T. L. Hughson, "Groups and Productivity: Analyzing the Effectiveness of Self Managing Work Teams," in J. P. Campbell and R. J. Campbell (eds.), *Productivity in Organizations: New Perspectives from Industrial and Organizational Psychology* (San Francisco: Jossey-Bass, 1988), pp. 295–237.

25. Robert E. Markland, Shawnee K. Vickery, and Robert A. Davis, *Operations Management,* 2nd ed. (Cincinnati, OH: Southwestern Publishing, 1998), p. 646.

26. Lee J. Kraijewski and Larry R. Ritzman, *Operations Management,* 5th ed. (Reading, MA: Addison-Wesley, 1989), pp. 158 159.

27. Ibid.

28. See Eryn Brown, "VF Corp. Changes Its Underware," *Fortune* (December 7, 1998), pp. 115–118; Edward Cone, "Inching Along," *Baseline* (October 2001), pp. 57–59.

29. See D. A. Garvin, "Building a Learning Organization," *Harvard Business Review* (July–August 1993): 78–91; and Danny Miller, "A Preliminary Typology of Organizational Learning: Synthesizing the Literature," *Journal of Management,* Vol. 22, No. 3 (1996), pp. 485–505.

30. Kirksman, Lowe, and Young (1998), pp. 6–7.

31. Macy, *Successful Strategic Change.*

32. Macy, Course Notes (Fall 2001).

33. See Macy, *Successful Strategic Change.*

34. Kirksman, Lowe, and Young (1998), pp. 7–12.

35. Ibid.

36. Ibid., p. 9.

37. Macy, Management 5371, Course Notes (Fall 2001).

38. Ibid.

39. Kirksman, Lowe, and Young (1998), pp. 10–12.

40. O'Toole, p. 15.

41. See B. A. Macy and J. Izumi, "Organizational Change, Design, and Work Innovation: A Meta-Analysis of 131 North American Field Studies—1961–1991," in W. A. Pasmore and R. W. Woodman (eds.), *Research in Organizational Change and Development,* Vol. 7 (Greenwich, CT: JAI Press, 1993), pp. 235–311.

42. Kirkman, Lowe, and Young (1998), pp. 11–12.

43. O'Toole.

44. Macy, *Successful Strategic Change.*

45. The discussion in this section is based on Howard D. Putnam, *The Winds of Turbulence* (New York: Harper Business, 1991); Christy E. Dockrey, *Southwest Airlines: A Texas Airline in an Era of Deregulation* (unpublished Master's thesis, Texas Tech

University, 1996); Kevin Frieberg and Jackie Frieberg, *Nuts* (Austin, TX: Bard Press, 1996); Joan M. Feldman, "IT, Culture and Southwest," *Air Transport World,* Vol. 37, No. 5 (May 2000), pp. 45–49; Perry Flint, "Back on Schedule," *Air Transport World,* Vol. 37, No. 11 (November 2000), pp. 47–51.

46. Mission Statement, *www.southwest.com/travel_center/ customer_service_commitment.html* (December 12, 2001), p. 1.

Source Notes

Pyramid from Thomas A. Stewart, "Planning a Career without Managers," *Fortune* (March 20, 1995), pp. 72–80.

Generation X values/preferences adapted from Barry A. Macy, *Successful Strategic Change* (San Francisco: Barett-Koehler, in preparation).

High performance organization components adapted from Bradley L. Kirksman, Kevin B. Lowe, and Dianne P. Young, "The Challenge of Leadership in High Performance Work Organizations," *Journal of Leadership Studies,* Vol. 5, No. 2 (1998), p. 8.

Effective Manager information developed from E. E. Lawler III, "Total Quality Management and Employee Involvement: Are They Compatible?" *Academy of Management Executive,* Vol. 8, No. 1 (1994), pp. 68–76.

CHAPTER 3

1. Kenichi Ohmae, *The Invisible Continent* (New York: Harper Business, 2000); *The Borderless World* (New York: Harper Business, 1989). Peter F. Drucker, "The Global Economy and the Nation-State," *Foreign Affairs* (September/October 1997).

2. See Michael Porter's three-volume series *The Competitive Advantage of Nations, Competitive Advantage,* and *Competitive Strategy* (New York: The Free Press, 1998).

3. Kenichi Ohmae, *The Evolving Global Economy* (Cambridge, MA: Harvard Business School Press, 1995); Kenichi Ohmae, "Putting Global Logic First," *Harvard Business Review* (January/February 1995), pp. 119–125; and, Jeffrey E. Garten, "Can the World Survive the Triumph of Capitalism?" *Harvard Business Review* (January/February, 1997), pp. 67–79.

4. William B. Johnson, "Global Workforce 2000: The New World Labor Market," *Harvard Business Review* (March/April 1991), pp. 115–127.

5. See Porter, op. cit.; Kenichi Ohmae *The End of the Nation State: The Rise of Regional Economies* (New York: The Free Press, 1995); and William Greider, *One World, Ready or Not: The Manic Logic of Global Capitalism* (New York: The Free Press, 1998).

6. For a discussion of FDI in the United States, see Paul R. Krugman, *Foreign Direct Investment in the United States,* 3rd ed. (Washington, DC, 1995). Statistics on FDI in the United States are available through the Bureau of Economic Analysis, International Accounts Data, [Online] *http://www.bea. doc.gov/bea/di1.htm.*

7. Michael E. Porter, "Clusters and the New Economics of Competition," *Harvard Business Review* (November/ December 1998).

8. "Europe Rising," *Business Week* (February 8, 1999), pp. 68–70.

9. Mzamo P. Mangaliso, "Building Competitive Advantage from Unbunfu: Management Lessons from South Africa," *Academy of Management Executive,* Vol. 15 (2001), pp. 23–33.

10. James A. Austin and John G. McLean, "Pathways to Business Success in Sub-Saharan Africa," *Journal of African Finance and Economic Development,* Vol. 2 (1996), pp. 57–76; Information from "International Business: Consider Africa," *Harvard Business Review,* Vol. 76 (January/February 1998), pp. 16–18.

11. Robert T. Moran and John R. Risenberger, *Making Globalization Work: Solutions for Implementation* (New York: McGraw-Hill, 1993); "Don't Be an Ugly-American Manager," *Fortune* (October 16, 1995), p. 225; and, "A Way to Measure Global Success," *Fortune* (March 15, 1999), pp. 196–197.

12. "Working Overseas—Rule No. 1: Don't Miss the Locals," *Business Week* (May 15, 1995), p. 8.

13. "Don't Be an Ugly-American Manager," op. cit., p. 225; Vanessa Houlder, "Foreign Culture Shocks," *Financial Times* (March 22, 1996), p.12.

14. Geert Hofstede, *Culture's Consequences: International Differences in Work-Related Values* (Beverly Hills, CA: Sage Publications, 1980); and, Fons Trompenaars, *Riding the Waves of Culture: Understanding Cultural Diversity in Business* (London: Nicholas Brealey Publishing, 1993). For an excellent discussion of culture, see also Chapter 3, "Culture: The Neglected Concept," in Peter B. Smith and Michael Harris Bond, *Social Psychology Across Cultures,* 2nd ed. (Boston: Allyn & Bacon, 1998).

15. Geert Hofstede, *Culture and Organizations: Software of the Mind* (London: McGraw-Hill, 1991).

16. A good overview of the world's cultures is provided in Richard D. Lewis, *When Cultures Collide: Managing Successfully Across Cultures* (London: Nicholas Brealey Publishing, 1996).

17. Benjamin L. Whorf, *Language, Thought and Reality* (Cambridge, MA: MIT Press, 1956).

18. Edward T. Hall, *Beyond Culture* (New York: Doubleday, 1976).

19. A classic work and the source of our examples is Edward T. Hall, *The Silent Language* (New York: Anchor Books, 1959).

20. Allen C. Bluedorn, Carol Felker Kaufman, and Paul M. Lane, "How Many Things Do You Like to Do at Once?" *Academy of Management Executive,* Vol. 6 (November 1992), pp. 17–26.

21. Edward T. Hall's book *The Hidden Dimension* (New York: Anchor Books, 1969; Magnolia, MI: Peter Smith, 1990) is a classic reference and the source of our examples. See also Edward T. Hall, *Hidden Differences* (New York: Doubleday, 1990).

22. The classic work is Max Weber, *The Protestant Ethic and the Spirit of Capitalism* (New York: Scribner, 1930). For a description of religious influences in Asian cultures, see S. Gordon Redding, *The Spirit of Chinese Capitalism* (New York: Walter de Gruyter, 1990).

23. Hofstede, op. cit. (1980). Geert Hofstede and Michael H. Bond, "The Confucius Connection: From Culture Roots to Economic Growth," *Organizational Dynamics,* Vol. 16 (1988), pp. 4–21.

24. Hofstede, op. cit. (1980).

25. Chinese Culture Connection, "Chinese Values and the Search for Culture-Free Dimensions of Culture," *Journal of Cross-Cultural Psychology,* Vol. 18 (1987), pp. 143–164.

26. Hofstede and Bond, op. cit., 1988: and Geert Hofstede, "Cultural Constraints in Management Theories," *Academy of Management Executive,* Vol. 7 (February 1993), pp. 81–94. For a further discussion of Asian and Confucian values, see also Jim Rohwer, *Asia Rising: Why America Will Prosper as Asia's Economies Boom* (New York: Simon & Schuster, 1995), and Chapter 3 on "China" in Lewis, op. cit. (1996).

27. For an example, see John R. Schermerhorn, Jr., and Michael H. Bond, "Cross-Cultural Leadership Dynamics in Collectivism + High Power Distance Settings," *Leadership and Organization Development Journal,* Vol. 18 (1997), pp. 187–193.

28. Nancy J. Adler, *International Dimensions of Organizational Behavior,* 2nd ed. (Boston: PWS-Kent, 1991).

29. Trompenaars, op. cit. (1993).

30. Alvin Toffler, *The Third Wave* (New York: William Morrow, 1980).

31. See Hofstede, op. cit. (1980, 1993); Adler, op. cit. (1991).

32. Adler, op. cit. (1991).

33. See J. Stewart Black and Hal B. Gregersen, "The Right Way to Manage Expats," *Harvard Business Review* (March/April 1999).

34. See Rosalie Tung, "Expatriate Assignments: Enhancing Success and Minimizing Failure," *Academy of Management Executive* (May 1987), pp. 117–126; and Adler, op. cit. (1991).

35. Nancy J. Adler, "Reentry: Managing Cross-Cultural Transitions," *Group and Organization Studies,* Vol. 6, No. 3 (1981), pp. 341–356; and Adler, op. cit. (1991).

36. For a discussion of international business ethics, see Thomas Donaldson and Thomas W. Dunfee, *Ties That Bind* (Boston: Harvard Business School Press, 1999); Thomas Donaldson, "Values in Tension: Ethics Away from Home," *Harvard Business Review* (September/October 1996), pp. 48–62; and, Debora L. Spar, "The Spotlight and the Bottom Line," *Foreign Affairs* (March/April 1998).

37. "Cracking Down on Overseas Bribes," *Business Week* (March 1, 1999), p. 41.

38. "Business Ethics: Sweatshops," *The Economist* (February 27, 1999), pp. 62–63.

39. Information from Council for Economic Priorities Accreditation Agency Web site: www.cepaa.org.

40. Donaldson, op. cit. (1996).

41. Ibid.; Thomas Donaldson and Thomas W. Dunfee, "Towards a Unified Conception of Business Ethics: Integrative Social Contracts Theory," *Academy of Management Review,* Vol. 19 (1994), pp. 252–285; and Donaldson and Dunfee, op. cit. (1999). For a related discussion see John R. Schermerhorn, Jr., "Alternative Terms of Business Engagement in Ethically Challenging Environment," *Business Ethics Quarterly* (1999), forthcoming.

42. Geert Hofstede, "Motivation, Leadership and Organization: Do American Theories Apply Abroad?" *Organizational Dynamics,* Vol. 9 (1980), pp. 43+; Hofstede, op cit. (1993).

43. Two classic works are William Ouchi, *Theory Z: How American Businesses Can Meet the Japanese Challenge* (Reading, MA: Addison-Wesley, 1981); Richard Tanner and Anthony Athos, *The Art of Japanese Management* (New York: Simon & Schuster, 1981).

44. See J. Bernard Keys, Luther Tray Denton, and Thomas R. Miller, "The Japanese Management Theory Jungle—Revisited," *Journal of Management,* Vol. 20 (1994), pp. 373–402; and "Japanese and Korean Management Systems," Ch. 13 in Min Chen, *Asian Management Systems* (New York: Routledge, 1995).

CHAPTER 4

1. J. Laabs, "Interest in Diversity Training Continues to Grow," *Personnel Journal* (October 1993), p. 18.

2. L. R. Gomez-Mejia, D. B. Balkin, and R. L. Cardy, *Managing Human Resources* (Englewood Cliffs, NJ: Prentice-Hall, 1995), p. 154.

3. John P. Fernandez, *Managing a Diverse Workforce* (Lexington, MA: D. C. Heath, 1991); D. Jamieson and Julia O'Mara, *Managing Workplace 2000* (San Francisco: Jossey-Bass, 1991).

4. T. G. Exner, "In and Out of Work," *American Demographics* (June 1992), p. 63, and A. N. Fullerton, "Another Look at the Labor Force," *Monthly Labor Review* (November 1993), p. 34; M. K. Foster and B. J. Orser, "A Marketing Perspective on Women in Management," *Canadian Journal of Administrative Sciences,* Vol. 11, No. 4 (1994), pp. 339–345: L. Gardenswartz and A. Rowe, "Diversity Q & A," *Mosaics* (March/April, 1998), p. 3.

5. Linda A. Krefting and Frank J. Kryzstofiak, "Looking Like America: Potential Conflicts Between Workplace Diversity Initiatives and Equal Opportunity Compliance in the U.S.," Working paper (Lubbock, TX: Texas Tech University, 1998), p. 10.

6. Krefting and Kryzstofiak, p. 10.

7. The following discussion is based on L. Gardenswartz and A. Rowe, *Managing Diversity: A Complete Desk Reference and Planning Guide* (Homewood, IL: Business One Irwin, 1993), p. 405.

8. Gardenswartz and Rowe, *Managing Diversity,* p. 405; Michelle N. Martinez, "Equality Effort Sharpens Bank's Edge," *HR Magazine* (January 1995), pp. 38–43.

9. See E. Macoby and C. N. Jacklin. *The Psychology of Sex Differences* (Stanford, CA: Stanford University press, 1974); G. N. Powell, *Women and Men in Management* (Beverly Hills, CA: Sage Publications, 1988): T. W. Mangione. "Turnover—Some Psychological and Demographic Correlates," in R. P. Quinn and T. W. Mangione (eds.), *The 1969–70 Survey of Working Conditions* (Ann Arbor: University of Michigan Survey Research Center, 1973); R. Marsh and H. Mannan, "Organizational Commitment and Turnover: A Predictive Study," *Administrative Science Quarterly* (March 1977), pp. 57–75; R. J. Flanagan, G. Strauss, and L. Ulman, "Worker Discontent and Work Discontent and Work Place Behavior," *Industrial Relations* (May 1974), pp. 101–23; K. R. Garrison and P. M. Muchinsky, "Attitudinal and Biographical Predictions of Incidental Absenteeism," *Journal of Vocational Behavior* (April

1977), pp. 221–230; G. Johns, "Attitudinal and Nonattitudinal Predictions of Two Forms of Absence from Work," *Organizational Behavior and Human Performance* (December 1978), pp. 431–44; R. T. Keller, "Predicting Absenteeism from Prior Absenteeism, Attitudinal Factors, and Nonattitudinal Factors," *Journal of Applied Psychology* (August 1983), pp. 536–540.

10. Gomez-Mejia, Balkin, and Cardy, p. 171.

11. "The Growing Influence of Women," *Workplace Visions* (Sept., Oct. 1998), p. 2.

12. American Association of Retired Persons, *The Aging Work Force* (Washington, DC: AARP, 1995), p. 3.

13. Nina Monk, "Finished at Forty," *Fortune* (February 1, 1999), pp. 50–58.

14. *Mosaics*, Vol. 3, No. 2 (March/April 1997), p. 3.

15. Paul Mayrand, "Older Workers: A Problem or the Solution?" *AARP Textbook Authors' Conference Presentation* (October 1992), p. 29; G. M. McEvoy and W. F. Cascio, "Cumulative Evidence of the Relationship Between Employee Age and Job Performance," *Journal of Applied Psychology* (February 1989), pp. 11–17.

16. See Fernandez, p. 236; *Mosaics*, Vol. 4, No. 2 (March/April, 1998, p. 4.

17. Fernandez; *Mosaics* (March/April, 1998).

18. See Taylor H. Co and Stacy Blake, "Managing Cultural Diversity: Implications for Organizational Competitiveness," *Academy of Management Executive*, Vol. 5, No. 3 (1991), p. 45.

19. Literature covering this topic is reviewed in Stephen P. Robbins, *Organizational Behavior*, 8th ed. (Englewood Cliffs, NJ: Prentice-Hall, 1998), Ch. 2.

20. Robbins, Ch. 2.

21. Krefting and Krzystofiak, p. 14.

22. Larry L. Cummings and Donald P. Schwab, *Performance in Organizations: Determinants and Appraisal* (Glenview, IL: Scott, Foresman, 1973), p. 8.

23. See J. Hogan, "Structure of Physical Performance in Occupational Tasks," *Journal of Applied Psychology*, Vol. 76 (1991), pp. 495–507.

24. R. Jacob, "The Resurrection of Michael Dell," *Fortune* (August 1995), pp. 117–128.

25. See N. Brody, *Personality: In Search of Individuality* (San Diego, CA: Academic Press, 1988), pp. 68–101; C. Holden. "The Genetics of Personality," *Science* (August 7, 1987), pp. 598–601.

26. See Geert Hofstede, *Culture's Consequences: International Differences in Work-Related Values,* abridged ed. (Beverly Hills: Sage Publications, 1984).

27. Chris Argyris, *Personality and Organization* (New York: Harper & Row, 1957); Daniel J. Levinson, *The Seasons of a Man's Life* (New York: Alfred A. Knopf, 1978); Gail Sheehy, *New Passages* (New York: Ballantine Books, 1995).

28. M. R. Barrick and M. K. Mount, "The Big Five Personality Dimensions and Job Performance: A Meta Analysis," *Personnel Psychology*, Vol. 44 (1991), pp. 1–26, and "Autonomy as a Moderator of the Relationships Between the Big Five Personality Dimensions and Job Performance," *Journal of Applied Psychology* (February 1993), pp. 111–118.

29. See Jim C. Nunnally, *Psychometric Theory,* 2nd ed. (New York: McGraw Hill, 1978), Ch. 14.

30. See David A. Whetten and Kim S. Cameron. *Developing Management Skills,* 3rd ed. (New York: Harper Collins, 1995), p. 72.

31. Raymond G. Hunt, Frank J. Krzystofiak, James R. Meindl, and Abdalla M. Yousry, "Cognitive Style and Decision Making," *Organizational Behavior and Human Decision Processes,* Vol. 44, No. 3 (1989), pp. 436–453. For additional work on problem-solving styles, see Ferdinand A. Gul. "The Joint and Moderating Role of Personality and Cognitive Style on Decision Making," *Accounting Review* (April 1984), pp. 264–277; Brian H. Kleiner, "The Interrelationship of Jungian Modes of Mental Functioning with Organizational Factors: Implications for Management Development," *Human Relations* (November 1983), pp. 997–1012; James L. McKenney and Peter G. W. Keen, "How Managers' Minds Work," *Harvard Business Review* (May/June 1974), pp. 79–90.

32. Some examples of firms using the Myers-Briggs Indicators are J. M. Kunimerow and L. W. McAllister, "Team Building with the Myers-Briggs Type Indicator: Case Studies," *Journal of Psychological Type,* Vol. 15 (1988), pp. 26–32; G. H. Rice, Jr. and D. P. Lindecamp, "Personality Types and Business Success of Small Retailers," *Journal of Occupational Psychology,* Vol. 62 (1989), pp. 177–182; and B. Roach, *Strategy Styles and Management Types: A Resource Book for Organizational Management Consultants* (Stanford, CA: Balestrand Press, 1989).

33. J. B. Rotter, "Generalized Expectancies for Internal versus External Control of Reinforcement," *Psychological Monographs,* Vol. 80 (1966), pp. 1–28.

34. Don Hellriegel, John W. Slocum, Jr., and Richard W. Woodman, *Organizational Behavior,* 5th ed. (St. Paul, MN: West, 1989), p. 46.

35. See John A. Wagner III and John R. Hollenbeck, *Management of Organizational Behavior* (Englewood Cliffs, NJ: Prentice-Hall, 1992), Ch. 4.

36. Niccolo Machiavelli, *The Prince,* trans. George Bull (Middlesex, UK: Penguin, 1961).

37. Richard Christie and Florence L. Geis, *Studies in Machiavellianism* (New York: Academic Press, 1970).

38. See M. Snyder, *Public Appearances/Private Realities: The Psychology of Self-Monitoring* (New York: W. H. Freeman, 1987).

39. Snyder.

40. Adapted from R. W. Bonner, "A Short Scale: A Potential Measure of Pattern A Behavior," *Journal of Chronic Diseases,* Vol. 22 (1969). Used by permission.

41. See Meyer Friedman and Ray Roseman, *Type A Behavior and Your Heart* (New York: Alfred A. Knopf, 1974). For another view, see Walter Kiechel III, "Attack of the Obsessive Managers," *Fortune* (February 16, 1987), pp. 127–128.

42. Viktor Gecas, "The Self-Concept," in Ralph H. Turner and James F. Short, Jr. (eds.), Vol. 8, *Annual Review of Sociology* (Palo Alto, CA: Annual Review, 1982), p. 3. Also see Arthur P. Brief and Ramon J. Aldag, "The Self in Work Organizations: A Conceptual Review," *Academy of Management Review* (January

1981), pp. 75–88; and Jerry J. Sullivan, "Self Theories and Employee Motivation," *Journal of Management* (June 1989), pp. 345–363.

43. Compare Philip Cushman, "Why the Self Is Empty," *American Psychologist* (May 1990), pp. 599–611.

44. Based in part on a definition in Gecas, p. 3.

45. Suggested by J. Brockner, *Self-Esteem at Work* (Lexington, MA: Lexington Books, 1988) p. 144; and Wagner and Hollenbeck, pp. 100–101.

46. See P. E. Jacob, J. J. Flink, and H. L. Schuchman, "Values and Their Function in Decisionmaking," *American Behavioral Scientist,* Vol. 5, Suppl. 9 (1962), pp. 6–38.

47. See M. Rokeach and S. J. Ball Rokeach, "Stability and Change in American Value Priorities, 1968–1981," *American Psychologist* (May 1989), pp. 775–784.

48. Milton Rokeach, *The Nature of Human Values* (New York: Free Press, 1973).

49. See W. C. Frederick and J. Weber, "The Values of Corporate Managers and Their Critics: An Empirical Description and Normative Implications," in W. C. Frederick and L. E. Preston (eds.), *Business Ethics Research Issues and Empirical Studies* (Greenwich, CT: JAI Press, 1990), pp. 123–144.

50. Gordon Allport, Philip E. Vernon, and Gardner Lindzey, *Study of Values* (Boston: Houghton Mifflin, 1931).

51. Adapted from R. Tagiuri, "Purchasing Executive: General Manager or Specialist?" *Journal of Purchasing* (August 1967), pp. 16–21.

52. Bruce M. Maglino, Elizabeth C. Ravlin, and Cheryl L. Adkins, "Value Congruence and Satisfaction with a Leader: An Examination of the Role of Interaction," unpublished manuscript (Columbia, SC: University of South Carolina, 1990), pp. 8–9.

53. Maglino, Ravlin, and Adkins.

54. Daniel Yankelovich, *New Rules! Searching for Self-Fulfillment in a World Turned Upside Down* (New York: Random House, 1981); Daniel Yankelovich, Hans Zetterberg, Burkhard Strumpel, and Michael Shanks, *Work and Human Values: An International Report on Jobs in the 1980s and 1990s* (Aspen, CO: Aspen Institute for Humanistic Studies, 1983); William Fox, *American Values in Decline: What We Can Do* (Gainesville, FL: 1st Books Library, 2001).

55. See Jamieson and O'Mara, pp. 28–29.

56. Compare Martin Fishbein and Icek Ajzen, *Belief, Attitude, Intention and Behavior: An Introduction to Theory and Research* (Reading, MA: Addison-Wesley, 1973).

57. See A. W. Wicker, "Attitude versus Action: The Relationship of Verbal and Overt Behavioral Responses to Attitude Objects," *Journal of Social Issues* (Autumn 1969), pp. 41–78.

58. Leon Festinger, *A Theory of Cognitive Dissonance* (Palo Alto, CA: Stanford University Press, 1957).

59. H. W. Lane and J. J. DiStefano (eds.), *International Management Behavior* (Scarborough, Ontario: Nelson Canada, 1988), pp. 4–5; Z. Abdoolcarim, "How Women Are Winning at Work," *Asian Business* (November 1993), pp. 24–29.

60. Michelle Neely Martinez, "Health Care Firm Seeks to Measure Diversity," *HR News* (October 1997), p. 6.

61. Martinez, p. 6.

62. See www.shrm.org/surveys for surveys available to SHRM members.

63. Jonathan Stutz and Randy Massengale, "Measuring Diversity Initiatives," *HR Magazine* (December 1997), pp. 84, 90.

Source Notes

Effective Manager information from Gary N. Powell, "One More Time: Do Male and Female Managers Differ?" *Academy of Management Executive,* Vol. 4, No. 3 (1995), p. 74.

Continuum excerpted from Chris Argyris, *Personality and Organization* (New York: Harper & Row, 1957).

Problem-Solving Summary based on R. P. McIntyre and M. M. Capen, "A Cognitive Style Perspective on Ethical Questions," *Journal of Business Ethics,* Vol. 12 (1993), p. 631; D. Hellriegel, J. Slocum, and Richard Woodman, *Organizational Behavior,* 7th ed. (Minneapolis: West Publishing, 1995), Ch. 4.

Effective Manager information from Michelle N. Martinez, "Health Care Firm Seeks to Measure Diversity," *HR News* (October 1997), p. 6.

CHAPTER 5

1. See Francis X. Clines, "Proud to be a Hillbilly," *Dallas Morning News* (April 8, 2001), p. 9A.

2. "Clark's Catch Engraved in NFL Lore," *Lubbock Avalanche-Journal* (January 11, 1992), p. D5.

3. H. R. Schiffmann, *Sensation and Perception: An Integrated Approach,* 3rd ed. (New York: Wiley, 1990).

4. Example from John A. Wagner III and John R. Hollenbeck, *Organizational Behavior* 3rd ed. (Upper Saddle River, NJ: Prentice-Hall, 1998), p. 59.

5. See M. W. Levine and J. M. Shefner, *Fundamentals of Sensation and Perception,* Georgia T. Chao and Steve W. J. Kozlowski, "Employee Perceptions on the Implementation of Robotic Manufacturing Technology," *Journal of Applied Psychology,* Vol. 71 (1986), pp. 70–76; Steven F. Cronshaw and Robert G. Lord, "Effects of Categorization, Attribution, and Encoding Processes in Leadership Perceptions," *Journal of Applied Psychology,* Vol. 72 (1987), pp. 97–106.

6. See Robert Lord, "An Information Processing Approach to Social Perceptions, Leadership, and Behavioral Measurement in Organizations," in B. M. Staw and L. L. Cummings (eds.), *Research in Organizational Behavior,* Vol. 7 (Greenwich, CT: JAI Press, 1985), pp. 87–128; T. K. Srull and R. S. Wyer, *Advances in Social Cognition* (Hillsdale, NJ: Erlbaum, 1988); U. Neisser, *Cognitive and Reality* (San Francisco: W. H. Freeman, 1976), p. 112.

7. See J. G. Hunt, *Leadership: A New Synthesis* (Newbury Park, CA: Sage Publications, 1991), Ch. 7; R. G. Lord and R. J. Foti, "Schema Theories, Information Processing, and Organizational Behavior," in H. P. Simms, Jr., and D. A. Gioia (eds.), *The Thinking Organization* (San Francisco: Jossey-Bass, 1986), pp. 20–48; S. T. Fiske and S. E. Taylor, *Social Cognition* (Reading, MA: Addison-Wesley, 1984).

8. See J. S. Phillips, "The Accuracy of Leadership Ratings: A Categorization Perspective," *Organizational Behavior and*

Human Performance, Vol. 33 (1984), pp. 125–138; J. G. Hunt, B. R. Baliga, an M. F. Peterson, "Strategic Apex Leader Scripts and an Organizational Life Cycle Approach to Leadership and Excellence," *Journal of Management Development,* Vol. 7 (1988), pp. 61–83.

9. D. Bilimoria and S. K. Piderit, "Board Committee Membership Effects of Sex-Biased Bias," *Academy of Management Journal,* Vol. 37 (1994), pp. 1453–1477.

10. Dewitt C. Dearborn and Herbert A. Simon, "Selective Perception: A Note on the Departmental Identification of Executives," *Sociometry,* Vol. 21 (1958), pp. 140–144.

11. J. P. Walsh, "Selectivity and Selective Perception: An Investigation of Managers' Belief Structures and Information Processing," *Academy of Management Journal,* Vol. 24 (1988), pp. 453–470.

12. J. Sterling Livingston, "Pygmalion in Management," *Harvard Business Review* (July/August 1969).

13. D. Eden and A. B. Shani, "Pygmalian Goes to Boot Camp," *Journal of Applied Psychology,* Vol. 67 (1982), pp. 194–199.

14. See B. R. Schlenker, *Impression Management: The Self-Concept, Social Identity, and Interpersonal Relations* (Monterey, CA: Brooks/Cole, 1980); W. L. Gardner and M. J. Martinko, "Impression Management in Organizations," *Journal of Management* (June 1988), p. 332; R. B. Cioldini, "Indirect Tactics of Image Management: Beyond Banking," in R. A. Giacolini and P. Rosenfeld (eds.), *Impression Management in the Organization* (Hillsdale, NJ: Erlbaum, 1989), pp. 45–71.

15. See H. H. Kelley, "Attribution in Social Interaction," in E. Jones, et al. (eds.), *Attribution: Perceiving the Causes of Behavior* (Morristown, NJ: General Learning Press, 1972).

16. See "Obese Women Finding Business Just Doesn't Pay," *Lubbock Avalanche Journal* (January 28, 2001), p. 2D.

17. See Terence R. Mitchell, S. G. Green, and R. E. Wood, "An Attribution Model of Leadership and the Poor Performing Subordinate," in Barry Staw and Larry L. Cummings (eds.), *Research in Organizational Behavior* (New York: JAI Press, 1981), pp. 197–234; John H. Harvey and Gifford Weary, "Current Issues in Attribution Theory and Research," *Annual Review of Psychology,* Vol. 35 (1984), pp. 427–459.

18. R. M. Steers, S. J. Bischoff, and L. H. Higgins, "Cross Cultural Management Research," *Journal of Management Inquiry* (Dec. 1992), pp. 325–326; J. G. Miller, "Culture and the Development of Everyday Causal Explanation," *Journal of Personality and Social Psychology,* Vol. 46 (1984), p. 961–978.

19. A. Maass and C. Volpato, "Gender Differences in Self-Serving Attributions About Sexual Experiences," *Journal of Applied Psychology,* Vol. 19 (1989), pp. 517–542.

20. See J. M. Crant and T. S. Bateman, "Assignment of Credit and Blame for Performance Outcomes," *Academy of Management Journal* (February 1993), pp. 7–27; E. C. Pence, W. E. Pendelton, G. H. Dobbins, and J. A. Sgro, "Effects of Causal Explanations and Sex Variables on Recommendations for Corrective Actions Following Employee Failure," *Organizational Behavior and Human Performance* (April 1982), pp. 227–240.

21. See F. Fosterling, "Attributional Retraining: A Review," *Psychological Bulletin* (Nov. 1985), pp. 496–512.

Source Notes

Data reported in Edward E. Lawler III, Allan M. Mohrman, Jr., and Susan M. Resnick, "Performance Appraisal Revisited," *Organizational Dynamics,* Vol. 13 (Summer 1984), pp. 20–35.

Information from John R. Schermerhorn, Jr., "Team Development for High Performance Management," *Training and Development Journal,* Vol. 40 (November 1986), pp. 38–41.

Information from B. R. Schlinker, *Impression Management: The Self Concept, Social Identity, and Interpersonal Relations* (Monterey, CA: Brooks Cole, 1980).

CHAPTER 6

1. See John P. Campbell, Marvin D. Dunnette, Edward E. Lawler III, and Karl E. Weick, Jr., *Managerial Behavior Performance and Effectiveness* (New York: McGraw-Hill, 1970), Ch. 15.

2. For a review article that identifies a still-relevant need for more integration among motivation theories, see Terrence R. Mitchell, "Motivation—New Directions for Theory, Research and Practice," *Academy of Management Review* 7 (January 1982): 80–88.

3. Geert Hofstede, "Cultural Constraints in Management Theories," *Academy of Management Executive* 7 (February 1993): 81–94.

4. Geert Hofstede, *Culture's Consequences: International Differences in Work-Related Values,* abridged ed. (Beverly Hills, CA: Sage Publications, 1984).

5. For good overviews of reinforcement-based views, see W. E. Scott Jr., and P. M. Podsakoff, *Behavioral Principles in the Practice of Management* (New York: Wiley, 1985); Fred Luthans and Robert Kreitner, *Organizational Behavior Modification and Beyond* (Glenview, IL: Scott, Foresman, 1985).

6. For some of B. F. Skinner's work; see his *Walden Two* (New York: Macmillan, 1948), *Science and Human Behavior* (New York: Macmillan, 1953), and *Contingencies of Reinforcement* (New York: Appleton-Century-Crofts, 1969).

7. E. L. Thorndike, *Animal Intelligence* (New York: Macmillan, 1911), p. 244.

8. Adapted from Luthans and Kreitner, op. cit. (1985).

9. This discussion is based on ibid.

10. Both laws are stated in Keith L. Miller, *Principles of Everyday Behavior Analysis* (Monterey, CA: Brooks/Cole, 1975), p. 122.

11. This example is based on a study by Barbara Price and Richard Osborn, "Shaping the Training of Skilled Workers," working paper (Detroit: Department of Management, Wayne State University, 1999).

12. See John Putzier and Frank T. Novak, "Attendance Management and Control," *Personnel Administrator* (August 1989): 59–60.

13. Robert Kreitner and Angelo Kiniki, *Organization Behavior,* 2nd ed. (Homewood, IL: Irwin, 1992).

14. These have been used for years; see K. M. Evans, "On-the Job Lotteries: A Low-Cost Incentive That Sparks Higher Productivity," *Compensation and Benefits Review* 20, No. 4

(1988): 63–74; A. Halcrow, "Incentive! How Three Companies Cut Costs," *Personal Journal* (February 1986), p. 12.

15. A. R. Korukonda and James G. Hunt, "Pat on the Back Versus Kick in the Pants: An Application of Cognitive Inference to the Study of Leader Reward and Punishment Behavior," *Group and Organization Studies* 14 (1989): 299–234.

16. See "Janitorial Firm Success Story Started with Cleaning Couple," *Lubbock Avalanche-Journal* (August 25, 1991), p. E7.

17. Edwin A. Locke, "The Myths of Behavior Mod in Organizations," *Academy of Management Review* 2 (October 1977): 543–553. For a counterpoint, see Jerry L. Gray, "The Myths of the Myths about Behavior Mod in Organizations: A Reply to Locke's Criticisms of Behavior Modification," *Academy of Management Review* 4 (January 1979): 121–129.

18. Robert Kreitner, "Controversy in OBM: History, Misconceptions, and Ethics," in Lee Frederiksen, ed., *Handbook of Organizational Behavior Management* (New York: Wiley, 1982), pp. 71–91.

19. W. E. Scott, Jr., and P. M. Podsakoff, *Behavioral Principles in the Practice of Management* (New York: Wiley, 1985); also see W. Clay Hamner, "Reinforcement Theory and Contingency Management in Organizational Settings," in Richard M. Steers and Lyman W. Porters (eds.), *Motivation and Work Behavior,* 4th ed. (New York: McGraw-Hill, 1987), pp. 139–165; Luthans and Kreitner, op. cit. (1985); Charles C. Manz and Henry P. Sims, Jr., *Superleadership* (New York: Berkeley, 1990).

20. Abraham Maslow, *Eupsychian Management* (Homewood, IL: Irwin, 1965), and *Motivation and Personality,* 2nd ed. (New York: Harper & Row, 1970).

21. Lyman W. Porter, "Job Attitudes in Management: II. Perceived Importance of Needs as a Function of Job Level," *Journal of Applied Psychology* 47 (April 1963): 141–148.

22. Douglas T. Hall and Khalil E. Nougaim, "An Examination of Maslow's Need Hierarchy in an Organizational Setting," *Organizational Behavior and Human Performance* 3 (1968): 12–35; Porter, op. cit. (1963); John M. Ivancevich, "Perceived Need Satisfactions of Domestic Versus Overseas Managers," 54 (August 1969): 274–278.

23. Mahmoud A. Wahba and Lawrence G. Bridwell, "Maslow Reconsidered: A Review of Research on the Need Hierarchy Theory," *Academy of Management Proceedings* (1974): 514–520; Edward E. Lawler III and J. Lloyd Shuttle, "A Causal Correlation Test of the Need Hierarchy Concept," *Organizational Behavior and Human Performance* 7 (1973): 265–287.

24. Nancy J. Adler, *International Dimensions of Organizational Behavior,* 2nd ed. (Boston: PWS-Kent, 1991), p. 153.; Richard M. Hodgetts and Fred Luthans, *International Management* (New York: McGraw-Hill, 1991), Ch. 11.

25. Clayton P. Alderfer, "An Empirical Test of a New Theory of Human Needs," *Organizational Behavior and Human Performance* 4 (1969): 142–175; Clayton P. Alderfer, *Existence, Relatedness, and Growth* (New York: Free Press, 1972); Benjamin Schneider and Clayton P. Alderfer. "Three Studies of Need Satisfaction in Organization," *Administrative Science Quarterly* 18 (1973): 489–505.

26. Lane Tracy, "A Dynamic Living Systems Model of Work Motivation," *Systems Research* 1 (1984): 191–203; John Rauschenberger, Neal Schmidt, and John E. Hunter, "A Test of the Need Hierarchy Concept by a Markov Model of Change in Need Strength," *Administrative Science Quarterly* 25 (1980): 654–670.

27. Sources pertinent to this discussion are David C. McClelland, *The Achieving Society* (New York: Van Nostrand, 1961); David C. McClelland, "Business, Drive and National Achievement," *Harvard Business Review* 40 (July/August 1962): 99–112; David C. McClelland, "That Urge to Achieve," *Think* (November/December 1966): 19–32; G. H. Litwin and R. A. Stringer, *Motivation and Organizational Climate* (Boston: Division of Research, Harvard Business School, 1966), pp. 18–25.

28. George Harris, "To Know Why Men Do What They Do: A Conversation with David C. McClelland," *Psychology Today* 4 (January 1971): 35–39.

29. David C. McClelland and David H. Burnham, "Power Is the Great Motivator," *Harvard Business Review* 54 (March/April 1976): 100–110; David C. McClelland and Richard E. Boyatzis, "Leadership Motive Pattern and Long-Term Success in Management," *Journal of Applied Psychology* 67 (1982): 737–743.

30. P. Miron and D. C. McClelland, "The Impact of Achievement Motivation Training in Small Businesses," *California Management Review* (Summer 1979): 13–28.

31. The complete two-factor theory is well explained by Herzberg and his associates in Frederick Herzberg, Bernard Mausner, and Barbara Bloch Synderman, *The Motivation to Work,* 2nd ed. (New York: Wiley, 1967); and Frederick Herzberg, "One More Time: How Do You Motivate Employees?" *Harvard Business Review* 46 (January/February 1968): 53–62.

32. From Herzberg, op. cit. (1968), pp. 53–62.

33. See Robert J. House and Lawrence A. Wigdor, "Herzberg's Dual-Factor Theory of Job Satisfaction and Motivation: A Review of the Evidence and a Criticism," *Personnel Psychology* 20 (Winter 1967): 369–389; and Steven Kerr, Anne Harlan, and Ralph Stogdill, "Preference for Motivator or Hygiene Factors in a Hypothetical Interview Situation," *Personnel Psychology* 27 (Winter 1974): 109–124; Nathan King, "A Clarification and Evaluation of the Two-Factor Theory of Job Satisfaction," *Psychological Bulletin* (July 1970): 18–31; Marvin Dunnette, John Campbell, and Milton Hakel, "Factors Contributing to Job Satisfaction and Job Dissatisfaction in Six Occupational Groups," *Organizational Behavior and Human Performance* (May 1967): 143–174; R. J. House and L. Wigdor, "Herzberg's Dual Factor Theory of Job Satisfaction and Motivation: A Review of the Evidence and a Criticism," *Personnel Psychology* (Summer 1967): 369–389.

34. Adler, op. cit. (1991), Ch 6; Nancy J. Adler and J. T. Graham, "Cross Cultural Interaction: The International Comparison Fallacy," *Journal of International Business Studies* (Fall 1989): 515–537; Frederick Herzberg, "Workers Needs: The Same around the World," *Industry Week* (September 27, 1987), pp. 29–32.

35. See, for example, J. Stacy Adams, "Toward an Understanding of Inequality," *Journal of Abnormal and Social Psychology* 67 (1963): 422–436; and J. Stacy Adams, "Inequity in Social Exchange," in L. Berkowitz (ed.), *Advances in Experimental Social Psychology,* Vol. 2 (New York: Academic Press, 1965), pp. 267–300.

36. Adams, op. cit. (1965).

37. These issues are discussed in C. Kagitcibasi and J. W. Berry, "Cross-Cultural Psychology: Current Research and Trends," *Annual Review of Psychology* 40 (1989): 493–531.

38. Victor H. Vroom, *Work and Motivation* (New York: Wiley, 1964).

39. See Vroom (1964).

40. See Terence R. Mitchell, "Expectancy Models of Job Satisfaction, Occupational Preference and Effort: A Theoretical, Methodological, and Empirical Appraisal," *Psychological Bulletin* 81 (1974): 1053–1077; Mahmoud A. Wahba and Robert J. House, "Expectancy Theory in Work and Motivation: Some Logical and Methodological Issues," *Human Relations* 27 (January 1974): 121–147; Terry Connolly, "Some Conceptual and Methodological Issues in Expectancy Models of Work Performance Motivation," *Academy of Management Review* 1 (October 1976): 37–47; Terrence Mitchell, "Expectancy-Value Models in Organizational Psychology," in N. Feather (ed.), *Expectancy, Incentive and Action* (New York: Erlbaum & Associates, 1980).

41. See Lyman W. Porter and Edward E. Lawler III, *Managerial Attitudes and Performance* (Homewood, IL: Irwin, 1968).

42. See Adler (1991).

43. See William E. Wymer and Jeanne M. Carsten, "Alternative Ways to Gather Opinions," *HR Magazine* 37, 4 (April 1992): 71–78.

44. The Job Descriptive Index (JDI) is available from Dr. Patricia C. Smith, Department of Psychology, Bowling Green State University; the Minnesota Satisfaction Questionnaire (MSQ) is available from the Industrial Relations Center and Vocational Psychology Research Center, University of Minnesota.

45. Barry M. Staw, "The Consequences of Turnover," *Journal of Occupational Behavior* 1 (1980): 253–273; John P. Wanous, *Organizational Entry* (Reading, MA: Addison-Wesley, 1980).

46. Charles N. Greene, "The Satisfaction-Performance Controversy," *Business Horizons* 15 (1972): 31; Michelle T. Iaffaldano and Paul M. Muchinsky, "Job Satisfaction and Job Performance: A Meta-Analysis," *Psychological Bulletin* 97 (1985): 251–273; Greene, op. cit. (1972), pp. 31–41; Dennis Organ, "A Reappraisal and Reinterpretation of the Satisfaction-Causes-Performance Hypothesis," *Academy of Management Review* 2 (1977): 46–53; Peter Lorenzi, "A Comment on Organ's Reappraisal of the Satisfaction-Causes-Performance Hypothesis," *Academy of Management Review* 3 (1978): 380–382.

47. Porter and Lawler (1968).

48. This integrated model is consistent with the comprehensive approach suggested by Martin G. Evans, "Organizational Behavior: The Central Role of Motivation," in J. G. Hunt and J. D. Blair (eds.), *1986 Yearly Review of Management of the Journal of Management* 12 (1986): 203–222.

CHAPTER 7

1. For a good discussion of human resource management strategy and its linkage to overall management strategy, see A. J. Templer and R. J. Cattaneo, "A Model of Human Resources Management Effectiveness," *Canadian Journal of Administrative Sciences,* Vol. 12, No. 1, (1995) pp. 77–88.

2. See J. R. Schermerhorn, Jr., *Management,* 5th ed. (New York: Wiley, 1996), Ch. 12; G. M. Bounds, G. H. Dobbins, and O. S. Fowler, *Management: A Total Quality Perspective* (Cincinnati: South-Western, 1995), Ch. 9; L. R. Gomez-Mejia, D. B. Balkin, and R. L. Cardy, *Managing Human Resources* (Englewood Cliffs, NJ: Prentice-Hall, 1995), chs 2, 6.

3. Bounds, Dobbins, and Fowler, pp. 313–318.

4. Bounds, Dobbins, and Fowler, p. 315.

5. Bounds, Dobbins, and Fowler, p. 317; Gomez-Mejia, Balkin, and Cardy, pp. 97–98.

6. Summarized from Bounds, Dobbins, and Fowler, pp. 319–321; Gómez-Mejia, Balkin, and Cardy, Ch. 6; Schermerhorn, pp. 290–293.

7. See "Blueprints for Service Quality: The Federal Express Approach," *AMA Management Briefing* (New York: AMA Publications, 1991).

8. Based on A. Uris, *Eighty-eight Mistakes Interviewers Make and How to Avoid Them* (New York: AMA Publications, 1988).

9. G. C. Thornton, *Assessment Centers in Human Resource Management* (Reading, MA: Addison-Wesley, 1992).

10. B. B. Gaugler, D. B. Rosenthal, G. C. Thornton, and C. Bentson, "Meta-Analysis of Assessment Center Validity," *Journal of Applied Psychology,* Vol. 72 (1987), pp. 493–511; G. M. McEvoy and R. W. Beatty, "Assessment Centers and Subordinate Appraisals of Managers: A Seven-Year Study of Predictive Validity," *Personnel Psychology,* Vol. 42 (1989), pp. 37–52.

11. P. M. Muchinsky, "The Use of Reference Reports in Personnel Selection: A Review and Evaluation," *Journal of Occupational Psychology,* Vol. 52 (1979), pp. 287–297; "Background checks on the Rise," *Dallas Morning News* (November 11, 2001), pg. L.

12. This training discussion based on Bounds, Dobbins, and Fowler, pp. 326–329; Schermerhorn, pp. 294–295; S. R. Robbins, *Organizational Behavior,* 7th ed. (Englewood Cliffs, NJ: Prentice-Hall, 1996), pp. 641–644.

13. See Rob Muller, "Training for Change," *Canadian Business Review* (Spring 1995), pp. 16–19.

14. Much of the initial discussion in this section is based on Daniel C. Feldman, "Careers in Organizations: Recent Trends and Future Directions," *Journal of Management,* Vol. 15 (June 1989), pp. 135–156; Irving Janis and Dan Wheeler, "Thinking Clearly about Career Choices." *Psychology Today* (May 1978), p. 67; Walter Kiechel III, "How We Will Work in the Year 2000," *Fortune* (May 17, 1993), pp. 38–52.

15. Charles Handy, *The Age of Unreason* (Boston: Harvard Business School Press, 1991).

16. This discussion combines earlier and later career development literature based on Janis and Wheeler, p. 67; Daniel J. Levinson, *The Seasons of a Man's Life* (New York: Knopf, 1978): Douglas T. Hall, *Careers in Organizations* (Santa Monica, CA: Goodyear, 1975); Lloyd Baird and Kathy Krim, "Career Dynamics: Managing the Superior-Subordinate Relationship," *Organizational Dynamics* (Spring 1983), p. 47; Paul H. Thompson, Robin Zenger Baker, and Norman Smallwood, "Improving Professional Development by Applying the Four-Stage Career Model," *Organizational Dynamics* (Autumn 1986), pp. 49–62; Thomas P. Ference, James A. F. Stoner, and E. Kirby Warren, "Managing the Career Plateau." *Academy of Management Review,* Vol. 2 (October 1977), pp. 602–612; Gail Sheehy, *New Passages: Mapping Your Life across Time* (New York: Ballantine Books, 1995).

17. "Strategic Issues in Performance Appraisal, Theory and Practice," *Personnel,* Vol. 60 (Nov./Dec. 1983), p. 24; Gómez-Mejia, Balkin, and Cardy, Ch. 8; "Performance Appraisal: Current Practices and Techniques," *Personnel* (May/June 1984), p. 57.

18. See G. P. Latham and K. N. Wexley, *Increasing Productivity Through Performance Appraisal* (Reading, MA: Addison-Wesley, 1981), p. 80.

19. See R. J. Newman, "Job Reviews Go Full Circle," *U.S. News and World Report* (November 1, 1993), pp. 42–43; J. A. Lopez, "A Better Way?" *Wall Street Journal* (April 13, 1994), p. R6; M. S. Hirsch, "360 Degrees of Evaluation," *Working Woman* (August 1994), pp. 20–21; B. O'Reilly, "360 Degree Feedback Can Change Your Life," *Fortune* (October 17, 1994), pp. 93–100; see *Leadership Quarterly;* Vol. 9, No. 4 (1998), special issue on "360-Degree Feedback in Leadership Research," pp. 423–474; Stephen P. Robbins, *Organizational Behavior,* 8th ed. (Upper Saddle River, NJ: Prentice Hall, 1998, p. 568.

20. Robert C. Hill and Sara M. Freedman, "Managing the Quality Process: Lessons from the Baldrige Award Winner," *Academy of Management Executive,* Vol. 6 (February 1992), p. 84.

21. For more details, see Latham and Wexley, op. cit. (1981); Stephen J. Carroll and Craig E. Schneier, *Performance Appraisal and Review Systems* (Glenview, IL: Scott, Foresman, 1982).

22. See George T. Milkovich and John W. Boudreau, *Personnel/Human Resource Management: A Diagnostic Approach,* 5th ed. (Plano, TX: Business Publications, 1988).

23. For a detailed discussion, see S. J. Carroll and H. L. Tosi, Jr., *Management of Objectives: Application and Research* (New York: Macmillan, 1976); A. P. Raia, *Managing by Objectives* (Glenview, IL: Scott, Foresman, 1974).

24. For discussion of many of these errors, see David L. Devries, Ann M. Morrison, Sandra L. Shullman, and Michael P. Gerlach, *Performance Appraisal on the Line* (Greensboro, NC: Center for Creative Leadership, 1986), Ch. 3.

25. E. G. Olson, "The Workplace Is High on the High Court's Docket," *Business Week* (October 10, 1988), pp. 88–89.

26. Based on J. J. Bernardin and C. S. Walter, "The Effects of Rater Training and Diary Keeping on Psychometric Error in Ratings," *Journal of Applied Psychology,* Vol. 61 (1977), pp. 64–69; see also R. G. Burnask and T. D. Hollman, "An Empirical Comparison of the Relative Effects of Sorter Response Bias on Three Rating Scale Formats," *Journal of Applied Psychology,* Vol. 59 (1974), pp. 307–312.

27. W. F. Cascio and H. J. Bernardin, "Implications of Performance Appraisal Litigation for Personnel Decisions," *Personnel Psychology,* Vol. 34 (1981), pp. 221–222.

28. See David Shar, "Comp Star Adds Efficiency and Flexibility to Performance Reviews," *HR Magazine* (October 1997), pp. 37–42.

29. For complete reviews of theory, research, and practice, see Edward E. Lawler III, *Pay and Organizational Effectiveness* (New York: McGraw-Hill, 1971); Edward E. Lawler III, *Pay and Organization Development* (Reading MA: Addison-Wesley, 1981); Edward E. Lawler III, "The Design of Effective Reward Systems," in Jay W. Lorsch (ed.), *Handbook of Organizational Behavior* (Englewood Cliffs, NJ: Prentice-Hall, 1987), pp. 255–271.

30. As an example, see D. B. Balkin and L. R. Gómez-Mejía (eds.), *New Perspectives on Compensation* (Englewood Cliffs, NJ: Prentice-Hall, 1987).

31. Jone L. Pearce, "Why Merit Pay Doesn't Work: Implications from Organization Theory," in David B. Balkin and Luis R. Gómez-Mejía, pp. 169–178; Jerry M. Newman, "Selecting Incentive Plans To Complement Organizational Strategy," in Balkin and Gómez-Mejía, pp. 214–224; Edward E. Lawler III, "Pay for Performance: Making It Work," *Compensation and Benefits Review.* Vol. 21 (1989), pp. 55–60.

32. See Daniel C. Boyle, "Employee Motivation that Works," *HR Magazine* (October 1992), pp. 83–89. Kathleen A. McNally, "Compensation as a Strategic Tool," *HR Magazine* (July 1992), pp. 59–66.

33. S. Caudron, "Master the Compensation Maze," *Personnel Journal* (June 1993), pp. 640–648.

34. N. Gupta, G. E. Ledford, G. D. Jenkins, and D. H. Doty, "Survey Based Prescriptions for Skill-Based Pay," *American Compensation Association Journal.* Vol. 1, No. 1 (1992), pp. 48–59; L. W. Ledford, "The Effectiveness of Skill-Based Pay," *Perspectives in Total Compensation,* Vol. 1, No. 1 (1991), pp. 1–4.

35. See Brian Graham-Moore, "Review of the Literature," in Brian Graham-Moore and Timothy L. Ross (eds.), *Gainsharing* (Washington, DC: The Bureau of National Affairs, 1990), p. 20.

36. S. E. Markham, K. D. Scott, and B. L. Little, "National Gainsharing Study: The Importance of Industry Differences," *Compensation and Benefits Review* (Jan./Feb. 1992), pp. 34–45.

37. Gómez-Mejía, Balkin, and Cardy, pp. 410–411.

38. Gómez-Mejía, Balkin, and Cardy, pp. 409–410.

39. C. O'Dell and J. McAdams, "The Revolution in Employee Benefits," *Compensation and Benefits Review* (May/June 1987); pp. 68–73.

Source Notes

Effective Manager information from A. Uris, *Eighty-eight Mistakes Interviewers Make and How to Avoid Them* (New York: AMA Publications, 1988).

Performance Review Form adapted from Andrew D. Szilagi, Jr., and Marc J. Wallace, Jr. *Organizational Behavior and Performance,* 3rd ed. (Glenview, IL: Scott, Foresman, 1983), pp. 393–394.

Adapted from J. P. Campbell, M. D. Dunnette, R. D. Arvey, and L. V. Hellervik, "The Development Evaluation of Behaviorally Based Rating Scales," *Applied Psychology,* Vol. 57 (1973), p. 18.

Copyright 1973 by the American Psychological Association.

Reprinted by permission of publisher and authors.

Effective Manager information from J. Zignon, "Making Performance Appraisal Work for Teams," *Training* (June 1994), pp. 58–63.

CHAPTER 8

1. Information from Jessica Guynn, "Peet's Brews Successful Blend for Retaining Workers," *The Columbus Dispatch* (October 26, 1998), pp. 10–11; company Web site: www.peets.com.

2. Frederick W. Taylor, *The Principles of Scientific Management* (New York: W.W. Norton, 1967).

3. Frederick Herzberg, "One More Time: How Do You Motivate Employees?" *Harvard Business Review* 46 (January/February 1968), pp. 53–62.

4. Paul J. Champagne and Curt Tausky, "When Job Enrichment Doesn't Pay," *Personnel*, Vol. 3 (January/February 1978), pp. 30–40.

5. For a complete description, see J. Richard Hackman and Greg R. Oldham, *Work Redesign* (Reading, MA: Addison-Wesley, 1980).

6. See J. Richard Hackman and Greg Oldham, "Development of the Job Diagnostic Survey," *Journal of Applied Psychology*, Vol. 60 (1975), pp. 159–170.

7. Hackman and Oldham, op. cit. For forerunner research, see Charles L. Hulin and Milton R. Blood, "Job Enlargement Individual Differences, and Worker Responses," *Psychological Bulletin*, Vol. 69 (1968), pp. 41–55; Milton R. Blood and Charles L. Hulin, "Alienation, Environmental Characteristics and Worker Responses," *Journal of Applied Psychology*, Vol. 51 (1967), pp. 284–290.

8. Gerald Salancik and Jeffrey Pfeffer, "An Examination of Need-Satisfaction Models of Job Attitudes," *Administrative Science Quarterly*, Vol. 22 (1977), pp. 427–456; Gerald Salancik and Jeffrey Pfeffer, "A Social Information Processing Approach to Job Attitude and Task Design," *Administrative Science Quarterly*, Vol. 23 (1978), pp. 224–253.

9. George W. England and Itzhak Harpaz, "How Working Is Defined: National Contexts and Demographic and Organizational Role Influences," *Journal of Organizational Behavior* (July 1990), pp. 253–266.

10. William A. Pasmore, "Overcoming the Roadblocks to Work-Restructuring Efforts," *Organizational Dynamics*, Vol. 10 (1982), pp. 54–67; Hackman and Oldham, op. cit. (1975).

11. See William A. Pasmore, *Designing Effective Organizations: A Sociotechnical Systems Perspective* (New York: Wiley, 1988).

12. Michael Hammer, "Reengineering Work: Don't Automate, Obliterate," *Harvard Business Review* (July/August 1990), pp. 104–112.

13. See Thomas M. Koulopoulos, *The Workflow Imperative: Building Real World Business Solutions* (New York: Van Nostrand Reinhold, 1995).

14. For a good overview, see Michael Hammer and James Champy, *Reengineering the Corporation* (New York: Harper Business, 1993); and Michael Hammer, *Beyond Reengineering* (New York: Harper Business, 1997).

15. Edwin A. Locke, Karyll N. Shaw, Lise M. Saari, and Gary P. Latham, "Goal Setting and Task Performance: 1969–1980," *Psychological Bulletin*, Vol. 90 (July/November 1981), pp. 125–152; Edwin A. Locke and Gary P. Latham, "Work Motivation and Satisfaction: Light at the End of the Tunnel," *Psychological Science*, Vol. 1, No. 4 (July 1990), pp. 240–246; and Edwin A. Locke and Gary P. Latham, *A Theory of Goal Setting and Task Performance* (Englewood Cliffs, NJ: Prentice-Hall, 1990).

16. Gary P. Latham and Edwin A. Locke, "Goal Setting—A Motivational Technique That Works," *Organizational Dynamics*, Vol. 8 (Autumn 1979), pp. 68–80; Gary P. Latham and Timothy P. Steele, "The Motivational Effects of Participation versus Goal-Setting on Performance," *Academy of Management Journal*, Vol. 26 (1983), pp. 406–417; Miriam Erez and Frederick H. Kanfer, "The Role of Goal Acceptance in Goal Setting and Task Performance," *Academy of Management Review*, Vol. 8 (1983), pp. 454–463; and R. E. Wood and E. A. Locke, "Goal Setting and Strategy Effects on Complex Tasks," in B. Staw and L. L. Cummings (eds.), *Research in Organizational Behavior* (Greenwich, CT: JAI Press, 1990).

17. See E. A. Locke and G. P. Latham, "Work Motivation and Satisfaction," *Psychological Science*, Vol. 1, No. 4 (July 1990), p. 241.

18. Ibid.

19. For a good review of MBO, see Anthony P. Raia, *Managing by Objectives* (Glenview, IL: Scott, Foresman, 1974).

20. Ibid.; also, Steven Kerr summarizes the criticisms well in "Overcoming the Dysfunctions of MBO," *Management by Objectives*, Vol. 5, No. 1 (1976).

21. For overviews, see Allan R. Cohen and Herman Gadon, *Alternative Work Schedules: Integrating Individual and Organizational Needs* (Reading, MA: Addison-Wesley, 1978); and Jon L. Pearce, John W. Newstrom, Randall B. Dunham, and Alison E. Barber, *Alternative Work Schedules* (Boston: Allyn & Bacon, 1989). See also Sharon Parker and Toby Wall, *Job and Work Design* (Thousand Oaks, CA: Sage, 1998).

22. C. Latack and L. W. Foster, "Implementation of Compressed Work Schedules: Participation and Job Redesign as Critical Factors for Employee Acceptance," *Personnel Psychology*, Vol. 38 (1985), pp. 75–92.

23. "Aetna Life & Casualty Company," *Wall Street Journal* (June 4, 1990), p. R35; (June 18, 1990), p. B1.

24. Getsy M. Selirio, "Job Sharing Gains Favor as Corporations Embrace Alternative Work Schedule," *Lubbock Avalanche-Journal* (December 13, 1992), p. 2E.

25. Ibid.

26. "Making Stay-at-Homes Feel Welcome," *Business Week* (October 12, 1998), pp. 153–155.

27. T. Davenport and K. Pearlson, "Two Cheers for the Virtual Office," *Sloan Management Review* (Summer 1998), pp. 51–64.

28. "Making Stay-at-Homes Feel Welcome," op. cit.

29. Guynn, op. cit. (1998).

30. Daniel C. Feldman and Helen I. Doerpinghaus, "Missing Persons No Longer: Managing Part-Time Workers in the '90s," *Organizational Dynamics* (Summer 1992), pp. 59–72.

CHAPTER 9

1. Information from David Kirkpatrick, "The Second Coming of Apple," *Fortune* (November 9, 1998), pp. 86–92. See also Brent Schlender, "The Three Faces of Steve," *Fortune* (November 9, 1998), pp. 96–104; www.apple.com.

2. For a good discussion of groups and teams in the workplace, see Jon R. Katzenbach and Douglas K. Smith, "The Discipline of Teams," *Harvard Business Review* (March/April, 1993), pp. 111–120.

3. Harold J. Leavitt and Jean Lipman-Blumen, "Hot Groups," *Harvard Business Review* (July/August 1995), pp. 109–116.

4. See, for example, Edward E. Lawler, III, *High-Involvement Management* (San Francisco: Jossey-Bass, 1986).

5. Marvin E. Shaw, *Group Dynamics: The Psychology of Small Group Behavior*, 2nd ed. (New York: McGraw-Hill, 1976).

6. Bib Latane, Kipling Williams, and Stephen Harkins, "Many Hands Make Light the Work: The Causes and Consequences of Social Loafing," *Journal of Personality and Social Psychology*, Vol. 37 (1978), pp. 822–832; E. Weldon and G. M. Gargano, "Cognitive Effort in Additive Task Groups: The Effects of Shared Responsibility on the Quality of Multi-attribute judgments," *Organizational Behavior and Human Decision Processes*, Vol. 36 (1985), pp. 348–361; John M. George, "Extrinsic and Intrinsic Origins of Perceived Social Loafing in Organizations," *Academy of Management Journal* (March 1992), pp. 191–202; and W. Jack Duncan, "Why Some People Loaf in Groups While Others Loaf Alone," *Academy of Management Executive*, Vol. 8 (1994), pp. 79–80.

7. D. A. Kravitz and B. Martin, "Ringelmann Rediscovered," *Journal of Personality and Social Psychology*, Vol. 50 (1986), pp. 936–941.

8. A classic article is by Richard B. Zajonc, "Social Facilitation," *Science*, Vol. 149 (1965), pp. 269–274.

9. Rensis Likert, *New Patterns of Management* (New York: McGraw-Hill, 1961).

10. For a good discussion of task forces, see James Ware, "Managing a Task Force," Note 478-002, Harvard Business School, 1977.

11. See, for example, Leland P. Bradford, *Group Development*, 2nd ed. (San Francisco: Jossey-Bass, 1997); Greg L. Stewart, Charles C. Manz, and Henry P. Sims, *Teamwork and Group Dynamics* (New York: John Wiley & Sons, 1999).

12. J. Steven Heinen and Eugene Jacobson, "A Model of Task Group Development in Complex Organization and a Strategy of Implementation," *Academy of Management Review*, Vol. 1 (October 1976), pp. 98–111; Bruce W. Tuckman, "Developmental Sequence in Small Groups," *Psychological Bulletin*, Vol. 63 (1965), pp. 384–399; and Bruce W. Tuckman and Mary Ann C. Jensen, "Stages of Small Group Development Revisited," *Group & Organization Studies*, Vol. 2 (1977), pp. 419–427.

13. See J. Richard Hackman, "The Design of Work Teams," in Jay W. Lorsch (ed.), *Handbook of Organizational Behavior* (Englewood Cliffs, NJ: Prentice Hall, 1987), pp. 343–357.

14. David M. Herold, "The Effectiveness of Work Groups," in Steven Kerr, ed., *Organizational Behavior* (New York: Wiley, 1979), p. 95; see also the discussion of group tasks in Stewart, Manz, and Sims, op. cit. (1999), pp. 142–143.

15. Ilgen, et al., op. cit. (1997); and Warren Watson, "Cultural Diversity's Impact on Interaction Process and Performance," *Academy of Management Journal*, Vol. 16 (1993).

16. L. Argote and J. E. McGrath, "Group Processes in Organizations: Continuity and Change" in C. L. Cooper and I. T. Robertson (eds.), *International Review of Industrial and Organizational Psychology* (New York: Wiley, 1993), pp. 333–389.

17. See Daniel R. Ilgen, Jeffrey A. LePine and John R. Hollenbeck, "Effective Decision Making in Multinational Teams," in P. Christopher Earley and Miram Erez (eds.), *New Perspectives on International Industrial/Organizational Psychology* (San Francisco: New Lexington Press, 1997), pp. 377–409.

18. William C. Schultz, *FIRO: A Three-Dimensional Theory of Interpersonal Behavior* (New York: Rinehart, 1958).

19. William C. Schutz, "The Interpersonal Underworld," *Harvard Business Review*, Vol. 36 (July/August, 1958), p. 130.

20. Katzenbach and Smith, op. cit. (1993).

21. E. J. Thomas and C. F. Fink, "Effects of Group Size," in Larry L. Cummings and William E. Scott (eds.), *Readings in Organizational and Human Performance* (Homewood, IL: Irwin, 1969), pp. 394–408.

22. Shaw, op. cit. (1976).

23. George C. Homans, *The Human Group* (New York: Harcourt Brace, 1950).

24. For a discussion of intergroup dynamics, see Schein, op. cit. (1988), pp. 106–115.

25. "Producer Power," *The Economist* (March 4, 1995), p. 70.

26. The discussion is developed from Schein, op. cit. (1988), pp. 69–75.

27. Ibid., p. 73.

28. Developed from guidelines presented in the classic article by Jay Hall, "Decisions, Decisions, Decisions," *Psychology Today* (November 1971), pp. 55–56.

29. Norman R.F. Maier, "Assets and Liabilities in Group Problem Solving," *Psychological Review*, Vol. 74 (1967), pp. 239–249.

30. Ibid.

31. Irving L. Janis, "Groupthink," *Psychology Today* (November 1971), pp. 33–36; Irving L. Janis, *Groupthink*, 2nd ed. (Boston: Houghton Mifflin, 1982). See also J. Longley and D. G. Pruitt, "Groupthink: A Critique of Janis' Theory," in L. Wheeler (ed.), *Review of Personality and Social Psychology* (Beverly Hills, CA: Sage Publications, 1980): Carrie R. Leana, "A Partial Test of Janis's Groupthink Model: The Effects of Group Cohesiveness and Leader Behavior on Decision Processes," *Journal of Management*, Vol. 11, No. 1 (1985), pp. 5–18. See also Jerry Harvey, "Managing Agreement in Organizations: The Abilene Paradox," *Organizational Dynamics* (Summer 1974), pp. 63–80.

32. Janis, op. cit. (1982).

33. Gayle W. Hill, "Group versus Individual Performance: Are N1 1 Heads Better Than One?" *Psychological Bulletin*, Vol. 91 (1982), pp. 517–539.

34. These techniques are well described in George P. Huber, *Managerial Decision Making* (Glenview, IL: Scott, Foresman, 1980); and Andre L. Delbecq, Andrew L. Van de Ven, and David H. Gustafson, *Group Techniques for Program Planning: A Guide to Nominal Groups and Delphi Techniques* (Glenview, IL: Scott, Foresman, 1975); and William M. Fox, "Anonymity and Other Keys to Successful Problem-Solving Meetings," *National Productivity Review*, Vol. 8 (Spring 1989), pp. 145–156.

35. Delbecq et al., op. cit. (1975); Fox, op. cit. (1989).

36. R. Brent Gallupe and William H. Cooper, "Brainstorming Electronically," *Sloan Management Review* (Fall 1993), pp. 27–36.

CHAPTER 10

1. *Fortune* (May 7, 1990), pp. 52–60. See also Ronald E. Purser and Steven Cabana, *The Self-Managing Organization* (New York: Free Press, 1998).

2. Susan Albers Mohrman, Jay R. Galbraith, Edward E. Lawler III, and Associates, *Tomorrow's Organization: Crafting Winning Capabilities in a Dynamic World* (San Francisco: Jossey-Bass, 1998).

3. Jon R. Katzenbach and Douglas K. Smith, "The Discipline of Teams," *Harvard Business Review* (March/April 1993a), pp. 111–120; and Jon R. Katzenbach and Douglas K. Smith, *The*

Wisdom of Teams: Creating the High-Performance Organization (Boston: Harvard Business School Press, 1993b).

4. Jay A. Conger, *Winning 'em Over: A New Model for Managing in the Age of Persuasion* (New York: Simon & Schuster, 1998).

5. Ibid., p. 191.

6. Katzenbach and Smith, op. cit. (1993a and 1993b).

7. See also Jon R. Katzenbach, "The Myth of the Top Management Team," *Harvard Business Review,* Vol. 75 (November/December 1997), pp. 83–91.

8. Katzenbach and Smith, op. cit. (1993a and 1993b).

9. For a good overview, see Greg L. Stewart, Charles C. Manz, and Henry P. Sims, *Team Work and Group Dynamics* (New York: Wiley, 1999).

10. Katzenbach and Smith, op. cit. (1993a), p. 112.

11. Developed from ibid. (1993a), pp. 118–119.

12. See Stewart et al., op. cit. (1999), pp. 43–44.

13. See Daniel R. Ilgen, Jeffrey A. LePine and John R. Hollenbeck, "Effective Decision Making in Multinational Teams," in P. Christopher Earley and Miriam Erez (eds.), *New Perspectives on International Industrial/Organizational Psychology* (San Francisco: New Lexington Press, 1997), pp. 377–409.

14. Ilgen, et al., op. cit. (1997); and Warren Watson, "Cultural Diversity's Impact on Interaction Process and Performance," *Academy of Management Journal,* Vol. 16 (1993).

15. For an interesting discussion of sporting team see Ellen Fagenson-Eland, "The National Football League's Bill Parcells on Winning, Leading, and Turning Around Teams," *Academy of Management Executive,* Vol. 15 (August 2001), pp. 48–57; and, Nancy Katz, "Sports Teams as a Model for Workplace Teams: Lessons and Liabilities," *Academy of Management Executive,* Vol. 15 (August, 2002), pp. 56–69.

16. For a good discussion of team building, see William D. Dyer, *Team Building,* 3rd ed. (Reading, MA: Addison-Wesley, 1995).

17. Developed from a discussion by Edgar H. Schein, *Process Consultation* (Reading MA: Addison-Wesley, 1969), pp. 32–37; Edgar H. Schein, *Process Consultation: Volume I* (1988), pp. 40–49.

18. The classic work is Robert F. Bales, "Task Roles and Social Roles in Problem-Solving Groups," in Eleanor E. Maccoby, Theodore M. Newcomb, and E. L. Hartley (eds.), *Readings in Social Psychology* (New York: Holt, Rinehart & Winston, 1958).

19. For a good description of task and maintenance functions, see John J. Gabarro and Anne Harlan, "Note on Process Observation," Note 9-477-029 (Harvard Business School, 1976).

20. See Daniel C. Feldman, "The Development and Enforcement of Group Norms," *Academy of Management Review,* Vol. 9 (1984), pp. 47–53.

21. See Robert F. Allen and Saul Pilnick, "Confronting the Shadow Organization: How to Select and Defeat Negative Norms," *Organizational Dynamics* (Spring 1973), pp. 13–17; Alvin Zander, *Making Groups Effective* (San Francisco: Jossey-Bass, 1982), Ch. 4; Daniel C. Feldman, op. cit. (1984).

22. For a summary of research on group cohesiveness, see Marvin E. Shaw, *Group Dynamics* (New York: McGraw-Hill, 1971), pp. 110–112, 192.

23. Information from Stratford Shermin, "Secrets of HP's 'Muddled' Team," *Fortune* (March 18, 1996), pp. 116–120.

24. See Jay R. Galbraith and Edward E. Lawler III, "The Challenges of Change Organizing for Competitive Advantage," in Susan Albers Mohrman, Jay R. Galbraith, Edward E. Lawler III, and Associates, *Tomorrow's Organization: Crafting Winning Capabilities in a Dynamic World* (San Francisco: Jossey-Bass, 1998).

25. See Kenichi Ohmae, "Quality Control Circles: They Work and Don't Work," *Wall Street Journal* (March 29, 1982), p. 16; Robert P. Steel, Anthony J. Mento, Benjamin L. Dilla, Nestor K. Ovalle, and Russell F. Lloyd, "Factors Influencing the Success and Failure of Two Quality Circles Programs," *Journal of Management,* Vol. 11, No. 1 (1985), pp. 99–119; Edward E. Lawler III, and Susan A. Mohrman, "Quality Circles: After the Honeymoon," *Organizational Dynamics,* Vol. 15, No. 4 (1987), pp. 42–54.

26. See Jay R. Galbraith, *Designing Organizations* (San Francisco: Jossey-Bass, 1998).

27. Jerry Yoram Wind and Jeremy Main, *Driving Change: How the Best Companies Are Preparing for the 21st Century* (New York: The Free Press, 1998), p. 135.

28. Jessica Lipnack and Jeffrey Stamps, *Virtual Teams: Reaching Across Space, Time, and Organizations with Technology* (New York: Wiley, 1997).

29. For a review of some alternatives, see Jeff Angus and Sean Gallagher, "Virtual Team Builders—Internet-Based Teamware Makes It Possible to Build Effective Teams from Widely Dispersed Participants," *Information Week* (May 4, 1998).

30. Christine Perey, "Conferencing and Collaboration: Real-World Solutions for Business Communications," *Business Week* special advertising section (1999).

31. R. Brent Gallupe and William H. Cooper, "Brainstorming Electronically," *Sloan Management Review* (Fall 1993), pp. 27–36.

32. For early research on related team concepts, see Richard E. Walton, "How to Counter Alienation in the Plant," *Harvard Business Review* (November/December 1972), pp. 70–81; Richard E. Walton, "Work Innovations at Topeka: After Six Years," *Journal of Applied Behavior Science,* Vol. 13 (1977), pp. 422–431; Richard E. Walton, "The Topeka Work System: Optimistic Visions, Pessimistic Hypotheses, and Reality," in Zager and Rosow (eds.), *The Innovative Organization,* Ch. 11.

CHAPTER 11

1. The bulk of this chapter was originally based on Richard N. Osborn, James G. Hunt, and Lawrence R. Jauch, *Organization Theory: Integrated Text and Cases* (Melbourne, FL: Krieger, 1985).

2. For recent but consistent views, see Lex Donaldson, "The Normal Science of Structural Contingency Theory," in Stewart R. Clegg, Cynthia Hardy, and Walter R. Nord (eds.), *Handbook of Organizational Studies* (London: Sage Publications, 1996), pp. 57–76.

3. The view of strategy provided here is a combination of perspectives drawn from several sources including Alfred D. Chandler, *The Visible Hand: The Managerial Revolution in America* (Cambridge, MA: Belnap, 1977); Michael E. Porter, *Competitive Strategy* (New York: Free Press, 1980); L. R. Jauch and R. N.

Osborn, "Toward an Integrated Theory of Strategy," *Academy of Management Review* 6 (1981): 491–498; B. Wernefelt, "A Resource-based View of the Firm," *Strategic Management Journal* 5 (1984): 171–180; J. B. Barney, "Firm Resources and Sustained Competitive Advantage," *J. Management* 17 (1991): 99–120; Michael A. Hitt, R. Duane Ireland, and Robert E. Hoskisson, *Strategic Management: Competition and Globalization* (Cincinnati, OH: Southwestern, 2001).

4. H. Talcott Parsons, *Structure and Processes in Modern Societies* (New York: Free Press, 1960).

5. See Terri Lammers, "The Effective and Indispensable Mission Statement," *Inc.* (August 1992): 1, 7, 23, for instance, and I. C. MacMillan an A. Meshulack, "Replacement versus Expansion: Dilemma for Mature U.S. Businesses," *Academy of Management Journal* 26 (1983): 708–726.

6. See Stewart R. Clegg and Cynthia Hardy, "Organizations, Organization and Organizing," in Clegg, Hardy, and Nord (eds.), *Handbook of Organizational Studies* (1996), pp. 1–28 and William H. Starbuck and Paul C. Nystrom, "Designing and Understanding Organizations," in P. C. Nystrom and W. H. Starbuck (eds.), *Handbook of Organizational Design: Adapting Organizations to Their Environments* (New York: Oxford University Press, 1981).

7. See Jeffery Pfeffer, "Barriers to the Advance of Organization Science," *Academy of Management Review* 18, No. 4 (1994): 599–620; Richard M. Cyert and James G. March, *A Behavioral Theory of the Firm* (Englewood Cliffs, NJ: Prentice-Hall, 1963). A good discussion of organizational goals is also found in Charles Perrow, *Organizational Analysis: A Sociological View* (Belmont, CA: Wadsworth, 1970) and in Richard H. Hall, "Organizational Behavior: A Sociological Perspective," in Jay W. Lorsch (ed.), *Handbook of Organizational Behavior* (Englewood Cliffs, NJ: Prentice-Hall, 1987), pp. 84–95.

8. See Osborn, Hunt, and Jauch (1985).

9. Janice Beyer, Danta P. Ashmos, and R. N. Osborn, "Contrasts in Enacting TQM: Mechanistic vs. Organic Ideology and Implementation," *Journal of Quality Management* 1 (1997): 13–29, and for an early treatment, see Paul R. Lawrence and Jay W. Lorsch, *Organization and Environment* (Homewood, IL: Irwin, 1969).

10. Chandler, op. cit. (1977).

11. For reviews, see Osborn, Hunt, and Jauch (1985); Clegg, Hardy, and Nord (1996).

12. See Prashant C. Palvia, Shailendra C. Palvia, and Edward M. Roche, *Global Information Technology and Systems Management: Key Issues and Trends* (Nashua, NH: Ivy League Publishing, 1996).

13. For instance, see J.E.M. McGee, M. J. Dowling, and W. L. Megginson, "Cooperative Strategy and New Venture Performance: The Role of Business Strategy and Management Experience," *Strategic Management Journal* 16 (1995): 565–580 and James B. Quinn, *Intelligent Enterprise: A Knowledge and Service Based Paradigm for Industry* (New York: Free Press, 1992).

14. See P. Candace Deans, *Global Information Systems and Technology: Focus on the Organization and Its Functional Areas* (Harrisburg, PA: Ideal Group Publishing, 1994) and Osborn, Hunt, and Jauch (1985).

15. Haim Levy and Deborah Gunthorpe, *Introduction to Investments,* 2nd ed. (Cincinatti, OH: South-Western, 1999).

16. William G. Ouchi and M. A. McGuire, "Organization Control: Two Functions," *Administrative Science Quarterly* 20 (1977): 559–569.

17. This discussion is adapted from W. Edwards Deming, "Improvement of Quality and Productivity Through Action by Management," *Productivity Review* (Winter 1982): 12, 22; and W. Edwards Deming, *Quality, Productivity and Competitive Position* (Cambridge, MA: MIT Center for Advanced Engineering, 1982).

18. For related reviews, see W. Richard Scott, *Organizations: Rational, Natural, and Open Systems,* 2nd ed. (Englewood Cliffs, NJ: Prentice-Hall. 1987): Osborn, Hunt, and Jauch (1985); Clegg, Hardy, and Nord (1996).

19. See Osborn, Hunt, and Jauch (1985), pp. 273–303 for a discussion of centralization/decentralization.

20. Ibid.

21. For reviews of structural tendencies and their influence on outcomes, also see Scott (1987); Clegg, Hardy, and Nord (1996).

22. Ibid.

23. For a good discussion of the early use of matrix structures, see Stanley Davis, Paul Lawrence, Harvey Kolodny, and Michael Beer, *Matrix* (Reading, MA: Addison-Wesley, 1977).

24. See P. R. Lawrence and J. W. Lorsch, *Organization and Environment: Managing Differentiation and Integration* (Homewood, IL: Richard D. Irwin, 1967).

25. See Osborn, Hunt, and Jauch (1985).

26. Max Weber, *The Theory of Social and Economic Organization,* translated by A. M. Henderson and H. T. Parsons (New York: Free Press, 1947).

27. These relationships were initially outlined by Tom Burns and G. M. Stalken, *The Management of Innovation* (London: Tavistock, 1961).

28. See Henry Mintzberg, *Structure in Fives: Designing Effective Organizations* (Englewood Cliffs, NJ: Prentice-Hall, 1983).

29. Ibid.

30. Ibid.

31. See Osborn, Hunt, and Jauch (1984) for an extended discussion.

32. See Peter Clark and Ken Starkey, *Organization Transitions and Innovation—Design* (London: Pinter Publications, 1988).

CHAPTER 12

1. See *www.IBM.com,* CEO's comments on 2000 financial performance and www.Ford.com.

2. The view of strategy as a process of co-evolution was drawn from several sources, including Alfred D. Chandler, *The Visible Hand: The Managerial Revolution in America* (Cambridge, MA: Belnap, 1977); Michael E. Porter, *Competitive Strategy* (New York: Free Press, 1980); L. R. Jauch and R. N. Osborn, "Toward an Integrated Theory of Strategy," *Academy of Management Review* 6 (1981): 491–498; B. Wernefelt, "A Resource-based View of the Firm," *Strategic Management Journal* 5 (1984): 171–180; J. B. Barney, "Firm Resources and Sustained Competitive Advantage," *J. Management* 17 (1991): 99–120; Ross Marion, *The Edge of Organization: Chaos and Complexity*

Theories of Formal Social Systems (London, Sage, 1999); Arie Lewin, Chris Long, and Timothy Caroll, "The Coevolution of New Organizational Forms," *Organization Science* 10 (1999): 535–550; Michael A. Hitt, R. Duane Ireland, and Robert E. Hoskisson, *Strategic Management: Competition and Globalization* (Cincinnati, OH: Southwestern, 2001).

3. R. N. Osborn, J. G. Hunt, and L. Jauch, *Organization Theory Integrated Text and Cases* (Melbourne, FL: Krieger, 1984), pp. 123–215.

4. See Henry Mintzberg, *Structure in Fives: Designing Effective Organizations* (Englewood Cliffs, NJ: Prentice-Hall, 1983).

5. For a comprehensive review, see W. Richard Scott, *Organizations: Rational, Natural, and Open Systems,* 2nd ed. (Englewood Cliffs, NJ: Prentice-Hall, 1987).

6. See Peter M. Blau and Richard A. Schoenner, *The Structure of Organizations* (New York: Basic Books, 1971); Joan Woodward, *Industrial Organization: Theory and Practice* (London: Oxford University Press, 1965).

7. Ibid.

8. Gerardine DeSanctis, "Information Technology," in Nigel Nicholson (ed.), *Blackwell Encyclopedic Dictionary of Organizational Behavior* (Cambridge, MA: Blackwell Publishers, Ltd., 1995), pp. 232–233.

9. James D. Thompson, *Organization in Action* (New York: McGraw-Hill, 1967).

10. Woodward (1965).

11. For reviews, see Osborn, Hunt, and Jauch (1984); and Louis Fry, "Technology-Structure Research: Three Critical Issues," *Academy of Management Journal* 25 (1982): pp. 532–552.

12. Mintzberg (1983).

13. Charles Perrow, *Complex Organizations: A Critical Essay,* 3rd ed. (New York: Random House, 1986).

14. Mintzberg (1983).

15. Prashant C. Palvia, Shailendra C. Palvia, and Edward M. Roche, *Global Information Technology and Systems Management: Key Issues and Trends* (Nashua, NH: Ivy League Publishing, 1996).

16. DeSanctis (1995).

17. P. Candace Deans, *Global Information Systems and Technology: Focus on the Organization and Its Functional Areas* (Harrisburg, PA: Ideal Group Publishing, 1994).

18. Osborn, Hunt, and Jauch (1984).

19. David A. Nadler and Michael L. Tushman, *Competing by Design: The Power of Organizational Architecture* (New York: Oxford University Press, 1997).

20. David Lei, Michael Hitt, and Richard A. Bettis, "Dynamic Capabilities and Strategic Management," *Journal of Management* 22 (1996): pp. 547–567.

21. Melissa A. Schilling, "Technological Lockout: An Integrative Model of the Economic and Strategic Factors Driving Technological Success and Failure," *Academy of Management Review* 23, No. 2 (1998): 267–284.

22. Jack Veiga and Kathleen Dechant, "Wired World Woes: www.help," *Academy of Management Executive* 11, No. 3 (1997): 73–79.

23. Jaana Woiceshyn, "The Role of Management in the Adoption of Technology: A Longitudinal Investigation," *Technology Studies* 4, No. 1 (1997): 62–99.

24. Janice Beyer, Danta P. Ashmos, and R. N. Osborn, "Contrasts in Enacting TQM: Mechanistic vs Organic Ideology and Implementation," *Journal of Quality Management* 1 (1997): 13–29.

25. Veiga and Dechant (1997).

26. Michael A. Hitt, R. Duane Ireland, and Robert E. Hoskisson, *Strategic Management: Competitiveness and Globalization* (Cincinnati, OH: South-Western College Publishing, 2001).

27. This section is based on R. N. Osborn and J. G. Hunt, "The Environment and Organization Effectiveness," *Administrative Science Quarterly* 19 (1974): 231–246; and Osborn, Hunt, and Jauch (1984).

28. See R. N. Osborn and C. C. Baughn, "New Patterns in the Formation of U.S. Japanese Cooperative Ventures," *Columbia Journal of World Business* 22 (1988): 57–65.

29. R. N. Osborn, *The Evolution of Strategic Alliances in High Technology,* working paper (Detroit: Department of Management, Wayne State University, 2001); and Shawn Tully, "The Modular Corporation," *Fortune* (February 8, 1993).

30. G. Huber, "Organizational Learning: The Contributing Process and the Literature," *Organization Science* 2, No. 1 (1991): 88–115.

31. J. W. Myer and B. Rowan, "Institutionalized Organizations: Formal Structure as Myth and Ceremony," *American Journal of Sociology* 83 (1977): 340–363.

32. Bandura, *Social Learning Theory* (Englewood Cliffs, NJ: Prentice-Hall, 1977).

33. See, for example, A. M. Morrison, R. P. White, and E. Van Velsor, *Breaking the Glass Ceiling* (Reading, MA: Addison-Wesley, 1987); J. D. Zalesny and J. K. Ford, "Extending the Social Information Processing Perspective: New Links to Attitudes, Behaviors and Perceptions," *Organizational Behavior and Human Decision Processes* 47 (1990): 205–246; M. E. Gist, C. Schwoerer, and B. Rosen, "Effects of Alternative Training Methods of Self-Efficacy and Performance in Computer Software Training," *Journal of Applied Psychology* 74 (1989): 884–91; D. D. Sutton and R. W. Woodman, "Pygmalion Goes to Work: The Effects of Supervisor Expectations in a Retail Setting," *Journal of Applied Psychology* 74 (1989): 943–950; M. E. Gist, "The Influence of Training Method on Self-Efficacy and Idea Generation among Managers," *Personnel Psychology* 42 (1989): 787–805.

34. See M. E. Gist, "Self Efficacy: Implications in Organizational Behavior and Human Resource Management," *Academy of Management Review* 12 (1987): 472–485; A. Bandura, "Self Efficacy Mechanisms in Human Agency," *American Psychologist* 37 (1987): 122–147.

35. J. March, *Decisions and Organizations* (Oxford: Basil Blackwell, 1988).

36. R. N. Osborn, and D. H. Jackson, Leaders, "Riverboat Gamblers on Purposeful Unintended Consequences in the Management of Complex Technologies," *Academy of Management Journal* 31 (1988): 924–947.

37. See A. L. Stinchcombe, *Economic Sociology* (New York, Academic Press, 1983).

38. Ibid.

39. Osborn and Jackson (1988).

40. Ibid.

41. O. P. Walsch and G. R. Ungson, "Organization Memory," *Academy of Management Review* 16, No. 1 (1991): 57–91.
42. A. A. Marcus, *Business and Society: Ethics Government and the World of Economy* (Homewood, IL: Richard D. Irwin, 1993).
43. Ibid.

CHAPTER 13

1. For a recent discussion of the resurgence of interest in individuals within organizations, see Jeffery Pfeffer, *The Human Equation: Building Profits by Putting People First* (Boston: Harvard Business School Press, 1998).
2. Edgar Schein, "Organizational Culture," *American Psychologist*, Vol. 45 (1990), pp. 109–119; and E. Schein, *Organizational Culture and Leadership* (San Francisco: Jossey-Bass, 1985).
3. Schein (1990).
4. See www.dellapp.us.dell.com.
5. This example was reported in an interview with Edgar Schein, "Corporate Culture Is the Real Key to Creativity," *Business Month* (May 1989), pp. 73–74.
6. For early work, see T. Deal and A. Kennedy, *Corporate Culture* (Reading, MA: Addison-Wesley, 1982); and T. Peters and R. Waterman, *In Search of Excellence* (New York: Harper & Row, 1982), while more recent studies are summarized in Joanne Martin and Peter Frost, "The Organizational Culture War Games: The Struggle for Intellectual Dominance," in Stewart R. Clegg, Cynthia Hardy, and Walter R. Nord (eds.), *Handbook of Organization Studies* (London: Sage Publications, 1996), pp. 599–621.
7. Schein (1985).
8. For an extended discussion, see J. M. Beyer and H. M. Trice, "How an Organization's Rites Reveal Its Culture," *Organizational Dynamics* (Spring 1987), pp. 27–41.
9. A. Cooke and D. M. Rousseau, "Behavioral Norms and Expectations: A Quantitative Approach to the Assessment of Organizational Culture," *Group and Organizational Studies* 13 (1988), pp. 245–273.
10. Martin and C. Siehl, "Organization Culture and Counterculture," *Organizational Dynamics* 12 (1983), pp. 52–64.
11. Ibid.
12. See R. N. Osborn, "The Aftermath of the Daimler and Detroit," Working Paper, Department of Management, Wayne State University 2001.
13. See Pfeffer (1998).
14. Taylor Cox, Jr., "The Multicultural Organization," *Academy of Management Executive*, Vol. 2, No. 2 (May 1991), pp. 34–47.
15. Carl Quintanilla, "DU-UDE: CEOs, Feeling Out of Touch with Junior Employees, Try to Get 'Within,'" *Wall Street Journal*, (November 10, 1998), p. 1.
16. Schein (1985), pp. 52–57.
17. Peters and Waterman (1982).
18. Schein (1990).
19. H. Gertz, *The Interpretation of Culture* (New York: Basic Books, 1973).
20. Beyer and Trice (1987).
21. *Business Week* (November 23, 1992), p. 117.

22. H. M. Trice and J. M. Beyer, "Studying Organizational Cultures Through Rites and Ceremonials," *Academy of Management Review*, Vol. 3 (1984), pp. 633–669.
23. J. Martin, M. S. Feldman, M. J. Hatch, and S. B. Sitkin, "The Uniqueness Paradox in Organizational Stories," *Administrative Science Quarterly*, Vol. 28 (1983), pp. 438–453.
24. Deal and Kennedy (1982).
25. Osborn and Baughn (1994).
26. R. N. Osborn and D. Jackson, "Leaders, River Boat Gamblers or Purposeful Unintended Consequences," *Academy of Management Journal*, Vol. 31 (1988), pp. 924–947.
27. G. Hofstede and M. H. Bond, "The Confucius Connection: From Cultural Roots to Economic Growth," *Organizational Dynamics*, Vol. 16 (1991): 4–21.
28. This section is based on R. N. Osborn and C. C. Baughn, *An Assessment of the State of the Field of Organizational Design* (Alexandria, VA: U.S. Army Research Institute, 1994).
29. Martin and Frost (1996).
30. Warner Burke, *Organization Development* (Reading, MA: Addison-Wesley, 1987); Wendell L. French and Cecil H. Bell, Jr., *Organization Development*, 4th ed. (Englewood Cliffs, NJ: Prentice-Hall, 1990); Edgar F. Huse and Thomas G. Cummings, *Organization Development and Change*, 4th ed. (St. Paul, MN: West, 1989).
31. Warren Bennis, "Using Our Knowledge of Organizational Behavior," in Lorsch, pp. 29–49.
32. Excellent overviews are found in Cummings and Huse (1989), pp. 32–36, 45; and French and Bell (1990).
33. Richard Beckhard, "The Confrontation Meeting," *Harvard Business Review*, Vol. 45 (March/April 1967), pp. 149–155.
34. See Dale Zand, "Collateral Organization: A New Change Strategy," *Journal of Applied Behavioral Science* 10 (1974): 63–89; Barry A. Stein and Rosabeth Moss Kanter, "Building the Parallel Organization," *Journal of Applied Behavioral Science*, Vol. 16 (1980), pp. 371–386.
35. J. Richard Hackman and Greg R. Oldham, *Work Redesign* (Reading, MA: Addison-Wesley, 1980).

Source Notes

Copyright 1969 by the Regents of the University of California.

Reprinted from *California Management Review* 12, No. 2 (1996), p. 26. Figure 1, by permission of the Regents.

CHAPTER 14

1. See J. P. Kotter, *A Force for Change: How Leadership Differs from Management* (New York: Free Press, 1990).
2. See Bernard M. Bass, *Bass and Stogdill's Handbook of Leadership*, 3rd ed. (New York: Free Press, 1990).
3. See Alan Bryman, *Charisma and Leadership in Organizations* (London: Sage Publications, 1992), Ch. 5.
4. Ralph M. Stogdill, *Handbook of Leadership* (New York: Free Press, 1974).
5. Based on information from Robert J. House and Ram Aditya, "The Social Scientific Study of Leadership: Quo Vadis?" *Journal of Management*, Vol. 23 (1997), pp. 409–474; Shelley A. Kirkpatrick and Edwin A. Locke, "Leadership: Do Traits Matter?" *The Executive*, Vol. 5, No. 2 (1991), pp. 48–60; Gary

Yukl, *Leadership in Organizations,* 3rd ed. (Upper Saddle River, NJ: Prentice-Hall, 1998), Ch. 10.

6. Rensis Likert, *New Patterns of Management* (New York: McGraw-Hill, 1961).

7. Bass, op. cit. Ch. 24.

8. Yukl, op. cit.; George Graen, "Leader-Member Exchange Theory Development: Discussant's Comments," *Academy of Management 1998 Meeting,* San Diego, August 7–12, 1998.

9. Yukl, op. cit.; Peter G. Northouse, *Leadership Theory and Practice* (Thousand Oaks, CA: Sage, 1997), Ch. 7.

10. See M. F. Peterson, "PM Theory in Japan and China: What's in It for the United States?" *Organizational Dynamics* (Spring 1988), pp. 22–39; J. Misumi and M. F. Peterson, "The Performance-Maintenance Theory of Leadership: Review of a Japanese Research Program," *Administrative Science Quarterly,* Vol. 30 (1985), pp. 198–223; P. B. Smith, J. Misumi, M. Tayeb, M. F. Peterson, and M. Bond, "On the Generality of Leadership Style Measures Across Cultures," paper presented at the *International Congress of Applied Psychology,* Jerusalem, July 1986.

11. G. B. Graen and M. Uhl-Bien, "Relationship-Based Approach to Leadership: Development of Leader-Member Exchange (LMX) Theory of Leadership Over 25 Years: Applying a Multi-Level Multi-Domain Perspective," *The Leadership Quarterly,* Vol. 6 (Summer 1995), pp. 219–247.

12. R. J. House and R. Aditya, "The Social Scientific Study of Leadership: Quo Vadis?" *The Journal of Management,* Vol. 23 (1997), pp. 409–474.

13. Kirkpatrick and Locke; Yukl, Ch. 10; J. G. Hunt and G. E. Dodge, "Management in Organizations," *Handbook of Psychology* (Washington, DC: American Psychological Association, 2000).

14. This section is based on Fred E. Fiedler and Martin M. Chemers, *Leadership* (Glenview, IL: Scott-Foresman, 1974).

15. This discussion of cognitive resource theory is based on Fred E. Fiedler and Joseph E. Garcia, *New Approaches in Effective Leadership* (New York: Wiley, 1987).

16. See L. H. Peters, D. D. Harke, and J. T. Pohlmann, "Fiedler's Contingency Theory of Leadership: An Application of the Metaanalysis Procedures of Schmidt and Hunter," *Psychological Bulletin,* Vol. 97 (1985), pp. 274–285.

17. Yukl, op. cit.

18. F. E. Fiedler, M. M. Chemers, and L. Mahar. *Improving Leadership Effectiveness: The Leader Match Concept,* 2nd ed. (New York: Wiley, 1984).

19. For documentation see Fred E. Fiedler and Linda Mahar, The Effectiveness of Contingency Model Training: A Review of the Validation of Leader Match," *Personnel Psychology* (Spring 1979), pp. 45–62; Joseph E. Garcia, Cecil H. Bell, Martin M. Chemers, and Dennis Patrick, "Increasing Mine Productivity and Safety through Management Training and Organization Development: A Comparative Study," *Basic and Applied Social Psychology* (March 1984), pp. 1–18; Arthur G. Jago and James W. Ragan, "The Trouble with Leader Match Is that It Doesn't Match Fiedler's Contingency Model," *Journal of Applied Psychology* (November 1986), pp. 555–559.

20. See Yukl, op. cit.; R. Ayman, M. M. Chemers, and F. E. Fiedler, "The Contingency Model of Leadership Effectiveness: Its Levels of Analysis," *The Leadership Quarterly,* Vol. 6 (Summer 1995), pp. 147–168.

21. This section is based on Robert J. House and Terence R. Mitchell, "Path-Goal Theory of Leadership," *Journal of Contemporary Business* (Autumn 1977), pp. 81–97.

22. House and Mitchell, op. cit.

23. C. A. Schriesheim and L. L. Neider, "Path-Goal Theory: The Long and Winding Road," *The Leadership Quarterly,* Vol. 7 (1996), pp. 317–321; M. G. Evans, "Commentary on R. J. House's Path-Goal Theory of Leader Effectiveness," *The Leadership Quarterly,* Vol. 7 (1996), pp. 305–309.

24. R. J. House, "Path-Goal Theory of Leadership: Lessons, Legacy, and a Reformulated Theory," *The Leadership Quarterly,* Vol. 7 (1996), pp. 323–352.

25. See the discussion of this approach in Paul Hersey and Kenneth H. Blanchard, *Management of Organizational Behavior* (Englewood Cliffs, NJ: Prentice Hall, 1988) and Paul Hersey, Kenneth Blanchard, and Dewey E. Johnson, *Management of Organizational Behavior,* 8th ed. (Upper Saddle River, NJ: Prentice Hall, 2001).

26. R. P. Vecchio and C. Fernandez, "Situational Leadership Theory Revisited," in M. Schnake (ed.), *1995 Southern Management Association Proceedings* (Valdosta, GA: Georgia Southern University 1995), pp. 137–139; Claude L. Graeff, "Evolution of Situational Leadership Theory: A Critical Review," *The Leadership Quarterly,* Vol. 8 (1997), pp. 153–170.

27. The discussion in this section is based on Steven Kerr and John Jermier, "Substitutes for Leadership: Their Meaning and Measurement," *Organizational Behavior and Human Performance,* Vol. 22 (1978), pp. 375–403; Jon P. Howell, David E. Bowen, Peter W. Dorfman, Steven Kerr, and Phillip M. Podsakoff, "Substitutes for Leadership: Effective Alternatives to Ineffective Leadership," *Organizational Dynamics* (Summer 1990), pp. 21–38.

28. Phillip M. Podsakoff, Peter W. Dorfman, Jon P. Howell, and William D. Todor, "Leader Reward and Punishment Behaviors: A Preliminary Test of a Culture-Free Style of Leadership Effectiveness," *Advances in Comparative Management,* Vol. 2 (1989), pp. 95–138; T. K. Peng, "Substitutes for Leadership in an International Setting," unpublished manuscript, College of Business Administration, Texas Tech University (1990); P. M. Podsakoff and S. B. MacKenzie, "Kerr and Jermier's Substitutes for Leadership Model: Background, Empirical Assessment, and Suggestions for Future Research," *The Leadership Quarterly* (1996).

29. See T. R. Mitchell, S. G. Green, and R. E. Wood, "An Attributional Model of Leadership and the Poor Performing Subordinate: Development and Validation," in L. L. Cummings and B. M. Staw (eds.), *Research in Organizational Behavior,* Vol. 3 (Greenwich, CT: JAI Press, 1981), pp. 197–234.

30. James G. Hunt, Kimberly B. Boal, and Ritch L. Sorenson, "Top Management Leadership: Inside the Black Box," *The Leadership Quarterly,* Vol. 1 (1990), pp. 41–65.

31. C. R. Gerstner and D. B. Day, "Cross-cultural Comparison of Leadership Prototypes," *The Leadership Quarterly,* Vol. 5 (1994), pp. 122–134.

32. Hunt, Boal, and Sorenson, op. cit.

33. See J. Pfeffer, "Management as Symbolic Action: The Creation and Maintenance of Organizational Paradigms," in L. L. Cummings and B. M. Staw (eds.), *Research in Organizational Behavior,* Vol. 3 (Greenwich, CT: JAI Press, 1981), pp. 1–52.

34. James R. Meindl, "On Leadership: An Alternative to the Conventional Wisdom," in B. M. Staw and L. L. Cummings (eds.), *Research in Organizational Behavior,* Vol. 12 (Greenwich, CT: JAI Press, 1990), pp. 159–203.

35. Compare with Bryman; also see James G. Hunt and Jay A. Conger (eds.), Special issue, Part 1, *The Leadership Quarterly,* Vol. 10, No. 2 (1999), entire issue.

36. See R. J. House, "A 1976 Theory of Charismatic Leadership," in J. G. Hunt and L. L. Larson (eds.), *Leadership: The Cutting Edge* (Carbondale, IL: Southern Illinois University Press, 1977), pp. 189–207.

37. R. J. House, W. D. Spangler, and J. Woycke, "Personality and Charisma in the U.S. Presidency," *Administrative Science Quarterly,* Vol. 36 (1991), pp. 364–396.

38. R. Pillai and E. A. Williams, "Does Leadership Matter in the Political Arena? Voter Perceptions of Candidates Transformational and Charismatic, Leadership and the 1996 U.S. Presidential Vote," *The Leadership Quarterly.* Vol. 9 (1998), pp. 397–416.

39. See Jane M. Howell and Bruce J. Avolio, "The Ethics of Charismatic Leadership: Submission or Liberation," *Academy of Management Executive,* Vol. 6 (May 1992), pp. 43–54.

40. Jay Conger and Rabindra N. Kanungo, *Charismatic Leadership in Organizations* (San Francisco: Jossey-Bass, 1998).

41. Conger and Kanungo, op. cit.

42. B. Shamir, "Social Distance and Charisma: Theoretical Notes and an Exploratory Study," *The Leadership Quarterly,* Vol. 6 (Spring 1995), pp. 19–48.

43. See B. M. Bass, *Leadership and Performance Beyond Expectations* (New York: Free Press, 1985); A. Bryman, *Charisma and Leadership in Organizations* (London: Sage Publications, 1992), pp. 98–99.

44. B. M. Bass, *A New Paradigm of Leadership* (Alexandria, VA: U.S. Army Research Institute for the Behavioral and Social Sciences, 1996).

45. Bryman, op. cit., Ch. 6; B. M. Bass and B. J. Avolio, "Transformational Leadership: A Response to Critics," in M. M. Chemers and R. Ayman (eds.), *Leadership Theory and Practice: Perspectives and Directions* (San Diego, CA: Academic Press, 1993), pp. 49–80; Kevin B. Lowe, K. Galen Kroeck, and Nagaraj Sivasubramanium, "Effectiveness Correlates of Transformational and Transactional Leadership: A Meta-Analytic Review of the MLQ Literature," *The Leadership Quarterly,* Vol. 7 (1996), pp. 385–426.

46. See Bradley L. Kirman, Kevin B. Lowe, and Dianne P. Young, "The Challenge in High Performance Organizations," *The Journal of Leadership Studies,* Vol. 5, No. 2 (1998), pp. 3–15.

47. Charles C. Mantz and Henry P. Sims, Jr., "Leading Teams to Lead Themselves: The External Leadership of Self-Managed Work Teams," *Administrative Science Quarterly,* Vol. 32 (1987), pp. 106–128; Susan G. Cohen, Lei Chang, and Gerald E. Ledford, Jr., "A Hierarchical Construct of Self-Management Leadership and Its Relation to Quality of Work Life and Perceived Work Group Effectiveness," *Personnel Psychology,* Vol. 50 (1997), pp. 275–308.

48. Manz and Sims, op. cit.

49. Cohen, Chang, and Ledford, op. cit.

50. Bass, *New Paradigm;* Bass and Avolio, op. cit.

51. See Jay A. Conger and Rabindra N. Kanungo, "Training Charismatic Leadership: A Risky and Critical Task," in Jay A. Conger, Rabindra N. Kanungo, and Associates (eds.), *Charismatic Leadership: The Elusive Factor in Organizational Effectiveness* (San Francisco: Jossey-Bass, 1988), Ch. 11.

52. See J. R. Kouzes and B. F. Posner, *The Leadership Challenge: How to Get Extraordinary Things Done in Organizations* (San Francisco: Jossey-Bass, 1991).

53. Marshall Sashkin, "The Visionary Leader," in Conger and Kanungo, *Charismatic Leadership: The Elusive Factor in Organizational Effectiveness,* Ch. 5.

Source Notes

Trait-based information from Robert J. House and Ram Aditye, "The Social Scientific Study of Leadership: Quo Vadis?" *Journal of Management,* Vol. 23 (1987), pp. 405–474; Shelby A. Kirkpatrick and Edwin A. Locke, "Leadership: Do Traits Matter?" *The Executive,* Vol. 5, No. 2 (1991), pp. 48–60; Gary Yukl, *Leadership in Organizations* (Upper Saddle River, NJ: Prentice Hall, 1998), Ch. 10.

Fiedler model based on F. E. Fiedler and M. M. Chemers, *Leadership and Effective Management* (Glenview, IL: Scott, Foresman, 1974).

Path-goal adapted from Richard N. Osborn, James G. Hunt, and Lawrence R. Jauch, *Organization Theory: An Integrated Approach* (New York: Wiley, 1980), p. 464.

From Paul Hersey and Kenneth H. Blanchard, *Management of Organizational Behavior* (Englewood Cliffs, NJ: Prentice Hall, 1988), p. 171. Used by permission.

Based on Steven Kerr and John Jermier, "Substitutes for Leadership: Their Meaning and Measurement," *Organizational Behavior and Human Performance,* Vol. 22 (1978), p. 387; Fred Luthans, *Organizational Behavior,* 6th ed. (New York: McGraw-Hill, 1992), Ch. 10.

Close and Distant based on Boas Shamir, "Social Distance and Charisma: Theoretical Notes and an Exploratory Study," *The Leadership Quarterly,* Vol. 6 (1995), pp. 19–48.

Effective Manager based on B. M. Bass, *Leadership and Performance Beyond Expectations* (New York: Free Press, 1985).

Leader behavior information from Charles C. Manz and Henry P. Sims, "Leading Workers to Lead Themselves: The External Leadership of Self-Managed Work Teams," *Administrative Science Quarterly,* Vol. 32 (1987), pp. 106–128; and Susan G. Cohen, Lei Chang, and Gerald E. Ledford, Jr. "A Hierarchical Construct of Self-Management Leadership and Its Relationship to Quality of Work Life and Perceived Work Group Effectiveness," *Personnel Psychology,* Vol. 50 (1997), pp. 275–308.

Self-Directing Work Teams information from Delphi Packard Electric Systems, Brookhaven Facility, *Summary Managers Network Information Packet* (Lubbock, TX: Center for Productivity and Quality of Work Life, Texas Tech University, May 1995).

Effective Manager information from Jay A. Conger and Rabindra N. Kanungo, "Training Charismatic Leadership: A Risky and Critical Task," In J. A. Conger, R. N. Kanungo and Associates (eds.), *Charismatic Leadership: The Elusive Factor in Organizational Effectiveness* (San Francisco: Jossey-Bass, 1988), Ch 11.

CHAPTER 15

1. See "Microsoft and the Browser Wars," *Seattle Times* (November 18, 1998), pp. C1–3; "ASAP Interview with Bill Gates," *Forbes ASAP* (1992), p. 84; "Identity Crises," *Forbes Magazine* (May 25, 1992), p. 82; "Microsoft Aims Its Arsenal at Networking," *Business Week* (October 12, 1992), pp. 88–89; "The PTC and Microsoft," *Business Week* (December 28, 1992), p. 30; "The PC Wars Are Sweeping into Software," *Business Week* (July 13, 1992), p. 132; Top 10 reasons to get Windows XP Home Edition, www.microsoft.com/windowsxp; Eric Wildstrom, "Microsoft: How it Became Stronger than Ever," businessweek.com/magazine/ content/01-23/63735001.htm.

2. We would like to thank Janice M. Feldbauer, Michael Cakrt, Judy Nixon, and Romuald Stone for their comments on the organization of this chapter and the emphasis on a managerial view of power.

3. Rosabeth Moss Kanter, "Power Failure in Management Circuit," *Harvard Business Review* (July/August 1979): 65–75.

4. John R. P. French and Bertram Raven, "The Bases of Social Power," in Dorwin Cartwright (ed.), *Group Dynamics Research and Theory* (Evanston, IL, Row, Peterson, 1962), pp. 607–623.

5. We have added process, information, and representative.

6. John P. Kotter, "Power, Success, and Organizational Effectiveness," *Organizational Dynamics* 6 (Winter 1978): 27; David A. Whetten and Kim S. Cameron, *Developing Managerial Skills* (Glenview, IL: Scott, Foresman, 1984), pp. 250–259.

7. David Kipinis, Stuart M. Schmidt, Chris Swaffin-Smith, and Ian Wilkinson, Patterns of Managerial Influence: Shotgun Managers, Tacticians, and Bystanders," *Organizational Dynamics* 12 (Winter 1984): 60, 61.

8. Ibid., pp. 58–67; David Kipinis, Stuart M. Schmidt, and Ian Wilkinson, "Intraorganizational Influence Tactics: Explorations in Getting One's Way," *Journal of Applied Psychology* 65 (1980): 440–452.

9. Warren K. Schilit and Edwin A. Locke, "A Study of Upward Influence in Organizations," *Administrative Science Quarterly,* 27 (1982): 304–316.

10. Ibid.

11. Stanley Milgram, "Behavioral Study of Obedience," in Dennis W. Organ (ed.), *The Applied Psychology of Work Behavior* (Dallas: Business Publications, 1978), pp. 384–398. Also see Stanley Milgram, "Behavioral Study of Obedience," *Journal of Abnormal and Social Psychology* 67 (1963): 371–378; Stanley Milgram, "Group Pressure and Action Against a Person," *Journal of Abnormal and Social Psychology* 69 (1964): 137–143; Some Conditions of Obedience and Disobedience to Authority," *Human Relations* 1 (1965): 57–76; Stanley Milgram, *Obedience to Authority* (New York: Harper & Row, 1974).

12. Chester Barnard, *The Functions of the Executive* (Cambridge, MA: Harvard University Press, 1938).

13. Ibid.

14. See Steven N. Brenner and Earl A. Mollander, "Is the Ethics of Business Changing?" *Harvard Business Review* 55 (February 1977): 57–71; Barry Z. Posner and Warren H. Schmidt, "Values and the American Manager: An Update," *California Management Review* 26 (Spring 1984): 202–216.

15. Although the work on organizational politics is not extensive, useful reviews include a chapter in Robert H. Miles, *Macro Organizational Behavior* (Santa Monica, CA: Goodyear, 1980); Bronston T. Mayes and Robert W. Allen, "Toward a Definition of Organizational Politics," *Academy of Management Review* 2 (1977): 672–677; Gerald F. Cavanagh, Dennis J. Moberg, and Manuel Velasquez, "The Ethics of Organizational Politics," *Academy of Management Review* 6 (July 1981): 363–374; Dan Farrell and James C. Petersen, "Patterns of Political Behavior in Organizations," *Academy of Management Review* 7 (July 1982): 403–412; D. L. Madison, R. W. Allen, L. W. Porter, and B. T. Mayes, "Organizational Politics: An Exploration of Managers' Perceptions," *Human Relations* 33 (1980): 92–107.

16. Mayes and Allen, "Toward a Definition of Organizational Politics," p. 675.

17. Jeffrey Pfeffer, *Power in Organizations* (Marshfield, MA: Pitman, 1981), p. 7.

18. Michael Sconcolfi, Anita Raghavan, and Mitchell Pacelle, "All Bets Are Off: How the Salesmanship and Brainpower Failed at Long Term Capital," *Wall Street Journal* (November 16, 1998), pp. 1, 18–19.

19. B. E. Ashforth and R. T. Lee, "Defensive Behavior in Organizations: A Preliminary Mobel," *Human Relations* (July 1990): 621–648; personal communication with Blake Ashforth, December 1998.

20. See Pfeffer (1981); M. M. Harmon and R. T. Mayer, *Organization Theory for Public Administration* (Boston: Little, Brown, 1984); W. Richard Scott, *Organizations: Rational, Natural and Open Systems* (Englewood Cliffs, NJ: Prentice-Hall, 1987).

21. Developed from James L. Hall and Joel L. Leldecker, "A Review of Vertical and Lateral Relations: A New Perspective for Managers," in Patrick Connor (ed.), *Dimensions in Modern Management*, 3rd ed. (Boston: Houghton Mifflin, 1982), pp. 138–146, which was based in part on Leonard Sayles, *Managerial Behavior* (New York: McGraw-Hill, 1964).

22. See Jeffrey Pfeffer, *Organizations and Organization Theory* (Boston: Pitman, 1983); Jeffrey Pfeffer and Gerald R. Salancik, *The External Control of Organizations* (Englewood Cliffs, NJ: Prentice-Hall, 1978).

23. R. N. Osborn, "A Comparison of CEO Pay in Western Europe, Japan and the U.S.," working paper (Detroit: Department of Management, Wayne State University, 1998).

24. Source: Pamela L. Perrewe, Gerald R. Ferris, Dwight D. Frink, and William P. Anthony, "Political Skill: An Antidote for Workplace Stressors," *Academy of Management Executive* 14:3 (2001): 115–120.

25. Amy J. Hillman and Michael A. Hitt, Corporate Political Strategy Formulation: A Model of Approach Participation and Strategy Decisions," *Academy of Management Review* 24:3 (1999): 825–842.

26. Douglas A. Schuler, "Corporate Political Strategy and Foreign Competition: The Case of the Steel Industry," *Academy of Management Journal* 29:3 (1996): 720–732.

27. Op. cit. Hillman and Hitt, 1999.

28. See the early work of James D. Thompson, *Organizations in Action* (New York: McGraw-Hill, 1967) and more recent studies by R. N. Osborn and D. H. Jackson, "Leaders, Riverboat Gamblers, or Purposeful Unintended Consequences in Management of Complex Technologies," *Academy of Management Journal* 31 (1988): 924–974; M. Hector, "When Actors Comply: Monitoring Costs and the Production of Social Order," *Acta Sociologica* 27 (1984): 161–183; T. Mitchell and W. G. Scott, "Leadership Failures, the Distrusting Public and Prospects for the Administrative State," *Public Administration Review* 47 (1987): 445–452.

29. J. J. Jones, *The Downsizing of American Potential* (New York: Raymond Press, 1996).

30. This discussion is based on Cavanagh, Moberg, and Velasquez (1981); and Manuel Velasquez, Dennis J. Moberg, and Gerald Cavanagh, "Organizational Statesmanship and Dirty Politics: Ethical Guidelines for the Organizational Politician," *Organizational Dynamics* 11 (1983): 65–79, both of which offer a fine treatment of the ethics of power and politics.

CHAPTER 16

1. Bill Gates, "Bill Gates' New Rules," *Time* (March 22, 1999), pp. 72–84. This is an excerpt from Bill Gates, *The Speed of Thought: Using a Digital Nervous System* (New York: Warner Books, 1999). See Henry Mintzberg, *The Nature of Managerial Work* (New York: Harper & Row, 1973); Morgan W. McCall, Jr., Ann M. Morrison, and Robert L. Hannan, *Studies of Managerial Work: Results and Methods, Technical Report No. 9* (Greensboro, NC: Center for Creative Leadership, 1978); and John P. Kotter, *The General Managers* (New York: Free Press, 1982).

2. Surveys reported on line at the American Management Association Web site (www.amanet.org): "The Passionate Organization" (September 26–29, 2000) and "Managerial Skills and Competence" (March/April, 2000).

3. Baseline survey reported in Lucent Technologies, *1998 Annual Report.*

4. See Angelo S. DeNisi, and Arraham N. Kluger, "Feedback Effectiveness: Can 360-degree Appraisals Be Improved?" *Academy of Management Executive* 14 (2000): 129–139.

5. See Richard L. Birdwhistell, *Kinesics and Context* (Philadelphia: University of Pennsylvania Press, 1970).

6. Edward T. Hall, *The Hidden Dimension* (Garden City, NY: Doubleday, 1966).

7. See D. E. Campbell, "Interior Office Design and Visitor Response," *Journal of Applied Psychology* 64 (1979): 648–653; P. C. Morrow and J. C. McElroy, "Interior Office Design and Visitor Response: A Constructive Replication," *Journal of Applied Psychology* 66 (1981): 646–650.

8. M. P. Rowe and M. Baker, "Are You Hearing Enough Employee Concerns?" *Harvard Business Review* 62 (May/June 1984): 127–135.

9. This discussion is based on Carl R. Rogers and Richard E. Farson, "Active Listening" (Chicago: Relations Center of the University of Chicago).

10. Modified from an example in ibid.

11. Richard V. Farace, Peter R. Monge, and Hamish M. Russell, *Communicating and Organizing* (Reading, MA: Addison-Wesley, 1977), pp. 97–98.

12. The statements are from *Business Week* (July 6, 1981), p. 107.

13. See A. Mehrabian, *Silent Messages* (Belmont, CA: Wadsworth, 1981).

14. See C. Barnum and N. Woliansky, "Taking Cues from Body Language," *Management Review* 78 (1989): 59; S. Bochner (ed.), *Cultures in Contact: Studies in Cross-Cultural Interaction* (London: Pergamon, 1982); A. Furnham and S. Bocher, *Culture Shock: Psychological Reactions to Unfamiliar Environments* (London: Methuen, 1986); "How Not to Do International Business," *Business Week* (April 12, 1999); Yori Kagegama, "Tokyo Auto Show Highlights," Associated Press (October 24, 2001).

15. See Gary P. Ferraro, "The Need for Linguistic Proficiency in Global Business," *Business Horizons* 39 (May/June, 1966): 39–46.

16. This research is reviewed by John C. Athanassiades, "The Distortion of Upward Communication in Hierarchical Organizations," *Academy of Management Journal* 16 (June 1973): 207–226.

17. F. Lee, "Being Polite and Keeping MUM: How Bad News is Communicated in Organizational Hierarchies," *Journal of Applied Social Psychology* 23 (1993): 1124–1149.

18. Thomas J. Peters and Robert H. Waterman, Jr., *In Search of Excellence* (New York: Harper & Row, 1983).

19. Portions of this section are adapted from John R. Schermerhorn, Jr., *Management*, 5th ed. (New York: Wiley, 1996), pp. 375–378. Used by permission.

20. Networking is considered an essential managerial activity by Kotter (1982).

21. Peters and Waterman (1983).

22. *Business Week* (May 16, 1994), p. 8.

23. The concept of interacting, coacting, and counteracting groups is presented in Fred E. Fiedler, *A Theory of Leadership Productivity* (New York: McGraw-Hill, 1967).

24. Research on communication networks is found in Alex Bavelas, "Communication Patterns in Task-Oriented Groups," *Journal of the Acoustical Society of America* 22 (1950): 725–730. See also "Research on Communication Networks," as summarized in Marvin E. Shaw, *Group Dynamics: The Psychology of Small Group Behavior* (New York: McGraw-Hill, 1976), pp. 137–153.

25. See "e.Biz: What Every CEO Should Know about Electronic Business," *Business Week,* Special Report (March 22, 1999).

26. Information from Alison Overholt, "Intel's Got (Too Much) Mail, *Fortune* (March 2001): 56–58.

27. Deborah Tannen, *Talking 9 to 5* (New York: Avon, 1995).

28. Deborah Tannen, *You Just Don't Understand: Women and Men in Conversation* (New York: Ballantine Books, 1991).

29. Deborah Tannen, "The Power of Talk: Who Gets Heard and Why," *Harvard Business Review* (September/October, 1995): 138–148.

30. Reported by *Working Woman* (November 1995), p. 14.

31. Ibid.

32. For an editorial opinion, see Jayne Tear, "They Just Don't Understand Gender Dynamics," *Wall Street Journal* (November 20, 1995), p. A14.

33. Reported in "Big Brother Inc.," www.pccomputing.com (March 2000), p. 88. See "My Boss, Big Brother," *Business Week* (January 22, 1996), p. 56.

CHAPTER 17

1. We would like to thank A. Levi for his critical comments on this chapter.

2. For concise overviews, see Susan J. Miller, David J. Hickson, and David C. Wilson, "Decision-Making in Organizations," in Stewart R. Clegg, Cynthia Hardy, and Walter R. Nord (eds.), *Handbook of Organizational Studies* (London: Sage Publications, 1996), pp. 293–312; George P. Huber, *Managerial Decision Making* (Glenview, IL: Scott, Foresman, 1980).

3. This section is based on Michael D. Choen, James G. March, and Johan P. Olsen, "The Garbage Can Model of Organizational Choice," *Administrative Science Quarterly* 17 (1972): 1–25 and James G. March and Herbert A. Simon, *Organizations* (New York: Wiley, 1958), pp. 137–142.

4. See KPMG, "Enterprise Risk Management Services," www.kpmg.com.

5. This traditional distinction is often attributed to Herbert Simon, *Administrative Behavior* (New York: Free Press, 1945), but an available source is Herbert Simon, *The New Science of Management Decision* (New York: Harper & Row, 1960).

6. Ibid.

7. Also see Mary Zey (ed.), *Decision Making: Alternatives to Rational Choice Models* (Thousand Oaks, CA: Sage Publications, 1992).

8. Simon, *Administrative Behavior*.

9. For discussions, see Cohen, March, and Olsen (1972); Miller, Hickson, and Wilson (1996); and Michael Masuch and Perry LaPontin, "Beyond Garbage Cans: An AI Model of Organizational Choice," *Administrative Science Quarterly* 34 (1989): 38–67.

10. Weston H. Agor, *Intuition in Organizations* (Newbury Park, CA: Sage Publications, 1989).

11. Henry Mintzberg, "Planning on the Left Side and Managing on the Right," *Harvard Business Review* 54 (July/August 1976): 51–63.

12. See Weston H. Agor, "How Top Executives Use Their Intuition to Make Important Decisions," *Business Horizons* 29 (January/February 1986): 49–53; and Agor (1989).

13. The classic work in this area is found in a series of articles by D. Kahneman and A. Tversky, "Subjective Probability: A Judgment of Representativeness," *Cognitive Psychology* 3 (1972): 430–454; "On the Psychology of Prediction," *Psychological Review* 80 (1973): 237–251; "Prospect Theory: An Analysis of Decision under Risk," *Econometrica* 47 (1979): 263–291; "Psychology of Preferences," *Scientific American* (1982): 161–173; "Choices, Values, Frames," *American Psychologist* 39 (1984): 341–350.

14. Definitions and subsequent discussion based on Max H. Bazerman, *Judgment in Managerial Decision Making*, 3rd ed. (New York: Wiley, 1994).

15. Cameron M. Ford and Dennis A. Gioia, *Creative Action in Organizations* (Thousand Oaks, CA: Sage Publications, 1995).

16. G. Wallas, *The Art of Thought* (New York: Harcourt, 1926). Cited in Bazerman (1994).

17. E. Glassman, "Creative Problem Solving," *Supervisory Management* (January 1989): 21–26; and B. Kabanoff and J. R. Rossiter, "Recent Developments in Applied Creativity," *International Review of Industrial and Organizational Psychology* 9 (1994): 283–324.

18. Information from Kenneth Labich, "Nike vs. Reebok," *Fortune* (September 18, 1995), pp. 90–106.

19. James A. F. Stoner, *Management*, 2nd ed. (Englewood Cliffs, NJ: Prentice-Hall, 1982), pp. 167–168.

20. Paul C. Nutt, "Surprising but True: Half the Discussions in Organizations Fail," *Academy of Management Executive* 13:4 (1999): 75–90.

21. Ibid.

22. Victor H. Vroom and Philip W. Yetton, *Leadership and Decision Making* (Pittsburgh: University of Pittsburgh Press, 1973); Victor H. Vroom and Arthur G. Jago, *The New Leadership* (Englewood Cliffs, NJ: Prentice-Hall, 1988).

23. Barry M. Staw, "The Escalation of Commitment to a Course of Action," *Academy of Management Review* 6 (1981): 577–587; Barry M. Staw and Jerry Ross, "Knowing When to Pull the Plug," *Harvard Business Review* 65 (March/April 1987): 68–74. See also Glen Whyte, "Escalating Commitment to a Course of Action: A Reinterpretation," *Academy of Management Review* 11 (1986): 311–321.

24. Joel Brockner, "The Escalation of Commitment to a Failing Course of Action: Toward Theoretical Progress," *Academy of Management Review* 17 (1992): 39–61; J. Ross and B. M. Staw, "Organizational Escalation and Exit: Lessons from the Shoreham Nuclear Power Plant," *Academy of Management Journal* 36 (1993): 701–732.

25. Bazerman (1994), pp. 79–83.

26. See Brockner (1992); Ross and Staw (1993); and J. Z. Rubin, "Negotiation: An Introduction to Some Issues and Themes," *American Behavioral Scientist* 27 (1983): 135–147.

27. See "Computers That Think Are Almost Here," *Business Week* (July 17, 1995): 68–73.

28. A. R. Dinnis and J. S. Valacich, "Computer Brainstorms: Two Heads Are Better Than One," *Journal of Applied Psychology* (February 1994): 77–86.

29. For an expanded discussion of such ethical frameworks for decision making, see Linda A. Travino and Katherine A. Nelson, *Managing Business Ethics* (New York: Wiley, 1995).

30. B. Kabanoff and J. R. Rossiter, "Recent Developments in Applied Creativity," *International Review of Industrial and Organizational Psychology* 9 (1994): 283–324.

31. Fons Trompenaars, *Riding the Waves of Culture: Understanding Cultural Diversity in Business* (London: Nicholas Brealey Publishing, 1993), p. 6.

32. See ibid., pp. 58–59.

33. For a good discussion of decision making in Japanese organizations, see Min Chen, *Asian Management Systems* (New York: Routledge, 1995).

34. Nancy J. Adler, *International Dimensions of Organizational Behavior,* 2nd ed. (Boston: PWS-Kent, 1991).

35. See Miller, Hickson, and Wilson (1996).

36. We would like to thank Kristi M. Lewis for emphasizing the importance of identifying criteria and weighing criteria and urging us to include this section on ethics.

37. Stephen Fineman, "Emotion and Organizing," in Clegg, Hardy, and Nord, *Handbook of Organizational Studies,* pp. 542–580.

38. For an expanded discussion of ethical frameworks for decision making, see Linda A. Travino and Katherine A. Nelson, *Managing Business Ethics* (New York: Wiley, 1995); Saul W. Gellerman, "Why 'Good' Managers Make Bad Ethical Choices," *Harvard Business Review* 64 (July/August 1986): 85–90 and Barbara Ley Toffler, *Tough Choices: Managers Talk Ethics* (New York: Wiley, 1986).

Source Notes

S.S. Harrington, "What Corporate America is Teaching About Ethics," *Academy of Management & Education 11* (1991): 21–30; Don Hellreigel, John Slocum and Richard Woodman *Organizational Behavior* (Minneapolis: West Publishing, 1999).

Reprinted from Victor H. Vroom and Arthur G. Jago, *The New Leadership* (Englewood Cliffs, NJ: Prentice-Hall, 1988), p. 184. Used by permission of the authors.

CHAPTER 18

1. Information from "From 'Blank Looks' to Blank Checks," *Business Week Enterprise* (December 7, 1998), pp. Ent 18–20; Organization Web site: www.capitalacrossamerica.org.

2. See, for example, Henry Mintzberg, *The Nature of Managerial Work* (New York: Harper & Row, 1973); and John R.P. Kotter, *The General Managers* (New York: Free Press, 1982).

3. One of the classic discussions is by Richard E. Walton, *Interpersonal Peacemaking: Confrontations and Third-Party Consultation* (Reading, MA: Addison-Wesley, 1969).

4. Kenneth W. Thomas and Warren H. Schmidt, "A Survey of Managerial Interests with Respect to Conflict," *Academy of Management Journal* 19 (1976): 315–318.

5. For a good overview see Richard E. Walton, *Managing Conflict: Interpersonal Dialogue and Third Party Roles,* 2nd ed. (Reading, MA: Addison-Wesley, 1987) and Dean Tjosvold, *The Conflict-Positive Organization: Stimulate Diversity and Create Unity* (Reading, MA: Addison-Wesley, 1991).

6. Walton (1969).

7. Ibid.

8. Richard E. Walton and John M. Dutton, "The Management of Interdepartmental Conflict: A Model and Review," *Administrative Science Quarterly* 14 (1969): 73–84.

9. Geert Hofstede, *Culture's Consequences: International Differences in Work-Related Values* (Beverly Hills: CA: Sage Publications, 1980), and Geert Hofstede, "Cultural Constraints in Management Theories," *Academy of Management Executive* 7 (1993): 81–94.

10. These stages are consistent with the conflict models described by Alan C. Filley, *Interpersonal Conflict Resolution* (Glenview, IL: Scott, Foresman, 1975); and Louis R. Pondy, "Organizational Conflict: Concepts and Models," *Administrative Science Quarterly* 12 (September 1967): 269–320.

11. Information from "Capitalizing on Diversity: Navigating the Seas of the Multicultural Workforce and Workplace," *Business Week,* Special Advertising Section (December 4, 1998).

12. Walton and Dutton (1969).

13. Rensis Likert and Jane B. Likert, *New Ways of Managing Conflict* (New York: McGraw-Hill, 1976).

14. See Jay Galbraith, *Designing Complex Organizations* (Reading, MA: Addison-Wesley, 1973); David Nadler and Michael Tushman, *Strategic Organizational Design* (Glenview, IL: Scott, Foresman, 1988).

15. E. M. Eisenberg and M. G. Witten, "Reconsidering Openness in Organizational Communication," *Academy of Management Review* 12 (1987): 418–426.

16. R. G. Lord and M. C. Kernan, "Scripts as Determinants of Purposeful Behavior in Organizations," *Academy of Management Review* 12 (1987): 265–277.

17. See Filley (1975); and L. David Brown, *Managing Conflict at Organizational Interfaces* (Reading, MA: Addison-Wesley, 1983).

18. Ibid., pp. 27, 29.

19. For discussions, see Robert R. Blake and Jane Strygley Mouton, "The Fifth Achievement," *Journal of Applied Behavioral Science* 6 (1970): 413–427; Kenneth Thomas, "Conflict and Conflict Management," in M. D. Dunnett (ed.), *Handbook of Industrial and Organizational Behavior* (Chicago: Rand McNally, 1976), pp. 889–935; and Kenneth W. Thomas, "Toward Multi-Dimensional Values in Teaching: The Examples of Conflict Behaviors," *Academy of Management Review* 2 (1977): 484–490.

20. For an excellent overview, see Roger Fisher and William Ury, *Getting to Yes: Negotiating Agreement Without Giving In* (New York: Penguin, 1983). See also James A. Wall, Jr., Negotiation: Theory and Practice (Glenview, IL: Scott, Foresman, 1985).

21. Roy J. Lewicki and Joseph A. Litterer, *Negotiation* (Homewood, IL: Irwin, 1985), pp. 315–319.

22. Ibid., pp. 328–329.

23. Following discussion is based on Fisher and Ury (1983); and Lewicki and Litterer (1985).

24. This example is developed from Max H. Bazerman, *Judgment in Managerial Decision Making,* 2nd ed. (New York: Wiley, 1991), pp. 106–108.

25. For a detailed discussion, see Fisher and Ury (1983), and Lewicki and Litterer (1985).

26. Developed from Bazerman (1991), pp. 127–141.

27. Fisher and Ury (1983), p. 33.

28. Lewicki and Litterer (1985), pp. 177–181.

CHAPTER 19

1. Michael Beer and Nitin Mitra, "Cracking the Code of Change," *Harvard Business Review* (May/June, 2000), p. 133.

2. Tom Peters, *Thriving on Chaos* (New York: Random House, 1987); Tom Peters, "Managing in a World Gone Bonkers," *World Executive Digest* (February 1993), pp. 26–29; and Tom Peters, *The Circle of Innovation* (New York: Alfred A. Knopf, 1997).

3. See David Nadler and Michael Tushman, *Strategic Organizational Design* (Glenview, IL: Scott, Foresman, 1988);

and Noel M. Tichy, "Revolutionize Your Company," *Fortune* (December 13, 1993), pp. 114–118.

4. Jerry I. Porras and Robert C. Silvers, "Organization Development and Transformation," *Annual Review of Psychology,* Vol. 42 (1991), pp. 51–78.

5. The classic description of organizations on these terms is by Harold J. Leavitt, "Applied Organizational Change in Industry: Structural, Technological and Humanistic Approaches," in James G. March (ed.), *Handbook of Organizations* (Chicago: Rand McNally, 1965). This application is developed from Robert A. Cooke, "Managing Change in Organizations," in Gerald Zaltman (ed.), *Management Principles for Nonprofit Organizations* (New York: American Management Association, 1979). See also David A. Nadler, "The Effective Management of Organizational Change," in Jay W. Lorsch (ed.), *Handbook of Organizational Behavior* (Englewood Cliffs, NJ: Prentice-Hall, 1987), pp. 358–369.

6. Beer and Mitra (2000), op cit., p. 133.

7. John P. Kotter, "Why Transformation Efforts Fail," *Harvard Business Review* (March/April, 1995), pp. 59–67.

8. Kurt Lewin, "Group Decision and Social Change," in G. E. Swanson, T. M. Newcomb, and E. L. Hartley (eds.), *Readings in Social Psychology* (New York: Holt, Rinehart & Winston, 1952), pp. 459–473.

9. Tichy and Devanna (1986), p. 44.

10. The change strategies are described in Robert Chin and Kenneth D. Benne, "General Strategies for Effecting Changes in Human Systems," in Warren G. Bennis, Kenneth D. Benne, Robert Chin, and Kenneth E. Corey (eds.), *The Planning of Change*, 3rd ed. (New York: Holt, Rinehart & Winston, 1969), pp. 22–45.

11. Example developed from an exercise reported in J. William Pfeiffer and John E. Jones, *A Handbook of Structural Experiences for Human Relations Training*, Vol. II (La Jolla, CA: University Associates, 1973).

12. Ibid.

13. Ibid.

14. Donald Klein, "Some Notes on the Dynamics of Resistance to Change: The Defender Role," in Bennis et al. (eds.), *The Planning of Change* (1969), pp. 117–124.

15. See Everett M. Rogers, *Communication of Innovations*, 3rd ed. (New York: Free Press, 1993).

16. Ibid.

17. John P. Kotter and Leonard A. Schlesinger, "Choosing Strategies for Change," *Harvard Business Review*, Vol. 57 (March/April 1979), pp. 109–112.

18. A classic work in this area is Peter F. Drucker, *Innovation and Entrepreneurship* (New York: Harper, 1985).

19. Edward B. Roberts, "Managing Invention and Innovation," *Research Technology Management* (January/February 1988), pp. 1–19. For an extensive case study, see John Clark, *Managing Innovation and Change* (Thousand Oaks, CA: Sage Publications, 1995). For a comprehensive update on innovation in industry, see "Innovation in Industry," *The Economist* (February 20, 1999), pp. 5–18.

20. Quotes from Kenneth Labich, "The Innovators," *Fortune* (June 6, 1988), pp. 49–64.

21. Arthur P. Brief, Randall S. Schuler, and Mary Van Sell, *Managing Job Stress* (Boston: Little, Brown, 1981).

22. A review of research is available in Steve M. Jex, *Stress and Job Performance* (Thousand Oaks, CA: Sage, 1998).

23. "Couples Dismayed at Long Workdays, New Study Finds," *Columbus Dispatch* (January 23, 1999), p. 5A.

24. See Orlando Behling and Arthur L. Darrow, *Managing Work-Related Stress* (Chicago: Science Research Associates, 1984).

25. Meyer Friedman and Ray Roseman, *Type A Behavior and Your Heart* (New York: Alfred A. Knopf, 1974).

26. See H. Selye, *The Stress of Life,* rev. ed. (New York: McGraw-Hill, 1976).

27. Jeffrey Pfeffer, *The Human Equation: Building Profits by Putting People First* (Boston: Harvard Business School Press, 1998).

28. Quotes are from Alan M. Webber, "Danger: Toxic Company," *Fast Company* (November 1998), p. 152.

29. See John D. Adams, "Health, Stress, and the Manager's Life Style," *Group and Organization Studies*, Vol. 6 (September 1981), pp. 291–301.

30. Information from Mike Pramik, "Wellness Programs Give Businesses Healthy Bottom Line," *Columbus Dispatch* (January 18, 1999), pp. 10–11.

31. Ibid.

32. Pfeffer (1998).

SUPPLEMENTAL MODULE

1. C. William Emory, *Business Research Methods*, rev. ed. (Homewood, IL: Irwin, 1980).

2. John B. Miner, *Theories of Organizational Behavior* (Hillsdale: Dryden Press, 1980).

3. See Richard L. Daft, "Learning the Craft of Organizational Research," *Academy of Management Review* Vol. 8 (October 1983), pp. 539–546; Eugene Stone, *Research Methods in Organizational Behavior* (Santa Monica, CA: Goodyear, 1978), p. 21.

4. Stone, op. cit. (1978), p. 26.

5. Duane Davis and Robert M. Casenza, *Business Research for Decision Making* (Belmont, CA: Wadsworth, 1993), p. 134.

6. Davis and Casenza, op. cit. (1993), Ch. 5.

7. Davis and Casenza, op. cit. (1993).

8. Davis and Casenza, op. cit. (1993), p. 174.

9. Davis and Casenza, op. cit. (1993), p. 125.

10. This section based on Davis and Casenza, op. cit. (1993), Ch. 5.

11. This section based on Stone, op. cit. (1978).

12. See G. Pinchot, *Intrapreneuring* (New York: Harper, 1985).

13. See A. D. Aczel, *Complete Business Statistics* (Homewood, IL: Irwin, 1989) for further discussion.

14. Davis and Casenza, op. cit. (1993).

15. Davis and Casenza, op. cit. (1993), Ch. 14.

Glossary

Ability   A person's existing capacity to perform the various tasks needed for a given job.

Accommodation or **smoothing**   Involves playing down differences and finding areas of agreement.

Achievement-oriented leadership   Emphasizes setting challenging goals, stressing excellence in performance, and showing confidence in people's ability to achieve high standards of performance.

Action research   The process of systematically collecting data on an organization, feeding it back for action planning, and evaluating results by collecting and reflecting on more data.

Active listening   Encouraging people to say what they really mean.

Adhocracy   An organizational structure that emphasizes shared, decentralized decision making; extreme horizontal specialization; few levels of management; the virtual absence of formal controls; and few rules, policies, and procedures.

Affective component   The component of an attitude that reflects the specific feelings regarding the personal impact of the antecedents.

Anchoring and adjustment heuristic   Bases a decision on incremental adjustments to an initial value determined by historical precedent or some reference point.

Aptitude   The capability of learning something.

Arbitration   When a neutral third party acts as judge with the power to issue a decision binding on all parties.

Artificial intelligence (AI)   Studies how computers can be programmed to think like the human brain.

Associative choices   Decisions which can be loosely linked to nagging continual problems but which were not specifically developed to solve the problem.

Attitude   Predisposition to respond in a positive or negative way to someone or something in one's environment.

Attribution theory   The attempt to understand the cause of an event, assess responsibility for outcomes of the event, and assess the personal qualities of the people involved.

Authoritarianism   The tendency to adhere rigidly to conventional values and to obey recognized authority.

Authoritative command   Uses formal authority to end conflict.

Authority decisions   Made by the manager or team leader without involving others using information he or she possesses.

Automation   Allows machines to do work previously accomplished by people.

Availability heuristic   Bases a decision on recent events relating to the situation at hand.

Avoidance   Involves pretending the conflict does not really exist.

Bargaining zone   The zone between one party's minimum reservation point and the other party's maximum reservation point in a negotiating situation.

Behavioral component   An intention to behave in a certain way based on a person's specific feelings or attitudes.

Behavioral decision theory   Views decision makers as acting only in terms of what they perceive about a given situation.

Behaviorally anchored rating scales (BARS)   A performance appraisal approach that describes observable job behaviors, each of which is evaluated to determine good versus bad performance.

Behavioral perspective   Assumes that leadership is central to performance and other outcomes.

Beliefs   Ideas about someone or something and the conclusions people draw about them.

Benefit cycle   A pattern of successful adjustment followed by further improvements.

Brainstorming   Generating ideas through "freewheeling" discussion and without criticism.

Bureaucracy An ideal form of organization whose characteristics were defined by the German sociologist Max Weber.

Case study An in-depth analysis of one or a small number of settings.

Career planning Creates long-term congruence between individual goals and organizational career opportunities.

Career planning and development Working with managers and/or HR experts on career issues.

Career plateau A position from which someone is unlikely to move or advance to a higher level of responsibility.

Career stages Different points of work responsibility and achievement through which people pass during the course of their work lives.

Causality The assumption that change in the independent variable has caused change in the dependent variable.

Cellular form An organizational structure that emphasizes quasi-independent clusters of self-organizing components.

Central tendency error Occurs when managers lump everyone together around the average, or middle, category.

Centralization The degree to which the authority to make decisions is restricted to higher levels of management.

Centralized communication networks Networks that link group members through a central control point.

Certain environments Provide full information on the expected results for decision-making alternatives.

Change agents People who take action to change the behavior of people and systems.

Changing The stage in which specific actions are taken to create a change.

Channels The pathways through which messages are communicated.

Charismatic leaders Those leaders who, by force of their personal abilities, are capable of having a profound and extraordinary effect on followers.

Classical conditioning A form of learning through association that involves the manipulation of stimuli to influence behavior.

Classical decision theory Views decision makers as acting only in terms of what they perceive about a given situation.

Coercive power The extent to which a manager can use the "right of command" to control other people.

Cognitive components The components of an attitude that are the beliefs, opinions, knowledge, or information a person possesses.

Cognitive dissonance Describes a state of inconsistency between an individual's attitude and behavior.

Collaboration Involves recognition that something is wrong and needs attention through problem solving.

Communication The process of sending and receiving symbols with attached meanings.

Communication channels The pathways through which messages are communicated.

Competition Seeks victory by force, superior skill, or domination.

Compressed work week A work schedule that allows a full-time job to be completed in less than five full workdays.

Compromise Occurs when each party involved in a conflict gives up something of value to the other.

Conceptual skill The ability to analyze and solve complex problems.

Confirmation trap The tendency to seek confirmation for what is already thought to be true, and to not search for disconfirming information.

Conflict Occurs when parties disagree over substantive issues or when emotional antagonisms create friction between them.

Conflict resolution Occurs when the reasons for a conflict are eliminated.

Confrontation meeting An OD intervention designed to help determine how an organization might be improved and to start action toward such improvement.

Conglomerates Firms that own several different unrelated businesses.

Consensus A group decision that has the expressed support of most members.

Consideration A highly considerate leader is sensitive to people's feelings and tries to make things pleasant for the followers.

Constructive stress Stress that has a positive impact on attitudes and performance.

Consultative decisions Decisions made by one individual after seeking input from or consulting with members of a group.

Content theories Profile different needs that may motivate individual behavior.

Contingency approach Seeks ways to meet the needs of different management situations.

Continuous improvement The belief that anything and everything done in the workplace should be continually improved.

Continuous reinforcement A reinforcement schedule that administers a reward each time a desired behavior occurs.

Contrast effects Occur when an individual's characteristics are contrasted with those of others recently encountered who rank higher or lower on the same characteristics.

Control The set of mechanisms used to keep actions and outputs within predetermined limits.

Controlling Monitoring performance and taking any needed corrective action.

Coordination The set of mechanisms used in an organization to link the actions of its subunits into a consistent pattern.

Countercultures Patterns of values and philosophies that outwardly reject those of the larger organization or social system.

Creativity Generates unique and novel responses to problems and opportunities.

Critical incident diary A method of performance appraisal that records incidents of unusual success or failure in a given performance aspect.

Cross-functional team Brings together persons from different functions to work on a common task.

Cultural relativism The suggestion that ethical behavior is determined by its cultural context.

Cultural symbol Any object, act, or event that serves to transmit cultural meaning.

Culture The learned and shared ways of thinking and acting among a group of people or society.

Decentralization The degree to which the authority to make decisions is given to lower levels in an organization's hierarchy.

Decentralized communication networks Networks that link all group members directly with one another.

Decision making The process of choosing a course of action to deal with a problem.

Deficit cycle A pattern of deteriorating performance that is followed by even further deterioration.

Delphi technique Involves generating decision making alternatives through a series of survey questionnaires.

Demographic characteristics Background variables (e.g., age, gender) that help shape what a person becomes over time.

Destructive stress Stress that has a negative impact on both attitudes and performance.

Developmental approaches Systematic models of ways in which personality develops across time.

Directive leadership Spells out the what and how of subordinates' tasks.

Distributed leadership The sharing of responsibility for meeting group task and maintenance needs.

Distributive justice The degree to which all people are treated the same under a policy.

Distributive negotiation Negotiation in which the focus is on positions staked out or declared by the parties involved who are each trying to claim certain portions of the available pie.

Diversity-consensus dilemma The tendency for diversity in groups to create process difficulties even as it offers improved potential for problem solving.

Divisional departmentation The grouping of individuals and resources by product, territories, services, clients, or legal entities.

Dogmatism Leads a person to see the world as a threatening place and regard authority as absolute.

Domestic multiculturalism Cultural diversity within a national population.

Dysfunctional conflict Works to the group's or organization's disadvantage.

E-corporation Utilizes the Internet and information technologies to support enterprisewide computer integration of all aspects of operations.

Effective communication When the intended meaning equals the perceived meaning.

Effective groups Groups that achieve high levels of task performance, member satisfaction, and team viability.

Effective manager Leader of a team that consistently achieves high performance goals.

Efficient communication Communication that is low cost in its use of resources.

Electronic commerce Where business is transacted through the Internet.

Emotional adjustment traits These traits measure how much an individual experiences emotional distress or displays unacceptable acts.

Emotional conflict Conflict that involves interpersonal difficulties that arise over feelings of anger, mistrust, dislike, fear, resentment, and the like.

Employee involvement The amount of decision making delegated to employees.

Employee involvement teams Members of such teams meet regularly to examine work-related problems and opportunities.

Empowerment The process that allows individuals and groups to make decisions affecting themselves and their work.

Environmental complexity   The magnitude of the problems and opportunities in the organization's environment as evidenced by the degree of richness, interdependence, and uncertainty.

Equity theory   Adams' theory, which posits that people will act to eliminate any felt inequity in the rewards received for their work in comparison with others.

ERG theory   Alderfer's theory, which identifies existence, relatedness, and growth needs.

Escalating commitment   The tendency to continue a previously chosen course of action even when feedback suggests that it is failing.

ESOPs   Like profit sharing, ESOPs are based on the total organization's performance, but measured in terms of stock price.

Ethical absolutism   Assumption that a single moral standard applies to all cultures.

Ethical behavior   Behavior that is morally accepted as "good" and "right."

Ethical dilemmas   Situations that require a person to choose among actions that offer possible benefits while also violating ethical standards.

Existence needs   Desires for physiological and material well-being.

Expatriate   A person who works and lives in a foreign country for an extended time.

Expectancy   The probability that work effort will be followed by performance accomplishment.

Expectancy theory   Vroom's theory that argues that work motivation is determined by individual beliefs regarding effort/performance relationships and work outcomes.

Expert power   The ability to control another's behavior because of the possession of knowledge, experience, or judgment that the other person does not have but needs.

External adaptation   Reaching goals and dealing with outsiders. Issues concerned are the tasks to be accomplished, the methods used to achieve the goals, and methods of coping with success and failure.

Extinction   The withdrawal of the reinforcing consequences for a given behavior.

Extrinsic rewards   Rewards given to the individual by some other person in the work setting.

Feedback   The process of communicating how one feels about something another person has done or said.

Field survey   A research design that relies on the use of some form of questionnaire for the primary purpose of describing and/or predicting some phenomenon.

FIRO-B theory   Examines differences in how people relate to one another based on their needs to express and receive feelings of inclusion, control, and affection.

Flexible benefit plans   Pay systems that allow workers to select benefits according to their individual needs.

Flexible manufacturing system   Uses adaptive technology and integrated job designs to easily shift production among alternative products.

Flexible working hours   Work schedules that give employees some daily choice in scheduling arrival and departure times from work.

Forced distribution   A method of performance appraisal that uses a small number of performance categories, such as "very good," "good," "adequate," and "very poor" and forces a certain proportion of people into each.

Formal channels   Communication pathways that follow the official chain of command.

Formal groups   Officially designated groups for a specific organizational purpose.

Formalization   The written documentation of work rules, policies, and procedures.

Functional conflict   Results in positive benefits to the group.

Functional departmentation   The grouping of individuals by skill, knowledge, and action yields.

Functional silos problem   When persons working in different functions fail to communicate and interact with one another.

Fundamental attribution error   The tendency to underestimate the influence of situational factors and to overestimate the influence of personal factors in evaluating someone else's behavior.

Gain sharing   A pay system that links pay and performance by giving the workers the opportunity to share in productivity gains through increased earnings.

Garbage can model   Views the main components of the choice process—problems, solutions, participants, and choice situations—as all mixed up together in the garbage can of the organization.

Generation X (Gold-Collar) workers   Workers born between 1965 and 1977 who are knowledge workers in short supply.

Glass ceiling effect   A hidden barrier limiting advancement of women and minorities in organizations.

Globalization   Involves growing worldwide interdependence of resource suppliers, product markets, and business competition.

Global manager   A manager who has the international awareness and cultural sensitivity needed to work well across national borders.

Global organizational learning   The ability to gather from the world at large the knowledge required for long-term organizational adaptation.

Goal setting   The process of developing and setting motivational performance objectives.

Grafting   The process of acquiring individuals, units, and/or firms to bring in useful knowledge to the organization.

Grapevine   The network of friendships and acquaintances that transfers information.

Graphic rating scale   A scale that lists a variety of dimensions thought to be related to high performance outcomes in a given job and that one is expected to exhibit.

Greenfield sites   Those HPO sites started from scratch at a new site.

Group decisions   Decisions that are made by all members of the group.

Group dynamics   The forces operating in groups that affect the ways members work together.

Groups   Involves two or more people working together regularly to achieve common goals.

Groupthink   The tendency of cohesive group members to lose their critical evaluative capabilities.

Growth needs   Desires for continued personal growth and development.

Halo effect   Occurs when one attribute of a person or situation is used to develop an overall impression of the person or situation.

Halo error   Results when one person rates another person on several different dimensions and gives a similar rating for each one.

Heuristics   Simplifying strategies or "rules of thumb" used to make decisions.

Hierarchy of needs theory   Maslow's theory that offers a pyramid of physiological, safety, social, esteem, and self-actualization needs.

High-context cultures   Words convey only part of a message, while the rest of the message must be inferred from body language and additional contextual cues.

Higher-order needs   Esteem and self-actualization in Maslow's hierarchy.

High performance organization (HPO)   An organization that is intentionally designed to bring out the best in people and produce sustainable organizational results.

Hindsight trap   A tendency to overestimate the degree to which an event that has already taken place could have been predicted.

Horizontal specialization   A division of labor through the formation of work units or groups within an organization.

House's path-goal theory of leadership   Assumes that a leader's key function is to adjust his or her behaviors to complement situational contingencies.

HPO islands   Those HPO units engulfed by organizations or units that do not function as HPOs and may even be opposed to them.

Human resource strategic planning   The process of hiring capable, motivated people to carry out the organization's mission and strategy.

Human resources   The people who do the work that helps organizations fulfill their missions.

Human skill   The ability to work well with other people.

Hygiene factors   Factors in a job context, the work setting, that promote job dissatisfaction.

Individualism-collectivism   The tendency of a culture's members to emphasize individual self-interests or group relationships.

Influence   A behavioral response to the exercise of power.

Informal channels   Do not follow the chain of command.

Informal groups   Unofficial groups that emerge to serve special interests.

Information power   Access to and/or control of information.

Information technology   The combination of machines, artifacts, procedures and systems used to gather, store, analyze, and disseminate information to translate it into knowledge.

Initiating structure   This kind of leader is concerned with spelling out the task requirements

Innovation   The process of creating new ideas and putting them in practice.

Instrumental values   Values that reflect a person's beliefs about the means for achieving desired ends.

Instrumentality   The probability that performance will lead to various work outcomes.

Integrated production technologies   Focus on providing flexibility in manufacturing and services and involve job design and information systems as part of the technology.

Integrative negotiation   Negotiation in which the focus is on the merits of the issues, and the parties involved try to enlarge the available "pie" rather than stake claims to certain portions of it.

Intellectual capital   The sum total of knowledge, expertise, and energy available from organizational members.

Interactional justice   The degree to which people are treated with dignity and respect.

Interfirm alliances   Announced cooperative agreements of joint ventures between two independent firms.

Intergroup conflict   Occurs among groups in an organization.

Intergroup team building   Helps groups improve their working relationships with one another and experience improved group effectiveness.

Intermittent reinforcement   A reinforcement schedule that rewards behavior only periodically.

Internal integration   The creation of a collective identity and way of working and living together within an organization.

Interorganizational conflict   Occurs between organizations.

Interpersonal conflict   Occurs between two or more individuals in opposition to each other.

Intrapersonal conflict   Occurs within the individual because of actual or perceived pressures from incompatible goals or expectations.

Intrinsic rewards   Rewards received by the individual directly through task performance.

Intuition   The ability to know or recognize quickly the possibilities of a situation.

Job analysis   The procedure used to collect and classify information about tasks the organization needs to complete.

Job characteristics theory   Identifies five core job characteristics of special importance to job design—skill variety, task identity, task significance, autonomy, and feedback.

Job design   The process of defining job tasks and the work arrangements to accomplish them.

Job enlargement   Increases task variety by adding new tasks of similar difficulty to a job.

Job enrichment   Increases job content by giving workers more responsibility for planning and evaluating duties.

Job redesign   Creates long-term congruence between individual goals and organizational career opportunities.

Job rotation   Increases task variety by shifting workers among jobs involving tasks of similar difficulty.

Job satisfaction   The degree to which individuals feel positively or negatively about their jobs.

Job sharing   Allows one full-time job to be divided among two or more persons.

Job simplification   Standardizes tasks and employs people in very routine jobs.

KISS principle   Stands for "keep it short and simple."

Knowledge workers   Employees whose major task is to produce new knowledge, typically through computer-oriented means.

Law of contingent reinforcement   The view that, for a reward to have maximum reinforcing value, it must be delivered only if the desired behavior is exhibited.

Law of effect   The observation that behavior which results in a pleasing outcome is likely to be repeated; behavior that results in an unpleasant outcome is not likely to be repeated.

Law of immediate reinforcement   The more immediate the delivery of a reward after the occurrence of a desirable behavior, the greater the reinforcing effect on behavior.

Leader match training   Leaders are trained to diagnose the situation to match their high and low LPC scores with situational control.

Leadership   A special case of interpersonal influence that gets an individual or group to do what the leader wants done.

Leadership prototype   An image people have in their minds of what a model leader should look like.

Leading   Creates enthusiasm to work hard to accomplish tasks successfully.

Least preferred coworker (LPC) scale   A measure of a person's leadership style based on a description of the person with whom respondents have been able to work least well.

Legitimate power   The extent to which a manager can use the "right of command" to control other people.

Leniency error   The tendency to give relatively high ratings to virtually everyone.

Line units   Work groups that conduct the major business of the organization.

Long-term/short-term orientation   The degree to which a culture emphasizes long-term or short-term thinking.

Low-context cultures   Cultures in which messages are expressed mainly by spoken and written words.

Low differentiation errors   What occurs when raters restrict themselves to a small part of the rating scale.

Lower-order needs   Physiological, safety, and social needs in Maslow's hierarchy.

Lump-sum increase   A pay system in which people elect to receive their wage or salary increases in one or more "lump-sum" payments.

Maintenance activities   Activities that support the emotional life of the group as an ongoing social system.

Management by objectives (MBO)   A process of joint goal setting between a supervisor and a subordinate.

Management philosophy   A philosophy that links key goal-related issues with key collaboration issues to come up with general ways by which the firm will manage its affairs.

Managers   People who are formally responsible for supporting the work efforts of other people.

Masculinity-femininity   The degree to which a society values assertiveness or relationships.

Matrix departmentation   A combination of functional and divisional patterns wherein an individual is assigned to more than one type of unit.

MBWA   Involves getting out of the office to directly communicate with others.

Mechanistic type (machine bureaucracy)   Emphasizes vertical specialization and control with impersonal coordination and a heavy reliance on standardization, formalization, rules, policies, and procedures.

Mediation   A neutral third party tries to engage the parties in a negotiated solution through persuasion and rational argument.

Merit pay   A compensation system that bases an individual's salary or wage increase on a measure of the person's performance accomplishment during a specific time period.

Mimicry   The copying of the successful practices of others.

Mission statements   Written statements of organizational purpose.

Mixed messages   Misunderstandings that occur when a person's words say one thing while his or her nonverbal cues say something else.

Monochronic culture   Cultures in which people tend to do one thing at a time.

Motivating potential score   The extent to which the core characteristics of a job create motivating conditions.

Motivation   Forces within an individual that account for the level, direction, and persistence of effort expended at work.

Motivator factors   In job content, the tasks people actually do, are sources of job satisfaction.

Multinational corporation   A business with extensive international operations in more than one country.

Multiskilling   Team members are trained in skills to perform different jobs.

Mum effect   Occurs when people are reluctant to communicate bad news.

Need for achievement (nAch)   The desire to do better, solve problems, or master complex tasks.

Need for affiliation (nAff)   The desire for friendly and warm relations with others.

Need for power (nPower)   The desire to control others and influence their behavior.

Negative reinforcement   The withdrawal of negative consequences, which tends to increase the likelihood of repeating the behavior in similar settings; also known as avoidance.

Negotiation   The process of making joint decisions when the parties involved have different preferences.

New leadership   Emphasizes charismatic and transformational leadership approaches and various aspects of vision related to them, as well as self-directing work teams.

Noise   Anything that interferes with the effectiveness of communication.

Nonprogrammed decisions   Decisions created to deal uniquely with a problem at hand.

Nonverbal communication   Communication that takes place through facial expressions, body movements, eye contact, and other physical gestures.

Norms   Rules or standards for the behavior of group members.

Open systems   Systems that transform human and material resources into finished goods and services.

Operant conditioning   The process of controlling behavior by manipulating, or "operating" on, its consequences.

Operations technology   The combination of resources, knowledge, and techniques that creates a product or service output for an organization.

Organic type   A professional bureaucracy that emphasizes horizontal specialization, extensive use of personal coordination, and loose rules, policies, and procedures.

Organization charts   Diagrams that depict the formal structures of organizations.

Organizational behavior (OB)   The study of individuals and groups in organizations.

Organizational behavior modification (OB Mod)   The systematic reinforcement of desirable work behavior and the nonreinforcement or punishment of unwanted work behavior.

Organizational communication   The process by which information is exchanged in the organizational setting.

Organizational (or corporate) culture   The system of shared actions, values, and beliefs that develops within an organization and guides the behavior of its members.

Organizational design   The process of choosing and implementing a structural configuration for an organization.

Organizational development (OD) The application of behavioral science knowledge in a long range effort to improve an organization's ability to cope with change in its external environment and increase its problem-solving capabilities.

Organizational development interventions Activities initiated to support planned change and improve work effectiveness.

Organizational governance The pattern of authority, influence, and acceptable managerial behavior established at the top of the organization.

Organizational learning The process of acquiring knowledge and using information to adapt successfully to changing circumstances.

Organizational myth A commonly held cause-effect relationship or assertion that cannot be empirically supported.

Organizational politics The management of influence to obtain ends not sanctioned by the organization or to obtain sanctioned ends through nonsanctioned means and the art of creative compromise among competing interests.

Organizational strategy The process of positioning the organization in the competitive environment and implementing actions to compete successfully.

Organizations Collections of people working together to achieve a common purpose.

Organized anarchy A form or division in a firm in a transition characterized by very rapid change and a lack of a legitimate hierarchy.

Organizing Dividing up tasks and arranging resources to accomplish them.

Output controls Controls that focus on desired targets and allow managers to use their own methods for reaching defined targets.

Output goals The goals that define the type of business an organization is in.

Paired comparison A comparative method of performance appraisal whereby each person is directly compared with every other person.

Participative leadership Focuses on consulting with subordinates and seeking and taking their suggestions into account before making decisions.

Perception The process through which people receive, organize, and interpret information from their environment.

Performance appraisal A process of systematically evaluating performance and providing feedback on which performance adjustments can be made.

Permanent part-time work Permanent work of fewer hours than the standard week.

Personal bias error Occurs when a rater allows specific biases, such as racial, age, or gender, to enter into performance appraisal.

Personality Represents the overall profile or combination of characteristics that capture the unique nature of a person as that person reacts and interacts with others.

Personality dynamics The ways in which an individual integrates and organizes social traits, values and motives, personal conceptions, and emotional adjustment.

Planned change Intentional and occurs with a change agent's intentional direction.

Planning Sets objectives and identifies the actions needed to achieve them.

Polychronic culture A culture in which people tend to do more than one thing at a time.

Positive reinforcement The administration of positive consequences that tend to increase the likelihood of repeating the behavior in similar settings.

Power The ability to get someone else to do something you want done or the ability to make things happen or get things done the way you want.

Power distance The willingness of a culture to accept status and power differences among its members.

Problem solving Uses information to resolve disputes.

Procedural justice The degree to which policies and procedures are properly followed.

Process consultation Helps a group improve on such things as norms, cohesiveness, decision making methods, communication, conflict, and task and maintenance activities.

Process controls Controls that attempt to specify the manner in which tasks are to be accomplished.

Process innovations Innovations introducing into operations new and better ways of doing things.

Process power Control over methods of production and analysis.

Process reengineering The total rethinking and redesign of organizational process to improve performance and innovation; involves analyzing, streamlining, and reconfiguring actions and tasks to achieve work goals.

Process theories Theories that seek to understand the thought processes determining behavior.

Product innovations Innovations that introduce new goods or services to better meet customer needs.

Programmed decisions Decisions that are determined by past experience as appropriate for a problem at hand.

Profit-sharing plans Reward employees based on the entire organization's performance.

Projection   The assignment of personal attributes to other individuals.

Punishment   The administration of negative consequences that tend to reduce the likelihood of repeating the behavior in similar settings.

Quality circle   Members of a quality circle meet regularly to find ways for continuous improvement of quality operations.

Quality of work life (QWL)   The overall quality of human experiences in the workplace.

Ranking   A comparative technique of performance appraisal that involves rank ordering of each individual from best to worst on each performance dimension.

Rational persuasion   The ability to control another's behavior because, through the individual's efforts, the person accepts the desirability of an offered goal and a reasonable way of achieving it.

Rational persuasion strategy   Uses facts, special knowledge, and rational argument to create change.

Realistic job previews   Previews which provide applicants with an objective description of a job and organization.

Recency error   A biased rating that develops by allowing the individual's most recent behavior to speak for his or her overall performance on a particular dimension.

Recruitment   The process of attracting the best qualified individuals to apply for a job.

Referent power   The ability to control another's behavior because of the individual's desire to identify with the power source.

Refreezing   The stage in which changes are reinforced and stabilized.

Reinforcement   The administration of a consequence as a result of behavior.

Reinforcement theories   They emphasize the means through which operant conditioning takes place.

Relatedness needs   Desires for satisfying interpersonal relationships.

Reliability   The consistency and stability of a score from a measurement scale.

Representative power   The formal right conferred by the firm to speak for and to a potentially important group.

Representativeness heuristic   Bases a decision on similarities between the situation at hand and stereotypes of similar occurrences.

Resistance to change   An attitude or behavior that shows unwillingness to make or support a change.

Restricted communication networks   Link subgroups that disagree with one another's positions.

Reward power   The extent to which a manager can use extrinsic and intrinsic rewards to control other people.

Risk environments   Business environments that provide probabilities regarding expected results for decision-making alternatives.

Rites   Standardized and recurring activities used at special times to influence the behaviors and understanding of organizational members.

Rituals   System of rites.

Role   A set of expectations for a team member or person in a job.

Role ambiguity   Occurs when someone is uncertain about what is expected of him or her.

Role conflict   Occurs when someone is unable to respond to role expectations that conflict with one another.

Role negotiation   A process through which individuals clarify expectations about what each should be giving and receiving as group members.

Role overload   Occurs when too much work is expected of the individual.

Role underload   Occurs when too little work is expected of the individual.

Romance of leadership   People attribute romantic, almost magical qualities to leadership.

Sagas   Embellished heroic accounts of the story of the founding of an organization.

Satisficing   Decision making that chooses the first alternative that appears to give an acceptable or satisfactory resolution of the problem.

Scanning   Looking outside the firm and bringing back useful solutions to problems.

Schemas   Cognitive frameworks that represent organized knowledge about a given concept or stimulus developed through experience.

Scientific method   A key part of the OB research foundations, which involves four steps: the research question or problem, hypothesis generation or formulation, the research design, and data gathering, analysis, and interpretation.

Selection   The series of steps from initial applicant screening to hiring.

Selective perception   The tendency to single out for attention those aspects of a situation or person that reinforce or emerge and are consistent with existing beliefs, values, and needs.

Self-concept   The view individuals have of themselves as physical, social, and spiritual or moral beings.

Self-directing work teams Teams that are empowered to make decisions about planning, doing, and evaluating their work.

Self-fulfilling prophecy The tendency to create or find in another situation or individual that which one has expected to find.

Self-managing teams Same as self-directing work teams.

Self-monitoring Reflects a person's ability to adjust his or her behavior to external, situational (environmental) factors.

Self-serving bias The tendency to deny personal responsibility for performance problems but to accept personal responsibility for performance success.

Shamrock organizations Firms that operate with a core group of permanent workers supplemented by outside contractors and part-time workers.

Shaping The creation of a new behavior by the positive reinforcement of successive approximations to the desired behavior.

Shared-power strategy Uses participative methods and emphasizes common values to create change.

Simple design An organization configuration involving one or two ways of specializing individuals and units.

Situational control The extent to which leaders can determine what their groups are going to do and what the outcomes of their actions and decisions are going to be.

Skill-based pay A system that rewards people for acquiring and developing job-relevant skills in number and variety relevant to the organization's need.

Social facilitation The tendency for one's behavior to be influenced by the presence of others in a group.

Social information processing An approach that believes that individual needs and task perceptions result from socially constructed realities.

Social loafing Occurs when people work less hard in groups than they would individually.

Social responsibility The obligation of organizations to behave in ethical and moral ways.

Social traits Surface-level traits that reflect the way a person appears to others when interacting in various social settings.

Socialization Orienting new employees to the firm and its work units.

Societal goals Goals that reflect the intended contributions of an organization to the broader society.

Sociotechnical systems Organizational systems that integrate people and technology into high performance work settings.

Sources and types of values Parents, friends, teachers, and external reference groups can all influence individual values.

Span of control The number of individuals reporting to a supervisor.

Staff units Groups that assist the line units by performing specialized services to the organization.

Status congruence The consistency between a person's status within and outside of a group.

Stereotyping Occurs when one thinks of an individual as belonging to a group or category (e.g., elderly person) and the characteristics commonly associated with the group or category are assigned to the individual in question.

Stimulus Something that incites action.

Strategy The process of positioning the organization in the competitive environment and implementing actions to compete successfully.

Stress Tension from extraordinary demands, constraints, or opportunities.

Stress management An active approach to deal with stress that is influencing behavior.

Stress prevention Minimizing the potential for stress to occur.

Stressors Things that cause stress.

Strictness error Occurs when a rater tends to give everyone a low rating

Structural redesign Involves realigning the structure of the organization or major subsystem in order to improve performance.

Subcultures Unique patterns of values and philosophies within a group that are not consistent with the dominant culture of the larger organization or social system.

Substantive conflict Fundamental disagreement over ends or goals to be pursued and the means for their accomplishment.

Substitutes for leadership Make a leader's influence either unnecessary or redundant in that they replace a leader's influence.

Supportive leadership Focuses on subordinate needs, well-being, and promotion of a friendly work climate.

Survey feedback Begins with the collection of data via questionnaires from organization members or a representative sample of them.

Synergy The creation of a whole that is greater than the sum of its parts.

Systems goals Goals concerned with conditions within the organization that are expected to increase its survival potential.

Task activities   Actions that directly contribute to the performance of important group tasks.

Task performance   The quantity and quality of work produced.

Team building   A collaborative way to gather and analyze data to improve teamwork.

Teams   People working actively together to achieve a common purpose for which they are all accountable.

Teamwork   Occurs when group members work together in ways that utilize their skills well to accomplish a purpose.

Technical skill   An ability to perform specialized tasks.

Telecommuting   Working at home or in a remote location that uses computer and telecommunication linkages with the office.

Temporary part-time work   Temporary work of fewer hours than the standard week.

Terminal values   A person's preferences concerning the "ends" to be achieved.

Theory   A set of systematically interrelated concepts, definitions, and hypotheses that are advanced to explain and predict phenomena.

360-degree evaluation (also called 360-degree feedback)   A comprehensive approach that uses evaluations of bosses, peers, and subordinates but also self-ratings, customer ratings, and others outside the work unit.

Total quality management (TQM)   A total commitment to high-quality results, continuous improvement, and meeting customer needs.

Training   Provides the opportunity to acquire and improve job-related skills.

Trait perspectives   Assume that traits play a central role in differentiating between leaders and nonleaders or in predicting leader or organizational outcomes.

Transactional leadership   Involves leader-follower exchanges necessary for achieving routine performance agreed upon between leaders and followers.

Transformational leadership   Occurs when leaders broaden and elevate followers' interests and followers look beyond their own interests for the good of others.

Transformational change   Radically shifts the fundamental character of an organization.

Two-factor theory   Herzberg's theory that identifies job context as the source of job dissatisfaction and job content as the source of job satisfaction.

Type A orientation   A personality orientation characterized by impatience, desire for achievement, and perfectionism.

Type B orientation   A personality orientation characterized by an easygoing and less competitive nature than Type A.

Uncertain environments   Business environments that provide no information to predict expected results for decision-making alternatives.

Uncertainty avoidance   The cultural tendency to be uncomfortable with uncertainty and risk in everyday life.

Unfreezing   The stage of the change process at which a situation is prepared for change.

Unplanned change   Change that occurs spontaneously and without a change agent's direction.

Valence   The value to the individual of various work outcomes.

Validity   The degree of confidence one can have in the results of a research study.

Value congruence   Occurs when individuals express positive feelings upon encountering others who exhibit values similar to their own.

Values   Broad preferences concerning appropriate courses of action or outcomes.

Vertical specialization   A hierarchical division of labor that distributes formal authority.

Virtual groups   Groups that work together via computer networks.

Virtual team   A work team that convenes and operates with its members linked together electronically via networked computers.

Wellness   Maintaining physical and mental health to better deal with stress when it occurs.

Whistleblower   Someone within the organization who exposes the wrongdoings of others in order to preserve high ethical standards.

Workforce diversity   Differences based on gender, race and ethnicity, age, and able-bodiedness.

Work-life balance   Deals with the demands from one's work and personal affairs.

Zone of indifference   The range of authoritative requests to which a subordinate is willing to respond without subjecting the directives to critical evaluation or judgment.

Index